LET'S GO!

www.letsgo.com

ISRAEL

AND THE PALESTINIAN TERRITORIES

researcher-writers
Richard Fegelman
Victoria Liu
Alexander Traub

staff writers

Audrey Anderson	Mikia Manley
Beatrice Franklin	Dorothy McLeod
Lexie Perloff-Giles	Taylor Nickel
Rachel Granetz	Emily Pereira
Ammar Joudeh	Eleanor Reagan
Devi Lockwood	

research manager
Amy Friedman

editor
Leah Schulson

managing editor
Sarah Berlow

CONTENTS

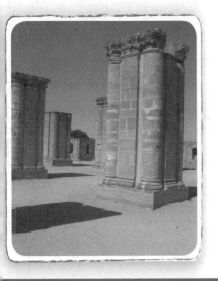

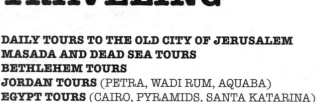

RESEARCHER-WRITERS

RICHARD FEGELMAN. Richard Fegelman really takes the biscuit when it comes to travel stamina. From his impeccable copy and anecdotes from club hopping, it was evident that Ricky was a Research-Writer on a *Let's Go* mission. He's also one of the only guys around who could stick out his thumb to pick up a ride and happen to stop one of the nation's best brewers.

VICTORIA LIU. Delightful and eager to go anywhere and everywhere, Victoria was road-ready from day one. Fluent in the language of haggling and full of ingenious tricks like decoy wallets, she braved buses, dusty car rides, and Jewish holidays to find all the best deals in Israel. Oh, and some darn good falafel.

ALEXANDER TRAUB. Truly a bro who has never known a stranger, Alex made new friends the nation over all for the sake of bringing authenticity to the book—and finding a free meal. With an abounding love for new cultures and green meats, Traub trekked from the Old City streets of Jerusalem to the deserts of the Negev and all the way through the West Bank, with wit and iced coffee always on hand.

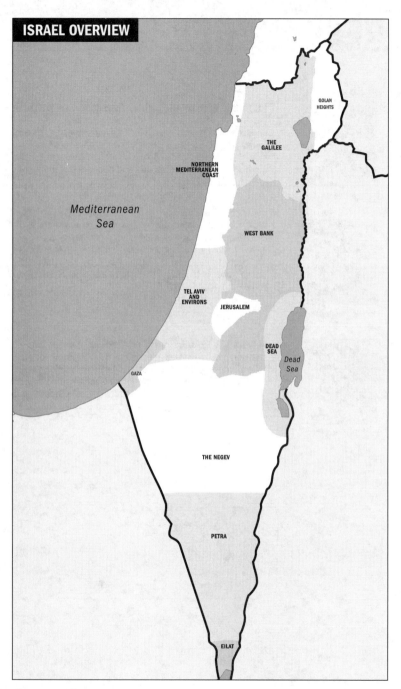

ISRAEL OVERVIEW

Mediterranean Sea

GOLAN HEIGHTS

THE GALILEE

NORTHERN MEDITERRANEAN COAST

WEST BANK

TEL AVIV AND ENVIRONS

JERUSALEM

DEAD SEA

Dead Sea

GAZA

THE NEGEV

PETRA

EILAT

DISCOVER

ISRAEL

AND THE PALESTINIAN TERRITORIES

Factions fight for it. Lackadaisical Hebrew School dropouts dream of sharing Birthright funds to explore it. Heck, Moses dragged his people around a desert for 40 years to get to it. It's clear Israel is not your ordinary travel destination. This may be because of its incredible diversity; home to four climates, three major religions, two stock exchanges, and at least one partridge in a pear tree, the country can sound more like a *Sesame Street* lesson than a real place. And that's exactly why you should go—where else in the world can you both prostrate and party, dive and debate?

Be prepared, though. Israel changes you, and you can't always predict how that will happen. You'll find yourself tanner for sure, but you may also discover new ways to understand your political views, your religion, and yourself. The traditionally brash inhabitants of this beautiful, conflict-ridden country will help you along, whether you want them to or not. We recommend that you embrace it all—as a student, as a pilgrim, as a historian, as an adventurer. Just don't forget to pack your sunscreen.

1

when to go

Unless an angel descends and tells you to head into the northern mountains in late December, you're not going to be worrying about which heavy coat to bring to Israel. While winter is both cooler and emptier than the summer months, it's also rainier, meaning you may just want to grin and bear the crowds that flock to Israel from April to September—though if you head to the northern region a little earlier, you'll get to appreciate the lush springtime greenery. A little heat never hurt anyone, particularly when you're in a country that borders four eminently swimmable seas.

The bigger concern when visiting Israel is the holidays—whole cities may shut down in observance or, alternatively, overflow with pilgrims. September and October are particularly big holiday months for Jews and Muslims. Generally, it's an exercise in common sense. Not much will be happening on Yom Kippur, the Jewish Day of Atonement. Ditto for Ramadan. And only go to Bethlehem on Christmas if you enjoy claustrophobia, plastic imitations of the newborn Jesus, and a lot of pushy pilgrims.

what to do

dancing with the (gold)stars

- **TEL AVIV.** When it comes to nightlife in Israel, it's a no-brainer. You go to Tel Aviv, where the trance is louder, the clubs cooler, and the skirts shorter. Where else in Israel are you going to find megaclubs, chill bars, and a dance floor/sex shop all in the same place? Nowhere, we promise (p. 119).

- **EILAT.** Show off your new tan as you make your way though the more touristy clubs and bars of Israel's southern tip (p. 332).

- **BE'ER SHEVA.** Forget Abraham's Well—Be'er Sheva's quirky student bars and hookah lounges are the real watering holes for those wandering in the desert (p. 306).

- **RAMALLAH.** Trap a bunch of rich people in a small city, and they're going to figure out a killer way to unwind. More specifically, one that involves large quantities of Taybeh (Palestinian beer) and *arak* (p. 267).

ROCKS OF AGES

For a country that's less than a century old, Israel is pretty hoity-toity about its ruins. Of course, it's located in a region that's been inhabited for over four millennia, so maybe there's a reason for that pride. Israel is crammed with places whose names you've heard of but never quite believed were real. Well, they are. And you can see them all, and usually for less than NIS40.

- **JERICHO.** Tell es-Sultan, in the West Bank, is the oldest city in the region—if Joshua made those walls crumble, it was only because they'd already been there for more than 1000 years (p. 273).

- **JERUSALEM.** While the Old City is clearly, well, old, it's the outskirts that really have the heavy-hitters, including the City of David and the Mount of Olives (p. 34).

- **PETRA.** Word's still out on who managed to lose a city this big for 700 years...

especially since it's been around since the sixth century BCE (p. 335).

- **CAESAREA.** Caesarea's national park is home to everything from Herod's mansion to the Roman take on the Indy Motor Speedway. You can also dive beneath the port and pretend you're discovering Atlantis (p. 187).

- **MASADA.** The 150 BCE fortress gained fame in the 66 CE Roman siege. Just because the Jewish Zealots burned every building within the walls in order to psych out the Romans doesn't mean there's nothing left to see (p. 289).

PRACTICE WHAT YOU BEACH

From the luscious Sea of Galilee and the salaciously saline Dead Sea in the east to the Mediterranean coast in the west, Israel boasts a wide variety of opportunities to be a little beach(y).

- **TIBERIAS.** The beaches of Tiberias proper can get a little crowded, but the city is also the gateway to the 55km-stretch of Sea of Galilee shore. If it was good enough for St. Peter, it's good enough for us (p. 219).

- **EILAT.** Resort-central for Israel, Eilat has the brightest reefs, boldest dolphins, and most bronzed bodies. Think Cancun, but with a little less Friday-night action (p. 327).

- **HERZLIYA.** Nearby Netanya might have the better beach buzz, but at least one man thinks Herzliya's shores are good enough to merit a life-size sand castle. Check out Kakhalon's structure, then head to a nearby secluded strip of sand (p. 141).

- **EIN GEDI.** Hike out a little bit and rinse off from the traditional Dead Sea float-and-coat with a dip in one of Ein Gedi's nearby springs (p. 291).

FALA-FULL

Depending on your affinity for the power pea, you'll quickly find yourself either worshipping the chickpea or having anxious nightmares about it. Garbanzo is god here, where you can find its progeny—hummus and falafel—on literally every corner. But, like any country with a few decent cities, Israel also has a burgeoning international eating scene and some of the best seafood you'll ever find. Take that, kosher laws.

- **TEL AVIV.** There may be a few other places in Israel where you can find burgers, smoothies, and sushi at any time of day and night. There is nowhere else in Israel, however, where they will taste even half as good (p. 113).

- **JAFFA.** It may be just a glorified suburb of Tel Aviv, but that hasn't stopped Jaffa from carving out its own restaurant niche where you can find what is widely considered to be the best hummus in Israel (p. 132).

- **JERUSALEM.** That pizza oven has probably been around since the destruction of the Second Temple. Same for that falafel stand. The greasy-spoon food in the Muslim Quarter is some of the best in the country, while West Jerusalem offers fancier options for those unwilling to dine without a cloth napkin (p. 66).

- **RAMALLAH.** Bastion of the West Bank's glitzy and glamorous, Ramallah has food that ranges from cheerfully cheap to I-can't-afford-that good (p. 265).

BEYOND TOURISM

There are only so many times that you can pretend to be excited about a millennium-old rock that some Ottoman stole from some Byzantine church that was built on top of some ancient temple. Take a break from the sightseeing and leave your own mark on the country with one of the many volunteer, study, and work opportunities. If all else fails, you can just go save that kid who's drowning in the ocean. Yes, that one. Right there. What are you waiting for?!

- **ULPANIM.** These intensive Hebrew programs, offered at most of the country's universities, get you ready to negotiate the mean streets of Israel in no time (p. 379).
- **KIBBUTZIM.** Feel like a Zionist, learn about conservation, or just learn how to milk a cow at one of Israel's many collective farms (p. 380).
- **B'TSELEM.** There's, like, some dispute going on or something? Do your part in the Palestinian-Israeli conflict by helping increase cross-cultural understanding (p. 382).

student superlatives

- **BEST PLACE TO WATCH A BRAWL:** Jerusalem's **Church of the Holy Sepulchre** has been a bone of contention between rival Christian sects, who all want to present Jesus's love in their own way (p. 48).
- **MOST SCARVES PER CAPITA:** In **Ein Hod,** the expression "artists' colony" is taken quite seriously (p. 174).
- **BEST PLACE TO BUILD THE DEATH STAR:** Rehovot, where the **Weizmann Institute** has got that futuristic look down to an art...er, science (p. 145).
- **BEST PLACE TO GET SMASHED:** Head to Tel Aviv's **70 Pilim**—liquor boutique by day and a boozefest by night (p. 119).
- **BEST DESERT DATE:** Rent alpacas and head into the nearby forest for some quality time with your camelids in **Mitzpe Ramon** (p. 318).
- **MOODIEST STATUE:** The Virgin Mary in Ramallah's **Church of Transfiguration** supposedly sheds tears of oil (p. 264).

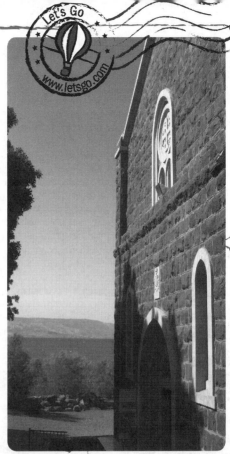

suggested itineraries

CITY SLICKERS

Just because Israel is about the size of New Jersey doesn't mean that it's home to the Newarks and Hobokens (Chobokens?) of the Middle East. Israel has a cosmopolitan side, so if you prefer bougie-bored to boogie boards, hit up these cities.

1. TEL AVIV: One of the few places in the world where house blasts from Bauhaus, Tel Aviv deserves its party-hard reputation. If you think your horn-rims will attract glares at the clubs, take refuge in the artsy alleyways of the south (p. 103).

2. HAIFA: It may be a little lacking in the skinny-jean department, but Haifa is still home to plenty of cafes, and museums cover all the usual suspects: science, contemporary art, and clandestine immigration (p. 159).

3. JERUSALEM: Forget the old stuff—stick around West Jerusalem for the city's best restaurants, shopping, and neighborhood snooping. Check out the Temple Mount only if you're feeling particularly retro (p. 13).

4. RAMALLAH: Once a vacation spot for the Arab elite, Ramallah is now their home. And they've brought the requisite theater, university, and classy bars along with them (p. 261).

5. BE'ER SHEVA: Its location in the desert might mean that culture is a little lacking. But, as home to Ben-Gurion University, Be'er Sheva has more than its fair share of food, nightlife, and co-eds. What more do you want? (p. 299)

6. EILAT: Eilat in a nutshell? Surf, ski, swim, snorkel, or suntan by day. Get schwasted by night (p. 323).

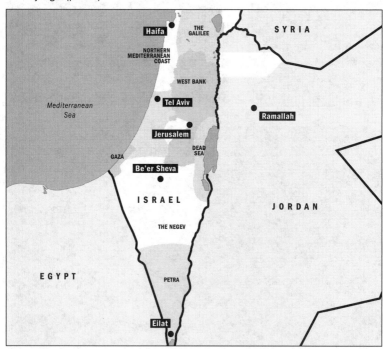

WANDERING IN THE WILDERNESS

Hiking through ethereal craters. Scuba diving in reefs. Biking where Jesus once walked (minus that "on water" part). Shimmering springs. Arma-freaking-geddon. We could go on listing these, or we could just remind you—when it comes to outdoor activities, Israel has a Summer-Olympics-worthy list of possible activities.

1. EIN GEDI: Do the obligatory Dead Sea stuff, then retreat to the muggy hikes—and refreshing pools and waterfalls—of the Ein Gedi Nature Reserve (p. 291).

2. SDE BOKER: Desert, schmesert. The ferns and tropical trees in Ein Avdat's steep canyons may cause you to forget that the sand stretches for miles (p. 310).

3. MITZPE RAMON: Stay in a hut made from mud and recycled materials, snack on some home-cooked quiche, and then head into the world's largest crater for a day of colored sand and otherworldly outcroppings (p. 314).

4. BEIT GUVRIN: Wander through the 2000-year-old caves in the national park, then watch the sunset from the nearby kibbutz (p. 138).

5. CAESAREA: Even if the actual national park has more Roman ruins than rock formations, the city's southern beaches have some of the best swimming, parasailing, and jet-skiing in the country (p. 189).

6. SEA OF GALILEE: Training for a triathlon? Swim at one of Tiberias's beaches, bike along the 55km shore, and finish with a trek up Mt. Arbel (p. 228).

suggested itineraries

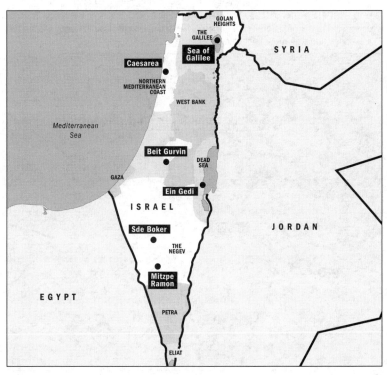

TRAVELERS WITHOUT BORDERS

We know, we know: you were raised on Pokemon. You gotta catch 'em all. Here are, hands down, the best places to go in Israel and the West Bank. Leave no stone unturned (and no **Charizard** uncaught).

1. BETHLEHEM: It's where Jesus began, and so should you to get your first taste of the religious sights, cheap falafel, and Israeli-Palestinian conflict (p. 251).

2. JERUSALEM: Come for the religion and history, stay for the food. And the views. And the people. And the caves (p. 13).

3. MASADA: Beautiful mountain views meet dramatic historical significance—and there's a cheesy sound and light show to ensure you're aware of both (p. 289).

4. MITZPE RAMON: As you cut through Be'er Sheva, you may want to do a quick look around, but the real jewel of the Negev is Mitzpe Ramon, home to the world's largest crater and Israel's hippiest hikers (p. 314).

5. TEL AVIV: Even if you weren't coming from the desert, Tel Aviv would still feel like an oasis—of modernity in the land of history, Maccabee in the land of monks, and sushi in the land of kosher (p. 103).

6. CAESAREA: Tear yourself away from the chill kibbutz to explore Roman ruins at their most extravagant (p. 184).

7. HAIFA: Stop and smell the roses at the Baha'i Gardens, then catch some contemporary art before sunbathing at one of the best beaches in the country (p. 159).

8. TZFAT: Maybe it's all the Kabbalists, maybe it's the clear mountain air—all we know is that Tzfat is one of the best places in Israel to find your inner spark (p. 230).

9. TIBERIAS: The gateway to the Sea of Galilee and the Golan Heights, Tiberias has the layers of history typical of an Israeli town. Less typical, however, are the hot springs and waterfront light extravaganza (p. 215).

discover israel

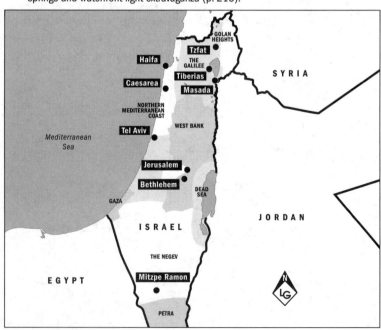

HOLIER-THAN-WOW!

If you suffer from spheniscipobhia, you should probably just turn around now. Nuns—and, for that matter, every other type of religious figure you could imagine—are everywhere in Israel. To get a full tour of all the different funny hats, head to these cities.

1. JERUSALEM: You gotta start here: Dome of the Rock, Western Wall, and the Church of the Holy Sepulchre (p. 34).

2. BETHLEHEM: See where Jesus was born, Rachel died, and the entire monastic order may have begun (p. 253).

3. TZFAT: It's clear why Tzfat became Israel's home for Kabbalah: with views this beautiful, it's impossible not to have a spiritual experience (p. 230).

4. NAZARETH: Not only is this where Jesus went through his awkward pubescence (high school is hard when you keep performing miracles), but you're also near the White Mosque and Tel Meggido, better known as Armaggedon (p. 208).

5. SEA OF GALILEE: This is where the magic happened. Literally. Check out the sites where Jesus walked on water, multiplied the loaves and fishes, and gave the Sermon on the Mount (p. 226).

6. HAIFA: You don't have to be a Baha'i to find tranquility in their Haifa gardens, the second holiest site of this inclusive religion (p. 163).

suggested itineraries

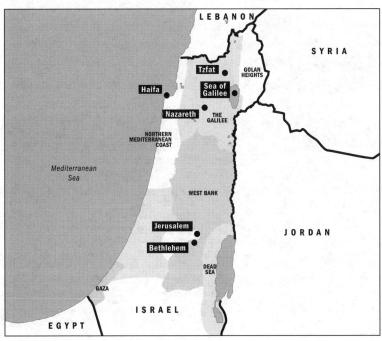

how to use this book

CHAPTERS

In the next few pages, the travel coverage chapters—the meat of any *Let's Go* book—begin with **Jerusalem**. Because religion just isn't as good if you don't have something to atone for, we follow that with **Tel Aviv** and the surrounding towns before working our way up the **Northern Mediterranean Coast** and into the **Galilee.** From lush hills, we then move to the politically contentious **West Bank**. And after that? Death, in the form of the **Dead Sea** and Israel's largest desert, the **Negev.** Coverage wraps up with **Eilat,** a resort town at the country's southern tip, and ancient **Petra** in nearby Jordan. Due to unrest at time of writing, there were certain regions of Israel that we were not able to cover.

But don't worry, folks. We still have a few extra chapters for you to peruse:

CHAPTER	DESCRIPTION
Discover Israel	Discover tells you what to do, when to do it, and where to go for it. The absolute coolest things about any destination get highlighted in this chapter at the front of all *Let's Go* books.
Essentials	Essentials contains the practical info you need before, during, and after your trip—visas, regional transportation, health and safety, phrasebooks, and more.
Israel 101	Israel 101 is just what it sounds like—a crash course in where you're traveling. This short chapter on Israel's history and culture makes great reading on a long plane ride.
Beyond Tourism	As students ourselves, we at *Let's Go* encourage studying abroad, or going beyond tourism more generally, every chance we get. This chapter lists ideas for how to study, volunteer, or work abroad with other young travelers in Israel to get more out of your trip.

LISTINGS

Listings—a.k.a. reviews of individual establishments—constitute a majority of *Let's Go* coverage. Our Researcher-Writers list establishments in order from **best to worst value**—not necessarily quality. (Obviously a five-star hotel is nicer than a hostel, but it would probably be ranked lower because it's not as good a value.) Listings pack in a lot of information, but it's easy to digest if you know how they're constructed:

ESTABLISHMENT NAME type of establishment $$$$
Address ☎phone number; website
Editorial review goes here.
🧭 Directions to the establishment. ℹ Other practical information about the establishment, like age restrictions at a club or whether breakfast is included at a hostel. $ Prices for goods or services. ⏰ Hours or schedules.

ICONS

First things first: places and things that we absolutely love, sappily cherish, generally obsess over, and wholeheartedly endorse are denoted by the all-empowering 👍**Let's Go thumbs-up.** In addition, the icons scattered at the end of a listing (as you saw in the sample above) can serve as visual cues to help you navigate each listing:

👍	*Let's Go* recommends	☎	Phone numbers	🧭	Directions
ℹ	Other hard info	$	Prices	⏰	Hours

OTHER USEFUL STUFF

Area codes for each destination appear opposite the name of the city and are denoted by the ☎ icon. Finally, in order to make the book as accessible as possible, we've used a few **major transliterations and translations.** For example, rather than using such transliterations as *derech*, *sderot*, and *kikar*, we've given you their English counterparts: road, avenue, and square. Be aware that, since Hebrew uses a different alphabet, most names are merely transliterations. It's important to bear in mind that these English spellings—if available at all—may vary widely in Israel. We try and make note of other common spellings throughout the book.

PRICE DIVERSITY

A final set of icons corresponds to what we call our "price diversity" scale, which approximates how much money you can expect to spend at a given establishment. For **accommodations,** we base our range on the cheapest price for which a single traveler can stay for one night. For **food,** we estimate the average amount one traveler will spend in one sitting. The table below tells you what you'll *typically* find in Israel at the corresponding price range, but keep in mind that no system can allow for the quirks of individual establishments.

ACCOMMODATIONS	RANGE	WHAT YOU'RE LIKELY TO FIND
$	under NIS80	Campgrounds, hostel dorms, and rooftop mattresses. Expect bunk beds (if that) and a communal bathroom. You may have to bring your own towels, sheets, and positive attitude.
$$	NIS80-260	Most Israeli accommodations fall in this range. Unless you're in the middle of nowhere, $$ will get you anything from a nice dorm bed to a relatively spacious private room.
$$$	NIS260-400	Typically, a $$$ has decent amenities: A/C, TV, maybe even free breakfast. But some places in Israel are more expensive than others, and in a city like Tel Aviv, you may pay $$$ to get the same perks (or lack thereof) as a small town's $$.
$$$$	over NIS400	This is saved for beachside resorts and hotels that double as sought-after sights. If it's this expensive and doesn't exceed your weary backpacker dreams, you've paid too much.
FOOD	RANGE	WHAT YOU'RE LIKELY TO FIND
$	under NIS32	Like falafel? How about shawarma? Here you're going to find mostly street food and small cafes, as well as some astonishingly good dives. As long as you're not a total germaphobe, you can eat relatively well for this price.
$$	NIS32-80	Sandwiches, pizza, or low-priced entrees. Most ethnic eateries are $$. The food will be a little better, the decor a little nicer, and the seating will be more than just four rickety tables squeezed next to the oven.
$$$	NIS80-145	A somewhat fancy restaurant. Entrees tend to be heartier or more elaborate, but you're really paying for decor and ambience. Few restaurants in this range have a dress code, but some may look haughtily upon T-shirts and sandals.
$$$$	over NIS145	Your meal might cost more than your room, but there's a reason—it's fabulous and/or comes in staggeringly gigantic portions. You can usually, however, get a delish dish for much less; only spend this much if you're really trying to get laid.

JERUSALEM

This is a tough town. Steely eyed nuns can melt nosy tourists with a facial expression. Orthodox Jews have been known to beat up the "immodestly dressed" who mistakenly wander into their neighborhoods. Palestinian kids in the Silwan sometimes trash foreigners' cars because they're hyped up after Friday services. You might begin to perceive every sight as just a flashpoint of political conflict and the very archaeology of Jerusalem, its stacks upon stacks of burned remains, as the casualties of a never-ending controversy. You might start to see politics in everything, and feel yourself caught in a cultural maze, stuck between competing stories of hardship and violence. Whose story is real?

And then, on the day you realize you'll have to leave, you might become extremely sad; that retreat to Tel Aviv might not look so necessary after all. The fact is these people are tough because there is something deeply worth fighting for here. It's in the ground itself; the Temple Mount has been one of the holiest places in the world for both monotheistic and pagan religions for centuries. The most elemental and human battles about the most elemental and human beliefs have been waged here, and all it takes is a dig to discover them. Many of Jerusalem's stories remain subterranean, too fought over to be found—yet you are walking on them all the time. Instead of trying to pick a side, you might step back and see the testament to devotion and heritage that is at the center of all these loyalties. Abandoning the conflict and the shaky compromises they have struck—that is, Jerusalem itself—will feel like you're abandoning everything. You'll have no choice but to marry a falafelist and move here permanently.

greatest hits

- **EAT.** Eat the food of your ancestors at Eucalyptus (p. 74). Biblical food only; no devil's food cake allowed.

- **PRAY.** Crowds not your thing? Go to the Ethiopian Monastery (p. 49) in the Christian Quarter of the Old City.

- **LOVE.** Celebrate the fact that you aren't reading a certain cheesy book by buying yourself a present at the *souq* (p. 36).

- **REVOLT.** See the beginnings of the Israeli army in Latrun (p. 95).

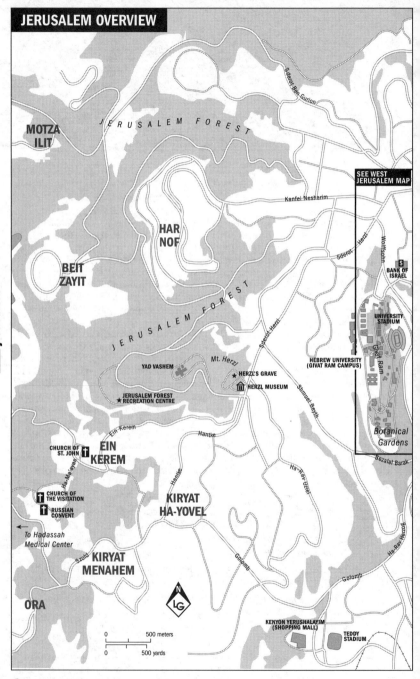

JERUSALEM OVERVIEW

MOTZA ILIT

JERUSALEM FOREST

Sderot Ben Gurion

SEE WEST JERUSALEM MAP

Kanfei Nesharim

HAR NOF

Sderot Herzl

Wolfsohn

BANK OF ISRAEL

BEIT ZAYIT

JERUSALEM FOREST

UNIVERSITY STADIUM

Sderot Herzl

Givat Ram

YAD VASHEM

Mt. Herzl

HERZL'S GRAVE

HERZL MUSEUM

HEBREW UNIVERSITY (GIVAT RAM CAMPUS)

JERUSALEM FOREST RECREATION CENTRE

Shmuel Beyth

Ein Kerem

Hantke

Botanical Gardens

CHURCH OF ST. JOHN

EIN KEREM

Ha-Ma'ayan

Hantke

Ha-Rav Uriel

Bazalet Barak

CHURCH OF THE VISITATION

RUSSIAN CONVENT

KIRYAT HA-YOVEL

To Hadassah Medical Center

Stolb

KIRYAT MENAHEM

Golomb

Ha-Rav Herzog

Golomb

ORA

N LG

0   500 meters

0   500 yards

KENYON YERUSHALAYIM (SHOPPING MALL)

TEDDY STADIUM

jerusalem

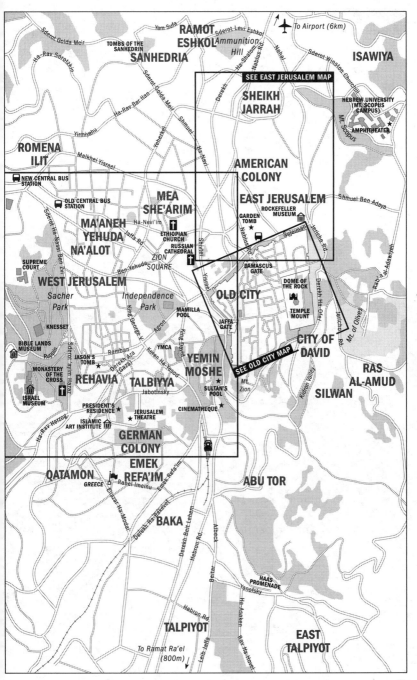

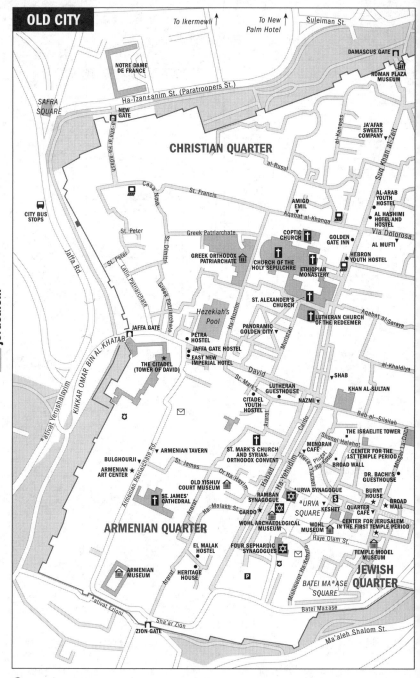

OLD CITY

To Ikermewli
To New
Palm Hotel
Suleiman St.

DAMASCUS GATE
ROMAN PLAZA
MUSEUM

NOTRE DAME
DE FRANCE

SAFRA
SQUARE

Ha-Tzan±anim St. (Paratroopers St.)

NEW
GATE

JA'AFAR
SWEETS
COMPANY

a-Sha'ar ha-adash

al-Kanayes

Suq Khan az-Zeit

CHRISTIAN QUARTER

al-Rusul

CITY BUS
STOPS

Casa Nova

St. Francis

AL-ARAB
YOUTH
HOSTEL

AMIGO
EMIL

Jaffa Rd.

jerusalem

St. Peter

Greek Patriarchate

Aqabat al-Khanqa

AL HASHIMI
HOTEL AND
HOSTEL

Via Dolorosa

St. Dimitri

St. Peter

COPTIC
CHURCH

GOLDEN
GATE INN

AL MUFTI

Greek Patriarchate

GREEK ORTHODOX
PATRIARCHATE

CHURCH OF THE
HOLY SEPULCHRE

ETHIOPIAN
MONASTERY

HEBRON
YOUTH HOSTEL

ativat Yerushalayim

Latin Patriarchate

Hezekiah's
Pool

Ha-Nozrim

ST. ALEXANDER'S
CHURCH

Muristan

Aqabat al-Saraya

JAFFA GATE

PANORAMIC
GOLDEN CITY

LUTHERAN CHURCH
OF THE REDEEMER

KIKKAR OMAR BIN AL-KHATAB

PETRA
HOSTEL

JAFFA GATE HOSTEL

THE CITADEL
(TOWER OF DAVID)

EAST NEW
IMPERIAL HOTEL

David

al-Khaldiya

St. Mark's

SHAB

LUTHERAN
GUESTHOUSE

KHAN AL-SULTAN

CITADEL
YOUTH
HOSTEL

NAZMI

Bab al-Silsilah

Ararat

Cardo

ARMENIAN TAVERN

ST. MARK'S CHURCH
AND SYRIAN-
ORTHODOX CONVENT

Shonei Halahot

THE ISRAELITE TOWER

MENORAH
CAFE

CENTER FOR THE
1ST TEMPLE PERIOD

Magare ha-Dach

Armenian Patriarchate Rd.

BULGHOURJI

ARMENIAN

St. James

Or Ha-Harim

Hahad

Ha-Yehudim

Hurat Plugat

Ha-Yehudim

BROAD WALL

DR. BACHI'S
GUESTHOUSE

ART CENTER

OLD YISHUV
COURT MUSEUM

Ararat

Ha-Malakh St

RAMBAN
SYNAGOGUE

URVA SYNAGOGUE

BURNT
HOUSE

ST. JAMES'
CATHEDRAL

CARDO

URVA
SQUARE

KESHET

URVA
CAFE

QUARTER
CAFE

BROAD
WALL

ARMENIAN QUARTER

WOHL ARCHAEOLOGICAL
MUSEUM

WOHL
MUSEUM

CENTER FOR JERUSALEM
IN THE FIRST TEMPLE PERIOD

Haye Olam St.

ARMENIAN
MUSEUM

EL MALAK
HOSTEL

FOUR SEPHARDIC
SYNAGOGUES

TEMPLE MODEL
MUSEUM

JEWISH
QUARTER

HERITAGE
HOUSE

Ararat

BATEI MAªASE
SQUARE

Mishmaot Ha-kohanim

ativat Ezioni.

Sha'ar Zion

Batei Ma±ase

ZION GATE

Ma'aleh Shalom St.

16 www.letsgo.com

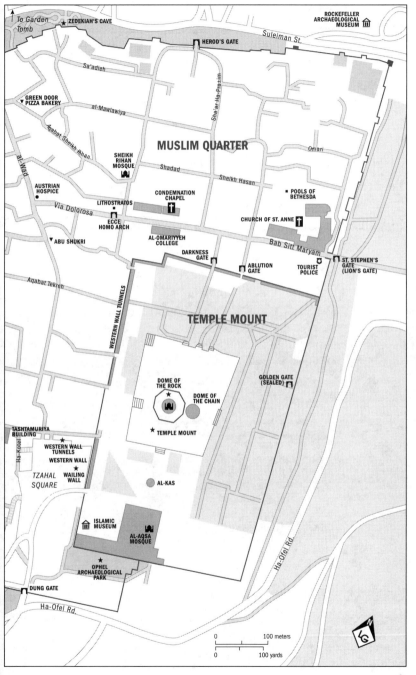

To Garden Tomb

★ ZEDEKIAH'S CAVE

ROCKEFELLER ARCHAEOLOGICAL MUSEUM 🏛

Suleiman St.

🏳 HEROD'S GATE

Sa'adieh

Sha er Ha-Pratim

▼ GREEN DOOR PIZZA BAKERY

al-Mawlawiya

Aqabat Sheikh Rihan

al-Wad

MUSLIM QUARTER

Omari

SHEIKH RIHAN MOSQUE ♨

Shadad

Sheikh Hasan

AUSTRIAN HOSPICE ●

LITHOSTRATOS

CONDEMNATION CHAPEL ✝

■ POOLS OF BETHESDA

Via Dolorosa

ECCE HOMO ARCH

CHURCH OF ST. ANNE ✝

▼ ABU SHUKRI

AL-OMARIYYEH COLLEGE

Bab Sitt Maryam

Aqabat Tekreh

DARKNESS GATE 🏳

ABLUTION GATE 🏳

TOURIST POLICE ♨

🏳 ST. STEPHEN'S GATE (LION'S GATE)

WESTERN WALL TUNNELS

TEMPLE MOUNT

DOME OF THE ROCK ♨

DOME OF THE CHAIN ●

GOLDEN GATE (SEALED) 🏳

★ TEMPLE MOUNT

TASHTAMURIYA BUILDING

Ha-Kotel

★ WESTERN WALL TUNNELS

WESTERN WALL

TZAHAL SQUARE

★ WAILING WALL

● AL-KAS

ISLAMIC MUSEUM 🏛

AL-AQSA MOSQUE ♨

★ OPHEL ARCHAEOLOGICAL PARK

Ha-Ofel Rd.

🏳 DUNG GATE

Ha-Ofel Rd.

0   100 meters

0   100 yards

jerusalem

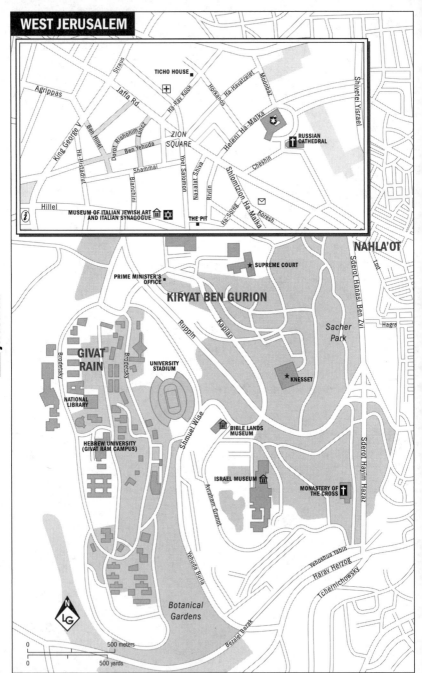

WEST JERUSALEM

Agrippas

Straus

TICHO HOUSE

Jaffa Rd.

Ha-Rav Kook

Horkenos

Ha-Havatzelet

Monbaz

Shivetei Yisrael

King George V

Ben Hillel

Dorot Rishonim

ZION
SQUARE

Heleni Ha-Malka

RUSSIAN
CATHEDRAL

Ben Yehuda

Yoel Salomon

Nazarat Shiva

Cheshin

Ha-Histadrut

Shammai

Rivlin

Shlomtzion Ha-Malka

Bianchini

Koresh

Hillel

MUSEUM OF ITALIAN JEWISH ART
AND ITALIAN SYNAGOGUE

THE PIT

Ha-Sorek

NAHLA'OT

★ SUPREME COURT

PRIME MINISTER'S
OFFICE

KIRYAT BEN GURION

Sderot Hanasi Ben Zvi

Hagra

Ruppin

Kaplan

Sacher
Park

GIVAT
RAIN

Brodetsky

UNIVERSITY
STADIUM

★ KNESSET

NATIONAL
LIBRARY

Shmuel Wise

BIBLE LANDS
MUSEUM

HEBREW UNIVERSITY
(GIVAT RAM CAMPUS)

Abraham Granot

ISRAEL MUSEUM

Sderot Hayim Hazaz

MONASTERY OF
THE CROSS

Yehuda Burla

Bezalel Borak

Yehoshua Yabin

Harav Herzog

Tchernichowsky

*Botanical
Gardens*

N
LG

0 _____ 500 meters

0 _____ 500 yards

jerusalem

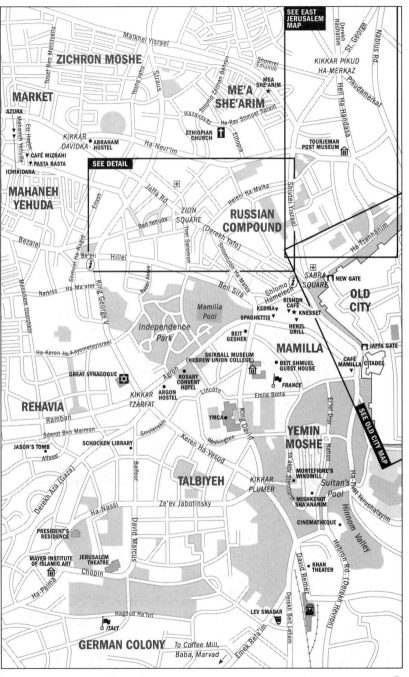

jerusalem

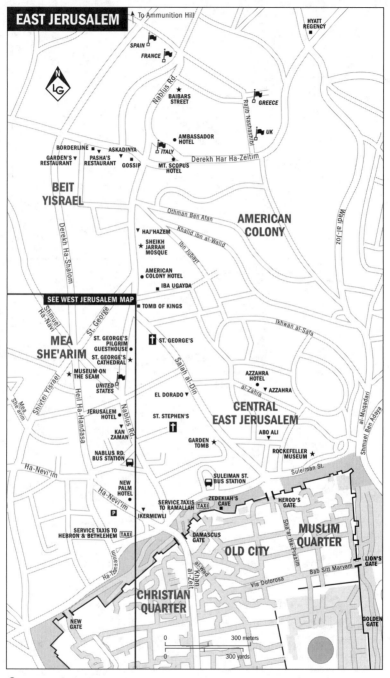

EAST JERUSALEM

To Ammunition Hill

HYATT REGENCY

SPAIN
FRANCE

Nablus Rd.

BAIBARS STREET

GREECE

Rajib Nashashibi

UK

AMBASSADOR HOTEL

BORDERLINE   ASKADINYA
GARDEN'S   PASHA'S
RESTAURANT   RESTAURANT   GOSSIP

ITALY

Derekh Har Ha-Zeitim

MT. SCOPUS HOTEL

BEIT YISRAEL

Derekh Ha-Shalom

Othman Ben Afan

AMERICAN COLONY

Wadi al-Joz

HAJ'HAZEM

Khalid ibn al-Walid

SHEIKH JARRAH MOSQUE

Ibn Jubayr

AMERICAN COLONY HOTEL
IBA UGAYDA

SEE WEST JERUSALEM MAP

TOMB OF KINGS

Ikhwan al-Safa

MEA SHE'ARIM

Shmuel Ha-Navi

St. George

ST. GEORGE'S PILGRIM GUESTHOUSE
ST. GEORGE'S CATHEDRAL

ST. GEORGE'S

Shitrei Yisrael

MUSEUM ON THE SEAM
UNITED STATES

Mea She'arim

Heil Ha-Handasa

Salah al-Din

AZZAHRA HOTEL
al-Zahra   AZZAHRA

EL DORADO

CENTRAL EAST JERUSALEM

JERUSALEM HOTEL

Nablus Rd.

KAN ZAMAN

ST. STEPHEN'S

ABO ALI

NABLUS RD. BUS STATION

GARDEN TOMB

ROCKEFELLER MUSEUM

Shmuel Ben Adaya

al-Muqadari

Ha-Nevi'im

NEW PALM HOTEL

SULEIMAN ST. BUS STATION

Suleiman St.

Ha-Nevi'im

SERVICE TAXIS TO RAMALLAH   TAXI
IKERMEWLI

ZEDEKIAH'S CAVE

HEROD'S GATE

Sha'ar Ha-Zahira

MUSLIM QUARTER

P

DAMASCUS GATE

SERVICE TAXIS TO HEBRON & BETHLEHEM   TAXI

Ha-Tzanhanim

al-Wad
Khan al-Zeit

OLD CITY

LION'S GATE

Bab Sitt Maryam

Via Dolorosa

CHRISTIAN QUARTER

NEW GATE

GOLDEN GATE

0   300 meters
0   300 yards

Jerusalem is more about the Bible than the brew. References to the Holy Book come in the form of names like **Abraham Hostel** (which will plan out a full Jerusalem experience for you) and sights like the **Stations of the Cross,** the **Temple Mount,** and the **Western Wall** (which are free to all visitors). If you're looking for a more debaucherous time, even the Holy City has a semi-wild West side. West Jerusalem has plenty of packed houses and GLBT-friendly bars. Check out a live show at **Uganda** or stop into **Toy Bar** to hobnob with the Israeli rich and gorgeous. But do go over to East Jerusalem for a foreign discount and big student crowd at **Gossip.** Not to mention the shawarma, fries and 0.5L beer deal—now that's a rumor worth spreading around.

orientation

Considering that whole civilizations have devoted their energies to claiming Jerusalem, it's a surprisingly small city. You will inevitably get lost trying to find your way around the **Old City,** but it's so densely packed that you will also (eventually) find your way again. The lack of street signs—and, even worse, the many names each street has acquired over the last few millennia—make this the hardest part of Jerusalem to navigate. Outside, everything has been built up in the last 100 years to follow a more logical grid. Jaffa Rd. and Ben-Yehuda St. are the main streets in **West Jerusalem,** while **East Jerusalem** is centered on Nablus Rd. and Salah ad-Din.

OLD CITY

In all of Israel, it is the Old City that best exhibits the different cultures and events that have molded the Holy Land into its present form. This is why visitors pass through the Old City walls, but it's also why they then spend days—years, some say—wandering around side streets begging passersby for directions. Most streets have multiple names, turn into a variety of streets, and run in all kinds of directions. Worse, the many different wars and territorial expansions that have ravaged this uneven square kilometer make the neighborhood's grid about as comprehensible as artifacts from the First Temple Period.

You should still try, of course, to find your way around, and *Let's Go* is here to help. There are two main gates, **Jaffa Gate** and **Damascus Gate,** each of which leads into the Old City's two busiest quarters: the **Christian Quarter** and the **Muslim Quarter** respectively. The Old City consists of these and two other quarters—a quieter and more spacious **Jewish Quarter** and a very small **Armenian Quarter**—which together serve as useful subdivisions of the Old City. To most residents, however, these names are hopelessly general. **Souq Khan az-Zait** and **al-Wad,** two of the area's main streets, both begin at Damascus Gate. **David Street,** which runs through the Christian and Jewish Quarters, is the thoroughfare immediately accessible from Jaffa Gate. If you hang right after Jaffa Gate, you wind up at **Armenian Orthodox Patriarchate Road**, the principal (perhaps only) street in the Armenian Quarter.

All right, now quit reading and get walking. You'll get lost, no matter how hard you try not to, but in that moment of sheer confusion you may just begin to understand the endlessly perplexing place around you.

WEST JERUSALEM

Sprawling across an area larger than the rest of Jerusalem put together, the western part of the city is big by any standard. Luckily, it rarely becomes a tangle of alleys like the Old City, and a number of major roads pass through, making it easily navigable. West Jerusalem is best approached as three main regions, each of which contain smaller, well-defined neighborhoods.

zion square

Sitting northwest of the Old City, Zion Sq. is the indisputable center of West Jerusalem. Running diagonally through it is **Jaffa Road,** the main thoroughfare that connects the Central Bus Station to Jaffa Gate and the Old City. Heading out of Zion Sq. is **Ben-Yehuda Street,** a packed pedestrian road filled with shops and food stalls. Heading southeast along Jaffa Rd. from Zion Sq., other popular streets are the parallel **Rivlin Street** and **Feingold Garden,** both of which are lined with restaurants and bars. Jaffa Rd. forks soon after it passes through the main square; the part that remains Jaffa Rd. runs along the Old City walls before it hits Jaffa Gate, while **Shlomtsiyon HaMalka** splits off to the south until it converges with five other streets in a large intersection marking the end of the Zion Sq. area.

eastern portion

South of the Zion Sq. area is the city's eastern portion, which encompasses the small neighborhoods of **Yemin Moshe, Mamilla,** and **Talbieh.** East of the large Shlomtsiyon Ha-Malka intersection is **Mamilla Avenue,** a pedestrian street that serves as the Israeli Fifth Ave., complete with designer boutiques. It heads east, eventually hitting Jaffa Gate. Heading away from the intersection are **Agron Street** and **King David Street.** Agron runs along Independence Park for about 1km until it reaches a junction with four other roads. A right here will take you onto **King George Street,** which in turn goes north, eventually intersecting with Jaffa Rd. just northwest of Zion Sq. King David St., on the other hand, runs south along the top of a valley to its east. This valley, bounded by Mamilla to the north and the Old City to its east, is home to **Yemin Moshe,** one of the first Jewish settlements outside of the Old City and the site of the Artists' Colony.

west jerusalem outskirts

Next to the foot of Yemin Moshe, King David St. meets a large crossroads which marks the end of the eastern area and the beginning of the southern half of West Jerusalem's outskirts—an area that encompasses many of the neighborhoods outside of Jerusalem, including **Mahane Yehuda, Mea She'arim, the German Colony, Ein Kerem,** and **Givat Ram.** Heading west from this junction is **Jabotinsky Street,** which borders the top of a rectangular residential neighborhood known as Talbieh. If you bear left instead and remain on King David St., you head south, past Talbieh. Going right at the two subsequent forks takes you onto **Emek Refa'im,** the main thoroughfare of the **German Colony,** which is a tranquil neighborhood packed with upscale cafes and restaurants. There's not much in this area that isn't on Emek Refa'im.

The outskirts also includes a portion of the city north of Zion Sq. Past the intersection of Jaffa Rd. and King George St. is **Davidka Square,** which marks the beginning of Mahane Yehuda. This neighborhood's main draw is its *shuk*, which is contained by Jaffa Rd. and the parallel **Agrippas Street.** The two major streets connecting those roads, **Mahane Yehuda Street** and **Etz Haim Street,** are home to most of the market. Past Mahane Yehuda along Jaffa Rd. is the **Central Bus Station,** and below it is Givat Ram, a large green area running the length of the city and containing the country's main political institutions. Finally, running east from Davidka Sq. is **HaNevi'im Street,** which reaches the Old City wall. Highly religious **Mea She'arim** is in this area as well.

EAST JERUSALEM

There are two major streets in East Jerusalem, **Nablus Road** and **Salah ad-Din.** Easy enough, right? They both begin at **Sultan Suleiman,** the street that encircles the edge of the Old City. Even on these main streets, not all buildings have numbers, which does makes life a little tougher, but fear not: **Central East Jerusalem,** the area closer to the Old City, is not that big, and it's hard to get lost for more than about 5min., unless, that is, you're particularly gifted. Once you get into **Sheikh Jarrah,** things may get a bit more complex. Keep Nablus Rd. as a compass; where it ends, Shimon HaTsadik (the restaurant row), is on the left, and most of the hotels, consulates, and health services are on the right on Har HaZeitim Rd. and where Nablus Rd. reappears. The **American Colony Hotel,** midway down Nablus, is a major landmark and is just a bit past the beginning of Sheikh Jarrah, though the unofficial line separating Sheikh Jarrah from the central part of East Jerusalem is blurry. Here, we've decided that Sheikh Jarrah begins with St. George's Church and the guesthouse attached to it. Now go forth and explore.

accommodations

Each neighborhood in Jerusalem has a distinct set of accommodations. In East Jerusalem, cheap (and dingy) hotels come by the plenty, and those who don't have the money to waste—or the stomach to rub knees with other guests in a shared dorm—will find themselves at home. At the same time, the **American Colony,** perhaps the most glamorous hotel in Jerusalem, is just off Nablus Rd., the main street in East Jerusalem. A haven for leftist Europeans and expats, it's a great place to empty your wallet and get in some prime people-watching.

Of course, some people want to hit up the actual sights. In the midst of the religious monuments of the Old City, you can find a wide variety of accommodations. The **Austrian Hospice,** the Old City's ritziest and prettiest option, is along the Stations of the Cross path, while the **Citadel Youth Hostel,** centrally located in a 750-year-old building near Jaffa Gate, is a lively student hub with a roof you can sleep on for only NIS45 a night. The neighborhood's nighttime curfew, though, can leave the Old City eerie at night, making West Jerusalem the best place to stay for nightlife and Jerusalem's cafe scene. However, most of the lodgings here are a little pricey, with only a few neighborhoods offering places for the truly budget-conscious to crash. To stay close to the action, you'll want to be in Zion Sq., home to a number of restaurants and bars—the hotels in the area may not leave you well-rested, but they certainly won't leave you bored. Though a bit secluded, **Abraham Hostel** in Davidka Sq. is quickly becoming one of the most talked about hostels in the Holy City.

OLD CITY

Rowdy from 6am to 4pm and a ghost town for the rest of the evening, the Old City is not the obvious pick for staying the night. But even if you find those religious places creepy at night (if Jesus rose from the dead there, what's to stop zombies from doing the same?), you'll still eventually realize that the Old City is perhaps the best place to stay in Jerusalem. Centrality and nighttime quiet come with every hotel, and you're almost always within a 15min. walk of the more modern city. This is especially true if you stay near the bustling Jaffa Gate in the Christian Quarter, the best neighborhood for hotels. Throw in the fact that you're sleeping in some of the most sacred territory in the world, and you realize that the Old City really can accommodate most of the diverse travelers who come here to find faith, themselves, or simply excellent falafel.

Although few of the establishments are five-star quality by, say, Gossip Girl standards, several offer large gardens with spectacular views and comfortable rooms for a price that may surpass usual Old City rates. For those less interested in chilling with the pious elderly—an inevitable consequence of staying at hospices and guesthouses—the **Citadel Youth Hostel** is unquestionably the premier spot in the Old City. Only NIS45 for a mattress on the roof is a sweet deal, and students crowd the weaving staircases and duplex dormitories that make up the hostel. From here, things can get even cheaper, but that is only for the truly brave—or truly Jewish, in the case of the free **Heritage House.**

stairway to heaven?

The **Chords Bridge** towers over Jerusalem's eastern skyline, right next to the Central Bus Station. This $73 million brainchild of the Spanish architect Santiago Calatrava was erected in 2008 to the cries of skeptical citizens and cheering politicians alike. The contentious steel support tower was the tallest addition to the city at a whopping 387 ft. and is supported by 66 cross-strung steel cables that light up at dusk. The distinctive structure has elicited a lot of theories about what it most closely resembles. Our favorites:

- **THE BREAST OF A LONG-NECKED BIRD:** Classy....we think.
- **A HUMAN ARM:** Reaching up to the heavens, or down to the underworld?
- **AN ARROW IN A TAUT BOW:** Let's just hope it doesn't snap.
- **A CLOTHESLINE:** This nickname was coined by unhappy locals at the bridge's opening ceremony. Hey, not everyone loves his skyline steel-clad.
- **DAVID'S HARP:** A tribute to the biblical king, this was the theory favored by then-mayor Uri Lupolianski.

muslim quarter

HEBRON YOUTH HOSTEL
HOSTEL $
8 Aqabat at-Takiya St.
☎02 628 1101

Above a serene cafe and inside a small honeycomb-colored archway, with the names of former travelers written on various stone octagons, sits the unimpeachably reasonable and well-located Hebron Youth Hostel. It costs no more than NIS35-50, depending on the season, to stay in a dorm, most of which have lots of space and a sufficient amount of natural light, though the mattresses are as thin and tough as cafeteria steak. Depending on your priorities, the fact that the hotel is sometimes run by two kids in their mid-teens will either be fun or discouraging.

⚑ *Walk down Souq Khan az-Zait from Damascus Gate for about 10 min.; Hebron Youth Hostel is on the right after you pass Aqabat at-Takiya St.* ⓘ *Free Wi-Fi in cafe.* ⓢ *Dorms NIS35-50; private rooms NIS180-200; 5-bed family rooms NIS250. Cash only.* ⌚ *Reception daily 7am-1am.*

AL HASHIMI HOTEL AND HOSTEL
HOTEL $$
73 Souq Khan az-Zait
☎02 628 4410; www.alhashimihotel-jerusalem.com

While its design is fairly corporate for a 400-year-old building, and its prices are above average, Hashimi is the most comfortable hotel in the Muslim Quarter. The roof, with large shaded sections and cutesy tree-trunk tables, affords an excellent view of the Muslim Quarter. Every room has a TV, air-conditioning, and ensuite bathroom, and one triple even has its own kitchen. A variety of services, including laundry and free coffee and tea, makes it much more manageable to be staying in an area that shuts down by sunset. The Saleh family brothers who own and operate the hotel are always around to chat with guests.

 # From Damascus Gate, walk about 5min. down Souq Khan az-Zait. It is on the left just past Al-Arab Hotel. i Consumption of alcohol is not permitted in the hotel, and unmarried couples cannot sleep in the same room. Laundry NIS50 per load. Computer NIS15 per hour. Free Wi-Fi in rooms. Tours of Jerusalem offered by the hotel. [S] Single-sex dorms US$30, with breakfast US$35; doubles US$120; triples US$150. Those not staying in a dorm get breakfast free. Prices subject to change during high season. Cash only. ⏰ Reception 24hr.

GOLDEN GATE INN — HOTEL $

10 Souq Khan az-Zait — ☎02 628 4317; www.goldengate4.com

Though not still in its glory days, this 850-year-old hostel is worth a stay. While some rooms have a strange and somewhat see-through plastic-encased bathroom that doesn't seem like it was designed to be its own room, all bathrooms are at least appropriately sized, and most rooms have them with proper doors. If catching eyes with your new best friend while you're on the toilet isn't really your style, there is a small sitting area outside that looks onto the *souq*, and the well-equipped kitchen is also a communal gathering space. The brown-and-pink design may not be the most appealing choice for non-tweens, but everything is usually extremely clean.

 # From Damascus Gate, the hotel is on Souq Khan az-Zait after the intersection with Aqabat al-Batiq. i Free Wi-Fi in lobby. Breakfast included. Single-sex dorms unless hotel is full or there are special requests. [S] High-season dorms NIS80; singles NIS200; doubles NIS300. Low-season dorms NIS70; singles NIS150; doubles NIS250. Cash only. ⏰ Open 24hr.

AL-ARAB YOUTH HOSTEL — HOSTEL $

Souq Khan az-Zait — ☎02 628 3537; al_arab@netvision.net.il

It is impossible to get more quintessentially budget than Al-Arab. With dorm beds priced at an unbeatable NIS40, it barely matters that none of the staffers speak English and that, when *Let's Go* visited, the only apparent guests were a French couple who had wandered in off the street. The old building is clean and has some attractive touches, like a traditional Arabic design on the floor of the common space and well-trodden stone in the dormitory. There is a small kitchen on the roof, but only one, albeit large, shower. Single rooms do not necessarily have windows, but you get what you pay for.

 # From Damascus Gate, walk 5min. down Souq Khan az-Zait. Right before Al Hashimi. [S] Dorms NIS40, singles NIS60. ⏰ Reception morning-midnight.

armenian quarter

CHRIST CHURCH GUESTHOUSE — GUESTHOUSE $$$

Jaffa Gate — ☎02 627 7727; www.cmj-israel.org

A stately retreat open to everyone, though geared mainly toward religious officials and pilgrims, the Christ Church Guesthouse is one of the most peaceful hotels in the Old City. Guests get breakfast free in the hotel's cafe and may eat their food in a tranquil outdoor garden. Rooms are appointed in traditional Ottoman style (read: red and gold...lots of red and gold) with large, comfortable beds and classy wooden floors. Students might not appreciate that most of the guests are aging, serene religious folk, but if you're looking for an escape from the bustle of the city, this guesthouse is the place to be—there's even a prayer garden available, on request, for reflection, study, and prayer.

 # From Jaffa Gate, it is on the way to Armenian Orthodox Patriarchate Rd. near the Tower of David bridge. i Free Wi-Fi in some rooms. [S] Singles NIS295; doubles NIS465; suites NIS525. Prices subject to change during high season. ⏰ Reception 7am-7pm, but flexible.

EAST NEW IMPERIAL HOTEL HOTEL $$

Greek Orthodox Patriarchate Rd. ☎02 628 2261; www.newimperial.com

The upstairs living room says it all: a large Swedish flag hangs near two reproductions of the Mona Lisa side-by-side and above a 12 ft. long Syrian couch (or is it a throne?). You wouldn't be surprised to see Professor Trelawney at the concierge desk of this antiquated hotel, with its photographs of bygone religious officials and other bizarre decorations and shrines that take over the building. Unfortunately, the quality of the decor outpaces that of the rooms: in one, a garish tiger rug clashes with white floors, the view is of wires and the back of another building, and a small TV is oddly perched on top of a bureau. Throw in the childish fish designs on the shower floor, and you feel like you're in the room of a sad 14-year-old whose parents don't understand him. Another room, however, has two levels, more cohesive decorations, and a small bar area. Really, the only guarantee at the East New Imperial Hotel is that you'll never think it's lacking in character. The Swedish flag, for example, commemorates writer Selma Lagerlôf's stay in the hotel, where she wrote some of the manuscripts that would later make her the first woman to win the Nobel Prize for Literature in 1909.

⇟ Inside Jaffa Gate, the hotel is at the end of the 2nd street to the left. ℹ Free Wi-Fi available. [S] Singles US$70; doubles US$100; triples US$140. Cash only. ⏰ Open 24hr.

JAFFA GATE HOSTEL HOSTEL $

Jaffa Gate ☎02 627 6402; www.jaffa-gate.hostel.com

Though there is a nice foyer with a TV, the rest of Jaffa Gate Hostel is a bit depressing. It is sometimes empty during the low season, the ceiling is a tad low, and the color composition of the decor ranges from muted to faded. However, the staff is kind and helpful, and even during the high season, rooms can sometimes be booked up to two weeks in advance.

⇟ When you enter the Old City from Jaffa Gate, walk toward David St., but instead of taking it, make a right. Continue walking to the next street over and follow signs. ℹ Small kitchen. Free luggage storage, fans, and heaters. Free Wi-Fi on 1st floor only. Max. 1-week stay. [S] Dorms NIS65; private rooms NIS120-150. Prices negotiable in groups of 3-4 or more and when the hotel is fairly empty. ⏰ Reception in high season 8am-10pm; in low season 9am-9pm. Guests provided with key.

jewish quarter

HERITAGE HOUSE HOSTEL $

Women's Hostel at 7 HaMalakh St., Men's Hostel at 2 Or HaHayim St.; Office at 90 Habad St.
☎Men's 02 627 2224, Women's 02 628 1820; www.heritage.org.il

For those who like to milk that vaguely Jewish background for all it's worth, Heritage House is an opportunity to use your hypothetical religious roots to their fullest. You must apply for lodgings, but, if you're accepted, you score a stay that includes a free bed and connections to local Jewish families for meals—especially on Shabbat—as well as the intimate community of a house and its common spaces. Don't relax too much, however: maximum lengths of stay are determined by how long you are having a productive experience exploring Jerusalem and your own Jewish identity. Basically, think of the Heritage House as your Jewish mother away from home, with a little less pressure to take care of it in its old age.

⇟ Walking on Habad toward Zion Gate past Hurva Sq., take a left at HaMalakh and continue until the next left to the Women's Hostel. With your back to the Women's Hostel, go right, take the first left, and then turn right again to arrive at the Men's Hostel. ℹ Must be Jewish and from a fairly secular background. Some applications are turned down, and reservations are tentative until completion of in-person interview. Free Wi-Fi. [S] Free. ⏰ Check-in Su-Th 8am-9am and 5pm-midnight, F-Sa 8am-9am. Afternoon and night check-in times differ each week. Curfew midnight.

EL MALAK HOSTEL $$

18 HaMalakh St. ☎02 628 5362

El Malak is a clean, orderly, and dark lair under the apartment of last year's winner of the Israeli National Sweetest Lady Championship in the over-60 category. After newcomers have rung the bird-chirp doorbell, Claire Ghawi dangles a key out the window with a string to let them in. She makes one of her sons clean her basement-turned-hostel and change the sheets of each bed daily while she lies in bed watching TV (back problems, she says) and gossiping. The rooms that do not get natural light are on the sadder side, the place can be completely empty during low season, and the price is noticeably higher than that of other, more cheerful hostels, but Claire is really fun.

🚶 With your back to the Women's Hostel of the Heritage House, El Malak is the beige door to your left with black angels painted on it. ℹ Kitchen available 24hr. Some Fridays, the place is rented out by a school whose students enjoy Claire's cooking and spend the night at El Malak. $ Adults NIS100, students NIS75. Cash only. ⏰ Doors open 24hr.

DR. BACHI'S GUESTHOUSE GUESTHOUSE $$$$

11 Misgav Ladach St. ☎02 628 6668; www.jerusalemguesthouse.com

Highly overpriced for what it offers, Dr. Bachi's Guesthouse is nonetheless a beautiful place to stay. Rooms are flooded with natural light and have great views of the Old City, which only get better with the two patios and access to the roof. One room has its own entrance and exit, but most mean living alongside the very sweet Dr. Bachi.

🚶 Walk on Bab al-Silsila toward the Dome of the Rock and take a right on Misgav Ladach St. Buzz to get into Dr. Bachi's, which is on the left. ℹ Guests get their own key to enter and exit. $ Single person NIS450-500, but prices may be negotiable. Family NIS600. Cash only. ⏰ Open 24hr.

christian quarter

👍 **CITADEL YOUTH HOSTEL** HOSTEL $

20 St. Mark's Rd. ☎02 628 4494; citadelhostel@mail.com

A heavily bearded 20-something in a white cloth onesie is on the roof playing a guitar, staring at the most beautiful view of the Old City imaginable, high enough up that the city—kneeling nuns, haggling shopkeepers, and all—is clear from his perch. For years he has paid NIS40 a night to sleep on this canopy at the Citadel Youth Hostel, but the allure of this hostel has not been confined to the roof: in the kitchen, a fully veiled teen is baking brownies; between the corridors and staircases of the 750-year-old building's many levels, students and backpackers brush past each other, exchanging hellos and joking with the manager; and someone who just wants some privacy is kicking back in the common room watching TV. With reasonable prices, an almost comically upbeat atmosphere, and a location on simultaneously peaceful and central St. Mark's Rd., Citadel Youth Hostel is where heaven-bound backpackers go after they die.

🚶 After entering David St. from Jaffa Gate, take first right onto St. Mark's Rd. ℹ 2-week max. stay, but they tend to be flexible. No air-conditioning, but fans are free. Heaters NIS10 per night. Lockers available for a fee. Free luggage storage. Free Wi-Fi in the 2 common areas, and a computer available. $ Rooftop single night NIS45; multiple nights NIS40. Dorms single night NIS65; multiple nights NIS60. Singles from NIS140, depending on size of room, privacy of bathroom, and presence of window. Cash only. ⏰ Doors open 24hr.

👍 **AUSTRIAN HOSPICE** HOSPICE $$

37 Via Dolorosa ☎02 626 5800; www.austrianhospice.com

In a large and beautiful building at the intersection of major Old City avenues al-Wad and the Via Dolorosa, the Austrian Hospice has a garden on its second level and a Viennese cafe on the roof that serves a famous apple strudel. Though the staff may not be supremely friendly, and the hospice is officially for pilgrims, the place generally attracts older guests from a variety of different backgrounds to stay in its spacious dorms (NIS110). Those with larger wallets may reserve classy tile-floor singles (NIS313), which have large comfortable beds and views of the garden and the street below. While it might be surprising that a place with these rates does not accept credit cards, Israeli shekels, US dollars, and euros are all fair game.

✱ *At intersection of al-Wad Rd. and the Via Dolorosa.* i *Some rooms air-conditioned. Reservations may be needed as much as a year in advance for high season and a few months in advance for low season. Walk-ins charged small fee. Substantial breakfast buffet included.* Ⓢ *Dorms (single-sex) NIS110; singles NIS313; doubles NIS522; triples NIS678 per person. For longer stays, it is possible to work in exchange for room and board; see website for details. Cash only.* ⚑ *Reception 7am-10pm, but guests can enter at all times with a key.*

LUTHERAN GUESTHOUSE
GUESTHOUSE $$$

St. Mark's Rd. ☎02 626 6888; www.luth-guesthouse-jerusalem.com

One of the most beautiful hotels in the Old City, the Lutheran Guesthouse has a gorgeous outdoor garden containing a small cafe. Guests sip lattes (NIS12) and glasses of wine (NIS20) from little tables near the central garden fountain or on benches looking over the Old City. Rooms are cozy with comfortable beds, usefully sized desks, and a good deal of natural light. Although the crowd isn't as explicitly religious as other guesthouses where Jesus is their main homeboy, don't expect to meet many wanderlustful backpackers or hip night owls here.

✱ *Coming from Jaffa Gate, enter David St. and take a right on St. Mark's Rd. The Lutheran Guesthouse is about 1min. walk down St. Mark's on the left.* i *Upstairs rooms have better views and cost the same. Breakfast included. Free Wi-Fi in some rooms.* Ⓢ *Singles NIS284; doubles NIS466.* ⚑ *Open 24hr.*

PETRA HOSTEL
HOSTEL $

Jaffa Gate ☎02 628 6618; www.newpetrahostel.com

The dorm rooms here have the benefit of a small desk, a standing-room-only terrace, and air-conditioning. Though the bathrooms are windowless, there is enough space to take a comfortable shower. There is a small kitchen that is open from 8am to 9pm, as well as roof access.

✱ *To the left on David St. after entering Jaffa Gate* i *Bring a sleep sack or sleeping bag. To guarantee a room, reserve 2-3 weeks in advance. Lockers are free.* Ⓢ *Dorms NIS70; singles NIS180; doubles NIS250.* ⚑ *Open 24hr.*

outskirts of old city

▨ ST. ANDREW'S GUESTHOUSE
GUESTHOUSE $$$

1 David Remez St. ☎02 673 2401 ; www.scotsguesthouse.com

Like most Israeli hotels set up by Western European Christians, St. Andrew's Guesthouse (known to friends as "The Scottie") is prim, pretty, and reasonable. A garden overlooking the Old City and parts of West Jerusalem has a few tables and umbrellas, though the old-fashioned indoor sitting rooms may be more comfortable. A long driveway separates St. Andrew's from its urban surroundings. As long as you're shelling out over US$100 for a room, go ahead and pay the extra US$10 for a view: this usually means that you'll get a terrace, which is unquestionably worth it.

✱ *Coming from Lavan, cross the footbridge and walk uphill. St. Andrew's is on the left.* i *Breakfast included. Free Wi-Fi in rooms. Free parking. Call to ask about the 2-bedroom apartment available for families.* Ⓢ *High-season singles US$115, with a view US$125; doubles US$150/165. Low-season singles US$105, with a view US$115; doubles US$140/150.* ⚑ *Open 24hr.*

MT. ZION HOTEL
HOTEL $$$$

17 Hebron Rd. ☎02 568 9555; www.mountzion.co.il

Outside the *hamam* (steam bath), a couple canoodles lazily, covered in intersecting towels as they doze in a sated haze. Near them, there is a hot tub, pool, gym, and small massage room. This is Mt. Zion Hotel, a gorgeous six-story marble slab of a hotel on an avenue with an overpriced corporate accommodation every 15 ft. Mt. Zion may be the best of this bunch: not only is it the least far uphill (clearly an important consideration), but it also includes a coffee shop, bar, restaurant, and rooms with beds so comfortable that they could probably solve the whole Middle East peace process. That the entrance to the first-floor garden is almost definitely artificially scented represents the tackier side of this equation, and don't be looking to run into many fellow *Let's Go* readers here. This stay is strictly for those looking to be pampered after a bit of Israeli rough and tumble.

✇ *Coming from the restaurant Lavan, take a left once you reach the street above the Cinematheque and keep walking uphill. After about 5min., Mt. Zion Hotel is on the left.* ℹ *Breakfast included. Pool, spa, and hamam also included.* ⓢ *Singles US$240; doubles US$267.* ⌚ *Open 24hr.*

WEST JERSUALEM

The Old City may be what you came for, but the "character" (read: grime, cramped spaces, and funky smell) that comes with it is not for everyone, especially when it comes to spending the night. For something a bit cleaner—and more familiar—you can't go wrong with West Jerusalem, where the slightly more upscale lodgings are rarely more than a 15min. walk from the Old City. Accommodations are generally distributed over two main areas, one centered on **King David Street** and the other on **Zion Square.** The former might see you scrabbling for extra change, but the latter has a good selection of cheaper beds. On the border of the Zion Sq. region and Mahane Yehuda, it has swiftly become the most popular hostel in Jerusalem for good reason.

zion square

▨ JERUSALEM HOSTEL   HOSTEL $$
44 Jaffa Rd.   ☎02 623 6102; www.jerusalem-hostel.com

Jerusalem Hostel's location simply can't be beat—smack dab in the middle of the square, the hostel guarantees that you're no more than a 20min. walk from most other places in the city. This means that it can get a little loud on weekends, but that's all part of the fun. The hostel itself is centered on a magnificent spiral staircase, and the staff is happy to dish out tips on the area (or let you pet the family pug). The rooftop terrace, made lounge-worthy with scattered mattresses, offers great views of the bustling square.

✇ *On the northern side of Zion Sq.* ℹ *A/C and ensuite bathroom. Free Wi-Fi.* ⓢ *Dorms NIS80; singles NIS230-310; doubles NIS250-340.*

HOTEL NOGA   HOTEL $$
4 Bezalel St.   ☎02 625 4590; http://hotelnoga.com

Noga may be removed from Zion Sq. proper, but it's still only a few minutes from the hubbub of Ben-Yehuda St. The simple rooms are clean and entirely habitable. A small rooftop terrace provides a refreshing—though somewhat obstructed—view of the city.

✇ *Follow Ben-Yehuda St. away from Zion Sq. and turn left onto Shmu'el HaNagid. Walk about 100m, and turn right onto Bezalel St.* ℹ *Min. 2 night stay.* ⓢ *Singles NIS150; doubles NIS210.*

KAPLAN HOTEL   HOTEL $$$
1 Havazelet St.   ☎02 625 4591

The building may look a little dilapidated from the outside, but a quick climb up the faded staircase will take you to the cordial owner, pastel yellow and blue walls, and rooms that run the elbow-room gamut from tiny to spacious.

✇ *Turn north off Jaffa Rd., 1 block east of Zion Sq.* ℹ *A/C, TV, and ensuite bathroom. Free Wi-Fi.* ⓢ *Singles NIS150-250; doubles NIS260-280.*

ZION HOTEL   HOTEL $$$
10 Rishonim Ave.   ☎02 623 2367; www.hotelzion.com

A full-fledged hotel perched above a lively cafe just off Ben-Yehuda St., Zion has a lot going for it. If your pocket can take the plunge, you'll get to enjoy the multitude of nearby restaurants and shops, regal red carpets, spotless rooms, and great views of the bustling area. Unfortunately, said bustle can continue late into the night, courtesy of raucous Birthrighters and local barhoppers, so don't expect an early bedtime on weekends unless you have some earplugs handy.

Off Ben-Yehuda St., above the Rimon restaurant. i A/C, TV, and ensuite bathroom. Free Wi-Fi. $ Singles NIS250, with breakfast NIS280; doubles NIS300/340. Cash only.

JERUSALEM INN HOTEL
HOTEL $$$

7 Horkanos St. ☎02 625 2757

The most high-end of the lodgings listed here, the Jerusalem Inn has got your back when the thought of another cramped hostel makes you shudder. The elegance of the glass-walled reception is only matched by the capacious, carpeted rooms. But the best perk is the location—only a block from Zion Sq., the quieter scene gives you all the advantages of the city without the drag of loud, drunk patrons come nightfall.

From Jaffa Rd., turn onto Heleni HaMalka St., then take the 2nd left. Jerusalem Inn is 50m down on the left. i A/C, TV, safe, and ensuite bathroom. Free Wi-Fi and computers available. $ High-season singles US$125; doubles US$156; triples $185. Low-season US$6 less.

birthwrong?

Taglit-Birthright's free, 10-day trip to Israel for young Jews is enough to have some crossing their fingers that great-aunt Hilda's marriage to Morris Goldstein will be enough to score them a place. (In fact, at least one of your parents must be Jewish in order for you to be eligible.) But the program isn't all about candids and camels, and Birthright has been criticized by some for advocating a clearly biased position on the Palestinian-Israeli conflict.

It was in response to this perceived propaganda that **Birthright Unplugged** was created. This option may not be free, but it attempts to present a less one-sided view of the conflict. During the six- to 10-day trips, participants of all ages travel through West Bank cities, villages, and refugee camps, speaking both to Palestinians and Israeli Jews. While, in its own way, Birthright Unplugged might be just as biased as its more famous counterpart, it's still an interesting choice for those who like their whirlwind tours political.

eastern portion

AGRON GUEST HOUSE
HOSTEL $$

6 Agron St. ☎02 594 5522; agron@iyha.org.il

A member of the Israel Youth Hostel Association, Agron has features similar to its cousins across Israel: a big building, clean and non-descript rooms, and a focus on groups. However, it does have a more historical building next door, which provides a better space for those hoping for some character. The hostel is across the street from the large Independence Park should you feel the need for an impromptu picnic or sunbathing session.

On the western end of the street, near the intersection with Keren Hayesod St. i Breakfast included. TV and ensuite bathroom. A/C in most rooms. Free Wi-Fi in lobby, ethernet connection in older rooms (bring a cable). $ Dorms NIS118; singles NIS276; doubles NIS388. ⏰ Reception Su-Th 7am-11pm, F 7am-sunset, Sa sunset-11pm.

BEIT SHMUEL GUEST HOUSE
HOTEL $$$$

6 Eliyahu Shama St. ☎02 620 3445; www.beitshmuel.co.il

Sequestered in the quiet part of town bordering Yemin Moshe, Beit Shmuel is centered on an appropriately serene courtyard covered in greenery, and many of the modern, airy rooms sport views of the Old City across the valley. Peace and quiet ain't cheap round these parts, so you'll need to fork it over in order to join the mostly middle-aged clientele.

*Walk south down King David St. and take the left directly after the David Citadel Hotel. Beit Shmuel is just after the bend on the right. **i** Breakfast included. A/C, TV, and ensuite bathroom. Free Wi-Fi. $ High-season singles US$115; doubles US$135. Low-season singles US$100; doubles US$120. Additional bed US$30 per person.*

ROSARY CONVENT HOTEL — HOSTEL $$$

14 Agron St. — ☎02 622 2087

No, we aren't trying to trick you into becoming a nun—though Rosary Convent Hotel is tacked onto a Catholic church, should the (Holy) spirit move you in that direction. The magnificently domed church, which holds a Sunday mass, makes this reasonably large hostel a hotspot for groups of pilgrims, although such sinful activities as drinking, smoking, and being of a different religion are still allowed on the premises. The rooms themselves are sizable affairs with high ceilings, thick mattresses, and the odd painting of Madonna—the virgin one, not the one with the scary arms.

*About 400m from the intersection with King David St. **i** Ensuite bathroom. Kitchen access. Free Wi-Fi. $ Singles NIS250; doubles NIS400. Cash only.*

YMCA THREE ARCHES HOTEL — HOTEL $$$$

26 King David St. — ☎02 569 2692; www.ymca3arch.co.il

It makes sense that the YMCA would be high quality in the birthplace of the C. The Three Arches is nothing like the ratty place where your mom does water aerobics—this YMCA is downright palatial, with a grand central tower flanked by two massive domes (yes, from above it probably looks like a giant dick). Designed by the same architect who did the Empire State Building, it's got grandeur in spades, with a mosaic-clad interior and sprawling lawns. The rooms are equally luxurious—admittedly, more often home to diplomats than grimy backpackers like you—but if you can spare eating for a few days, it's probably worth it. After all, there's a pool. And you can always just load up at the breakfast buffet, right? If scrounging for scraps isn't your style, still drop by and climb the 152 ft. tower for one of the best views of the Old City.

*On King David St. **i** Breakfast included. A/C, TV, and ensuite bathroom. Free Wi-Fi in lobby; in rooms US$7 per hr., US$15 per day. $ Singles US$150; doubles US$164. ⏰ Tower open daily 7am-11pm.*

BEIT GESHER GUEST HOUSE — HOSTEL $$$

10 King David St. — ☎02 622 8070

A labyrinth of clean dorms, Beit Gesher is used more by groups than by staggeringly attractive backpackers like you. The hostel itself is actually part of the same-named institute that occupies the entire building, which also houses a synagogue and classrooms for seminars about Israeli and Jewish life. The complex is tucked away on King David St., but, as of July 2011, a luxury Waldorf is rising at the mammoth construction site next door, so don't expect a lazy, Sunday morning lie-in.

*Walk south on King David St. past the intersection with Agron St., then make the next right. The road begins forking back in the opposite direction, and the hostel is on the left. Enter through the door up the steps just before the alley turns left. **i** Breakfast included for groups. A/C and ensuite bathroom. $ Singles Su-Th NIS220, F NIS250, Sa NIS220; doubles NIS280/300.*

west jerusalem outskirts

ABRAHAM HOSTEL — HOSTEL $

67 HaNevi'im St. — ☎02 650 2200; www.abraham-hostel-jerusalem.com

The biblical Abraham was apparently the first backpacker around (all that desert camping), and this eponymous hostel has set out to provide the ultimate experience for the independent wanderer. Abraham Hostel was only a few months old as of July 2011, but it's already making waves, pretty much doubling the number of dorm beds in West Jerusalem and quickly becoming the city's premier hostel. Not only are the rooms large, spotless, and cheap, but Abraham is also more than a place to sleep. A huge common area complete with a bar, a kitchen, a pool table, and hammocks and beanbags sits at the hostel's heart, and groups of 20-somethings hang out here around the clock. The space also hosts regular events, including lectures on language and culture, happy hours, Shabbat dinner, film screenings, and a very popular open-mic night. The phenomenally attentive staff are well-versed in the neighborhood and eager to dole out tips or go one step further and take you out themselves.

Indie Travelers, an agency geared specifically toward backpackers, has set up shop in the lobby and runs inexpensive excursions to the Dead Sea, Jordan, and various spots around the country. Larger and even more ambitious works are still in the pipeline for Abraham, and we could spend a great deal longer yammering about the hostel—or just tell you to spend a few nights, and the place will sell itself.

Right off Davidka Sq. by the intersection with Jaffa Rd. i A/C and ensuite bathrooms. Weekly pub crawls and daily Old City tours. $ Dorms from NIS65; singles from NIS240; doubles from NIS270.

EAST JERUSALEM

The famous hotel might be called the "American Colony," but don't let that fool you—aside from a tiny group of settlers and expats, East Jerusalem has been fully Palestinian since it became almost completely autonomous in 1967. Some Jews have never even been inside East Jerusalem and cannot understand why someone would want to go. While they may be missing out on the warm interactions possible with shopkeepers and civilians, their reluctance is understandable, considering that the neighborhood can be unsafe for the visibly Jewish and, particularly, for men in *kippot.*

Although at night it can be similarly dangerous for tourists, some of the fanciest hotels are in East Jerusalem, including the aforementioned **American Colony Hotel,** one of the most famous in Jerusalem and a hub for expats. Unfortunately, it's hard to find quality accommodations that aren't ridiculously expensive: unless you want to really splurge for marble halls and beds more comfortable than your mother's shoulder, you're going to end up in a cheap place long on character but short on comfort, such as the **New Palm Hostel.** For nice cheap or mid-range options, it's best to look for lodgings elsewhere in the city.

central east jerusalem

NEW PALM HOSTEL/NEW PALM HOTEL/FAISAL HOSTEL HOTEL $

6 HaNevi'im St. ☎02 627 3189; newpalmhotel@gmail.com

Walk through an indoor fruit and vegetable stand identical to half a dozen others on the same block and climb up a nondescript staircase to find yourself at a single hotel that boasts three different names and 300 beds. The singles and doubles may be beige, undecorated, and often windowless; the bathrooms sometimes consist solely of a toilet and a daunting square foot of tile that, along with a drooping shower head, makes for an acrobatic bathing experience. Nonetheless this triple-titled flophouse is still the best deal in East Jerusalem. Its prices (NIS50 for a bed in a dorm) are unmatched in the neighborhood, and coffee, tea, and breakfast from the hotel's cafe come free. As of most recent research, its owner, Alex, also plans to open a rooftop hookah bar and restaurant in the summer of 2011.

Midway down HaNevi'im St. on the way to the Old City walls i A/C in singles and doubles but not in dorms. 2 computers available. Free Wi-Fi in the rooms. $ Dorms NIS50; singles NIS140; doubles NIS200. Prices subject to moderate change during high season. Students receive a 10-15% discount. ⏰ Doors open 24hr.

JERUSALEM HOTEL HOTEL $$$$

12 Nablus Rd. ☎02 628 3282 or +1-800-657-9401; www.jrshotel.com

The Jerusalem Hotel has all the luxurious peace of the 19th-century palace it was designed to resemble. Its high-ceilinged rooms are made from classic gray Jerusalem stone, which helps keep rooms cool in the thick heat of summertime. The medieval elegance of this stone contrasts with the handsomely carved wooden bureau and large desk in each room. These antique adornments sit beside flatscreen TVs, Wi-Fi connections, and two separate phone lines. Best of all may be the complimentary breakfast in the adjoining Kan Zaman restaurant, whose vine trestle roof and view of Nablus make for a great summer dining experience. Slightly less exciting is the unfortunately steep price of this high-class establishment.

⛿ Across the street from the Nablus bus station; take a left off Nablus Rd. for entrance on Antara Ben-Shadad St. **i** *Reservations up to 2-3 months in advance may be needed during the high season. Free Wi-Fi.* $ *High-season singles US$160; doubles US$220. Low-season singles US$120; doubles US$160. 10% discount for large groups.* ⏰ *Gates close at 1:30am. Building open 24hr.*

AZZAHRA HOTEL HOTEL $$

13 Azzahra St. ☎02 628 2447; www.azzahrahotel.com

Hidden on a nondescript side street off Salah ad-Din, Azzahra Hotel is a cheerful and spacious world unto itself. Away from the din of the main drag, Azzahra has a broad marble lobby that opens into a large and bright dining room where guests receive a 10% discount on lunch and dinner and get breakfast free. Rooms have big windows that cast a full glow of natural light, and some afford views of the manic scramble of East Jerusalem.

⛿ Coming from the Old City, take the right off Salah ad-Din just before the Archaeological School and the Ministry of Justice. Azzahra is a small side street, and the hotel is halfway down it. **i** *Ask for a room with a balcony; they are the same price and have much better views. Reservations should be made 1-2 months in advance during high season.* $ *High-season singles $110; doubles $160; triples $210. Low-season singles $85; doubles $135; triples $150. Otherwise, singles $95; doubles $145; triples $180.* ⏰ *Doors open 24hr.*

sheikh jarrah

THE AMERICAN COLONY HOTEL HOTEL $$$$

1 Louis Vincent St. ☎02 627 9777; www.americancolony.com

Probably the single classiest joint in Jerusalem, the American Colony is home to regular book readings, a gourmet (yet cozy) garden restaurant, a large pool and well-equipped sauna, and, sometimes, Tony Blair. The rooms are large and cheery, especially if you spring for a "Superior Room" (US$380). The price may imply gaudy, but the room is simple and perfect, with pretty yellow and blue decorations, a wide terrace, and a small sitting area. The American Colony prides itself on being more than just a place to stay, and the shops in the courtyard—including a famous bookstore that foreign correspondents say is the place to go for books on the Middle East—help make the hotel a prominent hangout for sophisticated expats. Even if you can't afford a room, make time in your schedule to stop by for a tasty and overpriced drink.

⛿ Walk up Nablus Rd. from Damascus Gate for 5-10min. After 2 intersections, the American Colony is on the right. **i** *Breakfast included. Pool, sauna, business center, and fitness center included. Free Wi-Fi in rooms. Massage US$80.* $ *High-season singles from US$235; doubles from US$315. Low-season singles from US$215; doubles from US$275.* ⏰ *Open 24hr.*

ST. GEORGE'S PILGRIM GUESTHOUSE GUESTHOUSE $$$

20 Nablus Rd. ☎02 628 3302; stgeorges.gh@j-diocese.org

The rooms may be a little dark and lack good views, but an ample garden and quiet grounds make this guesthouse one of the best lodgings in East Jerusalem that you can stay in for under NIS400 a night. Sip a drink while reading in the shade of the garden courtyard near St. George's Cathedral and enjoy the fact that, other than the rooms, this hotel is bright and pleasant.

After crossing Na'omi Kiss on Nablus Rd., the guesthouse and the cathedral to which it is connected are on the left. *i* *Breakfast included.* $ *Singles US$110; doubles US$150; triples US$190.* ⏰ *Open 24hr.*

AMBASSADOR HOTEL HOTEL $$$$

56 Nablus Rd. ☎02 541 2222; www.jerusalemambassador.com

On a tier between St. George's and the American Colony, the Ambassador Hotel is pricey and pleasant, with an outdoor tent for summer dining, a cafe in the lobby, and a terrace in nearly every room with views over the sprawl of Sheikh Jarrah. Don't let the brown carpet in some singles get you down; snuggle in one of the gigantic beds at night and just sit on the terrace while you're awake.

Walk uphill on Nablus Rd. until it forks and going up any farther would lead to a dead end, and then take a right. After passing Mount Scopus Hotel, take the next left to backtrack and walk uphill. The Ambassador Hotel is on the right. *i* *Breakfast included. Free Wi-Fi in rooms.* $ *High-season singles US$180; doubles US$200. Low-season singles US$160; doubles US$180.* ⏰ *Open 24hr.*

MOUNT SCOPUS HOTEL HOTEL $$$

10 Sheikh Jarrah St. ☎02 582 8891; www.mtscopus.com

Most rooms have a desk, small terrace, tiny sitting area, and two beds whose gaudily patterned covers clash strangely with the funky 1970s-style carpet. Although this room probably resembles the bedroom of your friend's tasteless bachelor pad (yes, *that* friend), Mount Scopus is cheaper than a lot of the competition and is thoroughly clean. Though the staff don't speak English very well—or at all—they will at least be nice and make an effort.

Walk uphill on Nablus Rd. until it is about to dead-end, then take a right and walk until you reach Mount Scopus (there will be a big sign). *i* *Breakfast included. Free Wi-Fi in lobby.* $ *Singles US$90; doubles US$120; triples US$180.* ⏰ *Open 24hr.*

sights

Jerusalem's sights come in two chief varieties, the religious and the archaeological, and share a common significance: they are way old. The **Church of the Holy Sepulchre** claims to be the site of the Crucifixion, and the holy walk to reach it (the Stations of the Cross) has been performed since the 15th century. The **Temple Mount,** which has been religiously important pretty much since opposable thumbs became hip, hides such archaeological treasures as the Ark of the Covenant, according to some. Unlike dusty European cathedrals, these significant stones have managed to remain highly relevant. Sights like the **City of David** are vastly controversial today both in their treatment of present residents and in the stories they construct of the past. It's in part a reflection on how history works here—if people treat the wars of the 20th century like they occurred in the last hour, then the events of 2000 years ago were only yesterday.

OLD CITY

The pun is almost too obvious: when it comes to sights, the Old City, well, rocks. In the **Church of All Nations,** the Rock of Agony marks the spot where Jesus prayed to the point of sweating blood. At the **Western Wall,** the underground bottom layer, site of the oldest rocks, is the point of greatest significance. The Dome of the Rock contains the stone from which Muslims believe Muhammad rose to heaven and at which God supposedly convinced Abraham to nearly sacrifice his son. Today, housewives drape drying clothes on ancient Mamluk rocks in the Muslim Quarter, tourists and soldiers amble about the reconstructed rocks of the Jewish Quarter, and pilgrims furiously rub the rock slab inside the **Church of the Holy Sepulchre.** But while the presence of ancient history—and God—may be, well, boulder here than anywhere else in the world, the Old City has also changed enormously from its original form, and markets sell more cell phone chargers than spices or religious icons. Snow globes aside, though, the Old City is still built from the very rocks whose meanings have been invented, debated, stolen, faked, and fought over for thousands of years, making its very existence a landmark in itself. Wherever you walk, you're looking at human history.

muslim quarter

Perhaps the most fun section of the Old City, the Muslim Quarter has both the best food and the most vibrant local life. Souq Khan az-Zait and al-Wad, the two main *souqs*, and Damascus Gate all have an endless variety of shops that don't cater to tourists. Rather than Judaica trinkets and dumb T-shirts, most salespeople hawk Middle Eastern sweets, clothes, spices and nuts, electronics, and pretty much anything else a human could want to buy. The Ayyubid and Mamluk architecture has been almost completely preserved through the many wars that have rocked Jerusalem over the last few hundred years, which means narrow streets and dense networks of alleys. Don't go off on madcap adventures at night, but stumble by daylight down offshoot streets and find the most memorable parts of the Old City.

qur'an quiz

Interested in touring the Dome of the Rock while visiting Jerusalem? Unless you're all about Allah, you may have trouble gaining access to the inner sacred sanctum—all visitors are allowed to tour the sprawling gardens of the Temple Mount, but only Muslims may enter the actual temple. But how do they separate the believers from the non-believers? As racial profiling isn't really PC, visitors are required to answer quiz questions based on the Qur'an before they can enter. Those with sufficient knowledge of Islamic practice are permitted to enter and pray; those who aren't up to snuff must do a walk of shame back to the courtyard full of other visitors. Let's hope you studied before your trip!

TEMPLE MOUNT   RELIGIOUS SITE
Temple Mount

The Temple Mount (*al-Haram al-Sharif* in Arabic and *Har HaBayit* in Hebrew) is probably the most diversely holy site in the world. In addition to countless pagan traditions associated with the place, the hill—better known as Mt. Moriah—for Jews is the spot where God asked Abraham to sacrifice his son Isaac, and for Muslims is the place where Muhammad ascended to heaven.

In the early years, construction on the site followed a pretty clear pattern, starting with King Solomon's building of the First Temple in the 10th century BCE: temple gets built, temple gets destroyed by invaders, builder gets exiled, repeat. The destruction by the Romans in 70 CE was a particular doozy—the resultant diaspora lasted until the creation of the Israeli state. Proving once and for all that karma's actually a, well, you know, the Roman temple to Jupiter on the site was destroyed by the Byzantines, who respectfully placed a sewage center there. The story goes that when Caliph Omar conquered Jerusalem in 638 CE, he ascended the Mount, cleared away the muck with his bare hands, and began rebuilding. The final products were Al-Aqsa Mosque and the Dome of the Rock, both of which still stand today.

As with most sights considered holy by the two religions, there has been a little ensuing drama. Although all are technically welcome on the Mount, only Muslims are allowed to pray there. For some Jews, that's okay—many Orthodox actually believe that no one should be on the Mount, for fear that they'll walk on certain holy sections of the Temples. After all, when it's possible that the Ark of Covenant (the Holy of Holies that was lost with the First Temple) is still somewhere under the Temple Mount, it's better to be safe than sorry, right? But, if you're okay with risking the wrath of God, the Temple Mount, with its large patches of shade and vast empty space, can be a good spot for a picnic or a lounging afternoon. Thirty-five acres in total, gardens cover most of the Mount and function as a spiritual public park. Veiled women sit and meditatively munch on falafel as they chat and occasionally glance up around one of the holiest places in Islam. Kids use ancient arches as goal posts for games of pickup soccer, while their parents watch and talk on cell phones. Tourists walk around snapping photographs and get ripped off buying protective coverings for their legs and heads. Whatever you choose to do here, it's good to keep a low profile: violence has followed unintended insults around the Mount in the past and despite its laconic appearance, it is still a place of inestimable spiritual gravitas. So it might be a good idea to find a different spot to make out with that soldier you met on Rivlin St. last weekend.

✣ Coming from Dung Gate, enter the line leading into the above-ground passageway to the right of the line to the Western Wall. If you're Muslim, you can also access the Mount from the end of Bab al-Silsila St. and other Muslim Quarter roads that feed into it. *i* Dress conservatively. The Mount can close suddenly without warning. Ⓢ Free. Leg and head coverings around NIS50. ☑ Open daily in summer 7:30-11am and 1:30-2:30pm; in winter 7:30-10:30am and 12:30-1:30pm. Subject to change for Islamic holidays.

DOME OF THE ROCK AND AL-AQSA MOSQUE   MOSQUES
Temple Mount

At the center of the Dome of the Rock is the spot where Abraham supposedly almost sacrificed his son (Ishmael for Muslims, Isaac for Jews and Christians), and the complex as a whole is considered the third-holiest sight in Islam. According to Muslim tradition, this is also where Muhammad began the Night Journey (*miraj*) before ascending to heaven. Both mosques are considered so sacred that the visit of then-prospective Prime Minister Ariel Sharon with a thousand Israeli soldiers in 2000 is seen by some as having caused the subsequent *intifada*. Though others point out that the *intifada* had been planned months earlier, the result is that only Muslims may now enter Al-Aqsa and the Dome of the Rock.

Since most visitors can only admire from afar, it's good to have your facts about the exterior down: the Dome of the Rock is the one with the golden dome (Al-Aqsa sports the silver), but in this case, all that glitters is not, well, gold. Although the dome was once made of solid gold, it was gradually melted down to pay caliphs' debts and eventually replaced with aluminum-bronze alloy, before being recoated with a layer of 24-karat gold in 1993. Some of the ceramic work on the outside is also a 20th-century addition, but many of the tiles were installed by Sultan Suleiman in the 16th century.

Between the Dome of the Rock and Al-Aqsa is **al-Kas**, a fountain where Muslims perform ablutions. Originally built in 709 CE, it is connected to an underground cistern that can hold 10 million gallons of water. At the exact center of the Temple Mount also stands the small **Dome of the Chain**, a place where Muslims believe a chain used to hang from heaven that could be held only by the righteous.

SOUQ   MARKET

Whether you're looking for atmosphere or anise, the markets of the Muslim Quarter are the place to go. Because they cater to locals as well as tourists, harassment is comparatively low and quality is high, meaning that there are about as many pottery places as there are vendors hawking snow globe versions of the Dome of the Rock. One of the most prominent of these specialized commercial zones is **Souq al-Qattanin,** a famed cotton market that was recently renovated. If you do enough asking around, you may be able to get to the roof when it's open and snatch a supposedly unrivaled view of the Temple Mount.

Once you've braved the chaotic *souq* during the day, return at night. Stick to the safer main roads, but even the most cursory walk will allow you to appreciate what the Old City looks like when it is unadorned by commerce. The architecture becomes more apparent, the layout of the streets more comprehensible, and the beauty of this ancient walled-in square reveals itself in an entirely new way.

legends of the rock

Most of those visiting the Dome of the Rock already know the basics: Jews think Abraham almost killed his son on the stone, and Muslims believe Mohammad ascended into heaven from there. But the "foundation stone" has spawned lesser-known legends as well. Here are some of the more entertaining ones:

- **SOURCE OF WATERS:** According to Arab tradition, the source of all the world's water and wind lies beneath the stone. We imagine this looks something like what you saw in the last season of *Lost*.

- **ANGELS LEAVE FINGERPRINTS TOO:** When Mohammed ascended into heaven, he stepped on the foundation stone, and it started to come up with him. According to the Qur'an, the Archangel Gabriel gripped the stone and pulled it back to earth as Mohammed continued to rise. His grip was so strong that you can still see where he made indents on the stone. Elementary, my dear Watson.

- **UNIDENTIFIED FLOATING STONE:** During the Middle Ages, popular belief held that the foundation stone hovered between heaven and earth. It was said that if a pregnant woman gazed upon the levitating rock, she would miscarry. Add that to the list of things you can't do while preggers.

- **MESSIAH O'CLOCK:** Going off of the hovering legend, the Ottoman Turks specifically believed that when the stone fell to earth, the Jewish Messiah would have arrived. In a trick totally outsmarting God, they built a support below the stone to ensure it could never fall.

ZEDEKIAH'S CAVE   CAVE
Sultan Suleiman St.   ☎02 627 7962; davidson@pami.co.il

Coffee is one good way to wake yourself up in the middle of a hot and busy Jerusalem day, but a better way may be a trip through the eerie hidden cavernous nooks and ancient gloom of Zedekiah's Cave, which should give goose bumps to even the most burly traveler. It is fitting that Freemasons held meetings in this damp, dripping hole, which was likely created by King Herod as a quarry for his massive construction projects. Also possible, however, is that the cave has been a quarry since the First Temple Period. With a history almost as murky as its dark inner chambers, this legend-shrouded cave is worth a visit.

✈ *When you walk to the Old City side of Sultan Suleiman from HaNevi'im St., continue past Damascus Gate. The cave's entrance is along the Old City walls.* ℹ *Brochures and signs in English.* Ⓢ *NIS16, students and elderly NIS10.* ☾ *Open Su-Th 9am-5pm, Sa 9am-5pm; in summer Su-Th 9am-4pm, Sa 9am-4pm.*

old city

The Temple Mount, the Church of the Holy Sepulchre, the Western Wall. Blah, blah, blah, we get it: Jerusalem is bursting with sights so significant that just looking at them makes you feel slightly transcendent. But once you've gotten the heavy-hitters out of the way, take a stroll (or, if you're directionally challenged, a progressively more and more frantic weave) through the alleyways of the Old City and check out these smaller sights. The tour will take about 2½hr.

1. ZEDEKIAH'S CAVE. You can walk through the Muslim Quarter later. For now, walk *under* it; start your tour at the ancient Zedekiah's Cave, which sprawls the length of five blocks beneath the quarter. The tiny entrance can be found just north of Damascus Gate, and remember: bonus points if you track down a stray Freemason.

2. DAMASCUS GATE. From Zedekiah's Cave, walk about 150m to reach the busy 16th-century Damascus Gate, perhaps the grandest of the many gates into the Old City. If you need a snack to settle your nerves after the cave, head to the nearby Green Door Pizza Bakery.

3. SOUQ. See that mess of booths in front of you? Keep to Al-Wad Rd. and dive into the fray of the *souq*—or, if you'd prefer, stand back and watch the pros haggle for anything from quality cotton to Dome-of-the-Rock-shaped bottle openers.

4. BURNT HOUSE. Al-Wad ends just before the Western Wall; take a right, and then go left on Misgav Ladach. After a few blocks, the Burnt House is on the right. Destroyed by the Romans around the same time they took out the Second Temple— yeah, rough week—it's yielded a wealth of artifacts. It may be pretty fireproof now, but the place still lights up frequently with an audiovisual display.

5. HERODIAN QUARTER. From the Burnt House, head south on HaKara'im St. and follow it as it bends to reach the Wohl Archaeological Museum, which displays restorations of some of ancient Jerusalem's finest mansions. Expect mosaics, *mikva'ot*, and many laughs... well, maybe not the last one.

6. ST. JAMES' CATHEDRAL. Continue following HaKara'im St. and take a left when you hit the Y-junction. Take a slight left onto Gil'ad to reach HaT'kuma Garden. Pray for a little shade as you turn right onto Batei Mahase and follow it as it becomes first Habad and then Armenian Orthodox Patriarchate Rd. You may have to dodge a few cars as you make your way up the road, so take a breather at St. James' Cathedral. If you're there between 3 and 3:30pm, you can check out its murky interior; otherwise, just look for the exterior inscription that proves that Armenians have been believing in Jesus since long, long before you were born.

7. TOWER OF DAVID. Continue along the traffic-heavy Armenian Orthodox Patriarchate Rd. to reach the final stop: the Tower of David Museum, right next to Jaffa Gate. The dioramas may be decent, but the namesake tower has views that are out-of-this-world. Be sure to take a sweaty and unattractive picture from the top, then reward yourself with a relaxing dinner in West Jerusalem. Or just collapse into a heap and refuse to move until your friends bring you a Maccabee.

CHURCH OF ST. ANNE CHURCH

Lion's Gate Rd. ☎02 628 3285; mafrepo@steanne.org

Initially dedicated to the Madonna and considered to be her birthplace, this simple church was rebuilt by the Crusaders in 1130 and survived the Islamic period intact as a Quranic school. It now stands as a monument to St. Anne and contains what are believed to be the ruins of the Pool of Bethesda, where invalids would come to be healed by angels. Perhaps because that method wasn't exactly foolproof, Jesus reportedly stepped in and healed a man here as well. The church allows you to walk around these bath ruins, meaning you may be standing on the same spot as Jesus Christ once did. There is a garden where you can sit and ponder the deep philosophical revelations you will inevitably have as a result.

⌖ Enter St. Stephen's Gate; the church is a 3min. walk down on your left through big wooden doors. $ NIS7, students NIS5. ⏰ Open daily 8am-noon and 2-5pm.

ROMAN SQUARE MUSEUM MUSEUM

Damascus Gate ☎02 627 7550

Most of this dank and claustrophobic museum is in the unfortunate position of having uninteresting artifacts and infinitely more interesting reproductions. Unless you really care about oil pressing, the relevant thousand-year-old instruments will not be particularly compelling. On the other hand, the photographic representations of the Old City, which start in the mid-1800s, are interesting, even if they're just pieces of plastic. The best part of the museum, though, is when it manages to combine old and new—if you pay an extra NIS2, you are allowed go upstairs and walk around the Old City walls, which is a fun way to survey the history and gain some insight into the labyrinthine layout of the area.

*⌖ In the courtyard before the entrance to Damascus Gate and the Old City, turn right and walk down the stairs. Continue straight to reach the museum. **i** Neither English brochures nor tours offered. $ NIS10, students NIS6. Cash only. ⏰ Open in summer Su-Th 9am-5pm, Sa 9am-5pm; in winter Su-Th 9am-6pm, Sa 9am-6pm.*

armenian quarter

To the untrained eye, the Armenian Quarter is more like one-sixteenth of the city than a full quarter, but that's only because people don't...ok, even to the eye of a trained *Let's Go* traveler, it is really just one street—**Armenian Orthodox Patriarchate Road**—and the small residential neighborhood that extends out from St. James Rd. Only 1200 Armenians remain in the quarter, many having fled during the Turkish genocide of Armenians during World War I. Most of the remaining Armenians in Israel live in the Armenian Compound, which tourists cannot enter. *Let's Go* has therefore chosen to include the courtyard immediately outside Jaffa Gate, which belongs to no explicit neighborhood, in our coverage of the quarter. Yes, we do love the power.

TOWER OF DAVID MUSEUM MUSEUM

Jaffa Gate ☎02 626 5333; www.towerofdavid.org.il

Probably the best starting place for learning about Jewish history and culture, the Tower of David Museum attempts to recount Jewish history in its entirety—even if it has to resort to little toy figures in dioramas to accomplish this feat. Though the museum extends from the Canaanite Period (before the First Temple!) to a 19th-century model of Jerusalem, the most interesting stuff is in the courtyard, where a First Temple Period stone quarry, a Hasmonean-era wall, and remains of Herod's palace are all on display. Best among these artifacts is the museum's namesake, a Herodian tower that was transformed into an Ottoman minaret, then named the Tower of David centuries later. It is not only an interesting historical symbol but also one of the highest points in the city and, therefore, a great place to take pictures for that "SB2012:IsrealEdishun!!!" Facebook album with the Old City spread beneath you. Also, there is a night show in which, according to the brochure, "the story of Jerusalem unfolds in a majestic blaze of breathtaking images and sounds" projected onto the ancient city walls. With a description like that (and a NIS40 price tag), how could it not be impressive?

✦ *Bear right when you enter Jaffa Gate, and cross the bridge on the right.* ⓢ *Museum entry NIS30, students NIS20; night show NIS55/45; combined ticket NIS70/55.* ⓓ *Open Sept-June Su-W 10am-4pm, Th 10am-6pm, Sa and holidays 10am-2pm; July-Aug Su-Th 10am-5pm, F 10am-2pm, Sa 10am-5pm. Free English tours Su-Th at 11am. Call ahead to find out the time for the night show.*

▨ ST. JAMES' CATHEDRAL

CATHEDRAL

Armenian Orthodox Patriarchate Rd. ☎02 628 2331

Like hipsters who claim to have been into a band when it was just a small part of the local scene with only a homemade EP to its name, Armenians take great pride in the fact that theirs was the first state to embrace Christianity (in 301 CE). In fact, as they love to tell you, evidence shows that there were Armenian bishops doing research in the Holy Land as early as 154 CE. All right, Bromenians, real authentic. But this lineage does have documentation to back it up: outside of the main entrance of St. James' Cathedral, the central site for the Armenian Orthodox in Jerusalem, is an Arabic inscription casting protection on the church from 1450 CE. Inside, the cathedral is covered in faded paintings of biblical scenes, shrouded in the mist of incense and the constant chanting of monks. A remarkable number of unlit oil lamps are suspended from the ceiling; the only light in this perpetually dim cathedral comes from the tallow candles that dot the place. St. James the Apostle is buried in a small chapel inside the Cathedral, where he is believed to have been entombed after his execution in 44 CE. Much later in history, St. James' functioned as a safe haven and bomb shelter during the 1948 War.

✦ *Coming from Jaffa Gate, walk down Armenian Orthodox Patriarchate Rd., following the traffic. Walk about 10min. The cathedral is on the left.* ⓘ *Legs must be covered. Be sure to pick up a brochure on your way in.* ⓢ *Free.* ⓓ *Open M-F 6:30-7:30am and 3-3:30pm, Sa 8:30-10:30am and 3-3:30pm.*

ARMENIAN CERAMIC SHOPS

CERAMICS

Armenian Orthodox Patriarchate Rd.
Armenian Art Centre ☎02 628 3567; www.sandrouni.com
Armenian Ceramics Gallery ☎02 626 1212; www.garosandrouni.com

Unlike the mass-produced potentially plastic crap sold by most vendors on David St., the ceramics found in the Armenian Quarter are handmade using methods that have remained essentially unchanged for centuries. At the Armenian Art Centre, Harout will take you into the back and show you the drawing, painting, and glazing processes and tell you about his kiln. He will also expound at great length on his categorization of the history of Armenian ceramics into three discrete sections—a Christian religious period, a symbolic period focused on certain animals (particularly deer), and a period influenced by the Ottoman patrons who requested Armenian bowls, plates, and plaques that incorporated the geometrical designs common to Arabic artwork. Harout's employees are all friendly and some speak English. At the nearby Armenian Ceramics Gallery, Garo will tell you about how he and his wife Sonia make their work by hand on a wheel. Of particular note are his Jerusalem skyline clocks and the brochure he offers guests that gives a detailed explanation of the process and history of Armenian ceramics. It is easy to treat these two places as museums and not shops, but that isn't what Harout and Garo would like you to think.

✦ *The Art Centre is on the right-hand side of Armenian Orthodox Patriarchate Rd., behind you after you pass through the tunnel. The Ceramics Gallery is the 7th storefront on the right-hand side of Armenian Orthodox Patriarchate Rd. from Zion Gate.* ⓢ *Entry free. Small jars NIS50. Tiles NIS100.* ⓓ *Both shops open M-Sa 9am-7pm.*

sights

ST. MARK'S CHURCH AND SYRIAN ORTHODOX CONVENT CHURCH, CONVENT

Ararat St. ☎02 628 3304

Although visitors aren't allowed in the upstairs convent, the main attraction of this site is clearly the church. The nuns in residence endow it with as much religious significance as possible—it's the first church in Christianity, it's the site of the Last Supper, it's where Jesus sent the Holy Ghost to talk to the apostles, etc. If you want to hear "first-person" accounts of many of these events as they would be told by the people involved and also learn about the modern-day miracles associated with the church, you have to be lucky enough to chance upon one of the nuns giving a tour. If you do, you are in for an hour-long lecture, by turn enlightening and hilarious, depending on your point of view and appreciation for nuns who sound eerily like John Cleese.

➜ Coming from Jaffa Gate, go onto Armenian Orthodox Patriarchate Rd., take a left onto St. James Rd., and then a left at the dead end. ***i*** *Women should cover their legs. Call in advance to schedule a tour. $ Free. ⏰ Open daily 10am-3pm; can be opened later if you call in advance.*

jewish quarter

In the Old City, it is paradoxically the Jewish Quarter that has the fewest intact historical sights. Though the Jews have been soaking in the milk and honey for nearly 3000 years, their religious and cultural sights have fared particularly badly in the many wars that have ravaged Jerusalem—much like the Jews, come to think of it. Gobs of cash from philanthropists and the government have helped to compensate, and there is now a ton for tourists to do in this section of the Old City. So, although the Western Wall may be the closest thing to an authentic been-here-for-centuries sight, you can still find plenty of museums with ruins, reconstructed synagogues, and educational centers that put forward their interpretation of Israel's history.

👍 WESTERN WALL RELIGIOUS SITE

☎02 627 1333; www.english.thekotel.org

In a town where many people cling to artifact fragments as profound connections to their deepest historical roots, the Western Wall is the ultimate fragment. *HaKotel*, as it is often called, is a 67m-long, 15m-tall structure that is one of the few surviving remnants of the wall built by King Herod around the Second Temple. It may not sound like much, but, barring a miraculous recovery of the Ark of the Covenant (Indiana Jones, we're still waiting...), the Western Wall is the holiest site in Judaism, the closest most Jews are willing to get to the highly significant Foundation Stone and the remains of the Second Temple. Many therefore believe that praying at the wall is the best substitute for praying at the Second Temple and that the wall affords a direct link to God. Because of that, it's traditional to leave little messages to the Big Guy in the crevices between stone blocks. If you're one of the lazy or lapsed, you can also just visit the wall's website, where you can write up notes that will then be printed by the Western Wall Heritage Foundation and put in the wall for you. The notes are periodically collected and buried as dictated by Jewish law.

The time to visit the Western Wall is definitely Friday night, when crowds gather around it in anticipation of Shabbat—or maybe just because all Jewish shops are closed anyway and these hoodlums have nothing better to do. In accordance with Orthodox Jewish practice, a small wall separates men's and women's prayer sections, and Torah scrolls have to be picked up on the men's side, but the Western Wall remains the most accessible major site in Jerusalem: as long as a man's head is covered and a woman isn't flashing leg, anyone can participate in many of the rituals practiced around the wall without having to wait in line—or even, really, having much prior understanding of Judaism. Once called the Wailing Wall in honor of those who came to mourn the destruction of the Second Temple, the wall represents pain, loss, and human cruelty and can be a highly spiritual experience for the religious and secular alike. But it's also become a social spot for international Jews to congregate, compare their experiences exploring Israel, and do some modern-day kvetching about the lack of air-conditioning.

Go through Dung Gate, follow the signs in the Jewish Quarter, or take either al-Wad Rd. or Bab al-Silsila to their ends as they move away from Jaffa and Damascus Gates. [i] Coverings for head and legs can be found at the Western Wall. $ Free. ⏰ Open 24hr.

WESTERN WALL TUNNEL TOUR — TUNNELS

☎02 627 1333; www.english.thekotel.org

An old Jewish lady presses a button, and a model of the Second Temple lights up with whirrs and flashes as parts of the miniature street disappear and reconstitute themselves. She explains the multiple evolutions of the Temple Mount and the Western Wall and tells how "all the treasures were schlepped out" of the Second Temple for residents to marvel at a few times a year so they would continue paying taxes to the powers at be. Once this is over, the tour group walks down a staircase to the underground base of the Western Wall, where the original stones from Herod's time remain connected and perfectly intact. The tour also covers some of the ancient streets and reservoirs still visible from the Second Temple Period while weaving a narrative that ties together these disparate elements. Overall, it is the best way to understand the importance of the Western Wall from a Jewish perspective.

Once you have entered the Western Wall plaza, the waiting area for the tour is near the bathrooms on a lifted platform just before the men's prayer area. [i] Call a day in advance to reserve. $ NIS25, students NIS15. ⏰ Call to find out times.

are you there, god?

Forget prayer; God's a big fan of handwritten letters. When at the Wailing Wall, look for the folded paper shoved between the cracks. While most of these prayers are placed by the devout themselves, the Israel Post also receives letters addressed to God. Under international law, mail carriers are obliged to deliver the prayer to the "dead letter" office. Postal workers then place letters to God in a special box that will be hand-delivered (by a rabbi, if you're lucky) to the Wailing Wall.

Only letters addressed "To God, Jerusalem" will make it to the Western Wall. Jesus Christ, the Virgin Mary, and King David may be reached at other addresses.

OPHEL JERUSALEM ARCHAEOLOGICAL PARK — RUINS, GARDEN

☎02 627 7550; www.archpark.org.il

Part of what makes the Western Wall a fascinating sight to visit is its material simplicity: the fact that it is invested with incalculable spiritual meaning does not prevent you from slipping it notes, banging on it, coming to see it at 4:51am so the two of you can have a private moment—really, whatever you're into. The same can be said for the Archaeological Park, which contains a collection of ruins unmatched in size, quality of preservation, and intimacy. A lack of metal fences and white ropes means you can walk around ancient *mikva'ot* (ritual baths), the ruins of old Byzantine residences, and even the remains of an Umayyad palace from the early Islamic Period. There is also a beautiful and peaceful garden area with ample shade and a tower that offers a view of the towns just outside Jerusalem.

From the Western Wall, exit the security checkpoint and walk toward Dung Gate. The Archaeological Park is just before the gate on your left. $ NIS30, students NIS16. 1hr. guided tour NIS160, audio guide NIS5. ⏰ Open Su-Th 8am-5pm, F 8am-2pm.

WOHL ARCHAEOLOGICAL MUSEUM — MUSEUM

1 HaKara'im St. ☎02 626 5900; www.rova-yehudi.org.il

Only the swankiest palaces and districts get their ruins preserved. Here, the remains of three mansions from the Herodian Quarter (ancient Jerusalem's Upper East Side) have been found and restored in surprising completeness. Three meters below the present-day quarter, the old nobility's spacious *mikva'ot*, intricate mosaics, and many extra rooms are available for visitors to explore amidst the dank smell of exhumed stone. Even stoves and frescoes have been preserved. There are many helpful signs that explain, in English, the former uses and meanings of each object and room. A few artifacts are also on display at the museum, including a statuette from the First Temple Period of a woman with breasts so cartoonishly large that she holds them up with her fists. Forget amphorae—ancient jugs don't get much better than this.

⇞ In the square which Ramban and Hurva synagogues look onto. With your back to the synagogues, it is in the top right corner of the square. ℹ Combined ticket options for the Wohl Archaeological Museum, Burnt House, and Alone on the Walls exhibit are available. $ NIS15, students NIS13. ⏰ Open Su-Th 9am-5pm, F 9am-1pm.

BURNT HOUSE — MUSEUM

2 HaKara'im St. ☎02 628 7211; www.jewish-quarter.org.il/atar-saruf.asp

In 70 CE, Romans destroyed the Second Temple and pillaged Jerusalem, causing the dispersion of the Jews for almost two subsequent millennia. Among the wreckage left from that day is the Burnt House, the former residence of the Kathros family—specifically called out as corrupt gonifs in the New Testament—that was set on fire. The excavation that led to the Burnt House's discovery found it under layers of ash, and the breakdown of stone and wooden beams was such that certain artifacts and rooms in the house were preserved. Proof of its destruction during the Roman siege was found in the date of coins discovered at the site, a burned spear, and the skeleton of a young girl's arm. Eerie, right? A movie reminiscent of a Lifetime "real-time depiction" animates the house's remnants by setting them in a historical and cultural context.

⇞ At the intersection of HaKara'im and Tiferet Yisra'el, across the square and 1 block down from the Wohl Archaeological Museum. ℹ A movie in English plays periodically, taking up the whole museum. There is a tour in English twice a day; call in advance to find out times. Combined ticket options for the Wohl Archaeological Museum, Burnt House, and Alone on the Walls exhibit are available. $ NIS25, students NIS20. ⏰ Open Su-Th 9am-5pm, F 9am-1pm.

ALONE ON THE WALLS EXHIBIT — MUSEUM

The Cardo ☎02 627 3916; www.jewish-quarter.org.il/atar-acharon.asp

A politicized look at the 1948 War that ended in the expulsion of Jews and the destruction of the Jewish Quarter. The many photographs taken by legendary *Life* correspondent John Phillips tell a great war narrative, and the captions put alongside them are fascinating. The fall of the Jewish Quarter is on full display here, from the point when Jewish forces had only an hour of ammunition left and decided to surrender, to when residents were given an hour to collect their belongings and depart for an unknown future. As many Jewish Quarter sights are reconstructions of buildings destroyed in the aftermath of this war, the perspective offered by the Alone on the Walls Exhibit helps to further put them in context.

⇞ On your left once you enter the Cardo and begin walking toward David St. ℹ Combined ticket options for the Wohl Archaeological Museum, Burnt House, and Alone on the Walls exhibit are available. $ NIS12, students NIS10. ⏰ Open Su-Th 9am-5pm, F 9am-1pm.

YISHUV COURT MUSEUM — MUSEUM

6 Or HaHayim St. ☎02 628 4636

A representation of 19th- to early 20th-century Jewish Quarter life through period furniture and clothing, facts, and firsthand accounts that help explain everything from how locals dealt with high infant mortality to what possessions normal residents tended to have and why. The museum is just small enough that each room is focused but still substantial. If you are cripplingly jetlagged or generally an overenthusiastic person, come early to see the two synagogues that were found empty but undamaged after the Six-Day War and have since been redesigned to match their former appearances.

*⇞ On the right when coming from St. James Rd. from Jaffa Gate. **i** Call ahead to find out what is on display for the changing exhibit. $ NIS18, students NIS14. ⏰ Open Su-Th 10am-5pm, F 10am-2pm. Attached synagogues open daily 7-8am.*

HURVA SYNAGOGUE SYNAGOGUE

HaYehudim Rd. ☎02 626 5900; www.jewish-quarter.org.il/atar-hurva.asp

Only officially reopened in 2010, the Hurva Synagogue has gone through five incarnations since it was first built in the First Temple Period. More than any other sight, persistent attempts at reconstruction have been met by equally persistent attacks: after its 1864 rebuilding, Hurva was seen as the most important synagogue in Israel, until it was destroyed along with everything else in the Jewish Quarter in 1948. Today, sixth-century *mikveh* ruins and the remnants of a street that once led to the Cardo sit under the renovated synagogue. Most of the tour guides are wide-eyed Jewish post-adolescents who tell you about the "legend, dream, myth" of Jerusalem and are nice to the grandparently Jews who go on these tours.

*⇞ On the right side of HaYehudim if you walk from the nearby square toward the Cardo. Adjacent to Ramban Synagogue. **i** Either call ahead for a reservation or buy a ticket at the Alone on the Walls Exhibit. $ NIS25, students NIS15. ⏰ Open Su-Th 9am-4pm, F 9am-1pm.*

CENTER FOR JERUSALEM IN THE FIRST TEMPLE PERIOD MUSEUM

Bonei HaHomah St. ☎02 628 6288; www.ybz.org.il

Although a lack of facts and artifacts means that our understanding of the First Temple Period is pretty fuzzy, this museum manages to still have some success in depicting its history. The museum may not capture the spirit of Jerusalem, as it promises, but it does have a full model of ancient Jerusalem based on archaeological findings and biblical account, so we're not complaining. There is also a movie and exhibits dedicated to daily life and the evolution of the Hebrew language, but be warned: the heavy presentation of facts may bore those lacking an extremely analytical attitude.

*⇞ Facing the Broad Wall from the gate in front of it, make a right and then bear left. It is just around the corner from the Broad Wall and at the corner of Bonei HaHomah St. and Plugat HaKotel St. **i** Call in advance to find out when there will be tours for individuals or to schedule a group tour. $ NIS18, students NIS14. ⏰ Open Su-Th 9am-4pm.*

RAMBAN SYNAGOGUE SYNAGOGUE

HaYehudim Rd.

The oldest active synagogue in the Old City, Ramban was built in 1267 and then went through a series of other uses until Jews regained control of the quarter exactly 700 years later. A letter written by founder Rabbi Moshe Ben-Nahman ("Ramban" is an acronym for his name) detailing the medieval Jewish Quarter is framed inside the synagogue. A lack of English brochures or tourist officials can make this a tough place to visit, but it is worth a peek inside if only to witness Hebrew school antics and get a sense of what a functioning synagogue in the Old City feels like.

⇞ On the right side of HaYehudim if you walk from the nearby square toward the Cardo. $ Free.

FOUR SEPHARDIC SYNAGOGUES SYNAGOGUES

HaTuppim Rd. and Misherot HaKehuna

Originally 15th-century synagogues built by Mediterranean Jews, these four connected synagogues—Yochana Ben-Zakai, Eliyahu HaNavi, Kahal Zion, and

Istanbuli—were destroyed in the 1948 War. Faithfully reconstructed in 1967, they are now mostly empty and dusty, although religious services are still held here twice per day, and a Portuguese *minyan* is held every Shabbat in the Istanbuli synagogue. Without English-speaking employees or English brochures, this place can be unintelligible to tourists unless they've done immense prior research or have an extraordinarily powerful imagination. On the plus side, the sight can be uninhabited enough that you can use that imagination to pretend you're a rabbi and gesture at an imaginary congregation without risking public shame.

Walk on HaYehudim Rd. toward David St. and take a right on HaTuppim. $ NIS10, students NIS7. ⏰ Open Su-Th 9am-4pm, F 9am-1pm.

BROAD WALL WALL

Plugat HaKotel Rd.

A former boundary line for the City of David, the Temple Mount, and Herodian Quarter, the Broad Wall is a 7m-thick block of stone you can see from about two stories up. Don't expect any hand-holding: this is just a wall in a ditch. But it is very old. So, yeah. There's that.

Right after passing Ramban and Hurva Synagogues on HaYehudim. $ Free. ⏰ Open 24hr.

CARDO OLD STREET

The Cardo www.jewish-quarter.org.il/atar-kardo.asp

Descend a flight of stairs, and you will find yourself in the Roman Cardo, the main market boulevard that once ran through the length of the Old City. Replaced today by a series of dense and coiling markets, the Cardo signified the centralization of commerce and rule brought by the Romans. Walking on the modern reconstruction, notice the huge pillars that suggest its once great size. Near the entrance is another staircase that leads to the excavated remains of some First Temple Period buildings. Unfortunately, the shops on this new Cardo bear no comparison to that of its predecessor, unless you really like spending 15 extra shekels on the same Judaica trinkets sold everywhere else. Though to be fair, we hear Romans were really into "My boyfriend pillaged Jerusalem and all he got for me was this stupid T-shirt" T-shirts.

*Past the end of Souq Khan az-Zait nearest to the Jewish Quarter with a staircase off of HaYehudim Rd. **i** No English brochures, but a few signs give some historical explanation. $ Free. ⏰ Open 24hr.*

christian quarter

It's called the Christian Quarter for a reason. Churches litter the neighborhood, in which structures are packed together like presents in a Christmas stocking. The holiest of these is the Church of the Holy Sepulchre: the sight of Jesus's crucifixion, burial, and resurrection. Leading up to this are the Stations of the Cross, the 14 points of interest during Jesus's final walk. The neighborhood has always been a thriving testament to religious devotion, and the many wars and reconstructions in this part of Jerusalem have all involved religious identity. Today, the Christian Quarter plays host to the most secular practices as well—Darwinian struggle among small businesses and wide-eyed tourism governed more by exploration than adoration. The collision of ethnicities, ideologies, and classes that erupts here functions to obscure each discrete element of the Christian Quarter, but also reinforces its position as one of the most historic sites in the world.

STATIONS OF THE CROSS

The 14 Stations of the Cross represent the events leading up to Jesus's crucifixion, beginning with his condemnation and ending with his death. Though historical and religious disputes surround the exact placement and activity of just about every station, most pilgrims and tourists follow a similar formula. That is, they wander around Old City side streets for three to 19 hours, hire an overpriced tour guide, or (if they are in the know) use *Let's Go*. The route is covered with churches and religious gift shops that increase in number and grandeur until it reaches the Church of the Holy Sepulchre. The intimacy of following Jesus's footsteps—and witnessing the modern-day reverence—can be astounding, but, for those unacquainted with the meaning behind the Stations of the Cross, it can also be unintelligible and underwhelming. There is little official explanation because the Franciscan Order, charged by the Pope to maintain religious sites in the Holy Land since the Crusaders were expelled, has left them as close to their historical forms as possible. Hence, 15min. of prior reading goes a long way. Then again, so does a lifetime of prior reading.

FIRST STATION
HOLY WALK

The First Station, at the Tower of Antonia in the center of the Al-Omariya College courtyard, is usually inaccessible to tourists and totally unmarked. It is where Pontius Pilate, the Roman governor, condemned Jesus.

⚜ *Enter St. Stephen's Gate, and continue straight for about 10min. until you see a faded bronze plaque that commemorates the Stations of the Cross on the left and the entrance to a courtyard on the right. The 1st Station is beyond the school to the right.*

SECOND STATION
HOLY WALK

There are two chapels: the Chapel of Condemnation and the Chapel of the Flagellation. The Second Station is the former, where Jesus was sentenced to be crucified. He was then beaten by Roman soldiers at the latter. Inside the Chapel of the Flagellation on the right-hand side, there is a crown of thorns sitting atop the dome.

⚜ *At the Chapel of Condemnation, across the way from the 1st Station.*

THIRD STATION
HOLY WALK

This is where the Stations become a wildly confusing hunt through sweaty and tourist-crowded streets, but, once you've found this one, you'll be happy to learn that signs mark most of the remaining Stations. The Third Station is where Jesus first fell to his knees. Notice how, inside the chapel, the pavement has changed size and shape. These stones are segments of a road from the Second Temple Period that were found by archaeologists below street level. They have been reconstructed here in their original form.

⚜ *Walk left for about 40sec. immediately after al-Wad appears as a left turn and the Via Dolorosa changes direction. You will see stairs leading down to a chapel and a circular dark sign above it on the left that reads "III."*

FOURTH STATION
HOLY WALK

This is where Jesus reportedly saw the Virgin Mary, although some argue that, while Mary's presence at the Crucifixion is mentioned in John, there is no biblical indication that she was present during Jesus's walk.

⚜ *When you exit the chapel that holds the 3rd Station, look left and you will see the entrance to the courtyard that is the 4th Station.*

FIFTH STATION
HOLY WALK

At the Fifth Station, Simon of Cyrene helped Jesus carry his cross. There is a sign reading "V." Some see the moment as an act of kindness on the part of Simon, but others argue that the Romans forced him to do so.

⚜ *Turn right on the Via Dolorosa from the 4th Station.*

SIXTH STATION
HOLY WALK

This is where Veronica, a local woman, wiped Jesus's perspiring face with a cloth. Jesus's face then appeared on the shroud, which is now on display at Turin Cathedral in Italy.

⚜ *Walk 5-10min. farther down the street, and you should see a small column knee-level on the left-hand wall and a "VI" sign above it.*

sights

SEVENTH STATION   HOLY WALK

This is where Jesus fell down from exhaustion for a second time. You've only reached the halfway point, so try not to do the same.

⚑ *Continue walking until the intersection with Souq Khan az-Zait; in front of you will be a "VII" sign.*

EIGHTH STATION   HOLY WALK

By this point, a procession had developed behind Jesus. Here he said to the women mourning his imminent death, "Daughters of Jerusalem, do not weep for me, weep rather for yourselves and for your children" (Luke 23:28). This was, unsurprisingly, not very comforting.

⚑ *Cross Souq Khan az-Zait and climb al-Khanqa St. Look left, past the Greek Orthodox Convent, to the Latin cross that marks the 8th Station.*

NINTH STATION   HOLY WALK

Here, Jesus fell for a third time. The last five Stations of the Cross are located inside the Church of the Holy Sepulchre.

⚑ *Go back to Souq Khan az-Zait, take a right, and continue walking through the market until you see a staircase leading upward on your left. There should be a large sign in front of it and another at the first landing that says "Mike's Center." Walking through the street that appears after the stairs, you will eventually reach the Coptic Church.*

CHURCH OF THE HOLY SEPULCHRE   HOLY WALK, CHURCH

The Church of the Holy Sepulchre is the believed site of Jesus's crucifixion, burial, and resurrection. Proving that mother always knows best, it was actually Eleni, mother of Roman Emperor Constantine, who encouraged the initial excavation of the area in 331. The subsequent discovery of Joseph of Arimathea's tomb and three crosses led Constantine to build the first Church of the Holy Sepulchre two years later. Like most major sights in Jerusalem, it was then destroyed and rebuilt a few times. The form that stands today, erected by the Crusaders in 1099, has managed to survive almost a millennium, but not without sustaining significant damages from earthquakes and fires in the 19th and early 20th centuries. Unfortunately, renovation has been a laborious process, particularly since 1852 when the Ottomans divided control of the church between the Franciscans and the Greek Orthodox and Armenian Orthodox Churches, whose interactions bring to mind three David St. shopkeepers fighting over an unsuspecting Iowan. By 1935, wooden reinforcements had to be used to keep the church standing because no agreement could be reached regarding reconstruction. Renovations have since ensured the structural integrity, but the church remains a battered and mostly illogical chaos of tourists, pilgrims, monks, and priests.

To continue with the **Stations of the Cross,** turn left the instant you enter the Church of the Holy Sepulchre. Up crowded and creaking stairs you will find two chapels: on the right, the Franciscan Chapel, and on the left, the Greek Orthodox Chapel. The entrance to the Franciscan Chapel marks the **Tenth Station,** where Jesus was stripped of his clothing, and the far end represents the **Eleventh Station,** where he was nailed to the cross. The Greeks, on the other hand, have the prime real estate: to the right of their chapel is the **Twelfth Station,** the official site of the Crucifixion. Strangely, the **Thirteenth Station,** where Mary received Jesus's body, falls somewhere between Stations Eleven and Twelve. If you've been examining these stations too carefully, you have inevitably let a huge line grow at the **Fourteenth Station,** the Holy Sepulchre itself, the marble structure in the main room where Jesus was buried and from which he was resurrected. Head down the stairs in front of the Greek Orthodox Chapel to go to the Holy Sepulchre. On the way, you will see the **Stone of Unction,** a slab traditionally held to be the spot on which Jesus's body was prepared for burial by Joseph of Arimathea. Pilgrims wipe it with handkerchiefs to take some holiness with them. (Note: *Let's Go* does not support the theft of sanctity.)

Below the Franciscan and Greek Orthodox Chapels is the Chapel of Adam, which contains the **Rock of Calvary.** Some believe that Jesus was buried above the spot of Adam's burial, which leads to a variety of traditional stories: namely that Jesus's blood ran down the cross onto the Rock of Calvary, purifying Adam's sins, and that the crack in the Rock of Calvary was produced by the earthquake that was a result of the Crucifixion.

✠ *From the 9th Station, walk through the courtyard opposite the Coptic Church and down the stairs of the Ethiopian Monastery at the right-hand corner. If not entering from the Ethiopian Monastery, walk to the end of Christian Quarter Rd. or Souq ed-Dabbagha.* **i** *It is advised to wear long pants, or at least cover your knees.* ⑨ *Free.* ⏰ *Open daily Apr-Sept 9am-5pm, Oct-Mar 8am-4pm.*

OTHER SIGHTS

ETHIOPIAN MONASTERY   MONASTERY
Holy Sepulchre Courtyard

The monastery provides a dark and obscure relief from the madness in and around the Holy Sepulchre Church. Scattered monks pray, prostrate themselves, or simply sit on the monastery's two levels, which are connected by a tiny, blackened staircase. Faded rugs and icons litter the church with no apparent rhyme or reason, bringing a sense of peace to the place. The only reminder that you are not in the mists of Christian history is a lone mid-century clock that, battered, hangs from above the upstairs doorway. Open the door to get to the sunny and quiet roof.

✠ *Facing the Church of the Holy Sepulchre, a small door at the bottom right corner of the courtyard leads into the Ethiopian Church.* ⑨ *Free.* ⏰ *Open daily dawn-dusk.*

COPTIC CHURCH   CHURCH
Holy Sepulchre Surroundings

Although cisterns may not be your usual idea of a good time, the one at the Coptic Church is worth a visit. Walking down a damp and fly-filled staircase with a ceiling that is only 4 ft. high in some places, you eventually reach a great opening that reveals another level of stairs and a giant dark pool. Other than a few lights that dimly light the staircase and a railing put up near it, the cistern and its immediate environment have been left unchanged since its heyday in the fourth century.

✠ *Continue straight past the courtyard after exiting the Ethiopian Monastery. The door to the Coptic Church is directly in front of you. Alternatively, turn off Khan az-Zait to the stairway that leads to the 9th Station and turn right once you reach its end.* ⑨ *NIS5.* ⏰ *Open daily dawn-dusk.*

ST. ALEXANDER'S CATHEDRAL   CHURCH
25 Souq ed-Dabbagha   ☎02 628 6866

Remnants of the city wall from the time of Christ are the main attraction at this site operated largely by Russian nuns. Of the sacred wall fragments in the Old City (of which there are surprisingly many), these are not the most interesting unless you're a history nerd or Christianity buff.

✠ *Coming from Jaffa Gate on David St., take a left on Muristan Rd. and continue until it ends at Souq ed-Dabbagha. Take a right and ring the doorbell.* **i** *Anyone wearing shorts will probably have to put on the baggy long pants they provide at the door.* ⑨ *NIS5.* ⏰ *Open daily 9am-6pm.*

outskirts of old city

So, you thought the Old City was old. Puh-lease. Those walls weren't built until 1538—in a city where there's still controversy surrounding the 100 BCE expulsion of the Jebusites, that's nothing. Some of these more ancient ruins can be found in the area right outside the Old City, partly because it is the *old* Old City, but also because it's more uninhabited and, therefore, more accessible to archaeologists. Of course, there's always got to be some controversy, and here is no exception: in the City of David—which Palestinians view as a present-day part of their neighborhood—aggressive Israeli organizations have taken control of much of the archaeological agenda, bringing an overtly biblical and political agenda to their digging and interpretation of sites which some consider to be occupied territory. That isn't to say the City of David isn't worth going to; it is so old that it is impossible to be mortal and not think it is unbelievably awesome. For Old Testament nerds, it can be a revelatory experience. Just keep in mind that Jebusites, Babylonians, Ottomans, Palestinians, and scholars might all interpret the area differently. The decidedly less controversial Mount Zion has at least equal religious significance, as Christians view it to be the site of some of the most significant events surrounding Jesus's life.

CITY OF DAVID

Although some consider the methodology of City of David archaeologists a little suspect, it's pretty widely accepted that this site is the probable location of Jebus, the original Canaanite city that King David is said to have captured and made his capital in the 11th century. With a prime location on an elevated plane in the mountains above the Kidron Valley, the City of David has amazing views—oh, and was extremely strategically important, which is probably more the reason that David chose to make it his capital. Throw in a good water supply (Gihon Spring) and, boom: ancient habitation becomes a given. Here, you can see house foundations from the First Temple Period to burial grounds that may date to the seventh century BCE.

To get to the City of David, exit Dung Gate from the Western Wall and take a left, then follow signs. While the 3hr. tour offered at the sight is a helpful and comprehensive introduction (☎02 626 8700; www.cityofdavid.org.il *i* Call a day in advance to reserve a spot.), visitors are also welcome to explore the sights listed below on their own. (⑨ Admission to the park includes all sights. NIS27, students NIS22, seniors and under 18 NIS14. ⏰ Open in summer Su-Th 8am-7pm, F 8am-2pm; in winter Su-Th 8am-5pm, F 8am-noon. Last tickets sold 2hr. before close.)

portman power

Looking for a little Hollywood glam amidst the somber religious symbolism in Jerusalem? Screen star Natalie Portman was actually born in the biblical city—a little girl named Natalie Hershlag immigrated to the United States in 1984 at the age of 3. A dual citizen, she attended Jewish elementary school stateside and even learned to speak Hebrew. After landing her first film role in 1994, she adopted her grandmother's maiden name as a pseudonym in order to protect her family's privacy. In 2004, the celebrity brainiac returned to Israel to complete graduate courses at the Hebrew University of Jerusalem. In the religious spirit of the city, make a pilgrimage to the school in order to pay homage to one of the most powerful (and beautiful) women in Hollywood.

⚑ HEZEKIAH'S TUNNEL   TUNNEL

Provided that you aren't afraid of tiny spaces, darkness, being buried alive, drowning, jagged stone, or things that are soul-blowingly cool, Hezekiah's Tunnel—some combination of theme park, legend, and ancient wonder of the world—is one of the best sights in Jerusalem. As the threat of an Assyrian invasion of Jerusalem grew, King Hezekiah sought to prepare for a siege by channeling water from the Gihon Spring into the city walls, expanding a shaft that may have been originally used in King David's original attack on Jebus. The result: human desperation and ingenuity displayed in their rawest forms, as you can see where the men furiously chipping away at stone with simple sharp objects went off-path, went entirely too high for water to run down and had to start over, and met midway through the tunnel, as left-leaning and right-leaning chink marks converge. Water, however, does manage to run throughout Hezekiah's Tunnel (still, in fact), and the Jews survived the Assyrian attack. Some sections of the tunnel are less than 5 ft. tall and 2½ ft. wide, which means that you don't only read about the increasing fear builders felt as the Assyrians approached but can actually get to see and experience its results.

✣ Follow the steps down from the Observation Point, turn right, and head down Warren's Shaft.

𝒊 Wear waterproof shoes and pants you don't mind getting dirty and wet. Bring a flashlight. The tunnel is extremely dark and the water can reach your thighs.

"THE LAST RESORT" AND "PILGRIM'S WAY"   OLD STREETS

Beneath the broken parts of this street, archaeologists discovered intact cooking utensils and Roman coins from the Second Temple Period. They surmised that the last remaining Jewish residents during the Roman siege of Jerusalem went underground and managed to live there for some time before Romans smashed through the sidewalk and hunted them down. This chilling backstory is not apparent in the simple appearance of the street, which is a remnant from the Second Temple Period, including a staircase that presumably led up to the Temple Mount. Notice how the stairs are spaced out with two steps and then a landing? This is probably because some worshippers would carry water from the Shiloach Pool all the way to the Temple and needed to rest every once in a while. It's a 120m climb up—give the poor schlubs a break.

✣ Just outside the exit of Hezekiah's Tunnel.

BEIT HATZOFEH OVERLOOK   VIEW

A great view of the area surrounding Jerusalem from which you can see lots of potential Old Testament sights. Apparently if you look to the right, you can see where one of Solomon's brothers held a shmancy party, figuring that if he got people drunk and announced his claim to the throne, then he would actually *have* a claim to throne. Unsurprisingly, this attempt to usurp Solomon's place in the succession failed. If you peer straight ahead into a small hole in a rock formation, you can see an ancient Jewish burial site. Or just relax and enjoy the unforgettable 360-degree view.

✣ To the left when you first enter the archaeological part of the City of David, up a staircase. It's on top of the room where the movie is screened.

ROYAL QUARTER   NEIGHBORHOOD

Here, the foundations of one house date from the First Temple Period, or, as we prefer to think of it, the Really Damn Old Period. Through locating a hole in a slab of stone (translation: a toilet) archaeologists have discovered that the residents were eating grasses and uncooked meat, indicating that they were probably in the middle of a siege—not that they were dining on steak tartare and wheatgrass shakes. This toilet and the remains of furniture imported from Lebanon both indicate that this was once a well-to-do neighborhood. Even though little of this structure is left, it is truly amazing to be able to look at this rubble and still get significant historical understanding from it, ancient bowel movements and all.

✣ After passing the palace (below) take a left and continue walking until you see the placards.

THE PALACE   RUINS

Here, the ruins of a large structure may very well be King David's palace. Two seals of documents were hardened—presumably in a fire that burned the documents— and are inscribed with the names of two disciples of the prophet Jeremiah. The age, size, and location of the structure all point to the possibility that it was once David's palace, though there is no definitive proof.

✣ Facing the visitors center, turn left and go down the wide metal staircase descending beneath the center itself.

WARREN'S SHAFT SHAFT

Charles Warren, Jerusalem's most important 19th-century archaeologist (or at least the one with the most important namesakes), discovered and made a series of now disproved conjectures about this tunnel. Though it may just be a natural shaft, some believe this unearthing provides historical evidence for Old Testament stories about the many underground tunnels and fortifications under Jerusalem. Regardless, walking down this eerie passageway is fun for anyone who appreciates treacherous and dank subterranean tunnels or wants to make jokes about how it's not difficult to stay erect in such a large shaft.

 # Follow the path left from the Observation Point, then turn right.

ANCIENT TOMBS OBSERVATION POINT VIEW

Ancient burial grounds dating to the seventh and eighth century BCE can be seen from here. Some people believe that David is buried in one of these crypts, but, seeing as there's a lot of controversy about whether or not David is even a real historical figure, we're really not sure where he was buried. Even if we did, we're not telling.

 # Walk up the pottery path from the Royal Quarter.

SHILOACH POOL RUINS

Archaeologists believe that the water from the once-gigantic Shiloach Pool was carried all the way up to the Second Temple when, you know, the Temple still existed. As most of the site now lies under private land, little of the pool is visible, making it bad for swimming, but still good for oohing and ahhing.

 # Facing out from the steps adjacent to the entrance to "The Last Resort."

MOUNT ZION

Supposedly the site of such mildly important things as the Last Supper, King David's Tomb, and the descent of the Holy Spirit at Pentecost, Mt. Zion sits just outside the Old City walls. During the 1948 War, Mt. Zion was a flashpoint for armed conflict, and bullet holes and bombshell pockmarks function as their own commemorations. To get there, exit the Old City through Zion Gate and go straight along the short path opposite the gate, bearing right at the Franciscan Convent. At the next fork, a left leads to the Cenacle and David's Tomb, while a right takes you to Dormition Abbey.

COENACULUM (CENACLE) RELIGIOUS

The Cenacle is best for those with a vivid imagination. Startlingly sparse due to British efforts to avoid sectarian disputes during their mandate, the room where Jesus supposedly had his last supper is unmarked and unadorned. In fact, a *mihrab* (prayer niche) from the mosque that once stood here is still visible in the southern wall. So, if you're planning on a reenactment, it's probably best to bring your own table. And wine. And disciples.

 # Take a left at the Franciscan Convent and climb the stairs through the Diaspora Yeshiva door on the left. The church is on the 2nd floor. If all else fails, follow the tourist groups led by men with Bibles in their fannypacks. $ Free. ⏰ Open daily 8:15am-5:15pm.

DAVID'S TOMB BURIAL SITE

King David was almost definitely not buried here initially, as the Bible says kings were buried within the walls of the city, and it is unclear how David's tomb could have wound up in this location. Nevertheless, mysterious references in the New Testament to the whereabouts of David's body, the remains of churches surrounding Mount Zion, and a legacy of calling this place David's Tomb has caused some to believe that this is his original burial spot. Some whisper David's psalms in the room, and in a dark recess in the wall sits a

Torah cover blackened with age. Regardless of historical authenticity, witnessing this tradition can be powerful, even for non-believers.

After taking a left at the fork in Mount Zion, go straight. You will see an open entrance to a building and a list of the times that the tomb is open. Take a right once in that room. $ Free. ⏰ Open Su-Th 7am-5pm, F 7am-4pm, Sa 6am-4pm.

BASILICA OF THE DORMITION ABBEY ABBEY

☎02 565 5330; www.dormitio.net

Having recently celebrated its 100th birthday, Dormition Abbey, which commemorates the death of the Virgin Mary, is one of the youngest basilicas in Jerusalem. On the first floor, a series of mosaics depict biblical stories with painstaking artistry (if you look closely at the gold scene above the apse, you can see that three different colors of tile have been used just to texture the figures' clothing). Downstairs, allegedly the home of the Madonna after the resurrection (and the site of her death), a central coffin has a spooky three-dimensional inlay of a resting Mary. Surrounding this sculpture are examples of religious art from around the world, including a *Virgen de Guadalupe* (Virgin of Guadalupe) from Mexico. If you head down to the bathrooms, you can see the excavated ruins of a Byzantine church.

Once you enter Mount Zion, take a right at the fork. It will lead into Dormition Abbey. [i] Call ahead about occasional classical music concerts, which may be held monthly in coming years. $ Free. ⏰ Open Su around 10:30am-noon and 12:30-5:30pm, M-Sa 8:30am-noon and 12:30-5-:30pm. Mass Su-W 7:15am, Th 5:45am, F-Sa 7:15am.

not for prophet

If you're wandering through the streets of Jerusalem and have the sudden urge to don a toga, it doesn't mean you're going crazy. Or, at least, you're not alone in that desire—Jerusalem syndrome, which affects about 50 visitors to the Holy City each year, is a condition marked by the belief that you are actually a prophet. Sufferers perform such specific actions as "preparation of a toga-like gown" (always white, apparently) and "the delivery of a sermon at a holy place."

While most sufferers come to Jerusalem with delusions already solidly in place, a small fraction spontaneously develop them. Once removed from the city, symptoms disappear, and the ashamed tourists prefer not to discuss the experience. And you thought you only had to worry about getting some bad shawarma.

CHAMBER OF THE HOLOCAUST (MARTEF HASHOAH) MEMORIAL

☎02 671 5105

In the wake of the Holocaust, survivors in Israel did not have a place to mourn for their dead loved ones and their lost way of life. So, a year after Israel's independence, Israel's first Chief Rabbi, Isaac Herzog, traveled to death camps in Europe to collect the ashes of the dead and brought them back to be buried at this memorial. Initially a symbolic graveyard where people went to mourn and pay respect to gravestones representing more than a thousand Jewish communities extinguished by the Holocaust, the Chamber of the Holocaust is now a museum. Among the haunting memorabilia from death camps are reconstructed gas chambers and desecrated Torah scrolls which have been put to rest as dictated by Jewish law.

Across the street from the back entrance to David's Tomb. [i] Guided tours for groups require prior arrangement. $ Suggested donation NIS12, students NIS6. ⏰ Open Su-Th 9am-3:45pm, F 9am-1:30pm. Closed on Jewish holidays.

MOUNT OF OLIVES AND KIDRON VALLEY

An apocalyptic Jewish prophecy says God will stand on top of this mountain and it will split in two, some of King Solomon's wives prayed to idols on the mountain, and Jesus is said to have taught his disciples here before being arrested in the Garden of Gethsemane on the mountain's slopes. A chapel around the peak marks the spot where Jesus supposedly ascended to heaven. Basically, this place is kind of a big deal. Walk to the Mount of Olives (*Har HaZeitim* in Hebrew and *Jabal al-Zeitoun* in Arabic) while the sun sets, and its significance becomes clear to believers and non-believers alike: it is a special place. Important Jews have been buried on the mountain since the time of biblical kings, and an ancient necropolis on the southern ridge marks the burial spot of elites from the ninth to seventh centuries BCE.

When visiting, it's best to start early (particularly in the summer, when afternoons get hot) and begin at the top at the Church of Ascension. Either take a cab (which should be under NIS30) or go to the end of Rub'a el-Adawiya St., where the Church of the Pater Noster is. You can begin a bit before this at the Church of Ascension, but to find the main road down Kidron Valley, face the Pater Noster and take a right at the end of the street. Keep going downhill until you see a staircase and then a path down on the right. To start from the bottom and walk up, exit St. Stephen's Gate and walk straight until Jericho Rd., then take a left and you should see the path upward on the left.

CHAPEL OF CHRIST'S ASCENSION — CHAPEL

First built in 392, the Chapel of Christ's Ascension commemorates Jesus's entry to heaven. Its spareness feels holy, as nuns, believers, and tourists stare at a litter box-like marble container of a sacred footprint (illegible after centuries of adoration) and a few candles. The small dome, built by Salah ad-Din in the 12th century, protects monks (and roosting pigeons) from rain. Nine hundred years later, the sight is still owned and operated by Muslims. Unless you go on or around Ascension Day (in May or June, depending on the year), when the Chapel of Ascension becomes mainstream and pilgrims set up shop in the surrounding courtyard, it is usually fairly empty and quiet.

🚶 Walk down Rub'a el-Adawiya St. toward its end at Pater Noster. The Chapel of Christ's Ascension is marked by a yellow sign with blue lettering on the left. It is less than 1min. from Pater Noster. $ NIS5. ⏰ Open daily in summer 8am-6pm; in winter 8am-4:30pm.

CHURCH OF THE PATER NOSTER — CHURCH

Said to be the site of the grotto where Jesus foretold the sacking of Jerusalem and his own Second Coming, the Church of the Pater Noster commemorates the first telling of the Lord's Prayer (*pater noster* is Latin for "our father"). By way of proving what a big deal the Lord's Prayer is, the church displays it in more than 140 different languages, including Mpoo, Quechua, and Provençal. In the middle of the Church lies the body of the former Princesse de la Tour d'Auvergne, who financed the reconstruction of the Church and tried to find the grotto where the Pater Noster was first taught. An urn above the tomb holds the ashes of Italian politician and poet Baron de Bossi, the princess's father. The church, which is run by French Catholics to this day, is surrounded by gardens and, usually, amateur photographers.

🚶 From the Chapel of Ascension, take a left and continue down Rub'a el-Adawiya St. until the dead end. There is a sign. $ NIS7. ⏰ Open M-Sa 8:30am-noon and 2:30-5:30pm.

SANCTUARY OF DOMINUS FLEVIT — CHAPEL, GARDEN

Built in 1955 to commemorate where Jesus wept for Jerusalem, the imminent destruction of the Second Temple, and the oncoming Jewish diaspora (*Dominus flevit* literally means "the Lord wept"), Dominus Flevit has a small chapel with a beautiful mosaic floor and a couple of stone engravings of biblical scenes. The chapel itself is shaped like a teardrop. The sanctuary also includes a surprisingly romantic garden, which has seats overlooking the Old City and the Dome of the Rock.

➜ Exit Pater Noster, make a left, and follow the road as it turns left. Keep going downhill until you see a staircase on the right. Walk down, and pass the Tombs of the Prophets on your left, at which point you can begin to make out the black dome of Dominus Flevit. Walk downhill and take a right through a driveway to enter the courtyard. ℹ Legs and shoulders must be covered. $ Free. ⏰ Open daily 8-11:45am and 2:30-5pm.

RUSSIAN CHURCH OF MARY MAGDALENE — CHURCH

Though the Russian Church is open only 2hr. per day, it's worth changing your schedule around for. Hell, even break into it; the possible jail time is worth the sight of the seven Russian onion domes, golden glories in the sun that look even grander when set in relief by the many columns and arches of its facade. In contrast to the modest chapels that dot the Mount of Olives, this church has a grandiose flair in the most fun Orthodox tradition. Noblewomen such as the Grand Duchess Elizabeth Feodorovna, whose body was smuggled into Jerusalem via Beijing after the Russian Revolution, and Princess Alice of Greece, who helped Jews during the Nazi occupation, are interned at the church. It is very much a monument to the women of Christianity: Mary, its namesake, was Jesus's most prominent female disciple, and Tsar Alexander III built the church for his mother, the Empress Maria Alexandrovna. Women and gardens don't really go well together in the Bible, but this church has some of the lushest and most incredible greenery in the valley.

➜ Continuing downhill, the church is past the Sanctuary of Dominus Flevit on the right. ℹ Legs and shoulders must be covered. $ Free. ⏰ Open Tu 10am-noon, Th 10am-noon, Sa 10am-noon.

GARDEN OF GETHSEMANE AND CHURCH OF ALL NATIONS — CHURCH, GARDEN

The Garden of Gethsemane is the location of Jesus's betrayal and arrest, as well as his lamentation the previous night. The eight olive trees in the Garden today are said to have been witnesses to Jesus's tragedy. In fact, Gethsemane is actually a combination of *gat*, which in Hebrew means wine press, and *shmnanin*, meaning oils, which could only indicate that there was an Italian restaurant in this spot around the fifth century BCE. The church adjacent to this garden was initially built by the Byzantines in 380 CE, though it was destroyed in 614. The "Rock of Agony," which was once the centerpiece of the apse, marks the place where Jesus is said to have sweat blood during prayer has survived to the church's present incarnation. Rebuilt by the Crusaders in the 12th century, it was destroyed again in 1200, and only in 1924 was the basilica fully rebuilt. It is now one of the most impressive churches in Jerusalem, as its hulking dark interior is dramatically lit by small symmetrically aligned lamps hanging from the ceiling. Look up and see if you can find the US state department logo amidst the deep blue roof that was designed to resemble the midnight sky.

➜ Continuing downhill from the Russian Church, Gethsemane is on your left side at the bottom of the path. ℹ Legs and shoulders must be covered. $ Free. ⏰ Open daily Apr-Sept 8am-noon and 2-6pm; Oct-Mar 8am-noon and 2:30-5pm.

TOMB OF THE VIRGIN MARY — TOMB

Mary's supporters are said to have buried her inside this cavernous church and crypt in the first century. You almost have to brush aside the incense with your hands as you try to dodge the treacherously low lamps that hang from the inky ceiling. Maybe it is just that nobody has cleaned this place in 2000 years; apparently it's too holy for a Swiffer.

➜ At the bottom of the main path on the right, across the street from the Church of All Nations. $ Free. ⏰ Open daily 6am-7pm.

WEST JERUSALEM

Don't lie: you came to Jerusalem for the Old City. Fair enough. Who's going to come all this way and not get an awkward, sweaty picture in front of the Dome of the Rock? But if you can get over the wonder of millennia-old sights, West Jerusalem is good for more than just food, shut-eye, and happy hour. It may not merit more than a few days of exploration, but there's more than enough history and charm now that settlers have ventured outside the safety of the Old City walls. Unfortunately, the sights are not condensed into a manageable chunk: Givat Ram has the seat of Israeli democracy and the stunning Israel Museum, but you'll have to travel farther afield for the Chagall House or Mt. Herzl in the far western outskirts. Yad Va-Shem, the Holocaust museum, is similarly a good bus ride away (though it certainly merits the journey). Closer to the city, sightseeing is often just about getting a feel for the hodgepodge of different neighborhoods. A stroll through Mamilla, Mea She'arim, or Mahane Yehuda might not provide much in the way of specific sights, but the character of each neighborhood offers a fascinating glimpse into different modes of modern Israeli life. Basically, get ready for prime people-watching: reach for some comfortable shoes, bring a book that you can pretend to read, and stop for a lot of coffee.

zion square

👍 GREAT SYNAGOGUE OF JERUSALEM — RELIGIOUS SITE

56 King George St. ☎02 623 0628; www.jerusalemgreatsynagogue.com

A veritable newborn when it comes to Israeli sights, this 25-year-old synagogue is dedicated to those lost in the Holocaust and during the subsequent wars for the Israeli state. Renowned for their stained glass windows and excellent cantor and choir, the synagogue encourages visitors, advertising itself as a "home away from home" for the soul-searching and skeptical alike. If you're not entertained by the occasional awkward Bar Mitzvah, take a look at the Dr. Belle Rosenbaum Mezuzah Collection, which is one of the largest such collections in the world.

🚏 From Zion Sq., turn left onto HaHistadrut. Take a right onto Hillel St. and then a left where Hillel intersects with King George St. The synagogue is a few blocks down. ℹ Check website for weekly service times. $ Free. ⏰ Group tours can be arranged Su-Th 9am-noon.

ETHIOPIAN CHURCH — CHURCH

Ethiopia St.

The centerpiece of the city's Ethiopian neighborhood, this huge blue-domed structure was constructed in 1874. A similarly grand blue sanctum sits in the center, surrounded by walls lavishly adorned with vivid murals and inscriptions in Ge'ez (ancient Ethiopian). While perhaps a little faded, the decorum is still opulent enough to give your ordinary Papist a run for his money. Combine this with the fact that the church is usually fairly empty, and you've got a prime spot for quiet reflection. Or, at least, a place to practice your thoughtful face.

🚏 Head east down HaNevi'im St. and make a left onto Ethiopia St. The church is 100m down through the gate on the right. ℹ Shoulders and knees must be covered. Remove shoes before entering the church. Services in Ge'ez daily 5am and 5pm. ⏰ Open daily 5am-5pm.

TICHO HOUSE — MUSEUM

9 Harav Kook St. ☎02 624 5068; www.english.imjnet.org.il

Artist Anna Ticho and her husband built one of the first houses outside the walls of the Old City. From here, she drew the stunning landscapes surrounding Jerusalem and, after her death, she bequeathed the house to Israel. Today the museum and gardens display Ticho's work, in addition to some temporary exhibits, and create a small slice of serenity outside the Old City's walls. There are concerts every Friday morning and all-you-can-take-in wine, cheese, and jazz every Tuesday at 8:30pm.

🚏 From Jaffa Rd., turn onto Harav Kook St. $ Free. ⏰ Open Su-M 10am-5pm, Tu 10am-10pm, W-Th 10am-5pm, F 10am-2pm.

U. NAHON MUSEUM OF ITALIAN JEWISH ART — MUSEUM

27 Hillel St. ☎02 624 1610; www.jija.org

Two of the great food cultures collide at this museum of Italian Jewry. The museum houses artifacts dating from the Middle Ages to modern times, as well as a synagogue that is open to the public on Friday nights and Saturday mornings for services.

 # Take Shamai St. from Zion Sq. and turn onto Bianchini. Take a left onto Hillel St., and the museum is near the corner. $ NIS15, children NIS10. ⏰ Open Su 9am-5pm, M 9am-2pm, Tu-W 9am-5pm, Th-F 9am-1pm.

eastern portion

HUTZOT HAYOTZER ARTISTS' COLONY — NEIGHBORHOOD

Hutzot Hayotzer 24 ☎02 622 1163; www.jerusalem-art.org/artist-colony

The Artists' Colony stands at the head of Yemin Moshe, burrowed into the valley that separates the Old City from the rest of Jerusalem. For the last 40 years, the 26 art galleries and workshops on this small street have been displaying some of the city's most intricate Judaica—silver jewelry reigns supreme, but glass, embroidery, and painting all make appearances as well. The quality is staggering, and the prices match. While many artists keep their private workshops out back, most are more than content to talk you through their displays or just chat. That said, the area is pretty much deserted during the day; other tourists are a rare sight, so many artists have highly irregular hours during the week. Nevertheless, you can usually count on at least half the galleries being open at any point.

 # Located in Yemin Moshe. Go south along Jaffa Rd. until it turns into Hativat Yerushayalim (after the intersection with Yitzhak Kariv). ⏰ Open Su-Th 10am-5pm, F 10am-2pm.

HOUSE OF QUALITY — GALLERIES

12 Hebron Rd. ☎02 671 7430; www.art-jerusalem.com

While it once served as a hospital—and now sounds like a brothel—this beautiful century-old building is home to a set of galleries and workshops. Again, the emphasis is on Judaica, but the workshops centered around this sun-drenched courtyard tend to be smaller and more intimate than those in the Artists' Colony. Prices stay high, however, meaning it's another place where you can look but probably shouldn't touch. Events are regularly held here, so be sure to check the website for what's coming up.

 # Make a left from the west end of the Artists' Colony and go straight past the gate and through the parking lot. Stay to the right and after about 500m in total you will come to Hebron Rd. Continue on the right side of the street about 200m up from the pedestrian bridge across the road. ⏰ Open Su-Th 10am-4pm, F and holiday eves 10am-1pm.

KING DAVID HOTEL — HOTEL

23 King David St. ☎02 620 8888; www.danhotels.com

If you want to live vicariously through Israel's rich and luxurious, the King David Hotel will convince you that you've died and gone to swank heaven. Though you may be looking up in order to thank Jehovah for the powerful air-conditioning, be sure to look down at the famous red carpets, which are lined with gold. Though many of the hotel's amenities are closed to the public, some rooms are open for the viewing pleasure of the lowly likes of you. You can continue to fuel your voyeurism by heading a few doors down to the **YMCA Three Arches Hotel,** which has a 152 ft. tower that offers amazing views of the Old City.

 # Located on King David St. a few blocks south of Hebrew Union University. ⏰ Public areas open daily 10am-10pm. YMCA Tower open daily 7am-11pm.

LIBERTY BELL PARK PARK

King David St.

Yes, it's exactly what it sounds like. A replica of America's Liberty Bell sits in the middle of this sprawling park, looking realistic enough to make T-Jeff proud. However, since this bell lacks the fanfare and fanaticism of the one that hangs in Philadelphia, the park is more a picnic spot than a glorious monument to truth and justice. If the sculptures, basketball courts, walking paths, playgrounds, and frequent festivals aren't enough to keep you entertained, start writing the script for *National Treasure 3*. We're sure it'll be better than the one they're currently working on.

Located in Talbieh and Yemin Moshe, straddling southern King David St. Begins where King David St. meets Beit Lechem Rd. $ Free.

MONTEFIORE WINDMILL WINDMILL

Yemin Moshe

Who says that all Jews who wander are lost? Some are just quixotically looking for the right place to build their windmills. Sir Moses Montefiore found that place in Yemin Moshe in the 1850s, and the windmill bearing his name has since been converted into a museum commemorating his life. Montefiore also built **Mishkenot Sha'ananim,** the first Jewish settlement outside the walls of the Old City. The original buildings have since been converted into a municipal guesthouse, a snooty French restaurant, and a profusion of studios and galleries.

In the Bloomfield Garden. $ Free. ⏰ Open Su-Th 9am-4pm, F 9am-1pm.

MAMILLA NEIGHBORHOOD

Israel has a penchant for paradoxes, and Mamilla is no doubt one of its most quintessential: hugging the walls of the highly spiritual Old City, Mamilla is a promenade of pricey restaurants, designer labels, and even a Rolex shop. Here you easily find the juxtaposition of the old and the new, the secular and the orthodox, the rich and the poor, and almost every other tricky dichotomy that helps define Israel. While Mamilla is your average exercise in superficial mall culture branded with familiar logos, you'll find a cross-section of Jerusalem here—intrigued locals here for the novelty, cellphone-wielding yuppies, aspiring young mallrats and, naturally, homesick American tourists. If you're not keen on this strange little slice of social commentary—or simply not rolling in dough—Mamilla has little to offer. In itself, it's little different from what you'd find back home, albeit in cleaned-up Mamluk architecture. The end of the road leads right up to Jaffa Gate and sports lovely views of the southern city on the way, so at the very least Mamilla is worth a brief stroll for some modern relief after the claustrophobic alleys of the Old City.

west jerusalem outskirts

CHAGALL WINDOWS WINDOWS

Hadassah Medical Center, Kiryat Hadassah ☎02 677 6271

Quick! Get yourself to the hospital. Not because you're hurt (God willing), but because the synagogue in the Hadassah Medical Center in Ein Kerem has breathtaking windows. Stop yawning, already: these are world-renowned masterpieces by Marc Chagall that depict scenes from Genesis and Deuteronomy in his signature swirling style. The stained-glass windows, which use as many as three colors in a single pane, were installed in 1962 but damaged during the 1967 War. Chagall told the hospital not to worry: "You take care of the war," he said, "I'll handle the windows." If you look closely, you can still see bullet holes in three of the panes. Works of art are actually scattered throughout the halls of the medical center; according to Hadassah, they keep the buildings surrounded in art because they "convey the message that soothing the soul is as important to us as healing the body."

Buses #12, 19, or 27. i Best to call before visiting. ⏰ Open Su-Th 8am-1pm and 2-3:45pm.

ISRAELI SUPREME COURT   GOVERNMENT BUILDING

Sha'arei Mishpat St.   ☎02 675 9612; www.court.gov.il

The Supreme Court building, like most Israeli sights, is a strange mix of old and new: it's barely 20 years old, as the postmodern decor indicates, but there are also motifs of the Old City Quarters. If this art talk is already boring you, get straight to business and sit in on one of the trials. (Your Hebrew may not be up to scratch, but you can still nod wisely.) The Supreme Court is connected to the Knesset by the **Wohl Rose Garden,** a meticulously trimmed stretch of rose beds and verdant greens with a wide vista of the city.

⚑ *Take bus #9 from the Central Bus Station. The building is toward the north end of the large park.* *i Must bring passport for entry.* ⌚ *Open Su-Th 8:30am-2:30pm. English tours at noon.*

KNESSET   GOVERNMENT BUILDING

☎02 675 3416; www.knesset.gov.il

Check out the Israeli parliament building for a look into the heart of the country's democracy. Sessions are open to the general public, and free tours are available twice a week; highlights include a short film, the titanic Marc Chagall embroideries adorning the Main Hall, and a peek at the chamber itself.

⚑ *Take bus #9 from the Central Bus Station. The Knesset is toward the middle of the park on Eliezer Kaplan St.* *i Must bring passport for entry.* ⌚ *1hr. tour in English Su and Th 8:30am and noon.*

YAD VA-SHEM   MUSEUM

Mt. Herzl   ☎02 644 3802; www.yadvashem.org

Yad Va-Shem is the largest of Israel's Holocaust museums—in fact, Yad Va-Shem itself is a collection of many museums, including a history museum, art museum, exhibitions pavilion, learning center, and synagogue. Built around the belief that a fitting memorial of the Holocaust cannot be accomplished with a single medium, Yad Va-Shem has filled its walls with countless tributes, including Nazi records, first-person testimonies from victims, and documentation of resistance. The resulting experience is powerful and disturbing. Start your visit at the **Historical Museum,** which traces the Holocaust through photographs, documents, and relics before ending with a simple but powerful image: symbolic tombs show the number of Jews killed in each country, and there is a tiny shoe that belonged to one of the Holocaust's 1.5 million child victims. Next, the **Hall of Names** houses the names of every known Holocaust victim; visitors to the museum may fill out a Page of Testimony recording the name and circumstances of death of family members killed by the Nazis. The names of many of the concentration camps are engraved into the floor of the **Hall of Remembrance,** which also houses a *ner tamid,* the eternal flame traditionally seen at Jewish altars. The nearby **art museum** displays drawings and paintings composed by Jews in the ghettos and concentration camps, while the aptly named **Children's Hall** displays the toys

sights

and dolls that outlived their young owners. In the same room are guest books in which visitors may share their impressions; reading through the thoughts and reflections left by others is at least as powerful as the curated exhibits.

By far the most haunting part of Yad Va-Shem is the **Children's Memorial,** where a recorded voice recites the names and ages of young victims as you look into mirrors that have been positioned to create the illusion of an infinite sea of candles. The **Avenue of Righteous Among the Nations** honors non-Jewish Europeans who risked their lives to aid Jews fleeing Europe, and the **Valley of the Communities** is an enormous labyrinthine memorial dedicated to the destroyed villages of Europe, where family members may wander through the carved names of these *shtetls* that are no more, searching for their ancestral towns. Don't plan to do too much right after a visit; the museum's several buildings deserve some time and take an emotional toll.

🚌 Take bus #13, 18, or 20 and get off at the red arch just past Mt. Herzl. Turn around and take a left on Ein Kerem St., then follow the signs down HaZikaron St. for about 10min. ℹ Tours in English or Hebrew daily 11am. $ Entry free. Tours NIS30. Audio tour NIS20. ⏰ Open Su-W 9am-5pm, Th 9am-8pm, F 9am-2pm.

MOUNT HERZL AND THE HERZL MUSEUM MUSEUM, MOUNTAIN

Herzl Blvd. ☎02 632 1515; www.herzl.org

At the summit of Mt. Herzl is, appropriately, a cemetery and museum dedicated to Theodor Herzl—the man, the myth, the legendary father of modern Zionism. The museum, along with a short video, follows Herzl's intellectual journey and his attempts to create a Jewish state. Zionists can sometimes be quite zealous, and the site is mainly focused on promoting the goals of the movement, particularly those yet to be reached. The mountain also acts as Israel's National Cemetery, containing the resting place of Herzl as well as those of such legendary Israeli leaders as Golda Meir and Yitzhak Rabin. If you wish to memorialize one of the many graves, keep in mind that in the Jewish faith it's traditional to leave rocks, not flowers.

🚌 Bus #13, 14, 18, 20, 21, 27, or 33. $ NIS25, under 6 free. Students, soldiers, seniors, and children NIS20. ⏰ Open Su-W 8:45am-6pm, Th 8:45am-8pm, F 8:45am-12:15pm. Last tour 1hr. before close.

JERUSALEM FOREST FOREST

If you've seen enough weathered stone and gold leaf to last a lifetime, go west, young man. Or, more specifically, take a trip out to Ein Kerem—though its Jerusalem Forest has shrunk from 4 sq. km to about 1.5 sq. km, it still boasts gorgeous views and short hikes.

🚌 Buses #12, 27, 42, or 19. Located in Ein Kerem, just west of Mt. Herzl.

ISRAEL MUSEUM MUSEUM

Ruppin Blvd. ☎02 670 8811; www.english.imjnet.org.il

Want to nourish the budding numismatist in you? The Israel Museum has ancient coins galore. Prefer contemporary and Asian art? It's got that covered too. With an extensive collection of antiquities, sculptures, ancient and modern art, and books, as well as a children's section with hands-on exhibits, the museum has nearly as many facets as the country itself. But the biggest draw of the museum is undoubtedly its ownership of the **Dead Sea Scrolls,** which are located in the Shrine of the Book section of the museum. The scrolls, which date back to the second century BCE, were hidden for thousands of years in the caves around Qumran. Rediscovered in 1947, they contain prayers and stories that are almost identical to those in the modern Talmud and have therefore been used to support claims of Judaism's ancient roots. In addition to the scrolls, the museum houses over 500,000 other pieces that range from fine art to archaeological artifacts. Extensive renovations during 2010 have brought the museum upgraded public facilities and surrounding landscapes; in particular, be sure not to miss the **Billy Rose Art Garden,** widely considered to be one of the world's finest outdoor sculpture gardens.

Though the museum undoubtedly puts an emphasis on Judaica, the **Ruth Young Wing for Art Education** frequently hosts programs to promote intercultural understanding between Arab and Jewish students in addition to many art-based activities for children.

🚏 Buses #9, 9a, 17, 17a, 24, or 24a. $ NIS48, students NIS36. Seniors, disabled, and ages 5-17 NIS24. Soldiers free. Ages 5-17 free on Tu and Sa. Repeat visit within 3 months NIS24. ⏰ Open Su-M 10am-5pm, Tu 4-9pm, W-Th 10am-5pm, F and holiday eves 10am-2pm, Sa and holidays 10am-5pm.

BIBLE LANDS MUSEUM — MUSEUM

25 Granot St. ☎02 561 1066; www.blmj.org

Sure, all of Israel can be treated like a field trip into the Bible, but this museum really makes that concept come to life. Mixing religious and academic history, the museum attempts to tell the story of the Bible using artifacts collected by Dr. Elie Borowski, who founded the museum in 1992 after his wife convinced him not to build the museum in Toronto. Each area of land mentioned in the Bible gets a spot, and the museum contains everything from coins to scale models of ancient Jerusalem.

🚏 On Museum Row in Givat Ram between the Israel Museum and the Bloomfield Science Museum. ℹ Tours Su-Tu and Th-Sa in English 10:30am, in Hebrew 11am. Tours W in English 10:30am and 5:30pm, in Hebrew 11am and 8pm. $ NIS40, students, soldiers, new immigrants, seniors, and ages 5-18 NIS20. ⏰ Open Su-Tu 9:30am-5:30pm, W 9:30am-9:30pm, Th 9:30am-5:30pm, F and holiday eves 9:30am-2pm, Sa 10am-3pm.

L.A. MAYER MUSEUM FOR ISLAMIC ART — MUSEUM

2 HaPalmach St. ☎02 566 1291; www.islamicart.co.il

Located near Talbieh, this museum puts the "art" into artifact: a dazzling display of Islamic work is arranged by chronology rather than genre, allowing visitors to use the changing images of art and culture as a study of Islamic history and tradition. The exhibits include a gigantic collection of clocks from around the world, as well as a variety of Islamic historical artifacts, ranging from weaponry to chessboards.

🚏 In the German Colony. Bus #13 from the Central Bus Station via city center stops on HaPalmach St. Buses #9, 19, 22, 31, and 32 stop on Aza Rd., a short walk from the museum. $ NIS40; students, children, seniors, soldiers, and police NIS30. ⏰ Open Su-M 10am-3pm, Tu 10am-7pm, W 10am-3pm, Th 10am-7pm, F and holiday eves 10am-2pm, Sa and holidays 10am-4pm.

BLOOMFIELD SCIENCE MUSEUM — MUSEUM

Hebrew University, Givat Ram ☎02 654 4888; www.mada.org.il

Cue the Bill Nye music: science rules. At least, the Bloomfield Science Museum certainly does. Like most museums of its kind, Bloomfield seems geared for elementary school field trips, but that's not to say big kids and adults can't have fun. Frequently changing exhibits, a huge IMAX Theater, and a prime location near the rest of Givat Ram's museums ensure that it's worth the visit. All of the exhibits have English labels, and most of the staff speaks English.

🚏 Egged bus #9, 24, or 28 to Givat Ram, Hebrew University. The museum is a 5min. walk from there. $ NIS34, on holidays and school vacations NIS40. Families (parents and under 18) NIS110/145. Students, soldiers, police, and disabled NIS27/34. Seniors NIS17/20. Under 5 free. ⏰ Open M-Th 10am-4pm, F 10am-2pm, Sa 10am-4pm.

CHURCH OF THE VISITATION — CHURCH

Off HaMa'ayan ☎02 641 7291

According to lore, Mary visited her cousin Elizabeth here when both women were pregnant. As the two were complaining about swollen feet and weird cravings (at least, we think so), Elizabeth's baby—soon to be John the Baptist—apparently recognized the unborn savior and leapt with joy in her womb. Elizabeth was then filled with the Holy Spirit and realized that her cousin was carrying the miniature deity; in response, Mary spoke the **Magnificat,** her famous speech honoring God. The Church of Visitation now stands at the home of Elizabeth and her husband, and the Magnificat is printed in 57 languages on one side. If this highly specific event doesn't hold quite enough clout for you, follow the tunnel near one side of the altar to find an ancient well and the rock behind which John hid to save himself from the Romans. Also be sure to get a look at the stunning mosaic that depicts Mary's journey to the Church.

In western Ein Kerem, just above the Spring of Virgin. $ Free. ⏰ Open daily 8-11:45am and 2:30-6pm.

ARDON WINDOW LIBRARY

Edmond Safra campus, Givat Ram ☎02 658 5027; www.jnul.huji.ac.il

Get your nerd on—and see some gorgeous sights—at the Jewish National and University Library in Givat Ram. Unlike most stained-glass pieces, the windows here show different Judaic symbols rather than biblical figures. Make up your own story out of the symbols, or be a spoilsport and check out a few books to learn the real story. Either way, we recommend a walk around the Hebrew University campus; wax poetic about "important topics" and clear your throat frequently in order to blend in with the studious crowd here.

Buses #9, 24, or 28 to the main entrance of the Givat Ram, Hebrew University–Edmond Safra campus. There is an intercampus bus service for students. ℹ *To enter the campus by car, you need a special permit from security, located near the main entrance. $ Free. ⏰ Open Su-Th 9am-8pm, F 9am-1pm. Loan desk open Su-Th 9am-6pm.*

JASON'S TOMB TOMB

10 Alfasi St.

In a city where Jesus walked, Jason really isn't that big of a deal—he bought his way into being named High Priest, then quickly lost the job after a rival outbid him. Come to think of it, his tomb isn't that big of a deal either, but it's a nice place to find some peace away from the city. One of the better preserved tombs in Israel, this rock-cut resting place contains a simple courtyard and a single Doric column along with a few charcoal drawings and inscriptions.

Walking south on Gaza Rd., turn left onto Radak St. Take a left onto Alfasi St., and the tomb is on the right. $ Free. ⏰ Open M-Th 10am-1pm.

MAHANE YEHUDA NEIGHBORHOOD

Looking to hone your haggling skills? Or just tired of all that extra elbow room people keep giving you? Mahane Yehuda, the Arabic quarter of the modern city, has your back when it comes to low prices under the high sun. While the Old City's *souq* has its fair share of touristy knick-knacks, the knock-off fezzes don't make it over here: this is a market for the locals (read: groceries galore). Row upon row of stalls flank **Mahane Yehuda Street** and the parallel **HaHayim Street** and sell everything from standard fruits and vegetables for a couple shekels to some of the best *halva* that (not much) money can buy. On Friday afternoons, the market gets swamped with the Shabbat rush as Jews from all over the city, including the top-hatted droves from Mea She'arim who rarely leave their neighborhood, descend upon the market to get all the ingredients necessary to make a meal that will keep the mother-in-law happy. By far the best time to swing by is during closing hours, when the prices are driven ridiculously low as vendors try to get rid of their day's wares.

If your idea of cooking is picking up the phone for Domino's, well, Mahane Yehuda doesn't have Domino's—but you can easily find someone to wait on you. Punctuating the throngs of stands are hip cafes and some of the quirkiest restaurants you'll find in the city. Sip your coffee and leave the vicious bartering to the plebes—at the end of the day, darling, it's just an eggplant. You can easily make a sport out of people-watching here, so go ahead and unleash your voyeurism on the masses.

🕐 *Market open Su-Th early-7pm, F early-1pm.*

GERMAN COLONY   NEIGHBORHOOD

Good work there, Einstein. The German Colony was indeed founded by German immigrants—they set up shop in the 1870s with luxurious European-style homes, beautiful stonework, and plenty of the good old green stuff (trees, not absinthe). Nowadays, there's little German about the area, but the upscale character has made it through the century, and the main thoroughfare, **Emek Refa'im,** has become a restaurant and cafe haven. Some of the city's best mid-range restaurants have found their way down here, while a rabble of cafes sprawls onto the pavements. Because it's down south and a little out of the way (the walk from Zion Sq. is at least 45min.) the area never gets too crowded, nor is it too tainted by the tourist swarms. Rather it's a serene sanctum for expats and the middle-class Israeli crowd, who take in lazy afternoons with an aimless stroll. While enjoying your own walk-and-gawk time, mosey over to the **Haas Promenade,** where you'll get an amazing view of the Old City—and even as far as the Dead Sea.

🚌 *Buses #21 or 4 go between the area around Zion Sq. and Emek Refa'im.*

MEA SHE'ARIM   NEIGHBORHOOD

Without a doubt, Mea She'arim is the most religious patch of land in Jerusalem. Spanning about six blocks, the neighborhood is a final remnant of the *shtetls* (small communities) that lived in Eastern Europe before the Holocaust. Now imported into the Middle East, it feels kind of like a big, black-and-white-clad, wig-wearing anachronism. Mea She'arim is home to a few thousand Ultra-Orthodox Jews who live stringently by religious doctrine: expect to hear Yiddish on the streets (Hebrew being too holy for common conversation), prepare yourself for plenty of funny hats, and don't plan to visit during Shabbat, as inhabitants have been known to literally barricade all entrances into the village. To put it simply, it's probably the last place on earth that you're going to find a McRib.

A word of warning: the "Ultra" in Ultra-Orthodox is there for a reason. People here don't take lightly to remarks against their way of life (even if they weren't meant to be offensive) and have been known to throw stones, or, more recently, dirty diapers at anyone they deem to be in violation of doctrine. Huge red signs near the neighborhood entrances warn you about the stringent dress code; while men can get away with just covering their knees, women should avoid tight clothing and cover up as much as possible. Pants are prohibited for women, so it's best to stick to loose blouses and long skirts that cover at least the knees. It's also best to enter individually: the area is above all residential, so loud tourist groups are just going to make residents feel like zoo animals.

If someone hasn't doused you in baby poop within 5min., chances are you're doing fine. Granted, much of the area's hostile reputation is thanks to a small minority known as the **Neturei Karta (City Keepers),** who have gone so far as to oppose the Israeli state, claiming it is illegitimate until the Messiah shows up. Signs proclaiming a modern "Israeli Holocaust" and vehement accusations of racism, though uncommon, are not unheard of in the area, and they even once asked Yasser Arafat to accept them as a minority in any future Palestinian state. Nevertheless, the majority of residents will leave you alone as long as you don't let them know you've got a thong on under that skirt. Indeed, some might even be so friendly as to (gasp) talk to you.

Once inside, safe and sound, you'll quickly realize that Mea She'arim is just as residential as the signs claim. The main street, **Mea She'arim Street,** has a small band of stores that includes a bakery serving up some of the best challah in town and a cluster of kiosks, fishsellers, and the odd Judaica store—books and clothing are particularly prominent. A small market sometimes congregates one street over along **Ein Ya'akov,** where fruit, vegetables, and cheap CDs are on display. The streets stay relatively quiet and the nicest thing to do is simply take a quiet stroll and people-watch... just make sure not to stare. In fact, maybe just stick to people-glancing.

EAST JERUSALEM

Sure, the best reasons to come to East Jerusalem are the food, the fun of walking around, and the chance to soak in the texture of Palestinian life interspersed with nervously hurrying Hasids, but the area also has a few worthwhile sights. The quirky historical array includes the **Garden Tomb,** the supposed location of Christ's burial; **Ammunition Hill,** a museum trumpeting Israel's victory in the Six-Day War; and a mosque with roots in the 13th century.

central east jerusalem

👍 ROCKEFELLER MUSEUM — MUSEUM

27 Sultan Suleiman St. — ☎02 628 2251; www.img.org.il

Exhibiting a chronologically organized history of the Holy Land, the Rockefeller Museum embodies a narrative of Jerusalem and the area around it in a series of half-sculptures, fresco fragments, and trinket remains. In fact, the museum itself is a story of broken pieces put back together: built on top of some of the first structures erected outside the Old City walls in the early 18th century, it is an inheritance from the time of the British mandate in the 1930s. Some of the best pieces in the museum are in its collection of ancient Egyptian art, with one room full of intact sculptures of kings from the 13th century BCE.

🚏 Continue down Sultan Suleiman St. past Salah ad-Din; after another 5min. of walking you will see a driveway leading uphill and a closed gate. ℹ Brochures and signs in English. $ Free. ⏰ Open Su-M and W-Th 10am-3pm, Sa 10am-2pm.

GARDEN TOMB — GARDEN, RELIGIOUS SITE

Schick St. — ☎02 627 2754; www.gardentomb.com

Unverified biblical connections, large rock formations, and the historical remnants of the garden of Joseph of Arimathea—a wealthy Jerusalem resident who, according to the New Testament, donated his own tomb to Jesus—have effectively convinced a small group of Western European Christians that this spot is the site of the Crucifixion. Whether or not the facts behind the tomb are historically accurate, the garden around it is a beautiful place to sit. All denominations come out to enjoy the spot: American teenagers sit in circles and play Christian rock, Portuguese men play keyboards they have brought along with them, and tours are conducted in everything from Japanese to Hebrew to Dutch. If the people-watching isn't enough, these tours can also be fun, as long as you don't mind unsubtle insertions of Gospel and occasional outbursts of the devout speaking in tongues.

🚏 Enter Nablus Rd. from Sultan Suleiman St. and take the 2nd right onto Schick St. Follow signs. ℹ Guided tours can usually be organized on arrival by a member of the staff, but it is good to call ahead. Not wheelchair-accessible. $ Free. ⏰ Open M-Sa 8:30am-noon and 2-5:30pm.

MUSEUM ON THE SEAM — MUSEUM

4 Hel Handasa St. — ☎02 628 1278; www.mots.org.il

Of the many Jerusalem museums that try to find a way to approach ethnic and sectarian conflict in the Middle East, this may be the only one that does so exclusively through contemporary art. The Museum on the Seam seeks to showcase a variety of viewpoints expressed by artists with different backgrounds who work in different media.

🚏 Cross from Nablus Rd. to Hel Handasa via either Na'omi Kiss or Antara Ben-Shadad St. Continue

walking up Hel Handasa. The museum is on the left, with the entrance up a flight of stairs and through large glass doors. *i* *Closed when installing a new exhibition. Be sure to call ahead.* $ *NIS25; students, soldiers, and seniors NIS20.* ⏰ *Open Su-Th 10am-5pm, F 10am-2pm.*

sheikh jarrah

SAINT GEORGE'S CATHEDRAL — CATHEDRAL

20 Nablus Rd. ☎02 627 1670; www.j-diocese.org

Officially consecrated in 1898 as the home of Anglicanism in the Middle East, St. George's is now an excellent example of (middle) east meets west: heavy incense swirls in the arched vaults, and services are held in Arabic and English with musical accompaniment from an impressively gigantic organ. Faded plaques commemorating 19th- and early 20th-century figures hang outside the cathedral, and, on the outer western wall, you can find the block that people would use to mount their horses. During World War I, the site was also used as a base for the Ottoman army; the surrender of Jerusalem to the British in 1917 was signed in the bishop's residence.

Walk uphill on Nablus Rd. past the intersection with Na'omi Kiss. The cathedral is on the right through an open gate. $ *Free.* ⏰ *Open M-Sa 8am-5pm. The cathedral sometimes closes at 4pm, so call ahead if you plan on coming late.*

SHEIKH JARRAH MOSQUE — MOSQUE

Nablus Rd.

Though it's barely more than a century old, the Sheikh Jarrah Mosque is said to have been built on the site of a Salah ad-Din mosque from the 13th century, and a tomb inside is supposedly that of Hussam al-Din al-Jarrahi, an emir who was Salah ad-Din's personal physician and the namesake of the Sheikh Jarrah neighborhood. The real appeal of the place, though, particularly for those interested in Muslim culture, is that it's a functioning mosque that provides a perspective on Muslim life in modern Jerusalem. It's a simple place of worship, with a few men kneeling on the floor and others standing around to chat. Though foreigners are not technically allowed inside, you can usually gain entry by asking politely.

Right after passing the American Colony on Nablus Rd., take a right and walk into the large entryway adjacent to the minaret. *i* *To get inside, it helps to be conservatively dressed and not wearing anything identifiably Jewish. Try to enter with a Muslim, or ask 1 of the people milling outside or in the nearby restaurant, Haj'hazem, to ask permission to enter.* $ *Free.* ⏰ *Open daily sunrise-sunset. If you hear calling in Arabic through a loudspeaker, it's prayer time, and you should hold off on entering.*

AMMUNITION HILL — MILITARY MEMORIAL, MUSEUM

5 Shagrai St. ☎02 582 9392; www.givathatachmoshet.org.il

Now a bare sandy outcropping bordering the highway, Ammunition Hill was a flashpoint of violence during the 1967 Six-Day War. One of the key strategic outposts captured by Israel in order to unite Jerusalem under its flag, the hill has since been dedicated to the Israeli soldiers who died in the fighting. The plaques remembering the dead are very detailed—to the level of "even as a child he was good at chess"—and make the battle more accessible to outsiders. Walking on the grounds can be chilling or boring, depending on your enjoyment of battle sites. The nearby museum has some interesting models of rockets used during the war and pictures of Israel before and during the conflict.

From the Ambassador Hotel, continue walking uphill on Nablus Rd. until you get to Clermont Ganneau, then take a left and cross the highway onto Shagrai St. Walk on Shagrai, and the museum entrance is to the right. It's about 5min. outside Sheikh Jarrah. $ *Free. Pamphlets NIS5. Guided tours NIS450.* ⏰ *Open in summer Su-Th 9am-6pm, F 9am-2pm; in winter Su-Th 9am-5pm, F 9am-1pm.*

Baibars St.

It is fitting that Belgium, stiff competitor in quality-of-life country rankings and historic exporter of chocolate and waffles, has its embassy on Baibars St., the prettiest boulevard in central Sheikh Jarrah. On a quiet side street in this luxurious neighborhood, homeowners have constructed a memorable row of beige brick mini-mansions with large courtyards and a surprising variety of trees, from your basic palms and to the decidedly more deciduous. As long as a barking guard dog doesn't find a way to bite your head off and the exclusivity of the hoity-toity gates doesn't bother you (it shouldn't—they're the only thing between you and that guard dog), this is a great place to gawk at the finery of Sheikh Jarrah living.

✠ *Walk uphill past the Ambassador Hotel on Nablus Rd. and take the 1st right.*

food

If you have an endless appetite for hummus, Jerusalem is worth a culinary pilgrimage in its own right. You'll find the best cheap eats in Arab districts: **Ikermewli** in East Jerusalem is superb, and the small shops of the **Muslim Quarter** (particularly Shab) abound with the sweet grease of street food at its best. The generalization may break down as you hit the more upscale places in East Jerusalem, but it's indisputable that the best restaurants go to West Jerusalem, where every cuisine imaginable awaits. Be sure to spend ample time close to city center in the small alleys of **Rivlin Street** and the **Feingold Garden**—or just head straight for the intellectual coffeehouse mecca that is **T'mol Shilshom.** Then venture away from the touristy areas; while **Zion Square** may have enough international restaurants to feed you for a year, a trip to the bakeries of religious Mea She'arim or to the modernized Jewish fare in the German Colony is definitely worth it.

a sauce for the bold

Amba, a popular Israeli condiment, should be treated with due caution: rumor has it that eating large quantities can cause an unusual body odor for up to a week. Originally from India, this pickled mango sauce was brought to Israel by Iraqi Jews. The key ingredient to its smelly magic is the spice fenugreek, which is somewhat bitter when raw. But, when toasted, it is said to taste like maple syrup, and it is this sweet smell which you will supposedly exude from your pores. *Amba* is found in most restaurants that sell shawarma and falafel, so if smelling like pancakes tickles your fancy—and seriously, whose fancy would not be tickled?—go ahead and load it on.

OLD CITY

The land of milk and honey's land of falafel and kebab. **Amigo Emil** is about your only bet for the sit-down, waitstaff, fork-and-knife experience, but if that's the experience you're looking for, you should probably have just dropped your canvas shoulder bags somewhere back in West Jerusalem. The best food you'll find in the Old City is the kind that involves not only your bare hands but also the bare hands of a possibly sweaty and definitely frantic chef/acrobat with a cafeteria spoon. **Shab** and the **Green Door Pizza Bakery,** both in the Muslim Quarter, cook up some of the best street fare in town, though it's hard to go wrong if you just keep searching the various closet-sized food stands of the Muslim Quarter. Basically, if you think unwashed hands and

Jerusalem

leftover vegetables add a subtle seasoning to your food, then you can have a religious experience without ever going to the Temple Mount. But if you're convinced Purell is the only thing that stands between you and certain death, then it's probably best to eat before entering the Old City.

muslim quarter

▨ SHAB
KEBAB $

3 al-Attarin St.

Two men knead a mound of green meat with their bare hands as if it were clay; strangers huddle together to eat side by side at four tiny tables; the crackling of fire in the oven can be heard from the street. This is Shab (meaning "young man" in Arabic), a claustrophobic and austere scoop-in-the-wall kebab shop that has remained utterly undiscovered by the frantic tourists of the Christian Quarter. A kebab plate (NIS22) comes with four delicate green meat pipes—each browned to an ideal crisp and spiced with subtlety—grilled onions and tomatoes, and standard Arabic bread. And that's it: Shab makes nothing other than these essentials. In a neighborhood dedicated to the commercial and religious experience of outsiders, Shab remains an enclave of sweet simplicity.

✚ *At the intersection of Khan az-Zait and Souq ed-Dabbagha right in front of St. Alexander's Church, continue in the direction of Khan az-Zait as it becomes al-Attarin St. Shab is the 2nd storefront on the left* **i** *Cash only. Restaurant very hot during summer. Dress conservatively.* ☒ *Open daily 9am-5pm.*

▨ AL MUFTI
CAFE $

12 Via Dolorosa ☎02 628 8463; Almufticafe@gmail.com

A spanking two-and-a-half months old at the time of writing, Al Mufti is the cafe to go to. Its founder and manager, Omar, is a financial analyst who went to high school and college in the United States and rightly realized that tourists and caffeine-addled locals needed a place in the Old City to go to for decent drinks. The result? A simple, posh spot for cappuccino (NIS10) and conversation. Omar's upbringing in the Muslim Quarter means he also knows the signless side streets and can tell you the history of the neighborhood. The menu continues to grow by the day.

✚ *From Damascus Gate, walk on Khan az-Zait. Turn left on the Via Dolorosa, and Al Mufti is a few shops down on the left.* **i** *Free Wi-Fi. A/C. Nice bathrooms.* Ⓢ *Coffee drinks NIS10-15, small food items under NIS25. Cash only.* ☒ *Open daily 9am-9pm.*

▨ JA'FAR SWEETS COMPANY
SWEET SHOP $

Souq Khan az-Zait ☎02 628 3582

Thin and doughy layers of *konafah* (NIS3) come drenched in a sweet, sticky goo and filled with sugary cream. Widely reputed to be the best dessert place in town, Ja'far attracts locals who buy by the bundle and a few stray tourists. It's a great place to go to stash up on sweets, as 0.25kg of *konafah* is only NIS12. The gray plastic tables and similarly dull walls may make Ja'far less than ideal for passing the time, but, after eating here for a few minutes, it'll probably be best that you walk it off anyway.

✚ *From Damascus Gate, walk 5min. Ja'far is on the right after passing the 3rd Station of the Cross.* Ⓢ *Baklava NIS1, boxes of sweets NIS12-130. Cash only.* ☒ *Open daily 8am-7:30pm.*

GREEN DOOR PIZZA BAKERY
PIZZA $

Between al-Wad, Sheih Reihan St., and Risas St. ☎02 627 6171

Arabic pizza combines some of the most profound things humans have ever created—the hamburger, the omelette, and the pizza—into one revelatory meal. This fast-food ambrosia for the gods is served in all its primordial glory at Green Door Pizza Bakery. The restaurant is so committed to pizza that it is actually shaped like a pizza oven itself, with walls of blackened, breaking plaster and a tiny entrance. Okay, to be honest, the grime doesn't stop there: this place is

food

probably best for those who believe that a slightly overflowing trash bin, a putrid refrigerator, and ingredients littered on the floor add some perverse and wonderful taste. For the more rational, less budget-obsessed: you could miss out, or just blindfold yourself and dig in.

Enter al-Wad from Damascus Gate and take an immediate left. It's one of the first things on the left. If you start walking down al-Wad, you've missed the turn. ***i*** *Vegetarian pizza available.* [$] *Pizza NIS15.* ⏰ *Open daily 10am-10pm.*

ABU SHUKRI FALAFEL $

Al-Wad ☎02 627 1538

Abu Shukri is perhaps the only restaurant that has managed to make it with the tourist crowd despite having a menu that includes nothing more than a good falafel and a handful of other dishes. That is, it has been well-reviewed in enough guide books that fanny-packers and backpackers alike now sample some of this falafel greatness alongside a few locals. The falafel is above average in quality, but truly exceptional in terms of value at a meager NIS10. Also try the exceptionally good baklava.

Walk on al-Wad toward the Dome of the Rock. Abu Shukri will be on the left soon after the 3rd Station of the Cross. [$] *Falafel NIS10. Hummus plate NIS20. Cash only.* ⏰ *Open daily 8am-4pm.*

NAZMI MIDDLE EASTERN $

Souq el-Khawajat

Considering its inconspicuous streetside slop-stop status, Nazmi probably has the best falafel sandwich in the area. Sit among chatting local families in a surprisingly large room, and pita bread will be nonchalantly placed right on your table along with piping hot and crunchy falafel and, really, not much else: they even give you the option of a falafel sandwich without hummus, which is strikingly rare. Unlike some other local restaurants, however, Nazmi makes it food fresh—nobody reaches into the familiar tin of stagnant sauces and chickpeas to deliver you ambiguously old food.

At the end of David St. near the Jewish Quarter, take a left onto Souq el-Khawajat. Nazmi will be on the right past some public toilets. ***i*** *Women might want to dress conservatively, but there is no rule.* [$] *Everything under NIS30.* ⏰ *Open daily 8am-4pm.*

armenian quarter

ARMENIAN TAVERN ARMENIAN $$

79 Armenian Orthodox Patriarchate Rd. ☎02 627 3854

The Armenian Tavern is a curiosity shop of chandeliers, pots, portraits, and icons, all of which hang without rhyme or reason from the restaurant's ceiling and across its walls. A uniformly tourist crowd gathers here for authentic Armenian cooking, including a wide variety of beef dishes. Its selected plate (NIS60) comes with *basturma*, *soujuk*, *kubbeh*, and *lahmajun*, all of which may sound like sneezes but are, in fact, just different ways of preparing beef. Their *kubbeh*—fried wheat balls packed with beef—is the highest form of dumpling. Vegetarians or those otherwise unsympathetic to cow-eating will find a variety of salads to their liking.

From Jaffa Gate, walk down Armenian Orthodox Patriarchate Rd. The Armenian Tavern is on the left right after you pass St. James Rd. [$] *Appetizers NIS15-35. Entrees NIS60. Salads NIS30.* ⏰ *Open M-Sa 11am-10pm.*

BULGHOURJI ARMENIAN, ITALIAN $$

6 Armenian Orthodox Patriarchate Rd. ☎02 628 2080; www.bulghourji.rest-e.co.il

Home to what may be the best restaurant garden in all of the Old City, Bulghourji puts many tables around a large spread of greenery that could make you forget that you're in a sardine tin of commercial and religious cacophony. Although the restaurant is primarily a destination for tourist groups, individuals can nonetheless stop by for dinner or, with a reservation, for lunch to try the range of high-priced Armenian meat options or one of the few Italian options. If it's too hot to enjoy the garden, Bulghourji also has excellent air-conditioning—a godsend in the land of sweaty tourism that is the Old City.

🪧 3 doors down from the Armenian Tavern on the opposite site of the street. ℹ Reservations often needed for lunch, as a lot of tour groups eat here. $ Meat entrees NIS75. Pasta NIS45. ⏰ Open daily noon-10pm

jewish quarter

MENORAH CAFE — JEWISH, INTERNATIONAL $$

87 HaYehudim Rd. ☎02 628 9944

For all the Jews that make the schlep to Israel, it appears that no one could find even a half-decent Jewish mother. Indeed, Menorah Cafe is clearly the best you can do foodwise in the Jewish Quarter, where an unmatched wealth of cultural artifacts is inexplicably set in a neighborhood where you can't get a decent pastrami on rye, let alone an edible falafel or potato latke. At Menorah, a well-appointed cafe covered in bottles of Israeli red wine, above-average Jewish classics come at reasonable prices (large homemade *bourekas*, eggs, and vegetables NIS35). Western fare is similarly good for value, like the pizza made with homemade dough (NIS48). You can also plant yourself under a big umbrella in the peaceful outdoor seating area and enjoy an iced coffee (NIS16) or a gooey chocolate soufflé (NIS27).

🪧 At the intersection between HaYehudim and Tiferet Yisra'el St. Walk down HaYehudim toward the Jewish Quarter wall and the City of David. Damascus Gate should be behind you. ℹ Free Wi-Fi. $ Entrees NIS36-48. ⏰ Open Su-Th 7am-8:30pm, F 7am-4pm.

QUARTER CAFE — JEWISH $$

11 Tiferet Yisra'el St. ☎02 628 7770; www.quarter-cafe.co.il

A single mediocre latke may cost NIS16, and the setting may consist of plastic tables surrounding a self-service buffet counter, but Quarter Cafe compensates for its flaws with its air-conditioning, a welcome relief from the crowded and sweaty Jewish Quarter. This cafeteria often hosts groups and can empty out later in the day, which makes it a nice place to just sit and appreciate the panoramic view of the area just outside of the Jewish Quarter's Old City walls. Either way, it beats the melted mozzarella bagels and overpriced kosher hamburgers that make up most of your other dining options in the Jewish Quarter.

🪧 Up the stairs at the end of Tiferet Yisra'el, with the Burnt House on its direct left. $ Coffee NIS15. Apple strudel and chocolate cake NIS25. Israel plate, which includes multiple salads and a falafel, NIS49. ⏰ Open Su-Th 9am-5:30pm, F 9am-3:30pm.

KESHET HAHURVA CAFE — ITALIAN, JEWISH $$

2 Tiferet Yisra'el St. ☎02 628 7515; www.keshethahurva.com

Birthrighters and their elder analogues, Semitic Floridians, congregate at this middling, overpriced restaurant. That the menu is largely conventional pasta and pizza dishes seems to indicate less authentic Italian cooking and more a desire to please the largest number of potential customers as possible. However, central placing on HaKhurba Sq. gives patrons a great view onto the buzzing social atmosphere of the Jewish Quarter, in which 20-somethings advertising gifts for Israeli soldiers, small religious marches, and individual pilgrims often intermingle. It's a nice place to sit and relax—now, if only the iced coffee (NIS20) were any good.

🪧 Coming from the Burnt House on Tiferet Yisra'el, Keshet is at the top right corner of HaKhurba Sq. $ Latkes with sour cream and apple sauce NIS50. Vegetable lasagna NIS45. St. Peter's fish NIS85. ⏰ Open Su-Th from 8 or 9am to 10 or 11pm depending on day and crowd, F from 8 or 9am to 3 or 4pm, depending on sunset.

christian quarter

👍 AMIGO EMIL — MIDDLE EASTERN, INTERNATIONAL $$

al-Khanqa St. ☎02 628 8090

Armed with a staff fluent in English, a cool stone interior with lots of empty space, and a tea room in the back with poufs and couches, Amigo Emil makes for a peachy pause during endless Old City treks. Guaranteed to be the best lemonade of your life, this thick and sweet treat (NIS12) provides an excellent reprieve from a hot Israeli day. Most Middle Eastern standards are also offered along with a few more creative house specialties and the usual pizza (NIS30) and hamburger (NIS35) imports. The crowd is a solid mix of lounging locals and fatigued foreigners.

*# Head to the end of Christian Quarter Rd. and turn left onto al-Khanqa. Amigo Emil is a few storefronts down on the left. **i** For dinner, make reservations sometime during the day. $ Entrees around NIS55. Cappuccino NIS15 ⏰ Open M-Sa 11am-9:30pm.*

PANORAMIC GOLDEN CITY — MIDDLE EASTERN, INTERNATIONAL $$

130 Aftimos Market ☎02 628 4433

Formerly known as Papa Andrea's, Panoramic Golden City is a well-trodden stomping ground for Holy Sepulchre sightseers. The *sfiha* (NIS40), or meat pie, is only a short step above street *sfiha* in quality but two or three steps above in price. Not only that, but street *sfiha* also arrives about 30min. faster. Gripes aside, the outdoor dining area on the third floor offers a great view of the Old City, and both the Dome of the Rock and the Church of the Holy Sepulchre are within clear sight. As its new name suggests, this view is really the highlight of the restaurant, so it might be better to come for drinks or coffee.

*# Walking on Muristan Rd. from David St., take the 2nd left, and the restaurant is on the right. **i** As long as you make a reservation in advance, this spacious restaurant is a good place to take a large group. $ Falafel NIS35. Shawarma NIS45. ⏰ Open daily 8am-10pm.*

outskirts of old city

👍 CAFE PARADISO — INTERNATIONAL $$

36 Keren Hayesod St. ☎02 563 4805; 2eat.co.il/cafeparadiso

It takes coming to a largely kosher country to understand the real power of the historic meat-dairy alliance. If your pork and shellfish diet has been thrown out of whack, then Cafe Paradiso is perhaps the best place to realize your dark Gentile fantasies. Its exterior is a small, friendly garden where locals smoke and drink late into the afternoon, munching on some of the excellent snack options (half roast beef sandwich NIS26, 0.2L of beer NIS14) or diving headfirst into "gentle" pork ribs (NIS87). It's a hike from the sights in this area, but, then again, so is pretty much everything.

 # From Lavan (below), walk up to the road above and opposite the Old City and cross the footbridge. Keep going uphill until you see St. Andrew's Guesthouse on the left, then take a right and walk uphill for another 5min. Cafe Paradiso is past the intersection on the left. $ Entrees NIS60-105, though small, cheaper options are available. ⏰ Open M-Th noon-midnight, F 10am-midnight, Sa 1pm-11pm.

👍 LAVAN BA'CINEMATHEQUE — ITALIAN $$$

11 Hebron Rd. ☎02 673 7393

It's enough just to look at it: thin roasted asparagus sit between the plate and a bed of polenta, and a baked salmon fillet drizzled with citrus butter sauce sits atop the whole three-storied entree (NIS92). Less extravagant options—such as whole wheat pasta with ricotta (NIS62)—may be equal in taste, if not splendor, at this spacious and cheerily designed restaurant where the staff may enter into meal-long banter with the patrons-turned-audience-members. Make sure to grab a table in the room to the right so you can go glossy-eyed as you stare into a broad view of the valley. That is, unless you'd rather lose yourself in the eyes of that special someone sitting across from you.

*⯁ Walking from West Jerusalem alongside the Old City walls past Jaffa Gate, take a left when the road forks to Hebron Rd. Lavan is in the Cinematheque, the lone building set into the hillside. Just keep walking until you get there. **i** Best to make reservations for dinner on Friday. $ Main courses NIS62-94, but closer to NIS94. Pizzas around NIS56. ⏰ Open daily 10am-midnight.*

TERASA ITALIAN $$

6 Nachon St. ☎02 671 9796; www.terasa.co.il

Another great option for views, Terasa is an elevated perch directly facing the Old City. Its extremely large rooms and white-and-gray surfaces may mirror the corporate feel of the neighboring overpriced hotels, but the well-priced Italian fare and relatively convenient location make this a good place to stop for lunch. The sweet potato croquettes with crispy almonds and goat yogurt dip is only NIS35.

*⯁ Coming from Lavan, Terasa is in the Begin Heritage Center, across the highway. Follow the footbridge, and you will see its outdoor tables 1 story above street level. **i** Reservations for dinner recommended. $ Focaccia NIS39. Tagliatelle alfredo NIS48. Fish and chips NIS65. Norwegian salmon fillet NIS90. ⏰ Open Su-Th 9am-10pm, F 9am-2pm.*

WEST JERUSALEM

The Old City may make you spiritually whole, but until you manage to figure out how to transcend your corporeal body, you're going to have to depend on West Jerusalem to keep you going. Here, you can find every major cuisine covered for whatever price you're willing to spend. The main thing to remember is that, though West Jerusalem is huge, the eateries are clumped around four major areas: **Zion Square, German Colony, Mamilla,** and **Mahane Yehuda.** These places are positively packed with restaurants while the other areas of the modern city have next to nothing.

In particular, Zion Sq. is the city's culinary capital. Yes, you've got your falafel stands here, and the shawarma joints around **Ben-Yehuda Street** cover every end of the grease spectrum. However, mid-range restaurants dominate the scene and are mostly centered on the eastern end of **Jaffa Road,** though a huge number have taken over the small alleys of **Rivlin Street** and the **Feingold Garden.**

Mamilla, as Jerusalem's Fifth Ave., has enough overpriced (yet largely average) joints to keep the image-conscious busy, while Mahane Yehuda's got the intrepid chef's back—the huge market stocks everything from pickled herring to cow brains, often at ridiculously low prices. It's also punctuated by some of the choicest cheap restaurants in town. The German Colony, meanwhile, is a place pretty much exclusively cut out for eating (and, we suppose, for Germans): the tranquil cafes and mid- to high-range restaurants here won't do a foodie wrong.

zion square

☑ T'MOL SHILSHOM CAFE $

5 Yoel Moshe Solomon St. ☎02 623 2758; www.tmol-shilshom.co.il

Tucked behind a discreet staircase in the nether reaches of a quiet alley, T'mol Shilshom, with its rustic brick interior, may just look like your usual judgmental hipster joint. But if you can look past the square-framed glasses, you'll realize there are some brains behind them. The cafe is the undisputed hangout of the city's intelligentsia, where starving writers, esteemed artists, and the odd poser gather to shoot the breeze on poetry, politics, and everything in between. Or maybe they come to hang out on the tranquil balcony patio so they can literally and metaphorically be above the street-bound scurriers. Named after the protagonist of a book by Nobel Laureate Shai Agnon, the place is often frequented by famous authors, and all sorts of literary events are regularly held here. The cafe interior doubles as a small secondhand bookstore, which houses a particularly choice selection of GLBT literature.

✝ *From Zion Sq., head to Yoel Moshe Solomon St. behind the big HaPoalim tower. As you walk down, you'll see a series of small alleys on your left. Walk down any of them to reach a tiny courtyard. Take a left, head to the northern end of it, and climb the staircase on the left.* ⌚ *Open Su-Th 9am-late, F 9am-sunset, Sa sunset-late.*

▨ HUMMUS BEN-SIRA
3 Ben-Sira St.

HUMMUS $
☎054 229 6765

It's little more than a hole in a slightly-more-western wall, but Hummus Ben-Sira serves what may be the best chickpea paste in West Jerusalem. Generous portions of hummus are doled out from massive cauldrons that nearly fill the room, and the thick hummus comes with a delicious heavy dose of garlic and a good range of toppings—try the mushrooms for a real treat.

✝ *At the foot of Rivlin St., make a left onto Hillel St., which will turn into Ben-Sira St. The restaurant is on the left just before the parking garage.* ⑨ *Falafel NIS15. Hummus NIS22.* ⌚ *Open Su-Th 11am-2am, F 11am-5pm, Sa 11pm-2am.*

▨ MARAKIYA
4 Koresh St.

CAFE, BAR $
☎02 625 7797

Marakiya may mean "Soup Kitchen," but this low-key cafe is more for those who make a fashion statement out of being looking disheveled (i.e., *homo ironicus*, the common hipster) than for those who can't be choosers. The same could be said for the cafe itself: the blue-framed front window may be crammed with an old TV and a beat-up Christmas tree—and the ramshackle interior has peeling walls and a rusty chandelier—but Marakiya serves some of the best *shakshuka* in town. The young regulars swear by it, and the few who disagree can just take their coffees to the small garden out back. With character by the bucketload, it's a local favorite made even better thanks to the evening crowd, who down the cheapest Goldstar in the city until the wee hours.

✝ *Jaffa Rd. meets Shlomtsiyon HaMalka at a fork. From where they meet, take the latter and make the 1st left onto Koresh St. Marakiya is 50m down on the right.* ⑨ *Shakshuka NIS25. Soup du jour NIS28. Goldstar NIS14.* ⌚ *Open daily 6pm-late.*

▨ BABETTE
16 Shamai St.

CONFECTIONARY $
☎02 615 7004; www.2eat.co.il/babette

A pair of bright yellow shutters is the only exterior sign that this place serves the cheeriest waffles in Jerusalem and—according to them—the best hot chocolate in the world. Well, actually, the latter might be given away by the hordes of sweet-tooths flocking around the shop with chocolate sauce smeared around their smiling mouths. Step inside this tiny booth, adorned with a large poster of the joint's namesake movie, and join the throngs. The hot chocolate, served in shot glasses, goes down more easily than what's usually served in those tiny tumblers—it's piping hot, with the thick flavor of melted chocolate and the smooth texture of milk. The waffles, meanwhile, are huge and come liberally doused in anything from the usual maple syrup to cookie crumbs, thick chocolate sauce, chestnut cream, or *halva*.

✝ *From Zion Sq., head behind the big HaPoalim tower. Babette is at the foot of Shamai St. just across from the tower.* ⑨ *Waffles from NIS25. Hot chocolate shot NIS12. Credit card min. NIS30.* ⌚ *Open Su-Th noon-2am, F from 10am to 1hr. before sunset, Sa from 1hr. after sunset to 2am.*

▨ ALMA
16 Rivlin St.

ISRAELI $$
☎02 502 0069; www.alma-restaurant.co.il

Alma serves top-notch Israeli standards at the foot of the ever-mobbed Rivlin St. Rustic brick arches and a large chalkboard with the specials create an authenticity inside that contradicts the rabble of tourists who converge on the street.

Kebabs and hummus take a small step upmarket from the greasy street stands everywhere else, but that slightly higher price gets you some of the best Israeli food in town and a chill cafe vibe in which to enjoy it.

⚑ *Rivlin St. branches off from Jaffa Rd. 1 block east of Zion Sq. Alma is at the southern foot, by the smaller square with outdoor tables.* Ⓢ *Siniya in eggplant NIS36. Beef kebab NIS64.* Ⓩ *Open Su-Th 3pm-late, F 3pm-sunset, Sa sunset-late.*

ELDAD VEZEHU
31 Jaffa Rd.

FRENCH $$
☎02 625 4007

Kosher French cuisine? Only in Jerusalem. The stone-walled interior is reminiscent of a country inn—the place even faces a wood cabin toward the back and is packed with everything from faded metal chandeliers and bells to vintage radios. Meat is a real speciality here, and the portions manage to be generous while the prices stay low.

⚑ *In the Feingold Garden, which is a small alley off Jaffa Rd., 1 block east of the intersection with Rivlin St.* Ⓢ *Beef stroganoff NIS30. Chicken liver pasta NIS25.* Ⓩ *Open Su-Th noon-midnight, F noon-sunset, Sa 9pm-1am.*

ADOM
31 Jaffa Rd.

MEAT, FISH $$
☎02 624 6242; www.rest.co.il/sites/default.asp?txtRestID=616

Feingold Garden may be packed with restaurants, but Adom manages to distinguish itself from its bedfellows by being gloriously non-kosher. In fact, it downright basks in its status, even extending its hours during Shabbat and serving up an array of meat and fish that would make the Old Testament shudder. The prices may seem high, but the fact that its terrace is usually packed is a testament to some great food.

⚑ *In the Feingold Garden, at the southern end near the intersection with Rivlin St.* Ⓢ *Veal carpaccio NIS48. Chicken in honey sauce NIS82.* Ⓩ *Open Su-F noon-1pm and 6:30pm-11pm, Sa noon-11pm. Smaller menu only daily noon-1pm.*

GABRIELA CUCINA
5 Shim'on Ben-Shetach

ITALIAN $$
☎02 624 6261; www.gabriela-jerusalem.co.il

The small stretch of restaurants along Shim'on Ben-Shetach offers some of the higher-end dining in the area. Case in point: Gabriela. Not to be confused with Gabriel next door, Gabriela has some items that are ridiculously high, but the place is remarkably down-to-earth, and it's possible to eat more cheaply. The ambience is relaxed, and the pristine cream awnings shade just as many lackadaisical families as suit-clad yuppies.

⚑ *At the end of Rivlin St., make a left as the street curves back uphill, and continue straight at the T-junction. Gabriela is immediately on the right.* Ⓢ *Endive salad NIS49. Avocado sandwich NIS33. Fish risotto NIS74.* Ⓩ *Open Su-Th 8am-11:30pm, F 8am-5pm, Sa 1hr. after sunset-11:30pm.*

CAFE HILLEL
1 Heleni HaMalka

CAFE $
☎02 625 6552

On Jaffa Rd., cafes are as numerous as the stars in the sky, but Hillel dominates when it comes to location; it's only a block from Zion Sq., meaning that there are plenty of crowds for your viewing pleasure, but they're not so loud that your quiet cup of coffee is ruined. The young patrons usually take to the mess of tables sprawling onto Jaffa Rd., where they can shelter themselves under the large awnings.

⚑ *On the corner with Jaffa Rd.* 𝒊 *Free Wi-Fi.* Ⓢ *Eggs benedict NIS46.* Ⓩ *Open Su-Th 6:30am-midnight, F 6:30am-3pm, Sa 9pm-midnight.*

FOCACCETTA
4 Shlomtsiyon HaMalka

ITALIAN $$
☎02 624 3222

Just past the eastern end of Jaffa Rd., the large Focaccetta is a prime nighttime hangout. Appropriately hip, it's decked out with a glass-walled second floor, a stone oven behind a sleek black bar, a mascot oddly resembling a female Mi-

chelin Man, and a massive effigy of her looming over the restaurant's front.
🧭 Head east along Jaffa Rd. and make a right at the fork. Focaccetta is on the right about 50m down. [S] Focaccia NIS28. Steak sandwich NIS48. ⏰ Open daily noon-midnight.

SAKURA JAPANESE $$
31 Jaffa Rd. ☎02 623 5464
Another restaurant in the legion that has conquered Feingold Garden, Sakura will also conquer all your sushi desires with its pristine two floors, fish tanks, outdoor patio, and calligraphy-covered walls.
*🧭 In the Feingold Garden. **i** Takeout available. [S] Sushi combos from NIS42. Salmon teriyaki NIS58. ⏰ Open daily noon-11:30pm.*

HELENE, QUEEN OF HUMMUS HUMMUS $
1 Heleni HaMalka ☎02 500 0758
Yet another hummus joint amid the bustle of Jaffa Rd., this one has the distinction of not only an ambitious name, but also some novel twists on the traditional Israeli cookbook—*shakshuka* with beef jerky, anyone?
🧭 1 door over from the corner with Jaffa Rd. [S] Hummus NIS23. ⏰ Open Su-Th 9am-10pm, F 9am-5pm, Sa 9pm-late.

eastern portion

👍 **EUCALYPTUS** BIBLICAL $$$
14 Hativat Yerushalayim ☎02 624 4331
The type of restaurant that could only exist in Jerusalem, Eucalyptus exclusively serves dishes mentioned in the Bible—just in case you've been dying to try that red lentil stew for which Esau was willing to sell his birthright. (Really, Esau? Really?) Like in the good Old Testament days, the chefs concoct dishes with local ingredients and often use recipes from their childhoods. We have a feeling that it wasn't quite as biblically common for the chefs to come out to tell the story of each dish before you dig in.
*🧭 At the eastern end of the Artists' Colony in Yemin Moshe. **i** Reservations recommended. Call ahead on F to make sure it's open. [S] Stuffed figs with chicken NIS45. King David's Feast NIS167. ⏰ Open Su-Th 12:30pm-late, F 12:30pm-1hr. before sunset, Sa 1hr. after sunset-late.*

CAFE MAMILLA CAFE $$
14 Mamilla Ave. ☎02 548 2230
This upmarket cafe floats above the well-heeled bustle of the avenue below. The stylish black couches and tables scattered around the roof terrace allow you to enjoy a tranquil coffee and tasty morsel if all that designer-label shopping has left you exhausted (poor thing).
🧭 Up the staircase on the left, about halfway down Mamilla Ave. and just before the small square with Steimatzky. [S] Mediterranean lasagna NIS58. Shakshuka NIS52. Tapas from NIS38. ⏰ Open Su-Th noon-11pm, F noon-4pm, Sa 9:30pm-midnight.

"authentic" bagels

The best bagels come from Jewish bakeries–you only need a New York minute to figure that one out. So, following that logic, a country where over three-quarters of the population identifies as Jewish should have some pretty kick-ass bagel shops. If you're looking for a real Israeli bagel, called "beygls" here, you'll probably just end up with a hard biscuit. But don't cancel your trip just yet: die-hard bagel fans can get their fix at any Bonkers Bagel, a chain started by two Jewish immigrants from New York. It doesn't get more "authentic" than that.

KEDMA
BRASSERIE $$$

Mamilla Mall ☎02 500 3737; www.kedmamamila.co.il

Kedma serves plenty of high-priced, high-quality meat in a fittingly high place (the mall's top floor). You may just get a natural high from looking at the view from the large outdoor terrace, where chic black and white furniture seats patrons for a panorama of the Yemin Moshe valley, southern Jerusalem, and the towering walls and spires of the Old City. Should a native Israeli deign to let you take him or her on a date, a reservation here during sunset could do you some good.

🚏 On the top floor of the mall in the center of Mamilla Ave. Also accessible via Jaffa Rd. $ Corned beef NIS72. ⏰ Open Su-Th noon-midnight, F 11am-3pm, Sa sunset-midnight.

RISHON CAFE
CAFE $$

Mamilla Mall ☎159 950 1030

Always packed to the brim, Rishon Cafe has become a haunt for all sorts—laid-back locals, sweat-drenched tourists, and gadget-toting businessmen on their lunch breaks. Like many other restaurants in Mamilla, it sports a brilliant view over southern Jerusalem from its large outdoor terrace. Another branch of Rishon is located near Zion Sq.

🚏 Opposite the indoor section of the mall by the small amphitheater at the middle of the avenue. ℹ Free Wi-Fi. $ Mozzarella quesadilla NIS45. Salmon fillet NIS54. ⏰ Open Su-Th 8am-midnight, Sa 9pm-midnight, F 8am-4pm.

HERZL GRILL
MEAT $$

13 Mamilla Ave. ☎02 502 0555

Theodor Herzl's quite the big deal in Israel—he's basically the father of Israel and modern Zionism and all that. The man himself supposedly stayed in this building for a few nights when he visited Jerusalem; the eponymous restaurant was pretty much inevitable. The grill serves up basic fare (burgers, schnitzels, fries, etc.) for prices that somehow manage to evade that typical Mamilla mark-up.

🚏 Toward the middle of the avenue, in front of Steimatzsky's. $ Burgers NIS49. ⏰ Open Su-Th noon-midnight, F noon-1hr. before sunset, Sa 1hr. after sunset-late.

SPAGHETTIS
ITALIAN $$

Mamilla Mall ☎02 500 3636

Like its kosher brother Spaghettim (near Zion Sq.), Spaghettis serves up standard Italian pizza and pasta, complete with those trademark Mamilla views from the spacious balcony.

🚏 On the top floor of the mall in the center of Mamilla Ave. Also accessible via Jaffa Rd. behind. $ Margherita pizza NIS38. ⏰ Open Su-Th 11am-2am, F 11am-4pm, Sa 9pm-2am.

west jerusalem outskirts

👍 AZURA
ISRAELI $

8 Mahane Yehuda St. ☎02 623 5204

Maybe it's the old Jewish men playing backgammon and smoking *argilah* in the building next door; maybe it's the fact that it's smack in the middle of the market; or, of course, it might just be the food—regardless of reason, Azura is about as authentic as you're going to get. The eatery saves you the trouble of sweaty hours in the hostel kitchen by dishing out thick homemade stews and a mean hummus, all made with fresh produce from the surrounding market. The nosh here is locally famous—in fact, the softball-sized meatballs seem to have their own discipleship. The market around the small outside terrace is surprisingly quiet, making Azura a great spot to unwind after you've spent your heart and soul bargaining at the market and all you have left to care for is your stomach.

🚏 Not technically on Mahane Yehuda St. While it can be accessed via the Iraqi market, it's easier to climb the stairs halfway down HaEshkol St. on the northern side. Azura is on the left. $ Meatball NIS22. Calf's lung NIS40. Goulash NIS60. ⏰ Open Su-Th 8am-5pm, F 8am-4pm.

[icon] PASTA BASTA — ITALIAN $

8 HaTut St. ☎077 540 4633; www.2eat.co.il/pasta-basta

Set in the busiest part of the Mahane Yehuda market's indoor section, Pasta Basta offers primetime viewing of the crazy street scene. And the name may literally mean "Pasta, enough!" but we don't know how anyone could get tired of this place—not only are the startlingly large portions of pasta undoubtedly the cheapest in town (as little as NIS20), but they're also some of the best, featuring anything from beetroot to coconut milk in the sauces. The young crowd has turned the place into a local hangout, and it's easy to see why—with a sleek black bar, crates of pasta and wine piled high behind it, and framed menus with items marked as staff favorites, Pasta Basta walks the spaghetti-thin tightrope between hip and welcoming.

Enter Mahane Yehuda St. from the south and make the 1st right. Pasta Basta is 20m down on the right. $ Pasta from NIS19. Open Su-Th noon-midnight, F noon-5pm.

[icon] COFFEE MILL — CAFE $

23 Emek Refa'im ☎02 566 1665

Of the slew of cafes flanking the German Colony, Coffee Mill might just feel the most like home. The founders, who moved to Jerusalem from Chicago, have plastered the walls entirely in *New Yorker* covers and serve some of the best coffee in town, as well as less conventional drinks—Lemonama and Choco Mekupelet were simply made for those sweltering summer months. Unsurprisingly, the place has become a haven for American expats, who sip their poisons in the single small room.

On the east side of the road, north of the intersection with Masaryk St. $ Viennese coffee NIS20. Cream cake NIS22. Open Su-Th 7:30am-10:30pm, F 7:30am-1pm, Sa 9:30pm-midnight.

MEA SHE'ARIM BAKERY — BAKERY $

68 Mea She'arim St. ☎04 582 6037

Mea She'arim may have nothing in the way of restaurants—it's a little too devout to be a tourist hotspot—but this bakery is where the locals go to get their daily bread. It's no more than a single tiled room, but every morning sees the shelves covered with challah, bite-sized pastries, and other breads, all accompanied by the sumptuous aromas you'd expect. It's the kind of place that's only used to local shoppers; unless you speak Hebrew, you might be a little in the dark as to what you're eating, but all of it has the bonafide seal of neighborhood approval.

About halfway down the street at the apex of the bend. Locals will help point you in the right direction. $ Challah NIS9. Open Su-Th 8am-8pm, F 8am-2pm.

CAFE MIZRAHI — CAFE $$

12 HaShazif St. ☎02 624 2105

Another people-watchers' haven in the midst of Mahane Yehuda's market, Cafe Mizrahi's small terrace and window-covered interior keep you slightly apart from the haggling rabble. The tone is suitably modish yet unbuttoned—at any given hour you can find both 20-somethings getting their caffeine fix and local couples breaking up grocery trips with some homemade brioche (NIS22).

Located in Mahane Yehuda. Enter Mahane Yehuda St. from the south, take the 2nd right into the market, and Mizrahi is on the right. $ Bruce Lee rice noodles NIS52. Open Su-Th 7am-9pm, F 6:30am-sunset.

ICHIKIDANA — INDIAN, VEGETARIAN $$

4 HaEshkol St. ☎050 224 6060; www.2eat.co.il/ichikidana

Considering the avalanche of fresh produce in the market, it's surprising that Mahane Yehuda isn't packed with more vegetarian Indian restaurants. Decked out with prayer flags, posters of many-limbed gods, and tables plastered with collages, Ichikidana makes its presence known. This tiny joint specializes in *thali*, plates of rice, lentils, and vegetables doused in cool yogurt, making them the per-

fect response to the hot summer day. Check the chalkboard for the daily specials.
⚑ Located in Mahane Yehuda. HaEshkol is halfway along Mahane Yehuda St. on the west. Ichikidana is 50m down on the right. [$] Krishna thali NIS39. Cash only. ⏰ Open M-Th 8am-8pm, F 8am-1hr. before sunset.

BABA'S ISRAELI KITCHEN ISRAELI $

31 Emek Refa'im ☎02 566 2671

You know, you don't have to eat in the wretched squalor of a street booth in order to get an authentic fix of hummus and *shakshuka*. Baba's has recently been turning heads with its debonair wooden furniture and reggae soundtrack—and by looking more like an actual restaurant than a *shakshuka* shack while still serving the same fare for nearly the same price.

⚑ Located in the German Colony, near the intersection with Masaryk St. [$] Hummus NIS19. ⏰ Open Su-Th 11am-midnight, F 11am-4pm, Sa from 1hr. after sunset to 12:30am.

MARVAD HAKSAMIM YEMENITE $$

42 Emek Refa'im ☎02 567 0007

You might not usually eat at a place with as tacky a name as "Magic Carpet," but Marvad Haksamim has long dominated the Yemenite scene in the German Colony. The restaurant is perched at the area's major intersection, meaning it's a great place to watch the crowds mill on the other side of the wall-length windows and yellow facade. Take-out is extremely popular here—the stand in one corner of the restaurant sells the same generous portions for around NIS10-15 less, assuming you would be so kind as to get off their land once you've got your grub in hand.

⚑ On the corner with Rachel Imenu. [$] Yemenite meat soup NIS35. Stuffed eggplant NIS32. ⏰ Open Su-Th 11:30am-11pm.

cheap eats

Street food is ubiquitous in the Middle East, and Israel is no exception. We're not just talking about falafel and shawarma variety–here are some equally delicious options to try once you've exhausted the traditional chickpea ones.

- **SABICH.** This traditional Iraqi dish, meaning "morning" in Arabic, has been embraced by the Israeli population. The pita bread is filled with fried eggplant, egg, pickle, and tahini.
- **SHAKSHOUKA.** Traditionally a blue-collar breakfast, *shakshouka* consists of eggs fried in a spicy tomato sauce. It's usually served in the pan in which it's cooked with a side of white bread to sop up the sauce.
- **MALABI.** A creamy pudding originating in Turkish cuisine. It's sold in disposable cups with sweet syrup and various crunchy toppings (coconut or chopped pistachios, for example) and has become so popular that you can find swankier versions in fancy-pants restaurants.
- **JERUSALEM BAGELS.** These are not your mother's bagels...unless your mother is from Jerusalem. Unlike the ring-shaped bagels popularized by Ashkenazi Jews, Jerusalem bagels are oblong, chewy, sweet, and usually covered with sesame seeds.

EAST JERUSALEM

Try the cheap street food in East Jerusalem. You'll be able to find some ideal mid-range fare, but **Abo Ali** has the best sweet tea in town, and **Haj'hazem** dishes out a mean grilled (dead) chicken.

central east jerusalem

📵 IKERMEWLI   FALAFEL $
21 HaNevi'im St.   ☎02 626 1658

At Ikermewli—also the name of the family that owns and runs the restaurant—hummus is baptized in a dish brimming with olive oil. It comes rich and warm, with a savory tang that would be hard to find for NIS100, let alone the mere NIS22 that you pay for Ikermewli's only menu item: a collection of hummus, hot and crispy falafel, pita, uncooked onions, and pickles. But don't let this barebones approach deceive you: the sandwich that customers are left to make out of these ingredients is one of the best in town. Of the three solitary tables outside and three more inside, at least one is usually free for full falafel focus.

🍴 *Walk down HaNevi'im toward Damascus Gate; Ikermewli is one of the last storefronts before the street becomes Sultan Suleiman. The yellow awning has "since 1952" written on it in English.* Ⓢ *NIS22. Cash only.* 🕐 *Open daily 5am-2:30pm.*

KAN ZAMAN   MIDDLE EASTERN $$
12 Nablus Rd.   ☎02 628 3282; jrshotel.com

Part hotel restaurant for the Jerusalem Hotel, part daytime cafe, part Arabic music club, Kan Zaman is worthwhile as much for the people-watching as the food. It becomes especially sceney during weekly performances of the Arabic *oud*, with chic locals and wandering expats drinking and yakking, but the vine trellis ceiling and view of Nablus Rd. make the restaurant a great place to sit even with minimal evening buzz. Usually a greasy standard, the chicken shawarma (NIS38) takes on new life with Kan Zaman's gourmet interpretation.

🍴 *Across the street from the Nablus bus station. To get to the entrance, you actually must take a left off Nablus Rd. onto Antara Ben-Shadad St.* 𝒊 *Call ahead for performance dates and times.* Ⓢ *Entrees around NIS59.* 🕐 *Open daily 7am-midnight.*

ABO ALI   MIDDLE EASTERN $
10 Salah ad-Din   ☎02 628 4569

On a tiny side street, in a basement decorated like an abandoned hospital waiting room, and without a menu, Abo Ali is by all appearances the bottom of the barrel in East Jerusalem cafeteria fare. The joint is overrun by the mostly male crowd of locals at lunch for one reason: the falafel (NIS15). The pickles are bracingly briny, the hummus is stirred in a large pot visible to anyone at the counter, and the sandwich is superb. The tea is also exceptional: it's served with fresh mint leaves and extremely sweet. The place feels so perfectly Palestinian, you'll be sad that it's about to lose one of its staff to a job making hummus in New York City—no matter how close to home it means this delicious fare will soon be.

🍴 *With your back to the Old City, walk down Salah ad-Din to a street that runs between it and Nablus Rd. just before they connect.* 𝒊 *Dress conservatively.* Ⓢ *Dishes NIS15. Tea NIS4. Cash only.* 🕐 *Open daily 7:30am-4pm.*

AZZAHRA   ITALIAN $$
13 Azzahra St.   ☎02 628 2447; www.azzahrahotel.com

Though under the same ownership and roof as the Azzahra Hotel, the Azzahra restaurant is entirely its own beast. With a brick oven from a small village near Venice, a real Italian *pizzaiolo* (expert of the pizza pie), and a set of Italian recipes, the restaurant can now boast an expertly trained group of chefs who cook up to 32 different kinds of the real McCoy: thin-crust Italian pizza.

🍴 *Coming from the Old City, take a right off Salah ad-Din just before the Archaeological School* *and Ministry of Justice. Walk down Azzahra, a small side street. i Takeout available. Call to make a reservation for dinner the day you want to go. $\circledS$ Small pizzas NIS42. Large NIS59-67. $\boxed{\oslash}$ Open daily noon-11pm.*

east jerusalem rhyme

Eating shawarma at swanky Kan Zaman,
you might think, "I'm no trashy American."
But to 'get' EJ's food,
it takes more than an *oud*
and some expats sprawled on a divan.

EL DORADO CAFE
Salah ad-Din 19

CAFE $

☎02 626 0993; izhiman@gmail.com

For some Israeli tourists and *Let's Go* Researcher-Writers, iced coffee has an importance similar to that of water during the summer. Luckily, for addicts and appreciators alike, El Dorado really is the city of gold. The iced coffee (NIS15) has all the thick sweetness of a milkshake and all the caffeine of coffee. A small shop lined by walls of candy with an upstairs sitting area and stools at the coffee bar, El Dorado is a good place to sit and order a sandwich (NIS16-19) while enjoying the air-conditioning. As Arabic takes on Western fare go, this version of Western cafes is simultaneously accurate and successful on its own unique terms.

☀ *Walking up Salah ad-Din away from the Old City, El Dorado is on the left just past al-Isfahani on the right. i Wi-Fi accessible. $\circledS$ Drinks NIS12-15. Food under NIS20. Israeli students get 10% discount. $\boxed{\oslash}$ Open daily 9am-8pm.*

sheikh jarrah

🏷 ASKADINYA
11 Shimon HaTsadik

ITALIAN $$

☎02 532 4590

A huge tree grows right next to the register at this simple and elegant Italian trattoria that's become a quiet spot for chatting expats and a great place for a slow and pleasant meal. The Askadinya chicken (NIS58), though little more than grilled vegetables and chicken sauteed in a lemon and barbecue sauce, is unimpeachably tangy and tender. The pink stone floors and white tablecloths are tasteful while managing to avoid even the mildest hint of snootiness.

☀ *Walk uphill to the end of Nablus Rd. and take a left; Askadinya is in the middle of a row of restaurants and bars on the left. $\circledS$ Pizza and pasta around NIS55. Meat entrees NIS70-115. $\boxed{\oslash}$ Open daily noon-midnight.*

HAJ'HAZEM
32 Nablus Rd.

MIDDLE EASTERN $

Haj'hazem may just be the Monk's Cafe of Sheikh Jarrah: you may not spot Jerry and Elaine *kvetching* in the corner, but you will find a heartwarming feast for only NIS35. A largely Palestinian crowd squeezes in to get the best deal in expensive Sheikh Jarrah—mounds of grilled meat come stacked along with every Arabic salad you've ever heard of and a meal-worthy amount of pita and hummus. Haj'hazem is small, and the few tables are only big enough for two or three people, but the outdoor seating area is usually empty and a great place for solo travelers to bring a book—after they've skipped breakfast in anticipation, of course.

☀ *Walk uphill from the American Colony for about 50m. The restaurant is on the right, directly after the mosque. $\circledS$ Falafel NIS7, with salads and sides NIS16. Shawarma NIS20, with salads and sides NIS35. Grilled chicken with salads and sides NIS35. $\boxed{\oslash}$ Open Su-Th 10am-9pm, Sa 10am-9pm.*

food

GARDEN'S RESTAURANT MIDDLE EASTERN $$

6 Shimon HaTsadik ☎02 581 6463

Serving up traditional *taboon* pizzas—from the same type of oven that Arabs were using 1000 years ago—and other Arabic and international standbys, Garden's distinguishes itself with its beautiful outdoor seating. Forget the cramped or semi-roofed areas of most restaurants; here you sit directly on the grass and look up at the sky, and the dim lighting and ample space between tables create an atmosphere of a solo summer dinner on a terrace. This is an excellent place for romance and/or secret plotting.

⇆ Take your first left after the main row of restaurants on Shimon HaTsadik, and Garden's is down the road on the right. [$] Pizza NIS30-40. Grilled chicken NIS55. Argilah NIS30. ⏰ Open daily noon-midnight. Kitchen open noon-11pm.

PASHA'S RESTAURANT MIDDLE EASTERN $$

13 Shimon HaTsadik ☎02 582 5162; www.pashasofjerusalem.com

Winkingly under the same ownership as nearby Borderline (ask a waiter at one where else he'd suggest, and he'll likely mention the other), Pasha's is the somewhat more formal cousin. In the outdoor seating area, potted trees look bizarre on top of an ugly while tile floor, and a view of the sky is almost completely blocked by gigantic white umbrellas and a huge green sheet. The somewhat inconsiderate service can take awhile, and tourists and expats make up a good portion of the patronage, but the many lamb dishes are delicious and fairly priced.

⇆ Walk uphill to the end of Nablus Rd. and take a left; Pasha's is in the middle of a row of a few restaurants and bars on the left. [$] Grilled minced lamb NIS65. Lamb kebab NIS55. Mansaf NIS75. ⏰ Open daily noon-11pm.

nightlife

Some expect the Rapture to begin at an old rock (or a smooth old rock, or a pile of smooth old rocks, or whatever) but plenty of Jerusalemites prefer just *to* rock instead. While Jerusalem may not be as wild as Tel Aviv, the modern part of the city has a great bar scene and the occasional club. You'll find plenty to do come sunset, as long as you stick close to **Zion Square.** In particular, Israeli families mingle with noisy Birthrighters on **Ben-Yehuda Street,** where food stands are open late and yarmulke-donning break dancers bust their moves. **Rivlin Street** is packed with overpriced bars geared toward tourists, while locals crowd the area's **hipster bars.** You just have to take Jerusalem nightlife as it comes and realize that, unlike in Tel Aviv, posture doesn't go very far here. The see-and-be-seen type have all migrated west, leaving a bunch of happy-go-lucky 20-somethings who have just as much fun casually sipping beers in jeans and T-shirts as they do pounding their heads to dubstep in a sweaty basement.

OLD CITY

What, you want to go out looking like that? With that skirt? Who are you meeting, that boy again? Eh, meshugenah/majnooni, put your tights/headscarf back on and do your homework! As the religious center of Jerusalem, the Old City is not a good place to go out. In fact, it's barely possible to go out—shops start closing at 4pm, almost no restaurants are left open by 7pm, and there's hardly a single bar in the entire neighborhood. If you want to go out, why don't you go out to buy some yarn and sit here with me and knit? We can listen to *klezmer*/play the *oud*!

WEST JERUSALEM

The city of peace, huh? Sure, you probably won't see a tallit-clad Orthodox crowd double fisting Goldstars (unless it's Purim), but Jerusalem offers ample opportunities to get your shirt sweaty and eardrums damaged. With only a few exceptions, the party will be around **Zion Square,** which is popping pretty much nightly. If the crazed dance floor at clubs like **Sira** isn't your scene, bring your plaid shirt and foreign cigarettes to **Uganda.**

UGANDA BAR, GLBT-FRIENDLY

4 Aristobulus St. ☎02 623 6087; www.uganda.co.il

The undisputed king of Jerusalem's burgeoning hipster bar scene, this tiny Aristobulus St. bar sends the plaid-clad and tattooed into the night. This is not to say that the hordes overrunning the alleys are only hipsters—anyone who's in his 20s and wants a drink could conceivably be found in the crowd. The interior, which is slightly less packed, is a strikingly simple setup of white walls, a few sofas, and a bar with Israel's largest selection of *arak.* The building next door is often used as a concert venue or dance floor—bopping your head to reggae is only as ironic as you want to make it. During the day, the place is a hummus cafe and music and comic store.

From Heleni HaMalka St., make the first left. i Live music on Tu and Sa. DJs on Th and F. Buy 1 beer, get 1 free daily until 9pm. $ Goldstar NIS18. Open Su-F noon-late, Sa 3pm-late.

SIRA BAR, CLUB

4 Ben-Sira St. ☎02 623 4366; gootel@gmail.com

Hunkered down in a little alley off Ben-Sira St., Sira is the local go-to for a guaranteed great evening, whether you're looking for a casual cocktail or some shots and manic limb-flailing. Like Uganda, Sira is a place for anyone in town who's in the know and under 30. A small crowd gathers outside and orders drinks through a little window, but it's the intimate interior that really gets packed, with everyone taking to the small and sweaty dance floor as the night goes on.

In Mamilla, located off Hillel St. i Shows almost nightly. Different DJ nightly. Open daily 7pm-late.

nightlife

BASS CLUB, GLBT-FRIENDLY

1 HaHistadrut ☎077 512 3056; http://bassclub.wordpress.com

Bass may be right off of Ben-Yehuda St.—which is constantly jammed with rowdy Birthrighters—but it's hidden in a dark alley and up a staircase, ensuring that it's a place the locals can keep to themselves. The place may be a little grungy, with walls plastered in graffiti and a thick fog of cigarette smoke, but that's all part of Bass' charm. Expect funny hairdos, tight shirts, pounding music, riotous dancing, and a noticeable lack of Top 40 hits. Though not an exclusively GLBT club, Bass usually has a good turnout from the GLBT community. Should all the leg shaking get to be a little much, an outdoor terrace provides the perfect spot to recover.

Located in Zion Sq. between Ben-Yehuda St. and King David St. $ Cover NIS35. Open Th-F midnight-late.

TOY BAR BAR, CLUB, GLBT-FRIENDLY

6 Du Nawas St. ☎02 623 6666; www.thetoybar.com

Toy Bar is undoubtedly the favorite of stylish local 20-somethings—and by stylish, we mean those unwilling to wear the plaid required for the Jerusalem hipster scene. The interior of this voguish establishment, featuring a jet black bar, matte red walls, and a balcony, get packed to its metal-skirted brim nightly with a young and beautiful crowd. When the lack of elbow room becomes unbearable, head to the underground dance floor, where low ceilings and heavy bass make for some sweaty fun.

Opposite Uganda. Du Nuwas St. leads directly off of Jaffa Rd., 1 block to the west of Heleni HaMalka. i 23+. $ Cover NIS20-40. Open daily 9:30pm-late.

HAKATZE DANCE BAR, LIVE MUSIC, GLBT-FRIENDLY

4 Shushan St. ☎02 523 254310; www.hakatze.com

Located on secluded Shushan St., Hakatze ("The Edge") is a hotspot for alternative nightlife. Crowds gyrate under the retro disco ball to a pumping indie rock playlist where hipsters hangout at the small smoking booth out front. Hakatze also hosts a range of awesome events, including **Gevald!,** a famous drag comedy night that attracts divas from across Israel.

⚑ *Walk to the eastern end of Jaffa Rd. (past the Y-junction). Take a right down any street, then a left onto Shushan St. Hakatze is on the right.* *i* *Drag comedy night on M. Live music M-F, DJs Sa-Su. 18+.* Ⓢ *Beer NIS18. Chasers NIS8.* 🕐 *Open daily 9pm-late.*

CONSTANTINE
CLUB

3 HaHistadrut ☎02 622 1155

Another joint found near the tourist-run Ben-Yehuda St., Constantine is the closest Jerusalem has to a typical Tel Aviv club; think ultra-modern hall, roving strobe lights, bevies of short-skirted girls, and thumping trance and electro beats. However, it retains a Jerusalem vibe by channeling Roman hedonism with classical statues and white marble colonnade. It's a sight worth seeing—you just have to make it past the bouncers first.

⚑ *Located near Zion Sq. Take a right off Ben-Yehuda St.* *i* *Student night on M. Live performances on W. Enlisted men night on F.* 🕐 *Open daily 9pm-late.*

GLEN
BAR, GLBT-FRIENDLY

18 Shlomtsiyon HaMalka ☎054 901 0076; www.GLEN.co.il

Glen is a barman's bar with the vibe of an English pub and 17 beers on tap. Take some time to browse the sprawling menu, which offers an eye-widening and throat-whetting cornucopia of brews that may be impossible to find anywhere else in Israel. Glen also carries a wide selection of over 80 whiskies.

⚑ *Off Jaffa Rd. just before the intersection with King David St. in Zion Sq.* Ⓢ *Drinks from NIS19.* 🕐 *Open daily 7pm-late.*

JAFFA BAR 35
BAR

35 Jaffa Rd. ☎054 223 9253; lironkushnir@gmail.com

The entrance is hidden down a little alley off bustling Jaffa Rd. and up a flight of wooden stairs, meaning you can watch the sober tourists below from a small, packed balcony. Inside, the bar is tinged with blue light and, despite being right next to Rivlin St., keeps a mainly Israeli clientele.

⚑ *Just off Ben-Yehuda St. in Zion Sq. near Big Apple Pizza.* *i* *18+.* Ⓢ *Cover NIS45; includes 1 drink. Drinks around NIS40.* 🕐 *Open W-Th 11pm-late, Sa 11pm-late.*

EAST JERUSALEM

In the luxurious residential expanse that is Sheikh Jarrah—interrupted by only the occasional resort hotel or grandiose consulate—there hides the entertainment oasis of Shimon HaTsadik. Though the small street consists mostly of restaurants (and, tellingly, a fitness equipment shop) there are also two bars: **Borderline** targets expat intelligentsia and chilling Palestinian bros, while **Gossip** is the haven of high schoolers and Hebrew U students looking to dance themselves clean and score some free vodka.

🛡 GOSSIP
BAR, CLUB

3 Shimon HaTsadik ☎02 581 1922; www.gossip-jerusalem.com

A fixture in the Arab youth scene, Gossip also draws in some foreigners and local Jews. Thursdays—party night in the Arab community—usually involve a live DJ, jazz, blues, or *tarab*, Arabic music characteristically played with an *oud*. There are also karoake nights, chill-out nights (think *argilah* and old dudes), and bring-your-own-flashdrive events, where Gossip plays whatever music its customers have to offer. Saif, the ultra-friendly owner, built the bar in his old backyard and seems as interested in hanging out with patrons as he is with running a business. The large roof is opened for big events, such as when the Arabic reggae superstars Toot Ard play. For big groups (or, you know, whenever Saif feels like it), downing three or four vodka-based drinks may earn you a free bottle of vodka to take home.

⚑ *Walk uphill to the end of Nablus Rd. and then take a left; Gossip is in a row of restaurants and bars on the left.* $ *Beers and local liquors NIS20-30. Cocktails NIS25-45. Argilah NIS25. Shawarma, fries, Arabic salad, and 0.5L of beer NIS40. 10% discount for foreigners.* ⏰ *Open daily 4pm-late (doors usually close around 1am).*

BORDERLINE RESTAURANT, BAR

13 Shimon HaTsadik ☎02 532 8342; www.shahwan.org

Set in a beautiful open-air garden under tremendous eucalyptus trees, Borderline could be the perfect place to have a drink with friends—if only that 10% student discount compensated for the drink prices, which are astronomically high by Israeli standards. Whiskey and coke? NIS55. Gin and tonic? NIS40. In fact, for only a few shekels more than a cocktail, you can instead fill up on a delicious and generous serving of *mushakhan* (a chicken and bread dish; NIS65). Nonetheless, Borderline is popular with the cool kids of the expat community and with locals who come to enjoy a nice *argilah* (NIS40) outside, which doesn't burn too many shekels when shared with friends.

🚶 *Walk uphill to the end of Nablus Rd. and then take a left; Borderline is in the same building as Pasha's.* ℹ *Under the same management as Pasha's.* $ *Appetizers NIS12-35. Italian entrees around NIS50. 10% student discount.* ⏰ *Open daily noon-midnight, sometimes later.*

arts and culture

If Jerusalem's mix of irreconcilable political division, millennia-old religious struggle, and cultural segregation is no longer exciting enough for you, an escape into air-conditioned theaters and loud concerts is a solid backup plan. Jerusalem may not be on the same level as, say, Tel Aviv, but its art scene is colored by a distinctive tinge of political and religious motivation (surprised?), on display at such establishments as the Palestinian National Theater and the Jerusalem English-Speaking Theater. Lighter entertainment is also around, both at the artsier-than-thou performance space The Lab and at such music venues as Yellow Submarine. Just because this is the home of everyone's great-great-great-great-great-great grandmother doesn't mean you can't get your grind on.

THEATER

JERUSALEM ENGLISH-SPEAKING THEATER (JEST) EASTERN PORTION

Eliyahu Shama 6 ☎02 642 0908; www.jest-theatre.org

Formed in 1985 as a non-profit organization, JEST puts on three to four plays per year. While some plays seem intentionally geared to a Jewish audience (yes, they did recently do *The Diary of Anne Frank*), JEST puts on a wide variety of famous plays from the modern era as well as some lesser-known contemporary works. Plays are attended largely by expats.

🚶 *Coming from the city center, take Jaffa Rd. to Shlomtsiyon HaMalka St. Walk down Shlomtsiyon HaMalka to King David St. and take a left onto Eliyahu Shama.* ℹ *Ages 18-25 can get ½-priced rush tickets.* $ *Around US$20 per ticket.* ⏰ *Call ahead for showtimes.*

PALESTINIAN NATIONAL THEATER CENTRAL EAST JERUSALEM

Nuzha St. ☎02 628 0957; www.pnt-pal.org

A non-profit organization seeks to express the background of the Palestinian people through plays that are often political in nature. Because the Palestinian National Theater's goal is to raise the intellectual and artistic awareness of the Palestinian people, it is a great way to gain exposure to Palestinian culture and beliefs.

🚶 *Off Salah ad-Din St. just to the south of the American Colony Hotel.* ℹ *Performances in Arabic with subtitles in varying Western European languages, often French. Call in advance.* $ *NIS25.* ⏰ *Check website or call ahead for performance times.*

CINEMA

JERUSALEM CINEMATHEQUE OLD CITY OUTSKIRTS

11 Hebron Rd. ☎02 565 4356; www.jer-cin.org.il

Host of everything from Coen Brothers retrospectives to the extremely academic Anthropological Film Festival, the Jerusalem Cinematheque is the best place in Jerusalem for art-house, indie, classic, and critically-acclaimed films. And hipsters, of course.

🚏 Coming from West Jerusalem, walk past Jaffa Gate and continue along the road parallel to the wall until you can take a right. The Cinematheque is a large building standing alone on a mountainside. ℹ 4 screens, with different shows every night. Most films in English. [S] NIS37, students NIS31. ⏰ Open daily. Check website or call for showtimes.

GIL MOVIE THEATER WEST JERUSALEM OUTSKIRTS

Malha St. ☎02 678 8448

On the second floor of the gigantic Malha Mall, the Gil Theater shows the latest Hollywood films, sometimes including movies for kids, on its eight screens.

🚏 On the 2nd floor of the Malha mall. In the square surrounded by Agudat Sport Beitar Rd. [S] Nighttime shows US$5. Matinees US$5.50. ⏰ Call or check the newspaper for showtimes. Closed F night and Sa.

MUSIC

THE LAB EASTERN PORTION

28 Hebron Rd. ☎Office 02 629 2001, tickets 02 629 2000; www.maabada.org.il

An abandoned train station that has been turned into an intimate multimedia experimental artspace, The Lab exhibits music, performance art, theater, and dance. It also has a bar and draws Jerusalemites interested in the avant-garde alternative arts scene.

🚏 Hebron Rd. begins just below Sultan's Pool. Follow it for about 10min., and The Lab is on the right. ℹ Contact The Lab or check the website before going for more information.

EIN KEREM MUSIC CENTER WEST JERUSALEM OUTSKIRTS

HaMa'ayan 29 ☎02 641 4250; www.einkeremusicenter.org.il

All kinds of classical music *and* special events including celebrations of famous composers' birthdays: what could be better? As with most arts organizations that cater mainly to people whose sensibilities lie somewhere between the 16th and 19th centuries, the Ein Kerem Music Center offers a student discount.

🚏 Take Bus 17 from the Central Bus Station or Zion Sq. The Center is opposite Mary's Well in Ein Kerem. [S] Sa morning concerts NIS75; students, soldiers in uniform, and seniors NIS60. F morning concerts NIS35/25. Note: we do not advise that you buy an Israeli soldier costume. ⏰ Concerts F and Sa mornings. Check online for specific times and events.

SULTAN'S POOL EASTERN PORTION

☎02 629 9841

Just downhill from Jaffa Gate in Yemin Moshe (meaning right outside the Old City walls), this is probably the best place to hear music in Jerusalem. That is, when you can—Sultan's Pool is only open in the summer and puts on just a few shows per month. But seize the chance to look out over the Old City as you jam out to everything from opera to Matisyahu, Bob Dylan, and Sting.

🚏 Pass Jaffa Gate and take a left as you start walking downhill. ℹ Bimot (www.bimot.co.il) is the best place to learn what's going on at the Pool.

YELLOW SUBMARINE WEST JERUSALEM OUTSKIRTS

13 HaRechavim St. ☎02 679 4040; www.yellowsubmarine.org.il

Somewhat of a club when there is live music at night, Yellow Submarine showcases an eclectic mix of Israeli and American artists. Because few people are into both heavy metal and Israeli feel-good light-rock pop, you'll probably be happier if you check the website for the schedule and see what's being offered that night.

⇞ Across from the Mekor Chaim Garden and around the corner from Tel Aviv College. ⏰ Performances 3-4 nights per week.

JERUSALEM SYMPHONY ORCHESTRA WEST JERUSALEM OUTSKIRTS

☎02 561 1498; www.jso.co.il

The JSO has a concert series honoring specific composers and genres, as well as occasional concerts directed at kids.

*⇞ Performances often at the Jerusalem Theater on David Marcus St. or Henry Crown Symphony Hall on 5 Chopin St. **i** Check website for schedule. $ Tickets NIS130-140; students NIS45-90. ⏰ Concerts slow down during the summer and close entirely for July and Aug. Performances 8pm. Box office open Su-F 10am-1pm, on concert days 10am-1pm and 4-8pm.*

shopping

What kind of trip to Israel is complete without a novelty yarmulke embroidered with your college mascot? You can count on Jerusalem to provide some of the most unique Judaica in the universe. While the **Old City** offers the best quality, **Mea She'arim** has the best prices—though that also means lower standards and a smaller selection. You can find the kookiest Judaica stores along **Ben-Yehuda Street.**

The area around **Zion Square** is full of label brands, while bookstores and some cheaper apparel shops line **Jaffa Road.** While Israeli chain Steimatzsky's may have little more than Philip Roth and Elie Wiesel for the non-Hebrew speakers, some of the independent stores have rather impressive English-language selections. The well-heeled eschew Zion Sq. for **Mamilla,** a parody of Fifth Ave., meaning that everything you find here is also back home, but hey, if you feel the need for an Israeli Rolex, who are we to judge?

But if you're the type who would judge, get your haggle on in the *souqs* of the Old City or **Mahane Yehuda.** The markets of the **Muslim Quarter** sell everything from the mundane to the marvelous, while the Mahane Yehuda market has just about every type of food you can conceive of.

essentials

CITYWIDE

practicalities

- **EMBASSIES/CONSULATES: US Consulate.** (18 Agron St. ☎02 622 7230; www.jerusalem.usconsulate.gov.) **Austrian Consulate.** (Technology Park, 1 Manahat Building ☎02 649 0649; www.bmeia.gv.at/en/embassy/tel-aviv.) **Greek Consulate.** (31 Rachel Imenu St. ☎02 561 9583.) **Italian Consulate.** (60 Nablus Rd. ☎02 582 2170; www.consgerusalemme.esteri.it ⏰ Open M 11am-1pm, W 11am-1pm.) **Spanish Consulate.** (53 Ramban ☎02 582 8680.) **Turkish Consulate.** (87 Nablus Rd. ☎02 532 1087; jerusalem.cg.mfa.gov.tr ⏰ Open M-F 9am-6pm.) **UK Consulate.** (19 Nashashibi St. ☎02 541 4100; ukinjerusalem.fco.gov.uk ⏰ Open M-Th 7:30am-3:30pm, F 7:30am-1:30pm.) **French Consulate.** (24 Mount Scopus St. ☎02 540 0423; www.consulfrance-jerusalem.org.)
- **GLBT RESOURCES: Jerusalem Open House** provides community support and hosts events and marches. (2 HaSoreg St. ☎02 625 0502; www.joh.org.il ⇞ Walk on Shlomtsiyon HaMalka St. Just before Jaffa Rd., take a left onto HaSoreg St. ⏰ Open Su 1-4:30pm, M-Tu 1-8pm, W 1-5pm, Th 1-8pm.)

- **TICKET AGENCY: Bimot** is the major ticket agency for festivals, shows, and sports events in Israel. (8 Shamai St. ☎02 623 7000; www.bimot.co.il 🧭 Walking uphill on Jaffa Rd. from Safra Sq., take a left on Lunz St. and then a right on Shamai St.)
- **PUBLIC TOILETS:** In West Jerusalem, public toilets can be found at the intersection of Jaffa Rd. and Ben-Yehuda. In East Jerusalem, go to the bus station in front of the Jerusalem Hotel. In the Old City, go from Jaffa Gate to the end of David St.
- **INTERNET: Cafe Net** has coffee, sandwiches, pastries, and sweet, sweet Internet. (232 Jaffa Rd. ☎02 537 9192; www.cafenet.co.il 🧭 On the 3rd floor of the Central Bus Station. [S] Turkish coffee NIS6. Latte NIS7. Internet NIS15 per hr.; free drink after 3hr. ⏰ Open daily 5:30am-midnight.)

emergency

- **EMERGENCY NUMBERS: Police:** ☎100. **Ambulance:** ☎101. **Fire Department:** ☎102.
- **TOURISM POLICE:** Muristan Rd. ☎02 622 6282 🧭 On the left just before the Muristan Rd. entrance to the Holy Sepulchre Church.
- **POLICE STATION: Main Station.** (1 Salah ad-Din St. ☎02 620 7444 🧭 At the beginning of Salah ad-Din, off Sultan Suleiman St. ⏰ Open 24hr.) **Russian Compound Station.** (Russian Compound ☎02 539 1550 🧭 In Safra Sq. between Shivtei Yisra'el and Jaffa Rd. ⏰ Open 24hr.)
- **LATE-NIGHT PHARMACY: Super-Pharm** has the most comprehensive selection and best English-speaking staff. (In the Central Bus Station on Jaffa Rd. ☎02 538 8383; www.super-pharm.co.il. ⏰ Open Su-Th 8:30am-11pm, F 9am-4pm.) Other locations on HaHistadrut St., in West Jerusalem between King George St. and Ben-Yehuda, and on Mamilla Mall right outside Jaffa Gate.
- **HOSPITAL:** Tourist officials recommend the **Terem Emergency Medical Centers**; they are foreigner-friendly, highly competent, and have contact with hospitals. (80 Yirmeyahu St. in Romena; 6 Yanovksy St., East Talpiot in HaTayelet; 8 Tiltan St. in Modi'in. ☎1 599 677 7111, emergencies 125 5122.)

OLD CITY

practicalities

- **TOURIST OFFICES: Jaffa Gate Tourist Information Center** has knowledgeable, multilingual, and kind employees who offer free maps, brochures, information on tours, and advice. A great place to stop for directions or plan a trip. (Jaffa Gate ☎02 628 0382. 🧭 After walking through Jaffa Gate into the Old City it is the 2nd storefront on your left. ⏰ Open Su-Th 8:30am-5pm, F 8:30am-1pm.) The **Christian Information Centre** is the place to get information on pilgrimage sights, tours, and accommodations. (Jaffa Gate ☎02 627 2692; http://www.cicts.org/CICmainin.htm. 🧭 After walking through Jaffa Gate into the Old City it is the 1st storefront on your left. ⏰ Open M-F 8:30am-5:30pm, Sa 8:30am-12:30pm.) The **Jewish Student Information Center** has international Jewish travel guides, as well as information about Jewish Quarter sights. The center also offers counseling, yeshiva classes, outings, lectures on Jewish topics, and tours of the Western Wall. (5 Beit El St. ☎02 628 2634; http://jeffseidel.com/?page_id=8. 🧭 In Hurva Sq. ⏰ Open Su-Th 9:30am-4:30pm.)
- **ATM:** Adjacent to the Jaffa Gate Tourism Information Center on Latin Patriarchate St., behind the Hurva synagogue on Tiferet Yisra'el.
- **LOST PROPERTY:** It is very unlikely that you will recover anything lost in the Old City. If you think there may have been theft, ask to be transferred to the **tourist police**

(☎03 516 5382).

- **LAUNDROMAT: Mike's Center.** (172 Souq Khan az-Zait ☎02 628 2486 ⚡ Up the stairway on the way to the 9th Station of the Cross, the 2nd floor of the building across from you when you finish the 1st flight. There will be a sign. Ⓢ Wash and dry NIS35 per 2.5kg, NIS55 per 5kg. Ⓓ Open daily 9am-11pm.)

- **PUBLIC TOILETS:** Take an immediate left after entering the Old City through Jaffa Gate, and public toilets will be on the left at the end of David St. where it intersects with Souq el-Khawajat.

- **INTERNET: Old City Net** has computers with high-speed internet, cold drinks, and coffee. (Latin Patriarchate St. ☎02 627 5799 ⚡ The street adjacent to the Jaffa Gate Tourist Information Center. Toward the end of the street on the left. Ⓢ NIS7 per 15min., NIS10 per 30min., NIS15 per 1hr. Ⓓ Open Su-Th 10am-10pm, F 10am-midnight, Sa 10am-10pm.) There are also a few internet cafes on the Via Dolorosa around the 8th Station.

- **POSTAL CODES:** 97500 (Jewish and Muslim Quarters). 97600 (Christian and Armenian Quarters).

- **POST OFFICE: Jerusalem Central Post Office.** (23 Jaffa Rd. ☎02 629 0686 Ⓓ Su-Th 7:30am-2:30pm, F 8am-noon.)

emergency

- **POLICE:** Armenian Orthodox Patriarchate Rd. ☎02 622 6100.

- **LATE-NIGHT PHARMACY: Super-Pharm** is the largest pharmacy in Jerusalem with many English-speaking attendants. (9 King Solomon St. ☎02 636 6000 ⚡ Opposite the entrance to the Old City at Jaffa Gate, walk down to the Mamilla Promenade. Ⓓ Su-Th 8:30am-11pm, F 9am-4pm.)

- **HOSPITAL: Arab Orthodox Society Medical Center** offers, among other services, dental care, x-rays, skin care, and psychological care. (Greek Orthodox Patriarchate Rd. ☎02 627 1958 ⚡ Take a right off Latin Patriarchate Rd. onto Greek Orthodox Patriarchate Rd. It will be on the corner. Ⓓ Open M-F 9am-2:30pm, Sa 9am-1pm.)

WEST JERUSALEM

practicalities

- **ATM: Bank Leumi.** (23 Jaffa Rd. Ⓓ Open Su 8:30am-2pm, M 8:30am-1pm and 4-6:15pm, Tu-W 8:30am-2pm, Th 8:30am-1pm and 4-6:15pm.) There's a **2nd location** at 22 King George St.

- **LAUNDROMAT: Laundry Place.** (12 Shamai St. ☎02 625 7714 *i* Not self-service. Ⓢ NIS52 per load. Ⓓ Open Su-Th 8:30am-8pm, F 8:30am-3pm.)

- **INTERNET: Coffee Net.** (10 Agrippas St. ☎077 541 0348 Ⓢ NIS14 per hr. Ⓓ Open Su-Th 9am-3am, F 9am-5pm, Sa 9pm-3am.)

- **POST OFFICE:** 23 Jaffa Rd. Ⓓ Open Su-Th 10am-6pm, F 10am-2pm.

emergency

- **LATE-NIGHT PHARMACY: Super-Pharm.** (2 HaHistadrut Ⓓ Open Su-Th 8am-midnight, F 8am-4pm.) **Second location.** (10 Mamilla Ave. Ⓓ Open Su-Th 8:30am-11pm, F 8:30am-4pm, Sa 9pm-midnight.)

- **HOSPITAL: Hadassah University Hospital.** (Ein Kerem ☎02 677 7111, for emergencies ☎125 122.)

EAST JERUSALEM

practicalities

- **TOURIST OFFICE:** The office in **Safra Square** is the closest tourist office to East Jerusalem, but the staff is slightly less helpful than those in the Jaffa Gate office. (1 Safra Sq. ☎02 627 1422; www.jerusalem.muni.il/tourism ⇆ In the huge orange complex between Shivtei Yisra'el St. and Jaffa Rd. Entering from Shivtei Yisra'el, take an immediate left. ⏰ Open Su-Th 8:30am-5pm, F 8:30am-1:30pm, Sa 8:30am-5pm.)
- **ATM:** ATMs are generally found inside money exchanges. **Aladdin Money Changer** is a solid choice. (☎02 628 1077; assilabrothersltd@hotmail.com ⇆ On Salah ad-Din, about a 3min. walk from Sultan Suleiman just past the New Metropole Hotel. $ Surcharge NIS6. ⏰ Open Su-Th 8am-7pm, F 9am-3pm, Sa 8am-7pm.) There is another ATM on HaNevi'im St., just past Ikermewli on the way to Damascus Gate.
- **LAUNDROMAT: Ritz Laundry** is recommended by the locals. There's a significant difference between the quality of cleaning here and at other places, and you don't want to find out exactly what that difference is. (Ibn-Khalud St. ☎02 627 4889 ⇆ Just past the Educational Bookshop on Salah ad-Din. Take the 1st right, then the 1st left. Ritz is within sight of the Ritz Hotel. ⏰ Open Su-Th 9am-7pm, Sa 9am-7pm.)
- **PUBLIC TOILETS: East Jerusalem Central Bus Station** has probably the only public toilets in East Jerusalem (⇆ Across the street from the Jerusalem Hotel, where all the buses are. A left off of Nablus Rd.), though it's fairly easy to sneak into El Dorado Cafe, the Educational Bookshop, and other expat locales.
- **INTERNET: El Dorado Cafe** has coffee, candy, and free Wi-Fi. (19 Salah ad-Din ☎02 626 0993; izhiman@gmail.com ⇆ On the left side of Salah ad-Din, about a 3min. walk from Sultan Suleiman. ⏰ Open daily 9am-8pm.) **Educational Bookshop** has books, maps, coffee, and Wi-Fi, along with laptops to rent. (19 Salah ad-Din ☎02 627 5858; www.educationalbookshop.com ⇆ Adjacent to El Dorado. $ Laptops NIS20 per hr. ⏰ Open Su-Th 8am-8pm, F 8am-6pm, Sa 8am-8pm.)
- **POST OFFICE: Central East Jerusalem.** (☎159 950 0171 ⇆ On Salah ad-Din across from Herod's Gate near the Rockefeller Museum.)
- **POSTAL CODE:** 90908.

emergency

- **POLICE STATION:** 1 Salah ad-Din ☎02 620 7444 ⇆ Walk to the very beginning of Salah ad-Din, off of Sultan Suleiman St. ⏰ Open 24hr.
- **LATE-NIGHT PHARMACY: Balsalm Pharmacy.** (28 Salah ad-Din ☎02 627 3215 ⇆ Going up Salah ad-Din from Sultan Suleiman, the pharmacy is on the right after about 5-8min. of walking. ⏰ Open daily 8am-11pm.) You won't find a pharmacy open later than Balsalm in East Jerusalem, especially on Fridays.
- **HOSPITAL: St. Joseph Hospital** has X-ray machines, an intensive care unit, an outpatient clinic, and a lab. (13 Nashashibi St. ☎02 591 1911 ⇆ Take Nablus Rd. until it's about to dead end, then turn right, walk past Mount Scopus Hotel, and take a left to backtrack and walk uphill. Continue straight past the Ambassador Hotel. St. Joseph is on the right. ⏰ Open 24hr.)

GETTING THERE

If you're flying to Israel, you're flying into Tel Aviv. The best way to get to Jerusalem from David Ben-Gurion is probably by **sherut,** or shared taxi. These are relatively cheap and fast, albeit marginally disorienting as they whip through the city, dropping off each passenger at his desired stop. Even if you firmly believe that sharing is caring, it may still feel inconvenient to travel to the remotest reaches of Jerusalem (damn Israeli communist taxis), so you may want to consider a **private taxi,** which is expensive but faster and more comfortable. For the more cash-conscious, the **Egged bus** is your best option.

by taxi

NESHER TAXI SERVICE

☎02 625 7227

As recommended by the Israeli Airport Authority, the Nesher taxi service runs the most reliable sherut from Ben-Gurion to Jerusalem.

⌖ Directly outside the airport on the 2nd floor. Follow signs to the taxi area and take a left. $ NIS37.50 to city center and NIS58.40 for most other locations in Jerusalem. Cash only. ⏰ Open Su-F 24hr. Hours and prices can vary on Shabbat; call in advance for details.

BEN-GURION AIRPORT TAXI SERVICE

☎052 515 1791; benguriontaxi.com

It ain't cheap, but Ben-Gurion Taxi will dependably have a driver waiting outside your gate with your name on a placard, making it a comfortable way to get to Jerusalem that runs all day, every day (even Shabbat!).

⌖ Directly outside the airport on the 2nd floor. Follow signs to the taxi area and take a left. ℹ Must call 2hr. beforehand, so best to make an appointment before you land. Cash only. $ Any destination in Jerusalem NIS330. ⏰ Open 24hr.

by bus

EGGED BUS

☎*2800 or 03 694 8888; www.egged.co.il

You should just get used to seeing Egged everywhere. From its hub in the Jerusalem Central Bus Station, at the end of Jaffa Rd., Egged stops all over Jerusalem, throughout Israel, and at select destinations in Egypt and Jordan. You can also use Egged to get from the airport. (⌖ Bus #5 to Airport City El-Al Junction. $ NIS29.40. Students can usually get 10% discount with ID. ⏰ Around every 20min., 6:16am-10:42pm.)When boarding the bus, make sure to tell the driver your destination, then press the red button above your head when you approach it. In order to know when you're nearby, it's a good idea to look in advance at the estimated time of arrival and the number of preceding stops, although some stops may be skipped.

ℹ Arrive early at stops, especially when getting on in the middle of a route. Tickets can usually be purchased a few hours before departure, but it's best to buy online or at the Central Bus Station. Tickets can sometimes be purchased on the bus. Check website for information about student passes and discounts. $ Prices vary depending on time and duration of trip. ⏰ Hours vary based on route.

by train

ISRAEL RAILWAYS

☎03 577 4000; www.rail.co.il

The train can be a quicker alternative to bus travel, but has only two stops in Jerusalem, neither of which are convenient for much of the city.

⌖ Both stops in Jerusalem (at Malha and near Biblical Zoo) are far from city center. $ Prices vary depending on time and duration of trip. Students receive 10% discount. ⏰ Hours vary based on route.

GETTING AROUND

by bus

EGGED BUS

☎*2800 or 03 694 8888; www.egged.co.il

Egged has stops throughout Jerusalem and offers several different passes. Go online or call for details.

$ Monthly pass within Jerusalem NIS227. 1-day passes NIS7-11 (effective within Jerusalem city limits with a number of different geographical variations). For certain price codes, a 2-trip ticket can be

by taxi

Taxis are abundant along the wall past Damascus Gate, but usually can be spotted all around the center of the city. HaNevi'im St. on the way to Damascus Gate is also a good bet. Private cabs, called *special* (pronounced "spatial") can be expensive and use a meter. If you're told that you're getting a discount, it usually means you're being ripped off. If you seriously trust your ability to set a price without using the meter (*moneh*), make sure to do so before getting in the cab. Tips are not necessary.

by sherut

Sherut, or shared taxis, tend to be better deals than private taxis but aren't quite as reliable. Within the city, they have no set route and just drive around picking up pedestrians. Tell the driver your destination, **call a tourist office to determine price,** and cross your fingers. You'll most likely have to stop several places for other people to get on or off before you get to your stop (for more information about how sheruts work, see **Israel Essentials.**

near jerusalem

The towns around Israel are very small. The importance of their sights is dwarfed by the monuments of the Old City, and the quality of their food is shamed by the high-class West Jerusalem restaurant scene. But for those who don't travel just to see blockbuster sights, Latrun's **Armed Corps Museum** and monastery are worth a visit, and Abu Ghosh is a relaxing stop for those looking for some small town life and scenic walks. Just make sure you've prepared yourself for the excitement of taking the bus.

ABU GHOSH   ☎02

One of the only towns to support the Israeli independence movement in 1948, Abu Ghosh is renowned for being one of the most peaceful and friendly towns in Israel and is now home to the only soccer club in Israel under equal Jewish and Arab management. Don't be surprised if residents of Abu Ghosh ask you in for tea upon your asking them for directions or want to give you a ride up on one of the town's daunting hills. No, they're not trying to kidnap you: they're just bracingly kind people. There may not be any obvious draw for busy tourists, but it showcases the best of small-town life in Israel.

orientation

HaShalom, the major commercial street of Abu Ghosh, is actually two parallel streets connected by a road, a quirk you will notice if you walk from Caravan Inn to the pharmacy. Though the Crusader Church is fairly near the center of town, Notre Dame de l'Arche d'Alliance and the only hotel in town are both a pant-inducing climb uphill. Flip-flops, Birkenstocks, and bare feet are all grave mistakes.

accommodations

Abu Ghosh itself has no operating hotels at the time of writing. The closest and best option is **Ma'ale HaChamisha,** the hotel of a nearby kibbutz, which, though expensive, is located in a beautiful forest with many fine walking paths.

MA'ALE HACHAMISHA   HOTEL $$$$
Judean Hill   ☎02 533 1331; www.maale5.co.il

This scenic outpost is quite alone in the woods, which makes it well-suited for the reclusive and/or geriatric. The isolation unfortunately allows the hotel practically to extort you with its services: Wi-Fi is at least NIS15 per 15min. and NIS68 per day, the gym is NIS30 per entrance, and even the massage chairs oddly placed in the lobby cost NIS5-10 to be caressed by worn leather. For some, the interior of the hotel might even appear a little shabby; the ugly tile floor of the lobby collects wrappers and dirt, and the rooms have cheap wood floors, small desks, and three small, low-lying beds. But the isolation is also what makes a stay at Ma'ale HaChamisha worth it. Their vast outdoor sitting area with its high perch offers views over the surrounding towns, and it provides access to the nearby, serene forests. Though you will be more than an easy walking distance away from civilization, the best reason to come here might be the escape from civilization.

Walking uphill from the Lebanese Food Restaurant, pass the Abu Ghosh Restaurant and continue until you reach the 1st roundabout (which is really a road extending downhill on the left), then take the next right. Keep walking uphill and bear left; you'll eventually reach the highway, where signs will direct you to the hotel. Continue going uphill and to the left; after you reach an intersection with a white statue, take a right and the hotel is 50m away. $ High-season singles US$194; doubles US$224; triples US$314, for 2 adults and a child US$280. Low-season singles US$123; doubles US$136; triples US$192/170. ⏰ Reception 24hr.

sights

Abu Ghosh may be a small and mostly residential town, but it remains an Israeli one—and therefore has a couple of important religious sites to offer. If you have a hankering for hanging around the French (one that watching *The Hunchback of Notre Dame* won't satisfy), be sure to check out Abu Ghosh's own version in the **Notre Dame de l'Arche d'Alliance.**

CRUSADER CHURCH OF THE RESURRECTION — CHURCH, CRYPT

☎monks 02 534 2798, nuns 02 534 3622; www.abbaye-abugosh.info

Within a colorful garden tended by caring and inconveniently robed nuns (imagine trying to weed in a wimple), the Crusader Church is both a historical treasure and a modern-day mini-park. One of a few sites identified as Emmaus, the ancient town where Jesus is said to have appeared after his resurrection, the church was built by Crusaders in 1143 and abandoned less than 50 years later. It was then used as a barn but somehow remained generally unharmed, meaning that the frescoes that have been destroyed at other sites are still visible here. Seeing the crude human forms and botched attempts at faces in the 12th-century artistry of this usually empty church does not help you communicate with the past, but it does give you a deep sense of its existence crumbling around you. Not to be a downer or anything.

Walk downhill on the road across from Caravan Inn and take a left. Walk toward the minaret of the nearby mosque and, before you reach it, you'll see a green gate on the right. Press the button near the door adjacent to the gate. $ Free. ⏰ Open M-Sa 8:30-11am and 2:30-5:30pm. Closed to tourists on feast days.

NOTRE DAME DE L'ARCHE D'ALLIANCE — CHURCH

It takes hearty quads and a will tougher than Jesus's abs to make it to this church, which is up more hills than is worthwhile for the fragile. However, those who do make the hike can appreciate the tranquility of the sight and the comprehensive birds-eye look over Abu Ghosh. Oh, yeah, and there's a church too. Beige and blue angels scatter their way across the ceiling, there are fifth-century mosaics built into the marble floor at the front right-hand side and in both of the chapels at the back, and the over-romantic white sculpture atop the church looks beautiful when set against a blue sky.

From the bus stop, walk until you see a sign for the Crusader Church. Take a left on that street to find a Muslim cemetery. Walk up the path adjacent to the cemetery and continue until you reach the Police Station 185 bus stop (the station is now defunct, but you can take the bus to this stop) and then take the path on the right leading uphill. Continue until you reach the church. $ Free. ⏰ Open M-Sa 8:30-11:30am and 2:30-5:30pm.

food

Around the central and never-ending HaShalom St., there are tight clusters of restaurants set far apart from each other. The best, **Lebanese Food Restaurant,** is the most solitary; it may be a short walk from the first Abu Ghosh bus station, but it's nearly a mile from the center of town. More convenient is the fairly touristy **Caravan Inn,** which serves up a mean kebab on a refined tablecloth. A variety of hummus places in town call themselves Abu Shukri—the New York City's Famous Ray's Pizza of this tiny mountain town—and all are similarly cheap and olive oily delicious.

▧ LEBANESE FOOD RESTAURANT   LEBANESE $$

88 HaShalom St.   ☎02 570 2397; www.abo-gosh.co.il

Sit under the ancient and mysterious mulberry tree, which produces green fruit on one side and black on the other, and enjoy the cool breeze from a horde of fans as you feast on the fearsome portions. It's just better than anything around it. The bread is thicker and richer; the cucumbers and tomatoes (NIS12) are juicier; and the chicken *shishlik* (NIS45) is simultaneously crunchy and tender. Elderly Arab locals and dedicated patrons from Jerusalem and Tel Aviv alike will tell you that this food isn't just good, it's exceptional. And although former defense minister Moshe Dayan made some controversial policies, Israelis and Palestinians alike can get behind his decision to be a regular here.

✢ *Just across from the 1st bus stop in Abu Ghosh. From any other part of town, walk downhill on HaShalom St., following the signs for Jerusalem until you see the restaurant on the right, past the laundromat.* ⑨ *Hummus for 1 NIS18, for a family NIS46. Steak NIS50. Stuffed chicken NIS65.* ⓩ *Open daily 9am-11pm.*

CARAVAN INN RESTAURANT   MIDDLE EASTERN $$$

27 HaShalom St.   ☎02 534 2744; www.caravan-inn.co.il

Busy with tourists and pilgrims, the distracted and marginally rude staff serve up delicious, if slightly overpriced, kebabs that come on gigantic pikes over ample salads. Caravan Inn has the most centralized view of Abu Ghosh and is also the most comfortable (re: air-conditioned) restaurant in town.

✢ *Walking uphill on HaShalom St., the restaurant is on the right just beyond the road that leads to the pharmacy, Muslim cemetery, and Crusader Church.* ⑨ *Hummus NIS18. Veal and lamb shishlik NIS70. Steak fillet NIS110.* ⓩ *Open daily 10am-11pm.*

NAGI   MIDDLE EASTERN $$

2 Mahmoud Rashid St.   ☎02 533 6520

Of the many Arabic diners lining Mahmoud Rashid and the streets around it, Nagi is the one to go to according to locals. They offer a substantial amount of free falafel with each table, a wonderful attribute that actually applies to a few other places in Abu Ghosh as well.

✢ *Walking toward the Crusader Church, continue past it and take a right after the mosque. Nagi is the 1st in a row of restaurants on a street going uphill. It can be hard to differentiate from the others; if in doubt, ask someone.* ⑨ *Nagi kebab NIS49. Ribeye steak NIS49. Mixed grill NIS85.* ⓩ *Open daily 9am-10pm.*

shopping

The limited shopping opportunities in Abu Ghosh offer household goods with varying levels of quality and specificity.

CRUSADER CHURCH OF THE RESURRECTION SHOP   CERAMICS, LIQUOR

☎02 534 2798; www.abaye-abugosh.info

At the gift shop of the Crusader Church, the monks and sisters sell the fruit of their labors—Emmaus commemorative plates and specialty liquors, including limoncello, verveine, and nut liquor.

✢ *Adjacent to the Crusader Church.* ⑨ *Large bottle €40. Ceramic plates start at €11.* ⓩ *Open M-Sa 2:30-5:30pm.*

KASSEL

HaShalom St.   ☎02 579 6587; www.kasselcandles.com

Though shopping at Kassel does not afford you the opportunity to hang out with monks, it does offer handmade goods of a slightly higher quality. Kassel's candles, its main focus, come in a huge range of shapes, sizes, colors, smells, and prices (NIS10-211). The store also has a wide selection of oils and scents.

Ⓢ *Body lotions NIS45-60. Body spray NIS50. Perfumes NIS45.* Ⓗ *Open Su-Th 10am-7pm, F 10am-5pm, Sa 10am-7pm.*

essentials

PRACTICALITIES

- **ATM:** On HaShalom immediately uphill from, and on the same side of the street as, the Lebanese Food Restaurant. Another ATM is across the street from Caravan Inn and downhill at a convenience store.

- **LAUNDROMAT: Dry Clean Abu Ghosh** offers dry cleaning, washing, and drying. (☎052 636 2955 ⚲ About 200m away from the Lebanese Food Restaurant, on the same side of the street. *i* There may be nobody around who speaks English well. Ⓢ Wash NIS40. Dry NIS40.)

- **POSTAL CODE:** 90845.

EMERGENCY

- **EMERGENCY NUMBERS: Police:** ☎100. **Ambulance:** ☎101. **Fire:** ☎102. **Tourism Police:** ☎03 516 5382.

- **PHARMACY: Abu Ghosh Pharmacy.** (33 HaShalom St. ☎02 533 3623 ⚲ Walk on the road going downhill from Caravan Inn and take the 1st right. Ⓗ Open daily 8am-9pm.)

GETTING THERE

The best way to get to Abu Ghosh is on the **185 Superbus line,** even if its non-Egged status means you'll have to catch the bus at a minimally marked stop. To get to the stop, cross the street at the Central Bus Station in Jerusalem, continue straight past the railroad, and then take a left when you reach the highway. Keep walking until you see a series of bus stops; the one going to Abu Ghosh says "185" on its sign (thus the clever line name) and is the farthest from you. The trip costs NIS8.80 and takes less than 15min.; get off at the first stop to eat at the **Lebanese Food Restaurant,** or wait until the second if you want to begin at the **Crusader Chapel**.

GETTING AROUND

Getting around Abu Ghosh requires (or builds) quite the calf muscles. Cabs are a rare species in this town, so if you're not game for walking up and down rugged hills, you should plan your trip strategically around the schedule of the **185 Superbus,** which has four different stops in town. Note: the first and last stops are more than 2 mi. away from each other (and that's a tough 2 mi. to walk), so feel no shame if you decide to use the bus instead.

LATRUN   ☎09

Like a bowl of milk in which only a few Cocoa Puffs are left floating, Latrun is a roadside town dotted with four precious sights and not much else. But just as those plucky Puffs soak up the milk and grow richer with time, so too have Latrun's cultural offerings settled and grown with decades of peace. Peace, of course, hasn't always been the norm for Latrun—a key strategic prize in battles since the time of Salah ad-Din (and most recently in the 1948 War), the town is home to the Armored Corps Museum, a fascinating and somewhat aggressive tribute to the wars Israel has won to secure its place in the Middle East. The Latrun Monastery exhibits a similar degree of seriousness: its garden was built specifically for quiet reflection, and its vineyard and wine shop seem to encourage stimulated contemplation more than hammered hijinks. Walking around Latrun may not be as fun as drinking that cereal-sweetened, vaguely brown milk, but the proverbial Puffs are worth a thoughtful munch.

orientation

If you're facing the **gas station** from the road, the monastery and guesthouse are on the right. The Armored Corps Museum and restaurant are beyond the station, and the market, which also has ATMs and public toilets, is inside. That the town is oriented around the gas station is a hint that it's much more convenient if you have a car here, but it's not impossible to walk around and enjoy the highways...we mean, sights.

accommodations

Latrun is a roadside stopping ground, and, as such, there is no hotel within Latrun proper. However, Neve Shalom Wahat al-Salam Guesthouse is nearby, and outdoor adventurers can camp out in Canada Park.

NEVE SHALOM WAHAT AL-SALAM GUESTHOUSE — GUESTHOUSE $$$

☎02 999 3030; www.nswas.org/hotel

A short drive, or bearable walk, from the gas station, Neve Shalom Wahat al-Salam Guesthouse is the premier (okay, only) hotel in the Latrun area. Even without considering its lack of competition, Neve Shalom is a fine place to rest your head, although its price may be a little steep for the standard stay it offers.

⇅ Facing the gas station from the road parallel to it, take a left. Continue, then follow sign on the right for Neve Shalom. Shortly afterward there is a sign on the left for the guesthouse. ℹ Free Wi-Fi in lobby. Ⓢ High-season singles US$105; doubles US$140. Low-season singles US$85; doubles US$110. ⏰ Reception daily 7am-10pm. After 10pm, call phone number on gate to be let in.

sights

Historically a hotly contested (yet empty) strategic outpost in Israel, Latrun is now home to the Israeli Army's major museum and two religious sights, one beautiful and one biblical. This may sound like a stern little group, but each sight is highly interesting and embodies part of what makes Latrun a small but crucial dot on Israel's map.

☑ ARMORED CORPS MUSEUM — MUSEUM

☎08 925 5268; www.yadlashiryon.com

Provided you have at least some interest in military history, the Armored Corps Museum's unbelievable collection of weaponry and enthusiastic Israeli soldier tour guides makes for a great visit. A Hotchkiss tank manufactured by France in 1939, then captured by the Germans and emblazoned with a tiny swastika, now sits on the tarmac after having been stolen by the Israelis after World War II for use in the 1948 War. In fact, the first tank the Israelis ever had is here as well, a machine stolen from the British in a bizarre and hilarious stunt involving a movie director and a bottle of scotch. Infamous Merkava 4 tanks—which some consider to be the most intimidating tanks in the modern world—are also on display and can be climbed on and played with (but, unfortunately, not driven) by any visitor. Although the museum has everything from maps to military cartoons, the best part is probably the chance to walk on the Suez Canal bridge, the actual structure Israeli soldiers walked on during the 1967 war. Promotional movies with a 1980s aesthetic and the hyper gung-ho tour guides do make the museum feel unavoidably propagandistic, but that doesn't really have an effect on how awesome all of it is.

⇅ Facing the gas station from the road parallel with it, walk uphill and to the right. ℹ Call in advance to reserve a free tour, which makes the experience more comprehensible and fun. Ⓢ NIS30; ages 3-16, students, and seniors NIS20; families with kids 16 or under NIS100. ⏰ Open Su-Th 8:30am-4:30pm, F 8:30am-12:30pm, Sa 9am-4pm.

LATRUN MONASTERY MONASTERY, VINEYARD

☎08 925 5180

Built by the French Trappist Order as a place for quiet reflection, the Latrun Monastery offers a tranquil garden and a view over all of Latrun—religious sites, gas stations, and military complexes alike. Famous for its wine, the Monastery sells reasonably priced bottles at their shop, to the left when you first enter the building. The Garden of Brotherhood, on the monastery premises, is dedicated to Jewish scholar Rashi of Troyes, the famous Arab ruler Salah ad-Din, and Crusader and nobleman Bernard de Clairvaux. Unfortunately, the garden's message is more beautiful than its grounds, which are weedy and sparse in comparison to the garden inside the monastery.

⇆ Facing the gas station on the road parallel to it, take a right, cross the highway, and continue walking uphill. Signs point to the monastery; its driveway is on the left. $ Entry free. Fontaney dry white wine NIS25. Bottle of brandy NIS140. ⏰ Open daily in summer 8:30am-noon and 2:30-5pm; in winter 8:30-11am and 2:30-4pm. Shop open 8:30am-5:30pm.

EMMAUS (NIKOPOLIS) RELIGIOUS SITE

☎08 925 6940

Supposedly Jesus appeared to two of his disciples on this sight after his resurrection. What's left are ruins from around the third century, including an ancient apse; fifth-century mosaics; and a first-century tomb. Jesus, unfortunately, is nowhere to be seen. However, there is a modern chapel in honor of the event farther up the hill.

⇆ On the way to the monastery from the gas station, before crossing the highway take a left and walk uphill along the highway. You will pass an overpass after 5-10min., and Emmaus will be on the right after another 1-2min. $ NIS5, under 16 free. ⏰ Open M-Sa 8:30am-noon and 2:30-5:30pm.

star power

It may look like just a blue six-pointed star, but that design on the Israeli flag is actually known as the "Shield of David" in Hebrew. Widely recognized as a symbol of the country and Jewish culture as a whole, the star has been used on Jewish flags since the 14th century. But ever wondered where it comes from? It's speculated to be a relatively new addition to the religion—in the sense that 600 years is nothing when compared to millennia. Early instances show its use as a decorative symbol, particularly in architecture and calligraphy, but no one is entirely sure how it became associated with Judaism. One theory suggests that this arose from the design of protective amulets, called *segulot*, which illustrations have been found in early medieval Kabbalistic manuscripts. Maybe we should ask Madonna.

the great outdoors

CANADA PARK PARK

Yes, this is called Canada Park. No, we didn't accidentally put this in the wrong book—this park was built with donations from Canadian Jews. Now a popular place to picnic and camp, Canada Park is the site of controversy, as it was built over the rubble of Palestinian villages destroyed in the Six-Day War. But seeing as you probably won't be able to make peace in the Middle East while on vacation, it may be worthwhile to just try to enjoy Canada Park's many hiking and biking trails, various ancient ruins, and shady spots to sit and eat during the summer. In fact, it has been scientifically proven that wine from the Trappist

Monastery tastes better when poured from a Canada Park picnic bench. The Parks Authority advises that you stick to trails and avoid rock climbing.

➜ 1-2min. walk up from Emmaus. $ Free. ⏰ Open 24hr.

food

Gourmets, get out while there's still time. Latrun is more a stop for starving roadtrippers than anything else, and the eating options are limited, to say the least.

ASA

MEAT $$

☎08 924 9222

The *kebbeh* (NIS7) seem eerily like corndogs at this roadside Arabic meat diner where roadtrippers stop by for hearty helpings of protein, much-needed air-conditioning, and comfortable booth seating. The oriental kebab (NIS36) is deep fried to perfection, and it comes with a wide selection of pickles, cabbage, and other vegetables. For the purely vegetable- or kosher-minded, Asa serves a number of salads.

➜ In the courtyard behind the gas station. $ Goose liver NIS55. Sheep NIS48. Schnitzel NIS32. ⏰ Open Su-Th 9am-10pm, F 9am-5pm, Sa 9am-10pm.

SI ESPRESSO

CAFE $$

☎08 922 1513; www.siespresso.co.il

Part of an Israeli chain, this Si Espresso specializes in serving up just-above-average iced coffee to short-shorts-sporting cyclists and under-caffeinated drivers. Sip away at one of the outdoor tables to enjoy the charming view of the highway and gas station, or chill in the refreshing air-conditioning inside, where there are a few tables and stools around the bar.

➜ In the courtyard behind the gas station. ℹ Wi-Fi available, making it perhaps the only place to get internet in Latrun. Not kosher. $ Sandwiches NIS30-40. Medium iced coffee NIS21. ⏰ Open Su-Th 6am-11pm, F 6am-10pm, Sa 6am-11pm.

essentials

PRACTICALITIES

Since most visitors stays in Latrun last shorter than the lifespan of your average mayfly, the amenities are few. There is an **ATM** and **public toilets** in the gas station. If you need **Wi-Fi** so you can immediately friend that cute tour guide from the Armored Corps Museum, head next door to Si Espresso.

EMERGENCY

- **EMERGENCY NUMBERS: Police:** ☎100. **Ambulance:** ☎101. **Fire Department:** ☎103. All services come from Jerusalem.

GETTING THERE

The best way to get to Latrun is **by car,** but those who only want to come for the day will find that renting a car is not worthwhile. Daytrippers should opt for the beloved **Egged bus** (☎*2800; www.egged.co.il/eng. ➜ 404, 433, 434, or 448 lines. Which line to take depends on time of departure; check Egged website for more information. ⏰ Approximately 30min.). Once on the bus, it's always best to remind the driver of your destination and press the red button above you when you feel like Latrun should be approaching based on time lapsed and, well, the signs reading "Latrun." When you get out at what feels like the middle of nowhere, rest assured that you are only in the outer reaches of nowhere and, therefore, still somewhat close to civilization.

GETTING AROUND

Most people get around Latrun by car, but those woeful travelers who have taken the bus must go by foot along one of the two major highways. It ain't picturesque, but it'll do, pig. It'll do.

TEL AVIV AND ENVIRONS

Congratulations, you've made it to the most populated and un-Israeli part of the country: unabashedly liberal, modern, and—every now and then—utterly insane, Tel Aviv is a bastion of the West in the Middle East. Indeed, anything that reaches the country seems to pass through this area first, starting 70 years ago with the state of Israel itself, which began here. And though Jerusalem may have the Knesset, Tel Aviv takes the cake on designer labels, Bauhaus architecture, European-style megaclubs, and an odd penchant for '80s kitsch. In a land ravaged by ideological struggles between new and old, religious and secular, it's pretty clear where Tel Aviv sits on the spectrum. This propensity for the modern is also apparent in many of the surrounding cities. **Ashkelon** and **Herzliya** are both punctuated with top-notch beach resorts amid the urban grime, and, farther afield, **Beit Guvrin** gives a rural taste of a simpler life, with only the brightest of Tel Aviv's nighttime strobes glowing on the dusk horizon.

greatest hits

- **EVERYBODY SCREAM.** Iceberg's (p. 115) ice cream will have you screaming for more.
- **HERMIT'S HOUSE.** See a sandcastle 30 years in the making in Herzliya (p. 141).
- **BLACKOUT.** Experience eating blindly at Jaffa's pitch black restaurant, aptly named Blackout (p. 132). The best part? You'll remember the whole thing.
- **DIVINE SECRETS.** Check out Club Ya Ya (p. 120) in Tel Aviv and leave with a story you won't want to pass down to your daughter.

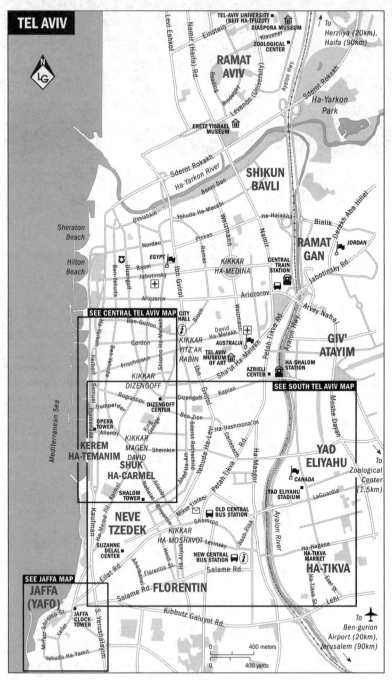

tel aviv and environs

TEL AVIV

To Herzliya (20km), Haifa (90km)

TEL-AVIV UNIVERSITY (BEIT HA-TFUZOT)
DIASPORA MUSEUM
Einstein
Klausner
ZOOLOGICAL CENTER
Levi-Eshkol
Namir (Haifa) Rd.
Raanan
Broedety
Ayalon Hwy.
Sderot Rokakh

RAMAT AVIV

Levanon (University)

ERETZ YISRAEL MUSEUM

Ha-Yarkon Park

Sderot Rokakh

Ha-Yarkon River

SHIKUN BAVLI

Benei Dan

Sheraton Beach

Ussishkin
Nordau
Basel
Dizengoff
Jabotinsky
Arlozorov
Ben-Yehuda

Hilton Beach

Yehuda Ha-Macabi

Pinkas

Remez

Werzmann

Namir

Ha-Halakha

Bialik

Derekh Aba Hillel

RAMAT GAN

JORDAN

EGYPT

Ibn Gvirol

KIKKAR HA-MEDINA

CENTRAL TRAIN STATION

Jabotinsky Rd.

Mediterranean Sea

SEE CENTRAL TEL AVIV MAP

Ben-Gurion
Gordon
Frischmann
Herbert
Ben-Yehuda

CITY HALL

Bloch

Arlozorov

Arvey Nahal

David Ha-Melekh

KIKKAR YITZ'AK RABIN

AUSTRALIA

TEL AVIV MUSEUM OF ART

Shaul Ha-Melekh

AZRIELI CENTER

Petah-Tikva Rd.

HA-SHALOM STATION

GIV' ATAYIM

KIKKAR DIZENGOFF

Dizengoff

Kaplan

SEE SOUTH TEL AVIV MAP

Moshe Dayan

Bograshov

DIZENGOFF CENTER

Ben-Zion

Allenby

King George

Sderot Rothschild

Ha-Hashmona'im

OPERA TOWER

Samuel Promenade

Trumpeldor

KIKKAR MAGEN DAVID

Sheinkin

Ahad-Ha-Am

Yehuda Ha-Levi

Ha-Carmel

Ha-Masger

To Zoological Center (1.5km)

YAD ELIYAHU

CANADA

KEREM HA-TEMANIM

SHUK HA-CARMEL

SHALOM TOWER

Nahalat Binyamin

Allenby

YAD ELIYAHU STADIUM

LaGuardia

Ayalon River

Kaufman

NEVE TZEDEK

KIKKAR HA-MOSHAVOT

OLD CENTRAL BUS STATION

Milka Yisrael

Shomron

Levinsky

Resh Pina

SUZANNE DELAL CENTER

NEW CENTRAL BUS STATION

Salame Rd.

Ha-Hagana

HA-TIKVA MARKET

HA-TIKVA

Eilat Rd.

Abarbanel

Florentin St.

Herzl

FLORENTIN

Salame Rd.

Ha-Tikva St.

Lehi

SEE JAFFA MAP

JAFFA (YAFO)

JAFFA CLOCK-TOWER

Mifratz Shlomo St.

Yefet

S. Yerushalayim

Kibbutz Galuyot Rd.

To Ben-gurion Airport (20km), Jerusalem (90km)

Yehuda Ha-Yamit

| 0 | 400 meters |
| 0 | 400 yards |

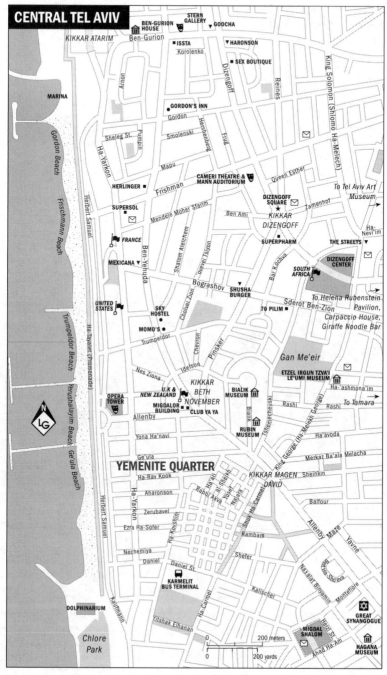

CENTRAL TEL AVIV

KIKKAR ATARIM

BEN-GURION HOUSE
Ben-Gurion

STERN GALLERY
GOOCHA

ISSTA
Korolenko

HARONSON

SEX BOUTIQUE

MARINA

Gordon Beach

GORDON'S INN
Gordon

Sheleg St.
Smolenski

Dizengoff

Reines

King Solomon (Shlomo Ha-Melech)

Arnon

Pumpin

Hershenberg

Frug

Ha-Yarkon

Mapu

HERLINGER

Frishman

CAMERI THEATRE & MANN AUDITORIUM

Queen Esther

Zamenhof

To Tel Aviv Art Museum

SUPERSOL

Mendeje Moher Sfarim

DIZENGOFF SQUARE
KIKKAR DIZENGOFF

Ben Ami

Ha-Nevi'im

FRANCE

Ben-Yehuda

Shalom Aletchem

Yosef Tsvon

SUPERPHARM

Bar KOchva

THE STREETS

DIZENGOFF CENTER

MEXICANA

Bograshov

SHUSHA BURGER

SOUTH AFRICA

To Helena Rubenstein Pavilion, Carpaccio House, Giraffe Noodle Bar

Frischmann Beach

Herbert Samuel

Chelouz Zion

70 PILIM

Sderot Ben-Zion

UNITED STATES

SKY HOSTEL

MOMO'S

Trumpeldor

Chevron

Pinsker

Gan Me'eir

ETZEL IRGUN TZVA'I LE'UMI MUSEUM

Ha-'ashmona'im

Trumpeldor Beach

Nes Ziona

Idelson

Ha-Tayalet (Promenade)

Ha-Yarkon

OPERA TOWER

U.K & NEW ZEALAND

MIGDALOR BUILDING

KIKKAR BETH NOVEMBER

CLUB YA YA

BIALIK MUSEUM

Bialik

Tshernehevski

Rashi

Rashi

To Tamara

Yerushalayim Beach

Allenby

Yona Ha'navi

RUBIN MUSEUM

King George (Ha-Melekh George)

Ha'avoda

Ge'ula Beach

Ge'ula

YEMENITE QUARTER

Ha-Rav Kook

KIKKAR MAGEN DAVID

Merkaz Ba'ala Melacha

Sheinkin

Aharonson

Rabot Akva

al-Shelhi

Shuk Ha-Carmel

Balfour

Zerubavel

Ha-Koyshim

Nailara

Ezra Ha-Sofer

Rambam

Allenby

Maze

Yavne

Nechemiya

Daniel

Shefer

Nazalat Binyamin

Montefiore

Rezalat Sha'eva

Herbert Samuel

Karlmann

Daniel St.

KARMELIT BUS TERMINAL

Kalischer

GREAT SYNAGOGUE

DOLPHINARIUM

Ha-Carmel

Yitshak Elhanan

MIGDAL SHALOM

Herzl St.

Ahad Ha-Am

HAGANA MUSEUM

Chlore Park

0   200 meters

0   200 yards

tel aviv and environs

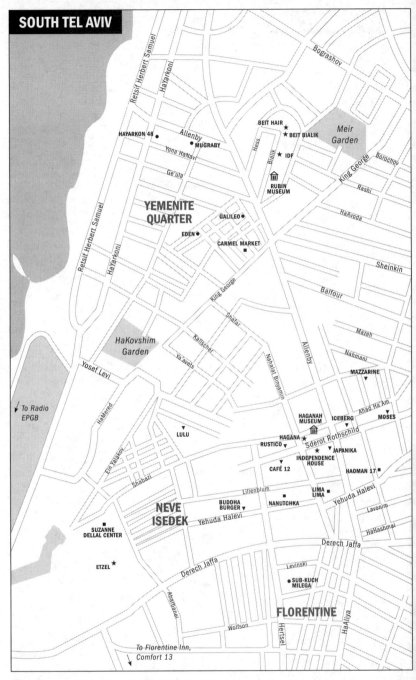

SOUTH TEL AVIV

tel aviv and environs

Bograshov

Retsif Herbert Samuel

HaYarkoni

Meir Garden

BEIT HAIR ★
★ BEIT BIALIK

HAYARKON 48 ● Allenby
● MUGRABY

Yona HaNavi

Hess

Bialik

★ IDF

King George

Borochov

Rashi

Ge'ula

🏛 RUBIN MUSEUM

Retsif Herbert Samuel

YEMENITE QUARTER

GALILEO ●

HaAvoda

EDEN ●

CARMEL MARKET ■

HaYarkoni

Sheinkin

King George

Balfour

Shafar

Mazeh

HaKovshim Garden

Kallscher

Nahmani

Yosef Levi

Ya'avets

Nahalat Binyamin

Allenby

MAZZARINE ▾

HaMered

▾ LULU

Ahad Ha'Am

HAGANAH MUSEUM 🏛

ICEBERG ▾

MOSES ■

Erin Ya'akov

HAGANA ★
RUSTICO ▾

Sderot Rothschild

▾ JAPANIKA

Shabazi

CAFÉ 12 ▾

INDEPENDENCE HOUSE ★

HAOMAN 17 ■

Lillenblum

LIMA LIMA ■

Yehuda Halevi

NEVE ISEDEK

BUDDHA BURGER ▾

NANUTCHKA ▾

Lavonim

Yehuda Halevi

HaHashmal

SUZANNE DELLAL CENTER ■

Derech Jaffa

ETZEL ★

Derech Jaffa

Levinski

Abarbanai

● SUB-KUCH MILEGA

FLORENTINE

Wolfson

Hertsel

HaAliya

To Radio EPGB ↓

To Florentine Inn, Comfort 13 ↓

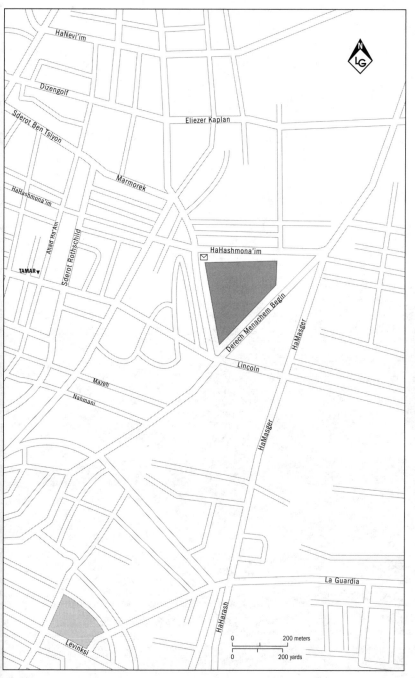

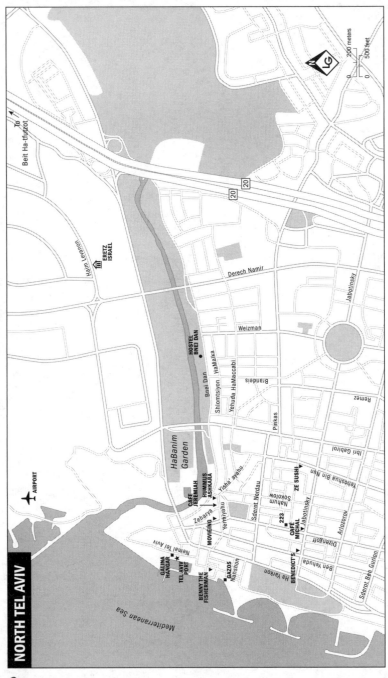

NORTH TEL AVIV

Mediterranean Sea

AIRPORT

To
Beit Ha-t'fuzot

Haim Levanon

ERETZ
ISRAEL

Derech Namir

Jabotinsky

20

20

Weizman

HOSTEL
BNEI DAN

Brandeis

Remez

Brei Dan

HaMalka

Shlomtsiyon

Yehuda HaMaccabi

Pinkas

Ibn Gabirol

HaBanim
Garden

Yisha'ayahu

Yehoshua Bin Nun

CAFÉ
EREMIAH

HUMMUS
ASHKARA

Sderot Nordau

ZE SUSHI

Zekarya

Nahum
Sokolow

Arlozorov

Yermiyahu

223

MOVIE&NG

CAFÉ
MICHAL

Jabotinsky

Nemal Tel Aviv

Dizengoff

GALINA
HANGAR

TEL AVIV
PORT

GAZOS
Nahshon

BENNY THE
FISHERMAN

BENEDICT'S

Ben Yehuda

Ha Yarkon

Sderot Ben Gurion

200 meters

500 feet

Tel Aviv is home of Tel Aviv University—and it doesn't get much more "student friendly" than that.

Florentine Hostel may be your best bet in terms of accommodation—cheap and with an under-40 age requirement, you know you'll be rooftop bonding and doing shots without your mom and pop doppelgangers.

If you're looking for a nice place to feel cool but act low-key, look no further than **Radio E.P. G.B.;** ignore the sketchiness of its location and waltz in. There is no cover, and you'll get a discount if you "attend" the event on Facebook. For a more balls-to-the-wall evening, try **70 Pilim** or get freaky at the sex boutique by day, club by night **Sex Boutique**. After your night on the town, stop off at Tel Aviv's famous breakfast place **Benedict's,** which is open 24hr., and cooks up late-night drunken snacks and morning hangover cures.

If you're looking to be more studious than smashed, take a quick trip to **Rehovot** and visit the **Weizmann Institute**, or hit up the *shuk* in Jaffa for some genuine Middle East knick-knacks.

tel aviv

Apparently Tel Aviv is sexy. Yeah, yeah, you've heard it all before. It's hard not to talk about the city without bouncing around the same old clichés about scantily clad beach-goers, short-skirted clubbers, and the conspicuous lack of anyone over the age of forty. But clichés exist for a reason: sometimes, things really do live up to the hype. Whether you find yourself in a cloud of dry ice at a trance club at 7am or holed up in a tragically hip or plain old cooler-than-thou bar come dusk, you'll soon realize that Tel Aviv is often over-the-top, somehow maintaining the sureality of a story that has always seemed just too crazy to be true. Stranger than fiction, sure—why not "cooler than" too?

While she may truly live and define herself by the night, Tel Aviv escapes a hangover in the morning as 20-somethings saunter toward the beaches or settle into the swanky cafes perched on every corner. This is not like the rest of Israel—Orthodox men are just as rare a sight as M16-toting teenagers—but more akin to a glamorous European Riviera town, with its laissez-faire approach to life. As the languid morning turns into late afternoon, the crowds migrate back toward the bars in preparation of the night ahead.

ORIENTATION

Tel Aviv sits at the center of Israel's Mediterranean coast, 60km northwest of Jerusalem and 90km south of Haifa. While the city is large by Israel's standards, much of it (the northern and central parts in particular) are organized in an easily navigable grid. Once you learn the main thoroughfares, it'll be almost impossible to get lost in the mess of cobbled streets that lie between—recognizable landmarks are never more than 5min. away. The city is most easily divided into three main sections: the city center, north Tel Aviv, and south Tel Aviv.

city center

The city center, which is a little grungy and a little dull, is built on a simple grid, which consists of five main roads running parallel to the coast. Along the coast is **HaYarkon Street.** Moving inland, **Ben-Yehuda Street** comes next, then **Dizengoff Street,** which swerves east past the Dizengoff Center and intersects with **King George,** which in turn cuts north toward Yitshak Rabin Sq., where it meets **Ibn Gvirol Street,** home to the city's performing arts scene. The southern boundary of Tel Aviv's city center begins at the intersection of **Allenby Street** and Ben-Yehuda St. A series of roads then cuts across perpendicularly as we progress north, including **Bograshov Street** (which eventually runs into the Dizengoff Center), **Frischmann Street, Gordon Street, Ben-Gurion Boulevard,** and **Arlozorov Street.**

north tel aviv

The major thoroughfares of the city center (the ones running parallel to the coast) all continue into the more high-end north, home to the city's chic. **Jabotinsky Street** and **Nordau Boulevard** are the two major roads cutting perpendicular to the thoroughfares, and the ritzy clubs in this area congregate in its northwest corner at the **Tel Aviv Port.** Just to the east of the port, **Little Tel Aviv** masses around the area where the major roads finally come together. **Ramat Aviv** and **Tel Aviv University** are located across the river.

south tel aviv

The grid breaks down as you descend into

TEL AVIV AND THE SOUTH COAST

the city's south, the more invitingly chaotic part of Tel Aviv. Ben-Yehuda St. turns into Allenby St., which leads into **David Magen Square,** the intersection of six roads and perhaps the busiest hub in all of Tel Aviv. To its west sits the **Yemenite Quarter** and the clamorous Carmel Market, while King George heads north and **Sheinkin Street** branches east. Cutting a large 'J' across the south is **Rothschild Boulevard,** which intersects both Sheinkin St. and Allenby St. to form a triangle that contains many of Tel Aviv's best restaurants and clubs. It eventually dead-ends at **Herzl Street,** which marks the edge of Neve Tsedek. Herzl St. meanwhile penetrates into the **Florentine,** the district bordered by Eilat St. to the north, Elifelet St. to the west, and Shlomo St. to the south, which leads to the New Central Bus Station in the east.

ACCOMMODATIONS

While the average Tel Avivian might tell you that sleep is for the weak, you'll probably want somewhere to work off that raging hangover. The city has a healthy number of hostels, but there are two or three that really outdo the competition. Naturally, this also makes them perennial favorites of the foreign and backpack-born, so it's generally a good idea to try and book ahead. The vast majority of beds are centered around the intersections of **Allenby Street** and **Ben-Yehuda Street.** The great news is that this is prime real estate, only a block away from the beach and with easy access to pretty much anywhere else in the city. The downside is that the area is loud, courtesy of city traffic, the nearby clubs, and their fairly vocal patrons (who are even louder and drunker in the wee hours of the morning). A handful of more intimate (and less costly) joints are scattered across the Florentine and elsewhere in **South Tel Aviv,** and, if you want to get away from it all, Jaffa is only a short bus ride away.

city center

For location, the city center can't be beat. Whether you're taking in the museums and markets by day or stumbling home at 7am after one Goldstar too many, you'll never be more than a 20min. walk from most of the city. Unfortunately, the area is filled mostly with expensive hotels, meaning budget-friendly hostels are few and far between. While Gordon Inn Guesthouse offers a great place to stay smack in the middle of town, most of the other inexpensive options are located on the border with South Tel Aviv.

GORDON INN GUESTHOUSE — HOSTEL $$

17 Gordon St. ☎03 523 8239; www.inisrael.com/gordon_inn/en

Occupying a unique position as the only hostel truly in central Tel Aviv, Gordon Inn is a great base camp from which to access most of the city. The immediate neighborhood is quiet, and older clientele create an especially relaxed mood. Rooms are spacious, clean, come with a fridge and iron, and have distinctly thick mattresses, but the best perk is probably the included breakfast buffet. Such amenities as a rooftop terrace and bar area with TV, pool table, and kitchen (all open until midnight) make Gordon Inn a very popular choice, so be sure to book about a month in advance to ensure a bed.

 # On the corner of Ben-Yehuda St. and Gordon St. by the flower stand. i Free Wi-Fi; computers can be rented for NIS10 per hr. Laundry service 50NIS per load. Free luggage storage. $ Dorms NIS90; singles NIS280-380; doubles NIS300-410; triples and quads available on advance request. ⏰ Doors locked daily 4-9am, but guests can still access via code.

MOMO'S HOSTEL — HOSTEL $$

28 Ben-Yehuda St. ☎03 629 7421; www.momoshostel.com

Straddling South Tel Aviv, Momo's provides an easy point of entry to both the city's center and the profusion of clubs and bars further south. While the rooms are clean and functional, the hostel best stands out for its homey vibe: staff are eager to show you around and crack a joke, a downstairs bar stays open until the last customer decides to stumble off to bed (beer and chasers NIS12), and Kebab, the cat-in-residence, will likely vie for your attention. The free breakfast of coffee and cake doesn't hurt either.

 # Take bus #4 from New Central Station. Between intersections with Allenby St. and Bograshov St. i Roof terrace closes at 10pm. Free Wi-Fi; computers available NIS8 per 30min; NIS12 per 1hr. Safety deposit box with NIS35 deposit. Lockers included, though locks aren't provided. $ May-Sept dorms NIS90; singles NIS135-200; doubles NIS185-270; triples NIS340.

SKY HOSTEL — HOSTEL $$

34 Ben-Yehuda St. ☎03 620 0044; www.sky1hostel.com

A few doors down from Momo's and under the same ownership, Sky Hostel has basic rooms with fans and linoleum floors, many overlooking the busy Ben-Yehuda St. A sparse lobby and roof terrace provide some social space for residents, but, if the atmosphere still seems dull, guests can head over to Momo's to claim their complimentary breakfast. When checking in, be sure to ask about the special bed and beer deal—two beers for NIS18 or three for NIS25.

 # Bus #4 from New Central Station. Sky is on Ben-Yehuda between Allenby St. and Bograshov St. i Lockers provided in rooms. $ Dorm NIS85; singles NIS160-260; doubles NIS280-320. ⏰ Reception 24hr.

south tel aviv

When it comes to cheap beds and free breakfasts, the south is the place to be. While most places are centered on the top of Allenby St. and the Yemenite Quarter, the more adventurous will be excited to find a curiosity or two in the Florentine as well.

HAYARKON 48 HOSTEL $$

48 HaYarkon St. ☎03 516 8989; www.hayarkon48.com

Cleaner than most and in a prime location, Hayarkon 48 is always full of American, English, and Canadian 20-somethings fresh off Birthright. But being the most popular hostel in Tel Aviv is a double-edged sword. Whether you're pre-gaming on the roof or playing pool in the lounge, you'll never be short of new friends; but between this same clientele at 2am and busy Hayarkon St. outside, the place is anything but restful. Staff are largely eager to help, but having to deal with a place this busy leaves them unafraid to strip your sheets in the morning if you haven't paid for the next night. Make sure to book in advance, especially for weekends, since this place always fills up.

Take bus #4 to the bottom of Ben-Yehuda St. and walk down Allenby toward the coast. Make a left on HaYarkon St. ℹ *Breakfast of coffee and toast included. Fans. Computer rental NIS15 per hr. Safe NIS1 per day with NIS50 deposit; lockers NIS15 per day. Self-service laundry and detergent NIS27.* $ *Dorms NIS90; private rooms NIS330-385. Weekly dorms NIS581. Prices rise in July.* ⏰ *Reception 24hr.*

FLORENTINE HOSTEL HOSTEL $

10 Elifelet St. ☎03 518 7551; www.florentinehostel.com

Teetering on the edge of the Florentine and on Tel Aviv's border with Jaffa, this hostel may be a little removed from most, but a tight community and great communal space make it a winner. Rooms are located on the top floor of the building and open up onto a huge rooftop terrace that has to be one of the best hangout spots in the area. It's scattered with hammocks, collected liquor bottles, and a technicolor hodgepodge of plush sofas. An under-40 age restriction (sorry, Dad) and limited number of rooms make sure that this place stays fresh.

From New Central Station, walk down Shalma St. for 1.25km before making a right onto Elifelet St. The hostel is on the right after 1 block. ℹ *Free Wi-Fi. Fans in all rooms. Large communal kitchen. Ages 18-40 only.* $ *Dorms NIS66; doubles from NIS176, additional person NIS50.* ⏰ *Reception Su-F 9am-2pm and 7-9pm.*

EDEN HOUSE HOTEL $$$

27 Kehilat Aden St. ☎052 746 9842; booking@edenhousetlv.com

A collection of buildings and houses scattered over the tranquil Yemenite Quarter, Eden House offers bright orange beds in pristine rooms. Take a glass of wine up to one of the shady vantage points in the complex of rooftop terraces and lazily enjoy the view of narrow, winding streets below. It'll be hard to believe that you're only a 5min. walk from boisterous Allenby St.

Take bus #4 up Allenby and get off just after David Magen Sq. Make a left onto Ge'ula St., then another left as it forks into HaAri. Take a right, then an immediate left, to get onto Kehilat Aden St. Eden House (unmarked) is behind the big gray door with the red stained-glass Star of David. ℹ *Fridge, kettle, Wi-Fi, A/C, and ensuite bathroom.* $ *Singles US$94; doubles US$106. Prices are subject to change based on season, so call ahead.*

SUB-KUCH MILEGA HOSTEL $

22 HaMashbir St. ☎03 681 3412; www.subkuchmilega.com

Everyone wants a place with "character," but when "character" means you're staying in an incense-laden hostel/vegan restaurant with a reggae soundtrack, are you really up for it? If so, you've just found a gem in the Florentine. (If not, the Florentine probably isn't for you anyway.) While the rooms may be dimly lit and a little cramped, Sub-Kuch Milega, draped in purple fabrics and Indian paraphernalia, may be the chillest place to stay in Tel Aviv. And if the eternal curry smell starts to get to you, you've got some of the cheapest beer in Tel Aviv downstairs (all-you-can-drink Maccabee for NIS40, anyone?) to distract you. At the very least, after staying at this place you'll have a story to tell at dinner parties.

Walk north on Herzl St. Take a right onto Matalon and the next left onto HaMashbir St. The hostel is on the left. ℹ *Breakfast and lockers included. Free Wi-Fi. Guests get 10% discount at restaurant.* $ *Dorms NIS70; private rooms NIS180-220.* ⏰ *Reception daily 11am-midnight.*

GALILEO HOTEL

HOTEL $$$

8 Hillel HaZaken St.   ☎03 516 0050; www.sun-hotels.co.il

With royal red carpets and Impressionist paintings, Galileo is certainly a world away from the dirt-caked, sweat-soaked world of backpacking. Right on the edge of the Yemenite Quarter, it's particularly quiet, yet remains only a 30sec. walk from Allenby St.

☂ *Take bus #4 up Allenby St. and make a left onto Beit Yosef, just after David Magen Sq. Galileo is on the corner with Hillel HaZaken.* *i* *A/C, bathroom, cable TV, safe, and coffee in all rooms. Free Wi-Fi. Light breakfast in nearby coffeeshop included.* ⓢ *Singles US$87, doubles US$109-150. Prices rise in Aug.*

MUGRABY HOSTEL

HOSTEL $

19 Allenby St.   ☎03 510 2443; www.mugraby-hostel.com

To get to your room from the lobby-cum-internet-cafe, you'll have to walk down a small alley and up a staircase. The place itself is noticeably bare; old-timey movie posters grace the walls, but they seem less vintage and more in tone with the unkempt nature of the place. The communal areas and kitchen are spacious but sparse.

☂ *Take bus #4 to the bottom of Ben-Yehuda. Walk down Allenby toward the sea for 1 block, and Mugraby will be a few doors down on the right.* *i* *Fans provided. Free Wi-Fi.* ⓢ *Dorms NIS75; singles NIS185; doubles NIS220.*

north tel aviv

Though the north of the city has enough bars and clubs to arguably outdo its southern cousins, you'll probably be passing out in the back of a taxi rather than staggering across the streets at 5am to get home. The bottom line is that if you're staying in Tel Aviv, you'll almost certainly be bunked up somewhere other than the north. **Hostel Bnei Dan** is the sole option, and, as it's located fairly far inland, it's at least a 20min. walk to reach anywhere of note.

▨ HOSTEL BNEI DAN

HOSTEL $$

36 Bnei Dan   ☎02 594 5655; telaviv@iyha.org.il

Hostel Bnei Dan straddles a strange accommodation-specific no man's land—hostel-style dorm rooms include the kinds of amenities you'd expect in a hotel at a price that fits somewhere between the two. The place itself is larger than most other hostels in town and is anything but homey. Tiled floors, sterile rooms, and long white corridors are more reminiscent of a hospital ward than a backpacker's inn. That said, it's as impeccably clean as a hostel could be, and the TV and bathroom in every room are notable perks.

☂ *Bus #24 or #25 from King George will take you to Bnei Dan, just past the intersection with Ibn Gvirol. From here the hostel is just past the intersection with Brandeis, heading east.* *i* *A/C. Wi-Fi in lobby NIS10 per hr. Breakfast included.* ⓢ *Dorms NIS140; singles NIS276; doubles NIS353.*

SIGHTS

Believe it or not, Tel Aviv keeps being a city during the day too. But as far as history is concerned, you're looking at barely a century of it, so save your synagogue visits for Jerusalem. While an explosion of modernist Bauhaus provides a real treat for those wacky for the white and straight-edged, Tel Aviv, as the former seat of government, is also home to monuments to—and museums about—Israel's founding. Indeed, museums are certainly a strength of the town; the best are located in the north by Tel Aviv University, where the **Diaspora Museum** can be found.

That said, Tel Aviv's daylight charm really stems from the hodgepodge of quirkiness bursting from its many different neighborhoods, particularly toward the south, where you can find the undeniable cool of **Sheinkin Street** and the gentrified elegance of **Neve Tsedek**, to name two. Both seem to have been constructed less for cars and more to accommodate a profusion of artsy cafes and dapper denizens. Meanwhile the bustle of **Carmel Market** and **David Magen Square** provide something for the more riot-ready. Heading up **Dizengoff Street** might be an exercise in urban grunge, but up north it blooms into a more refined affair, where designer shops and sequestered bars make up a little playground for the well-heeled. Needless to say, the beach is around a 10min. walk from wherever you find yourself.

city center

Sexy comes in many varieties here: the north has its Western chic, and the south revels in getting down and dirty. The city center, wedged between the two, is Western insofar as you can find McDonald's and Subways aplenty and only gets as dirty as is typically urban. Sure it might not have as much flair, but spend more than two hours in Tel Aviv and you'll inevitably be spending much of it here—forget posturing and take this place in. By day the easy-tempered cafes buzz around **Dizengoff Square** and King George, and the mammoth Dizengoff Center, burgeoning with name-brand chains and boutiques, provides respite to homesick mallrats. For the cultured, many of Tel Aviv's artistic institutions, such as the Opera House, Museum of Art, and the renowned Habima Theatre, are centered around Ibn Gvirol St. in the east.

TEL AVIV MUSEUM OF ART   MUSEUM
27 King Saul Blvd.   ☎03 607 7020; tamuseum.com

A colossal Lichtenstein adorns the main atrium of Tel Aviv's premier art museum, where the considerable permanent collection focuses on the last 150 years, covering everything from Impressionism to Modernism and contemporary. Think Picasso to Pollock, Monet and Matisse to Miró. Temporary exhibits run the gamut from installation art to photography, all by established artists of either international or Israeli renown. Winners of such prestigious Israeli awards as the Rappaport Prize, which generally goes to young artists, have their work on display here too. The auditorium and theater host a regular schedule of lectures, concerts, and film screenings, often in English. Make sure to check the website for listings.

✦ *Buses #9, 18, 28, 70, 90, or 111.* ⓘ *Free bag drop provided.* Ⓢ *NIS42, students NIS34, under 18 free.* ☒ *Open M 10am-4pm, Tu 10am-10pm, W 10am-4pm, Th 10am-10pm, F 10am-2pm, Sa 10am-4pm.*

HELENA RUBINSTEIN PAVILION OF CONTEMPORARY ART   MUSEUM
6 Tarsat Blvd.   ☎03 528 7196; tamuseum.com

An extension of the Tel Aviv Museum of Art, the Pavilion showcases work by up-and-coming Israeli artists. The space holds three or four different exhibitions per year. This means the exhibits are always fresh, but also that the space is unfortunately closed for long periods at least twice a year in order to set up the new ones, which are always...unique. Really, anything's game: from an exhibit on chair design to strobe-lit six-foot gravestones to a gargantuan graffitti display. The upstairs area is home to a permanent collection of intricate Meissen Porcelain.

✦ *Bus #63. The museum is between Ben-Tsiyon Blvd. and Dizengoff St.* Ⓢ *Free.* ☒ *Open M 10am-4pm, Tu 10am-10pm, W 10am-4pm, Th 10am-10pm, F 10am-2pm, Sa 10am-4pm.*

DIZENGOFF SQUARE   SQUARE

Surrounded by some of the best Bauhaus in town, Dizengoff Sq. is the heart of Tel Aviv's city center. The Fire and Water fountain (in the center of this center of the city center) was designed by famed Israeli artist Agam and originally wowed passersby with a revolving pyrotechnic display, before operational costs forced the city to turn off the gas—which means that it's now, well, just a water fountain, and not a particularly attractive one at that. A better reason to come to the square is the Antiques and Secondhand Fair (see **Shopping**), which is held every Tuesday and Friday.

south tel aviv

Home of the tragically hip, terminally chill and, naturally, the just plain weird, South Tel Aviv is where the young and idiosyncratic come out to play—or, at least, to look nonchalant behind Clark Kent glasses and the haze of smoke from their rollies. Whether it's the craziness of Carmel Market, the sleepy corners of the Florentine, or that guy with more tattoos than bare skin in the Yemenite Quarter, this place thrives on quirk. With that in mind, it's best just to wander. A day whiled away here grazing on cafe terraces is one lived well—after all, you're on vacation, right?

The more institutionalized sights of the area, however, fit a different mold. As the old seat of the Israeli government, Tel Aviv has enough monuments and statues to delight even the biggest nerds. The military has also established a number of museums in the area for those of you more into howitzers than history.

on the (bau)haus

After about two days in Tel Aviv, you'll most likely tire of hearing the word Bauhaus (assuming, that is, that you were sober for at least one of those days). That's because Tel Aviv is actually home to the world's largest collection of International buildings, an architectural style developed by students of the German Bauhaus School for Art. During the rise of Hitler, Jewish architects fled from Germany to the emerging Tel Aviv and put up these distinctive white buildings, which are usually marked by smooth balconies, asymmetry, and sharp angles. They may look like glorified parking garages, but it was the Bauhaus emphasis on functionality (and cheap materials) that made the style perfect for this new city.

▨ THE WHITE CITY   LANDMARK
21 Bialik St.   ☎03 620 4664; www.white-city.co.il

If you have a thing for Modernist architecture, South Tel Aviv will deliver. Earmarked as a UNESCO World Heritage Site as little as eight years ago, this area, located mainly in the triangle of Sheinkin St., Rothschild Blvd., and Allenby St., harks back to the '20s and '30s when flappers, talkies, and Bauhaus were all the rage. White walls, right angles, and boxy buildings swept their way through Tel Aviv. Unfortunately, many of the buildings have been poorly maintained, and water damage and smoke have made the structures in question a little more ashen than ivory. Nevertheless, a brief stroll down Rothschild Blvd. will reveal some gems. **Levin House,** on the corner with Shadal St., and **Lederberg House,** housing the restaurant Benedict's on the corner with Allenby St., are both highlights. If you can't get enough of the white stuff, your best bet is to take a tour—a free one leaves from 46 Rothschild Blvd. at 11am every Saturday morning. For more information on the interior design side of the Bauhaus, a small **center** (🕑 Open W 11am-7pm, F 10am-2pm) has been set up in the Bialik complex with a modest selection of chairs, clocks, and telephones designed under the tenets of the aesthetic.

ROTHSCHILD BLVD., ALLENBY ST., AND SHEINKIN ST.   NEIGHBORHOOD

Together, these three streets comprise what is possibly the busiest, most central part of Tel Aviv. Beyond the Bau, this is the place to find the highest concentration of bars, restaurants, and cafes—shawarma stands notwithstanding—in the whole city. While Allenby St. maintains much of the character of the city center from which it was birthed, Rothschild shoots for more urbane than urban. Art galleries and a collection of cafes are scattered among the skyscrapers and line the greenery running down its center. In recent years, Sheinkin St. has been attracting the most attention, with hip boutiques selling indie brands that wouldn't be cool if the likes of you had ever heard of them—it is about as hip as hip Tel Aviv gets. The area enclosed by the streets is strangely quiet but home to, you guessed it, yet more Bauhaus and a number of great galleries and bars.
Ⓢ Free. They're streets.

INDEPENDENCE HOUSE AND FOUNDERS' MONUMENT
16 Rothschild Blvd.

MUSEUM

☎03 510 6426

Here David Ben-Gurion, among others, signed Israel's Declaration of Independence and so founded the modern state that you're visiting today. A large hall replicates the house exactly as it was during the seminal event, while displays present the political and media reactions around the world. Directly outside stands the Founders' Monument, a small fountain overshadowed by a marble block on which is inscribed the names of the 66 Jewish families that first settled in Tel Aviv. Beside it is a bronze statue of the city's first mayor, Meir Dizengoff, on a horse. Mayor Meir on a mare, if you will.

✦ *1 block to the west of the intersection of Rothschild and Allenby.* Ⓢ *NIS20, students NIS15.* ⓣ *Open Su-F 9am-2pm.*

HAGANAH MUSEUM
23 Rothschild Blvd.

MUSEUM

☎03 560 8624

To say that an understanding of Israel's military is essential to an understanding of its history is an understatement. So, though a profusion of museums in the area might seem like propaganda overkill, the attention is deserved. The Haganah, Israel's military force before the IDF, is commemorated in this museum, a three-floor walk-through of displays, life-size replicas, videos, and antiques that is the best curated of the many military museums in the city. The house itself belonged to Eliahu Golomb, founder of the Haganah. His original quarters have been preserved in the building's atrium.

✦ *Opposite the Founders' Monument.* Ⓢ *NIS15, students NIS10. 1-month pass to all 5 military museums NIS20, students NIS15.* ⓣ *Open Su-Th 8am-4pm.*

don't hack me, bro

The Mossad, Israel's fearsome intelligence agency, has been known to be ruthless and uncompromising when it comes to protecting the Chosen People. Rumor, Wikipedia, and Steven Spielberg contend that, in the decades following the terrorist attacks on Israeli Olympians in Munich in 1972, the agency patiently and methodically hunted down and assassinated the terrorists responsible. In recent years, covert Israeli intervention has become less *James Bond* and more *Matrix* as the agency has shifted its focus to cyber warfare. In concert with the United States in 2010, Israel engineered the Stuxnet worm, a computer virus that infiltrated networks the world over, all in order to reach a very specific target: Iran's Natanz cluster of nuclear centrifuges. The worm took control of the facility, sending the centrifuges spinning wildly out of control and setting back Iran's nuclear by at least five years, with nary a shot fired.

BEIT HA'IR
27 Bialik St.

MUSEUM

☎03 724 0311; www.beithair.org

Crowning the Bialik complex at its center, this magnificent colonial-style building was the first city hall of Tel Aviv. Today it chronicles the city during its infancy. Highlights of the three-floor museum include the preserved office of Meir Dizengoff himself. While the displays aren't exactly lengthy, the house is an attraction in itself with a great terrace overlooking a garden.

✦ *Heading up Allenby St., make a right onto Bialik St. and head to the square at its helm.* Ⓢ *NIS20, students NIS10.* ⓣ *Open M-Th 9am-5pm, F-Sa and Jewish holidays 10am-2pm.*

BEIT BIALIK MUSEUM

22 Bialik St. ☎03 452 5430

This is the former home of Chaim Bialik, Israel's national poet who used his verse to articulate much of the collective angst and hope of the Jewish people following the founding of Israel. Attractions include some of Bialik's original manuscripts, his library, and the office where he composed many of his works. To continue the poetic tradition, the house holds Thursday poetry readings and other events. A lengthy English guide can be borrowed from the front desk.

 # Up Bialik St., just before the square. i Call ahead for information about events. $ NIS20, students NIS10. Cash only. ⏰ Open Su-Th 11am-5pm, F-Sa 10am-2pm.

BEIT RUBIN MUSEUM

14 Bialik St. ☎03 525 5961; www.rubinmuseum.org.il

Just down the street from the house of Israel's most prominent poet is that of its most celebrated painter. (Maybe Tel Aviv really is as artsy as it tries to appear.) The former house of Reuven Rubin displays a number of his works, bequeathed to the city at his death, and also includes some photo exhibitions and his former studio.

 # On the right before Beit Bialik. $ NIS20, students NIS10. ⏰ Open M 10am-3pm, Tu 10am-8pm, W-F 10am-3pm, Sa 11am-2pm.

YEMENITE QUARTER NEIGHBORHOOD

Drop all expectations. The only way to sum up the Yemenite Quarter is to declare it bipolar, as bonkers on one side as it is banal on the other. Bordering David Magen Sq., the descent into **Carmel Market** is without a doubt the most mobbed, crazed, and downright buzzing patch of the city, complete with throngs of tourists taking on local stalls and a soundtrack of an elderly woman bellowing in a laughably bad (yet strangely mesmerizing) falsetto over soft-rock muzak. But take a 30sec. walk north and the narrow streets empty out into one of the quietest parts of the city, with nothing but the occasional cafe stuck in a perpetual Sunday morning to remind you that humans actually live here.

NEVE TSEDEK NEIGHBORHOOD

Neve Tsedek might be the oldest Jewish neighborhood in the city, but the money here is definitely new. Its central thoroughfare, **Shabazi Street,** is lined with boutiques packed with things you can't afford, from ornate china to an antique refurbished Citroën. Indeed, gawking seems to be the order of the day; modish cafes fringe cobbled alleys where people-watching has become the choice sport of the discerning hipster. Toward the end of Shabazi St. is the **Suzanne Dellal Center,** which showcases a regular program of arts and culture events.

THE FLORENTINE NEIGHBORHOOD

Take the money out of Neve Tsedek and you'll have something along the lines of the Florentine, which lies just to the south of its bougie partner. Dilapidated Bauhaus scattered among disused warehouses and car repair shops make this neighborhood less an exercise in Mediterranean charm and more an untended maze. Of course, no self-respecting Tel Avivian is going to take that as an excuse and so, by night, keep an eye out for the noisy watering holes and some of the city's largest clubs as they blast the latest and hardest electro. The area can feel somewhat unsafe at night, so you may want to have a wingman to help you navigate those dodgy alleys, particularly on evenings when the clubs are closed.

IDF MUSEUM MUSEUM

HaMered St. ☎03 517 2913

Like guns? You'll love the IDF. This museum packs enough heat to start its own small war on the spot. Located just below the Florentine, this series of pavilions traces out the major achievements and history of the Israeli Defense Forces, but it seems more concerned with rubbing your nose in its firepower. With a tank shed, car-sized artillery pieces, and racks beyond racks of Uzis, M16s, and even antique hunting rifles, it's really an exhibition of the army's strength. Expect to see a fair number of soldiers jizzing themselves over this bazooka or that grenade, but, if you're not a gun person, this museum's probably not gonna be your thing.

🪧 Walk to the very end of Shabazi St. and turn left when you reach the large green area. Continue until you reach the museum. $ NIS15, students NIS10. 1-month pass to all 5 military museums NIS20, students NIS15. ⏰ Open Su-Th 8am-4pm.

ETZEL MUSEUM MUSEUM

Charles Clore Garden ☎03 517 7180

The Etzel (also called Irgun) was a controversial Jewish paramilitary force that broke off from the Haganah during the mandate to pursue a more confrontational policy toward Arab settlement in Palestine and the British, whom they viewed as oppressors. While the Israeli government today classifies them as an organization that committed terrorist acts, their contributions to Israeli independence are commemorated at this small museum.

🪧 On the coast, right on the border with Jaffa. The garden is at the intersection of Yehezkel Kaufmann and Nakhum Goldman. $ NIS15, students NIS10. 1-month pass to all 5 military museums NIS20, students NIS15. ⏰ Open Su-Th 8am-4pm.

north tel aviv

Tel Aviv is essentially a slather of grunge sandwiched between two slices of cool. The south may aim for an offbeat bohemian vibe, but the north trades in its skinny jeans for business casual—the area is probably the ritziest in Tel Aviv, and the neat rows of high-end shops, exclusive clubs, and dainty cafes pay homage to this. North across the river is Tel Aviv University, home to some of the city's best museums.

👍 **BEIT HATFUTZOT (DIASPORA MUSEUM)** MUSEUM

Klausner St. ☎03 6745 7808; www.bh.org.il

In the middle of the university campus, this brilliantly curated museum narrates the history of the Jewish people from their exile to Babylon to the eve of Israel's birth. With a colossal monument to the Holocaust at its heart, the museum tells the stories of Jewish people from Eastern Europe, Yemen, Spain, and other countries you might not have thought of (China? Really?) through a series of displays, relics, models of synagogues, and movies. Clearly, a lot of money and time have gone into this place, making it well worth the trip to the city's northern reaches.

🪧 Take bus #25 from King George. The entrance is through Matatia Gate at Tel Aviv University. $ NIS40, students NIS30. Audio guide NIS50 deposit. ⏰ Open Su-Th 10am-7pm, F 9am-2pm.

ERETZ ISRAEL MUSEUM MUSEUM

2 Levanon St. ☎03 641 5820; www.eretzmuseum.org.il

The logical counterpart to the Diaspora Museum—which tracks the history of the Israeli people—the Eretz Israel Museum traces the history of its land and archaeology. A shaded garden is surrounded by a series of pavilions, each dedicated to a specific aspect of local civilization, from ancient ceramics, coins, glasswork, and copper, to the more modern likes of the postal service and the Rothschild family. The range is pretty eclectic, with the highlight of the museum coming from the excavations of Tel Qasile, a 3000-year-old Philistine town, complete with temples and residential areas and sporting a phenomenal view of Tel Aviv from the north.

🪧 Take bus #24 or 25 from King George. $ NIS42, students NIS28. Map NIS1. ⏰ Open Su-W 10am-4pm, Th 10am-8pm, F-Sa 10am-2pm.

TEL AVIV PORT

NEIGHBORHOOD

Contrary to its name, the port is less industrial thoroughfare and more done-up local hangout, with seafood bistros and name-brand stores lining the waterfront. Evening often sees street performers taking to the boardwalk as crowds mill around the bars, a portent of the port's soon-to-bloom nightlife. The clubs here are some of the best, flashiest, and most well-known in the city. Liquor flows and subwoofers thunder until sunrise, but to appreciate it, you'll have to be cool enough to rub shoulders with the city's beautiful and haughtiest elite.

🚌 *Take bus #4 to the top of Ben-Yehuda St.*

LITTLE TEL AVIV

NEIGHBORHOOD

Past Jabotinsky St., the fast-food chains and megamalls give way to a collective of high-end cafes and designer boutiques. It's a great place to sip coffee with a raised pinky or—for the more easily tempted—max out your credit card.

🚌 *Take bus #5 to the top of Dizengoff St.*

beachy keen

Thriving urban centers don't exactly suggest pristine natural beauty, yet the long line of beaches that marks Tel Aviv's western border on the Mediterranean is shockingly lovely, with white sand and lapping turquoise waves. The more than half-dozen beaches reflect the diversity of the city itself: the GLBT beach sits not far from the "religious" beach, which holds separate bathing days for men and women so even the Orthodox can enjoy some sun and sea. Drum circles, surfing, and sunsets draw many to the shores, and the fun doesn't end when the sun goes down—groups of revelers from Tel Aviv's many clubs often end up on the sand in the early hours of the morning. Probably not the wisest time of day to be drunk like a fish and try to swim like one.

tel aviv

FOOD

The good news is that Tel Aviv is a culinary hotspot with a truly cosmopolitan character: Chinese diners, German sausage houses, and sandwich shops share the streets with the usual falafel and hummus stands. The bad news is that these restaurants can be pretty expensive. Many are worth the money—sushi and burgers are particularly popular in the city, so competition has really upped quality—but sit-down dining should be more an occasional treat than default choice for the budget conscious.

That said, your typical fast food fare isn't especially cheap either—Subway and Mickey D's can be pretty expensive, thanks to their kosher menus; the holy trinity in this city is falafel (about NIS10), shawarma (about NIS25), and hummus (about NIS20). As you can see, you'll be eating mashed chickpeas in more ways than you ever thought possible. Walk a block in any direction and you can usually find a stand selling at least one of these, but the largest concentration can be found along **Ben-Yehuda Street** and **Allenby Street.** Pizza is another common fixture and usually goes for NIS15 per slice. Periodically you'll also find small stands selling bagel panini (about NIS15).

For the more well-bred (or hummus-weary), Tel Aviv provides plenty of options to cook for yourself. The best bet for groceries, as for pretty much anything else under the sun, is the outdoor **Carmel Market** where a vast array of spices, vegetables, and meats are consistently for sale. For something more conventional, a couple supermarkets can be found by the northern tip of Allenby St. and along Ben-Yehuda St., and **am:pm** supermarkets are found every few blocks and, as the name implies, are open 24hr.

city center

👍 TAMARA JUICE BAR — SMOOTHIES $

At the intersection of Dizengoff St. and Ben-Gurion Blvd. ☎03 523 4445

The smoothie must have been invented for scalding Tel Avivian days. When the relentless Middle Eastern sun becomes too much, stop by Tamara to sip fruity manna that could only have come from the very hands of God. Decked in bouquets of fruit, this loud orange booth has built up a sizable discipleship among locals as it grants grace to the thirsty throngs. Indeed, branches are popping up all over the city in order to spread the good news. With the main stand near a small park and open all day, every day, Tamara is the perfect daytime pit stop *and* the best place to go at 3am when you're looking for that particularly refreshing mixer. Hallelujah!

🚶 Corner of Dizengoff St. and Ben-Gurion Blvd. $ Small smoothie NIS20, large NIS23. Juices from NIS20. ⏰ Open 24hr.

👍 SHU SHA BURGER — BURGERS $$

45 Bograshov St. ☎03 525 1331

Tel Aviv is a fierce battleground for burger joints, but this new kid on the block is deservedly turning heads. Recently quitting his day job, the chef started this restaurant with the simplest of missions—a quest for the perfect burger—and it looks like he may have found it, since the place is seldom empty. The smell alone may drag you inside, but the best burger in Tel Aviv will make sure you stay.

🚶 Corner of Zafat Rd. and Bograshov St. $ Burger NIS26. Noon-5pm burger, fries, and drink NIS40. ⏰ Open daily noon-midnight.

👍 THE STREETS — CAFE $$

70 King George ☎03 620 1070; www.2eat.co.il/thestreets

While the selection of salads, sandwiches, burgers, and schnitzels is largely standard fare, Streets has mastered the sacred art of the hang-out space. Wicker couches and shaded porch swings sprawl across the square outside, while a quick climb up the wooden staircase leads to a quiet study haven. Open 24hr., it becomes the prime post-game spot by night, offering a beer plus burger, grilled cheese, and other munchies into the wee hours. Regardless of the time, you can be sure of finding the young and beautiful here.

🚶 At intersection of King George and HaNevi'im St. ℹ Free Wi-Fi. Great selection of magazines. Laptops loaned free of charge. $ Business lunch of sandwich or salad and drink NIS42. Night special NIS46 ⏰ Open 24hr. Business lunch noon-6pm. Night special 11:30pm-6am.

GIRAFFE NOODLE BAR — ASIAN $$

49 Ibn Gvirol St. ☎03 691 6294; www.giraffe.co.il

Giraffe Noodle Bar takes the idea of pan-Asian seriously: the menu spans everything from Malaysian and Thai to Filipino and Japanese. If you want to quench the sizzle of Indian curry with some reasonably priced sushi, this is the place to go. The jet-black facade lets you know this place is more chic than chintz, and a staple for the shekel-smart hipster.

🚶 Bus #63 to the bottom of Ibn Gvirol St. Walk north toward city hall for 2 blocks, and it'll be on the left between Netsach Israel and HaShoftim St. $ Small sushi combo NIS48. Kashmir chicken NIS52. ⏰ Open daily noon-1am.

HARONSON — SANDWICHES $$

164 Dizengoff St. ☎170 070 5507; www.haronson.rest-e.co.il

The concept is simple but brilliant: pick a meat (or meat-substitute, for the faint of heart or strong of moral code) and then decide whether you want it on a salad, pizza, or considerably stocky sandwich. Anyway you like it, it won't cost more than NIS40. With sleek platters served on canteen trays, this is fast food a la mode. Make sure to snag the meal deal for a sandwich, drink, and bowl of chunky potato wedges (NIS45).

☩ *On Dizengoff St., just south of intersection with Ben-Gurion Blvd.* 🕃 *Open Su-Th 11am-midnight, F 11am-3pm, Sa 7pm-midnight.*

CARPACCIO HOUSE
CARPACCIO $$

8 Ibn Gvirol ☎03 609 8118; www.2eat.co.il/eng/carpaccio/

Adorned with chalk portraits, this is a rare species of restaurant serving that haughtiest of dishes, carpaccio, for a price that won't leave your pockets similarly raw. Doused in olive oil, the signature dish of raw meat or fish makes the perfect Mediterranean accompaniment to the countless sweltering days— a contrast that will be eminently clear as most seating, other than the bar, is outdoors. The business lunch offers soup, juice, salad, and doughy bread for as little as NIS39, and after 8pm on Sunday nights is aperitifs night, with drinks served from a wooden bar lined with a variety of cocktails and wines, including the house-brewed white sangria (NIS26 per glass).

☩ *Take bus #63 to the base of Ibn Gvirol. Walk north 1 block and the restaurant is on the right, before Eliezer Kaplan St.* 🕃 *Open Su-Th noon-1am, F-Sa noon-3am. Business lunch Su-Th noon-5pm.*

GOOCHA
SEAFOOD $$

171 Dizengoff St. ☎03 648 2999

Shellfish is always going to be a rare commodity in this kosher land, so satisfy your goyish seafood cravings here, just a block over from the sea where the fish on your plate was caught. Wall-length windows, lots of outdoor seating, and a Clash soundtrack complement reassuringly large portions of such local favorites as butter and garlic shrimp and coconut, coriander, and chili curry (both NIS54).

☩ *On intersection of Dizengoff St. and Ben-Gurion Blvd.* 🕃 *Open Su-W noon-1am, Th-F noon-2am, Su noon-1am.*

MEXICANA
MEXICAN $$

7 Bograshov St. ☎03 517 9420; www.mexicana.rest-e.co.il

Neither decor nor food are anything special at Mexicana, where patrons eat typical Tex-Mex grub surrounded by pastel pink walls covered with strange masks and other paraphernalia. But none of that really matters, because the real crowd-pleaser here is the happy hour, which blesses the hungry and sober masses in the form of unlimited margaritas with any main course every day from 5 to 7pm.

☩ *On the intersection of Ben-Yehuda St. and Bograshov St.* Ⓢ *Tacos from NIS55. Quesadillas from NIS40.* 🕃 *Open daily noon-midnight.*

south tel aviv

🅜 ICEBERG
ICE CREAM $

31 Rothschild Blvd. ☎03 566 1588; www.iceberg.co.il

Though the number of names ending in "berg" in Israel rivals the grains of sand in the Negev, this establishment manages to distinguish itself with the "ice" component. After a trip to Iceberg, you'll realize that saying that ice cream was made for sunny days is an understatement; pairing this baby-blue booth with that blazing Middle Eastern sun was the easiest 1+1 of the century. And the stand is anything but vanilla. The "100% low-tech" Iceberg offers such flavors as "Nutella Baby," strawberries and cream, deep-dish cheesecake, and "Banana King." The joint is so popular with locals that a new branch has opened in the city center, now accompanied by the whitewashed, classier, and even more Jewish-sounding Wineberg bar.

☩ *On the corner of Rothschild Blvd. and Allenby St.* Ⓢ *Small cone or cup NIS15, medium NIS19, large NIS25.* 🕃 *Open daily 10am-2am.*

BUDDHA BURGER
VEGAN **$$**

21 Yehuda HaLevi St. ☎03 510 1333; www.buddhaburgers.co.il

The premier veggie eatery in the city, if not the country, Buddha Burger is famous for helping locals stay true to their love for animals (or, possibly, vendetta against plants). Swathed in all things green, the restaurant is normally packed to the brim with a healthy clientele grazing on a large buffet. While classics such as eggplant parmesan (NIS39) and that eponymous burger (NIS25) are mainstays, curiosities such as the vegan roast beef will leave you either puzzled or enlightened. The smoothies, with a refreshing parsley kick, are another must (NIS17).

✝ *On the corner of Herzl St. and Yehuda HaLevi, 1 block over from Rothschild Blvd.* ⏱ *Open Su-Th 11am-midnight, F 11am-5pm, Sa 8pm-midnight.*

CAFE 12
CAFE **$$**

12 Rothschild Blvd. ☎03 510 6430

The coolest cafe in Tel Aviv? It's a bold claim, but this place is certainly on the top of a lot of lists. A creaky, run-down hovel has outer walls plastered with outdated bill stickers and gig posters, plus a patio ever-jammed with people who will inevitably be younger, hipper, and more plaid-covered than you. But a sleek black-and-white interior is a clue-in that this place is more *derelictique* than derelict. Overlooking the bustling boulevard, it offers the perfect vantage point to sip a coffee and sneer at the masses. You know, the ones not wearing vintage Goodwill sweaters.

✝ *Right by the foot of Rothschild Blvd.* Ⓢ *Coffee NIS12. Roast beef sandwich NIS34.* ⏱ *Open Su-Th 7am-late, F-Sa 8am-late. Bar open until about 5am.*

TAMAR CAFE
CAFE **$**

57 Sheinken St. ☎03 685 2376

If Cafe 12 has got the cool, Tamar has the name. It has even been immortalized in the canon of cheesy '80s synth-pop by the big-haired New Romantic band Mango—and, if you ask nicely, the staff might give you an a cappella rendition of the song. The cafe is owned by local legend Sarah Stern, who stars in the glut of political cartoons adorning the walls, taking on the world as she indiscriminately kisses, chases, or bitch-slaps her way through decades of presidents, prime ministers, and their aides.

✝ *On the corner with Ahad HaAm.* Ⓢ *Coffee NIS10. Bagel NIS25. Cash only.* ⏱ *Open Su-F 7:30am-8pm.*

MAZZARINE
DESSERT **$$**

42 Montefiore St. ☎03 566 7020; www.mazzarine.com

It's just as posh as you would expect of an old-style colonial house decorated with chandeliers and the sort of furniture you know you're messing up just by sitting on. And that's only where the decadence starts; every day, Mazzarine imports a guilt-inducing selection of macaroons, cakes, biscuits, and, of course, chocolates from its central patisserie in Herzliya. Make sure to check out the elegant, shaded garden out back, with white wicker chairs to laze (and get fat) on.

✝ *On the corner with Zahani St.* Ⓢ *Slice of cake NIS28.* ⏱ *Open Su-Th 7:30am-10pm, F 7:30am-3:30pm. Business lunch noon-5pm.*

RUSTICO
ITALIAN **$$**

15 Rothschild Blvd. ☎03 510 0039; www.rustico.co.il

Stand aside, Olive Garden. Rustico actually achieves the feel of a small Italian country kitchen without seeming tacky. Browse the wine bottles covering the walls or watch your pizza as it's cooked in the massive stone hearth at the back of the bar. The prices make this a favorite with the student crowd, whose pockets are usually pinched by Italian cuisine in this city.

✝ *By the foot of Rothschild Blvd. just behind the Founders' Monument.* Ⓢ *Margherita pizza NIS47.* ⏱ *Open Su-W noon-midnight, Th-Su noon-1am. Business lunch M-F noon-5pm.*

JAPANIKA

SUSHI $$

Intersection of Rothschild Blvd. and Allenby St.   ☎03 546 6666; www.japanika.net

A small booth perched at the center of the major intersection of the southern region, Japanika knows just how good sushi looks to drunk revelers making their way back from the clubs at 4am. Serving up the standard Maki and Nigiri from a bar counter, the place has limited seating, and it isn't uncommon to wait up to 20min., even during the wee hours. The wait is perhaps the most brilliant ploy conceivable to tease their customers, as the hammered and hungry must stand and watch others get their raw fish fill first. The novel sushi sandwich—fish wedged between crispy tempura chips—is a first for many and a must-try.

🍴 Open-air booth in the middle of the intersection. Ⓢ Sushi sandwich NIS29. Cash only. 🕐 Open Su-F noon-late, Sa 2pm-late.

MOSES BURGER

BURGER $$

35 Rothschild Blvd.   ☎03 566 4949; www.mosesrest.co.il

Tel Aviv is a battleground for burger joints, and Moses has always been the one to beat. A true local institution, it's the undoubted hometown hero that any self-respecting resident is bound to champion. While new kid on the block **Shu Sha Burger** up north seems to have outdone it, Moses is still a popular late-night pit stop that has a knack for the kind of stocky patties and thick, doughy buns that will leave even an American satisfied.

🍴 On Rothschild Blvd., a block up from the intersection with Allenby St. Ⓢ Burgers from NIS39. 🕐 Open Su-W 10:30am-4am, Th-F 10:30am-4:30am, Sa 10:30am-4am.

the most important meal

Although lunch is the heaviest meal of the day for most Israelis, breakfast is not something to be taken lightly. Cheese, salad, olives, and bread—in addition to the more typical yogurt and fruit—can all be found on the Israeli breakfast table. If you're staying in someone's home, expect to be served *shakshuka* (a spicy egg and tomato dish) alongside *labane* (tangy Israeli yogurt). These lavish spreads have religious origins: Jewish hospitality stems from Abraham and Sarah's habit of heartily feeding anyone who wandered into their desert home.

LULU

SEAFOOD $$$

55 Shabazi St.   ☎03 516 8793

It's just another chichi cafe breaking up the boutiques and bookshops of urbane Neve Tsedek, with another glossy black-and-white bar affair on the inside and a large patio expanding into the narrow street outside. But, hey—sometimes, you've just got to gorge on mollusks and crustaceans to dulcet Samba tones.

🍴 On the corner with Tachkemoni St. Ⓢ Shrimp on rock salt NIS32. 🕐 Open daily 8am-midnight. Breakfast served Su-Th 8am-12:30pm, F 8am-4pm, Sa 8am-1pm.

north tel aviv

🔲 BENEDICT'S

BREAKFAST $$

171 Ben-Yehuda St.   ☎057 944 3406; www.rest.co.il/_Intros/benedict/

Since breakfast is the most important meal of the day, Benedict's has taken the logical step and ensured that you can have it as every meal of the day (and the night—it's open 24hr.). Whether it's serving the post-clubbing throngs or, you know, people actually having breakfast, the restaurant is a huge hit in Tel Aviv, where it now has two branches. While eggs benedict is the obvious go-to dish, Benedict's specializes in eggs served every which way: its innovation, the egg ball, may sound strange and unappetizing, yet is actually anything but. The champagne cocktail that comes with many of the dishes is the cherry on top—it's free, after all, so you have to drink that 9am Bellini. Lines are common, so be prepared for a short wait during peak hours.

✽ *On the corner with Jabotinsky St. Bus #4 stops nearby.* Ⓢ *Spinach and goat cheese egg balls NIS58. Pancakes NIS35.* Ⓩ *Open daily 24hr.*

▨ HUMMUS ASHKARA HUMMUS $
45 Yermiyahu St. ☎03 546 4547

You might have noticed a conspicuous dearth of Israeli food in these listings—in the end, hummus, shawarma, and falafel taste basically the same, regardless of which street-side cafe or vendor they come from. Hummus Ashkara is a clear exception. While it may look unimpressive from the outside, its thick, garlic-laden hummus has earned a cult following among locals. Generous bowls of hummus are served with hard-boiled eggs, thick-cut chips and an assortment of spices you shouldn't even begin to try and pronounce.

✽ *1 block after the intersection of Yermiyahu St. and Dizengoff St.* Ⓢ *Hummus bowl NIS20, with egg NIS23.* Ⓩ *Open Su-Th 24hr, F midnight-5pm, Sa 7pm-midnight.*

CAFE JEREMIAH CAFE, BAR $$
306 Dizengoff St. ☎077 793 1840

Like **Cafe 12** or **The Streets** below it, Cafe Jeremiah is a slightly plainer take on the staple cafe hangout patronized by Tel Avivians younger and better looking than you. While most coffee-sippers take to the large patio on the surprisingly quiet intersection with Yermiyahu St., the interior is dominated by a large bookcase stacked with trinkets. The case conveniently evolves into a bar as it reaches the height of those nonchalantly slouched over it.

✽ *On the southern corner with Yermiyahu St.* Ⓢ *Shakshuka NIS38. Business lunch deal NIS54.* Ⓩ *Open daily 7am-2am. Business lunch Su-Th noon-5pm.*

CAFÉ MICHAL CAFE $$
230 Dizengoff St. ☎03 523 0236

For a cafe experience with a marginally stiffer upper lip, Café Michal secludes its clientele from the bustling hubbub of Dizengoff St. behind a row of plants punctuated only by a little gate. The clientele reclining among the white and pastel olive scenery might be a little older, but the tone is all the more quiet for it.

✽ *On the intersection with Jabotinsky St.* Ⓢ *Carpaccio baguette NIS44. Calamari bruschetta NIS19.* Ⓩ *Open Su-Th 8am-midnight, F 8am-6pm.*

MOVIEING CAFE $$
308 Dizengoff St. ☎03 544 4434

Cafe, bar, and DVD rental store: the vowel-heavy Movieing really is a triple threat. If your friends seem too boring, Movieing has got your back with a huge DVD library sprawled across its upper floor. After all, what could be more nonchalant than not just sneering at passersby, but positively ignoring them as you engross yourself in some Godard or Truffaut on the cafe patio? That said, the selection is perhaps more Hollywood than hipster, with a particularly extensive selection of action films. No players are provided so be sure to bring your own computer if you plan to watch there.

✽ *On the northern corner with Yermiyahu St.* *i Free Wi-Fi. All English films are subtitled.* Ⓢ *DVD rental NIS20 for the night. Hamburger NIS52. Beer NIS17.* Ⓩ *Open daily 24hr.*

ZE SUSHI JAPANESE $$
16 Ishtori HaParhi ☎03 602 3249; www.zesushi.co.il

Another part of Tel Aviv, another sushi joint: Ze Sushi might be small, but, overlooking Bazel Sq. as it does, it's got location on its side. The stone-walled interior can seat only a few, either at black booths or at the bar. A fountain trickles serenely in the corner. Make sure to check out one of the signature dishes: the inexplicably monikered Ocean's 11—maki with fish and seaweed, no rice—or the sushi sandwich, constructed with slivers of sashimi wedged between bread-crumb-encrusted sushi rice.

✈ *A few doors down from the corner with Bazel St.* Ⓢ *Small combo NIS48.* 🕐 *Open daily noon-midnight.*

BENNY THE FISHERMAN
SEAFOOD $$$

Hangar 8, Namal St. ☎03 544 0518

Several seafood restaurants inevitably line the port waterfront, but Benny really pulls in the catch. Once a local favorite in Jaffa, the eponymous Benny recently moved up north to set up shop in this swankier part of town. The food has apparently only gotten better, and Benny offers some of the cheapest and most popular seafood in the port.

✈ *Along Namal St. Bus #4 stops nearby at the top of Ben-Yehuda.* Ⓢ *Bass NIS84. Shrimp NIS120.* 🕐 *Open daily noon-midnight.*

NIGHTLIFE

It's okay. You can admit it: you skipped everything else and turned here first, didn't you? There's no need to hide it. Tel Aviv is a city that unabashedly lives and defines itself by the night. When the homeward club-goers mingle in the streets with work-bound yuppies, and you're more likely to encounter a minyan of mesh-tops than yarmulkes, you figure out fairly quickly that Tel Avivians clearly put partying high on their list of daily activities. And by daily, we mean daily: Thursdays and Fridays are certainly the biggest nights of the week, but the streets explode every evening into short-skirted, neon-strobed, and tobacco-clouded pandemonium. Although the trance doesn't usually start blasting until past midnight, it's a testament to that renowned Israeli zeal that the volume only falls once the moon does. Nor is the drinking culture especially big—how can you flail your limbs like a rabid maniac until 6am if you're drowsy from daiquiris? As you head out, keep in mind age limits (often 25+), which aren't always strictly adhered to, and how to win over the "selectors" at the door (turning up with a bevy of beautiful women will always better your chances). Nightlife here will also be hard on your wallet; covers, drinks, and taxis really do add up, so don't be surprised if you spend NIS100 or more on a night out.

That the joints will be loud, sweaty, and packed with people cooler than you is basically guaranteed. But everything else about Tel Aviv nightlife runs the gamut on a spectrum that uncannily follows geography. Clubs in the city's north, centered on the discotheque mecca of **Namal Street,** border on pretentious. Smattered over a collection of hangars, the beautiful and Versace-clad come here to be seen by those lucky enough to get in and join their 🎴**martini-sipping ranks.** Heading south, the attitude is considerably more laissez-faire. Door policies become looser, tables become dance floors, and nonchalant posturing just becomes awkward. The bars and clubs centered around **Rothschild Boulevard** take on a more bohemian flavor, while the warehouses and hangars of the Florentine haven't even bothered with renovations, using the dingy atmosphere to host to some of the most riotous bacchanals this side of Ibiza.

city center

▨ 70 PILIM
BAR

70 Bograshov St. ☎03 629 1777; 70pilim.co.il

While by day it's a high-end liquor boutique, by night you can stumble through the deserted shop and descend a back staircase to find this alcoholic Narnia. With stone walls and a central mahogany bar, Pilim (Hebrew for elephant) has got a serious case of the Goldilocks: the young and beautiful crowd is cool, but not cooler-than-thou; the place is packed, but not uncomfortable; and something you've never noticed in a bar until now—the music volume—is eerily perfect, just quiet enough to allow for conversation, but loud enough to make awkward silence a thing of inferior establishments.

On Bograshov St. between Bar Kokhva and Tchernichovski. $ Chasers from NIS12. Beer from NIS24. i Ages 25+. Be sure to tip. ⏰ Bar open Sa-Th 9pm-late, F noon-late. Store open daily 11am-1am.

beat it, beatles

In past years, concerts and partying were seen as antithetical to the serious Zionist ethic. Former Prime Minister Golda Meir even refused to let The Beatles perform, claiming that their music might corrupt Israeli youth. Today, however, international DJs regularly perform in Israel and revelers dance until morning at local clubs. Tel Aviv in particular is famous for its wide range of music venues, from megaclubs blasting house music to alternative underground lounges.

CLUB YA YA — CLUB

3 Ben-Yehuda St. ☎054 588 8915

Owned by the same guys as the now-famous **Club Dizengoff,** Ya Ya is coming into the ring with a serious pedigree. After all, while most of Tel Aviv is burrowing underground, this club is strutting its stuff on the fifth floor of a skyscraper. Bob to the latest American mainstream under pink-tinged chandeliers while looking at one of the best views of the Mediterranean in the city. Off of the dance floor, a chiller scene emerges on the large outdoor balcony. But why are we telling you this? If you're cool enough to get in, this should all come naturally to you anyway.

In the big tower on the corner of Allenby St. and Ben-Yehuda. Enter on the north side of building. i Most nights 25+, Sa 22+. Usually a line and not always easy to get in—come before 10pm to be safe. $ Cover NIS20 on F. Beer NIS28. Vodka Red Bull NIS54. ⏰ Open Su-Th 9pm-2am, F 2pm-late, Sa 6pm-late.

SEX BOUTIQUE — BAR

122 Dizengoff St. ☎ 03 544 4555

So while most of Tel Aviv is bringing the proverbial sexy back, Sex Boutique is going the extra mile and doing it literally. Sex shop by day, the bar comes out at night as its boozed-up superhero alter ego. Beneath the dim lights and neon pink, expect plenty of indie music and a crowd covered in tattoos and piercings. Perhaps the best part are those golden three hours when both sex shop and bar are open; trying to chat up a member of the opposite sex when there's a three-foot long contraption hovering by your face is either going to be the best kind of ice-breaker or the worst kind of cockblock.

On Dizengoff St., the block before Gordon St. Bar is on the right. $ Beer from NIS21. ⏰ Sex shop open Su-Th 11am-1am, Sa 11am-1am. Bar open Su-Th 9pm-late, Sa 9pm-late.

HERLINGER — BAR

69 Ben-Yehuda St. ☎054 238 3687

Herlinger may not have the glitz of its neighbors, but it's just that lack of pretense that seems to have made it a local favorite. Jet black inside and out, the bar is frequented by the kinds of guys for whom dress codes are best left to weddings and funerals—of course, the obligatory pool table also makes an appearance. The scene won't go crazy, but that's not what you're looking for here.

Up Ben-Yehuda, on the left before the corner with Frishman St. i Happy hour daily 4-8pm; buy a beer and get a free glass of wine. ⏰ Open daily 4pm-late.

HAOMAN 17

CLUB

88 Abarbanel St. ☎03 681 3636; www.myspace.com/haoman_17

If bigger really is better, then Haoman deserves a top spot on Tel Aviv's laundry list of nightlife must-sees. Two sprawling dance floors and a massive outside area make the city's only megaclub the default stop for the world's biggest DJs. With the kind of sound setup that's more weapon than entertainment system and a vast mural of the Virgin Mary looking helplessly on, Haoman is not for shmoozers and drunks, but a place to simply go crazy. Five times a year, the club holds its famous "T-Bar": a swimming pool is set up and the party starts at 4am (yes, starts). Every other Friday is FFF line, the largest gay night in Tel Aviv. But, whatever the party, if things don't go your way, the suggestively titled Babydoll's next door will be able to sort you out pronto...one way or another.

 # At the end of Abarbanel St., coming off of Shlomo St. i Men 24+, women 22+. Tickets for all events must be bought in advance online. Go to http://mrticket.co.il for tickets. For FFF line, purchase at http://bin.co.il. $ Ticket around NIS80. Beer NIS28. Vodka mixers NIS45. ⏰ Hours vary depending on night. Club open only on weekends.

RADIO E.P.G.B.

BAR, GLBT-FRIENDLY

7 Shedal St. ☎03 560 3636

It's not often that *Let's Go* will advise you to go down a dark, unmarked alley and descend a dingy staircase, but we're making an exception here—this is just one of those places you would never find unless you did. That said, if you get over how badass you feel making that entrance, Radio is actually one of the chillest joints in town. The queues are run democratically, and even though the bar is seriously indie—with local artsy types plastered in plaid, a variety of punk posters, and even a vintage "Tommy" pinball machine—the vibe is supremely welcoming.

 # Shedal runs off of Rothschild Blvd. Walk down and make a left into the alley just before the falafel stand. There might be a line. If not, walk to the end of the alley, turn right and walk down the staircase. i 22+. Frequent live music. $ No cover. Beer NIS21. Free chaser if "attending" event on Facebook. ⏰ Open daily 10:30pm-late.

COMFORT 17

CLUB, GLBT-FRIENDLY

13 Comfort St. ☎054 773 7237; www.comfort13.co.il

Nestled in the heart of the Florentine, by day Comfort may look like just another rusty abandoned warehouse in the labyrinth of autoshops and bungalows. But at night, it transforms into one of the city's rowdiest venues, a massive bar spilling across its side and the dance floor taking center stage. For music, expect anything from the latest dubstep to the cheesiest nostalgia. Comfort is also home to a fortnightly "Glamorama" gay night.

 # Heading south on Herzl St., make a left onto Jaffa St., which turns onto Eilat St., and a right onto Abarbanel St. After 300m, make a right onto HaMekhoga. Comfort will be on your second right. i 18+. The Florentine is not well lit at night, so don't travel there and back alone. $ Cover NIS40-60. Beer NIS16. ⏰ Open Th 11:30pm-5am, F midnight-5am, Sa 10pm-5am.

NANUTCHKA

BAR, GLBT-FRIENDLY

30 Lilienblum St. ☎03 516 2254

A Georgian restaurant by day, complete with mannequin heads decked out in military apparel and an expansive back garden, any semblance of table manners disappears by night as Nanutchka transforms into what can only be described as the Israeli Coyote Ugly, with riotous crowds of 30-somethings dancing on tables.

 # On Lilienblum between Herzl St. and Nahalat Binyamin. i 25+. M 80s night, Su Live Georgian music. Call ahead to reserve a place at the bar. $ No cover. Beer NIS30. ⏰ Kitchen open daily noon-late. Bar around 9pm-late.

LIMA LIMA   CLUB, GLBT-FRIENDLY
42 Lilienblum St.   ☎03 560 0924

A veteran of the Tel Aviv club circuit, Lima Lima keeps it simple with a single sweaty, packed dance floor skirted by plush red couches. Local funk cover band Groove Redemption plays every Sunday, and there's live reggae on Wednesdays. There's also gay and hip-hop night (Monday) and a Sunday dubstep set—quotations from the American Psychological Association flit across the walls, telling you it's okay to get a little angry now and then...blow off some steam, why don't you?

✦ On Lilienblum between Allenby St. and Nahalat Binyamin. *i* 23+. Ⓢ Cover M and Th-F NIS15; Su, Tu-W, and Sa NIS30. Beer NIS26. Chasers NIS9. Beer and chaser on Sa NIS29. ◫ Open daily 9:30pm-late.

north tel aviv

🏆 GALINA HANGAR   CLUB
Nemal St.   ☎03 544 5553; www.galinabar.co.il

Hangar is probably Tel Aviv's most popular club. Even among the bars and pounding warehouses that throng the port, it still stands out with its ever-so-slightly-better-dressed crowd. The vibe, however, manages to stay looser than most, due mainly to a huge outdoor area as large as the club itself. Here the sweaty, tranced-out masses can recline for a pit stop before heading back in.

✦ ½-way up Nemal St. on the right. ◫ Open daily 9pm-late.

---

where's the *hufla* at?

For centuries, the ancient language of Hebrew survived only through religious texts and the works of intellectuals. It was resurrected as a living, breathing language with the emergence of Zionism in the late 19th century. Pretty cool, except that the rabbis and other smarty-pants who kept Hebrew alive somehow managed to lose a few key everyday words and phrases along the way. Luckily, Israeli youth stepped in to fill in the gaps. Here are some potentially useful ones:

- **ASHKARAH:** "Like, totally," as in, "Another shot? *Ashkarah.*"

- **BALAGAN:** "A total mess," a good way to describe your room after a rager.

- **FRECHA:** "Floozy," best used if you're looking to be slapped in the face.

- **HOMEL:** "Drugs," usually marijuana.

- **HUFLA:** "Party," Usually the *hufla* precedes the *balagan*.

- **YALLA:** "Let's go!" A loveable travel guide series, of course.

---

223   BAR, GLBT-FRIENDLY
223 Dizengoff St.   ☎03 544 6537

Founded by a group of local bartenders, 223 has expectedly excellent cocktails—the 17 options include everything from a standard mojito (NIS39) to a chili-passion fruit margarita (NIS42). The joint itself isn't large, but it's certainly ornate, with plush couches, gold-framed pictures, and a chandelier all neatly distributed across the two-floor space. Expect an older crowd with the sort of bespectacled sophistication which that entails—and yes, that does include suspender-clad barmen.

✦ Just north of the intersection with Jabotinsky St. *i* 18+. Ⓢ Beer from NIS23. ◫ Open daily 7pm-late.

GAZOS   CLUB
Yordei Hasira St.   ☎050 422 2444; www.gazozbar.co.il

Toward the southern end of the Port district, Gazos is the new hangout for a younger crowd who would never deign to travel farther south and swap their high heels for Converse. The club may not be as big as others, but this serves as an excuse to keep the dance floor, flanked by two bars, absolutely chockablock. The more chill waterfront area, requisite of any Port club, is sequestered in bamboo and festooned with pink lights.

☆ At the southern end of the port, 1 block below the foot of Nemal St. ℹ Men 25+, women 23+. Ⓢ Beer NIS20. Cocktails NIS50. Ⓣ Su-F 9pm-late, Sa 5:30-late.

SHABLUL JAZZ CLUB
LIVE MUSIC

Hangar 13, Nemal St.   ☎03 546 1891; www.shabluljazz.com

What do you mean you're sick of trance? Well, if it's all starting to sound kind of the same, Shablul Jazz provides a more relaxed affair at the heart of Tel Aviv's clubbing central. The venue is small enough to be intimate, big enough not to get too clogged with smoke, and famous enough to bring in some of the biggest names in jazz on a regular basis. This is the go-to place for anything smooth and funky. From blues to beebop, something's brewing here every night of the week.

☆ About 200m walk up Nemal St. on the right. Ⓢ Tickets NIS50-150. Ⓣ Concerts daily 9pm. Doors open at 8pm. Matinees F-Sa 4pm. Jam session M 10:30pm.

ARTS AND CULTURE

If you feel like sitting down to music rather than raging to it, Tel Aviv has you covered. In this most liberal part of Israel, the arts scene flourishes. Many large dance and music institutions have found their home here, but the visual arts are the real strength of the city, from the large **Tel Aviv Museum of Art** to the cornucopia of smaller galleries scattered throughout the city.

music and dance

Should awkwardly shuffling your feet among the throngs of footloose and fancy-free Israelis at the clubs get to be too much, you can always watch someone else dance instead. As Israel's de facto culture capital, Tel Aviv has become a home for the arts. **The Israeli Philharmonic** has taken up residence here, and the **Suzanne Dellal Center** is the bonafide hub of Israeli dance, so go get yourself some honest-to-goodness culture—that way you'll have a few stories you can actually tell mom.

🏛 SUZANNE DELLAL CENTER
SOUTH TEL AVIV

5 Yechiely St.   ☎03 510 5656; www.suzannedellal.org.il

Occupying regal premises in the heart of Neve Tsedek, the Suzanne Dellal Center hosts the best of Israeli dance. The internationally renowned **Batsheva Dance Company** (☎03 517 1471; www.batsheva.co.il) puts on regular shows in its auditorium. They also often take to the streets—or, more specifically, the promenades and ports, where it's not uncommon to see an array of scantily clad men and women shimmying the sunset hours away to jazz or clambering over impromptu sets dressed as marionettes. Be sure to check the website for upcoming performances.

☆ From Allenby St., walk about 500m along Shabazi St. in Neve Tsedek. The Center is at the very end on the left. Ⓢ Ticket prices vary. Batsheva performances around NIS100. Ⓣ Box office open Su-Th 9am-7pm, F 9am-1pm. Center open 2hr. before every performance.

ISRAELI PHILHARMONIC ORCHESTRA
CITY CENTER

Mann Auditorium, 1 Huberman St.   ☎03 621 1777; www.ipo.co.il

The country's premier orchestral ensemble offers shows running the aural gamut from classical staples to more contemporary and experimental fare.

☆ On the corner of Huberman and Dizengoff St., on the same block as Habima Theatre and Helena Rubinstein Pavilion. ℹ Check the website for more information about specific concerts. Ⓣ Box office open Su-Th 9am-7pm, F 9am-1pm, Sa 9am-7pm.

cinema

TEL AVIV CINEMATHEQUE — SOUTH TEL AVIV

2 Sprinzak St. ☎03 606 0800; www.cinema.co.il

An independent movie theater, Tel Aviv Cinematheque is about as pretentious as its name sounds, focusing on international films ranging from the latest documentaries to golden oldies. Most films are only subtitled in Hebrew, so it's best to check before you buy that ticket.

➔ By HaShoter Square. Bus #63 stops 1 block away. $ Tickets from NIS20. ⏰ Open daily 9am-10pm.

RAV-HEN CINEMA — CITY CENTER

Dizengoff Sq. ☎03 528 2288; www.rav-hen.co.il

Watch all the typical Hollywood fare, plus other popular movies from France and Israel, on the largest movie screen in Israel. Most films are shown in the original language, with only kids' films dubbed in Hebrew, meaning English-speakers will be able enjoy all the linguistic nuances of *Not Another Teen Movie*, though the lack of English subtitles for foreign films may pose a problem. This cinema is part of a chain that includes other branches near Rabin Sq. and the Opera House.

$ Matinees NIS34, evening showings NIS37. 3D films NIS41/45. ⏰ 4 screenings per day, usually starting at 2:30pm and a final showing at 10pm.

visual arts

You thought all those cardigans and horn-rimmed spectacles were just for show? Tel Aviv has a burgeoning community of small galleries which showcase talent both local and international. There are two major clusters: one in the city center along **Gordon Street** and the other between **Rothschild Boulevard** and **Sheinken Street** in the south.

👍 CHELOUCHE GALLERY FOR CONTEMPORARY ARTS — SOUTH TEL AVIV

7 Mazeh St. ☎03 620 0068; www.chelouchegallery.com

Housed in a Neoclassical marble building designed by Joseph Berlin, the three-floor Chelouche specializes mostly in prominent Israeli artists. The roof salon hosts regular cultural events, while a secluded cafe can be found in the basment.

➔ Heading up Allenby, make a right onto Mazeh. Gallery is on the corner with Yavne St. $ Free. ⏰ Open Jan-July M-Th 11am-7pm, F 10am-2pm, Sa 11am-2pm; Sept-Dec M-Th 11am-7pm, F 10am-2pm, Sa 11am-2pm.

ART GALLERY 39 — SOUTH TEL AVIV

39 Nachmani St. ☎03 566 6631; www.artgallery39.com

A somewhat smaller affair than Chelouche, Art Gallery 39 focuses on young, emerging Israeli talent but also hosts the odd international exhibition.

➔ Heading up Rothschild Blvd., make a right on Nachmani St. The gallery is within 1 block, on the left before Yehuda HaLevi. $ Free. ⏰ Open M-Th 11am-7pm, F 10am-2pm, Sa 11am-1pm.

SHOPPING

As the most Western patch of land in Israel, Tel Aviv unsurprisingly brings you consumer culture in all its big, brash, label-clad wonder. Malls litter the cityscape, offering everything you're used to: familiar brand names, lamentable muzak, multiplex cinemas, teenage mallrats, and the inevitable food courts. While there are dozens of malls in the city, a good number of these are small, lame, or largely empty, and the ones listed are the only ones worth your time. For those seeking something outside their air-conditioned comfort zone, Tel Aviv's markets, like Carmel Market, are a great option for your wallet, assuming your diplomatic skills are up to snuff.

Certain areas maintain very particular characters too. While the south of **Dizengoff Street,** lying in the wake of the Dizengoff Center, is predominantly inhabited by all the basic chains, it emerges into a bevy of designer wear and similarly classy fare as it heads toward the port. Just south of it, the stores along **Bograshov Street** focus on cheaper surfwear and raunchy T-shirts. Finally, **Sheinken Street** is the place for urban-chic wear, with the odd designer shop interrupting the rows of vogue boutiques.

malls

▨ AZIRIELI CENTER
132 Petach Tikva Rd.

CITY CENTER
☎03 608 1199

The mother of Israeli malls, Azirieli has cineplexes and every shop, chain, and cuisine you could think of to boot. A massive panorama of Tel Aviv is offered from the observation deck. The mall also has Israel's only H&M, which attracts a different breed of pilgrim than most sights (more pay, less pray).

✤ Bus #127 from New Central Bus Station. ⌚ Open Su-Th 10am-10pm, F 9:30am-3:30pm, Sa 8:45-11pm.

DIZENGOFF CENTER
50 Dizengoff St.

CITY CENTER
☎03 621 2400; www.dizengof-center.co.il

As the most centrally located mall by a long shot, Dizengoff Center is easy to find from the outside. But beware: once inside, it's easy to get lost in the maze of cinemas, food courts, and all those brand-name stores you thought you'd left behind.

✤ On the intersection with King George. Bus #5 goes here directly. ⌚ Open Su-Th 10am-10pm, F 10am-5pm, Sa 8:15-10pm.

RAMAT AVIV MALL
40 Einstein St.

NORTH TEL AVIV
☎03 643 1666; www.ramat-aviv-mall.co.il

Up in the secluded north, Ramat Aviv provides more upscale fare than its southern counterparts, offering some of the most exclusive fashion in the city.

✤ Opposite Eretz Israel Museum. Bus #127 goes there directly. ⌚ Open Su-Th 9:30am-9:30pm, F 8am-4pm, Sa sunset-11pm.

markets

▨ CARMEL MARKET

SOUTH TEL AVIV

In stark opposition to the chic boutiques and haute couture that pervade the rest of the city, Carmel Market is a bonafide Tel Aviv institution, the sort of gloriously riotous market that you've seen in so many movie chase scenes. Cries of "Yalla!" and the smell of cumin wafting from spice stands choke the swarthy air; a vendor is more excited about an eggplant than you ever thought was humanly possible; and, all at once, your childhood Indiana Jones fantasies feel fulfilled. So pick up your whip and weave your way through the stall-packed street to find everything from novelty T-shirts and "Foakley" sunglasses to corncob pipes and pig entrails. Be prepared to sacrifice elbow room and test your haggling mettle.

✤ Leads directly off of Magen David Sq. ⌚ Open daily 8am-sunset (closes earlier on Fridays).

NAHALAT BENYAMIN ARTS AND CRAFTS MARKET

SOUTH TEL AVIV

After the fray of Carmel Market, take a breather and check out the more laid-back Nahalat Benyamin Market one street over. The phrase "arts and crafts" may bring to mind the macaroni picture frames of your youth, but the artisans lining this wide pedestrian thoroughfare proudly peddle high-quality jewelry, fabrics, clocks, and figurines. Numerous cafes and buskers, including, occasionally, a samba troupe, give you all the more reason to stroll through.

✤ Runs parallel to Carmel Market, off of Magen David Sq. ⌚ Open Tu 10am-5pm, F 10am-5pm.

TEL AVIV PORT AND FARMERS' MARKET

NORTH TEL AVIV

Overlooking the marina waterfront and the Mediterranean beyond, vendors hawk local produce including fresh-baked bread, artisanal cheeses, home-brewed beers, and unpronounceable spices. On Thursdays and Fridays an additional outdoor section opens up, and rumor has it that they occasionally have a cow that visitors may milk.

⇆ Bus #4 to top of Ben-Yehuda, then walk 5min. to the inlet of the port. ⏰ Port Market open M-Sa 7:30am-7pm. Adjacent Farmers' Market open Th 4pm-9pm, F 8am-sunset.

ANTIQUES AND SECONDHAND FAIR CENTRAL TEL AVIV

A cornucopia of everything and nothing in particular. Find a guy selling his machete collection and ninja stars, then mosey over to the next stall to find anything from Star Wars paraphernalia to antique wood carvings. Add in the wonderful confusion of the Creative Artists' Fair, a small section of local artists selling jewelry, paintings, and photo prints along Dizengoff St., and you're sure to find the perfect secondhand knickknack for you aunt. May the force be with you.

⇆ Located on Dizengoff Sq. ⏰ Antiques Fair open Tu noon-7pm, F 8am-3pm. Creative Artists' Fair open M noon-7pm, F 9am-4pm.

ESSENTIALS

practicalities

- **TOURIST OFFICE: Tourist Information Center** offers a huge array of free maps and brochures in a range of languages. Staff provide info on all the go-tos and must-sees in town. (46 Herbert Samuel Promenade ☎03 516 6188; www.visit-tlv.com ⇆ Located along the promenade between Ge'ula and HaRav Kook. ⏰ Open Su-Th 9:30am-5pm, F 9:30am-1pm.)
- **EMBASSIES/CONSULATES: UK.** (1 Ben-Yehuda St. ☎03 725-1222; www.ukinisrael.fco.gov.uk/en ⇆ On intersection with Allenby St. Bus #4 from New Central Station stops nearby. ⏰ Open M-Th 8am-4pm, F 8am-1:30pm.) **US.** (71 HaYarkon St. ☎03 519 7475; israel.usembassy.gov ⇆ Just north of intersection with Trumpeldor. ⏰ Available by phone only M-Th 10am-noon. For emergencies call ☎03 519 7551.)
- **BANKS: Bank HaPoalim.** (65 Allenby St. ☎03 520 0612; www.bankhapoalim.com ⏰ Open Su 8:30am-2pm, M 8:30am-2pm and 4-5pm, Tu-W 8:30am-2pm, Th 8:30am-2pm and 4-5pm.) **Bank Leumi.** (50 Dizengoff St. ☎03 954 4555; www.bankleumi.co.il ℹ ATMs can be found on almost every street corner. ⏰ Open Su 8:30am-4pm, M 8:30am-1pm and 4-6:15pm, Tu-W 8:30am-4pm, Th 8:30am-1pm and 4-6:15pm.)
- **LUGGAGE STORAGE:** On the 6th fl. of New Central Station. (☎03 639 3230 ℹ Most hostels also provide secure luggage storage. $ NIS12 per day. ⏰ Open Su-Th 5am-11pm, F 5am-4pm, Sa 8:30-11pm.)
- **GLBT RESOURCES/HOTLINES: Municipal GLBT Community Center** is a recently established center housing many local GLBT organizations and holding regular events. (22 Tchernichovsky St. ☎03 525 2896; gaycenter.org.il ⇆ By Meir Garden, 1 block from the intersection of King George and Allenby St.)
- **LAUNDROMATS: Mendele Self-Service.** (10 Mendele Mokher Safrim. ☎054 424 1964 ⇆ On intersection with Ben-Yehuda St. $ Wash NIS15 per load. Dry NIS1 per 2min. ⏰ Open 24hr.) **Laundry Millennium.** (26 Allenby St. ☎03 516 1323. ⇆ On intersection with Ben-Yehuda St. $ Wash NIS15 per load. Dry NIS5 per 15min. ⏰ Open 24hr.)
- **SWIMMING POOL: Ramat Aviv Swimming Pool** is available, but most people just go to the beach. (7 Haim Leveanon ☎03 641 2325 ⇆ Directly across from museum entrance. $ NIS46. ⏰ Open daily 6-8am and 7:30-10:30pm.)
- **INTERNET: Speilman.** (118 Dizengoff St. ☎03 529 1619 ℹ Cash only. $ NIS20 per 90min. and can be used over several visits. ⏰ Open daily 10am-2am.) **Cyberlink.** (20 Allenby St. ☎03 517 1448. $ NIS15 per hr. ⏰ Open daily 9am-3am.)
- **POST OFFICES:** 61 HaYarkon St. ⏰ Open Su-Th 8am-6pm, F 8am-noon. There are additional branches at 3 Mendele St. and 286 Dizengoff St.

emergency

- **EMERGENCY NUMBERS: Police:** ☎100. **Ambulance:** ☎101. **Fire:** ☎102.
- **POLICE:** 221 Dizengoff St. ☎03 545 4444; www.telaviv.police.gov.il *i* Multiple branches throughout city. Check website for nearest station. ⏰ Open 24hr.
- **LATE-NIGHT PHARMACIES: New-Pharm.** (75 Ben-Yehuda St. ☎03 529 0037 ⏰ Open Su-Th 8am-10pm, F 8am-3pm). **Second location.** (71 Ibn Gvirol St. ☎03 527 9318. ⏰ Open Su-Th 9am-9pm, F 9am-3pm.) **Super-Pharm.** (129 Dizengoff, on corner with Gordon St. ☎03 529 9566. ⏰ Open Su-Th 8am-midnight, F 8am-6pm, Sa 8am-midnight.)
- **HOSPITAL: Ichilov Hospital.** (6 Weizmann St. ☎03 697 4444; www.tasmc.org.il.)

getting there

BY PLANE

All flights come in and out of **Ben-Gurion Airport** (☎03 975 5555; www.iaa.gov.il/Rashat/en-US/Airports/BenGurion). Unfortunately, since the discontinuation of the airport shuttle to the city, **Egged** buses require a series of at least two largely confusing transfers to reach the city, so to reach Tel Aviv from the airport, your best bet is to take a train or taxi. **Taxis** are easy to get and most will offer a fixed rate of NIS100-110. A **train** into Tel Aviv can be taken from Level S of the airport. (🚏 Goes directly to main Savidor terminus. $ NIS14.50 ⏰ 20 min., every 20 min.)

BY TRAIN

All things rail run out of **Savidor Central Rail Station.** (10 al-Parshat Drachim St. ☎03 577 4000; www.rail.co.il/en ⏰ Open Su-Th 24hr., F midnight-3:30pm, Sa 8:30pm-midnight.) Trains go to Ashdod ($ NIS19. ⏰ 45min., every 45min.), Be'er Sheva ($ NIS29. ⏰ 1½ hr., every hr.), Haifa ($ NIS29.50. ⏰ 1hr., every 20min.), Jerusalem ($ NIS22. ⏰ 1hr. 40min., every hr.), and Netanya. ($ NIS15. ⏰ 20min., every 30min.)

BY BUS

All intercity buses run by **Egged** (☎*2880, www.egged.co.il/en ⏰ Open Su-Th 7am-11-pm, F 7am-3pm, Sa 30min. sunset-11pm) run through **New Central Station** (108 Levinsky St.). Buses also go to Be'er Sheva (🚏 Bus #370. $ NIS16.50. ⏰ 1½ hr., every 30min.), Eilat (🚏 Bus #394. $ NIS75. ⏰ 5½ hr., every 90min.), Haifa (🚏 Bus #910. $ NIS26.50. ⏰ 1½ hr., every hr.), Jerusalem (🚏 Bus #405. $ NIS20. ⏰ 1hr., every 20min.), Netanya (🚏 Bus #641. $ NIS17.20. ⏰ 2hr., every 30min.), and Tiberias. (🚏 Bus #835. $ NIS40. ⏰ 2½ hr., every 30min.)

BY CAR

Rent a car from **Avis.** (113 HaYarkon St. ☎03 527 1752; www.carrentalisrael.com $ From NIS49 per day for 2-6 days. NIS44 per day for 7-24 days. Additional US$7 per day for ages 21-25. Max. US$70. ⏰ Open Su-Th 8am-6pm, F 8am-2pm.)

getting around

BY FOOT

Aside from Ramat Aviv up north, Tel Aviv is easily accessible by foot, and, with a cool sea breeze for most of the year, walking is hardly torture. From north (the port) to south (the border with Jaffa) the city is about a 1½ hr. walk. Most of the places you'll want to visit are within a 20min. walk inland from the coast.

BY TAXI

Taxis in Tel Aviv are readily available. While certainly expensive, the service is not overpriced and shouldn't put you out more than NIS50 between any two points in the city. Drivers will inevitably try to rip you off by quoting a price, so make sure to ask for them to turn on the meter. There is no need to tip.

BY BUS

For only NIS6 per ride, 10min. of air-conditioning on a sweltering August day is worth the money alone—and you're being driven wherever you need to go. Everything bus-related orbits around the massive **New Central Bus Station** (108 Levinksy St.) in the south. **Egged** intercity buses leave from the seventh floor while **Dan** (☎03 639 4444; www.dan.co.il/english) is the intracity operator. For longer stays, check out the youth *kartisya*, which allows for 20 rides for NIS58 (over a 50% discount). There are no strict schedules, and routes are subject to change, but buses tend to come quite frequently. Unfortunately, bus maps are not available in English, so talk to a local, tour guide, or hostel owner about routes. **Sheruts** operate along the same routes for the same NIS6 price but can be a bit more flexible with stopping locations (make sure to shout *"Gai!"* when you want to get off).

As far as the lines go, **bus #4** goes from New Central Bus Station, makes a beeline to the coast, runs along Allenby St. onto Ben-Yehuda before reaching the port, then turns back. **Bus #5** also runs north from New Central Bus Station, going up Rothschild Blvd. before turning left onto Dizengoff St., passing Dizengoff Center and Square before eventually making a right onto Weizmann St. and then HaMedina Sq. to finish up at Savidor Central Railway Station. **Bus #9** originates in the port and travels diagonally southeast across the city, passing the hospital, Tel Aviv Art Museum, and Azrieli Center. **Bus #10** goes from Savidor Central Railway Station and works along Arlozorov toward the coast before heading down HaYarkon St. to reach Jaffa. **Bus #27** moves from New Central Bus Station and makes its way up the busy Namir St. thoroughfare to reach Ramlat Aviv and the university in the north.

jaffa ☎03

A Palestinian port city before Tel Aviv's founding, and the old Arab Quarter after, Jaffa—or Yafo—remains a place where Jews and Arabs live together largely in peace. To the fumbling backpacker without a care for politics, it just seems to be a more relaxed version of Tel Aviv: blasting electro has been replaced with periodic serenades from minarets, skyscrapers with clock towers, and pulsing strobe lights with streams of bulbs decking alleyways. Recent years have seen Jaffa undergo a major facelift, but this modernization is tinged with reminders of the area's past, from the ever-wafting aroma of hookahs to the Arabic music drifting through the streets. If you came to Israel hoping for something a little more alien than the brazenly Westernized Tel Aviv, the rustic charm of Jaffa might be just what you were looking for.

ORIENTATION

Lucky for you, Jaffa is small, largely uncomplicated, and easily navigable on foot—nothing will ever be more than a 15min. walk away. Coming in from Tel Aviv, **Herbert Samuel Street** leads directly to Jaffa's center, **the clock tower,** then uphill and farther south to Jaffa's main thoroughfare, **Yefet Street.** To the east is **Shuk HaPishpeshim** and a series of alleys flanked by old colonial buildings and shacks that end at **Yerushalayim St.,** Jaffa's eastern border. Through this block, the main thoroughfare is **Olei Tzion,** connecting both Yefet St. and Yerushalayim St. To the west of Yefet St. sits the large hill that is home to the HaPisga Gardens. The coast is bordered by **HaAliya HaSheniya Street,** which eventually coincides with the port. One block inland is **Mifratz Shlomo,** which runs into **Kedumim Square**—the central square of Jaffa's western side. The Church of St. Peter stands here, overlooking Tel Aviv.

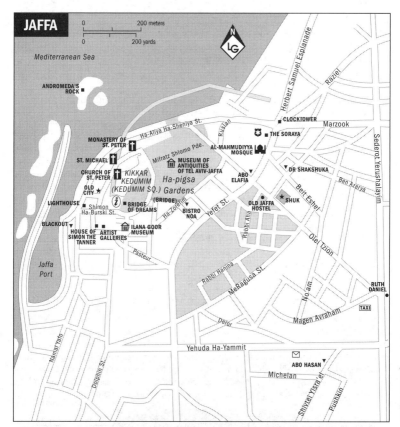

JAFFA

0 ___ 200 meters
0 ___ 200 yards

Mediterranean Sea

ANDROMEDA'S ROCK ■

Herbert Samuel Esplanade

Razíel

■ CLOCKTOWER   Marzook

Ha-Aliya Ha-Sheniya St.

Ruslan

■ THE SORAYA

Sederot Yerushalayim

MONASTERY OF ST. PETER

Mifratz Shlomo Pde.

AL-MAHMUDIYYA MOSQUE

ST. MICHAEL

MUSEUM OF ANTIQUITIES OF TEL AVIV-JAFFA

▼ DR SHAKSHUKA

CHURCH OF ST. PETER

KIKKAR KEDUMIM (KEDUMIM SQ.)

Ha-pigsa Gardens

ABO ELAFIA

Ben Azarya

OLD CITY

(BRIDGE)

Beit Esher

LIGHTHOUSE

Shimon Ha-Burski St.

■ BRIDGE OF DREAMS

Ha-Zorefim

Yefet St.

Rabbi Aha

★ SHUK

OLD JAFFA HOSTEL

BLACKOUT ▼

BISTRO NOA

HOUSE OF SIMON THE TANNER

■ ARTIST GALLERIES

ILANA GOOR MUSEUM

Olei Tzion

Pasteur

Jaffa Port

Rabbi Hanina

MeRagusa St.

No'am

RUTH DANIEL ●

Deror

Magen Avraham

TAXI

Nahmat Yafo

Dolphin St.

Yehuda Ha-Yammit

ABO HASAN ▼

Michelan

Shivtei Yisra'el

Pushkin

jaffa

ACCOMMODATIONS

Given the character of the locale, you might expect adorable guesthouses run by Betty White look-alikes. When considering Jaffa's size, though, it makes sense that budget-friendly bunks can be pretty hard to come by.

[✓] OLD JAFFA HOSTEL — HOSTEL $$

13 Amiad St. ☎03 682 2370

Located in a charmingly fatigued colonial house in the center of the *shuk*, Old Jaffa Hostel is clean but mildly quirky—hanging plants adorn its central staircase, and bright yellow doors veer off at head, shoulder, or waist height for no apparent reason. The real treat is the hostel's rooftop, replete with sofas and a fountain, which offers patrons a unique view of Jaffa, Tel Aviv, and the sea beyond.

➜ Walk south along Yefet St. Make a left onto Olei Tzion and follow it past the immediate square. The entrance to the hostel is on the right forking path. ℹ Free Wi-Fi. Breakfast included. Kitchen access. $ Dorms NIS80; singles NIS210-300; doubles NIS250-350.

RUTH DANIEL RESIDENCE — HOTEL $$$

47 Yerushalayim St. ☎03 526 4500; www.mishkenot-jaffa.co.il

Teetering on the eastern edge of Jaffa, Ruth Daniel is a slick modern building with spotless white rooms, many with views of the bungalows and shacks of Jaffa's flea market. While it does cost a good bit more than the Old Jaffa Hostel, places to stay in Jaffa are scarce enough that this might just be your next cheapest option short of catching the bus back to Tel Aviv.

➜ On Yerushalayim St. opposite the intersection with Olei Tzion. ℹ A/C, TV, and bathroom in all rooms. Breakfast included. $ Singles US$140; doubles US$165.

SIGHTS

As with much of Tel Aviv, the best sights you'll get out of Jaffa will not be the institutionalized museums and monuments, but rather the moments you catch while wandering the neighborhoods. The distinctly Arabic flavor to the areas around the clock tower and market are bound to be novel after Tel Aviv, and the serene **HaPisga Gardens** and the environs of **Kedumim Square** provide a quieter type of relief from the city.

lottery by the sea

Wars have been fought for the sake of land, but early Zionists found a slightly more practical way to divvy up the desert. In 1909, 66 families set up a lottery system to split the northern section of Jaffa. Each family wrote its name on a white seashell, while the portions of land were written on gray seashells. Shells were then matched up at random, and each family took their designated plot. Within a year, all the roads, homes, and water systems were constructed. Perhaps Israel and Palestine could learn a thing or two from these guys.

[✓] SHUK HAPISHPESHIM — MARKET

Sprawling across almost a quarter of Jaffa, Shuk HaPishpeshim might be, geographically speaking, the biggest market in the area, even rivaling the mighty Carmel Market in Tel Aviv. The fare here is true flea market: secondhand typewriters, shoes, *argilah* pipes, toys, CDs, German pornography, and much more. The market is spread out enough that it doesn't feel quite as manic and packed as Carmel Market, but it's certainly just as loud. Friday is the largest market day.

➜ From Yefet St. turn left heading south onto Beit Eshel or Olei Tzion. ⏰ Open Su-F 8am-7pm.

ILANA GOOR MUSEUM
MUSEUM

4 Mazel Digam St. ☎03 683 7676; www.ilanagoor.com

In the heart of the city's artists' colony is this burgeoning museum dedicated to the life and work of Israeli artist Ilana Goor. The museum is full of her bronze sculptures and installations teeming over the walls, ceilings, and furniture, from a medieval monk's table covered in metallic insects to a psychedelic piano and effigies of Christ. The top floor of the museum bursts forth into a glorious roof terrace that overlooks the Mediterranean and has a bird's-eye view of the Old City.

🚶 Walk to the south end of Kedumim Sq. and take a left onto Mazel Digam St. ℹ English guide available at front desk. $ NIS32, students NIS28. ⏰ Open Su 10am-4pm, Tu-F 10am-4pm, Sa 10am-6pm.

HAPISGA GARDENS
PARK

Until you reach HaPisga Gardens, you won't realize just how little grass you saw in Tel Aviv. Parks are a rare commodity in town, but this fastidiously manicured garden goes some way toward compensating the horticulturalist and picnicker within each of us. Relics include a reconstructed gate, Roman remains, and the Bridge of Dreams. If you are pure of heart and stand on the bridge, facing the sea and touching your astrological sign, you may just find your wishes granted. (Alternatively, you may just feel silly.) The top of the garden also sports probably the best view of the Tel Aviv coastline you're going to find.

on the market

Israel may have more malls per capita than any other country in the world (unless, perhaps, you decide to count New Jersey as its own nation), but that doesn't mean that all the best places to shop are climate-controlled. If you're in Tel Aviv, head to their famous flea market (*Shuk HaPishpeshim*), open every day except Saturday. These twisting lanes of stalls in the northeast corner of Jaffa's Old City house everything from vibrant textiles to kitschy antiques, brass menorahs to hand-carved rocking horses. But there's more to the surrounding neighborhood than prime haggling opportunities. Recent years have brought an explosion of development in the neighborhood, and new cafes, bakeries, and taverns with Greek mezze and cold beer abound. That's a far cry from getting a pretzel at the food court.

CHURCH OF SAINT PETER
RELIGIOUS SITE

Kedumim Square ☎03 682 2871

If you've spent more than a few seconds on the beaches of Tel Aviv, you've probably seen this church's famous white belfry, standing tall on the rocky promontory. Indeed, that belfry is so conspicuous that it became a symbolic beacon for pilgrims arriving by sea.

⏰ Open daily 8-11:45am and 3-5pm. English mass Sa 8pm and Su 9am.

THE OLD CITY
NEIGHBORHOOD

Descend the steps from Kedumim Sq. into Jaffa's old city, an intricate network of high-walled alleyways and heavenly, man-made shade where the sunlight only scrapes the tops of balconies above. The area has been cleaned up in recent years and is now home to a mass of upscale cafes and art galleries, which together make up the so-called artists' colony toward the southern end.

FOOD

Jaffa might be comparatively tiny, but you'll find an inordinately high concentration of the country's best eateries here. While Tel Aviv proper will rarely serve up Israeli dishes other than the standard hummus and falafel, Jaffa's kitchens dish up what you came to this country for: great traditional cuisine. Forget those Western wannabes farther north with their sushi, burgers and haute cuisine. Give yourself a taste of what Israeli cuisine is really all about.

👍 SAID ABOU ELAFIA AND SONS — BAKERY $

7 Yefet St. ☎03 681 2340

The word "institution" gets thrown around too much by restaurants, but this place is the real deal. Popularly regarded as the best bakery in the country, Abouelafia, as it's commonly known, has been serving up the best bagels and pastries in town since 1879. Try the eponymous Abouelafia (NIS12)—a sort of Cornish pasty with fried egg. It's so good that bakeries all over the country refer to their imitations with Abouelafia's name. The flatbreads and *souvlaki* are also divine. Do the rounds—Dr. Atkins can go suck it.

🧭 At the foot of Yefet St. by the clock tower. [$] Bagel NIS5. Bagel panini NIS20. Cash only. ⏰ Open 24hr.

👍 ABU HASSAN — HUMMUS $

14 Shivtai Israel St. ☎03 682 0387

Not content with the best bread in the country? How about its best hummus? This title may be a little more debatable, but Abu Hassan would certainly get a lot of votes. Indeed, even though it has recently spread out into two further branches across Jaffa, the original location is still positively swarming come meal time. Waiters scream at one another, and foot-high piles of pita are tossed around like footballs. Abu Hassan is a riot, but a particularly delectable one, so shove your way in and grab a free seat before someone else does.

🧭 Walk south along Yefet St. until you reach the intersection with Yehuda HaYamit St. Walk 500m and make a right onto Shivtai Israel St. [$] Hummus plate NIS16. ⏰ Open Su-F 6:45am-3am.

BLACKOUT — DINING IN THE DARK $$$

Nalaga'at Center ☎03 633 0808; www.nalagaat.org.il/blackout.php

No, this is not a restaurant for getting blindingly drunk. Though, now you say it, the first part of that is correct—part of the Nalaga'at Center for the blind and deaf, Blackout is a restaurant in absolute darkness. The completely blind waiters do more than just serve you food; they teach you how to do things as simple as pouring a drink or eating a meal, making it a truly once-in-a-lifetime experience. It's more than a gimmick though. Eating in the dark adds newfound elements of texture and smell to your food, and, should you choose the mystery menu, you may be surprised to find out what you've just been eating. Table manners somewhat go out the window when cutlery becomes impossible to operate, and there's no shame in making your ratatouille into finger food when no one can see you. Biggest bonus? You can finally pick your nose at the dinner table. By day, the warehouse becomes Cafe Kapish where all the waiters are deaf.

🧭 By Jaffa Port, 1 block behind the waterfront. ℹ Reservation required in advance. [$] Set menu NIS140. ⏰ Open Su-Tu 6:30-11pm, Th 6:30-11pm.

DR. SHAKSHUKA — ISRAELI $

3 Beit Eshel ☎03 682 2842; drshaksuka.rest-e.co.il

Shakshuka—chopped tomatoes, spices, and poached eggs in a piping hot skillet—doesn't get much better than this. While outwardly a Tripolian restaurant, this local joint serves up the traditional Israeli dish better than most. When you enter the restaurant, make sure to check out the mess of cauldrons, pots, and pans hanging from the obscured ceiling.

Heading south along Yefet St., make a left onto Beit Eshel right after the clock tower square. $ Shakshuka NIS30. Cash only. Open Su-Th 8am-midnight, F 8am-sunset, Sa 7pm-midnight.

BISTRO NOA FINE DINING $$

HaZorfim' 14 ☎03 518 4668; www.cordelia.co.il

Sister restaurant to Cordelia, the swankiest joint in Jaffa, Bistro Noa offers similar fare for much better prices. While the exterior might look like just another warehouse, inside it opens up into a wide alley, complete with a small wooden windmill by the bar, white garden furniture, and modern art hanging from the walls.

Heading south on Yefet St., make a right after number 30, then a left at the end of the alley onto HaZorfim. $ Gnocchi NIS49. Sirloin steak NIS82. Open daily 9am-midnight.

NIGHTLIFE

Let's get one thing straight. You're not coming to Jaffa to rage. Jaffa used to be home to Dungeon, the country's premier S and M joint, but it was shut down, apparently due to neighbors' complaints concerning the strange noises coming from the basement. So you'll have to save your whips and chains for elsewhere; in fact, clubs in the area are pretty much non-existent. Nevertheless, the bars of Jaffa certainly keep the place buzzing come nightfall. While not as riotous as their northern cousins, they're by no means boring, offering local socialites a place to drink (and occasionally dance).

SALOONA ART BAR BAR, GLBT-FRIENDLY

17 Tirza St. ☎03 518 1917; www.saloonabar.co.il

With high ceilings and the youngest crowd you'll find in Jaffa, Saloona is the closest the town gets to jumpin', jumpin' at night. The huge chandelier made out of sea sponges is worth the trip alone. The music's suitably loud, but the tone stays chill and nonchalant—knocking back a few shots here leads to casual conversation rather than shameless dancing.

Walk up Yerushalayim St. and take a right on Shlomo, then a left on Tirza. i Live shows on Su-Tu. Electronic music on 1st W of month. Fundraising evening for Beit Dror, a shelter for GLBT youth, on last W of month. $ Goldstar NIS22. Arak NIS12. Open daily 11pm-2am or later.

JAFFA BAR BAR, GLBT-FRIENDLY

30 Yefet St. ☎03 518 4668; www.cordelia.co.il

Owned by the posh joint Cordelia, Jaffa Bar keeps things looser than her sister and has become a local favorite over the past few years. The clientele is a little older than the crowd at Saloona, but the place keeps an impressive array of alcohols behind the bar. Make sure to try Jaffa Nights, the fruity house special made of *arak*, passion fruit liqueur, and grapefruit juice (NIS28).

Walk 300m up Yefet St. from the clock tower. Jaffa Bar is in the alley on the right. $ Beer from NIS18. Open daily 7pm-late.

ARTS AND CULTURE

In line with its slower, singular pace of life, Jaffa has its share of local bohemians that keep up a fairly lively arts scene. A large number of theaters have found their homes in the area, and the visual arts are championed by the artists' colony in the Old City.

NAGALA'AT CENTER THEATER

HaAliya HaShniya Dock ☎03 633 0808; www.nalagaat.org.il

The Nagala'at Center is most prominently home to a world-famous troupe of deaf-blind actors who perform in the 330-seat theater when they're not touring the world. The quality and intricacies of the performances are astounding. Also make sure to drop by Cafe Kapish or the Blackout Restaurant, both in the center. Check the website to see what is playing and to make post-show reservations for the restaurant.

➜ 1 block inland from the port. $ Tickets NIS60-150. ⏰ Shows are usually 3 times per week at 8:30pm.

ARTISTS' COLONY GALLERIES

Scattered around the southern end of the Old City, the artists' colony is a collection of galleries selling at prices generally cheaper than those in Tel Aviv proper but still probably beyond the range of the average backpacker. Among the more typical fare of painting and sculpture, highlights include a gallery of vintage posters and another plastered in pencil cartoons that seem to be the product of an especially vivid acid trip.

➜ Centered along Mazel Digam St. in the Old City at the south end of Kebumim Sq.

ESSENTIALS

Most services are easily found in nearby Tel Aviv, meaning that Jaffa proper may seem lacking in basic practicalities.

practicalities

- **ATM: Bank HaPoalim.** (16 Yerushalayim St. ⏰ Open Su 8:30am-1pm, M 8:30am-1pm and 3:45-5:45pm, Tu-W 8:30am-1pm, Th 8:30am-1pm and 3:45-5:45pm.)

emergency

- **EMERGENCY NUMBERS: Police:** ☎100. **Ambulance:** ☎101. **Fire:** ☎102.
- **LATE-NIGHT PHARMACY: Super-Pharm.** (49 Yerushalayim St. ⏰ Open Su-Th 8am-10pm, F 8am-4:30pm, Sa 8am-11pm.)

getting there

Major bus routes throughout Tel Aviv will take you to Jaffa—just look for lines which end at **Bat Yam Cemetery. Bus #8,** which comes from HaYarkon St., stops by the clock tower, and **bus #25** from King George stops at the northern end of Yerushalayim St.

getting around

Buses don't travel within Jaffa, so lace up those sneakers. Hell, even sandals will probably be okay—it's rare that you'll have to walk more than 15min. to get anywhere in Jaffa. If you're really pressed for time, you can call a cab, but they're not abundant down here.

ramla ☎08

The only town in modern Israel both founded and still populated by Arabs, Ramla (pronounced RAM-leh and not to be confused with Ramallah) is not simply a place of *yarmulkes* morphed into *keffiyehs* and cries of "Shalom!" replaced with "Salaam!" Sure, the great mosque and bustling *souq* pay homage to the town's Arabic character, but the city is a melting pot—a hub for Ethiopian and Russian Jews, African and Christian Arabs, and settlers from India. Shisha joints sit comfortably next to tandoors. A shopkeeper may have to cycle through five languages before he hits the right one. Despite all that culture and 13 centuries of backstory, Ramla's history has manifested more in dilapidation than in anything charming or old-timey. The city has garnered a national reputation for being grimy, ramshackle, and run-down—tell an Israeli you went to Ramla, and she may offer a little snigger in return. After all, the town's most prominent piece of modernity is a mammoth industrial plant towering over the city. Ramla is not exactly a tourist mecca, and there's really nowhere to stay, unless a jail cell is your style. Your best bet is to get to the city early enough to see the small crowd of churches, mosques, and ancient relics that huddle around the Old City, then grab some grub and get back to Tel Aviv by bedtime.

ORIENTATION

You'll enter Ramla via the **Central Bus Station,** which sits in the southeastern portion of the city, at the foot of **Herzl Street,** the town's main thoroughfare. The **Old City** is directly across the road along Herzl St. Unless you have an inexplicable desire to explore the vast industrial wastelands out east or the run-down neighborhoods in the north, everything you'll want to see—and everything listed in this book—is in the Old City and rarely more than a 15min. walk away. To the south of Herzl St., the Old City is contained within the two streets that branch off, **King Shlomo St.,** opposite the bus station and **Bialik Street,** just up the road. To the north, the crossroads formed by **Haganah Street** and **Chaim Weizmann St.** is about as far up the road as you'll ever need to go.

SIGHTS

Given Ramla's cosmopolitan nature, it's no surprise that the sights here really run the theological gamut, from Franciscan monasteries to mosques and crusader towers. The sights listed form a circuit around town that takes about 2hr. to complete.

RAMLA MUSEUM — MUSEUM

6 Herzl St. ☎08 929 2650; www.museum-ramla.org.il

Occupying the old municipal offices of the British consulate, the Ramla Museum traces the history of the town from its Arab origins. The museum isn't terribly large, only four rooms altogether, but a small collection of coins and mosaic fragments in conjunction with some extensive wall displays manages to pack a lot of history per square meter. Models of the local churches and Pool of the Arches foreshadow the sights you'll encounter farther along the trail. The museum also serves as the town's tourist office, and its staff are delighted to direct you to some of the best sights and eateries in town in the physically impossible case that your almighty *Let's Go* guide proves to be insufficient.

‡ Directly opposite the bus station. $ NIS7. ⏰ Open Su-Th 8:30am-4pm, F 8:30am-1pm.

SOUQ — MARKET

The centerpiece of Ramla's Old City, the *souq* runs down the pedestrianized Jabotinsky St. The market is mostly focused on groceries—olives by the kilogram, fruits you've likely never seen before, and glasses of lemonade ladled into empty Coke bottles for a shekel. A massive extension of the daily market takes over a nearby huge parking lot on Wednesdays. This section is less food-centric: the stalls offer everything under the sun, from bootleg kitchen appliances to a notably large selection of women's clothes you'd never expect to find in an Arabic market (think bikinis, tank tops, and heels).

‡ Jabotinsky St. branches off of Herzl St. to the south, about 1 block west of the museum. The market extension comes off of King Shlomo St., which is opposite the bus station. ⏰ Open Su-F. Times vary. Extension market open W sunrise-2pm.

THE GREAT MOSQUE — MOSQUE

Resh Zayin St. ☎08 929 2650

Originally dubbed the Cathedral of Saint John by the Crusaders who built it, the mosque gained its current moniker when Arabs recaptured Ramla and converted the spire into a minaret. The main building, however, was left untouched and still seems decidedly ecclesiastical. It may be a little disheveled on the outside, but the medieval vaults on the interior provide plenty of gawking material.

‡ Walk down King Shlomo St., opposite the bus station. Look for the minaret past the mosque's parking lot. ℹ Modest dress required. ⏰ Open Su-F 8-10am

CHURCH OF ST. NICODEMUS AND JOSEPH OF ARIMATHEA — CHURCH, MONASTERY

1 Bialik St. ☎08 912 7200

The Franciscan order has had a presence in Ramla since 1296, an influence which is evident in this large monastery. The parish's white spire dominates the skyline

ramla

of the Old City, dwarfing the so-called Little Mosque next to the church. The occasional robed monk scurries through the complex, but most of the monastery is now overshadowed by an elementary school that sits on the grounds next to the century-old church. If you manage to stop one of the monks for long enough, he might tell you that Napoleon slept in the monastery during his campaign here. Napoleon could not be reached for comment.

⚑ *On the corner of Herzl St. and Bialik St.* **i** *The monastery is guarded. Tours must be arranged in advance by phone.* ⏰ *Open M-F 8:30-11:30am.*

TOWER OF 40 MARTYRS   RUINS
Dani Mas St.

While a mammoth eighth-century tower used to stand on the grounds, only a few arches remain today; the lofty tower now present was a 14th-century addition. Napoleon purportedly directed his troops from the parapet, which offers so-ugly-they're-good views of the entire town, as well as of Ashkelon and even Tel Aviv on particularly clear days. Today, the tower's main residents are a coop of pigeons who have kindly demarcated the way to the top with plenty of guano—be careful not to veer off the staircase near the top, or you may find your face similarly splattered. Not that that happened to us or anything.

⚑ *Go west along Herzl St., take a left onto Dani Mas St., and walk for about 400m.* Ⓢ *NIS5.* ⏰ *Open Su-Th 8am-2pm, F 9am-1pm, Sa 9am-3pm.*

POOL OF THE ARCHES   RUINS
Haganah St.   ☎08 977 1595

An underground reservoir built at Ramla's founding a mere 1200 years ago—and largely untouched since—the pool is one of Ramla's most famous sights, in part thanks to the film *Hasamba and the Lost Youths*, in which the youths in question row through the cavernous underground arches. Visitors can tour the reservoir in the small rowboats moored at the pool's corner. Even if ridiculously old caves aren't your thing, they provide a brilliant excuse to cool down and cower from that scalding sun. The few rays that manage to peek through the portholes at the top of the cavern give the place an eerie beauty. It would be a perfect place for a swim, except that the water is stagnant due to a now-defunct spring.

⚑ *Walk west along Herzl St. Haganah St. is on the right after you pass Bialik St. on the left.* Ⓢ *NIS8.* ⏰ *Open Su-Th 8am-3:20pm, F 8am-2pm, Sa 8am-4pm.*

FOOD
As you might expect, haute cuisine is not Ramla's forte. But put up with a restaurant that may be faintly soiled and you may find a few diamonds in the rough.

🗹 SAMIR'S   HUMMUS $$
7 Kehilat Detroyt   ☎08 922 0195

Samir's is the closest thing Ramla has to an institution. Huddled between the little mosque and Franciscan monastery, it echoes its neighbors with monastery-worthy arched walls, and a mural of the Old City gives a nod to Ramla's presumably brighter days. In the cooler months, the restaurant opens its sizable roof terrace.

⚑ *Walk up Herzl St. from the bus station and take a left about 200m on Kehilat Detroyt.* Ⓢ *Hummus plate NIS15.* ⏰ *Open Su-Th 8am-8pm, F 8am-6pm.*

MAHARAJA   INDIAN $$
87 Herzl St.   ☎08 852 2064; www.maharaja.co.il

Another well-known local eatery, Maharaja caters to Ramla's sizable Indian population with the typical tandoori fare. The back of the restaurant is home to a sweet shop with all kinds of multi-colored and perfumed treats that go for as low as NIS2 a morsel.

⚑ *2 blocks up from the bus station on the right.* Ⓢ *Chicken masala NIS45. Plate of sweets NIS45.* ⏰ *Open Su-Th 9am-10pm, F 9am-5pm.*

tel aviv and environs

TUNISIA SANDWICH SANDWICHES $

3 King Shlomo St. ☎70 070 7133

After the legions of falafel and shawarma stands, you might be shocked to find a hole-in-the-wall that serves something not drenched in grease. Tunisia Sandwich may not look like much—it's a shack on the edge of a parking lot—but it's a perennial go-to for locals. The specialty is a tuna sandwich served in a particularly sweet bun (NIS20).

 # From the bus station, make a left onto King Shlomo St. Tunisia is on the left before the parking lot at the end of the 1st block. ⏰ Open Su-Th 7am-10pm, F 7am-4pm.

CAFE NECTAR CAFE $

Central Bus Station ☎08 923 7675

In the center of what may be the most banal bus station in the nation, Cafe Nectar really doesn't catch the eye—but it's the only cafe in town and, more importantly, the only free Wi-Fi you're going to find. Park yourself for coffee and a pastry and catch up on Neal Patrick Harris's Twitter.

 # You'll see it as soon as you get off the bus. $ Cheesecake NIS24. ⏰ Open Su-Th 7:30am-8pm, F 7:30am-2:30pm.

ESSENTIALS

practicalities

- **TOURIST OFFICE:** The **Ramla Museum** doubles as the town's tourist center, with staff that are more than eager to help out. (112 Herzl St. ☎08 929 2650.)
- **ATM: Bank Leumi.** (78 Herzl St. ⏰ Open Su 8:30am-2pm, M 8:30am-1pm and 4-6:15pm, Tu-W 8:30am-2pm, Th 8:30am-1pm and 4-6:15pm.)
- **INTERNET: Cafe Nectar** has free Wi-Fi. (Central Bus Station ☎08 923 7675 ⏰ Open Su-Th 7:30am-8pm, F 7:30am-2:30pm.)
- **POST OFFICE:** 2nd fl. of the Central Bus Station. ⏰ Open Su-M 9am-5pm, Tu 9am-4pm, W-Th 9am-5pm, F 9am-1pm.

emergency

- **POLICE: Local Station.** (80 Herzl St. ☎08 927 9444.)
- **LATE-NIGHT PHARMACY: Super-Pharm.** (2nd fl. of the New Central Bus Station. ⏰ Open Su-Th 8:30am-10:30pm, F 8:30am-5pm.)
- **HOSPITAL: Ichilov Hospital** in Tel Aviv is the closest facility. (6 Weizmann St. ☎03 697 4444; www.tasmc.org.il.)

getting there

A multitude of Egged routes are available to Ramla, but all involve at least one transfer. The quickest route is to take **bus #301** from Tel Aviv's New Central Bus Station to Rekhovot Center ($ NIS13.50. ⏰ 30min., every 10-15min.). From here, **bus #249** goes to Ramla's Central Bus Station ($ NIS9.80. ⏰ 20min., every 20min.). Returning from Ramla, **bus #174** ($ NIS13.50.) runs directly and daily, but only at the crack of dawn. So, unless you plan on roughing it in Ramla for the night—which *Let's Go* does not recommend—your best bet is to return via Rishon le-Tziyon. **Bus #433** goes to its station ($ NIS9.80. ⏰ 20min., every 30min.), and from there **buses #301, 201,** or **174** will be running at least every 5min. back to Tel Aviv.

getting around

The best way to get around small and industrial Ramla is by foot. If you're trying to go beyond the city center, or are just particularly tired, there are several **sheruts** that will take you around and should cost no more than NIS4.50.

beit guvrin ☎08

Tel Aviv is loud, busy, and proud of it—then there's Beit Guvrin. Consisting of a remote kibbutz and national park south of the city, it's a quick getaway that provides the most substantial fix of Israeli Arcadia you're likely to find in the area. With majestic views of the countryside—and magenta sunsets that throw the hilly terrain and roving Bedouin flocks into black relief—Beit Guvrin is a great spot for the nature-inclined (or, at least, for those who have been reading too much Wordsworth). During the winter, the area blooms into a thriving green, but even the sparser terrain during the summer—punctuated only by the odd vineyard—makes for quite a sight. The modern, privatized kibbutz is the only evidence of civilization in the area, while the park itself is home to a nationally famous network of underground caves containing two millennia of history from the likes of the biblical city of Maresha, a Roman settlement, and Crusader constructions. You don't need to be an outdoorsy person to visit; the kibbutz can provide a bed for the night, and, although most people tend to travel around the park by car, the equivalent hike isn't out of the question.

ORIENTATION

How many roads must a man walk down? For the citizens of Beit Guvrin, the answer is simple: one. The street cutting through the extremely small town is the only one for miles, so we feel confident telling you that you're unlikely to get lost—unless, of course, you decide to wander off-trail in the national park. **The kibbutz** is located to the north of the road while the **national park** is directly opposite it to the south.

ACCOMMODATIONS

Unfortunately, there are no designated campgrounds in the area. **Kibbutz Beit Guvrin,** however, offers free beds for the night to wandering souls.

KIBBUTZ BEIT GUVRIN — KIBBUTZ

Lachish Blvd. ☎08 687 4855

Perched on a hill facing the national park, Beit Guvrin is a mid-sized, privatized kibbutz, complete with an outdoor swimming pool, grocery store, and dairy farm. The extremely hospitable *kibbutzniks* are happy to offer travelers a free bed for a couple nights in one of the two dorms located at the edge of the complex. Dorms do have a sink, hot plate, and ensuite bathroom, but make sure to bring your own sheets or sleeping bag. Walk to the top of the hill in the evening to sit atop a dome by the radio tower and enjoy a magnificent 360-degree view of the sunset.

*🧭 Opposite Beit Guvrin National Park. **i** Make sure to call ahead to see whether beds are available. $ Free, but donations are welcome.*

THE GREAT OUTDOORS

Situated around the face of Tel Maresha, **Beit Guvrin National Park** (☎08 681 1020 $ NIS27. ⏰ Open daily 8am-4pm.) may be a little barren on the surface, but underground it bursts into a huge network of caves that seems more fitting for vampires than Hellenistic settlers. While hundreds of these caves are scattered across the landscape, a handful of the biggest have been equipped with iron walkways for visitors. The largest cluster of caves centers around the plateau of **Tel Maresha** at the northern end of the park, while others are spread more intermittently around with the ruins of the Roman-Byzantine city of Eleutheropolis. You can access all of the park's major sights easily from either the walking path or the road that runs a circuit of the entire park.

The most popular way to get around the park is by car (many of the sights are localized and have plenty of parking), but getting around by foot is relatively painless—a complete circuit of the park takes no more than 3-4hr. If walking, make sure to bring plenty of sunscreen and at least one or two liters of water, since the paths are all exposed to the sun and shade is lacking (water spigots are available by some caves).

a history of kibbutz

Kibbutzim (singular *kibbutz*) are agricultural collective communities in Israel. The first was founded in 1909, exactly a century before FarmVille made its debut. (Coincidence? We think not.) Combining the ideals of socialism and Zionism, kibbutzim originated as a way to create a utopian society via self-sustaining farming communities. Kibbutzim encouraged equality, mandating that members perform all aspects of the work on a rotating basis. Even the children of the community were shared, with different members taking shifts to care for all of them. This equality extended to relations between the sexes as well. Women referred to their husbands by the Hebrew word *ishi* ("my man") rather than by the traditional *ba'ali* ("my owner").Over the years, the socialist politics of kibbutzim have fallen out of favor, rendering fewer visitors and more closed communities. The advantage to this is that some kibbutzim are now more open to part-time visiting workers (for opportunities, see **Beyond Tourism**). These temporary *kibbutzniks* have included some pretty recognizable names: stars Jerry Seinfeld, Sigourney Weaver, and Sacha Baron Cohen all volunteered on kibbutzim as young adults. High five!

Upon entering the park, walk or drive up the road to the first parking lot, about 1.5km in. From here, the steps lead to the first set of caves, including the mammoth **Columbarium Cave**, pockmarked with over 2000 niches that were used in the third century BCE to raise pigeons for food, fertilizer, and mysterious "cultic purposes." From here, the road splits in two: a right leads to another series of caves around the back of the *tel*, while a left takes you up to the plateau of the *tel*. Once the site of a massive Crusader tower, the plateau offers breathtaking panoramic views of the countryside, including the Hebron mountains in the east and, on especially clear days, Tel Aviv and Ashkelon to the west. Either way, descending the *tel* will take you to another massive system of underground cisterns, baths, and an oil press by the next parking lot. At the foot of the valley, the **Sidonian Burial Caves** have been restored with reproductions of the paintings of musicians and mythical beasts that would have adorned them in biblical Maresha. A small pavilion here provides an ideal spot for lunch. From here, follow the road, and the pathway again splits near the **Bell Caves** toward the south of the park. The secluded walking path winds through a series of mountains and past the **Crusader Church of Saint Anne.** Follow the signs and make a right at the sign. The Bell Caves (so named since they consist of over 800 50 ft. high bell shaped caves) were originally employed as quarries by the Byzantines. Persecuted Christians later flocked to them for sanctuary—you can still see many crosses etched into the walls with the odd bit of graffiti. Indeed, in more modern times, the Italian Stallion himself dropped by to film part of the cinematic masterpiece *Rambo III*. From the Bell Caves, follow the road out to the park entrance.

ESSENTIALS

practicalities

Unfortunately, Beit Guvrin is pretty much a national park and nothing else, meaning it doesn't have very much in terms of emergencies services. Pack any medicine or toiletries you might need, and refer to Tel Aviv for all emergencies.

beit guvrin

getting there

Beit Guvrin can be reached via the nearby town of Kiryat Gat. Egged **bus #376** runs there from New Central Bus Station (Ⓢ NIS15. 🕓 1 hr., daily 2:30pm). From Kiryat Gat, **bus #11** runs to Beit Guvrin twice per day (Ⓢ NIS8.80. 🕓 25min., 8:11am and 5:15pm). Yet, beyond the inconvenient timing of the layover, bus #11 is notoriously irregular, so your best bet is to simply take a **taxi** from Kiryat Gat to Beit Guvrin. A taxi stand is located right next to the station and the trip costs NIS70, though you'll probably have to bargain the driver down from NIS100.

Unfortunately, the return journey is a bit trickier, as bus #376 only returns from Beit Guvrin to Kiryat Gat at 7:37am. Instead, take **bus #446** (Ⓢ NIS8.80. 🕓 25min., every hr.) to **Malak'hi Junction** and transfer to **bus #301** (Ⓢ NIS24.50. 🕓 80min., every 30min.) to New Central Bus Station.

getting around

Since Beit Guvrin is composed of only the kibbutz and national park, it is largely navigable by foot. However, the park consists of large exposed sections that are much more comfortably crossed in an air-conditioned car. Furthermore, given the difficulty and cost of getting there, a rental car might just be the best option for an exploration of Beit Guvrin. This would also, of course, let you do Beit Guvrin in one day rather than two since you don't need to work around the bus schedules. Road trip anyone?

herzliya ☎09

Named after Theodor Herzl, the father of Zionism, Herzliya goes some way toward fulfilling its namesake's idyllic dream—that is, if you think LA and Utopia have a lot in common. A definite contender for the coveted title of Israel's most beautiful beaches, this high-tech industry hub boasts the country's largest film studio and the spacious, whitewashed mansions of some of her richest residents. That said, as you go further inland, the city becomes more a matter of urban grunge than pastoral paradise. You're better off heading north along the secluded coast to visit such curios as a cliff-borne mosque and a hermit's house o' trash. Only a 40min. bus ride from Tel Aviv's center, Herzliya is an ideal daytrip—especially because the dearth of affordable accommodations prevents you from staying much longer anyway.

ORIENTATION

Herzliya is divided into two major sections: **Herzliya Pituach** running along the coast, and **Herzliya** (the city proper), just inland after a large empty area. The urban grunge of the latter is prevalent on two main streets, **Sokolov Street** and **Ben-Gurion Street,** which intersect at the center of town. Here you'll find all basic amenities. It's equally easy to find your way around the Pituach since almost everything gravitates toward the beach. The hub of this area is the square formed by **Galei Tchelet** and **Ramat Yam,** which branches off southward along the coastline until it reaches the marina. While most of the Pituach is residential, the overwhelming majority of Herzliya's malls, eateries, and shops can be found around the square formed by the highway, **Abba Eban Boulevard, Galgalei Haiplada,** and **Medinat HaYehudim** in the southeast corner of the Pituach.

ACCOMMODATIONS

It's unlikely you'll want to stay more than one night in Herzliya. The beach is the real attraction, and if you decide that you want more time there, the journey from Tel Aviv is so convenient that the 30min. commute is really your best option. Furthermore, spending the night in the playground of the rich and silver-screen-born is about as expensive as you would expect. Herzliya's accommodations are pretty much exclusively waterfront resorts that will cost the backpacking likes of you an arm and a leg (the loss of which would really put a damper on future travel).

HOTEL ESHEL HOTEL $$$$

3 Ramat Yam St. ☎09 956 8208; www.eshelhotel.com

One block from the waterfront, Hotel Eshel provides a series of double rooms with patios and balconies overlooking the Mediterranean. While the sun-burnished exterior and rugged front lawn may have seen better days, Eshel will provide a clean and comfortable stay for the most reasonable price in Herzliya. However, the management's choice to put chocolate waffles under "Sweat Snacks" on the room-service menu may be a little daunting to some.

⇞ Just at the northern end of Ramat Yam, as it comes out of the Pituach's central square. i A/C, TV, and ensuite bathroom. Breakfast included. Ⓢ Doubles US$125.

SIGHTS

Should the beach leave you too chilled out and sun-kissed—if that's possible—Herzliya offers distractions for those who simply can't sit still. And lucky for you, O restless ones, much of what the city has to offer is within walking distance of the coast (or on it). The **northern tip** of the Pituach is home to the ruins of ancient Apollonia, today a national park, and, more curiously, an eccentric hermit who has carved a functional home into the side of the cliff. The **city center** has little to offer except a small collection of museums and the largest TV studio in Israel. The starry-eyed are more than welcome to stroll through it, but, unless you're a nut for Israeli soap operas, there's little to do—no tour or information is available. For the liveliest area of Herzliya, check out the southeastern corner of the Pituach where restaurants, bars, and the city's young and beautiful congregate.

HERMIT'S HOUSE ARCHITECTURE

While most people are content to just build sandcastles, local recluse Nissim Kakhalon aspired to actually live in one. Kakhalon has been carving his domicile out of the sandstone cliffs overlooking the Mediterranean for over 30 years in contempt of both local authorities and (we can only assume) his own personal safety. While the barbed wire skirting the edges of his compound may seem unwelcoming, Kakhalon has been known to give impromptu tours of his handmade haven, constructed almost entirely from garbage, with walls made entirely out of empty Maccabee bottles and a loveseat constructed from mirror fragments. In the manner you might expect of an eccentric hermit, Kakhalon does intermittently disappear and might therefore not be nearby to offer a tour, but even the exterior provides quite a sight.

⇞ Up Yigael Yadin. The parking lot is on the left after the Sidna Ali Mosque, and the house is just downhill at the cliff edge. Bus #29 stops nearby.

SIDNA ALI MOSQUE MOSQUE

Yigael Yadin ☎052 332 8765

Perched on a cliff over the glassy Mediterranean, Sidna Ali is about as picturesque a 700-year-old mosque as you could hope to find. Built on the site of a holy man's grave, the mosque is still used for daily prayer and is inhabited by a friendly couple who are often happy to have a chat.

⇞ Near the bottom of Yigael Yadin. Bus #29 stops nearby. i Women must wear head coverings; no shorts permitted. ⏰ Open daily. Preferred if tourists come before sunset.

APOLLONIA NATIONAL PARK NATIONAL PARK

Just north of the mosque are the ruins of Apollonia, an excavated Crusader fortress. Over 800 years old, it has a moat, old munitions, a lookout point, and everything else you would conceivably need to defend yourself from an invading onslaught—you know, just in case. An even older Roman villa also stands on the site. The park itself is not large and centers mostly on the ruins, but it does offer stunning views of the sea and Mediterranean coast—a common theme in Herzliya.

✈ *At the end of Yigael Yadin. Bus #29 stops a 3min. walk away.* Ⓢ *NIS21, students NIS18.* Ⓞ *Open daily 8am-4pm.*

HERZLIYA MUSEUM OF CONTEMPORARY ART   MUSEUM
4 HaBanim St.   ☎09 955 1011; www.herzliyamuseum.co.il

Only a handful of sculptures smattered across the lawn hint that the building behind is a burgeoning art space, much of which is actually underground. The museum has no permanent collection, but rotating temporary exhibits showcase promising young Israeli and international artists, many of whom are barely out of school. The museum is often the first step toward future artistic stardom. It shuts down several times a year in order to set up new exhibitions, so make sure to call or check the website before going.

Ⓢ *NIS10.* Ⓞ *Open M 10am-2pm, Tu 4-8pm, W 10am-2pm, Th 4-8pm, F-Sa 10am-2pm.*

BEACHES

Herzliya lays claim to a stretch of prime Israeli coastline, with pristine sand, clear water, and enough space to ensure that it doesn't get too crowded. The wealthy neighborhood overlooking the water means that hoity-toits make sure the beaches are regularly cleaned—a real plus. Watch out for black flags: they signify unsafe waters, not a reunion tour.

🏖 HASHARON BEACH

The most centrally located beach, HaSharon splits off from Shalit Sq., thereby maintaining a vital artery to various eateries and, of course, ice cream booths. It's possibly the most crowded of the beaches here, but walk 5min. up the coast and you should be able to find a more secluded spot, with sandstone cliffs jutting out over the shore and some valuable shade. The waters stay relatively calm, but some offshore waves are no-brainers for surfers. Be careful though: the northern part of the beach isn't manned by lifeguards.

✈ *Leads off of Shalit Sq. where Bus #29 stops.*

ACCADIA BEACH

Just south of the marina, Accadia swaps the sleepy-town backdrop of HaSharon for one of towering hotel complexes—whether Accadia is Arcadian is, basically, pretty disputable. Offshore breaks keep the water calm here, meaning it's perfect for swimming. There's a wheelchair-accessible beach just south of it.

✈ *At the southern end of the coast, by the marina.*

APPOLOUN BEACH

It's the most secluded of the beaches for a reason—Appoloun has rough waters, and plenty of rocks lurking just under the surface ensure that it is perennially black-flagged. Furthermore, the cliffs in this area have been known to be susceptible to minor rockfalls. Nevertheless, its location at the foot of the mosque makes it one of the nicest-looking beaches, so—provided you don't die while there—it's a great place to get away and do a little brooding.

✈ *At the northern end of the Herzliya coast. Bus #29 stops 5min. away.*

FOOD

While the eating options in Herzliya proper are somewhat underwhelming, Herzliya Pituach has a good number in the industrial area in its southeastern corner, with many restaurants crowded along **Maskit Street.** While the malls here provide an array of Subways, you'll also find the obligatory seafood restaurants, the original patisserie for Tel Aviv's **Mazzarine,** and a surprising number of discount Chinese joints. One can only assume they're for the gentiles on the Sabbath—

the Jews' payback for Chinese food on Christmas, if you will. For finer dining, the upscale hotels along the beach provide suitably swanky fare for those with particularly high-angled noses.

OCEAN   SEAFOOD $$$
30 Maskit St.   ☎09 766 7674; www.rest.co.il/ocean

In Israel, any hope of keeping kosher seems to disappear as soon as the ocean comes into view. Touting the house specialty as the largest seafood dinner in Israel, which includes crustaceans that are literally measured by the kg (four to be exact; NIS799), Ocean is certainly keeping things secular. Watch your table manners as the huge Elizabethan-era portrait watches you work your way through the three-course meal (NIS89).

On Maskit St., just south of the intersection with Yad HaRutsim. Ⓢ *Grilled scallops and shrimp NIS108. Mullet NIS82.* Ⓞ *Open daily noon-midnight.*

PASTA FRESCA   ITALIAN $$$
27 Maskit St.   ☎09 957 0435

Making pasta from scratch in the basement kitchen every morning, the guys at Pasta Fresca make sure that it stays true to its name. While the place may seem bare, decorated with little more than the odd wine bottle, the smells wafting from the kitchen are more than enough to make you want to stay for a pie.

Technically on Sapir St, just by the intersection with Maskit St. Ⓢ *Pizza Bianca NIS35. Bolognese NIS46.* Ⓞ *Open daily 10am-10pm.*

ESSENTIALS
practicalities

- **ATM: Bank Leumi.** (2 Ben-Gurion St. *On corner of Sokolov and Ben-Gurion.* Ⓞ Open Su 8:30am-2pm, M 8:30am-1pm and 4-6:15pm, Tu-W 8:30am-2pm, Th 8:30am-1pm and 4-6:15pm.)

- **POST OFFICE:** 12 Sokolov St. *Take bus 29 to city center. Post office is about 300m west of intersection of Ben-Gurion and Sokolov.* Ⓞ Open Su 8am-6pm, M-Tu 8am-12:30pm and 3:30-6pm, W 8am-1:30pm, Th 8am-6pm, F 8am-noon.

emergency

- **EMERGENCY NUMBERS: Police:** ☎100. **Ambulance:** ☎101. **Fire Brigade:** ☎102.

- **POLICE:** 1 Shefayim ☎09 970 4444 *On the opposite side of motorway from industrial area. Cross the footbridge, make a right, and the station will be in front of you.*

- **LATE-NIGHT PHARMACY: Super-Pharm.** (21 Sokolov St. *About 200m west of intersection of Ben-Gurion and Sokolov St.* Ⓞ Open Su-Th 7:30am-11:30pm, F 7:30am-4pm, Sa sunset-11:30pm.)

getting there
BY BUS

Egged runs several regular services from the Tel Aviv Central Bus Station to Herzliya. While you can take **bus #531** (1½ hr.) or **bus #525** (1hr.), **bus #501** (Ⓢ NIS9.80. Ⓞ 30min., every 15min.) is the fastest way to get to Herzliya—though traffic may lengthen the trip by as much as 15min. To reach Herzliya Pituach, get off at the crossroads as soon as the bus leaves the motorway; to reach the city center, remain on the bus and it will take you directly to the intersection of Sokolov St. and Ben-Gurion St. Unlike other Eggeds, you do not pay for your ride at the ticket booth but instead buy your ticket on the bus.

getting around

BY FOOT

Each of Herzliya's two distinct neighborhoods is easily navigable by foot. While all areas of interest in the city center are conveniently located around the intersection of Sokolov St. and Ben-Gurion St., traversing the Pituach from the national park at the top to the marina in the south takes about 45min.

BY BUS

Crossing from the Pituach to the city center and back should be done by bus. By far the best and most regular route is **bus #29** (NIS6). Starting in the city center, it crosses to the top of the Pituach (near the national park) and then works down the coast until it reaches the southern industrial area, where it then backtracks to the city center.

rehovot   ☎08

If religion has found a home in Jerusalem, her mortal enemy—science—has conquered Rehovot. The brainchild of Israel's first chemist president, Chaim Weizmann, the eponymous **Weizmann Institute of Science** was erected when Rehovot was little more than a few rocks and a lot of sand. Strolling through the lawns of the Institute today, it's clear that his vision has come to fruition, to the delight of eggheads the country over. A huge complex of laboratories interrupted by the occasional tourist sight, Weizmann Institute is packed with the likes of particle accelerators, solar labs, and buildings that look like rocket ships primed for blast off. Naturally, these developments have pulled along the rest of the city. While Rehovot is certainly bustling with locals going about their daily shopping, there is still a dearth of much to see or do here, and, like many of the small towns that brush the outskirts of Tel Aviv, there are no places to stay, budget or otherwise. Poke around the Institute and the nearby kibbutz, snag a drink at a bar, then head back to Tel Aviv or to your next destination in time to rent a room.

ORIENTATION

Like practically every other city in central Israel whose name begins with an R, Rehovot is centered on a **Herzl Street** (incidentally, the same Herzl St. that connects Ramla and Rishon le-Tziyon). Herzl St. runs north to south through the town, becoming progressively grimier along the way. Nevertheless, everything of interest is on it, including the Weizmann Institute toward the northern end. The **Central Bus Station** is on Bilu St., which branches off Herzl St. in the south.

working for the weekend

Kids going to school, crazy ladies mumbling to themselves...and armed soldiers? Don't be surprised if your bus to Tel Aviv is packed with soldiers on their way home from the base for the weekend, or traveling back for the week. On Sundays in particular you may find yourself surrounded by uniforms, as soldiers try to get back to base before evening.

SIGHTS

Rehovot's sights invariably revolve around the Weizmann Institute, which should be enough to make nerds go bug-eyed behind their glasses. Other than that, Rehovot has few sights.

[✓] WEIZMANN INSTITUTE OF SCIENCE — SCIENTIFIC COMPLEX

Herzl St. — ☎08 934 4499; www.weizmann.ac.il

The jewel of Israel's scientific community, the Weizmann Institute was basically conjured from thin air when, in 1934, Chaim Weizmann established a chemistry lab in the middle of nowhere. Three quarters of a century later, a vast complex sprawls over the area, covering all the natural sciences in a futuristic melange of geometric sculptures, Japanese gardens, and Bauhaus. The Institute is worth at least a stroll through the boulevards of glass buildings and other structures that more resemble space stations than anything earthly. At time of writing, an ultra-modern visitors center was under construction that will house films, interactive exhibits, and information about all research conducted there. The **Clore Garden of Science** sits toward the east of the campus and provides games and hands-on displays to explain some of the more basic science.

*# At the northern end of Herzl St., just by the intersection with Yavne St. **i** All tours of the grounds must be arranged in advance, so make sure to call ahead.*

WEIZMANN HOUSE — MUSEUM

Weizmann Institute

Located on the very eastern edge of the Weizmann Institute, at Rehovot's highest point, lies the former house of the big man on campus, Chaim Weizmann himself. Unlike Tel Aviv's dilapidated Bauhaus, the house has been preserved as a specimen of modernist architecture par excellence, courtesy of famed architect Erich Mendelsohn. Spiral staircases, an opulent lounge, and a study housing thousands of books have all been meticulously conserved. Following a short video on the life and times of Dubya, a tour of the premises is given by curators who have every square inch of the house memorized.

*# At the eastern end of the Institute, at the end of HaNasi HaRishon St. **i** Tours must be booked in advance through the visitors center. $ NIS25. ⏰ Open Su-Th 8am-4pm.*

AYALON INSTITUTE — KIBBUTZ

Chaim Holtsman — ☎08 930 0585; ayalon@shimur.org.il

Sure, it may look like your typical sleepy kibbutz from the outside, but Ayalon was a bastion of Zionist resistance, hiding a large, subterranean munitions factory that supplied over two million bullets to the Haganah. Today, 1hr. tours of the underground facility are available by prior arrangement.

 # From the Weizmann Institute, turn right and walk down Herzl St. for 500m. Take a right onto HaMada St. and then a left onto Chaim Holtsman. $ NIS20. ⏰ Open Su-Th 8:30am-4pm, F 8:30am-2pm, Sa 9am-2pm.

FOOD

Like any other town in the country, Rehovot thrives off its cheap falafel scene. Moving up Herzl St. toward the Weizmann Institute, you'll find a growth of nicer, often quirky, stands and cafes.

CAFE LOOL — CAFE $$

202 Herzl St. — ☎077 663 0128

Though the name sounds uncannily similar to that place in Ghostbusters, the staff at Cafe Lool have no idea where the name came from. Drool perhaps? A particularly hearty laugh-out-loud? In any case, the quirk continues with a doorway covered in sketches of Bob Marley, Jimi Hendrix, and Ella Fitzgerald and a bar covered in the likes of Bob Dylan and the Fab Four—again for reasons seemingly unbeknownst to all. And perhaps most inexplicably, Yemeni food is the restaurant's specialty.

On the corner with Chaim Weizmann. $ Corn NIS23. ⏰ Open Su-Th 6:30am-late, F 6:30am-sunset.

techin' it to the next level

Israel has been at the forefront of technological development since its founding. We're not just talking about geeky gurus: Israel boasts the world's highest percentage of home computers per capita. However, those gurus don't do too badly for themselves either–here are a few things invented in a country that contains only 0.1% of the world's population.

- **VOICEMAIL.** An Israeli company called Comverse helped develop better voicemail systems, but that doesn't mean you can blame Israel for those regrettable late-night messages you left on your ex's phone.
- **AOL INSTANT MESSENGER.** Yeah, thought American Online Messenger must have been created in America? Think again. Four Israelis developed the technology, guaranteeing that middle-school drama could continue even after 3pm weekdays. OMG.
- **ANTI-VIRUS SOFTWARE.** While not the inventors, Israelis have taken great strides toward easing your cyber pop-up woes. Now we're just waiting on the cure for that other pesky virus, the common cold. Come on, Israel!
- **USB FLASH DRIVE.** Thanks to the Israelis' development of the memory stick, you can carry your work with you anywhere! Okay, maybe that's not a good thing.

ISHIMAKI SUSHI $$

191 Herzl St. ☎08 936 2022; www.rol.co.il/sites/ishimaki

Another town, another sushi joint. With a mascot intended to be a bright pink, scowling Asian face (but that instead looks sunburned and constipated), this small bar and patio is currently the flagship and only branch of a chain aiming to expand all over the country. Come for a raw fish fix.

2 blocks down from the Institute on the right. ℹ Free delivery. $ Maki from NIS15. Chicken tempura NIS39. ⏰ Open Su-Th noon-11pm, F 11am-3pm, Sa sunset-midnight.

MILSHTEIN CAFE $$

213 Herzl St. ☎077 514 1546

Named after one of Rehovot's founders, Milshtein is a chill cafe down by the Weizmann Institute. Lounge in the white furniture on its AstroTurf lawn and happily graze on one of their toothsome breakfasts.

Almost directly opposite the Weizmann Institute. $ Pizza from NIS35. Israeli breakfast from NIS41. ⏰ Open daily 7am-1am.

NIGHTLIFE

Only a stone's throw away from Tel Aviv, Rehovot doesn't really have a need for nightlife, but it seems even nerds want to get down occasionally (and a large soldier population doesn't hurt). Conveniently, Rehovot's finest four bars are on a single block—in fact, they're basically in the same building—so the scarce nightlife actually gets quite lively. While there are no clubs, the four bars are open nightly and each maintains a different character and has a different special night.

203 Herzl St. ☎054 551 4655; www.bar203.com

The smallest of the four bars, 203 is often the most packed—it's a place made for soldiers and those just out of their teens. A second floor opens on weekends to let the masses spill out. Also, check out **La Morse,** the bar next door, which is a favorite for the expat American scientist crowd. Their Woodstock night every Wednesday provides some of the most prime people-watching in all of Israel.

⚑ *Along Herzl St., just before the Weizmann Institute.* ***i*** *Special nights Tu. Happy hour buy 1 beer, get 1 free.* Ⓢ *Beer from NIS22. Chasers from NIS15.* ☒ *Open 8pm-late. Happy hour 8-10pm.*

ESSENTIALS

practicalities

- **ATM: Bank HaPoalim.** (179 Herzl St. ☒ Open Su 8:30am-1:15pm, M 8:30am-1pm and 4-6:15pm, Tu-W 8:30am-1:15pm, Th 8:30am-1pm and 4-6:15pm.)

emergency

- **POLICE:** 206 Herzl St. ☎08 937 1500.

- **LATE-NIGHT PHARMACY: Super-Pharm.** (182 Herzl St. ☒ Open Su-Th 8:30am-11-pm, F 8am-sunset, Sa sunset-11pm.)

- **HOSPITAL: Ichilov Hospital** in Tel Aviv is the closest facility. (6 Weizmann St. ☎03 697 4444; www.tasmc.org.il.)

getting there

Bus #301 (Ⓢ NIS13.50. ☒ 30min., every 15-25min.) runs a regular service to Rehovot's Central Bus Station. The bus stops at the Weizmann Institute before it reaches its final destination, so you can get off when you see the big white gates and save yourself a 20min. walk uphill. **Bus #201** (Ⓢ NIS13.50. ☒ 80min., every 15min.) will take you directly back to Tel Aviv.

getting around

Small and easily navigable, you can easily find your way to everything you could ever want to see in Rehovot on foot. If you're not in the mood for a 30min. schlep, the same bus that took you from Tel Aviv goes periodically by the Weizmann Institute.

ashkelon ☎07

Everyone wants a piece of Ashkelon. For the last 3000 years, between Israelites trying to steal it from the Philistines and Alexander the Great taking a piece out of Persia, Ashkelon has been at the top of many a civilization's territorial wish list. Even just a few years ago, the city was the target of a series of rocket attacks from nearby Gaza. The area is generally safe now, but it still leaves you wondering what all the fuss is about. You may be in for a small surprise—while strategic military location was a great attraction for the Ottoman Empire, that's less of a concern nowadays for all but the most megalomaniacal tourists. Unless you're here to spearhead the next Crusade, you'll find Ashkelon more desirable for its extensive archaeological sites, azure beaches, and serene national park, all of which provide a great respite from the hubbub of Tel Aviv. Now, if only those expensive accommodations didn't prohibit more than a couple days' stay...

ORIENTATION

The more visitor-friendly parts of Ashkelon can be divided into three adjacent areas. By the coast is **Afridar,** which is centered on Georgy Elyezer Sq. with its iconic clock tower. Ashkelon's beaches, hotels, and marina sprawl toward the waterfront, and the

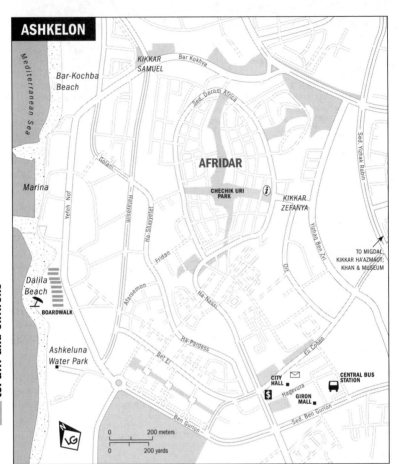

ASHKELON

Mediterranean Sea

Bar-Kochba Beach

KIKKAR SAMUEL

Bar Kokhva

Sed. Derom Africa

Sed. Yizhak Rabin

AFRIDAR

Marina

Golani

Yefeh Nof

Ha-avasim

Ha-Shayyetet

CHECHIK URI PARK

ⓘ

KIKKAR ZEFANYA

Yitzhag Ben Zvi

Fridan

Dalila Beach

Afasemon

Ha-Nassi

Ori

TO MIGDAL; KIKKAR HA'AZMAUT; KHAN & MUSEUM

BOARDWALK

Ashkeluna Water Park

Ha-Pardess

Bel El

Eli Cohan

CITY HALL

$

Hagevura

GIRON MALL

CENTRAL BUS STATION

Ben Gurion

Sed. Ben Gurion

0   200 meters

0   200 yards

bus station is located at the southern end, bordering the national park. A vast empty area sits to its east, the future site of a planned neighborhood, which is separated from **Neve HaHadarim** by Yizhak Rabin Blvd., a motorway running through the middle of the city. Finally, toward the city's eastern end are the **Artist's Quarter** and **Migdal**, where, after the high-rises and apartment blocks of the modern city, you'll find a labyrinth of bungalows, alleyways, and a pedestrianized area all centered on **Herzl. Eli Cohen Street** runs diagonally across the entire city, from the north end of Herzl toward the national park in the southwest corner.

ACCOMMODATIONS

There are two reasons why you probably won't spend more than a day in Ashkelon: there isn't much to see and the accommodations will run your pockets dry. Ashkelon is a resort town, and most of the places to stay are expensive waterfront hotels. While Golden Tower Hotel and Hotel Ganei Shimshom are the cheapest in town, your best bet for a frugal stay is camping in the **national park.** Unfortunately, though, that's only available on Fridays.

HOTEL GOLDEN TOWER	HOTEL $$$
28 Arakefet	☎08 673 4124; www.goldentower.co.il

While the tower in question is more faded orange than resplendent gold, Hotel Golden Tower offers the cheapest beds in Ashkelon. Spacious rooms equipped with air-conditioning, TVs, and ensuite bathrooms are centered around a courtyard and inside the eponymous tower. Weekends are usually booked, so make sure to reserve in advance.

⚐ *Arakefet leads off of Drom Afrika Blvd., the circular road enclosing Afridar on the western side. Walk down the road, past the bend, and it's on the right.* ⓘ *Breakfast included. Free Wi-Fi in the lobby.* ⓢ *Singles NIS280-390.*

HOTEL GANEI SHIMSHON	HOTEL $$$
38 HaTamar St.	☎050 547 5806; ganei_shimshom@walia.com

Nestled in the middle of Afridar, Shimshom provides a series of rooms and bungalows spattered along the street, many around a quiet garden perfect for a bit of zen meditation. The adjacent park, which gently slopes toward the ocean, seems to have been made for lazy Sundays spent on picnic blankets.

⚐ *Also leads off of Drom Afrkia Blvd., but into the island itself (i.e. a right if approaching from the south, clockwise).* ⓘ *Free Wi-Fi. Ensuite bathrooms.* ⓢ *High-season singles from NIS300. Low-season singles from NIS250.* ⏰ *Breakfast served 7:30-9am.*

SIGHTS

Ashkelon does it old school. Really old school. Forget what you learned about the three Rs; here they're rocks, ruins, and Romans. If fumbling around archaeological sites and contemplating the tragedy of human transience in the great theater of history doesn't appeal to you, then leave Ashkelon. You should probably just go chill on the beach.

⛰ **ASHKELON NATIONAL PARK**	PARK
	☎08 673 6444; www.parks.org.il

These aren't just old rocks, these are ancient rocks! Come for the world's oldest arch and stay for the remnants of a Roman basilica and dog cemetery, plus a church restored by Crusaders—that's three sites from three different millennia, all for the price of one. The park itself is quite a sight, with stunning Mediterranean vistas and walking paths along the cliffs. You almost don't notice that the world's largest desalination plant is a mere 2km down the coast. A large camping area near a secluded, pristine beach is open on Fridays and Jewish holidays.

⚐ *South of the city. Bus #6 goes there directly.* ⓢ *NIS27, students NIS22. Camping NIS40 per person.* ⏰ *Park open daily 8am-10pm. Beach open daily 8am-5:15pm.*

ASHKELON KHAN MUSEUM MUSEUM

Independence Sq. ☎08 672 7002

If you want the history without the exercise, the Ashkelon Khan Museum is the way to go. Unfortunately, the museum itself consists of only a single room with an unexpected (and unrelated) art gallery in the atrium. Highlights include the replica of a Canaanite silver cow totem that made headlines when it was discovered only 20 years ago. But the best attraction may be the building itself, a 700-year-old construction complete with bell spire and atrium.

 # At the top of Herzl St. Bus #6 stops 1 block away. $ Free. ⏰ Open Su-Th 9am-8pm, F 9am-noon, Sa 10am-1pm.

THE AFRIDAR CENTER MUSEUM

3 HaNassi St ☎08 673 4019

Come see the ancient dead guys who owned all those ancient dead dogs buried in the national park. Unlike their canine counterparts, the owners rest in two massive sarcophagi carved with detailed and incredibly well-preserved reliefs. These are undoubtedly the centerpiece of this courtyard museum.

 # Enter the shaded walkway of the small green just behind George Eliezer Sq. $ Free. ⏰ Open Su-Th 8:30am-3:30pm, F 8:30am-1:30pm.

MARINA LANDMARK

If you're looking for something closer to the end of this millennium, the marina might be your answer. Lined with yachts, seafood restaurants, and a few bars, it may not be big, but the marina seems to be closest thing Ashkelon gets to hip—or, at least, to "happening."

 # Toward the northern end of the Ashkelon coast, up Yefe Nof, past Delilah Beach.

THE GREAT OUTDOORS

Unless you're really into ancient rocks, you're probably coming to Ashkelon to escape the hubbub of Tel Aviv. Luckily for you, the beaches are quiet, large, and clean, and a great campground in the national park means you can stay in Ashkelon (at least on Fridays) and not break the bank.

DELILAH BEACH

☎08 673 6929

Though Ashkelon has a series of beaches along its coast, Delilah is surely the jewel. Young locals flock here for the small arcade with shops, food stands and bars and, of course, the swimming and tanning. Offshore breakwaters keep the sea calm.

 # Take bus #6 up HaTayassim. Get off before it turns inland and walk 5min. towards coast. ℹ Black flags signify dangerous water. $ Free.

FOOD

Restaurants in Ashkelon are centered largely on the **waterfront** or, out east, on **Herzl Street**—while the former is the domain of pricey seafood restaurants, the latter houses everything from your standard falafel stands to Nizharon, the local go-to for a daily dose of sheep's brain. A selection of chilled and reasonably priced cafes can also be found around **Georgy Elyezer Square.**

RESTAURANT NIZHARON ROMANIAN, JEWISH $$

33 Herzl St.

What do you mean there's Jewish food in Israel? While falafel and shawarma are literally on every corner, gefilte fish, and chopped liver are oddly rare in this country. So don't let the lace curtains fool you: Nizharon has been satisfying local cravings for more traditional fare since 1956. A large grill serves up everything from schnitzel and goose liver to spinal cord, brains, and calves' feet—if it's part of an animal, Nizharon will be glad to give it you. All meals come with a plentiful helping of bread, cabbage, and pickle, and are sure to leave you just as full as your bubbe could ever want you to be.

In the Migdal, just below the corner with Zahal St. $ Goulash NIS45. Gefilte fish NIS18. Chopped liver NIS18. ⏰ Open Su-Th 8am-10pm, Sa 8am-10pm.

LUNA FUSION $$

1 Herzl St. ☎08 672 2220; luna-cafe.co.il

Kosher surf and turf is, unsurprisingly, a lot more turf than surf. As with most fusion restaurants, the trend at Luna seems to be, well, trendy; it's a converted wine cellar with a jet black exterior and saucy, red-lit interior. Steaks are a specialty, so try the pulletsteak for NIS72, or go for the brilliantly named Luna Tuna Salad (NIS54).

At the top of Herzl St. by the Ashkelon Khan Museum. Bus #6 stops 1 block away. $ Business lunch (starter and pasta) NIS54. ⏰ Open Su-Th noon-late, Sa 8:30pm-late. Business lunch noon-5pm.

ESSENTIALS

practicalities

- **TOURIST OFFICE:** The tourist office staff offer a selection of maps, brochures, and tips in stilted English. (2 HaNassi St. ☎08 674 4677 Bus 6 stops right outside on Georgy Elyezer Sq. ⏰ Open Su-Th 8am-1pm and 5-7pm, F 8am-noon.)
- **ATM: Bank Leumi.** (4 HaNassi St. ☎03 514 9400 1 block over from the tourist office. ⏰ Open M 8:30am-1pm and 4-6:15pm, Tu-W 8:30am-2:30pm, Th 8:30am-1pm and 4-6:15pm, F 8:30am-12:30pm.)
- **SWIMMING POOL:** The **Municipal Swimming Pool** is usually segregated by gender due to religious concerns. (Ofer Blvd. ☎08 672 3903 From the Central Bus Station, turn left onto Ben-Gurion Blvd. and take a right onto Bialik. Walk down Bialik for 600m before taking a left onto Sederot Ofer. The pool is 300m down on the right. $ NIS35, students and children NIS30.)
- **POST OFFICE:** 5 Kibbutz Galuyyot Just behind the Central Bus Station. ⏰ Open Su-M 8am-12:30pm and 3:30-6pm, Tu 8am-1pm, W-Th 8am-12:30pm and 3:30-6pm, F 8am-12:30pm.

emergency

- **POLICE:** 80 HaNaim St. ☎08 677 1441.
- **LATE NIGHT PHARMACY: NewPharm.** (Hutzot Mall, 1 Hanahal St. ☎08 672 9961 ⏰ Open Su-Th 8am-10pm, F 8am-3pm, Sa 9-11pm.)
- **HOSPITAL: Hospital Barzilai.** (2 HaHistadrut ☎08 674 5555.)

getting there

BY BUS

Egged runs several regular services to Ashkelon via New Central Station. The Buses #300, 301 and 310 will all take you there, although only the #300 is the most direct and takes just under an hour. ($ NIS20, round-trip NIS35. ⏰ 1hr., leaves every 30min.) The other buses take anywhere between 1½ and 2hr.

getting around

By TAXI

Taxis and taxi stands are common in and around Ashkelon. Driving across the entire city from the waterfront to the eastern end by the Migdal should cost no more than NIS25, even at peak times, so be suspicious if you're asked for anything higher. Keep in mind that rates rise in the evenings and on Shabbat.

Egged runs a comprehensive service throughout the city for NIS4.10 per trip. **Bus #6** is by far the most useful route, running a circuit around the entire city and stopping within a 5min. walk of the best sights, food, and accommodations. Leaving from the Central Bus Station every 30min. on the hour, it runs to the national park before circling around Afridar and continuing toward Herzl St. (just off of the Remez terminal) before returning to the Central Bus Station.

rishon le-tziyon ☎03

Established by the Baron de Rothschild in 1882, Rishon Le-Tziyon literally means "first into Zion," and it was, in fact, the first modern Jewish settlement in the Holy Land. However, the local vibe has become less trailblazing spirit and more classic suburbia as Tel Aviv sprawled closer and closer. This proximity—Tel Aviv is now only 15min. away—is both a blessing (most of the tourist traps are drawn there) and a curse (there's nowhere to stay in the entire town). Rishon Le-Tziyon has a handful of historical sites peppered around a long, family-friendly *midrakhov* replete with ice cream stands and arts and crafts stalls. As it descends the large hill, the town evolves into a belt of industrial grunge, where most of her youth seem to have found asylum. This is particularly true along Moshe Beker St., a small cul-de-sac packed with bars, clubs, and flashy restaurants—including one of the country's most celebrated sushi shops.

ORIENTATION

Once again, **Herzl Street** serves as the city's main thoroughfare, cutting directly through Rishon Le-Tziyon from north to south. The bus station sits by the intersection with Tarmav Street. The *midrakhov*, or promenade, is perpendicular, one block to the south, heading east along **Rothschild Street**. While this is initially only for pedestrians, a road cuts in near the **Old Well** and intersects with Yehuda Leib Pinsker and Ahad Ha'am at the city's highest point. Heading south along Ahad Ha'am will take you along the **Pioneer's Walk,** and walking downhill along Yehuda Leib Pinsker for about a kilometer will take you directly to the foot of **Moshe Beker Street** where it intersects with **Tsvi Frank.** Heading east along Tsvi Frank, meanwhile, takes you right back to Herzl Street.

SIGHTS

Many of the town's best sights pay homage to Rishon Le-Tziyon's heritage as a trailblazer. In fact, it's only the Old Well and other sights along **Pioneer's Way** that remind you of a time when this place was a tad more edgy than its current sleepy self. For those who don't fancy crying over spilled milk (i.e. history), you can get yourself agreeably detached from time and space courtesy of the **Carmel Winery.**

RISHON LE-TZIYON MUSEUM
2 Ahad Ha'am St.

MUSEUM
☎03 968 2435

Back in the days when Aliyah had nothing to do with rhythm and blues, Zionists were making the famous pilgrimage to Israel, and Rishon Le-Tziyon was the first place to be settled. Located at the top of the city, the museum tells the story of the first settlers with a series of pavilions and audio tours (given in appropriately old-timey accents). Should you be traveling with family or boring friends, make sure to embarrass them by dressing up and having your photo taken in your turn-of-the-century pioneer duds.

✤ *At the very end of the midrakhov. Heading up it, turn right onto Ahad Ha'am. The museum is immediately to the right.* ☒ *Open Su 9am-2pm, M 9am-2pm and 4-7pm, Tu-Th 9am-2pm.*

PIONEER'S WAY
HISTORICAL WALK

Rishon Le-Tziyon's got more pioneer stories than you could shake a machete at, and they don't stop with the museum. Leading directly from the Rishon Le-Tziyon Museum, a yellow path takes you on a circuit round several blocks in the *midrakhov* area, highlighting the major sites of the first settlement, including **The Great Synagogue** at the city's highest point and the well where the pioneers first struck the good old blue stuff. The entire route, well-marked with signs in English, takes about 1hr.

CARMEL WINERY
WINERY

25 HaCarmel St.   ☎03 948 8801; www.carmelwines.co.il

Considering all the religious uses for wine (Passover, Communion, fancy-party courage, etc.) it's no surprise that Israel is wine country. The area below Tel Aviv is some of the country's most fruitful land, and Carmel—one of the country's largest vineyards—has its flagship winery just outside Rishon Le-Tziyon. While the facility is habitually closed to the public, it can offer tours upon advance booking; call ahead for details.

✦ *About 1km west along Herzl St. Take any of the many buses heading toward Tel Aviv for a couple of stops past the main station.*

FOOD

Food is the one area where Rishon Le-Tziyon goes above and beyond. A number of restaurants, including one of the country's most famous sushi gigs, are packed into the old industrial area around Moshe Beker St. Unbashedly trendy, the restaurants here follow the trademark New York-style conglomeration of bar/lounge/eatery and tend to be packed with as many well-dressed, cynical-looking young things as there are with ravenous clients. The places here are not cheap by any stretch of the imagination, but treat yourself—or try to convince that beach beauty that you're doing a little better than your dirty backpack implies.

kosher wine

When kosher rules are really followed, there's a lot more to consider than "no pork" and "no mixing meat and dairy." Wine, for example, seems like it would be fine. No animal products whatsoever. Done.

But apparently that's not enough. Since wine can be used by other religions, namely Christianity, it's possible that some wines could be made unclean through use in sacrilegious ceremonies. This unacceptable heresy resulted in the solution of declaring wines kosher only if a Sabbath-observant Jew has overseen the entire process, from grape to grocery. These kosher wines can then be used in Jewish religious ceremonies—as well as by guilt-free Israeli drunkards.

◪ SOHO
SUSHI $$$

15 Moshe Beker   ☎03 965 8395; www.soho-rest.com

Israel's sushi scene is burgeoning, and SOHO's in good enough standing to claim the country's title for best Japanese fare, if not best restaurant altogether, according to a number of proud locals. Decked out with fish tanks, bonsai trees, wall-sized LCD screens, and sultry purple lighting, the restaurant is certainly dressed to impress. Hell, even the bathrooms here are a joy, with urinals filled with ice and transparent stall doors that become opaque when locked. Naturally, the food is no joke, with a rotating menu of innovative ways to take your fish. With a phone ringing off the hook for reservations, SOHO is about as *au courant* as you can find.

✦ *At the foot of Moshe Beker.* Ⓢ *Maki from NIS23. Combos from NIS66.* Ⓩ *Open daily 10am-2am.*

MËAT LOFT
AMERICAN $$$

15 Moshe Beker ☎03 956 3216; www.meatloft.com

The promise of steak and umlauts? Coünt us in. So what if the name sounds like it would suit a slasher flick? Despite the pseudo-Germanic pretension, Mëat Loft is decidedly American in style, with large red chairs, booths, bare brick walls, and a polka dot display behind the bar. Nocturnal carnivores will appreciate the Friday deal of a hulking burger plus side (after 10:30pm; NIS38).

✦ *At the foot of Moshe Beker.* Ⓢ *Steak fillet NIS94.* Ⓩ *Open daily 10am-1am.*

CASA DO BRASIL
BRAZILIAN $$$

12 Moshe Beker ☎03 950 4100; www.casadobrasil.co.il

Okay, so the plastic parakeets, bull heads suited up with fancy hats, and waitresses sporting bright face paint may make the place look a little kooky. The real winner for whimsy, though, is the food, specifically their specialty, the *churrascaria*. At a massive grill by the bar, cooks skewer large hunks of all kinds of meat on a large spike before cavorting around the restaurant, skewer in hand, offering the drooling masses tasty morsels from their big stick. And it's all-you-can-eat. On Tuesdays and Thursdays, a Brazilian dancer joins the melee, shimmying along to some samba.

✦ *Toward the top of Moshe Beker.* Ⓢ *Churrascaria from NIS166.* Ⓩ *Open daily noon-late.*

ESSENTIALS

practicalities

- **ATM: Bank Leumi.** (65 Herzl St. Ⓩ Open Su 8:30am-2pm, M 8:30am-1pm and 4-6:15pm, Tu-W 8:30am-2pm, Th 8:30am-1pm and 4-6:15pm.)

emergency

- **POLICE:** 2 HaGvura HaYehudit, off Jablonsky St.

- **LATE NIGHT PHARMACY: Super-Pharm.** (On Herzl St., by the bus station. Ⓩ Open Su-Th 8am-11pm, F 8am-4pm, Sa sunset-11:30pm.)

- **HOSPITALS: Ichilov Hospital** in Tel Aviv is the closest facility. (6 Weizmann St. ☎03 697 4444; www.tasmc.org.il.)

getting there

Bus #163 runs directly to Rishon Le-Tziyon from Tel Aviv. (Ⓢ NIS9.80. Ⓩ 50min., every 30min.) Most of the buses heading down Herzl St. will be returning to Tel Aviv, including **bus #201.** (Ⓢ NIS9.80. Ⓩ 40min., every 15min.)

getting around

Following in the tradition of its two R-named sister cities before it, Rishon le-Tziyon is best traveled by foot.

NORTHERN MEDITERRANEAN COAST

Tel Aviv tiring you out? It's okay. If you've reached the point where a little chill time is imperative, it's time to take on the country's northern coast. With only one large city and a sprinkling of small towns, the area keeps its proverbial shirt untucked (and its top button undone). Political strife, religious friction, and even balls-to-the-wall partying seem far away when you've got an empty beach in front of you, rolling hills behind, and sunshine all around. Indeed, the main religious influence in the area is **Baha'i,** whose non-confrontational and all-accepting doctrine well sums up the area.

Despite the shared vibe, the towns themselves seem to have little in common—put the bustling *souq* in Akko against the haughty Caesarea port, or compare Haifa's splendid Baha'i Gardens with the encroaching tackiness of Nahariya. But you can always count on two things: the best beaches in the country and awesome archaeological sites. It may be a far cry from the hot debate that characterizes the rest of the country, but, after some time in Israel, it's just the kind of relief you'll need.

greatest hits

- **ZEN AND THE ART OF BOTANY.** Stroll through the endless Baha'i Gardens and learn a little about the Baha'i faith (p. 163).
- **HONEY BADGER DON'T GIVE A S***.** Meet him in person at the Haifa Zoo (p. 165).
- **HON HON HON.** Get your French fix at La Galette Creperie (p. 181).

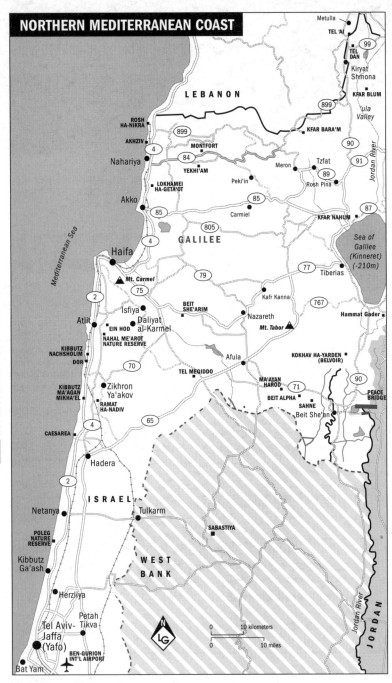

NORTHERN MEDITERRANEAN COAST

Metulla
TEL 'AI
99
TEL DAN
Kiryat Shmona
KFAR BLUM

LEBANON

ROSH HA-NIKRA
899
AKHZIV
4
Nahariya
MONTFORT
84
YEKHI'AM
LOKHAMEI HA-GETA'OT
Akko
85
4
GALILEE
805
Haifa
Mt. Carmel
2
75
79
Atlit
Isfiya
Daliyat al-Karmel
EIN HOD
NAHAL ME'AROT NATURE RESERVE
KIBBUTZ NACHSHOLIM
DOR
70
KIBBUTZ MA'AGAN MIKHA'EL
Zikhron Ya'akov
RAMAT HA-NADIV
4
65
CAESAREA
2
Hadera
ISRAEL
Netanya
POLEG NATURE RESERVE
Kibbutz Ga'ash
Herzliya
Petah Tikva
Tel Aviv-Jaffa (Yafo)
BEN-GURION INT'L AIRPORT
Bat Yam

KFAR BARA'M
90
Tzfat
89
91
Meron
Rosh Pina
Peki'in
85
Carmiel
KFAR NAHUM
87

Sea of Galilee (Kinneret) (-210m)
77
Tiberias

Kafr Kanna
767
BEIT SHE'ARIM
Nazareth
Hammat Gader
Mt. Tabor

Afula
KOKHAV HA-YARDEN (BELVOIR)
90
TEL MEGIDDO
MA'AYAN HAROD
71
PEACE BRIDGE
BEIT ALPHA
SAHNE
Beit She'an

Mediterranean Sea

Jordan River

Hula Valley

WEST BANK
Tulkarm
SABASTIYA

JORDAN

N
LG

0   10 kilometers
0   10 miles

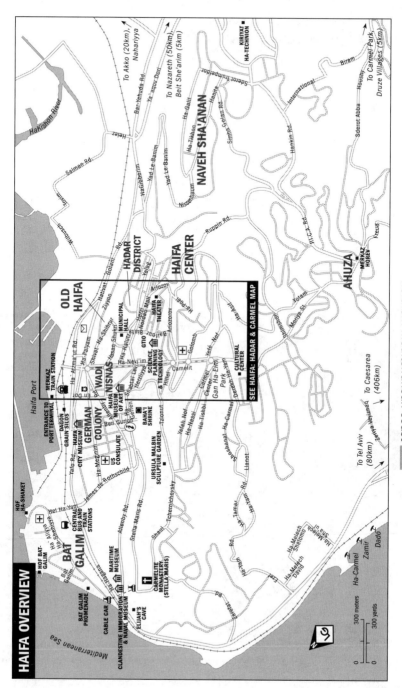

HAIFA OVERVIEW

northern mediterranean coast

SEE HAIFA: HADAR & CARMEL MAP

To Akko (20km), Nahariyya
To Nazareth (50km), Beit She'arim (5km)
To Carmel Park, Druze Villages (5km)

NAVEH SHA'ANAN

HADAR DISTRICT

HAIFA CENTER

OLD HAIFA

AHUZA

WADI NISNAS

GERMAN COLONY

BAT GALIM

MERKAZ HOREV

KIRYAT HA-TECHNION

Mediterranean Sea

Haifa Port

Entrance to Port Terminal

MERKAZ TRAIN STATION

HOF HA-SHAKET

HOF BAT-GALIM

BAT GALIM PROMENADE

CABLE CAR

CLANDESTINE IMMIGRATION & NAVAL MUSEUM

ELIJAH'S CAVE

CARMELITE MONASTERY (STELLA MARIS)

MARITIME MUSEUM

CENTRAL BUS AND TRAIN STATIONS

URSULA MALBIN SCULPTURE GARDEN

US CONSULATE

HAIFA CITY MUSEUM

DAGON GRAIN SILOS

HAIFA MUSEUM OF ART

BAHA'I SHRINE

MUNICIPAL HALL

HAIFA THEATER

SCIENCE PLANNING & TECHNOLOGY

CULTURAL CENTER

To Caesarea (406km)

To Tel Aviv (80km)

To Carmel Park

0 300 meters
0 300 yards

www.letsgo.com 157

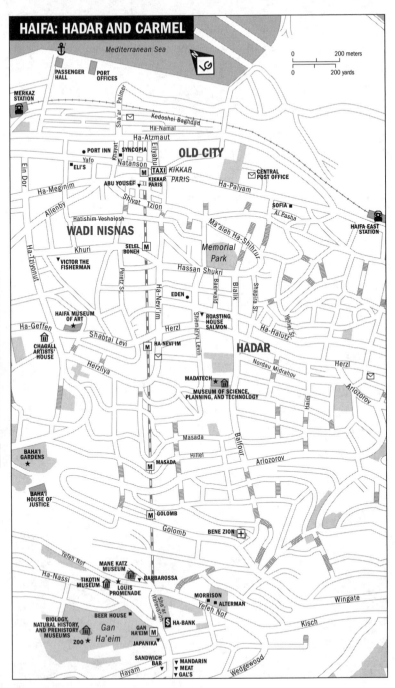

HAIFA: HADAR AND CARMEL

Mediterranean Sea

0   200 meters
0   200 yards

PASSENGER HALL
PORT OFFICES
MERKAZ STATION
Sha'ar Palmer
Kedoshei Baghdad
Ha-Namal
Ha-Atzmaut
PORT INN
SYNCOPIA
Natanson
Yafo
ELI'S
TAXI KIKKAR
KIKKAR PARIS
ABU YOUSEF
Shivat Tzion
Ein Dor
Ha-Meginim
Allenby
Hatishim Veshalosh
WADI NISNAS
Khuri
SELEL BONEH
Ha-Tzyonut
VICTOR THE FISHERMAN
Perez St.
HAIFA MUSEUM OF ART
Ha-Geffen
CHAGALL ARTISTS' HOUSE
Shabtai Levi
Herzliya
Ha-Nevi'im
EDEN
HA-NEVI'IM
Herzl
ROASTING HOUSE SALMON
Shematryu Levin
MADATECH
MUSEUM OF SCIENCE, PLANNING, AND TECHNOLOGY
BAHA'I GARDENS
BAHA'I HOUSE OF JUSTICE
Masada
Hillel
MASADA
GOLOMB
Golomb
BENE ZION
Yefeh Nof
MANE KATZ MUSEUM
Ha-Nassi
TIKOTIN MUSEUM
LOUIS PROMENADE
BARBAROSSA
Sha'ar Havadyon
MORRISON
ALTERMAN
Yefeh Nof
BEER HOUSE
BIOLOGY, NATURAL HISTORY, AND PREHISTORY MUSEUMS
Gan Ha'eim
ZOO
GAN HA'EIM
JAPANIKA
HA-BANK
SANDWICH BAR
MANDARIN
MEAT
GAL'S
Hayam
Wedgewood
Kisch
Wingate
Arlozorov
Herzl
Ha-Halutz
Yehiel St.
Shapira St.
Bialik
Baerwald
Nordau Midrahov
Halm
Balfour
Arlozorov
OLD CITY
CENTRAL POST OFFICE
Ha-Palyam
SOFIA
Al Pasha
HAIFA EAST STATION
Ma'aleh Ha-Shihrur
Memorial Park
Hassan Shukri
HADAR
Eliyahu
Khayat

northern mediterranean coast

If you're looking to recover from Tel Aviv, look no further than these sandy, serene beaches. With the intensity of the West Bank and Jerusalem to the east and the low-key quality to the south in Tel Aviv, the Northern Mediterranean Coast is a welcome break. Try the free beaches in **Haifa** or go a little down the coast to **Caesarea** for less crowded shores.

Next, head over to the artists' colony **Ein Hod,** where new Israeli artists showcase their work in houses and galleries, whose doors are often open to wandering travelers and curious art students. Make a pit stop at **Artbar,** the tourists' default hangout spot. Ask for Danny, one of the nation's best brewers, and try his homemade ales like the **Yo Mama's Ale.**

haifa ☎04

You might come away from Haifa struggling to describe the place, though not because it's so overwhelming that you're at a loss for words. It's just hard to figure out what, exactly, distinguishes Haifa: the parties are thumping, but never as out of control and wild as they are in Tel Aviv; the Baha'i have made it a hub of religious faith, but it hasn't got the same age-old aura as Jerusalem; the locals are polite, but mostly in an austere way; and the few hip boutiques and restaurants are well spread out in this swarm of non-descript urban sprawl over Mt. Carmel. The bottom line is that Israel's third largest city seems to be distinguished by its indistinguishability.

But the city's hardly a drag. The optimist could get a lot out of its straightforward nature; many locals refer to it as "the city that works," and this is undoubtedly true. The public transportation (including the country's only metro) adheres to its schedules, the streets are invariably clean, and the sights—while rarely irrepressibly awesome—are worth seeing. Even the inveterate pessimist has got to admit there are at least a few diamonds in this rough, including the spectacular Baha'i Gardens.

And therein lies the rub. Haifa will not disappoint, but it doesn't promise to bowl you over either. The city doesn't ooze character; you need to go looking for it. But the effort pays off more often than not for those who take the plunge.

ORIENTATION

Haifa looks nothing like it does on maps. This is largely due to the fact it sits on a large hill, **Mount Carmel,** and is surrounded by the ocean on three sides. On the peak is the appropriately titled **Carmel Center,** which revolves around **HaNassi Street,** home to many of the city's trendiest bars and restaurants before running farther west to the Baha'i Gardens. One block downhill, **Yefe Nof Street** runs parallel to this western section, sporting some of the best views of the city—as far as Lebanon on a clear day—from the **Louis Promenade.**

Below Carmel, things get a little more complicated, as the roads from it zigzag down into the **Hadar district.** While a sizable Russian and Eastern European community add a cool ethnic vibe to parts of the area, it's mostly grime and urban banality with a few lackluster sights. **HaNevi'im Street** and **Balfour Street** (which turns into Bialik St.) are the main downhill roads, while **Herzl Street,** cutting across the hill, is the site of most shops and cafes.

HaNevi'im ends on Solel Boneh Square, to the west of which is the Arab neighborhood of **Wadi Nisnas.** Meanwhile, the downtown area is directly south, sprawling out of **Paris Square** with **Haifa Port** toward the sea and the major thoroughfare

haifa

HaAtzma'ut Road running parallel to the waterfront just inland. Moving west along the coast from downtown will take you to the **German Colony,** a collection of posh cafes and restaurants almost exclusively centered on Ben-Gurion Blvd. with great views of the Baha'i shrine just above. Continuing further east along the coast, HaAzama'ut Rd. turns into **Haganah Road,** following the shore through the **Stella Maris** district with its museums and Elijah's Cave. Continuing to follow Haganah Rd. all the way to the southern end of the peninsula will bring you to the city's biggest beaches and Haifa's main bus station, **Hof HaCarmel.**

baha'ifa

Israel may seem to be all about sectarian conflict, but the Baha'i faith, whose world headquarters are in Haifa, is all about unity. Founded in 19th-century Persia, the religion focuses on acceptance: after all, it considers Abraham, Moses, Jesus, and Muhammad—as well as Zoroaster, Krishna, the Buddha, and their founder, Bahá'u'lláh—as manifestations of one God. The two big names to know are Bahá'u'lláh and Báb, the merchant who foretold the coming of this age of acceptance and tranquility. Israel, uh, may still be waiting on that last one.

ACCOMMODATIONS

Haifa has a good selection of cheap and cheerful accommodations, mostly located in the north and concentrated around downtown and the German Colony. The more expensive hotels keep closer to the sweeping panoramas of the southern Carmel area. While a good number of the budget stays in town do have religious ownership, most are very welcoming. Although there were surprisingly few Baha'i pilgrims at time of writing, it's smart to book your room in advance; the number of pilgrims can drastically increase.

PORT INN HOSTEL $$

34 Jaffa Rd. ☎04 852 4401; www.portinn.co.il

Port Inn is the default choice for the Haifa-bound backpacker, with good reason: it has clean and spacious rooms, ensuite bathrooms, air-conditioning, and prime real estate in the heart of the downtown. Despite the potentially noisy location, the area manages to avoid the city bustle, with a particularly serene shade-swathed garden patio where the odd cat meanders past. The staff are some of the friendliest you'll find, whether they're giving you a tour of the premises or sharing their near-encyclopedic knowledge of the town, eagerly pointing you in the direction of anything from a good bar to the nearest laundromat.

➡ Walk east along Jaffa Rd. Port Inn is on the left, 1 block after the intersection with ha'Bankim. $ Dorms NIS90, with breakfast NIS130. Singles NIS285, with bath NIS320; doubles NIS360/410. Wi-Fi NIS5 per hr., NIS10 per 3hr. Computer use 1st 15min. free, then NIS10 per 30min., NIS15 per hr., NIS30 per 3hr. ⏰ Check-in Su-Th 12:30pm-11pm, F 12:30pm-midnight, Sa 12:30pm-11pm. Check-out 11am.

HADDAD GUEST HOUSE HOSTEL $$$

26 Ben-Gurion Blvd. ☎077 201 0618; www.haddadguesthouse.com

Haddad Guest House is a family business, with all the warmth that "family" implies. It might be barely a stone's throw away from the foot of the Baha'i Gardens—and even has a Baha'i Gift Shop—but all religions are welcome, as the international clientele proves. It appears that spotless rooms, a prime location,

and blasting air-conditioning are a plus no matter whom you worship.

Along Ben-Gurion, about 2 blocks from the top. i Free Wi-Fi. Ensuite bathrooms. Non-smoking. $ Singles from NIS320; doubles from NIS380. Triples available. Discounts for stays longer than a week.

DARNA GUEST HOUSE HOSTEL $$

82 Jaffa Rd. ☎077 201 0618; www.haddadguesthouse.com

The new kid on the Haifa hostel block, Darna Guest House—located on a quiet edge of downtown—is actually owned by the Haddad Guest House and has inherited the experience and know-how of its well-established southern cousin. The immediate area might be a little dingy, but the spanking-new interior of Darna is anything but; especially spacious rooms and a balcony lounge overlook the large open-air courtyard that serves as the hostel's centerpiece.

At the western end of Jaffa Rd., by the intersection with Meir Rutberg i A/C. Free Wi-Fi. Ensuite bathrooms. Breakfast NIS25. $ Dorms NIS120; singles from NIS320; doubles from NIS380. Discounts for stays longer than a week.

BETHEL INN HOSTEL $$

40 HaGefen St. ☎077 450 6350

Another newcomer, Bethel Inn was a hostel long ago that has only recently been born again as a Christian inn—although all religions are welcome. The hostel roosts on a hill at the top of the German Colony, where a well-tended garden slopes down to the kitchen and public areas below. Rooms are usually reserved for larger groups, so make sure to call in advance.

From the top of Ben-Gurion Blvd., make a right and continue for 2 blocks. The hostel is on the right. i Fans in rooms. Kitchen access. No drinking or smoking allowed. $ Dorms NIS75. Cash or check only.

EDEN HOTEL HOSTEL $$

8 Shmaryahu Levin St. ☎04 866 4816

The only budget accommodation you'll find heading south up Mt. Carmel, Eden Hotel sits amid the midtown hubbub of Hadar. The lobby may be adorned with the odd picture of the owner surrounded by bikini-clad women, but the remainder of the hotel is rather more conservative, with somewhat small but certainly functional rooms.

On the corner with HeHaluz St. i All but the cheapest rooms have A/C. Free Wi-Fi and computer access. $ Singles from NIS150; doubles from NIS250; triples from NIS525.

SAINT CHARLES GUEST HOUSE HOSTEL $$

105 Jaffa Rd. ☎04 855 3705

Labeled as the German Hostel on some signs, St. Charles is just opposite Darna, but cloisters itself from the somewhat ramshackle street by a large gate. With a phenomenally quiet locale and a nun running the show, the colonial-style building is better for the pensive than the plastered. As with any of the religiously run lodgings in Haifa, all guests are welcome as long as they follow the rules—here that means no smoking or alcohol on the premises.

Directly opposite Darna Guest House. i A/C. Breakfast included. Internet NIS10 per hr. $ Singles NIS180; doubles NIS300. Cash only.

G38 APARTMENTS $$

38 HaGefen St. ☎054 522 4281; www.g38.co.il

Buildings which aren't either Bauhaus hovels or concrete monstrosities from the '70s can be a rare breed in Haifa, so G38's glass building covered with tessellated arrows definitely stands out. With pristine white rooms and modern art dispersed along the walls, G38 is certainly more vogue (and expensive) than many of the other options on this list, but it's great for longer stays. Sitting right next to Bethel Inn, it's still got the same great views over the German Colony and Wadi Nisnas.

 # About 2 blocks to the right after reaching the head of Ben-Gurion Blvd. i A/C, kitchenette, and free parking. $ Apartments from NIS200 per night.

SIGHTS

Haifa isn't wild. Sorry. You won't be finding über-hip neighborhoods or quirky holes in the wall. But the city does have the Israeli basics—religious sights and museums—and it does these well. Most sights are either in **Carmel Center** or by **Stella Maris,** which are helpfully connected by bus #115. To make a full circuit of the sights, start in **Hadar** before heading up to Carmel Center.

BAHA'I GARDENS

RELIGIOUS SITE

☎04 831 3131; www.ganbahai.org.il

If you're in Haifa, you have no choice but to see the Baha'i Gardens. The series of immaculate lawns dominates the northeastern face of Mt. Carmel by day, while meticulously arranged lights transform it into a neon crop circle at night. While most religious sites in Israel bask in storied dilapidation, the Baha'i Gardens—the second holiest site of the faith—are kept in pristine condition, with dainty fountains, brilliant floral arrangements, and lots and lots of gleaming white stairs. The garden is built in 19 levels, with each stage representing one of the faith's original disciples; the palatial, gold-domed shrine at the center is the burial place of Báb, the religion's forerunner, who prophesied the coming of its founder, Bahá'u'lláh. The entire area is open to the public, but it stays remarkably serene during the day.

 # If you value your calves, do not walk up the Gardens. Instead, begin at the top at the Yefe Nof entrance, which is at the end of the Louis Promenade. i Knees and shoulders must be covered. $ Free. ⏰ Gardens open daily 9am-5pm. Shrine open daily 9am-noon. Closed on Yom Kippur and Baha'i holidays. Free tours from top of Gardens Su-Tu noon, Th-Sa noon. Tours take first 60 to arrive, so it's best to come around 30min. in advance.

LOUIS PROMENADE

VIEW

Teetering on the peak of Mt. Carmel, the promenade boasts the best view in the city. Akko, Lebanon, and a good chunk of the Galilee are visible on any given day, and, when it's particularly clear, you can even see the snow-capped Mt. Khermon. The promenade itself is a far cry from the urban ruckus of nearby Carmel Center—a small and secluded affair, it's the perfect spot to snack on your falafel and drink up the vista.

 # The promenade is accessible from Yefe Nof St. about 200m down the road from where Sha'ar HaLevanon connects it to HaNassi St.

ELIJAH'S CAVE

RELIGIOUS SITE

230 Allenby St. ☎04 852 7430

The cave itself may not be especially large, but it only goes to show that size doesn't matter (right?). The prophet Elijah supposedly took shelter here after he managed to snuff 450 priests of Baal, an action which then-king Ahab was not that happy about. Since Elijah is an Old Testament Superman, the cave is a holy site for Christians, Muslims, and Jews alike; however, the latter have appropriated it, adorning the walls with scripture and a cornucopia of Judaica. The cave is split in two, with the women's entrance to the left and the men's to the right.

 # Located just above the Maritime Museum. Climb the staircase by the large wall where the hill becomes steep and follow the path to the cave. You can also take a path with breathtaking views of the Mediterranean, which begins across the road from Stella Maris. The trail is steep, so be sure to have comfortable shoes. i Head, shoulders, knees, (and toes, if you'd like) should be covered. Head coverings for women and yarmulkes available at entrance. $ Free. ⏰ Open in summer Su-Th 8am-6pm, F 8am-1pm; in winter Su-Th 8am-5pm, F 8am-1pm.

haifa

HAIFA MUSEUM OF ART MUSEUM

26 Shabtai Levi St. ☎04 852 3255; www.hma.org.il

While grimy Hadar might not scream culture, this museum fights that urban banality with some of the most far-out contemporary art in the country—think wacky installations, edgy sculptures, and a heavy dose of pop spread over three floors. The brilliantly curated permanent collection and temporary exhibits contain avant-garde pieces that manage to avoid the crass and breaking-convention-for-the-hell-of-it style that many expect from modern art. Closing time, on the other hand, is fairly in your face—a deafening siren erupts over the entire museum to let you know you're no longer welcome.

 # On Shabtai Levi St. just before the intersection with HaZiyonut St. $ NIS30, students NIS20. ⏰ Open Su-W 10am-4pm, Th 4-7pm, F 10am-1pm, Sa 10am-3pm.

STELLA MARIS CHURCH CHURCH, MUSEUM

Stella Maris Rd. ☎04 833 7758

When Christian monks were barred from Elijah's Cave, they moved up the hill and established this large church overlooking the Mediterranean. The interior bears all the fancy decorations that Catholics seem to love, from a marble chapel to a dome adorned with paintings of Elijah chilling in a fiery chariot and David jamming on his harp. A small museum in the monastery houses some Byzantine and Crusader artifacts found on Mt. Carmel.

*# Bus #31 or the Carmelit. **i** Shoulders and knees should be covered. $ Free. ⏰ Open daily 6:30am-12:30pm and 3-6pm.*

MADATECH SCIENCE MUSEUM MUSEUM

12 Balfour St ☎04 861 4444; www.madatech.org.il

It may not seem particularly different from your hometown science museum, but that just makes Madatech an even better place to feel like a kid—goodness knows you'll be surrounded by enough of them. While the adventurous can lie on the bed of nails, the more simple-minded can just play with the plasma ball for hours on end. If the exhibits aren't cool enough, marvel at the inadequacy of US curricula as you see 10-year-old Israelis learning about protein synthesis. One hall holds rotating exhibits; at the time of writing, it housed a sports science extravaganza that let you test everything from your speed on the running track to your ability to make soccer free kicks.

 # Buses #113, 114, or 115. Get off by the open area, just when leaving Hadar. $ NIS75, students NIS37.50. ⏰ Open Su noon-7pm, M-Th 9am-7pm, F 9am-4pm, Sa 9am-7pm.

smarty pants

Like Stewie Griffin, Israel is tiny and smart. Twenty-four percent of the Israeli workforce holds a university degree—more than any other industrialized nation except the United States and the Netherlands—and 12% hold advanced degrees. Here are a couple other facts that show just how much the Israelis are doing with all that book learnin'.

- **REVENGE OF THE NERDS.** The Israeli workforce has the largest percentage of scientists and technicians of any country by far.
- **WEIRD SCIENCE.** All these scientists apparently keep busy—the nation also produces the highest number of scientific papers per capita (about one per every 100 residents).
- **PATENT ME.** Israel has one of the highest per capita rates of patents filed.

CLANDESTINE IMMIGRATION AND NAVAL MUSEUM   MUSEUM
204 Allenby St.   ☎04 853 6249

This specifically named museum tells the story of *HaApala*, the secret immigration operation conducted by Zionists during the British mandate. While displays and videos present the historical details, the museum's highlight is a boat that was used for the actual smuggling. And what kind of Israeli naval museum would this be without some big guns? One hall details the navy's major victories, while captured Egyptian gunboats and a machine-gun-riddled jet ski used by terrorists sit outside. A huge missile boat and an entire submarine have also been hauled in for you to clamber through.

⚓ Bus #114 stops directly in front. *i* Passport required for entry. Ⓢ NIS15, students NIS10. ☼ Open Su-Th 8:30am-4pm.

TIKOTIN MUSEUM OF JAPANESE ART   MUSEUM
89 HaNassi St.   ☎04 911 5991; www.tmja.org.il

Yes, you read that correctly. It's Japanese art. In Israel. The museum keeps things simple with a single room of wood-and-paper sliding doors, although a second floor was under renovation at time of writing. The art itself runs the gamut from old-timey artifacts to up-to-date contemporary works and a *katana* (samurai sword) collection.

⚓ Bus #23 goes right past. The museum is to the west of the massive Dan Towers. Ⓢ NIS30, students NIS20. ☼ Open Su-Th 10am-4pm, F 10am-1pm, Sa 10am-3pm.

MARITIME MUSEUM   MUSEUM
198 Allenby St.   ☎04 853 6622; www.nmm.org.il

Haifa is by the sea. It's also pretty damn old. Put these things together, and you have the Maritime Museum. The ground floor displays a sturdy collection of well-preserved mosaics, and the basement tracks the history of Israeli shipping and piracy, complete with cheesy murals, a diorama, and cutlasses. Upstairs, things get a little more reserved with ancient artifacts that include a fisherman's boat dating back to biblical times.

⚓ Bus #114. Just above the Clandestine Immigration and Naval Museum. Ⓢ NIS30, students NIS20. ☼ Open Su-Th 10am-4pm, F 10am-1pm, Sa 10am-3pm.

MANÉ KATZ HOUSE   MUSEUM
89 Yefe Nof St.   ☎04 911 9372; www.mkm.org.il

Boasting the usual magnificent views from Yefe Nof St., the Mané Katz house remembers the famous Israeli painter in his former home with a small but varied selection of his works. His brilliantly colored art recalls the modernist leanings of his time, particularly Matisse and the Fauvists, but it also maintains an idiosyncratic Israeli flavor with depictions of Eretz Israel and recollections of the Shoah. For the even artsier, look out for a museum dedicated to Hermann Struck, renowned Israeli printmaker.

⚓ On Yefe Nof St., right by the intersection with Sha'ar HaLevanon. Ⓢ NIS30, students NIS20. Gold Mastercard holders free. ☼ Open Su-Th 10am-4pm, F 10am-1pm, Sa 10am-3pm.

HAIFA ZOO   ZOO
124 HaTishbi Street   ☎04 837 2390

Who doesn't enjoy depressed animals, corny dioramas, and the faint smell of manure? Haifa Zoo is actually pretty big for an urban zoo, with a selection of animals that ranges from the questionable (roosters roving the grounds) to the respectable (tigers, baboons, and leopards). Be sure to check out the hilarious—and highly aggressive—honey badgers.

⚓ In Gan Ha'em by Carmel Center. The zoo is directly opposite the park entrance. Ⓢ NIS30, students NIS25. ☼ Open Su-Th 9am-7pm, F 9am-4pm. Last entry 1hr. before close.

THE GREAT OUTDOORS

Haifa balances out its concrete jungle and industrial port with sandy beaches and the occasional patch of grass (suck on that, Tel Aviv). Most of these do require a small trek: the beaches skirt the peninsula's western coast, a bus ride from the city center; the greenery shrouds Mt. Carmel's western face, where downhill hikes offer stunning panoramas of the Mediterranean and steep hills.

beaches

The beach is the place to go in Haifa. On weekends, families, couples, and every bronzed 20-something take to the shores, meaning that—despite the huge expanse of coast—it gets crowded. The summer is also jellyfish season, and the slimy little bastards often take to the shallow waters in droves. Luckily, they're usually big enough to see and therefore avoid, but it's good to bring some vinegar to the beach just in case. Peeing on the wound will not work; it does not relieve pain, and you'll just be broadcasting the fact that you've been watching too many *Friends* re-runs.

☆ DOR — RUINS, MUSEUM

With one of the best beaches in the country, Dor is a placid getaway from the urban bustle of Haifa—think transparent waters and nearly white sands. Dor is enough out of the way that it doesn't get crowded, and the small offshore islands are within easy swimming distance. The one downside? The jellyfish seem to agree that this is a great beach. If stingers really aren't your style, head to the small peak of **Tel Dor,** seat of a large archaeological excavation that you can wander through (access from behind through the holiday resort). A 5min. walk to the peak, crowned with expansive Canaanite ruins, will offer you amazing views of the sea and of Caesarea farther down the coast. In the nearby resort, the **Hamizgaga Museum** (☎06 639 0950) showcases a panoply of finds, from 4000-year-old anchors to muskets ditched by Napoleon's retreating troops.

🚌 Bus #921 (NIS11.30) will take you here from Hof HaCarmel in 20min. Get off at Dor Junction and walk 5km through the sun-scorched vineyards. The walk is flat, but long and totally exposed. Some travelers say hitchhiking is common here, but Let's Go does not recommend hitchhiking. $ Beach NIS10. Museum NIS18. ⏰ Beach open 24hr. Lifeguards on duty daily 8am-5pm. Museum open Su-Th 8:30am-2pm, F 8:30am-1pm, Su 10:30am-3pm.

☆ HOF DADO

The largest and best of Haifa's shoreline retreats, Hof Dado is technically two beaches. The southern stretch, dubbed "the student beach" by locals, frees itself from lifeguards, amenities, and pretty much anyone over thirty. While it's certainly one of the more crowded beaches, the profusion of hip music and six-packed teens creates its own decidedly enjoyable atmosphere. Just north, the lifeguards return, bringing with them the small kids and square parents who make up probably the most crowded beach in the city. Public bathrooms and showers are available, as is a small grassy picnic area.

🚌 Directly accessible from Hof HaCarmel, the central bus station. Just leave the station and head for the water. ℹ Lifeguards on duty on northern beach daily 8am-5pm.

HOF HACARMEL

Heading a little upshore from Hof Dado, you'll reach Hof HaCarmel, where the promenade has exploded into full Western gaudiness—complete with the usual overpriced food stands, towering waterfront hotels, and crowds of families.

🚌 Just north of Hof Dado. Any of the buses heading to Hof HaCarmel bus station goes past.

BAT GALIM BEACH

Decidedly tattered—and possibly even grimy—Bat Galim is found in the very north of the city, at the end of a grungy promenade of the same name. Yes, you'll find some trash, but the breakwaters, free facilities, and growth

northern mediterranean coast

of cheap eateries help make up for the litter. A small playground reminds you that this is a beach for the kiddies.

Bus #16 goes along HaAliya HaShniya, which runs almost parallel to the beach 2 blocks over. The final stop, at the cable car station, is at the foot of the promenade.

hikes

KOKHAV HAYAM RANGE

Starting just opposite Stella Maris Church, this small gravel path winds down the steep valley of Kokhav Hayam Range. The path leads to a small peak where you'll find the **Sacre Coeur Convent**—a cinderblock cylinder with a cross on top—and a pair of dilapidated concrete lookouts with incredible views of the sea below. It's the perfect place to bring a bottle of wine and a date (or watch someone else with his bottle of wine and his date, if that's more your style). From the lookout, the path veers north, winding around the hill and through the small forest until it reaches Elijah's Cave.

The path is unmarked, and the entrance by Stella Maris is non-descript. Where the road bends, a small concrete plateau is just below the road. The gravel path leads off from it through the trees. The walk takes about 20min. ***i*** *The downhill path is not maintained and can be steep, so wear good shoes and bring water.*

NAHAL SIAH

A longer trail that's still pretty easygoing, Nahal Siah lazily weaves through the Carmeliya Valley. On the way, you'll pass the **Komotayim** (a 1000-year-old cave where monks once took refuge), the El Sik Monastery, and a prim garden. The trail—which takes approximately 1hr.—ends rather solemnly with the massive Sde Yehoshua Cemetery.

From Carmel Center, follow HaNassi south for 300m. After a bend, you'll take a right onto Wolfson and then the 2nd left onto Lotus St. The entrance is hidden behind some trees just after the intersection with Argaman St.

FOOD

Shawarma and falafel stands, while certainly not rare, are oddly scarce in Haifa—and those that do exist often close in the late afternoon, leaving you stranded when it comes to 2am munchies. But this is not to say that you'll have to empty your wallet to fill up your stomach: restaurants certainly prevail over fast-food booths in this city, and they're normally on the lower end of the price spectrum. The German Colony seems almost built to feed tourists, with its strip of posh restaurants and upscale cafes lining **Ben-Gurion Boulevard,** while the peak of **Mount Carmel** is packed with everything from sushi to pizza. These are the obvious places to hit up for a meal; downtown is pretty sparse, and the Hadar region seems to fail completely in providing anything worthwhile.

If your mother was nice enough to teach you how to fend for yourself, the markets provide plenty of material to work with. The **arab souq** in Wadi Nisnas has a great selection of exotica, while the huge and hectic **Sirkin Market** in the Hadar region is a must-go for the aspiring chef. A large **grocery store** is also located in Paris Square, directly opposite the Carmelit station.

ABU YOUSEF — HUMMUS $$

1 HaMeginim Ave. ☎04 866 3723

With its tile floor, self-service salad bar, and no-nonsense white walls, Abu Yousef may remind you of the high school cafeteria you foolishly thought you left behind. But if you can get past your pampered Western pretensions and concentrate on what's going into your mouth, you're in for a real treat: Abu Yousef is a local staple that serves some of the best hummus-based chow in Haifa. The crowd is invariably Arabic, and even though you might be the only tourist there, the extremely warm staff will make you feel right at home.

Head east from Paris Square, and it's immediately to the left. *[$] Hummus NIS20. Chicken shishlik NIS40.* *Open Su-Th 9am-9pm, F 9am-5pm.*

haifa

BARBAROSSA BURGERS, SUSHI $$
99 Yefe Nof St. ☎04 837 5602; www.barbarossa.co.il

One of the throng of restaurants in the trendy Carmel Center, Barbarossa is perched under the Louis Promenade, meaning it may just have the best view in the city. It feels like a happening Tel Aviv establishment thanks to the great burgers, extensive sushi menu, and jet black interior stylings, but your attention is going to be solely on the wall-sized window, which offers a sweeping panorama of Haifa, the Galilee, and the glassy Mediterranean lapping the Lebanese shore. Order the signature "Monica Be-lychee" and drink to that sunset.

➜ On the intersection of Yefe Nof and Sha'ar HaLevanon. [$] Burgers NIS52. Sushi combos from NIS38. ⏰ Open Su-Th noon-late, F-Sa 9am-late.

GAL'S BAKERY CAFE $
131 HaNassi St. ☎04 838 2928; www.galsbakery.co.il

Forget the Baha'i Gardens—Gal's may be the best-smelling place in the city, constantly swathed in the aromas of ambrosial icing, candied fruit, and a seemingly endless stream of freshly baked cakes, breads, and pastries. Divorced from the bustle of HaNassi St. by the nondescript alley that leads to the bakery, a large back garden is swaddled in a jungle of trees. Here, easy-tempered clientele munch on cake, a world away from the busy thoroughfare that is actually a mere 20m away.

➜ At the intersection with Wedgewood Ave. [$] Croissants NIS14. ⏰ Bakery open M-Th 5am-10pm, F 5am-2pm, Sa 5am-10pm. Cafe open M-Th 8am-9pm, F 8am-1pm, Sa 8am-9pm.

FATTOUSH CAFE $$
38 Ben-Gurion Blvd. ☎04 852 4930

Of the many tranquil upmarket restaurant-cafe-bars dotting Ben-Gurion, Fattoush is probably the most attractive. A large patio spills out onto the street, sequestered by short hedges and decked out with blue glass lanterns, a fountain, and garden furniture. It's also one of the few restaurants here that actually serves local cuisine. Right by the foot of the Baha'i Gardens, the spot is particularly quiet; your meditative coffee will be interrupted only by the occasional band of pilgrims scurrying past.

➜ On the left, 1 block north of the head of Ben-Gurion Blvd. [$] Shawarma NIS44. Breakfast NIS28. ⏰ Open daily 8am-1am.

ROASTING HOUSE SALMONA COFFEE $
14 HeHaluz St. ☎04 867 4467

Founded in 1946, Salmona is older than the state of Israel itself. The place may be small, but it's renowned throughout the city for some of the best and most distinctive coffee blends around—it's only a shop, though, so you'll have to brew your gourmet beans elsewhere. A whole anthology of nuts and candied fruits plaster the walls, allowing you to construct an excellent trail mix (and making it one of the only food places in Hadar). Salmona is a great pit stop for those hardy enough—or in desperate enough need of bragging rights—to walk up Mt. Carmel.

➜ By the intersection with Shmaryahu Levin St. [$] Candied fruits from NIS10. Cash only. ⏰ Open Su-Th 8am-7pm, F 8am-5pm.

VICTOR THE FISHERMAN SEAFOOD $$
22 Wadi St. ☎04 855 2301

Located in the middle of Wadi Nisnas' *souq*, Victor's is the go-to seafood place for those with the local know-how. A couple dolphins flank the entrance (but thankfully stay off the menu), and the otherwise spartan interior is brightened by a large mural of the coast. While almost every other fish joint in town is going to cost you a fin and a gill, Victor's is grilling up delicious marine cuisine at prices that simply can't be beat. Yet who is this great Victor? That remains a mystery.

✱ At the center of the souq, by the intersection with al-Hariri. Ⓢ St. Peter's fish NIS45. Fried calamari NIS50. 🕐 Open Su noon-7pm, M-Sa noon-10pm.

JAPANIKA   SUSHI $$
122 HaNassi St.   ☎04 838 6666; www.japanika.net

While Tel Aviv's Japanika is little more than a booth on the street, Haifa's branch of this small, top-notch sushi chain goes all out. A proper restaurant, Japanika boasts a pristine white interior with inky bars and crisp calligraphy etched on papyrus across the walls. A huge window dominates an entire side of the restaurant, affording great views of the serene park and amphitheater below. Yet prices remain pocket friendly, with a killer business lunch deal (appetizer plus a combo from NIS45).

✱ Right by the entrance to the Carmelit. Ⓢ Combos from NIS31. 🕐 Open Su-W noon-1am, Th noon-2am, F noon-3am, Sa noon-1am.

MANDARIN   CAFE $$
129 HaNassi St.   ☎04 838 0803; www.mandarin.org.il

Like Gal's Bakery just to the south, Mandarin eschews the bustle of HaNassi St. for a refreshingly tranquil patio, well-nestled behind crimson walls that keep the blaring traffic and loud-mouthed crowds out of sight—and therefore out of mind. Chill cafes are a rare commodity in Haifa, so those a little less tightly wound will be relieved to sip Mandarin's signature coffee in the sprawling shade.

✱ Mandarin is off the main street, but there's a small sign by the frozen yogurt stand. Follow it to a path that leads back through the block and eventually to Mandarin. Ⓢ Shakshuka NIS39. Sandwiches from NIS31. 🕐 Open Su-Th 8:30am-midnight, F 8am-1am, Sa 9am-1am.

MEAT, IN & OUT   MEAT $$
129 HaNassi St.   ☎04 837 3222

The name may strike excitement into the hearts of West Coast burger connoisseurs—or, conversely, apprehension into the hearts of readers of A Clockwork Orange. Meat, in any case, is a carnivore's heaven, which takes about half a second to figure out: the aroma of smoked meats and, perhaps, frying bacon (which means a lot more when you've been in Israel for a while) hits you the second you walk in. Slabs of mouthwatering meat are rustled up on the huge grill behind the bar, and a large patio spills into a garden as the dauntingly titled Meat Corruption—2kg of flesh—begs your attention.

✱ Just north of the intersection with Wedgewood Ave. Ⓢ Sirloin NIS77. Mini lamb kebabs NIS45. 🕐 Open daily noon-late.

CAFE FACES   ITALIAN $$
37 Ben-Gurion Blvd.   ☎04 855 2444

Another of the fancier joints along Ben-Gurion Blvd., Cafe Faces sports the street's signature great views of the Baha'i Gardens from a large shady patio out front. Inside, it's a swankier affair, with a chandelier and chic vermillion-on-black design. The menu is mainly Italian—with focaccia and pasta galore—though there's a choice selection of steaks for those with fatter wallets.

✱ Toward the middle of Ben-Gurion, just below the intersection with Allenby St. Ⓢ Lasagna NIS55. Steak NIS98. 🕐 Open daily 9am-late.

SANDWICH BAR   SANDWICHES $
128 HaNassi St.   ☎04 810 3103

Little more than a hole in the wall, the imaginatively named Sandwich Bar is about as eye-catching as your run-of-the-mill falafel stand. Yet the crowds prove that this place is a little more substantial. Meat and cheese, nicer and more authentic than you'll find elsewhere, are selected from a large deli counter and

stuffed into a sub which is then doused in coleslaw and grilled. Prepare to be assertive: the crowds will happily push in front of you as you try to navigate the cornucopia of cold cuts, and the staff may not be the nicest in the the world.
➜ At the intersection with HaYam Rd. $ Sandwiches from NIS28. ⏰ Open 24hr.

NIGHTLIFE

If you're planning an *arak* bender, you should probably head elsewhere. The few clubs in Haifa are very hit or miss—and seem to have a shelf life that can be measured in months. If you're looking to dance like a maniac, your options can be counted on one hand (one that's been in a woodshop accident, no less). On the plus side, this dearth of nightlife means all the partygoers are in one place, though the makeup of this crowd can be pretty suspect.

The bar scene is a little more developed, with plenty of old-timey pubs and taverns. The downtown area has a nice set of comfortable jazz bars and a wealth of live music, while the Carmel area is home to what little vogue can be found in Haifa. Friday is the biggest night for partying; however, public transportation is closed for the Sabbath, so you'll have to shell out NIS50 for a cab just to get to the action.

👍 MORRISON — CLUB

115 Yefe Nof St. ☎04 838 3828

Originally named after the shaggy-haired, eternally shirtless Doors frontman, Morrison has recently shed its rock bar roots in favor of a more up-to-date clubbing persona. You never know though: the booming electro, young crowd, and small balcony with stunning views of nighttime Haifa may still light that proverbial fire. While the place is often so packed that even dancing can be hard, Morrison knows how to put on a party—which, for Haifa, is saying a lot.
➜ On south Yefe Nof St., southeast of the Baha'i Gardens. ℹ Live music on Tu. Arab students night on W. Happy hour 8-11pm. ⏰ Open daily 8pm-late.

BEAR — BAR

135 HaNassi St. ☎04 838 1703; www.bears-pub.co.il

No, no, you haven't overdone the Goldstar—the man in a giant panda suit ushering you into this lively bar is very real. It only gets more hilarious with each successive Goldstar. In any case, 👍**Bear** is about as happening a bar as you're going to find in Haifa. The crowd tends a little more toward the older side, but the pumping music and flowing whiskey remind you that you're only as young as you think you are. The bar inside, decked out in football scarves from all over Europe, is usually packed into the wee hours.
➜ On southern HaNassi St. near the intersection with Shoshanat HaCaramel. ⏰ Open Su-W 4pm-3am, Th-F 11am-3am, Sa 5pm-3am.

SYNCOPA — BAR, CLUB

5 Chayat St. ☎050 918 8899; www.2eat.co.il/syncopa

The surest spot to find a party downtown, Syncopa comprises a typical pub on the ground floor (complete with a wooden bar and stools around high tables) and an upstairs that serves as an impromptu dance floor for the fleet-footed and poor conversationalists. Music ranges from dubstep to alt rock.
➜ From HaAtzma'ut Ave., walk about 1 block down Chayat St. Syncopa is on the corner of Natanzon and Chayat. $ Beer NIS24-35. No cover usually. Special events NIS20-40. ⏰ Open daily 9pm-late.

ALTERMAN — BAR

115 Yefe Nof St. ☎054 812 3801

Alterman is a place made for the post-game. Located next to the raucous Morrison, it features dim lights, a soundtrack of Coldplay, and a huge window offering a neon-tinged vista of Haifa. If you care to look away from that view for a second, you'll find some more unexpected sights, including a portrait of the

Queen picking her nose and one of a bare-bosomed Mona Lisa, who, apparently, had a penchant for nipple tassels.

⚑ *On south Yefe Nof St., southeast of the Baha'i Gardens.* ⓘ *20% off food and drink until 9pm.* ⏰ *Open daily 6:30pm-late.*

SOFIA
CLUB

5 al-Pasha St.   sofiaclub1@gmail.com

Sofia has an awesome location if nothing else—it's inside an old, dilapidated mosque. The bars are crammed into the ancient arches; the dance floor is sprawled beneath the large central dome. It's the kind of venue you see in movies, but secretly know that you're a little too lame to ever experience such a place yourself. Well, luck's on your side this time. Sort of. The building may be hip, but Sofia is only open two nights per week and often only for private events or 30+ nights. Make sure to check what's on: when this place does kick off, it's sweet.

⚑ *Located off HaPalyam Rd. near the eastern coast.* ⓘ *18+. Cover NIS30-40 on F.* Ⓢ *Beer from NIS23. Chasers from NIS10. Beer and chaser NIS28.* ⏰ *Open W-Th 11pm-late.*

ELI'S
BAR

35 Jaffa Rd.   ☎04 852 5550

Eli's is a cozy little downtown pub that's home to some great live music. Tourists and locals alike congregate for a regular slew of skittering drummers and elderly Serge Gainsbourg look-alikes on the piano. Expect everything from dulcet tones at jam sessions to freestyle odysseys over the course of the week.

⚑ *Located near HaShmona Station on the northern coast. From HaAtzma'ut Ave., take a right onto HaBankim, then left onto Jaffa Rd.* ⓘ *Jazz sessions on M. Acoustic performances on W and Sa.* ⏰ *Open daily 10pm-late.*

BEER HOUSE
BAR

116 HaNassi St.   ☎052 501 8889; www.beerhouse.co.il

Hoveled underground in what can only be described as a small cavern, Beer House would be better called "Beer Mansion" if we're going purely on the number of brews available (they have 120 types from around the world). The scene never gets too rowdy here, making it more a place for the connoisseur sipper rather than the rambunctious down-in-one-er.

⚑ *On southern HaNassi St., southeast of the Baha'i Gardens.* ⓘ *18+. Happy hour daily until 8pm.* Ⓢ *Beer from NIS20.* ⏰ *Open Su-Th 5pm-late, F 7pm-late, Sa 2pm-late.*

ARTS AND CULTURE

As Israel's third largest city, Haifa has its fair share of the artsy. Smaller galleries are strangely absent from the city, but the **Tikotin Museum of Japanese Art** and **Haifa Museum of Art** provide plenty of cultural eye candy. Theater is also particularly popular here, but it rarely caters to an English-speaking audience.

CINEMATHEQUE
FILM

142 HaNassi St.   ☎04 835 3530; www.ethos.co.il/cinema

While nothing with a name this French is likely to be featuring the latest Michael Bay masterpiece (*Transformers 4*, perhaps?), Cinematheque isn't just for those with a knack for obscure New Wave. A constant stream of international films, including many documentaries, is shown here, and many of the films are in English. Those that are not sometimes have English subtitles; make sure to call ahead for details if the Hebrew-only website is giving you a headache.

⚑ *On HaNassi St., just before it turns into Moriya St.* Ⓢ *NIS33, students NIS27.* ⏰ *Generally 2-3 films shown per day. First showing around 5:30pm and last at 9:30pm. Hours vary daily, so call ahead.*

HAIFA SYMPHONY ORCHESTRA
CLASSICAL MUSIC

6 Eliyahu Hakim St. ☎04 859 9499; www.haifasymphony.co.il

One of the country's premier orchestras, the HSO offers a range of shows that run the aural gamut from your more typical classical fare to that habitual crowd-pleaser, big band. The Friday Morning Classics series provides big-name sounds for lower prices.

⛳ Most performances at Haifa Auditorium at 138 HaNassi St. (in the middle of Carmel Center) or at the Krieger Center for the Performing Arts at 6 Elihayu Hakim St. $ Opera NIS150, reduced NIS135. Classics series NIS110/95, Friday Morning Classics NIS65. Jazz NIS100/80. Kids concert NIS70.

HAIFA MUNCIPAL THEATRE
THEATER

50 Yefe Nof St. ☎04 860 0500; www.ht1.co.il

Haifa's local theater puts on a range of Israeli plays that often deal with contemporary aspects of Jewish and national life. Unfortunately, the shows are almost always in Hebrew, and no provisions are made for English-speakers.

⛳ From Carmel Center, walk down Yefe Nof for about 1500m to reach the theater. $ Tickets from NIS100, but vary greatly.

SHOPPING

Haifa is not the place to shop 'til you drop. While the humble backpacker will find solace in the grimy *souq* and the silk-stockinged globetrotter will ferret out a few chic boutiques, the high and low ends of the consumer spectrum are otherwise absent. What's left is a series of shops catering to mid-range tastes, with items neither cheap enough to call a bargain nor special enough to merit a splurge. These shops are mostly centered on the **Hadar** neighborhood, which contains a cluster of clothing stores and booths chock full of tchotchke. Most locals do their shopping at the many malls that dot the area.

SIRKIN MARKET
MARKET

Nestled at the foot of Hadar, Sirkin may look busy from the outside. But even with fruit and vegetable stalls backing up traffic all over the block, that's only half the chaos—the market's heart is actually underground. Descend into the subterranean complex to find corridors swarming with shoppers browsing through wares that include homemade cheeses, watermelons as large as toddlers, and fish so fresh they're flopping. You're also likely to be the only tourist in sight. Many shopkeepers don't speak English, so be prepared to negotiate more with volume than wit.

⛳ Located just south of HeHaluz St. between Sokolov St. and Yehel St. The outside market lines Lunz St. The entrance to the underground portion is at the southern foot of the street. It's sometimes called Talpiyot Market. ⏰ Open Su-Th 8am-4pm, F 8am-1pm.

ARAB SOUQ
MARKET

The *souq* is the geographical and cultural nucleus of Wadi Nisnas. It may take over only a couple of short roads, but it's the loud and proud center of the Arab Quarter in the mornings. There are a few souvenir stands, but this one's really for the foodies; the exotic fruit and abundance of butchers will whet the culinary imagination of anyone with kitchen access.

⛳ On Yohanan and Wadi, the parallel streets leading off of Kouri St., about 500m down from the bottom of Hadar. ⏰ Open Su-F 9am-1pm.

GRAND CANYON MALL
MALL

54 Simha Golan Rd. ☎04 814 5115; www.grandcenyon.co.il

The name of Haifa's biggest megamall is no joke: it sits in a valley so massive that the roof of the three-floor building only reaches halfway up the valley. Unlike the actual Grand Canyon though, the mall holds every conceivable chain and big-name brand that you've missed so dearly.

⛳ Bus #16. ⏰ Open Su-Th 10am-10pm, F 10am-3pm, Sa sunset-11pm.

CINEMALL MALL

55 HaHistadrut ☎04 841 6090

A similar affair to Grand Canyon, Cinemall is a megamall located out in the boonies of the city's vast eastern industrial zone. While the selection of restaurants might be a little nicer here, the main attraction is the mammoth megaplex cinema.

🚌 Bus #114. ⏰ Open Su-Th 10am-10pm, F 9:30am-2pm, Sa sunset-11pm.

FESTIVALS

While Haifa may not be one for wild parties, it does put on a good festival. During the summer, a free block party takes place on the western end of Hanamal St. by the port every Friday at 5:30pm. A slightly cheesy Israeli band sets up on the huge stage, while the nearby hill is crowded with listeners sipping steins of strawberry beer bought from street vendors.

👍 **HAIFA INTERNATIONAL FILM FESTIVAL** CARMEL CENTER

☎04 810 3471; www.haifaff.co.il

Every year during Sukkot—around mid-October—silver-screen mania overtakes Carmel Center in the area immediately around Cinematheque. This gigantic film festival features everything from small-time documentaries to the bigwig blockbusters you'd be watching at the megaplex back home.

🚌 Take the Carmelit to the top of the line. $ NIS40, students NIS35. ⏰ Mid-Oct.

ESSENTIALS

practicalities

- **TOURIST OFFICE:** The **Haifa Tourist Office** offers a wide selection of maps, brochures, and tips, including a short film about Haifa's sights and history. (48 Ben-Gurion Blvd. ⏰ Open Su-Th 9am-4:30pm, F 9am-1:30pm, Sa 10am-3pm.)
- **ATM: Bank Leumi.** (21 Jaffa Rd. ⏰ Open Su-Th 8:30am-2:45pm, F 8:30am-noon.)
- **LAUNDROMAT: Brainwash.** (19 Masada St. ☎050 631 8397 $ Wash NIS15 per 7kg. Dry NIS15 per 7kg. ⏰ Open Su-Th 7:30am-midnight, F 7:30am-6pm, Sa 8pm-midnight.)
- **POST OFFICE:** 22 HaNevi'im ⏰ Open Su-Th 8am-6pm, F 8am-noon.

emergency

- **POLICE:** 82 HaAtzma'ut Rd. ☎04 835 4428.
- **LATE-NIGHT PHARMACY: New-Pharm.** (18 Herzl St. ⏰ Open Su 8am-5pm, M-Th 9am-8pm, F 8am-noon.)
- **HOSPITALS: Bnei Zion.** (47 Golomb St. ☎04 835 9359 ⏰ Open 24hr.)

getting there

BY TRAIN

Haifa has three train stations: **Hof HaCarmel, Merkaz,** and **Bat Galim.** Trains arrive from: Tel Aviv ($ NIS29.50. ⏰ 1¼hr., every 30min.), Akko ($ NIS15. ⏰ 25min., every 30min.), and Hadera. ($ NIS22.50. ⏰ 50min., every 30min.)

BY BUS

Haifa's two major bus stations are **Hof HaCarmel** in the southwest and **HaMifratz** in the northeast near the industrial area by **Kishon Junction.** There are two buses from Tel Aviv: the **#910** from city center ($ NIS26.50. ⏰ 1½hr., every hr.) and the **#947** from Ben-Gurion Airport ($ NIS36. ⏰ 2¼hr., every 30min.). The **#940** goes from Jerusalem to Haifa. ($ NIS40. ⏰ 2hr., every hr.)

getting around

Unfortunately for you, Haifa sits on a large hill, which means that it's not very navigable by foot. Be prepared to make public transportation your best friend—though be aware that this is one of those friends that refuses to emerge on Saturdays.

BY CARMELIT

Israel's only metro system is just one line with two actual trains. However, it does have six major stops going up Mt. Carmel: Paris Square, Solel Boneh, HaNevi'im, Massada, Golomb, and Gan HaEm. Tickets are NIS6, but for NIS10.40, you can get a bus ride in addition to the metro trip. Credit cards are accepted.

BY BUS

Bus is by far the easiest and most common way to get around the entire city. The central bus station is at **Hof HaCarmel** by the Haifa South Interchange at the southwestern edge of the city. All rides cost NIS6.40, with a second ride free if used within the next 80min. Bus **#16** starts out of Bat Galim, works its way across HaAtzma'ut Rd., then goes up through Hadar before terminating at Grand Canyon Mall; bus **#23** starts out of Bat Galim, goes up through the German Colony to Carmel Center, and also ends at Grand Canyon. Bus **#103** skirts the town's perimeter from Hof HaCarmel, taking you along HaAtzma'ut Rd., while bus **#113** connects Hof HaCarmel to HaMifratz via Hadar.

BY TAXI

Late at night, taxis are generally the easiest way to get around the city. A taxi from Carmel Center to downtown (which is the route you'll be taking for any nightlife fun-times) should not set you back more than NIS50.

northern mediterranean coast

honesty is the best policy

No beating around the bush here. Israelis tend to be very direct in conversations, to the point where some foreigners may find them blunt or even rude. The fact that conversations usually take place less than an arm's length apart can also be uncomfortable for a lot of Westerners. The key is to neither back away (it's considered rude) nor take offense: the preference is merely for honesty over insinuation. This seemingly prickly attitude has garnered native-born Israelis the nickname "sabra," which refers to a popular cactus fruit available in summer. Pick some up at a local market, and you'll quickly discover that both the fruit and the people are sweet on the inside.

ein hod ☎04

There are artists' colonies in quite a few Israeli cities, but Ein Hod takes it a step further: an artists' town. Every resident of this picturesque Mediterranean village had to undergo a stringent selection process before being allowed to move here and begin work. It should therefore come as little surprise that the place looks like it's straight out of a Dr. Seuss book—parks are swapped for sculpture gardens, gates for serpentine iron contraptions, and signposts for psychedelic ceramic shards. It's one of those places that simply has to be seen to be believed. Houses double as galleries for their inhabitants, who often keep their doors open for curious wanderers. Saturdays are both the best and worst days to visit: the town explodes with events and live music, but that means that it becomes similarly crowded with visitors.

Check the town's official website at www.ein-hod.info for upcoming events and more information about the colony.

ORIENTATION

If you manage to get lost in Ein Hod, congratulations! The place is so tiny that they haven't even bothered to name the streets. The town revolves around the **central square,** which is home to the **Main Gallery.** Pick up a map there to help you navigate the village's many smaller galleries.

ACCOMMODATIONS

For such a small town, Ein Hod has a surprisingly large number of places to stay. However, these are mostly local homes that rent out only a couple rooms each—staying in these might not be cheap, but it may well be luxurious.

HILLEL HOUSE

GUESTHOUSE $$$
☎054 728 3311

Coming in at a hefty century and a half, Hillel House is the oldest building in the village and certainly one of its most opulent—it was the home of the town's Arab chieftain before the creation of the artists' colony in 1953. In fact, the term "mansion" might be more appropriate given the sheer size of this place; the large rooms easily fit a double bed and a cot, making it perhaps the cheapest stay in town. In fact, during certain seasons the whole first floor can be rented out for up to four people, and the entire second floor, with its magnificent domed roof, is available for parties of six or seven. At Ein Hod's most western promontory, the terrace provides wide vistas of the Mediterranean below.

⌖ At the western end of town. From the central square, follow the road heading down from the Main Gallery to its very end. ℹ A/C and ensuite bathroom. $ 3-person room NIS400, for students NIS350; 1st fl. NIS600/500.

ARTREST

GUESTHOUSE $$$$
☎04 984 1560

ArtRest, which consists of two beautiful stone cottages in the middle of town, is about the most decadent stay you could ask for, with mosaic-tiled baths and views over the valley below. The price is at the higher end for Ein Hod, but if you're going to fork out for your visit, it's one of the few places that is specifically devoted to being an accommodation rather than just a spare room.

⌖ Walk out the eastern exit of Cafe Ein Hod, and ArtRest is just to the right, past the amphitheater. ℹ A/C, TV, kitchen, and ensuite bathroom. Call to book ahead. $ Rooms Su-W NIS500, Th-Sa NIS650.

SIGHTS

Ein Hod's sights are invariably its 70-odd galleries—if you see an open door, the place is usually fair game (though you should knock anyway). Even the three "larger" galleries consist of little more than a single room. A stroll around the entire village shouldn't take more than 2-3hr., even if you stop at these as well as the odd smaller gallery that catches your eye. The amphitheater near the center of town has a regular schedule of live music and performances.

NISCO MUSEUM OF MECHANICAL MUSIC

MUSEUM
☎052 475 5313

The only mechanical music museum in the Middle East—and only concert hall for it in the world—Nisco is undoubtedly unlike anything you've seen before. Before Edison invented the phonograph at the turn of the century, recorded music was available in music boxes, automated pianos, hurdy-gurdies, and the like from as early as 1850. Museum owner and curator Nisan Cohen has been collecting the contraptions for 50 years and displays the results of his quest here for your listening pleasure. The music may be mechanical, but Cohen's tours are anything but—he's quite the showman. He's also an artisan and sells his own music boxes and *mezuzot* for as little as NIS40.

⚑ *Toward the northern end of the village. From the central square, pass through the scultpure garden and continue down the steps. There are signs.* ⓘ *Concerts available for advance bookings of at least 15. Tours every hr. on the hr. assuming a few people are present. Last tour 4pm.* Ⓢ *NIS30.* ⌚ *Open daily 10am-5pm.*

JANCO DADA MUSEUM   MUSEUM
☎04 984 2350; www.jancodada.co.il

Established in honor of Dadaist Marcel Janco, the town's founder, the museum houses a large collection of his work as well as a basement housing exhibitions by contemporary Dadaists. It's more than just signed urinals, you know... at least, we think so. Maybe?

⚑ *Adjacent to the central square.* Ⓢ *NIS20, students NIS10.* ⌚ *Open Su-Th 9:30am-3:30pm, F 9:30am-2pm, Sa 10am-4pm.*

MAIN GALLERY   MUSEUM
☎04 984 2548

Housing a sizable collection of work by artists from all over the village, the Main Gallery provides a sampling of the work in town, spread out across four smaller galleries.

⚑ *On the central square.* ⌚ *Open Su-Th 10am-4pm, F 10am-2pm, Sa 11am-4pm.*

FOOD

There may be only a handful of cafes and restaurants in Ein Hod, but, like the rest of town, it's all about quality, not quantity.

▨ ARTBAR   CAFE $
☎052 836 2498

Where to start with a place like this? Artbar is the town's default hangout spot, run by local legend Danny Schlyfestone. He claims that his homemade beer and pizza are the best in the world, and, after a taste, even the most cynical, time-weathered travel writer has to agree. The place may not look like much, what with the door now propped against the wall (having fallen off its hinges) and a large vat of hops brewing outside, but the ales, served in old Coke bottles, are a real treat. Busy in the mouth, they cycle through a panoply of at least five flavors before settling on the tongue. Danny affectionately (and creatively) titles all his suds—make sure to check out the Yeasty Beasty or the undoubtedly best-named brew of all time, ▨Yo Mama's Ale. The place becomes packed every weekend, when live bands come to play.

⚑ *Just behind the central square, to the east.* ⓘ *Live music on Sa afternoon.* Ⓢ *Ale NIS20. Pizza NIS30.* ⌚ *Open daily 11am-midnight.*

ABU YA'AKOV   HUMMUS $
☎04 984 3377

Perched just over the amphitheater, Abu Ya'akov keeps it simple, with little more than a sparse, whitewashed kitchen and old plastic furniture on a shady outdoor terrace. But add an ice-cold beer and a plate of Abu's light hummus and you're in seventh heaven, with a sweeping view of the valley below and the Mediterranean beyond.

⚑ *Just above the amphitheater, to the east.* Ⓢ *Hummus NIS20.* ⌚ *Open M-Sa morning-3pm.*

DOÑA ROSA   ARGENTINE $$
☎049 543 777

About as upscale as Ein Hod gets, Doña Rosa certainly looks the part with its chandeliers, comically large steak knives, and, of course, that famous old-style meat grill sitting behind the bar. Enjoy your steak from the large veranda that overlooks the central square.

🍴 *On the east side of the central square.* *i* *Reservations suggested.* Ⓢ *Prime rib NIS88. Marisca-da NIS82.* 🕐 *Open M-Sa noon-11pm.*

ESSENTIALS

practicalities

Other than a **post office**—at which mail can only be received, not sent—Ein Hod lacks even the most basic amenities. In fact, the closest thing to civilization in the area is a prison. Therefore, you should refer to **Haifa** for all necessary services. There is a small **grocery store** in Ein Hod, but we recommend that you stock up on supplies beforehand if you plan on staying overnight.

getting there

If you don't have a car, the only way to get to Ein Hod is by **bus.** There are no direct routes, but Egged bus **#921** from Haifa (Ⓢ NIS9.80. 🕐 15min., every 30min.) will get you nearly there. After you pass the prison on the right, get out at the stop after the next major junction to the right. From here, Ein Hod is about a 2km walk up the steep road leading inland. *Let's Go* does not endorse hitchhiking under any circumstance, but some travelers say that doing so up this road to Ein Hod is a common practice.

getting around

Not only is Ein Hod tiny, but most of the roads aren't even accessible to cars. You're going to have to hoof it.

netanya ☎09

Netanya is famous for two things. The first is immediately obvious—a glorious 14km stretch of pristine Mediterranean beaches. These beaches actually brought about its second claim to fame—it's also home to some of Israel's most powerful families. Established in the 1920s as a collection of citrus farms and diamond factories (and, of course, those beaches), Netanya attracted boatloads of tourists, most of them French and Russian. Some of them stayed, and today Netanya has large French and Russian populations, meaning you're much more likely to hear French than English—and, perhaps, than Hebrew—as you stroll on the *midrak-hov* or sip your coffee in HaAtzma'ut Sq. That said, the city does generally observe Shabbat, with only a few restaurants remaining open then. Because of the many affluent, geriatric tourists, Netanya can strain the budget traveler's wallet, but it's worth paying for at least a night so you can enjoy the blue Mediterranean and the stunning purple sunsets.

ORIENTATION

Forming a long and skinny metropolis stretching along the Mediterranean coast, Netanya is actually pretty damn big. However, most of the goings-on are centered on the downtown area, and, in particular, on **Herzl Street,** which runs east to west in the northern part of the city. The **central bus station** is located in the middle of Herzl St. where it intersects **Weizmann Avenue,** which later turns into Binyamin Ave. Note that the area around the bus station may be unsafe after dark. Also, the neighborhood of Ne'ot Herzl, farther to the north, should be avoided at all times of day and night. At the western edge of Herzl St. is the *midrakhov*, **HaAtzma'ut Square,** and the most popular beaches. The other neighborhood of interest is the **New Industrial Area** (distinct from the Old Industrial Area), in the southeastern part of the city, where a lot of new cafes, shops, and bars are located. It's a bit of a schlep from downtown though—it takes about 25min. to get there by *sherut*.

netanya

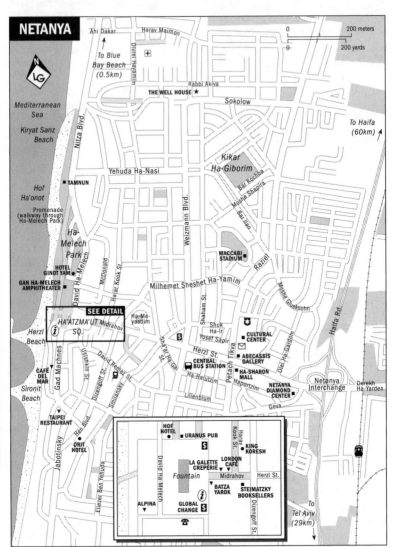

NETANYA

northern mediterranean coast

ACCOMMODATIONS

Beaches usually mean high prices, and Netanya is no exception. Most of its hotels cater to a much grayer and richer bunch; budget hotels are rare, and hostels are altogether nonexistent. To get a bed in one of the few reasonably priced places, make sure to call at least a couple weeks in advance.

HOTEL ORIT — GUESTHOUSE $$

21 Hen Blvd. ☎09 861 6818; www.hotelorit.com

This is truly a gem in the world of budget accommodations. Managed by a sweet Swedish couple who you'll wish were your grandparents, Orit is cozy without being cramped. Everything in the rooms seems carefully handpicked, from the woven rugs to the embroidered tablecloths to the little lamps—and, of course, it's all color-coordinated. Grab a book from the Swedish/English library to enjoy in the airy living room, or just bask on your sunny balcony to celebrate that you actually scored a room here.

Coming from HaAtzma'ut Sq., go south on Gad Machnes and continue on Jabotinsky Ave. Make a left on Hen Blvd. and the hotel is on the right. i Make sure to book well in advance. Breakfast included. Towels and soap included. Free Wi-Fi. $ 4-bed dorms NIS130; singles NIS208; doubles NIS292. ⏰ Reception 8am-2pm and 5-10pm.

KING KORESH — HOTEL $$

6 Harav Kook St. ☎09 861 3555; www.koreshotel.co.il

The lobby is decorated with a bizarre mix of large Oriental vases and painted portraits, and you might just find an old-school rotary telephone in your room. Don't let these eccentricities throw you off though—the rooms are perfectly comfortable, while the price is one of the cheapest in the area.

Going west on Herzl St., turn right on Harav Kook St. just before the square. The hotel is on the right. i Breakfast included. Free Wi-Fi. $ Singles NIS200; doubles NIS260; triples NIS300. ⏰ Check-in 2pm, check-out noon.

going for golda

When Golda Meir was elected Prime Minister on March 17, 1969, she became the first female Prime Minister of Israel and the third female prime minister in the world. Born in Russia, she grew up in the United States, where she became a committed Zionist, then moved to a kibbutz in Palestine. When the Israeli state was just starting out, the politically active Meir traveled to the United States to raise $50 million to purchase arms for the young nation. She then became one of 24 signatories of the Israeli declaration of independence and held the first Israeli passport when she was appointed ambassador to the Soviet Union. She may not be remembered as world's most amusing politician, but it turns out she had a surprising sense of humor:

- **ON ISRAEL.** "Let me tell you something that we Israelis have against Moses. He took us 40 years through the desert in order to bring us to the one spot in the Middle East that has no oil!"
- **ON POLICY.** "Our secret weapon: no alternative."
- **ON YOU.** "Don't be humble...you're not that great." (Ouch.)

HOF HOTEL
HOTEL $$

9 HaAtzma'ut Square ☎09 862 4422

Right in the middle of HaAtzma'ut Sq., Hof is close to all the action without actually getting too loud. The hotel feels a little run-down, with cigarette burns on the covers and fading mirrors, but the rooms are still very clean. Some travelers report being able to pick up Wi-Fi from the restaurant across the square, but good luck leaning out of your balcony to try and pick it up.

➡ On the north side of the square. ℹ Free Wi-Fi at reception desk. $ Singles NIS250; doubles NIS250. Extra person NIS100. Cash only. ⏰ Reception 24hr.

HOTEL GINOT YAM
HOTEL $$$

9 King David St. ☎09 834 1007

Located in a row of high-rise hotel clones, Hotel Ginot Yam has the least atrocious price of the bunch. It's as generic on the inside as it is on the outside, so don't expect any personal touches. Depending on your luck, your view might be of the stunning Mediterranean—or of the next high-rise hotel.

➡ Coming from the bus station, turn right at the end of HaAtzma'ut Square and go up King David St. The hotel is on the left. ℹ Free Wi-Fi in lobby. Breakfast included. $ Singles NIS340; doubles NIS370. ⏰ Check-in 11:30am, check-out 11am.

SIGHTS

Even though Netanya's beaches are its real sights, your skin can only peel so much before you start to resemble the Phantom of the Opera. At that point, it might be time to pack away the tanning oil and check out one of Netanya's few museums.

👍 BEIT HABE'ER
MUSEUM

17 Sokolov St. ☎09 832 9940; http://beit-habeher.biltiformali.org.il

If you'd like to do something besides laze on the beach while your brain atrophies, come here to learn something about Netanya beyond its tourist-filled coastline. Also known as the Well House, Beit HaBe'er was part of Netanya's first orchard, established in 1927. Today, the museum showcases Netanya's development from the Pardes Hagdud Orchard to present day.

➡ At the northeast corner of the intersection with Weizmann Ave. $ NIS10. ⏰ Open Su-W 8am-2pm.

CLIFF GALLERY
GALLERY

19 HaMa'apilm St. ☎09 833 5423

This gallery seems to have high ambitions, judging from the mini Louvre-style glass pyramid on its roof. Run by the municipality of Netanya, the two rooms of Cliff showcase traditional paintings and sculptures. It also has more modern art—at least, we're assuming that's why there's a skateboard sawed in half. From June through August, Cliff features artists from Netanya and the surrounding regions. Exhibitions change once a month.

➡ Go north on HaMa'apilm St. from the square. The gallery is on the left across from the King Solomon Hotel. $ Free. ⏰ Open M 10am-1pm and 5-10pm, Tu-W 5-10pm, Th 10am-1pm and 5-10pm, F 10am-1pm, Sa 10am-2pm.

BEACHES

There's no question about it. Netanya's raison d'être is its beaches. The surprisingly warm Mediterranean water and 14km of fine, soft sand blend seamlessly into each other to create what is basically paradise. Stock up on Coppertone and spend as much time on the beaches as humanly possible—skin cancer-shmancer, your melatonin will take care of things. Maybe? Right?

SIRONIT BEACH

Off Gad Machnes

This is the big boss of Netanya beaches. Sure, you could just take the stairs down to the shore, but why do that when there's a fancy elevator? Sure, you could just sit around on your beach towel, but why do that when you can rent a chair? And an umbrella? And a surfboard or kayak or jet ski? As if those weren't enough, there are also basketball courts, playgrounds, and soccer nets. Sironit Beach is also the only one open year-round

Just south of Herzl Beach. $ Free entry. Chairs NIS10. Umbrellas NIS20. Surfboards and kayaks NIS50 per hr. Jet skis NIS150 per 15min. ⏰ Lifeguard on duty 7am-7pm.

HAONOT BEACH

Off Nizza Ave.

Fighting over small areas is an Israeli tradition, but if warring with tourists and bratty kids over a patch of sand isn't your idea of a beach vacation, walk about 10min. north of Sironit and Herzl Beaches. At this quiet and less well-known beach, the sand is still pristine and the sun still glorious. However, self-pamperers beware: this smaller beach boasts fewer amenities, with only chairs and umbrellas available.

Behind the Four Seasons Hotel. i Also referred to as the Four Seasons Beach. $ Free. ⏰ Open only in summer. Lifeguard on duty 7am-7pm.

HERZL BEACH

Off Gad Machnes

Pretty much the mirror image of Sironit Beach, Herzl has all the same gimmicks, minus the fancy elevator. As the most conveniently located beach, it gets crowded with tourists.

Walk straight down Herzl, through HaAtzma'ut Sq., until you hit the sea. $ Free. ⏰ Open only in summer. Lifeguard on duty 7am-7pm.

FOOD

Like its hotels, food options in Netanya tend to be touristy and overpriced. The restaurants that hug the coastline and fill HaAtzma'ut Sq. will have no qualms about overcharging you. If you're looking for more budget-friendly options, the falafel and shawarma stands that line **Sha'ar HaGai Street** near the bus station cost less and taste better than their counterparts closer to the *midrakhov*. The health-conscious should head over to Weizmann Ave., where **Shuk Halr** (City Market), a block from the intersection with Herzl St., has excellent produce.

LA GALETTE CREPERIE — CREPERIE $

Herzl St. ☎09 887 0965

If you're looking for a cheap alternative to the wow-falafel-and-shawarma-again stands, stop by La Galette for some surprisingly unsnooty French eats. The little creperie is run by an adorable old man who doesn't speak much English but is willing to mime energetically to get his point across. The crepes themselves are equally adorable (and delicious as well).

On the right of the midrakhov when coming from the bus station. i Menu in French only. $ Nutella crepe NIS20; cheese crepe NIS25. Pizza NIS30-37. Cash only. ⏰ Open Su-Th 9am-8pm, F 9am-3:30pm.

BATZA YAROK — ITALIAN $$

12 Herzl St. ☎09 862 8883

Once your eyes get used to the electric pink walls and flickering chandeliers, they'll be glad to skim over a tasty menu, which includes a particularly nice salmon fettuccine in creamy alfredo sauce (NIS65). Otherwise, buy an overpriced iced coffee (NIS20) and make up for it by hogging a table as you take advantage of the free Wi-Fi.

On the left of HaAtzma'ut Sq. when coming from the bus station. i Free Wi-Fi. Kosher. $ Spicy tuna sandwich NIS59. ⏰ Open Su-Th 8am-1am, F 7am-6pm.

CAFE DEL MAR

CAFE $$

Gad Machnes

☎09 887 1277

The food here isn't particularly interesting, but don't come for the food—come for the jaw-dropping view of the Mediterranean. The prices are actually quite reasonable considering the prime real estate. When you're done with your meal and feeling satisfied, waddle five steps over to the Sironit Beach elevator and go nap it off by the water.

✈ *Just before the Sironit Beach elevator when walking toward the sea.* Ⓢ *Sandwiches NIS28-48. Entrees NIS42-52.* Ⓣ *Open Su-Th 8am-midnight, F 8am-6pm, Sa 8am-9pm.*

TAIPEI RESTAURANT

CHINESE $$

2 Jabotinsky Ave.

☎09 862 5135

This restaurant dishes up a tasty generic pan-Chinese selection. Sushi also somehow snuck onto the menu. The decorator clearly went a little overboard as he indulged himself in just about every Chinese stereotype—big red lanterns, golden ◢**dragons,** that obnoxious "bamboo" font, etc.

✈ *At the intersection of Jabotinsky and Gad Machnes.* Ⓢ *Noodles NIS35.* Ⓣ *Open daily noon-midnight.*

ALPINA

FRENCH $$$

2 Gad Machnes

☎09 882 9391

If you want to get a little classier, come to what is generally acknowledged to be one of the best restaurants in town. Be forewarned though: your wallet will be significantly lighter. The waitstaff here doesn't look too kindly on ragged backpackers either.

✈ *Across King David St. from the square, on your left when facing the sea.* Ⓢ *Shrimp in garlic butter NIS93. Fish of the day NIS82.* Ⓣ *Open daily noon-midnight.*

LONDON CAFE

ITALIAN $$

1 Herzl St.

☎09 833 8376

When it comes to suspect geography, London Cafe really takes the, um, biscuit. Serving mainly Italian food, they're best known for their large salads, which are roughly the same size as a small whale. The entrees may be a little pricey, but come before 6pm to take advantage of the lunch menu, which offers the same food at a reduced price. The outdoor seating is the best on the *midrakhov,* but plants, tents, and AstroTurf still make you feel like you're actually not where you paid such a large premium to be.

✈ *On the right of the midrakhov when facing the sea.* Ⓢ *St. Peter's fish NIS82; lunch NIS48. Burgers NIS56-62; lunch NIS48.* Ⓣ *Open daily 8am-1am. Lunch menu served Su-Th 8am-6pm.*

NIGHTLIFE

Since the French geriatric have taken over Netanya, downtown is pretty much dead by 9pm. The **New Industrial Area,** with all the newest bars and clubs, is where most locals go for their nightlife. Getting there is a bit of a haul though: you'll have to take either a taxi or a *sherut* from the central bus station, and at that point, you might as well just head to Tel Aviv.

TAMNUN

BAR

10 Nizza Ave.

☎052 540 8205; www.tamnun.net

Looking to rage like Raskolnikov? Mother Russia may be a little too far away, but Netanya does its best with Tamnun, an almost entirely Russian bar. The large outdoor patio, located right on the beach, is great for getting a little afternoon buzz by the sea, and there's an indoor bar for rainy days. On Thursday and Friday nights, Tamun brings in DJs from Tel Aviv and blasts house music across the beach. The grown-ups stay outside smoking on the patio, and the youngsters get grinding on the dance floor. The crowd here feels like a Russian crime syndicate stereotype, interspersed with the occasional outsider trying to pick up hot Russian chicks.

✦ On HaOnot Beach, just behind the Four Seasons Hotel. Ⓢ Cover Th-F NIS40. Bottle beer NIS20. Draft beer 0.5L NIS20. Ⓞ Open Su-W 9am-1am, Th-F 9am-5am, Sa 9am-1am. Th-F dancing begins at midnight.

URANUS   PUB
13 HaAtzma'ut Square   ☎09 882 9919

Other bars have come and gone, but Uranus has kept itself a downtown staple for over 30 years by modeling itself after a traditional English pub and steering clear of gimmicks. Purposefully hidden in a dark alley with no obvious signs, it's more difficult to find than the Room of Requirement, but that's half the fun. A laid-back crowd comes here, where locals (ages 18-80) all know the bartender.

✦ In HaAtzma'ut Sq., in the dark alley right before HaPaolim Bank. Turn right when facing the sea and continue to the end. Ⓢ Bottle beers NIS22-32. Draft beers NIS22-28. Liquor from NIS22. Ⓞ Open Su-Th 7pm-4am, F 9pm-6am, Sa 8pm-4am.

ARTS AND CULTURE

Folk dancing, art galleries, concerts—Netanya does its best to keep its citizens and tourists occupied, with the municipality frequently organizing free entertainment (check at the tourist office for a list of activities). In particular, we'd recommend the dreamy experience of sitting in the **Gan HaMelech Amphitheater,** watching the sun slowly set over the Mediterranean while being serenaded by classical melodies. Talented Russian musicians also perform **classical music** in HaAtzma'ut Sq. every Monday at noon (11 HaAtzmau't Square ☎09 884 0534 Ⓢ NIS25, includes refreshments. Ⓞ Concert M noon-1pm. Refreshments served 11-11:45am). On Saturday nights in the summer, join in the **folk dancing** in the square.

SHOPPING

Netanya is historically famous for its **diamonds.** However, if you can afford those diamonds, you probably have no need for this book (except maybe to point and laugh at us budget travelers in our cramped hostels). Those more like us will head over to the *midrakhov* and Herzl St., which are lined with little stands peddling trinkets. There is also a gigantic mall (HaSharon Mall) at the intersection of Herzl St. and Raziel Rd.

STEIMATZKY BOOKSELLERS   BOOKSTORE
4 Herzl St.   ☎09 891 7154

Steimatzky has books and magazines in Hebrew, English, and several other languages. It's also a good place to flip through *Us Weekly* and catch up on your celeb gossip. Once a year, in June, the store participates in a week-long discount book fair that takes place at night in HaAtzma'ut Square. Inquire at the store for details.

✦ On the left of the midrakhov when facing the sea. Ⓢ Magazines NIS30-40. Ⓞ Open Su-Th 8am-8pm, F 8am-2pm.

ESSENTIALS

practicalities

- **TOURIST OFFICE:** The staff at the **Tourist Information Center** can be extremely rude and unhelpful, although they do have information regarding seasonal events. Grab a free map and brochure quickly, then go find a friendly cafe proprietor or hotel manager if you need help. Also try the municipal website www.netanya.muni.il/Eng. (HaAtzma'ut Sq. ☎09 882 7286 ✦ Behind Batza Yarok, next to the post office. Ⓞ Open Su-Th 8am-4pm.)

- **ATM: Bank HaPaolim** has outdoor ATMs. (HaAtzma'ut Sq. ✦ At the northeast corner of HaAtzma'ut Sq., across from Batza Yarok. Ⓞ Open 24hr.)

- **LAUNDROMAT: Mileno** provides wash and dry services. (26 Dizengoff St. ☎052 624 8887, 09 882 5210 ✈ Walking on the *midrakhov* away from the sea, make a right at Dizengoff St. Mileno is on the right. *i* Min. 6kg. Ⓢ NIS40 per 6kg. Ⓩ Open Su-Th 6am-7pm, F 6am-3pm.)
- **INTERNET: Batza Yarok** has free Wi-Fi, which can be accessed in the restaurant or in the square. (12 Herzl St. ☎09 862 8883 ✈ On the southeast corner of HaAtzma'ut Sq. Ⓩ Open Su-Th 7am-1am, F 7am-6pm.)
- **POSTAL CODE:** 42438 (city center).
- **POST OFFICE:** 12 HaAtzma'ut Sq. ☎09 862 7797 ✈ In HaAtzma'ut Sq., next to the Tourist Information Center. Ⓩ Open Su 8am-6pm, M 8am-12:30pm and 3:30-6pm, Tu 8am-12:30pm and 3:30-6pm, W 8am-1:30pm, Th 8am-6pm, F 8am-noon.

emergency

- **POLICE: City Police.** (Raziel Rd. ☎09 886 4444 ✈ On the right, about ½ a block north of the intersection with Herzl St.)
- **LATE-NIGHT PHARMACY: HaMagen Pharmacy.** (13 Weizmann Ave. ☎09 882 2985.)
- **HOSPITAL/MEDICAL SERVICES:** Laniado Hospital. (Divrai Hayim St. ☎09 860 4666 ✈ From the central bus station, head north on Weizmann Ave. for about 1km. Turn left onto Rabbi Akiva then right onto Divrai Hayim. The hospital is on the right.)

getting there

BY BUS

The **Central Bus Station** is located at the corner of Herzl St. and Binaymin Ave. From **Tel Aviv** take Egged bus #641. (Ⓢ NIS17.20. Ⓩ 1¾hr.) From **Haifa,** take bus #947. (Ⓢ NIS23. Ⓩ 1¼hr.) From **Jerusalem,** take bus #947. (Ⓢ NIS29. Ⓩ 2hr.)

BY TRAIN

An **Israel Railway** station can be found off HaRakevet Rd. To get to Netanya from **Savidor Central Rail Station,** in Tel Aviv's city center, takes about 2hr. (Ⓢ NIS15.)

getting around

BY TAXI

The three main taxi services are **HaShahar** (☎09 861 4444), **HaSharon** (☎09 882 2323), and **Hen** (☎09 833 3333).

BY BUS

Nateev Express operates local buses. The most commonly used lines are **bus #4** for getting around the city center and **bus #84** to get to the New Industrial Area.

BY CAR

The most commonly used rental companies are **Sixt** (2 Ussishkin St. ☎09 887 2145 Ⓩ Open Su-Th 8am-5pm, F 8am-noon.) and **Budget.** (2 Gad Machnes ☎09 833 0618 Ⓩ Open Su-Th 8am-6pm, F 8am-2pm.)

caesarea   ☎04

There's no doubting Israel's a beautiful country, but in Caesarea, the milk's especially creamy and the honey's just a tad sweeter. Ask an Israeli where to find the most gorgeous beaches in the country, and you'll get Caesarea for an answer. Aside from the country's largest power plant looming to the south, the crystal waters here don't bother with such formalities as coastal urban grime, settling instead for sprawling ancient ruins. Herod the Great—yeah, the same one the New Testament mentions—

established a port here, and huge entertainment complexes, including a circus and hippodrome, soon flanked his palace over the Mediterranean. The city seems to have maintained this character today as a playground for the rich and famous. The ancient port has largely retreated underwater, leaving ruins now sprinkled with spotless cobbled paths and fancy restaurants. Cobblestones? Fancy restaurants? Alarm bells are doubtlessly going off in the heads of seasoned backpackers. Yes, the place is expensive, but farther south around the mellow Kibbutz Sdot Yam, barefoot kibbutzniks and a clan of diehard windsurfers take over. Caesarea also seems to thrive off weddings; expect to see no less than three every night.

ORIENTATION

Everything worth seeing in Caesarea—the ruins and the kibbutz—is within easy walking distance. The **kibbutz** sits adjacent to the **national park,** which is directly to the south. They are connected by the C-shaped road **Kvish HaTe'atron,** which juts out from the seaside **Rothschild Street.** Navigating within the kibbutz or national park is simple, with everything you could conceivably want to find clearly marked. The expensive chalets and condos that make up Caesarea's residential zones are located in two bunches—one about 1km inland and the other north of the aqueducts. Both are out of walking distance and would require a set of wheels to reach.

ACCOMMODATIONS

Caesarea's lodgings are generally expensive and far from the beach and ruins. Luckily, the two budget options available are prime real estate, right on the waterfront and only a few hundred meters from the national park.

⬛ KIBBUTZ SDOT YAM

KIBBUTZ $

☎054 666 9849; www.sdot-yam.org.il

Whatever would the sweat-drenched backpacker do without those hospitable kibbutzniks? Like many kibbutzim along the Mediterranean coast, Sdot Yam puts rooms aside for travelers. Normally that means Israelis hiking the length of the country, but they are often open to tourists for a single night given enough advance notice. The best part: they're free. The residents of the kibbutz are extremely friendly, and, while you might be sharing the room with a family of ants, the company, location, and price—or lack thereof—are all unbeatable.

⚑ Along Kvish HaTe'atron, directly adjacent to the national park. ⓘ Bathroom, TV, and A/C included. Fridge and kettle provided. Free tea and coffee. The phone number belongs to the proprietor, Shavide.

CAESAREA SEA CENTER

HOSTEL $$

Etrog Limon

☎04 636 4609

Just below the kibbutz is a complex of small apartments and stucco buildings reminiscent of your childhood summer camp. The staff might be as smug as that of some of the more expensive joints in town, but the place is located right on the beach and next to a water sports center. A large central lawn provides the perfect spot to chill out with an *argilah.*

⚑ Off Rothschild St., near the coast. Going north, turn right onto Hadar St. Caesarea Sea Center is located just past Etrog Limon St. ⓘ A/C, TV, and refrigerator. Free Wi-Fi.

SIGHTS

When it comes to sights, Caesarea's all about doing it old school. The port town is a regional hub and has found itself up for grabs multiple times over the last two thousand years. In fact, it has passed through the hands of no less than five civilizations, each of which left its mark on a coastline now littered with sights. On the more modern end of the things, the nearby kibbutz has a few museums.

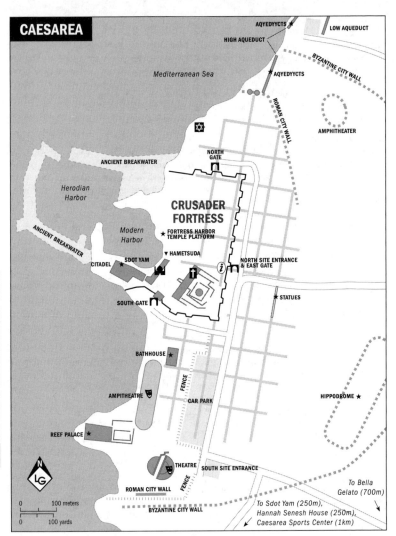

CAESAREA

Mediterranean Sea

AQYEDYYCTS ★
HIGH AQUEDUCT
LOW AQUEDUCT
AQYEDYYCTS
BYZANTINE CITY WALL

ROMAN CITY WALL

AMPHITHEATER

ANCIENT BREAKWATER

NORTH
GATE

Herodian
Harbor

CRUSADER
FORTRESS

★ FORTRESS HARBOR
TEMPLE PLATFORM

Modern
Harbor

▼ HAMETSUDA

ANCIENT BREAKWATER

CITADEL ★

SDQT YAM ★

NORTH SITE ENTRANCE
& EAST GATE

SOUTH GATE

★ STATUES

BATHHOUSE ★

FENCE

AMPITHEATRE ●

CAR PARK

HIPPODROME ★

REEF PALACE ★

N
LG

THEATRE
SOUTH SITE ENTRANCE

0   100 meters
0   100 yards

ROMAN CITY WALL

FENCE

BYZANTINE CITY WALL

To Bella
Gelato (700m)

To Sdot Yam (250m),
Hannah Senesh House (250m),
Caesarea Sports Center (1km)

mistaken identity

First your boss, then your mom, now even the country of Israel has its very own Twitter account. Although Israel has yet to reach Kim Kardashian status, its respectable number of followers are kept up-to-date on topics such as the Israeli Film Festival and the top 10 hikes in Israel. The Israel Twitter account wasn't always so family-friendly, however; the username was originally taken by Israel Meléndez, the owner of a Spanish porn site. The account was linked to X-rated content until the Israeli Foreign Ministry bought it from Meléndez in 2010 because it believed it could put the account to better use. Probably a smart move.

national park

The national park contains pretty much every historical sight in Caesarea, and, while it's too large ever to get packed, it does bear its fair share of tourists by the busload each day. **Free brochures and maps** are available at each of the park's three entrances, and a variety of paths can be taken through the park, depending on where you choose to begin. We recommend you begin in the south, by the Roman Theater, and work your way north in a route that takes about 3-4hr. If you need to save time, you can shave off an hour by cutting out the Byzantine Synagogue and aqueducts. While the area is quite exposed to the sun, the cool sea breeze and plethora of drink stands and restaurants by the port mean you can probably go quite light on the provisions (☎04 626 7080 $NIS38. ⏰ Open Apr-Sept Su-Th 8am-6pm, F 8am-5pm; Oct-Mar Su-Th 8am-4pm, F 8am-3pm).

ROMAN THEATER RUINS

The oldest theater in Israel, the Roman Theater was originally built by Herod to give some bread and circuses to more than 4000 local plebes by way of mock-marble flooring and a huge, multi-storied stage backdrop (now fallen). By the third century, the place had become a sort of ancient "Medieval Times," hosting war reenactments—until the battles became a little too real in the sixth century, when the theater was captured by the Byzantines and converted into a fortress. The building has today gone full circle and, in the original Herodian spirit of entertainment, offers a regular schedule of pop and classical music concerts, putting everyone from Eric Clapton to the Bolshoi on the stage. The **Time Trek video presentation** just to the north of the theater throws a comprehensive history of the port at you in 10min.

 # At the very southern end of the park. Enter the gate, and the theater is right there. ⏰ Movie showings Su-Th 8am-5pm, F 8am-3pm. English showing at quarter past and quarter of every hr.

HEROD'S REEF PALACE RUINS

The closest that the Romans ever got to the Playboy Mansion? Disputable. But the palace was certainly constructed with parties in mind. A large reception area for greeting the rich and famous dominates the upper half of the palace, with many of the original mosaics and foundations still intact. Jutting into the Mediterranean below are Herod's private quarters, where the remains of a freshwater pool (an early jacuzzi, perhaps?) are still visible. Today locals often sneak past the guardrails and perch over the sea to fish.

 # Just north of the theater. Walk through the architectural ruins garden just east of the theater. The palace is past the wall to its north.

HERODIAN AMPHITHEATER RUINS

We've all seen *Ben-Hur*, so we all know just how awesome Roman chariot races were. Herod seemed to have agreed—presumably bored with all that haughty culture business at the theater, he had this 250m-long hippodrome built in his backyard. In case the audience of 15,000 got tired of horses, the amphitheater would also host gladiatorial combats and other blood sports, which was pretty easy to do considering the steady supply of wild animals and hapless persecuted Christians and Jews in the area.

☨ *Directly adjacent to the Reef Palace.*

BYZANTINE BATHHOUSE   RUINS

Fast forward a few centuries to the Byzantine era. The amphitheater has fallen into disrepair, and Caesarea's new inhabitants use the northern end to build a large bathhouse complex, supplied with water from the Roman aqueducts. Fast forward quite a few more centuries, and the sauna, pool room, and public reception area are still identifiable among the warren of high walls and mosaics.

☨ *To the north, just behind the amphitheater.*

CRUSADER FORTRESS   RUINS

We feel almost disingenuous calling this place ruins—the Crusader Fortress is arguably the most intact and physically impressive sight in the park. A 900m-long, 13m-high wall encircles the entire city, surrounded by what was intended to be a moat (it never actually held water). While the walls are certainly daunting, they were still no match for Sultan Baibars's armies, who eventually penetrated them and razed the Crusader town, of which next to nothing remains. Nice try, walls.

☨ *Just north of the Herodian Amphitheater.*

SEBASTOS HARBOR   RUINS

The centerpiece of ancient Caesarea since its founding, the port was artificially constructed by a series of breakwaters filled with ash. It used to extend much farther into the Mediterranean, but centuries of wars and earthquakes have submerged large portions of the harbor; remnants are still visible as dark patches in the crystal clear sea and are accessible with scuba gear. If you feel the need to watch the Time Trek video again, there's another station on the promontory. This time, though, it's accompanied by a series of interactive holograms of various historical characters—talk to everyone from Herod to Hana Senesh to see what they say. A second video on top of the watchtower in the Art Nova Gallery provides a brief history of how the port itself was constructed. For those content to stick with modernity, chic restaurants line the waterfront, offering inordinately high prices and stunning views of the Mediterranean.

☨ *Within the Crusader Fortress, by the waterfront.*

TEMPLE PLATFORM   RUINS

Shameless sycophant that he was, Herod constructed a temple here in honor of his patron, Caesar Augustus—apparently it wasn't enough to name the town after him. The temple became a huge octagonal church in the Byzantine era, then a mosque, and finally a Crusader cathedral before it was just plain destroyed, leaving the immense elevated platform that exists today.

☨ *Toward the inland, southern portion of the Crusader Fortress.*

BYZANTINE SYNAGOGUE   RUINS

What kind of Israeli ruins would these be without just a little nod to the Jews of yore? While the structure itself had been largely decimated, the site yielded a treasure trove of menorahs and mosaics as well as the broken fragments of a grille listing the 24 priestly divisions. Unfortunately, most of that has been moved to museums, leaving little more than a nice view.

☨ *Exit the harbor (though not the fortress) on the inland side and continue up the road, heading north until you exit the fortress. There is a parking lot directly after the bridge that crosses the moat. The synagogue is just over the embankment by the coast.*

AQUEDUCTS RUINS

Since there was no freshwater in Caesarea, it had to be brought in from the faraway Shuni Springs, which feeds the northern aqueduct. Perched on arches, it houses three separate canals that were progressively added over its use. Thanks to a southern aqueduct built soon after by Hadrian, water flowed in on these 8m-high structures.

From the synagogue, the aqueducts should be just visible along the beach, about 600m away. They are more easily accessible by the road, which runs parallel to the coast about 100m inland.

STATUES SQUARE RUINS

When two kibbutzniks stumbled across what looked like the top of a statue, excavations revealed a whole Byzantine street, adorned by two massive statues supposedly depicting Roman emperors, one of which is carved out of striking red porphyry.

Head south along the main road. Turn left at the T-junction (the Crusader Fortress will be on the right). The square is on the left after 200m.

HIPPODROME RUINS

Those chariot races are big business. By the second century, Herod's amphitheater could no longer hold the crowds hoping for that NASCAR-style crash, and this 450m-long hippodrome was built in the east to hold up to 30,000 spectators. The arena was no doubt magnificent in its day—a 27m-high porphyry obelisk was uncovered on site—but is today swarmed with orange groves.

Continue up the road, heading inland from Statues Sq. for about 1km. An archway marks the entrance.

kibbutz sdot yam

This kibbutz, about 300m south of the national park, may be the chillest place in Israel. It's at least in the running: comfy bungalows are surrounded by manicured lawns and gardens, the residents go to the beach almost daily, and sweaty backpackers are invited in for a chat and a game of soccer. A clan of devoted windsurfers—including an **Olympic gold medalist**—has also taken up shop in the kibbutz. If just hanging out with these guys isn't exciting enough for you, check out one of the small museums on the grounds.

HANA SENESH HOUSE MUSEUM

☎04 636 4366; www.hannahsenesh.org.il

Hana Senesh was a paratrooper from Sdot Yam who, on a mission to save Auschwitz-bound Jews during WWII, was captured at the Hungarian border. Refusing to yield details of her mission, she was executed by firing squad. She is honored here with a short film and numerous displays.

Located in the center of the kibbutz. There are clear signs from the kibbutz's entrance. ***i*** *Film can also be shown in English.* $ *NIS13.* ⏰ *Open Su-Th 10am-4pm. It's best to call ahead.*

SDOT YAM ANTIQUE MUSEUM AND SCULPTURE GARDEN MUSEUM

☎04 636 4444

A large garden adorned with statues, friezes, and pillars divides the two rooms stuffed with coins, pottery fragments, and some very old urns. Extensive displays provide English commentary on many of the artifacts.

Directly opposite the Hana Senesh House. $ *NIS15.* ⏰ *Open M-Th 10am-4pm, F 10am-1pm.*

THE GREAT OUTDOORS

With azure waters and pristine beaches, the great outdoors is Caesarea's thing. The two major **beaches** are north and south of the national park. While the northern one has the dramatic backdrop of one of the aqueducts, it can get a little crowded, especially on weekends. The southern beach is more the domain of 20-something kibbutzniks; with no lifeguard on duty, it's a much less mobbed affair, though be sure to watch out for the jet-skiers and wind and kitesurfers who tear up the water in the area. Jellyfish are also a constant threat in these waters, but they're big enough that you'll probably spot them easily.

Not tired of ruins yet? The submerged remains of the port now constitute an **underwater archaeological park.** The Diving Center (☎04 626 5898) on the outermost reach of the port's promontory offers regular tours. While scuba certification is a prerequisite to see the majority of the port beyond the wharf, the 20% within can be seen using rented **snorkeling** gear. Tours last up to 45min. and start at NIS160 per person, with a minimum of three people required. Make sure to book in advance.

FOOD

Caesarea's culinary epicenter is the port, but—given the silver-spoon-bearing crowds who grace the area—these are the kinds of establishments you might treat yourself to, but probably won't frequent. Outside the city limits, the beachfront along Sdot Yam has a single bar that serves pretty shoddy fare for a pretty high price. However, the **refectory** at the Sea Center has a buffet for every meal for only NIS50, and a shack at the entrance to the park by the theater serves **cheap hot dogs and sandwiches**. Should you have a kitchen, check out the grocery store in the kibbutz where, though prices are 10% higher for non-residents, it's still the most economical way to get your daily bread.

◈ HAMETSUDA
SUSHI, MEAT $$$

Caesarea Port ☎04 610 0022; www.metsuda.co.il

Of those pricey waterfront restaurants, Hametsuda probably has the best view, roosting right on the promontory. It also serves up a great selection of meats and sushi at prices that seem reasonable for what you're getting. In particular, the sushi or meat all-you-can-eat deals (Su-Th until 8:30pm; meat NIS99, sushi NIS109) might strike you as both a challenge and a culinary experience, so go ahead and eat the bourgeoisie out of business.

⚓ At the promontory of the port. *i* As with all restaurants in the area, casual wear is acceptable. Ⓢ Burger and fries NIS55. Ⓐ Open daily noon-late.

BELLA GELATO
ICE CREAM $

Caesarea Port ☎04 626 5888; www.bellagelato.co.il

We've said it before, but ice cream is a godsend in this country. Bella might seem just as haughty as its next-door neighbors, but the prices suggest anything but. Flavors like bubble gum, limoncello, passion flower, and kiwi banana will awake your curiosity, while the paradox of diet chocolate ice cream will surely leave you puzzled.

⚓ At the northern end of the port, next to Aresto. Ⓢ Small ice cream NIS15, medium NIS19, large NIS23. Ⓐ Open Su-Th 9:30am-11:30pm, F-Sa 9:30am-12:30am.

AGENDA
CAFE $$

Rothschild St. ☎04 636 4444

The only eatery outside of the port might seem a little divey—after all, it's tacked onto a gas station—but Agenda is the only reasonably priced restaurant in the area. Be sure to check out **Minato Sushi,** owned by the same people, next to Agenda.

⚓ Driving into Caesarea from Hadera, you'll pass the gas station. Ⓢ Focaccia NIS32. Salmon carpaccio NIS55. Ⓐ Open Su-Th 8am-noon, F 8am-4pm, Sa 8am-noon.

northern mediterranean coast

ESSENTIALS

practicalities

Caesarea is oddly lacking in basic amenities. It's best to stock up on clean laundry, pharmaceuticals, and anything else you might need in the town of Hadera before you head over—many of the big chains are located around the central bus station.

- **ATM:** Caesarea's only ATM is located in the port in the same building as Bella Gelato.

emergency

- **POLICE: Or Akiva Police** (☎04 626 1630).

- **HOSPITAL: Hillel Yaffe Medical Center, Hadera** (☎04 630 4304).

getting there

BY BUS

It's difficult to get to Caesarea directly. Instead you'll have to go through the nearby city of Hadera. Unfortunately, the bus service from there to Caesarea is highly erratic. From either Haifa or Tel Aviv, the Egged #921 is the best and most direct route to Hadera. Buses run from Tel Aviv (Ⓢ NIS20. ☒ 1¼hr., every 20min.) and from Haifa. (Ⓢ NIS20. ☒ 45min., every 40min.)

BY TAXI

A taxi from Tel Aviv should not cost more than NIS50.

getting around

Although you would need to either rent a bike or drive in order to get to the swankier northern part of Caesarea, the rest of the city is walkable.

akko ☎04

Plopped on a small peninsula across the bay from Haifa, Akko simply oozes character—as you ignore the rather drab modern area in the north. The city's jewel is its Arab Old City, tucked behind the Crusader walls that defend it from the Mediterranean on three sides. This side of town has been around for a good millennium, and those magnificent walls now contain a labyrinth of Crusader buttresses, towering minarets, and serpentine alleys packed with spice stalls and the usual falafel stands. From the Templars' Tunnel burrowed underground to the church spires soaring overhead, the tiny area is packed with enough to keep you entertained for a few days. Tourists bewildered by the Gordian knot of alleys may not be an uncommon sight, but Akko is also a fully functioning Arab neighborhood, where the air is thick with wafting saffron and the cries of *muezzins*. It somehow manages to maintain the tough balance of being tourist-friendly while avoiding the inauthentic, and, while the area is certainly safe as a whole, *Let's Go* does not advise walking through the alleys at night. There'll be no reason to anyway—other than a few restaurants and *argilah* bars, the place essentially shuts down come sunset.

ORIENTATION

Akko's **Old City** is tiny, but labyrinthine. To make things even harder, the buildings don't have numbers, and only the larger roads have names. The best way to orient yourself is to use the major sights as landmarks and go from there. In any case, getting lost is never a biggie; walking 5min. in any direction is bound to take you to something you will recognize. This will most likely be the sea, as the Old City is surrounded by water on three sides. The main entrance is along **Weizmann Street,** which soon forks: to the right is the **Crusader Fortress,** while the left road follows the eastern wall of the city down to the head of **Salah ad-Din.** Salah ad-Din and Weizmann St. meet to form **Al-Jazzar Street**—the site

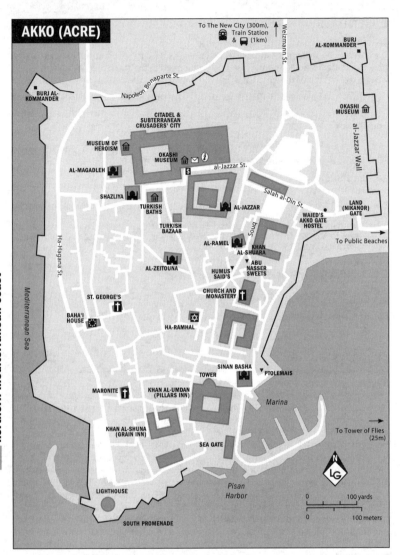

AKKO (ACRE)

To The New City (300m),
Train Station
& (1km)

Weizmann St.

BURJ
AL-KOMMANDER

BURJ AL-
KOMMANDER

Napoleon Bonaparte St.

OKASHI
MUSEUM

al-Jazzar Wall

CITADEL &
SUBTERRANEAN
CRUSADERS' CITY

MUSEUM OF
HEROISM

OKASHI
MUSEUM

al-Jazzar St.

AL-MAGADLEH

Salah al-Din St.

SHAZLIYA

LAND
(NIKANOR)
GATE

TURKISH
BATHS

AL-JAZZAR

WAIED'S
AKKO GATE
HOSTEL

TURKISH
BAZAAR

Souq

To Public Beaches

AL-RAMEL

KHAN
AL-SHUARA

AL-ZEITOUNA

HUMUS
SAID'S

ABU
NASSER
SWEETS

Ha-Hagana St.

CHURCH AND
MONASTERY

ST. GEORGE'S

BAHA'I
HOUSE

HA-RAMHAL

Mediterranean Sea

SINAN BASHA

PTOLEMAIS

TOWER

MARONITE

KHAN AL-UMDAN
(PILLARS INN)

Marina

To Tower of Flies
(25m)

KHAN AL-SHUNA
(GRAIN INN)

SEA GATE

N

LIGHTHOUSE

Pisan
Harbor

0   100 yards

0   100 meters

SOUTH PROMENADE

northern mediterranean coast

of many basic amenities and restaurants—after a quick kink in the road.

Al-Jazzar St. carries on west toward the Turkish Baths and eventually reaches **HaGanah Street**—the street running along the western wall of the city from an entrance to the Old City at its top to the **waterfront lighthouse** at its base, where it turns east to become **Salah el-Basri** that runs along the city's southern wall. The main thoroughfare of the central Old City is **Market Street.**

ACCOMMODATIONS

There aren't a large number of places to stay in Akko's Old City, but these two hostels do nicely.

▥ AKKO SAND HOSTEL   HOSTEL $
Salah ad-Din   ☎04 991 8636; akko.sand.hostel@gmail.com

Sand Hostel sits on prime real estate right by the *souq* in the middle of the Old City, but it still manages to stay quiet and serene. Consisting of three floors surrounding a small courtyard, Sand has a top-floor dorm that offers stunning views of the minarets and church steeples jutting above the maze of alleyways. Outdoor lounges and balconies provide shady chill-out spots, while the downstairs salon—adorned with everything from Bob Marley paraphernalia to a hat collection—is a center for the hostel community, offering live music and Tuesday open-mic nights.

✴ *Just behind Al-Jazzar Mosque. Coming from Weizmann St., pass the street with the mosque entrance and continue straight along the street bordering the mosque's eastern wall. The hostel is on the right. Signs point the way.* ℹ *Free Wi-Fi. Kitchen access. A/C and ensuite bathroom. Laundry NIS15 per load.* Ⓢ *Dorms NIS70; singles NIS200; doubles NIS297. Breakfast NIS25. Cash only.*

WALLED'S GATE HOSTEL   HOSTEL $
Salah ad-Din   ☎04 991 0410

Walled's Gate has claimed an especially quiet patch of the Old City right against its eastern wall, but it's still no more than 10min. from everything else. Recent renovations have seen the welcome addition of spotless dorms complete with extra-thick mattresses and bathrooms with—would you believe it—actual baths. For a cheaper sleep, you can opt to sleep on the back terrace, if you're willing to put up with a little dirt and the looming threat of insect bedfellows.

✴ *Enter the Old City on Weizmann St., make a right at the 1st fork, and then another right at the next fork. Follow the road to the corner and turn right. The hostel is on the right.* ℹ *Free Wi-Fi. A/C, TV, and fridge.* Ⓢ *Patio NIS50; dorms NIS70. Singles NIS200; doubles NIS300.*

SIGHTS

The town may be small, but there's a lot of depth to it—literally. When your city is surrounded by the ocean and Crusader walls, the only way to build is vertically, and so Akko has become an archaeological club sandwich of ancient, medieval, Byzantine, and modern sites. A large number of these are helpfully located at the **Citadel Complex** at 1 Weizmann St. (on your left as you enter the city). The local tourist authority also keeps your wallet happy by offering a combined ticket for a few of the sights.

▥ CRUSADER FORTRESS   HISTORICAL SITE
Citadel Complex   www.acre.org.il

Excavated almost in its entirety, this colossal fortress dominates the northern landscape of the Old City. The Knights Hospitaller built the fort in the 12th century to fight off the Mamluk hordes and to protect pilgrims en route to Jerusalem. Much of the site has been restored to its former magnificence, including the towering stone columns of the massive *Lord of the Rings*-esque halls, the vast refectory where feasts took place, and even the toilets.

✴ *Entrance just behind the ticket booths in the courtyard of 1 Weizmann St.* Ⓢ *Combined ticket with Okashi Museum and Templars' Tunnel NIS27, with Turkish Baths NIS46; students NIS24/39.* ⏰ *Open in summer Su-Th 8:30am-7pm, F 8:30am-5pm, Sa 8:30am-7pm; in winter daily 8:30am-5pm.*

akko

napoleon complex

Israel's all about the history—it's the only place where you can walk where Abraham walked, eat where Jesus ate... and sleep where Napoleon slept? During Bonaparte's campaigns in Egypt and Syria (he was heading toward India), he worked his way up the Mediterranean coast, seizing both Jaffa and Haifa before finally being stopped by the Turks at Akko, a defeat which many consider the turning point of the campaign. Despite having lost 1200 men—and an additional 600 to plague—Napoleon billed his retreat to Egypt as a triumphant return, fought a last battle there, and then did another "triumphant return" to France.

AL-JAZZAR MOSQUE
Al-Jazzar St.

RELIGIOUS SITE
☎04 991 3039

The third largest mosque in the country, Al-Jazzar Mosque was established in 1781 by the formidable Al-Jazzar, who ruled Akko and much of the surrounding area. The soaring green dome and matching minaret dominate the Old City skyline, and the brightly colored courtyard is a nice view from ground level. A hair from the beard of Muhammad himself is apparently housed in the mosque, but it's not on display.

⚵ *Make a right onto Al-Jazzar St. from Weizmann St. The entrance is opposite the post office.* ⓘ *Knees and shoulders must be covered. Shawls available for women at the door.* ⓢ *NIS10.* ☒ *Open sunrise-sunset, except during prayers.*

TURKISH BATHS
Al-Jazzar St.

HISTORICAL SITE
www.acre.org.il

After its construction by Al-Jazzar in 1795, the bathhouse was the social hub of the city for centuries. Although now its halls are frequented only by bronze figurines, the place has been meticulously restored. A corny audiovisual tour, courtesy of the "son of the last bathhouse attendant," guides you through the rooms. You'll learn some real history as you walk through—it'll just be interspersed with questionable accents and marginally hilarious acting.

⚵ *From Al-Jazzar St., go straight, passing the post office and the kink in the road. The entrance is at the T-junction immediately after.* ⓢ *NIS25, students NIS21. Combined ticket (also includes the Crusader Fortress, Okashi Museum, and Templars' Tunnel) NIS46, students NIS39.* ☒ *Open in summer Su-Th 8:30am-7pm, F 8:30am-5pm, Sa 8:30am-7pm; in winter daily 8:30am-5pm.*

MUSEUM OF THE UNDERGROUND PRISONERS
10 HaGanah St.

MUSEUM
☎04 991 1375

Long after the Crusaders had abandoned their looming fortress, the British moved into the area and found a suitable use for the impenetrable stone: a prison. Considering the excitement of the mandate, it's unsurprising that the building was home to scores of famous prisoners, most notably Bahá'u'lláh, founder of the Baha'i faith. The museum today focuses on the various resistance groups whose members did time there, the breakouts, and the lives of some of the more illustrious inmates. If the kids are acting up, take them to the solitary confinement cells—maybe that'll scare some sense into them.

⚵ *From the courtyard of the fortress, walk up the pathway at the northern end of the lawn, take a left, and continue for 50m. The entrance is on the left. Alternatively, enter the Old City via HaGanah St. and the museum is immediately on the left.* ⓘ *Passport required for entry.* ⓢ *NIS15, students NIS10.* ☒ *Open Su-Th 8:30am-4:30pm, F 8:30am-1:30pm.*

OKASHI MUSEUM

Al-Jazzar St.

MUSEUM

☎ 04 995 6710

Avshalom Okashi was an acclaimed Israeli artist who lived in Akko for most of his life. While he used some color in his lighthearted studies of Akko, he seemed to have had a deep obsession with black. Many of his intense compositions involve masses of black paint lashed onto the canvas in such quantities that it forms lumps.

✱ *On Al-Jazzar St., just past the post office on the right.* Ⓢ *NIS10, students NIS7. Combined ticket with Crusader Fortress and Templars' Tunnel NIS27, with Turkish Baths as well NIS46; students NIS24/39.* Ⓩ *Open in summer Su–Th 8:30am-7pm, F 8:30am-5pm, Sa 8:30am-7pm; in winter daily 8:30am-5pm.*

TEMPLARS' TUNNEL

HISTORICAL SITE

www.acre.org.il

This subterranean passage was dug out by the Knights Templar—yes, the ones of Dan Brown fame—to ensure a safe trip from the fortress to the nearby port. It was discovered in 1994, and hunched tourists can now tour a small portion while listening to the water running below the wooden walkways.

✱ *Entrance on HaGanah St., where it meets the sea—turn left just before the restaurant on the corner. Another entrance is just south of Khan al-Umdan.* Ⓢ *NIS10, students NIS7. Combined ticket with Crusader Fortress and Okashi Museum NIS27, with Turkish Baths as well NIS46; students NIS24/39.* Ⓩ *Open in summer Su–Th 8:30am-7pm, F 8:30am-5pm, Sa 8:30am-7pm; in winter daily 8:30am-5pm.*

TREASURE IN THE WALLS MUSEUM

2 Weizmann St.

MUSEUM

The name may sound romanticized, but it's completely literal—this museum (sometimes called the Ethnographic Museum) is located within the eastern wall of the Old City and displays artifacts from all over the Galilee. This new museum focuses on northern Israel in the past century and features a reconstructed smith's workshop and antique furniture.

✱ *Located within the eastern wall of the city and accessed through the top of it. Either climb the stairs by the city's main gate (on Weizmann St.) or take the large ramp farther south to reach the top of the walls.* Ⓢ *NIS15, students NIS12.* Ⓩ *Open Su–Th 10am-4pm, F 10am-2pm.*

BAHA'I SHRINE

North Akko Intersection

RELIGIOUS SITE

www.ganbahai.org.il/en/akko

Located halfway between Akko and Nahariya, this shrine houses the burial place of Bahá'u'lláh, the faith's founder. The holiest site of the religion, it may lack the pomp and circumstance of its cousin, the Baha'i Gardens in nearby Haifa, but it creates the same contagious serenity thanks to its lush, manicured greenery. The absence of a gigantic 19-stage staircase is an additional perk.

✱ *Take bus #971 to Nahariya and get off at the North Akko Intersection. The shrine is 300m up the access road toward Kibbutz Shomrat.* ℹ *Knees and shoulders must be covered.* Ⓩ *Shrine and inner gardens open M-F 9am–noon. Outer gardens open daily 9am-4pm.*

BEACHES

Akko's two beaches are located outside of the Old City, toward the east. They both sport beautiful views, but, thanks to the crowds and poor water conditions, you might be better off heading north to Nahariya.

PURPLE BEACH

The snails that were once used to produce a purple pigment may have disappeared, but bustling Purple Beach is now crawling with families as Akko's prime weekend spot.

✱ *From Salah ad-Din, leave the Old City through the eastern gate, go past Akkotel, and continue down the road for about 500m.*

ARGAMAN BEACH

Downshore from Purple Beach, Argaman has the same great views of the Old City. Unfortunately, the waters here are known for being a little dirty, thanks to the location of Haifa's industrial district just across the bay.

About 1km from Purple Beach.

FOOD

Another Arab Quarter means another collection of shawarma, falafel, and hummus. Akko comes out great in the cheap eats department, with the large quantity of food stands matched only by their incredible quality. The largest cluster of stands is located by the mosque entrance on Al-Jazzar St. The *souq*, which begins about 20m down the road, also has a good number of stands, as well as groceries and some hidden treats. As you get closer to the waterfront, pricier seafood restaurants begin to take over.

HUMMUS SAID — HUMMUS $

Souq ☎04 991 3945

Hummus Said has been in town since time immemorial. The huge crowds at its entrance have probably been there for just as long—forming a human roadblock at the center of the *souq*, the hungry patrons of this local favorite are the bane of pedestrian traffic. They're not here for the basic, white-walled interior; once you've tried that creamy hummus drenched in olive oil, you too will realize just how unimportant decor really is. Despite the lightning-fast service—and the possibility of using the back door to avoid some of the madness—crowds ensure that your wait will be at least 5min.

In the middle of the souq. Look for the green shutters and the crowd. $ Hummus plate NIS15. Cash only. ⏰ Open Su-F 6am-2:30pm.

KURDI AND BERIT — SPICES, COFFEE $

Souq ☎04 991 6188

Those who are really into the Israeli culinary scene know that Kurdi and Berit is an institution. For four generations, the Kurdi family has been mixing the best spices and Turkish coffee in the country, a distinction that has made them a mecca for the nation's gourmet chefs—and led to an article in *National Geographic*. Today, proprietor Hamudi and his son make the shop's signature cardamom coffee and concoct a flurry of paprikas, 12 types of curry, and much more. The swarm of odds and ends—from mandolins, sponges, and boomerangs lining the tables to pots strung across the ceiling—would look tacky anywhere else, but here it's all the real deal (although we're not quite sure about that portrait of Sharon Stone). Kurdi and Berit is only a shop, so you'll have to take your swag elsewhere to taste it.

Near the southern foot of the souq, on the right. $ 100g of cardamom coffee NIS25. Cash only. ⏰ Open daily 9:30am-6pm.

ABU CHRISTO — SEAFOOD $$$

Salah el-Basri ☎04 991 0065; www.abu-christo.co.il

The Greek-owned Abu Christo has been around since 1948, and, half a century later, its name has become almost synonymous with Old City eats. With its fish tanks, huge waterfront patio, and no-nonsense decor, the place may scream history, but the food is certainly fresh.

At the southeastern corner of the Old City, just past the eastern entrance to the Templars' Tunnel. $ Calamari NIS75. Shrimp NIS85. ⏰ Open daily noon-11pm.

ABU NASSER SWEETS — SWEETS $

☎04 991 7845

If you still have a little room after gorging on hummus at Said, head across the street to Abu Nasser Sweets, where baklava, *burma*, and all sorts of multi-colored treats on rows of trays will tempt you.

↯ Halfway down the souq, directly opposite Hummus Said. $ Sweets from NIS2 per piece, NIS14 per kg. ⏰ Open daily 6am-5pm.

FESTIVALS

ISRAEL FRINGE THEATER FESTIVAL

CRUSADER FORTRESS
www.accofestival.co.il

For the last 25 years, Israel's theater community has descended upon the Crusader Fortress each October for a four-day dramatic bonanza, during which small acting troupes and street performers strut their artsy stuff. International troupes also attend, but the majority of performances are in Hebrew.

↯ In the Crusader Fortress. $ Pre-competition performances NIS40. Competition shows NIS75; under 22, college and acting studio students, and soldiers NIS35. Advance orders by groups and workers' committees NIS60. ⏰ During Sukkot, in mid-Oct.

ESSENTIALS

- **TOURIST OFFICE:** The **Visitors Center** has a selection of brochures and maps and gives great advice. (1 Weizmann St. ☎04 995 6706; www.akko.org.il ↯ Inside the courtyard of the fortress. ⏰ Open Su-Th 8:30am-5:30pm, F 8:30am-4:30pm.)
- **ATM: Mercantile Bank.** (Al-Jazzar St. ⏰ Open M 8:30am-3pm and 4-6:15pm, Tu-W 8:30am-3pm, Th 8:30am-3pm and 4-6:15pm, F 8:30am-noon.)
- **POST OFFICE:** Al-Jazzar St., just opposite the mosque. ⏰ Open Su-M 8am-1pm and 1:30-6pm, Tu 8am-1:30pm, W-Th 8am-1pm and 1:30-6pm, F 8am-1:30pm.

emergency

- **POLICE:** 1 Weizmann St. ☎04 987 6736.
- **LATE-NIGHT PHARMACY:** Ben-Ami St. 27 ☎04 992 0027 ↯ On the intersection with Weizmann St. Leave the Old City and walk straight for 200m. ⏰ Open Su-Th 8am-8pm, F 8am-4pm.
- **HOSPITAL: Western Galilee Hospital** in Nahariya is the closest hospital. (Ben-Zvi St. ☎04 910 7107)

getting there

BY TRAIN

The train is both cheaper and quicker than the bus. The train **station** (☎08 854 4444), which is on David Remez St. at the intersection with Herzl St., is open 24hr. except during Shabbat—the station closes on Friday at 3pm and doesn't re-open until 7pm on Saturday. Trains arrive from Haifa ($ NIS15. ⏰ 25min., every 30min.) and from Tel Aviv. ($ NIS38. ⏰1½hr., every hr.)

BY BUS

The bus station is one block away from the train station, at the intersection of HaArba'a St. and Herzl St. (☎04 854 9555). Buses run from Haifa every 10min. ($ NIS13.50. ⏰ 35min.)

getting around

The Old City can be traversed by foot in no more than 10min. However, most visitors arrive at the bus or train station, which are both in the modern city. This area operates on a basic grid system, with the train station located at the intersection of David Remez St. and Herzl St., and the bus station located one block to the east. Walk about 400m east along Herzl St. to reach Weizmann St.; from here, the Old City is just another 400m to the south (left). The walk can be a little strenuous with some big bags. **Buses #61, 62, 64, 68,** and **69** leave from just outside the train station and will take you to the Old City for NIS4.90.

nahariya ☎04

"The Place for Fun Lovers" reads the gaudy turquoise and yellow sign that greets you as you drive in. But don't get too excited, Romeo—we have a sneaking suspicion that someone just forgot to put the hyphen in there. Although it's one of Israel's most famous seaside resorts, Nahariya is anything but saucy, especially after Lebanese rockets managed to pretty much take it off the map. It's generally safe today—albeit a little run-down—and it's now a place for families through and through (with the prices to match). The sands of **Galel Galil Beach** are packed with screaming kids and their somewhat jaded parents, and, come evening, the crowds head en masse to the promenade, where beachfront bars serve huge ice cream sundaes for the kids and cheeky nightcaps for the adults. The bottom line is that Nahariya wears its resort-town reputation with pride and has become a little garish and drab because of it. If you want secluded beaches, funky eateries, and the ever-present chance of adventure, head elsewhere. But if you can fork over the cash for a room at the Carlton and are looking for the basic seaside sojourn, Nahariya just might be your place.

ORIENTATION

Absolutely anything and everything you could ever want to find in Nahariya is either on the **beach** or on **HaGa'aton Street,** the main road which runs perpendicular until it hits **HaAzma'ut Road,** parallel to the shore. The train station is at the intersection of these two streets, while the the bus station is 100m down HaGa'aton. As HaGa'aton makes its way toward the shore, major landmarks include the **Carlton Hotel** on the south side of the street and the street's intersection with **Weizmann Street,** where you'll find most of the town's major amenities. When HaGa'aton reaches the shore, heading south will take you to **Sokolov Beach,** while heading north along **Ma'Apilim Street,** just before the promenade, will take you to **Galel Galil Beach.**

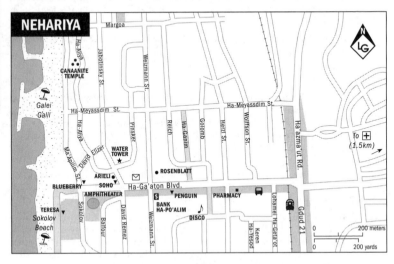

this land is my land

As if squabbles between Palestinians and Israelis weren't bad enough, there's another party that's entered the debate over this small strip of the Middle East: Eli Avivi. In 1952, the ex-fisherman was walking on a beach just north of Nahariya, saw a patch of land he loved, and claimed it as his own. When he declared himself ruler of Akhzivland in the '70s and started creating visas and marriage licenses, he was quickly jailed for "establishment of a country without permission," but, thanks to a friendly judge—and the fact that he wasn't really harming anyone—he was soon freed to go about the business of running his country.

Today, a white-robed Avivi still rules his micronation (population: two), which consists of his house, a few guest rooms, a small museum of odds and ends, and, of course, that glorious beach. Visitors are welcome to drive up the coast and say hello—just follow the many signs, and be sure to bring your passport. How else will you get it stamped with the traditional Akhzivland seal?

ACCOMMODATIONS

You won't want to stay in Nahariya for too long: budget accommodations are altogether absent, leaving low-end hotels as the cheapest option.

ROSENBLATT HOTEL HOTEL $$$
59 Weizmann St. ☎04 982 0069

The cleaning may be a little sub-par (you may find a few hairs in your bed from previous patrons), but the sheer size of the white rooms—and the location only a few blocks from the sea—makes up for it. If you can't speak Hebrew, be prepared to scrounge up your high-school Spanish in order to communicate with the owner.

⇞ By the intersection with HaGa'aton, just after the bar on the right. i Wi-Fi NIS50. A/C, TV, and ensuite bathroom. $ Singles NIS200. Cash only.

MOTEL ARIELI MOTEL $$$
1 Jabotinsky St. ☎04 992 1076

Just a block from the beach, Arieli offers the weary backpacker the cheapest beds in town in a small building just behind HaGa'aton St.

⇞ Near the SoGo Grill, just past the intersection of Jabotinsky and HaGa'aton. i A/C and ensuite bathroom. $ Singles NIS150; doubles NIS200. Cash only.

SIGHTS

Other than the beach, Nahariya is crushingly dull. As you head inland from the beach and promenade, there's pretty much nothing to see unless you have a strange obsession with restaurant decor. But as long as you're at the beach, you might as well spend 15min. at the nearby museum.

THE WATER TOWER MUSEUM
12 Jabotinsky St. ☎04 951 1214

A Nahariya landmark, the water tower has been in the town for decades and served every conceivable purpose from wartime lookout to, well, water tower. However, its history is not the focus of this museum; you can climb halfway up it if you'd like, but the real draw is the small art gallery on the ground floor.

⇞ Up Jabotinsky St., about 200m from the intersection with HaGa'aton St. ⏰ Open Su-M 9am-1pm, Tu 9am-1pm and 4-7pm, W 9am-1pm, Th 9am-1pm and 4-7pm, Sa 10am-2pm.

BEACHES

If you've come to Nahariya, you've come for the beaches. As one of the country's top seaside resorts, Nahariyia ensures that they're the main attraction. The shores can get a little crowded on weekends thanks to the Israeli families looking for a quick getaway, but the clear blue waters and pristine sands generally make up for the high-pitched squealing.

SOKOLOV BEACH

Reclining on the town's southern coast, this free beach consistently attracts crowds. However, they tend to cluster around the northern end, so head farther south to find a more secluded spot, where the calm waters make for great swimming and the crowd stays predominantly young and local.

Upon reaching the promenade, turn left and go south until it ends.

GALEL GALIL BEACH

With its jam-packed onshore pool and small number of food stands, Galel Galil is one for the families—and comes armed with the requisite screaming kids and old ladies in less-than-flattering swimsuits. The beach is the most popular in town, but it's also the most crowded.

Enter 100m along Ma'apilim St. from where it branches off of HaGa'aton St. $ Beach NIS12, with pool access NIS35. ⏰ Open daily 8am-6pm.

FOOD

You can count the number of falafel stands in Nahariya on a single hand. So, unless you're going to drop by—backpacking deities forbid—McDonald's (it's by the bus station, but we didn't tell you that), you should be prepared to spend a bit of money come meal time. The prices are about what you'd expect of a resort town—there's not much gourmet food, but even the lowliest focaccia costs more than it should.

PENGUIN CAFE — AMERICAN $$

31 HaGa'aton St. ☎04 951 0877

A comfortable cafe halfway along HaGaton, Penguin stays true to its name, with two large plastic penguins flanking the entrance. *Happy Feet* devotees, though, will be glad to know that flightless birds stay off the menu, which focuses more on the basic burger, pizza, and pasta fare. The large outdoor patio is smothered in cool air by a couple fans, giving you a comfortable front-row seat for watching the crowds scurrying around on the beach.

On the south side of the street, about 20m east of the intersection with Weizmann. ⏰ Open daily 8am-midnight.

golden arches go israeli

Need your fast food fix? Israeli McDonald's restaurants are all kosher, all the time (so forget about that cheeseburger). If the all-Hebrew menu isn't jarring enough, its uniquely Israeli highlights include the McShawarma (shawarma served in flatbread), the McKebab (kebab served on flatbread), and the McFalafel. Burgers are barbequed on charcoal rather than fried.

Dessert lovers take note: ice cream is definitely not off limits. In many McDonald's, a small door separates the dairy from the non-dairy sides of the restaurant. Since soft serve is virtually unheard of in Israel (and in fact goes by "American Ice Cream"), Mickey D's might be the best and only way to enjoy a taste of that manufactured, milky deliciousness.

TERESA

SNACKS $$

☎054 793 8283

Sitting on prime beachfront property, Teresa is the largest of the shoreside eateries, with a huge terrace and a few tables that hug large stone arches by the water. While hummus is a standard option, Teresa also serves more unusual fare, including watermelon with cheese (NIS31) and massive ice cream specials (NIS40) perfect for a beach break. If the looming Heineken signs aren't a clue, come evening the place transforms into a great place to watch the sunset as you nurse your beer.

 # On the south end of the promenade. Turn right after leaving HaGa'aton St. and Teresa is the penultimate restaurant on the left before Sokolov Beach. ⏰ Open Su-Th 6pm-late, F-Sa 10am-late.

SOGO GRILL

YEMENITE $$

1 Jabotinsky St. ☎04 900 0001

With a huge neon display plastered above it, SoGo is impossible to miss. Inside the sleek bar, purple lights, and MTV make it about as chic as Nahariya is going to get. Make sure to check out the Yemenite specials on the menu.

 # At the intersection with HaGa'aton. $ Beef tortilla NIS42. Bourbon shake NIS26. ⏰ Open daily 8am-late.

BLUEBERRY

ICE CREAM $

52 HaGa'aton St. ☎077 433 6063

A beach without an ice cream bar? God forbid. Blueberry is just a block off the beach and provides much nicer fare than the plastic-wrapped stuff you'll find at the stands on the promenade. Those extra three shekels are worth it.

 # At the end of HaGa'aton, 1 door down from where it becomes the promenade. $ Ice cream from NIS12. Frozen yogurt from NIS18. ⏰ Open Su-Th 9am-noon, F-Sa 9am-2am.

NIGHTLIFE

While Nahariya is certainly PG by day, a surprisingly vibrant bar scene emerges at night as the tourists retreat into their hotels and boozed-up young locals take over. Clubs and dance bars are nonentities in town, but many of the area's beachfront restaurants convert into sleek drinking holes. There are also a few places that are decidedly for drinking—and that makes them all the more popular with locals.

TOMMY BAR

BAR

43 HaGa'aton St. ☎054 798 0793

Not content to be packed with good-looking 20-somethings, Tommy Bar clearly felt compelled to plaster them over the walls—the narrow room is covered with huge Tommy Hilfiger advertisements. The atmosphere, however, is hardly one of pretentious models and martini-sippers; the crowd consists mostly of sweaty backpackers and relaxed locals. The huge bar takes up most of the room, leaving little space to stand, but the packed and noisy atmosphere is probably just what you've been missing in sleepy Nahariya.

 # Near the intersection with Weizmann St. ℹ 18+. Local workers night on M. Every 2nd drink ½-price on W. Electronic music on Th. $ Beer and chaser NIS35. ⏰ Open M-W 10pm-3am, Th-Sa 10pm-late.

LEVISON'S

BAR

Balfour 1 ☎052 236 1210

This dimly lit bar is a local staple where the music gets loud, the drinks flow freely, and the staff joke noisily. Whether the place is wild or chill, the vibe remains generally laissez-faire.

 # At the intersection of Balfour and HaGa'aton St. ℹ 18+. $ Beer and chaser NIS35. ⏰ Open daily 7:30pm-late.

ESSENTIALS

practicalities

- **ATM: Mercantile Bank.** (29 HaGa'aton St. ⏰ Open Su 8:30am-2:30pm, M 8am-1pm and 4-6:15pm, Tu-W 8:30am-2:30pm, Th 8am-1pm and 4-6:15pm.)
- **POST OFFICE:** 40 HaGa'aton St. ⏰ Open Su 8am-6pm, M-Tu 8am-12:30pm and 3:30-6pm, W 8am-1pm, Th 8am-6pm, F 8am-noon.

emergency

- **POLICE:** 5 Ben-Zvi St. ☎04 951 8444.
- **LATE-NIGHT PHARMACY: Super-Pharm.** (38 HaGa'aton St. ⏰ Open Su-Th 8am-noon, F 8am-4pm.)
- **HOSPITAL: Western Galilee Hospital** (☎04 910 7107).

getting there

Egged bus is by far the easiest way to get to Nahariya. Buses run from Akko ($ NIS8.80. ⏰ 40min., every 10min.) and Haifa. ($ NIS17.20. ⏰ 1½hr., every 10min.)

getting around

Absolutely everything you'll want or need to see in Nahariya is along **HaGa'aton Street** or on the beach itself, meaning you'll rarely have to walk more than 10min. The buses traveling around the city generally go back and forth between its suburbs.

THE GALILEE

Forget all those sand dunes you were going to cross in Israel—in the Galilee, at least, the only sand you'll find is that strip of beach between the water and the grass. From the mountains in Upper Galilee to the rolling plains of Lower Galilee, the region is coated with rich greenery and flowing rivers that feel more Amazonian than Old Testament. If you've ever touched a New Testament, you'll find that many of the town names here are familiar—Nazareth, anyone? As in, Jesus of? Also keep your eyes peeled for the sites of some of Jesus' first miracles and the Mount of Beatitudes (the Mount part of "Sermon on the Mount").

After almost a millennium of nonstop unrest and war, the Galilee now finds itself as one of the more peaceful regions in Israel. Most areas are out of reach of potential rockets, making the Galilee a tourist mecca, complete with tree huggers and bible thumpers and, of course, vendors everywhere hawking the requisite Jesus paraphernalia. Pilgrims flock to the Jordan River where John may have baptized Jesus, Indiana Jones wannabes scour the Roman ruins of Beit She'an and parasail over the sea, and tourists in Tiberias traverse the city in search of a great deal on tchotchke. The only downer in the region? You may need to be as rich as the greenery just to eat and sleep here.

greatest hits

- **THE GIFT OF LIFE.** Go vegetarian at Tree of Life (p. 237). Who knew benevolence came with dessert?

- **STRIP.** Put on an itsy-bitsy yellow polka dot bikini and experience the healing powers of Tiberias Hot Springs (p. 220).

- **I COULD REALLY USE A WISH RIGHT NOW.** Watch the Tiberium show light up the sky (p. 218).

- **LET THERE BE FISH.** Check out the many religious sights along the Sea of Galilee and don't miss the Church of the Multiplication of the Loaves and the Fishes (p. 227)—you never know when a miracle could repeat itself.

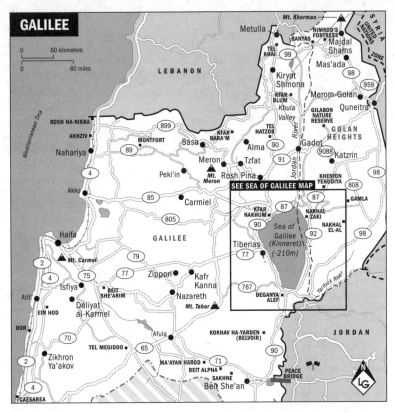

GALILEE

0 ____ 60 kilometers
0 ____ 60 miles

LEBANON

Mediterranean Sea

ROSH HA-NIKRA
AKHZIV
Nahariya
Akko
Haifa
Mt. Carmel
Isfiya
Daliyat
al-Karmel
EIN HOD
DOR
Zikhron
Ya'akov
CAESAREA
Atlit

Metulla
Mt. Kherman
NIMROD'S FORTRESS
BANYAS
Majdal Shams
Mas'ada
TEL KHAI
KFAR BLUM
Kiryat Shmona
Merom-Golan
Quneitra
Khula Valley
GILABON NATURE RESERVE
GOLAN HEIGHTS
Katzrin
TEL HATZOR
Gadot
Alma
Tzfat
Jordan River
KHENION YEHUDIYA
MONTFORT
Sasa
Meron
Mt. Meron
Rosh Pina
Peki'in
GAMLA
KFAR BARA'M
Carmiel
GALILEE
SEE SEA OF GALILEE MAP
KFAR NAKHUM
NAKHAL ZAKI
NAKHAL EL-AL
Sea of Galilee (Kinneret) (-210m)
Tiberias
Zippori
Kafr Kanna
BEIT SHE'ARIM
Nazareth
Mt. Tabor
DEGANYA ALEF
Yarmuk River
Afula
KOKHAV HA-YARDEN (BELVOIR)
TEL MEGIDDO
MA'AYAN HAROD
BEIT ALPHA
SAKHNE
Beit She'an
PEACE BRIDGE
JORDAN

SYRIA
UNIFIL ZONE

LG N

the galilee

The Galilee region mostly revolves around the **Sea of Galilee,** a gorgeous—albeit slightly difficult to navigate—lake and its surroundings. **Tiberias** is the main town that leads to the Sea and, though a stay there may include overpriced tourist attractions, you can save some money by staying at the comfortable **Hostel Aviv.** Most hostels in Tiberias also offer rental services for sightseeing around the Sea of Galilee.

Then it's time to lace up your hiking books and trek along the Jesus Trail. If that hasn't done you in, head to **Tzfat's** amazing (and free) **Alma Cave** for an extra workout and sightseeing opportunity.

nazareth   ☎04

Even though this is the childhood home of the possible Son of God and his adoptive family, don't expect a Christmas-card picture of pastoral churches and rolling fields dotted with grazing livestock. A center of Arab life in the Galilee, Nazareth (al-Nassra in Arabic, Natzeret in Hebrew) is gritty and commercial: devotees fill the quiet churches as droves of automobiles outside barrel through orange-coned construction.

Tour guides like to tell a story about how the roads of Nazareth's Old City were made by following a donkey's path as it wandered through the hills. After stepping into the Old City, you'll realize just how feasible that story is. But after a day of wandering around lost, you will suddenly, with a huff of pride, we imagine, realize you've come to know your way around this Diagon Alley. Just like in the wizarding world, it's best to be fully cloaked—visitors (women especially) should dress modestly to enter churches and avoid harassment on the streets. Though the city is only 30% Christian, expect the city to be pretty much shut down on Sundays.

ORIENTATION

Nazareth is actually two towns: downhill **Natzeret HaAtika** (Old Nazareth; largely Christian and Muslim) and the residential uphill **Natzeret Illit** (Upper Nazareth; largely Jewish). Most people arrive on buses, which stop on the busy **Paulus Street,** which divides Nazaret HaAtika into the Eastern Quarter, Latin Quarter, and Old City, where most of the sights are. Paulus St. intersects **Casa Nova Street** at a busy roundabout at the south end of town, then continues north to Mary's Well. Casa Nova St. also runs north until it hits the **souq,** where it becomes al-Bishara St., also known as Annunciation Rd. The changing names demonstrate that Nazareth is a biblical labyrinth, particularly in the Old City, where roads have four-digit numbers instead of names and street signs are few and far between. Grab a map from the **Tourist Information,** but be prepared to just enjoy getting lost.

ACCOMMODATIONS

In recent years, the city of Nazareth has worked hard to clean itself up and build up its tourist infrastructure. As the streets have gotten safer, the traditional accommodations offered by religious orders have gotten more expensive. Luckily, new budget accommodations have sprung up as well. Visitors flock to Nazareth around the Christian holidays, so you may want to call ahead unless you, too, want to end up sleeping in a manger.

nazareth

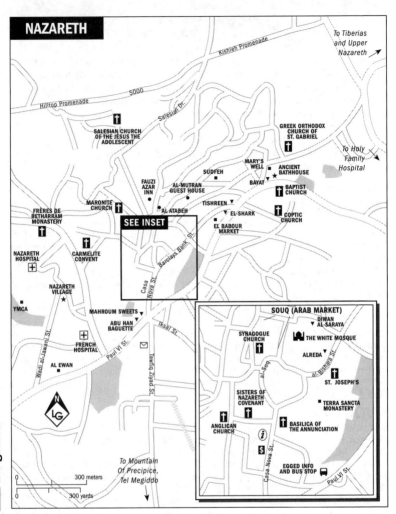

NAZARETH

To Tiberias
and Upper
Nazareth

Kishleh Promenade

5000

Hilltop Promenade

Salesian Dr.

SALESIAN CHURCH
OF THE JESUS THE
ADOLESCENT

GREEK ORTHODOX
CHURCH OF
ST. GABRIEL

To Holy
Family
Hospital

SUDFEH

MARY'S
WELL

ANCIENT
BATHHOUSE

FAUZI
AZAR
INN

AL-MUTRAN
GUEST HOUSE

BAYAT

BAPTIST
CHURCH

MARONITE
CHURCH

AL ATABEH

TISHREEN

COPTIC
CHURCH

FRÈRES DE
BETHARRAM
MONASTERY

EL-SHARK

SEE INSET

EL BABOUR
MARKET

Barclays Bank St.

NAZARETH
HOSPITAL

CARMELITE
CONVENT

Casa Nova St.

NAZARETH
VILLAGE

YMCA

MAHROUM SWEETS

ABU HAN
BAGUETTE

Tksal St.

Wadi al-Jawari St.

FRENCH
HOSPITAL

Paul VI St.

al-Bishara St.

AL EWAN

N

LG

SOUQ (ARAB MARKET)

DIWAN
AL-SARAYA

SYNAGOGUE
CHURCH

THE WHITE MOSQUE

ALREDA

al-Suq

ST. JOSEPH'S

SISTERS OF
NAZARETH
COVENANT

TERRA SANCTA
MONASTERY

ANGLICAN
CHURCH

BASILICA OF
THE ANNUNCIATION

To Mountain
Of Precipice,
Tel Megiddo

Casa Nova St.

EGGED INFO
AND BUS STOP

Paul VI St.

0   300 meters

0   300 yards

the galilee

FAUZI AZAR INN   HOSTEL $$

Off 6112 St.   ☎04 602 0469; www.fauziazarinn.com

Step through the small green door of Fauzi Azar Inn, and become enveloped in the tranquil, familial atmosphere created by the beautifully lit courtyard with sofas and a koi pond. The high hand-painted ceiling and marble floors of the upstairs salon provide further serenity, while motherly staff will offer you free cake, then remind you not to slouch. A Jewish entrepreneur and Arab family collaborated to restore this beautiful Old City mansion-turned-hostel, which recently expanded into the building next door. Revel in the history (which includes a dramatic conflagration) or just relax and enjoy the warmth of the herbal tea you just made in the fully stocked kitchen.

✤ Walk up Casa Nova St. and uphill through the souq, following the green and beige signs through the alleyways. *i* Breakfast included. Free internet and Wi-Fi. Free guided city tour M-F at 9:15am. ⑨ 5-bed dorm NIS90; singles NIS230, with private bath NIS300; doubles NIS440/500. ⏱ Reception 8:30am-10pm.

AL-ATABEH   HOSTEL $

6083 St.   ☎04 608 0031; www.alatabeh.com

This new kid on the block in the Nazareth hostel scene is owned and run by 26-year-old Kareem Hamad. Al-Atabeh has a youthful vibe, with regular movie screenings and Friday night performances by local bands that usually attract a crowd of both locals and visitors. The hostel also has a cafe area with outdoor seating that serves coffee and meals, as well as the only bar in town that has the Palestinian beer Taybeh on tap. It barely matters that the rooms are slightly cramped and the bathrooms small—it's worth it just to be a part of this scene.

✤ Walk uphill through the souq and follow the signs through the alleyways. Al-Atabeh is at the intersection with 6198 St. *i* Free internet and Wi-Fi. Kitchen available. ⑨ Dorms NIS60; doubles NIS180. Breakfast NIS20. Live music free for guests, NIS40-50 otherwise. ⏱ Reception noon-midnight. To check-in at other times, call ☎052 723 1818. Visual arts night on F 7:30-8:30pm. Live music on F 9pm. Happy hour daily 9-11pm.

AL-MUTRAN GUEST HOUSE   GUESTHOUSE $$

6090 St.   ☎04 645 7947, 052 722 9090; www.al-mutran.com

The rooms are lovely/ there's no need to spruce/ you may even get a pillowcase/ with pics of Doc Seuss! This little ditty expresses our satisfaction with this guesthouse's rooms, which are parts of larger suites that include a kitchen, dining space, lounge area, and balcony with a lovely view overlooking the town. The dorm room is a great bargain because it's really just a triple, but the three beds go quickly, so it's a good idea to reserve in advance.

✤ Walk uphill through the souq and continue on 6198 St. until you reach Bishop Sq. on the left. *i* Free internet for guests, NIS15 per hr. otherwise. ⑨ Dorm NIS100; singles NIS250, with private bath NIS280; doubles NIS350/400. Extra person NIS80. Breakfast NIS35. ⏱ Reception daily 9am-2pm and 5-7pm. Check-in 1-2pm.

SISTERS OF NAZARETH GUEST HOUSE   GUESTHOUSE $

6167 St.   ☎04 655 4304

The rooms in the Sisters of Nazareth Convent may be simple, but they're modern and clean, each including its own bathroom and that rare species of cheap-accommodation wildlife, the closet (*Wardrobus clausus*). There's also a common space and shared kitchen. With the front door always locked, and guests required to ring a buzzer for entry, the place feels very safe—unless, that is, you've never gotten over your childhood fear of nuns.

✤ Walk up Casa Nova St. and turn left on 6167 St. The guesthouse is on the right. *i* Internet. ⑨ Single-sex dorms NIS60; singles NIS190; doubles NIS230; triples NIS310. Cash only. ⏱ Reception 6am-10:30pm. Curfew 10:30pm.

SIGHTS

Think of all the photographs and home videos that your mother saved from your childhood. Sufficiently embarrassed? Okay, now imagine that over two billion people consider you to be the Son of God, and that your childhood has been commemorated with cathedrals rather than a Camcorder. That, basically, is Nazareth in a nutshell, although it's also near the sight of another monumental event—Armageddon.

BASILICA OF THE ANNUNCIATION — CHURCH

Casa Nova St. ☎04 657 2501; www.basilicanazareth.org

Consecrated in 1969, the Basilica of the Annunciation is the largest and most noticeable church in Nazareth—and in a town full of churches, that's saying something. The basilica was built on the site believed to be the Virgin Mary's home, where the angel Gabriel appeared to her to let her know that she would soon become the mother of Christ. The upper church is large and impressive, and the **Grotto of the Annunciation**—one of the holiest sites of Christianity—can be seen inside the lower church. The most interesting part, though, is the collection of mosaic murals honoring Mary, donated by Catholics around the globe. (Keep your eyes peeled for Japanese Jesus in the upper church.) Exiting the upper church, you'll also find excavations of churches from ancient Nazareth dating back to 356 CE.

Walk up Casa Nova St. from the intersection with Paulus St. ℹ *Modest dress required. The Pilgrims Office outside the gates has information and will loan scarves.* $ *Free.* ⏰ *Grotto open daily 5:45am-9pm. Upper basilica open daily 8am-6pm. Pilgrims Office open daily 9am-noon, 2-6pm. Silent prayer daily 6-9pm. Italian mass daily 6:30am. Arabic mass Su and holidays 7, 10am, 5, 6pm. Nazareth's Rosary Tu 8:30-9:30pm; Eucharistic Adoration Th 8:30-9:30pm; Candlelight Procession Sa 8:30-9:30pm.*

highway to heaven

As you make your way through Nazareth, you may see distinctive orange and white splotches near some of the major sights. No, it's not a University of Tennessee fan on the loose–these blazes mark the beginning of the **Jesus Trail,** a pathway that takes the whole "walking where Jesus walked" thing very literally. The 65km trail follows Roman roads and dirt tracks as it winds its way through the Galilee, going from Nazareth to Capernaum and stopping by such big-name places as the Mount of Beatitudes. It's not exactly rugged hiking–you pass through a number of small towns and could sleep in a bed nightly if you so wished–but it's a pleasant, four-day walk through the Galilee.

SALESIAN CHURCH OF THE ADOLESCENT CHRIST — CHURCH

Salesian St. ☎04 646 8954

Making it to the top of these steep 250 steps offers the treat of a spectacular view over Nazareth, and the Salesian Church is the giant, Neo-Gothic cherry on top. A present from the French government in 1923, the church was actually built on top of an existing church (if you look closely at the columns, you can even see where the stone changes color). In fact, the structure is all about combinations: while the walls have the classic Neo-Gothic arches on top, traditional Islamic horseshoe-shaped arches lie underneath. You can only see the church with a prior appointment, so call ahead and try to befriend your priest/tour guide—if you're extra persuasive, he may even show you the crypts in the lower church. There's also a statue of Jesus as a teenager, overlooking the city, as some believe he climbed these hills as a kid. Pop a squat and contemplate your own greatness, even if you aren't a deity.

✦ *Follow the Jesus Trail through the alleyways of the Old City and climb up the steps. Go through the gates of the school to reach the church.* ℹ️ *Modest dress required.* 💲 *Free.* ⏰ *By appointment only, so call ahead. Private mass available daily 24hr., by appointment only.*

SAINT JOSEPH'S CHURCH
CHURCH
Casa Nova St. ☎04 657 2500, 04 656 0001

Built in 1911 over the remains of a Crusader basilica, this church is thought to be on the site of Joseph's house. Inside the church is a famous painting of the Holy Family in Joseph's carpentry shop, and downstairs you can find excavations of pre-Byzantine stone houses, an ancient water cistern, a baptismal bath, and a mosaic floor.

✦ *Immediately uphill from the Basilica of the Annunciation.* ℹ️ *Modest dress required.* 💲 *Free.* ⏰ *Open daily 7am-6pm.*

MOUNTAIN OF PRECIPICE
MOUNTAIN
Off Rte. 60

The Mountain of Precipice, also known as the Mountain of the Leap, is where the people of Nazareth tried to push Jesus off a cliff after he declared himself Messiah (the nerve!), prompting him to utter the now-famous proverb, "Sticks and stones may break my bones, but pushing me off a mountain would definitely kill me." As they fell away in awe at his wisdom, he passed through them and went to Tiberias. From the top of this hill, there is a great view of Mt. Tabor, neighboring towns, and the Jezreel Valley. You can also see the large amphitheater constructed for Pope Benedict XVI when he came to give mass in front of 40,000 people.

✦ *From the intersection of Casa Nova St. and Paulus St., drive 10min. on Rte. 60 toward Afula. A round-trip taxi costs about NIS50. Although it is only a 1hr. walk, it's recommended that you find a ride.* ℹ️ *Let's Go does not recommend being here alone after dark.*

THE WHITE MOSQUE
MOSQUE
6133 St. ☎052 672 7944

Also known as Al-Abiad, this is the oldest mosque in Nazareth. From its tall white minaret (symbolizing peace and purity), the call to prayer rings over the *souq* five times a day. The white of the church symbolizes peace and purity. Inside is the tomb of Abdullah Ninawi, or "Al-Fahum," judge and governor of Nazareth in the early 19th century.

✦ *Follow Casa Nova St. uphill into the souq. Look for the green sign on the right.* ℹ️ *Modest dress required. Take shoes off inside.* 💲 *Free.*

SYNAGOGUE CHURCH
CHURCH
6120 St. ☎050 432 1250

This is the site of the synagogue where Jesus read from Isaiah 61 and declared himself the fulfillment of the prophecy. This ballsy move is commemorated by a humble church built in the 12th century by Crusaders. Devoted more to prayer and reflection than luring tourists, the church removes you from the kitschiness and makes it easy to picture Jesus actually living in Nazareth.

✦ *From the Sisters of Nazareth Convent, walk uphill and keep right. The church is on the right.* ℹ️ *Modest dress required.* 💲 *Free.* ⏰ *Open M-Sa 8am-5pm.*

GREEK ORTHODOX CHURCH OF SAINT GABRIEL   CHURCH
Church Sq.

The interior of the church is elaborately decorated with murals, chandeliers, and lots of shining coating. Follow the bubbling noise to the back of the church to find the spring that served the town of Nazareth in ancient times. Because Gabriel appeared to Mary as she was drawing water from the well, the Greek Orthodox believe that this is where the Annunciation actually occurred—though **Mary's Well,** the symbol of Nazareth, has been cut off and is now dry.

✦ *Left and uphill of Mary's Well.* **i** *Modest dress required.* Ⓢ *Free.* ☒ *Open Su 7am-2pm, M-Sa 7am-7pm.*

TEL MEGIDDO   DESTRUCTION
Off Rte. 66   ☎04 659 0316; megiddo.tau.ac.il

If the world's going to end in December anyway, might as well go check out the spot ahead of time, right? Bible nuts, headbangers, and Bruce Willis are all familiar with Armageddon, but few realize that the final battleground is actually Mt. Megiddo, an ancient *tel* (mound). Destruction has always been a focus of the mount: at the crossroads of trading routes between Egypt, Syria, and Mesopotamia, the ancient town here was the site of battles, involving everyone from the Canaanites to the Assyrians and the Israelites. In fact, the mound now contains 20 layers of ruins, ranging from the Neolithic Period (8000 BCE) to the end of the Persian Period (332 BCE).

Though the bloody history of Tel Megiddo and the future of Armageddon certainly does strike the imagination, the ruins themselves are at waist level and not that visually striking. It's therefore best to start at the museum at the site's entrance, which explains the history of the layers through a video and an interactive model that lights up and moves. Only then will you be able to appreciate such ruined beauties as a 20th-century BCE Canaanite temple, chariot stables from the time of Solomon, and a ninth-century BCE manmade tunnel engineered by King Ahab to allow for water access during a siege. If you'd prefer to just appreciate the present, relax and enjoy the view of the Jezreel Valley, Gilboa range, Mt. Tabor, and the hills of Nazareth. If you can avoid the crowds, the mount is a good place to marvel at the beauty of the Galilee, eat some dried pineapple, and contemplate the imminent end of the world. Or, like Britney, keep dancing until it does.

✦ *Take bus #823 from Nazareth to Tel Aviv, stopping at Megiddo (NIS18; 45 min., 5 per day). When the bus leaves Afula, remind the driver to stop at Megiddo Junction. From there, walk about 25min. north along the highway toward Haifa, then turn left at the brown sign. It's best to have a ride to the sight.* **i** *Bring a hat and water if you plan on walking. All materials in Hebrew. Movie in Hebrew and English.* Ⓢ *NIS27, students NIS22, ages 5-18 NIS14.* ☒ *Open daily 8am-5pm.*

NAZARETH ANCIENT BATHHOUSE   RUINS
Paulus St.   ☎04 657 8539, 050 538 4343; www.nazarethbathhouse.com

When a local couple began building a perfume shop, they started turning up architectural elements that the National Department of Antiquities declared were the ruins of a 19th-century Turkish *hamam* (bathhouse). Further investigation revealed that it was actually much, much older: certain decorative carvings suggest that this was the site of a Roman bathhouse from around 100 BCE. If you're feeling cheap, just enter the gift shop and look for the piping yourself. You'll have to pay for the tour if you want to see the really cool parts, including the maze-like underground hypocaust, which once channeled hot air beneath the marble floors.

✦ *In Cactus Gift Shop, just downhill from the Greek Orthodox Church of St. Gabriel and next to Mary's Well.* **i** *Tour lasts 30-45min. and includes refreshments.* Ⓢ *1- to 4-person tour NIS120. Bigger groups NIS28 per person. Adjoining restaurant serves combo lunches for NIS52.* ☒ *Open Su by appointment only, M-Sa 9am-7pm.*

NAZARETH VILLAGE VILLAGE

Al-Wadi al-Jawani St. ☎04 645 6042; www.nazarethvillage.com

Like an Israeli Colonial Williamsburg, this relatively recent addition to the Nazareth tourist market is a recreation of the town of Nazareth as it would have appeared when Jesus was alive (although we suspect there weren't quite as many tourists back then). Costumed villagers engage in such traditional activities as weaving, carpentry, and posing for photographs, and you too, can get in on the New Testament fun: depending on the season, visitors can help thrash wheat or pick olives. Otherwise, take the somewhat preachy tour or just enjoy poking through the stone houses, synagogue, furniture, tools, and replica tomb. Some exhibits, like the wine press, are genuine artifacts; others are reconstructions built using materials and techniques from the period.

⇞ Go up the hill toward Nazareth Hospital, on the left next to the YMCA. The sight shares a building with the YMCA; enter and go upstairs to find the reception desk. i Parking available. Tours last around 1hr. $ NIS50, students NIS32, volunteers NIS25, ages 7-18 NIS23, under 7 free. Min. credit card charge NIS150. ⏰ Open M-Sa 9am-5pm. Last tour 3pm.

FOOD

If low prices are your only requirement for a good dining experience, head toward the fast-food stands that line Paulus St. near its intersection with Casa Nova St., or stock up on groceries at **Heper Abu Khandra.** (☎04 655 9008 ⇞ Follow Paulus St. as it turns right past Mary's Well. Market is on the left. ⏰ Open M-Sa 7am-10pm.)

👍 **DIWAN AL-SARAYA** DESSERT $

6133 St. ☎04 657 8697

For 33 years, Abu Ashraf has been serving up his famous *kataifi* (pancake pockets stuffed with cinnamon and nuts or soft cheese) to locals and well-informed tourists. And by famous, we mean famous: the *kataifi*, fried fresh and drenched in syrup, have been featured in several books and documentaries. But the real gem in this single-room restaurant is Abu Ashraf himself. The grandfatherly proprietor speaks English well and will happily discuss the history of his establishment, his antiques collection, the coexistence of Arab Muslims and Christians in Nazareth, the best place to buy an Israeli mobile phone... anything really. He's always happy to help visitors find their way around town.

⇞ Going uphill in the souq, turn right onto the street immediately after the White Mosque. Diwan is on the right. $ 3 pancakes NIS12. Coffee NIS6. Cash only. ⏰ Open daily 8am-7pm, but pancakes aren't ready until about 10am.

ALREDA MIDDLE EASTERN $$$

Al-Bishara St. ☎04 608 4404

A beautiful restaurant with an outdoor garden seating area and homey feel inside, Alreda might not be cheap, but the food is worth every shekel. In addition to their meat dishes, they offer a good variety of vegetarian dishes besides the perpetual falafel and salad. Try the house special, eggplant, which comes stuffed with cheese, egg, and pesto (NIS55), and, if you're still hungry for dessert, order one of their homemade cakes.

⇞ Follow Casa Nova St. uphill. As it turns into al-Bishara, take the right fork and continue uphill. Alreda is on the left. $ Entrees NIS50-100. ⏰ Open M-Sa 1pm-2am, Su 7pm-2am.

MAHROUM SWEETS
DESSERT $

6 Paulus St.   ☎04 655 4470; www.mahroum-baklawa.com

Come here to satisfy your sweet tooth with a wide selection of desserts like gummies, candies, dried fruits, cakes, and *rahat lokum* (Turkish delight). The real draw for the locals has always been its baklava, flaky and covered in honey, though the glittering pink ceiling certainly enhances the experience—you'll feel like you've been transported to Willy Wonka's factory (sans the creepy Oompa Loompas).

⚲ *At the southwest corner of the intersection of Casa Nova St. and Paulus St.* Ⓢ *Baklava NIS80 per kg. Cookies NIS65 per kg. Candies NIS50 per kg. Coffee NIS10.* Ⓠ *Open daily 8am-11pm.*

EL-SHARK
FAST FOOD $

Paulus St.   ☎04 656 4012

At El-Shark, sink your jaws into some fin (oops, we meant *fine*) Middle Eastern fast food with refreshingly flexible prices—just ask owner Toamha about possible student discounts and group rates. The China Dumpling, despite its name, rather suspiciously resembles the traditional Arab *kofta*.

⚲ *Walk down Paulus St. away from Mary's Well. It's on the right near the taxi stand.* Ⓢ *Falafel NIS12-19. Meats NIS20-28. Cash only.* Ⓠ *Open Su 8:30am-6pm, M-Sa 8:30am-10pm.*

BAYAT
ITALIAN $$

Al-Bishara St.   ☎04 655 5146; www.bayat.co.il

Near Church Sq. and Mary's Well, Bayat serves up generous portions of cafe food to a mostly 30-something clientele. The calzones (NIS35) come with large salads on the side. Come in the evening and make friends with the locals who sit at outdoor tables to take in the sunset with one hand nursing a beer and the other a cigarette.

⚲ *When facing Mary's Well, go uphill and to the left.* Ⓢ *Entrees around NIS50. Seafood around NIS75. Min. credit card charge NIS50.* Ⓠ *Open Su 5pm-1am, M-Sa 8:30am-1am.*

TISHREEN
MIDDLE EASTERN $$$

6092 St.   ☎04 608 4666; www.rest.co.il/tishreen

Similar to Alreda, but not as well decorated and slightly more expensive, Tishreen has large tables that make it ideal for groups and families. The free bread—which comes piping-hot and loaded with garlic, sesame seeds, poppy seeds, and pine nuts—is a major draw after a long day of sightseeing and haggling.

⚲ *Walk down Al-Bishara St. away from Mary's Well. Tishreen is on the left.* Ⓢ *Entrees around NIS80.* Ⓠ *Open daily noon-midnight.*

ABU HANI BAGUETTE
FAST FOOD $

Paulus St.   ☎050 710 2844

This shawarma-only hole in the wall is one of many similar stands at the city's busiest intersection, but the prices here are slightly cheaper and include a soft drink.

⚲ *At the intersection of Casa Nova St. and Paulus St., on the right when walking away from Mary's Well.* Ⓢ *Shawarma in pita NIS24, in bread NIS25.* Ⓠ *Open M-Sa 9am-1am.*

NIGHTLIFE

Most restaurants and bars in Nazareth close down by midnight at the latest, so there's not much winding and grinding to be found within the city limits. That said, there are a few good places to lounge after dark, if you're so inclined: after all, if Jesus was able to turn his water into wine, you can surely find a drink here as well. Parts of Nazareth, especially those Old City alleyways, may be unsafe at night, so women and those traveling alone should use particular caution after dark.

SUDFEH
RESTAURANT, BAR

6083 St. ☎04 656 6611

Located in a converted mansion, this beautiful restaurant has lots of tables yet still feels intimate. The indoor courtyard's hanging flowers and twinkly lights only add to the sense of romance.. The dinners are a little pricey, so come for appetizers and drinks instead, while still getting to enjoy the ambience—and the excellent views of Nazareth. Try a cocktail with *arak* (around NIS30), a clear, licorice-tasting liquor that turns white when water is added. Call it science, call it magic, or just call the waiter for another round.

🪧 Walk uphill from al-Mutran. $ Arak cocktails around NIS30. Beer NIS15-24. ⏰ Open daily 12:30pm-midnight.

AL EWAN
CAFE, HOOKAH BAR

Paulus St.

This argilah cafe is patronized almost exclusively by locals, whom you can find lounging on the outdoor patio area throughout the day. No alcohol is served here, but Al Ewan does stay open later than most establishments in Nazareth.

🪧 Intersection of Paulus St. and 6153 St., just before Wadi al-Jawani St. On the right when walking away from Mary's Well. ℹ No alcohol. $ Argilah NIS15. Soft drinks NIS7. Snacks NIS10-20. Cash only. ⏰ Open daily 9am-2am.

SHOPPING

Shopping in Nazareth can be an endurance sport. Even if you manage to navigate the alleyways of the *souq* successfully, you'll need to stay on your toes to keep from being ripped of. Prices, whether at an outdoor market or inside a shop, tend to depend on the power of your bargaining skills more than anything else.

SOUQ
MARKET

Around 6133 St.

Sprawling through the winding alleyways of the Old City, the *souq* has pretty much everything you could ever want, as well as everything you never wanted: the market runs the gamut from refreshing, fresh-squeezed fruit juices to SpongeBob T-shirts. Just remember that you'll never be able to get that life-size Teletubby through customs (unless, perhaps, you buy it a plane ticket?). Be sure to keep an eye on your wallet as you join in the fray of Nazareth grannies haggling over the price of hookahs.

🪧 Head uphill past the Basilica of the Annunciation and take a left to follow the Jesus Trail, which brings you through the entrance of the souq. ⏰ Starts around 9am and shuts down by 7pm.

EL BABOUR
SPICE SHOP

al-Bishara St. ☎04 645 5596

If you get lost trying to find this place, just follow the enticing smell of spices, noticeable from blocks away. This spice mill, run for three generations by the Kanaza family, still sells spices, grains, nuts, and dried fruit of all kinds out of bulging sacks lined up along the floor like the good old days. Grab a plastic bag and make the best trail mix of your life from ingredients like dried pineapple, candied ginger, almonds, and crunchy peas. El Babour also sells spices, teas, herbs, and aromatic oils.

🪧 Follow Paulus St. uphill until it intersects with al-Bishara St. Turn left and go uphill. The store is on the left. $ Nuts NIS50 per kg. Dried fruit NIS75 per kg. ⏰ Open M-Sa 8:30am-7:30pm.

ESSENTIALS

practicalities

- **TOURIST OFFICE: Tourist Information** has free maps and useful brochures in English, Arabic, and Hebrew on the sights of interest in the city. (Casa Nova St. ☎04 657 3003 ⇆ On the left when walking away from the intersection of Casa Nova and Paulus St. ⏰ Open M-F 8:30am-5pm, Sa 9am-1pm.)
- **ATM: Israel Discount Bank** has an outdoor ATM. (Casa Nova St. ☎03 943 9111 ⇆ Just before tourist office. ℹ Other ATMs also available on Paulus St., across from the central bus stop. ⏰ ATM open 24hr. Bank open M 8:30am-1pm and 4-6pm, Tu-W 8:30am-2pm, Th 8:30am-1pm and 4-6pm, F 8:30am-12:30pm.)
- **LAUNDROMAT: Msalem.** (6053 St. ☎04 655 6817 ⇆ At the intersection of 6053 St. and 6077 St., near Mary's Well and across from the police station. Go through the parking lot, and it's on the left. $ Wash and dry NIS8 per kg. Cash only. ⏰ Open M-Sa 8am-6pm.)
- **INTERNET: Al-Atabeh Hostel** has Wi-Fi in its bar and cafe. (6083 St. ☎04 608 0031; www.alatabeh.com ⇆ Walk uphill through the *souq* and follow the signs on the walls. Near Fauzi Azar Inn. ℹ Free for customers. ⏰ Open daily noon-midnight.)
- **POSTAL CODE:** 16100.
- **POST OFFICE:** Tawfik Zayyad St. ☎04 646 8010 ⇆ Walking away from the intersection of Paulus St. and Casa Nova St., you'll see it on the right next to the gas station.

emergency

- **POLICE:** al-Bishara St. ☎100 ⇆ On the right when walking away from St. Gabriel's Church.
- **LATE-NIGHT PHARMACY: Super-Pharm.** (Paulus St. ☎04 641 0700, 07 788 8070 ⇆ Walking away from Mary's Well, you'll find it past the Basilica. ⏰ Open daily 9am-11pm.)
- **HOSPITAL: Nazareth Hospital.** (5112 St. ☎04 602 8888 ℹ Also known as the English Hospital or E.M.M.S. Nazareth has 2 other hospitals: French Hospital and Holy Family Hospital. All have English-speaking staff.)

getting there

When taking a **bus** to Nazareth, make sure it goes to Natzeret HaAtika (Old Nazareth), not Natzeret Illit (Upper Nazareth). The "bus station" in Nazareth consists of several stops on both sides of Paulus St., near the intersection with Casa Nova St.

Bus #823 will get you to Nazareth from Tel Aviv ($ NIS36. ⏰ 3hr., 5 per day.), **bus #331** from Haifa (⏰ 8 per day.), **bus #823** from Afula ($ NIS11.30. ⏰ 45min., 5 per day.), and **bus #995** from Jerusalem ($ NIS40. ⏰ 2 per day). **Bus #431** goes to and from Tiberias directly (⏰ 11 per day).

getting around

The city is small—and many places aren't accessible by vehicle—so most people just walk.

BY BUS

Buses with 1- and 2-digit route numbers stay in the area, mostly for making the steep trip uphill toward Salesian St. and Natzeret Illit.

BY TAXI

Mary's Well Taxis (☎04 655 5105, 04 656 0135) wait on Paulus St. near Mary's Well. **Taxi Diana** (☎052 770 3636) has cabs waiting on Wadi al-Jawani St.

tiberias   ☎04

If you know Venice Beach, you know Tiberias—just trade the weed for an excess of Jews. The main part of Tiberias, centered on the *midrakhov*, is loud and touristy, so embrace the kitsch. Befriend the angsty kid buying the "#1 *Nayfish*" T-shirt. Take a picture with the Christian pilgrims eager to poke through the city's many tombs. Say hello to the Ashkenazi Haredi men with long beards, black hats, and suits who sit on the *midrakhov* enjoying the sun while bare-chested boys and scantily clad girls sashay by. Worldly and commercialized, the city's wind-whipped streets don't get nearly as quiet for Shabbat as its neighbors to the north.

Travel back a few millennia, and you could easily have found some Sabbath peace: Rome's figurehead ruler of Judea, Herod Antipas (that cad), tried to bring settlers into this spic-and-span new town. But some rebellious Jews—including a rising star in the vigilante world, a certain J. Christ—defied Herod and refused to enter the town that had been built on Jewish graves. A century later, Rabbi Shimon Bar-Yokhai made a declaration neither ridiculous nor fishy saying that the town was now suddenly pure and could be inhabited. Although at one time the population was split almost evenly between Jews and Arabs, since the war in 1948, the population has remained almost entirely Jewish.

Today, Tiberias's fantastic location and cheap hostels make it a jumping off point for exploration of the Galilee and Golan Heights, as well as a hot spot in its own right. Sometimes that "hot" gets a little too literal, as the city's low elevation guarantees a sweaty and mosquito-filled summer. But plenty of street fairs, air-conditioning, and price gouging keep you distracted from all the humidity.

ORIENTATION

It's just as manageable as it was in 149 BCE: in **downtown Tiberias,** no two points are more than a 10-15min. walk from each other. The seaside part of this easily navigable square, the **promenade,** contains most of Tiberias's sights and restaurants, and the city's two main streets, HaBanim St. and HaGalil St. run parallel to it. Important for all comings and goings, the **central bus station** sits a few blocks from the sea at the intersection of HaShiloakh St. and HaYarden St., a quick walk from downtown. Farther from the city center, find beaches and campgrounds by following the shore up Gtdud Barak St.; in the opposite direction, Rte. 90 hugs Tiberias's southern coast. If you ever get lost, just find your way to the sea and you'll be able to find your way back again (yes, we realize how new-agey that sounds).

ACCOMMODATIONS

Tiberias's skyline is dominated by expensive resorts and even more expensive boutique hotels. Fortunately, it also has a range of other options, from simple private hotel rooms to dorms to rooftop accommodations. But cheap beds are often deservedly so: look before paying and pay for only one night in advance.

▨ HOSTEL AVIV   HOSTEL $
66 HaGalil St.   ☎04 672 3510, 04 672 0007; www.aviv-hotel.co.il

Most of the budget travelers who go through Tiberias stay at Hostel Aviv for its great quality at a reasonable price. Converted from a hotel, the hostel has unusually nice dorm rooms with spacious, pristine bathrooms, and the staff will happily befriend the lone traveler lounging around downstairs.

⚑ *Walk south on HaGalil St. from city center until it meets HaBanim St. The hostel is to the right.* **i** *Towels included for private rooms, NIS70 for dorms. Breakfast NIS30 next door at Hotel Aviv. Free internet access and Wi-Fi. Free parking.* ⓢ *Dorms NIS70; private rooms NIS200-250. Prices vary significantly with season. Bike rental NIS70 per day, includes lock and pickup service in case of a breakdown.* ⌚ *Reception 24hr.*

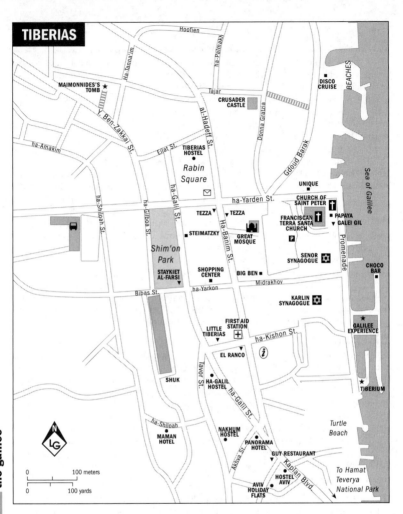

TIBERIAS

Hoofien
ha-Tanna'im
ha-Palmakh
MAIMONNIDES'S ★
TOMB
Tajar
DISCO
CRUISE
BEACHES
Y. Ben-Zakkai St.
Eilat St.
al-Hadefi St.
CRUSADER
CASTLE
Donna Grazia
Gdoud Barak
ha-Amakim
TIBERIAS
HOSTEL
Rabin
Square
ha-Yarden St.
UNIQUE
Sea of Galilee
CHURCH OF
SAINT PETER
ha-Shiloah St.
ha-Galil St.
TEZZA
TEZZA
Ha-Banim St.
FRANCISCAN
TERRA SANTA
CHURCH
PAPAYA
GALEI GIL
STEIMATZKY
GREAT
MOSQUE
Promenade
Shim'on
Park
SENOR
SYNAGOGUE
CHOCO
BAR
STAYKIET
AL-FARSI
SHOPPING
CENTER
BIG BEN
Midrakhov
Bibas St.
ha-Yarkon
KARLIN
SYNAGOGUE
FIRST AID
STATION
LITTLE
TIBERIAS
ha-Kishon St.
GALILEE
EXPERIENCE
EL RANCO
Tavor St.
SHUK
HA-GALIL
HOSTEL
ha-Galil St.
TIBERIUM
ha-Shiloah
Turtle
Beach
MAMAN
HOTEL
NAKHUM
HOSTEL
Akiva St.
PANORAMA
HOTEL
GUY RESTAURANT
To Hamat
Teverya
National Park
0   100 meters
0   100 yards
AVIV
HOLIDAY
FLATS
HOSTEL
AVIV
Kaplan Blvd.

the galilee

👍 HAGALIL HOSTEL — HOSTEL $

46 HaGalil St. ☎077 924 1404, 050 722 5181; gallilehostel@gmail.com

This hostel is a haven for weary backpackers. It may not be the shiniest—there are spots of peeling paint, and the showers in the dorms are separated from the beds by only a curtain—but it's quiet and cool and the prices are low for its great location near city center.

➤ Walk south on HaGalil St. past the intersection with HaKishon St. The hostel is to the right; look for a big red sign. ℹ Free internet access and Wi-Fi. Free parking. Laundry facilities in hostel, NIS30 per wash and dry. Linens and luggage storage included. Kitchen for guest use. $ Dorms NIS50; singles NIS150; doubles NIS200. ⏰ Reception 24hr.

TIBERIAS HOSTEL — HOSTEL $

Rabin Sq. ☎04 679 2611; m11111@012.net.il

This hostel has similar rooms and prices to Hostel Aviv, but it's slightly more cramped. Although its biggest selling point may be the presence of carpets (rare in the hostel world), it's also a bit more quiet here, with less foot traffic. Don't take that to mean it's lonely though: there's a bird in the reception area who's always willing to engage in conversation.

➤ In Rabin Sq., across from the post office and up the inside stairs. ℹ Breakfast included. Internet NIS10 per 30min. $ Dorms NIS70; singles and doubles NIS300. ⏰ Reception 24hr. Ring bell to be let in. Check-in 11am.

PANORAMA HOTEL — HOTEL $$

56 HaGalil St. ☎04 672 4811

Inexpensive rooms offer TV, air-conditioning, a small fridge, a private bathroom, and the solitude that dorms lack, but the quality of these concrete-walled rooms is mediocre. The panorama promised in the name depends entirely on the room: you may get a gorgeous view of the Sea of Galilee, or you may have to look over the wonders of commercial Tiberias. Guess which one you'll get if you want the best price quote.

➤ On the block before Hostel Aviv opposite the water. ℹ Free Wi-Fi. Large communal kitchen. Linens included. $ Singles NIS100; doubles NIS120-170. Prices vary by season. ⏰ Reception 24hr.

AVIV HOLIDAY FLATS — HOTEL $$$

66 HaGalil St. ☎04 671 2272, 04 671 2273, or 04 617 2274; www.aviv-hotel.co.il

Under the same management as Hostel Aviv, this well-run place will blow both mind and budget. All of the well-furnished rooms have kitchenettes, and some come with balconies, views of the Sea of Galilee, and jacuzzis (from NIS70). If you're intimidated by the three-story schlep, just take one of the hotel's elevators.

➤ Just behind Hostel Aviv in a white building with a "Hotel Aviv" sign. ℹ Breakfast NIS30. Linens included. Free internet access and Wi-Fi. Free parking. $ Doubles NIS300-500, depending on season. Extra beds NIS70. Bike rental NIS70 per day. ⏰ Reception 24hr. Check-in 2pm. Check-out 10am.

MAMAN HOTEL — HOTEL $

Atzmon St. ☎04 679 2986, 050 571 9786

Once a hostel, Maman converted many of its dorms to private rooms. The result: cheaply luxurious rooms in which, judging by noise level, no one seems to stay. The hotel's relative quiet does mean that you might get the bar area in the back and communal pool all to yourself. An unlocked back door means that there's no official curfew.

➤ From the central bus station, turn right on HaShiloakh St. and turn left onto Atzmon St. ℹ Breakfast NIS40. Linens included. Free Wi-Fi. $ Dorm NIS80; doubles NIS300. ⏰ Check-in noon, check-out 10am.

NAKHUM HOSTEL

HaTavor St.

HOSTEL $

☎056 642 0670

This hostel may have rusty pipes and miniscule bathrooms (and may even smell a little questionable), but it's one of the cheapest in town. In the warmer months, guests can even grab a mattress and stay on the roof (NIS35-40), yet still take advantage of the communal facilities downstairs. Dorms have kitchenettes with a sink and portable burner.

⚡ *Walk uphill on Ahva St. and turn right on HaTavor St. The hostel is on the right.* ⓘ *Linens included. Breakfast NIS20.* ⓢ *Dorms NIS40-45; doubles NIS150. Bike rental NIS60, includes lock, helmet, and pickup service.*

SIGHTS

Tiberias's actual tourist attractions are pretty limited: the real sights are the tourists themselves, who range from bronzed, bleached-blond beach bums to the similarly interesting (though less alliterative) disorganized tour groups. Watch all of them hit the *midrakhov* to shop for souvenirs and fight about where to eat dinner. If creepin' isn't your cup of tea, you can try a self-guided cellular tour around Tiberias's famous non-human sights (☎00 800 0222).

MAIMONIDES'S TOMB

Yokhanan Ben-Zakkai St.

TOMB

The signs at Maimonides's Tomb are all in Hebrew, so if you don't know your *aleph* from your *ayin*, you may need to wake up the man napping at the "reception desk." He'll take you over to the gender-appropriate side and translate the signs about Rabbi Moshe Ben-Maimon, better known as Moses Maimonides or by the acronym Rambam. A renaissance man before the Renaissance was even a thing, Maimonides was a hugely influential 12th-century physician, philosopher, and rabbi, who apparently had a little bit of Dr. Dolittle in him as well: according to legend, an unguided camel carried his coffin to Tiberias. We doubt the camel built the tomb though, as it's pretty difficult to carve in Hebrew "From Moses [the original] to Moses [Maimonides], there was no one like Moses [both]," when all you have are hooves.

⚡ *Walk up Yokhanan Ben-Zakkai St. from HaYarden St. Follow the signs for the tomb of Rambam. It is 2 blocks up on the right; go up the steps and through the snack stands.* ⓘ *Modest dress required.* ⓢ *Free.* ⏰ *Tomb open 24hr. Reception hours vary.*

TIBERIUM

Promenade

LIGHT SHOW

☎04 672 5666

Local families and tourists alike line the south end of the promenade several times per night to catch this 15min. show of lights, water jets, and music that will make even the greatest of fireworks displays look puny. The exact showtimes are often elusive, so just buy an ice cream and chill until the wonder starts—it'll be worth it.

⚡ *At the south end of the promenade.* ⓢ *Free.* ⏰ *A few shows per night. Times vary by season; call for information.*

CHURCH OF SAINT PETER

Promenade

CHURCH

☎07 730 8296

This church—also known as the Franciscan Terra Santa Church—is a bit oddly located, sandwiched between the frozen yogurt shops and tourist bars of the promenade. Built by 12th-century Crusaders, it's supposed to resemble an abandoned fishing boat, in honor of Peter, who ditched his own boat when he got hooked on the gospel and quit his day job to follow Jesus.

⚡ *Entrance on the promenade to the right of Papaya. Look for the nondescript brown gate facing the water.* ⓘ *Modest dress required.* ⓢ *Free.* ⏰ *Open Su by appointment only (min. 1 day in advance), M-Sa 8am-12:30pm and 2:30-5pm. Prayer by appointment only. Mass Su 8:30am, M-F 6pm.*

headgear hunt

Kippah, yarmulke, skullcap—call it what you want, Jewish men are all about covering their heads. Some Conservative and Reform women take part in the joy of yarmulke-wearing too, though usually only at times of prayer. See if you can identify the different varieties on your strolls through this Jewish state.

- **SATIN.** Sleek and shiny, these usually white yarmulkes are a favorite of Conservative and Reform Jews.

- **CROCHETED.** Look for the concentric circles and flamboyant colors typical of Zionist and Modern Orthodox Jews.

- **SUEDE.** The Modern Orthodox and Conservative variety is oh-so-soft.

- **BLACK VELVET.** Haredi Jews keep it classy.

- **WHITE CROCHETED.** You score an automatic 10 points for spotting a large and distinctive Breslov Hasidim kippah, which is often embroidered with scripture. Some even sport pom-poms or tassels on top!

HAMEI T'VERYA NATIONAL PARK PARK

Rte. 90 ☎04 672 5287

Hot springs are basically the hipsters of Tiberian history because, you know, beaches are just so mainstream. Unlike hipsters, though, Tiberias's hot springs actually did something for society—they allegedly possessed healing powers. In order to reap these benefits, the ancients built bathhouses, the remains of which you can see today, though bathing in them is quite impossible. Ancient ruins of bathhouses were discovered here in the early 1920s. The park also contains the remains of several small synagogues, some of which have extraordinary mosaics, including a gigantic zodiac calendar.

✣ *South of Tiberias on Rte. 90, just past Tiberias Hot Springs.* Ⓢ *NIS13, children NIS7.* ◷ *Open daily Apr-Sept 8am-5pm; Oct-Mar 8am-3pm.*

GALILEE EXPERIENCE MOVIE

Wharf ☎04 672 3620, 050 844 1116; www.thegalileeexperience.com

Shown on three screens and available in 12 languages, this 36min. film surveys 4000 years of history of the Galilee. Yup, it *is* exactly as boring as it sounds: the effect is similar to that of watching the History Channel in a dark movie theater, but the air-conditioning is a nice break from the heat of the promenade. If you realize you fell asleep halfway through and want to try again, just take the DVD version home with you (US$15).

✣ *In the center of the T-shaped wharf. Follow the HaKishon midrakhov to its end and climb the stairs.* 𝒊 *Reservations recommended.* Ⓢ *US$8, groups of 5 or more US$6 per person.* ◷ *Open Su-Th 9am-10pm, F 9am-1pm, Sa 7-10pm.*

THE GREAT OUTDOORS

Sadly, many of the beaches in the Galilee are BYOS—bring your own sand. At the very least, make sure you have some sturdy flip-flops in preparation for the dance you're about to do on the sizzling rocks. The beaches near the city that are actually good (and even some of the ones that aren't) are generally owned by the hotels, which charge non-guests bundles for admission.

Those who prefer steamy are in luck: Tiberias is home to the world's earliest-known mineral hot spring, Hamei T'verya. Some even say that Tiberias's hot springs were formed during the Great Flood, so, you know, that's gotta be good for the pores.

tiberias

Then again, other say that demons heat the water under standing orders from King Solomon, so... maybe not so much?

beaches

The beaches in the immediate vicinity of Tiberias are mostly private beaches that, in true Israeli fashion, seem to charge the price of your firstborn. **Hof HaSheket** (Quiet Beach) negates its name with a splash-happy kids' pool. (☎04 670 0800 *i* Owned by Leonardo Hotel. $ Free for guests. ⏰ Open Jul-Aug.) Next door, **Hof Hathelet** may have beautiful gardens and a huge swimming area, but it'll cost you NIS40. (☎04 672 0105 ⏰ Open daily 9am-5pm.) There are also two religious beaches, located on Gdud Barak St.: **Hof Mehadrin** is men-only (☎050 655 5291 $ NIS20. ⏰ Open Su-Th 9am-7pm.), and **Be'er Miriam** is women-only.

So, where do you go if you just want to swim? Your best bet for a free beach is to either leave the city altogether, or go to **Music Beach** on the north end of the promenade. (➔ Near the intersection of the promenade with HaYarden St. *i* No hookah or glass bottles allowed. ⏰ Open 24hr. Swimming 9am-5pm.) If you choose the latter, leave any big beach towels at the hostel—it's no more than a tiny strip of rocks, where you may have to dodge the flying pita coming from the waiters and families who throw their leftovers off the deck of the restaurant upstairs.

hot springs

So what if the ancient bathhouses in Hamei T'verya National Park have been defunct for centuries? You can still enjoy the "healing powers" of the springs in a relatively old building if you go to **Tiberias Hot Springs,** which offers single-sex baths. You can also head across the street to their newer spa, a less BC and more HC (haute couture) experience that has jacuzzis, fitness rooms, and an NIS145 massage. (☎04 670 0713 ➔ 2km south of town on the coastal road. Bus #5 runs from the central station and HaGalil St. $ NIS67, ages 3-12 NIS40. ⏰ Hot springs open Su-F 7am-1:35pm. Spa Open Su-M 8am-8pm, Tu 8am-10pm, W 8am-8pm, Th 8am-10pm, F-Sa 8am-2pm.)

FOOD

Heavy on tourist traps and low on delicious local fare, Tiberias's best dining may be that homemade picnic on the beach. The restaurant scene itself is overwrought with tourists and overpriced grilled fish, but the **souq** in the center of town, south of HaPrakhim St., sells cheap produce and baked goods everyday except Shabbat (when, come on now, you should be eating challah anyway). There's also a **Supersol** market on HaBanim St. (☎04 679 2588 ⏰ Open Su-Th 8am-8pm, F 8am-3:30pm). If you must stay indoors to protect that sunburn, try Guy's Restaurant for cheaper delicacies, or, if you're willing to shell out a little more dough, Little Tiberias.

✓ GUY RESTAURANT — MOROCCAN $

HaGalil St. ☎04 672 3036

This little family-run hut, easy to miss when walking by, is a great alternative to the perpetual shawarma stands (and about the same price!). No frills and no big bills will be found at this delicious Moroccan place, which bustles with locals throughout the day. The menu is full of small, cheap, and tasty dishes, so forgo the steak platters (NIS70) and order several smaller items instead. The eggplant stuffed with meat and nuts is delicious (NIS27), as are the winter soups. The servers can be a little distracted, but, once your food comes, you will be too.

➔ Walk south on HaBanim St. from city center. The restaurant is on the right before the intersection with HaGalil St. i Kosher. $ Stuffed vegetables NIS10-27. St. Peter's fish NIS52. Fried offerings and meatballs NIS7-15. Cash only. ⏰ Open Su-Th noon-10pm, F noon-5pm.

STAYKIET AL-FARSI GRILL $

HaGalil St. ☎050 986 6614

Presumably you didn't go to Israel for the same old, same old, so follow the locals to this hole-in-the-wall grill. Pick your meat out raw and watch it snap, crackle, and pop as the cook throws it onto the open grill. The restaurant is so hometown that English won't get you far with the people behind the counter: unless you've become a Semitic star, you'll have to find a local to help you order.

 # At the northwest corner of HaPrakhim St. and HaGalil St. i Cash only. $ Around NIS25. ⏰ Open Su-Th 8am-8pm, F 8am-3pm, Sa 8-10:30pm.

EL RANCHO ARGENTINIAN, ASIAN $$

HaKishon St. ☎052 802 6892

Throw away all kitschy Tex-Mex expectations that may arise at a name like El Rancho: this Argentinean grill and sushi place maintains a reputation for Asian fusion while simultaneously claiming the title of "Best Meat Restaurant in the North" (according to whom, we're not really sure). The sushi is overpriced, but the stir-fry, made in a big wok over the grill, is a good option for vegetarians.

 # Across from Little Tiberias on the HaKishon St. midrakhov. $ Combination entree/appetizer or dessert NIS59-119. Stir-fry NIS42-69. Sushi NIS42-69. ⏰ Open Su-Th noon-midnight, F 11am-4pm, Sa sunset-midnight.

TEZZA CAFE, BAR $$

HaBanim St. ☎054 443 2030

Cafes by the water are a staple for any seaside town. But the standard "cuppa joe" and panini come a little pricier at this slick and modern cafe/bar. Much like Starbucks, the draw to this local joint is less the food and more the free Wi-Fi. Unlike Starbucks, Tezza transforms into a bar at night, staying open later than the rest of the neighborhood.

 # Between HaYarkon St. and HaYarden St. 2 locations: a smaller branch across the street, and another to the right. i Free Wi-Fi. $ Coffee NIS9. Food around NIS43. Beer around NIS19. ⏰ Open Su-Th 7am-3am, F 7am-4pm, Sa sunset-3am.

GALEI GIL SEAFOOD $$

Alon Promenade

It's the perfect place for you and your sweetheart to share a bottle of wine. The long patio area stretches along the promenade, ensuring that the view of the Sea of Galilee from every table will take your breath away faster than that scene in *Dirty Dancing* (Patrick Swayze is so... so dreamy). It's also one of the few restaurants open on Friday night. So, forget about the area's deep religious significance and lose yourself in the ambience—or, if you'd prefer, in the delicious tilapia. The frugal and veggie-loving should dine elsewhere.

 # Walk south from the intersection with HaYarden St. Galei Gil is on the left. $ St. Peter's fish NIS62. Entrees NIS58-92. ⏰ Open daily 10am-11pm.

LITTLE TIBERIAS MIDDLE EASTERN, ITALIAN $$$

HaKishon St. ☎04 679 2148; www.rol.co.il/sites/little-tiberias

A great place for a drink or dessert, this Italian place may break the bank of more penny-pinching travelers. But if you're looking to splurge, this almost-rustic bistro allows for a huge meal and an escape from the tourist-laden *midrakhov*. To take in the vibe without overspending, sip your cocktail while pretending to leaf through the handwritten paper menu for as long as possible.

 # Off HaKishon St. on the midrakhov. i Reservations recommended. $ Meat NIS64-145. Pasta NIS57-73. Fish NIS59-94. ⏰ Open daily noon-midnight.

rolling with the chomies

Fear not if your only experience with Hebrew is a few "*Mazel Tovs*" at various bar and bat miztvahs—Israel has two official languages, so consider trying Arabic instead. Still a little rusty? We've compiled a list of important Yiddish slang terms that will have you chatting like a local in no time.

- **WALLA.** Translates to "Really?!" or "Say what?!"—also the name of a popular Israeli search engine and a travel website, and your response to the claim above. See, you're already learning.
- **BOKER TOV ELIYAHU.** The direct translation is "Good morning, Elijah," but the phrase is best employed when a traveling buddy arrives late, bedraggled, and utterly hungover after a long night out on the town. In this case, it's best to shout it out—might as well make the friend pay for that lost travel time!
- **EIZEH SERET.** The English translation means "What a movie!" but the phrase is best used as an exclamatory remark after recounting a particularly dramatic scenario. Like when you miss your plane. And your bus. And find out every bed in town is booked. And when you realize you forgot to pack underwear and your camera—*eizeh seret!*
- **HAFUCH.** This useful piece of slang has two meanings: "exhausted" and "cappuccino." Use both connotations in a sentence to get your caffeine fix while mildly confusing people. For example: "I'm so *hafuch*, that all I can think about is *hafuch*."

NIGHTLIFE

As with just about everything else in Tiberias, nightlife centers on the *midrakhov* and promenade. If bars and clubs aren't really your thing, simply stroll with some popcorn and listen to the street musicians.

👍 **CHOCO BAR** CLUB

Wharf ☎04 303 0234

Dangling at the edge of the wharf, this is where the music is loudest and the skirts are shortest. A young crowd jams itself into the high tables and stools under the reed umbrellas. This is definitely the place to be seen (but not heard), as hip-hop blasts so loudly that everyone on the *midrakhov* knows it's party time.

➜ At the left end of the wharf, coming down the HaKishon midrakhov. $ Draft beer NIS15-20. ⏰ Open daily 8pm-3am.

UNIQUE BAR

1 HaYarden St. ☎04 679 0358, 050 631 8888

The music at Unique may be American, but the football on the big projector definitely isn't. Soccer fans here aren't quite as rabid as in Europe though, which makes this tropical bar a friendly hangout, with pleasant, terraced tables on outdoor decks that are well-shaded by the trees.

➜ Walk up HaYarden St. away from the promenade. Unique is on the right. $ Beer NIS17-22. Mixed drinks NIS35-45. ⏰ Open daily 7pm-late.

BIG BEN PUB

HaKishon St. ☎04 672 2248, 050 525 6211

While the name of this faux-English pub screams London, the menu is all Israel: expect the usual hummus and shish kebabs rather than bangers and mash (maybe they made the right choice). While Birthrighters sometimes flock to the place for its cheap beer, Big Ben is also popular with those who just want a quiet drink and some food.

⇞ On HaKishon St. midrakhov, Big Ben is on the left when walking away from HaBanim St. $ Beer NIS20. ⏰ Open Su-Th 9am-2am, F-Sa 9am-late.

PAPAYA TAPAS

Alon Promenade ☎052 524 1205, 052 524 1210

The decor and clientele are a bit of a mismatch here. It's got that hip look of a club named after a tropical fruit, with a black-and-white courtyard and blue lights everywhere. But ever since this dance bar turned itself into a tapas bar, it's gotten, well, less fruity, and the costumers tend to be older.

⇞ On the promenade, between HaPerahim St. and HaYarden St. $ Beer NIS21-28. Cocktails NIS34-38. Tapas NIS10-32. ⏰ Open daily 5pm-2am.

DISCO CRUISE CRUISE

Lido Kinneret Beach ☎04 672 1538

If you believe that "booze" and "cruise" rhyme for a reason, finish your night partying where Jesus walked—on the water. These 30min. boat rides happen daily, complete with colored lights, music, and all the other trappings that should probably have stayed in the '70s. They're also the only way you can access the beach.

⇞ The first thing on Gdud Barak St. past HaYarden St. ℹ No entry without paying for disco cruise. 40 people per boat; you can request to join a group. $ NIS30. ⏰ Open daily 11am-late.

ESSENTIALS

practicalities

- **TOURIST OFFICE: Tourist Information** offers maps and brochures and is helpful with planning excursions around the Sea of Galilee. (HaBanim St. ☎04 672 5666 ⇞ In the archaeological park. ⏰ Open Su-Th 8am-4pm, F 8am-10am.)
- **ATM: Mizrahi Tefhot** has an outdoor ATM. (⇞ On the southeast corner of HaBanim St. and HaYarkon St. ℹ Other ATMs line the street.)
- **LAUNDROMAT: American Express Laundry** offers wash and dry within 3hr. (Rabin Sq. ☎04 672 2186. ⇞ Near the post office. $ NIS15 per load. Cash only. ⏰ Open Su-Th 7:30am-6pm, F 7:30am-2pm.)
- **INTERNET: Tezza** has free Wi-Fi. (HaBanim St. ☎054 443 2030)
- **POST OFFICE:** Rabin Sq. ☎04 672 2266. ⇞ Southwest corner of the square. ⏰ Open Su 8am-6pm, M-Tu 8am-12:30pm and 3:30-6pm, W 8am-1:30pm, Th 8am-6pm, F 8am-noon.

emergency

- **EMERGENCY NUMBERS: Police:** ☎100.
- **LATE-NIGHT PHARMACY: Pharmacy Schwartz.** (7 HaGalil St. ☎04 672 0994 ⏰ Open Su-M 8am-8pm, Tu 8am-7pm, W-Th 8am-8pm, F 8am-2pm.)
- **HOSPITAL: Magen David Adom.** (Corner of HaBanim St. and HaKishon St. ☎04 679 0111 ⏰ Open 24hr.)

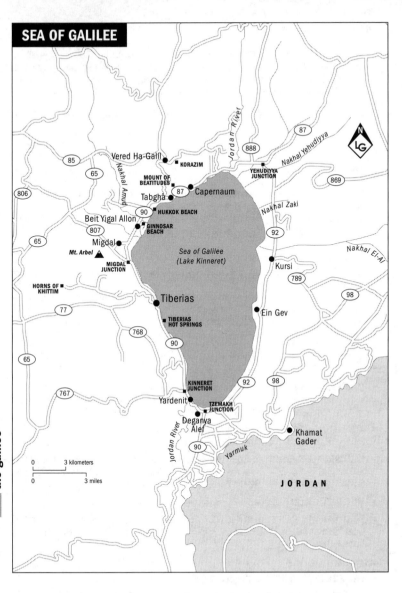

SEA OF GALILEE

85

65

806

65

Vered Ha-Galil

KORAZIM

Nakhal Amud

MOUNT OF
BEATITUDES

87

Capernaum

Tabgha

90

HUKKOK BEACH

Beit Yigal Allon

807

GINNOSAR
BEACH

Migdal

Mt. Arbel

MIGDAL
JUNCTION

Sea of Galilee
(Lake Kinneret)

HORNS OF
KHITTIM

77

Tiberias

768

TIBERIAS
HOT SPRINGS

90

65

767

KINNERET
JUNCTION

Yardenit

92

98

TZEMAKH
JUNCTION

Deganya
Alef

90

Khamat
Gader

Yarmuk

Jordan River

JORDAN

Jordan River

888

87

Nakhal Yehudiyya

YEHUDIYYA
JUNCTION

869

Nakhal Zaki

92

Kursi

Nakhal El-Al

789

Ein Gev

98

N

LG

0   3 kilometers

0   3 miles

the galilee

getting there

Undoubtedly, the best way to get to Tiberias is by bus. **Egged Bus** is generally used for more long-distance travel, while **Connex** runs local buses. Although it's possible to get to Tiberias using Egged, you'll have to go through Afula. If you're already in the area, it's easier to take local transport. From Nazareth take bus #431, which is run by **Nazarene** and departs from the bus stop across the street from Mary's Well.

getting around

Because it is so small, the best way to get around Tiberias is by foot or on bike.

BY BIKE

Rent a bike at **Hostel Aviv.** Fee of NIS70 per day includes bicycle, helmet, lock, and pickup service in case something happens. (HaGalil St. ☎04 672 3510, 04 672 0007. Ⓢ NIS70.)

sea of galilee ☎04

If you've spent your life looking for a place with serene beaches, scenic trails, and sacred sights all in a neat circumference of 55km, you've come to the right place. Ok, so the Sea of Galilee isn't actually a sea—whoever named it clearly wasn't paying attention in high school geography—but rather a beautiful lake (also known as Kinneret). Although a few sights are farther afield, most are along its shores, guaranteeing a constantly gorgeous view of the region. This area is particularly popular with Christian pilgrims because Jesus spent some time here performing miracles and the like—though turning water into wine sounds more like enlightened chilling to us.

ORIENTATION

We're defining the Sea of Galilee as everything around the lake except for the city of **Tiberias** (though most travelers come to the region via Tiberias). The Sea of Galilee is bordered on the west by **Route 90,** on the east by **Route 92,** and on the north by **Route 87.** Taking the bus in this area can be complicated, and walking in the summer heat would be an exercise in masochism, so the best way to get around is by renting a bike or car (see **Essentials**).

ACCOMMODATIONS

If you're trying to fulfill the *Let's Go* mission of budget travel, you'll probably end up staying in Tiberias. Accommodations around the lake (sorry, the "Sea") tend to be overpriced and hard to reach by bus. However, if you've got the wheels and bills, it can be worthwhile to escape the hot, sweaty mess that is a Tiberian summer. There's also the option of **camping** on the beaches surrounding the Sea of Galilee. The fee is small (usually in the form of a charge per car) and the setup perfect for those hardy of tent and constitution.

🕎 YMCA PENIEL-BY-GALILEE GUESTHOUSE $$
Off Rte. 90 ☎04 672 0685; www.ymca-galilee.co.il

If you're looking for luxury, this is the place—just pull off the dusty highway to enter what can only be described as heaven, Sea of Galilee style. Staying here feels like crashing in a wealthy private vacation home (which it actually once was). The sitting room is made of dark wood with hand-painted floral designs from the 1920s. The buildings are nestled in a lush garden overflowing with flowers and trees. There's a small chapel, a restaurant, a pool, and a private beach. Hell, there are even treadmills and ellipticals overlooking the water if, for some reason, you don't want to go run on the beach itself. Some rooms have balconies facing the lake as well, and bonus: somehow they smell fantastic. All of them. Don't question it— just enjoy.

⚔ About 5km north of Tiberias on Rte. 90. Turn right at the brown YMCA sign and enter via the small black front gate, hidden in the bushes. ⑤ Weekday singles NIS250; doubles NIS450; extra beds NIS100. Weekend singles NIS300; doubles NIS500; extra beds NIS130.

KAREI DESHE (HI)
HOSTEL $$

Near Hukkok Beach   ☎02 594 5633; kdeshe@iyha.org.il

The rooms at Karei Deshe may be a little cramped, but who cares? You'll be bronzing on the private beach anyway. That's right. Despite being large and somewhat impersonal, the hostel boasts an amazing private beach with a large lawn sloping down to the water—a real coup in an area where public beaches are crowded and private beaches are usually extremely expensive.

⚔ Follow signs indicating a right turn off Rte. 90 when traveling north from Tiberias. i Breakfast included. Internet access in lobby NIS5 per 30min., NIS25 per 24hr. ⑤ Dorms NIS97; doubles NIS431. Extra cot NIS100. ☒ Reception 24hr.

SIGHTS

Like religious sights throughout Israel, churches here mark the places that miracles might have happened. Maybe. The real draw of these places, though, is the sweeping panorama of the sea (yeah, again, it's a lake, but we'll play along). That's not to say that you can't get your introspection on—your epiphany may just come more from staring at the sea than from touching yet another potentially important rock.

🖼 MOUNT OF BEATITUDES
MOUNTAIN, CHURCH

Off Rte. 90

According to the New Testament, Jesus gave his Sermon on the Mount here—but that almost seems unimportant beside a view this beautiful. Follow the steep and narrow path up the mountain and chill on the benches inside the nearby cave. One observation point has a collection of memorabilia, including stones carved with the image of Jesus, a cross, and a list of the things that Jesus said were "blessed." If you're pretty sure that you won't be inheriting the earth anytime soon, at least use that boldness to make it to the top, where you'll find a Byzantine church.

⚔ To drive there, follow Rte. 90 as it turns north after Kfar Nahum Junction. The church is to the right. Alternatively, walk about 100m past the Church of the Primacy and climb the steps to the dirt path on the left. i Modest dress required. ⑤ Parking NIS10 per car. ☒ Church open daily 8:30am-noon and 2:30-5pm.

YIGAL ALLON MUSEUM
MUSEUM

Kibbutz Ginosar   ☎04 672 7700; www.jesusboatmuseum.com

In a story that VeggieTales would salivate over, falling water levels caused by a 1986 drought revealed the remains of an ancient boat. The ark perhaps? Probably not. The boat was restored and found to be a fishing boat from sometime between 100 BCE and 100 CE. The date, combined with the fact that fishing was kind of the disciples' thing, led devout Christians to call it the "Jesus Boat." (Jesus's people couldn't be contacted to confirm this naming.) However, most archaeologists believe that it's simply a vessel sunk during one of the many wars between the Romans and the Jews. Today, the boat rests in the Yigal Allon Museum along with a small art gallery that showcases local art.

⚔ Take bus #963 or 841 from Tiberias to the entrance to Kibbutz Ginosar, and walk the rest of the way. You can also take a boat from the Tiberias wharf, which will bring you directly to the museum. i Free parking. ⑤ NIS20, students NIS15. ☒ Open M-Th 8am-5pm, F 8am-4pm, Sa 8am-5pm.

CHURCH OF THE MULTIPLICATION OF THE LOAVES AND THE FISHES — CHURCH

Tabgha ☎06 667 8100

The story behind this church, if you haven't heard it already, is sort of awesome (and may induce hunger pangs): Jesus, being the omnipotent and benevolent cat that he was, found a way to feed 5000 of his followers with two small fish and a mere five loaves of bread. The sight itself, which focuses mainly on the rock where Jesus placed the bread, is less impressive. As in, it's basically a big rock under a humble altar. You may be better off skipping the crowds of tourists and just sitting outside, where you can listen to reverently singing tour groups and chow down on some bread of your own—in the Galilee, street vendors hawk their shawarma even outside places as holy as this church.

🚏 Take bus #963 or 841 from Tiberias to Kfar Nahum Junction. Walk toward the lake, following signs to Tabgha. [i] Modest dress required. $ Free. ⏰ Open M-F 8am-5pm, Sa 8am-3pm. Open Su only for Holy Mass. Pilgrims Office M-Sa 8:30am-noon.

CHURCH OF THE PRIMACY OF SAINT PETER — CHURCH

Tabgha ☎04 672 4767

Smaller and humbler than the Church of the Multiplication, this church marks the spot where Jesus called upon Peter to become an apostle. According to the story, Peter had just left on a fishing trip with some buds (read: the other apostles). Just before they cast their nets—and, we can only assume, while popping open their beers—a man on the beach called out and promised them a good catch. As soon as their nets hit the water, all the fish miraculously became suicidal and swam right in. Peter swam to shore and saw the man (oh, Jesus!) waiting for him, with dinner prepared for all of the apostles. This church is built mostly around the rock on which it is said they all broke bread and ate their catch. The church is next to a small beach, where swimming is prohibited, although some people wade in anyway.

🚏 About 100m past the Church of the Multiplication when coming from Tiberias. [i] Modest dress required. Pamphlets in 8 languages about the history of Tabgha available for NIS1. $ Free. ⏰ Open daily 8am-4:50pm.

MONASTERY OF THE TWELVE APOSTLES — MONASTERY

Off Rte. 87 ☎04 672 2282; capernaum1@gmail.com

Easily distinguishable by its bright red domes, this Greek Orthodox monastery honors the 12 Apostles who were chosen and called forth in nearby Capernaum. The inside of this church is decorated with murals depicting different scenes from the Bible, but the real draw is the lush and tranquil courtyard outside the monastery. The neighborhood cat often pops by to drink from the fountain. He has no official name, so *Let's Go* has dubbed him Sassy.

🚏 Past Capernaum on Rte. 87. Follow the brown signs that say "Orthodox." [i] Modest dress required. $ Free. ⏰ Open daily 9am-6pm.

LUNA GAL — WATERPARK

Golan Beach ☎04 667 8000; www.dugal.co.il

If all the churches are starting to bum you out, let Luna Gal, the mother of all water parks, wash your troubles away. This aquatic extravaganza has bumper boats, slides, pools, waterfalls, an inner tube ride, and an excellent beach.

🚏 Off Rte. 92 on the northeastern side of the lake. [i] Call ahead to make sure the park isn't closed for a religious holiday or group. $ NIS80. ⏰ Open Jun daily 10am-4pm; July-Aug Su 10am-4pm, M 9:30am-9pm, Tu 10am-4pm, Th 9:30am-9pm, F-Sa 10am-4pm; Sept daily 10am-4pm.

HAMAT GADER — HOT SPRINGS

Hamat Gader Junction ☎04 665 9965; www.hamat-gader.com

Another excellent secular alternative to the Christian-heavy sights around the sea, these hot baths were once used by the Romans in a town that straddled what is now the Israeli-Jordanian border. Sadly, Jordan got the more interesting half of the Roman ruins in the divorce settlement, but the remains on the Israeli side have been partially reconstructed and turned into a water park and spa. Hamat Gader contains all manners of self-pampering—a mud spring that cures skin ailments, a sulfur spring that relieves joints, and a spring so hot (51°C, or 124°F) that it's called "Ain Maqla," meaning "Frying Pool" in Arabic. It also boasts a small zoo, with parrots, baboons, pythons, and an alligator park, with sleepy gators from as far away as South America and Africa. If you get close enough you might may even hear a tick, tick, tick.

From Zemach Junction at the south end of the lake, take Rte. 92 to Ma'agan Junction, then turn right onto Rte. 98, which leads straight to the baths. $ NIS87. ⏰ Open Tu-W 9:30am-5pm, Th-F 8:30am-10:30pm, Sa 8:30am-5pm.

CAPERNAUM RELIGIOUS SITE

Capernaum

Not to be confused with Capernaum National Park, this ancient fishing village is Peter's birthplace and another spot where Jesus performed miracles—this time, the healing of Simon's mother-in-law and a Roman servant. Today, a modern church stands above the ruins of a fifth-century church that was originally built over the reputed ruins of Peter's home, where he and Jesus had many laughs, sleepovers, and miracles. Since the entire village is a holy site, visitors are asked to keep sinful influences out, including dogs, false idols, cigarettes, shorts, and, especially, jorts. God forbid.

From Tabgha, about 2km farther along the lakeshore, marked by a brown sign on the right. i Free parking. $ NIS3. ⏰ Open daily 8am-5pm. Last entry 4:30pm.

YARDENIT RELIGIOUS SITE

Off Rte. 90 ☎04 675 9111; www.yardenit.com

Christian pilgrims flock with their flocks to this spot where the Jordan River flows into the Sea of Galilee. Supposedly, John the Baptist baptized Jesus here, so people from around the world come here to have a little holy water sprinkled on them too. Though—like many sights on the Sea of Galilee—there's little hard evidence that Jesus actually did, well, anything here. An amphitheater, gift shop, frequent religious services, and a gorgeous view make up for any questions of veracity.

South of Kinneret Junction on Rte. 90. $ US$50 to rent a baptismal robe. Around US$5 for a vial of water from the Jordan River. ⏰ Open Mar-Nov Su-Th 8am-6pm, F 8am-4pm, Sa 8am-6pm; Dec-Feb Su-Th 8am-5pm, F 8am-4pm, Sa 8am-5pm.

THE GREAT OUTDOORS

Once you're bursting with religious and historical knowledge, you'll probably need a bit of fresh air. The Sea of Galilee boasts some of the most beautiful hikes in Israel, so lace up your tennies and clear your head at the **Mount Arbel National Park and Nature Reserve.** Complete with the ruins of a synagogue, an old lookout tree, and a cave fortress, Mt. Arbel may have the most fun (and most defensible) hikes in the Galilee. Northwest of the lake are two marked trails with handholds in the rock where climbing is necessary. The red trail leads to the Cave Fortress, and the black trail leads to the Carob Tree Lookout. (☎04 673 2904; www.parks.org.il It's best to drive. Take Rte. 77 northwest to Kfar Hitim Junction, then turn right onto Rd. 7717. Turn right toward Moshav Arbel, but don't enter the compound—instead, go left for 3.5km to the park entrance. $ NIS21, children NIS9. ⏰ Open daily in summer 8am-5pm; in winter 8am-4pm.)

FOOD

When it comes to traveling in Israel, there is one absolute: where the tourists go, the street carts follow. (Ok, there's another: you'll always wish you had brought one extra pair of underwear). In the Sea of Galilee, not even the churches have qualms about overcharging a fellow Christian for a bottle of Coke—it appears that "Thou shalt not price gouge my ice-cold deliciousness" is one of the more flexible commandments. But prices aside, the best fast food comes from the stands along Rte. 90 near the intersection with Rd. 8077. The only economical option is to buy groceries in Tiberias and take them on the road with you. There is a **Supersol** for that purpose on HaBanim St. (☎04 679 2588 ⏰ Open Su-Th 8am-8pm, F 8am-3:30pm.)

KTZE HANAKHAL LEBANESE $$

Rte. 90 ☎04 671 7776

One of the few places along Rte. 90 that isn't just a snack stand, this large restaurant serves up reasonably good Lebanese food, but the service can be pretty hands-off, especially if the waiters are busy pandering to large tour groups. If you're alone, you may have to light your head on fire to get your waiter's attention. Note: *Let's Go* does not recommend self-immolation.

#️ At the entrance to Kibbutz Ginosar, next to the gas station. [S] Entrees NIS70-90. ⏰ Open daily noon-9pm.

ESSENTIALS

practicalities

- **TOURIST OFFICE: Zemach Information Center** provides free maps and brochures, as well as information on hiking and accommodations. (Zemach Junction ☎04 675 2727; www.ekinneret.co.il #️ Inside the shopping center at Zemach Junction. ⏰ Open M-Th 8:30am-4:30pm, F 10am-noon.) For most other services, it's best just to head to Tiberias.
- **PUBLIC TOILETS:** You can find some in **Bet Gabriel,** a community center at the southern tip of the sea.
- **POSTAL CODE:** 14201.

emergency

- **POLICE:** ☎100.
- **LATE-NIGHT PHARMACY: Shop Supermarket.** (Zemach Junction ☎04 667 7369 #️ On Rte. 90, near Bet Gabriel. ⏰ Open daily 8am-8pm.)
- **HOSPITAL: Magen David Adom.** (In Tiberias, on the corner of HaBanim St. and HaKishon St. ☎04 679 0111 ⏰ Open 24hr.)

getting there

Tiberias is a few kilometers from the shore of the Sea of Galilee, so almost all visitors wishing to see the sights start their journey there.

getting around

BY FOOT

Not recommended, unless you're suicidal.

BY BIKE

It is possible to get to all the sights on the Sea of Galilee by bus, but renting a mountain bike is the most convenient (and scenic) option. Rent a bike in Tiberias at **Hostel Aviv,** and you'll also get a helmet, lock, and pickup service with a truck in case you run into trouble. (HaGalil St. ☎04 672 3510, 04 672 0007 [S] NIS70 per day. ⏰ Reception 24hr.)

A complete circuit of the lake is 55km and will take 5-7hr. It follows logically, then, that you'll be spending these hours in the sun. This area of Israel can get hellishly hot, so you should bring along your weight in water and leave as early in the day as possible for minimal *shvitzing* and heat stroke. It's better to circle the lake clockwise—the hilly area between Tiberias and Capernaum involves lots of huffing and puffing, and this way you'll hit them early so you'll still have the energy to make it through and the sun won't be John Wayne-ing at high noon.

BY CAR

If you prefer to sleep in (or just want to be more efficient and listen to your stereo), consider renting a car for the day. **Avis** in Tiberias will rent cars to drivers age 21 and over. (2 HaAmakim St. ☎04 672 2766; www.avis.com ☼ Open Su-Th 8am-5pm, F 8am-2pm.)

kabbalah

Kabbalah is a form of Jewish mysticism that emerged in France and Spain in the 12th and 13th centuries. It made its way to Palestine in the 17th century when a Kabbalah scholar named Sabbatai Zevi claimed that the Jewish messiah had arrived—himself. Zevi was later arrested by the Ottoman sultan for allegedly planning to rebuild the Temple in Jerusalem. In order to avoid execution, Zevi renounced Judaism and converted to Islam, making that whole "Jewish messiah" thing even more questionable than it already was. Fast forward a few centuries, and Kabbalah has a new champion: Madonna. The Material Girl has poured millions into the Los Angeles Kabbalah Centre and helped transform the once obscure sect into a celebrity trend.

tzfat ☎04

Easy, breezy, beautiful—Tzfat. Also known as Safed (and Tzfas and Zefas), this is a town of deep peace and tranquility and an easy place to fall in love with. Located on top of Mt. Canaan, it's the highest town in Israel, meaning it simply overflows with breathtaking views and cool mountain breezes. Everything here moves a little slower and people are a little calmer (but not much—they're still Israelis after all). There are two explanations for how Tzfat got its name: either it came from the Hebrew word meaning "to scout," because of its mountain vantage point; or from the word meaning "to anticipate," because the religious believe that the Messiah will pass through the town on his way from Mt. Meron to Jerusalem. In fact, according to Jewish tradition, Tzfat is one of Israel's four holy cities.

Unsurprisingly, religion has played a central role here. In the Middle Ages, the relatively tolerant Ottoman Empire conquered the area, and Jews started to arrive in Tzfat. The Spanish Inquisition drove more Jews to the area, setting off a Golden Age. One of the most prominent religious leaders during this time period was Rabbi Isaac Luria, also known as *HaAri*, who arrived here in 1572 and established the city as a center of Kabbalah, Jewish mysticism. (Urban legend says that Madonna tried to buy a piece of land here but was turned down by the city. Ouch, Madonna, you did that hand dance one too many times.) With a predominantly Jewish population since the 1948 War, the streets today are filled with Hasidic Jews and—because of the lack of Christian and Muslim holy sites—the tourists are almost all Jewish as well. This is definitely a place to stow those shorts, throw on a sweater, and relax as

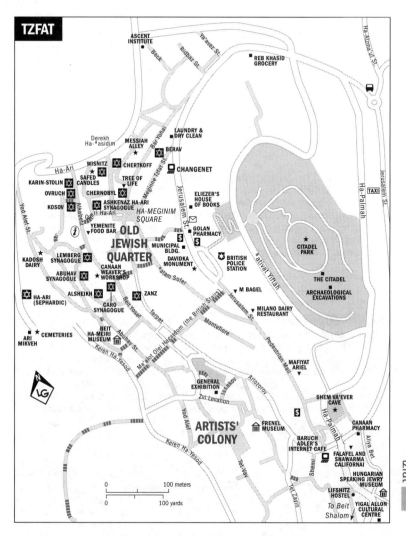

TZFAT

ASCENT INSTITUTE

Beck

Ridbaz St.

Ya'avez St.

Ha-Atzma'ut St.

■ REB KHASID GROCERY

Derekh Ha-ªasidim

MESSIAH ALLEY

LAUNDRY & DRY CLEAN

BERAV ★

Bar Yohai

Megune Tzfat St.

WISNITZ ✡ ★ CHERTKOFF ✡

Ha-Ari

💻 CHANGENET

KARIN-STOLIN ✡ SAFED ★ CANDLES TREE OF ▼ LIFE

OVRUCH ✡ CHERNOBYL ✡

Jerusalem St.

ELIEZER'S HOUSE OF BOOKS

Alkabetz

KOSOV ✡ ASHKENAZ HA-ARI ✡ SYNAGOGUE El Ha-Ari

HA-MEGINIM SQUARE

✉ GOLAN PHARMACY $

Yod Alef St.

ℹ YEMENITE ▼ FOOD BAR

OLD JEWISH QUARTER

MUNICIPAL BLDG. ■

DAVIDKA MONUMENT ★

✚ BRITISH POLICE STATION

Hativat Yiftah

CITADEL ★ PARK

Ha-Palmah

Jerusalem St.

TAXI 🚖

KADOSH DAIRY ■ LEMBERG ✡ SYNAGOGUE

CANAAN WEAVER'S WORKSHOP

Hatam Sofer

ABUHAV ✡ SYNAGOGUE

▼ M BAGEL

THE CITADEL ■

ARCHAEOLOGICAL ■ EXCAVATIONS

HA-ARI ✡ (SEPHARDIC) ALSHEIKH ★ CARO ✡ SYNAGOGUE

ZANZ ✡

Ben Yosef

Tarpat

Jerusalem St.

▼ MILANO DAIRY RESTAURANT

Pedestrian Mall

ARI ✡ MIKVEH ★ CEMETERIES

BEIT HA-MEIRI 🏛 MUSEUM

Abuhav St.

Montefiore

Ma'alot Olei Hagardom (the British Staircase)

Keren Ha-Yesod

N VG

ℹ GENERAL EXHIBITION

Zvi Levanon

Issakov

Artozorov

MAFIYAT ARIEL ▼

SHEM VA'EVER ★ CAVE

CANAAN PHARMACY

0   100 meters

0   100 yards

ARTISTS' COLONY

Yad Alef

Keren Ha-Yesod

$

FRENEL 🏛 MUSEUM

Ha-Palmah

Aliya Bet

BARUCH ADLER'S INTERNET CAFE

💻 FALAFEL AND SHAWARMA CALIFORNAI

Tel Zayin

Shemi

HUNGARIAN SPEAKING JEWRY MUSEUM 🏛

LIFSHITZ HOSTEL ■

To Beit Shalom ↓

YIGAL ALLON CULTURAL CENTRE

tzfat

everything closes down for Shabbat. But that doesn't mean that the hip and secular can't find their own sense of peace watching the sun rise in Citadel Park or meandering through the alleys of the Old City. The small but extremely vocal population of English-speaking expats who have made *aliyah* to the city makes getting understandable directions surprisingly easy, and every fourth conversation you overhear will be in English. After a day here, you may just find that you want to join their ranks.

ORIENTATION

Tzfat's most interesting places are squeezed into the compact **Old City,** where pedestrians maneuver easily and cars struggle to find enough space to move, let alone park. In contrast, Tzfat's suburbs are more accessible by bus or car. The Old City is arranged in curved terraces descending on the west side of the mountain, crowned by **Citadel Park** and encircled by **Jerusalem Street,** which follows the castle's old moat. Downhill from the park, the city can be divided into two regions: the **Artists' Colony** lies to the southwest, while the **Synagogue Quarter** is northwest. The two are separated by the steep **British Stairs** (officially called **Ma'alot Olei HaGardom Street**). The **bus station** is northeast of the mountain, next to a gas station and roundabout, so follow Jerusalem St. south around the mountain to get to the rest of the city, where it runs parallel to **HaPalmach Street** for a while, then goes under the stone **HaPalmach Bridge,** which is an easy landmark with which to orient yourself. It then turns into the *midrakhov* (pedestrian mall). Put away those stilettos, ladies, because there are a lot of stairs and the stone roads get slippery when went. Trust us, you'll just end up spraining your ankle and looking silly.

ACCOMMODATIONS

Budget accommodations in Tzfat are hard to come by, so if your great-aunt Ruthie was even remotely Jewish, dust off that old photo and bring it with you to the **Ascent Institute of Tzfat,** which allows Jewish travelers to stay in its cheap dorm beds. Everyone in town (and their mothers-in-law) rents out spare rooms, but these tend to be a bit pricier (around NIS300). To find available rooms, talk to the Tourist Information Center or just look for signs in the Old City. Some accommodations in town are more strictly religious and may not allow unmarried couples to share a room. Tzfat is an extremely popular Shabbat destination, so if you plan to visit then, book well in advance and be prepared to shell out more. Finding housing during the **Klezmer Festival** in August is particularly difficult.

✎ BEIT SHALOM — GUESTHOUSE $$

3 Janusz Korczak St. ☎04 697 0445, 050 771 6431

Beit Shalom, composed of a few separate units, is large and homey, with family photos decorating the walls. The rooftop is similarly homey, provided that your home happens to have a great view of the mountains. Some units at this guesthouse are older and may feel more neglected than others, but they also cost less. The elusive proprietor is often busy with his other shop, **Shalom Jewelry,** and may be difficult to track down. However, when you do find him, he's a friendly chap who's happy to help in any way he can, whether by providing some produce and eggs for you to cook dinner with or discussing neurobiology research.

⇞ From the bus station, go south on Jerusalem St. and make a left on Aliya Bet St. Continue through the roundabout as it turns into HaPalmach St., then make a right onto Janusz Korczak St. Look for a small wooden sign on a tree. ℹ Free Wi-Fi. Ensuite bathrooms. Large and well-stocked kitchen available. Gets booked by large groups on weekends, so call ahead. $ Dorms NIS100; singles NIS150-250; doubles NIS250-350. Prices higher on weekends and holidays. ⏰ No reception hours. Call the cell phone or find the proprietor at Shalom Jewelry on the midrakhov just north of the HaPalmach Bridge. Shalom Jewelry open Su-M 10am-2pm and 5-8pm, Tu 10am-2pm, W-Th 10am-2pm and 5-8pm, F 10am-2pm.

ASCENT INSTITUTE OF TZFAT
HOSTEL $

2 HaAri St. ☎04 692 1364, 1 800 304 070; www.ascentofsafed.com

This place is the frat club of hostels—but instead of a bro with a backward visor turning you away because you didn't bring enough chicks, it's the kindly reception desk lady telling you that you can't stay here if you're not Jewish. But if you're even a little bit Jewish, this is the place to stay (provided that you don't mind New-Agey expats trying to get you to "elevate the mystical spark within"). The beds are dirt cheap and the facilities quite reasonable.

*⇆ From the bus station, go north on Jerusalem St. and take a right on HaAri St. The Institute is on the left. **i** Jewish travelers only. Unmarried couples may not share rooms. Computers with internet access. Laundry facilities available. $ Dorms NIS60, students NIS50; on Shabbat NIS195. Attend a class and get NIS10 back (up to 2 classes). Prices higher during holidays and special seminar programs, so call ahead.*

LIFSHITZ HOSTEL
HOSTEL $$

Artists' Quarter ☎052 349 7055, 052 209 1563

You'll see signs proclaiming this hostel's slogan ("Lifshitz Hostel: Clean Rooms!") all around town. It may not be that creative, but it's definitely true: the rooms are indeed clean, and the dorm room is surprisingly comfortable and includes a futon and coffee table. Other amenities, such as the small kitchen with only a hot plate, aren't quite as nice. The clientele here may be a bit alternative—and by alternative we mean that, when *Let's Go* visited, we spotted a 60-something transvestite and a 20-something in his underoos smoking in the courtyard. To put it gently, this is a very different crowd from that at Ascent. But if that's your thing, puff away. Just put some pants on. Please.

*⇆ Walk south on HaPalmach St. Go past the bridge and look for a sign on the right that says Lifshitz Hostel. Turn right down the unmarked alley, and it's the green door on the left. **i** Communal bathrooms. $ Weekday dorms NIS100; singles NIS200. Shabbat dorms NIS120; singles NIS200. ⏰ No regular reception hours; just call.*

SIGHTS

As would be expected of the home of Jewish mysticism, Tzfat has a lot of synagogues. As in, there's a synagogue for every day of the week. But since some of these—notably Alsheikh, Chernobyl, and Chertkoff Synagogues—are closed to the public, you can use those days off to explore the city's museums and artisan workshops. If you really want to get away from it all, you can even go hide under a rock (well, cave). The Old City alleys can be tricky, but they are sporadically labeled with English and, if you're completely lost, just walk uphill. You'll eventually find yourself back on Jerusalem St.

👍 CITADEL PARK (GAN HAMETZUDA)
PARK

Hativat Yiftah Rd.

So, you got a little too out of breath on that short climb up the hill. Whatever. You'll have plenty of time to regain your composure as you appreciate this park's phenomenal view of the city and the surrounding mountains, with birds chirping around you and the wind whipping through your hair. Here, it's easy to feel the spirit of Tzfat. The park also includes the ruins of the 12th-century Crusader fortress that once controlled the main route to Damascus from this mountain and a monument to the "Meginei Tzfat" (Tzfat Defenders) who died in the 1948 War—check out their emblem of a hand holding a burning torch above the two peaks of Mt. Meron.

⇆ Climb up the stairs behind the British Police Station on Jerusalem St. and continue uphill on the park's road. $ Free.

👍 ASHKENAZI HAARI SYNAGOGUE — SYNAGOGUE

Israel Najara Alley ☎04 682 7798

This colorful synagogue was built in 1580, three years after the death of Rabbi Isaac Luria (also known as *HaAri*, as in "the lion"), to commemorate his contributions to Jewish mysticism. Okay, so even if those contributions were technically only a few poems, his influence was so great that an entire school of Kabbalistic thought is named after him. The altar at the front of the synagogue was made in Italy and doesn't quite fit—the top is too tall for the synagogue, so it's bent forward. Some say it was a mistake, but others hold that it was intentionally designed to show that the crown is reaching out to the people. Also look for the small, unmarked hole in the central pulpit, where visitors place notes for wishes and good fortune. Legend has it that this hole was the result of a miracle: in the 1948 War, a grenade landed outside the synagogue and the shrapnel flew in, zoomed just above the bowed heads of praying congregants, and landed in the pulpit. Lawrence, who staffs the synagogue, is always happy to discuss the synagogue's history.

🧭 From HaMeginim Sq., go west and downhill, then make a right onto Israel Najara Alley. The synagogue is to the right. ℹ Modest dress required. Kippahs and scarves on loan. $ Free, but donation requested. ⏰ Open Su-Th 9:30am-7pm, F 9:30am-1:30pm, Sa 9:30am-7pm.

👍 MESSIAH ALLEY — ALLEY

Intersects with Shimon Bar-Yehai St.

This narrow alley is barely wide enough to fit one person, but, then again, it was designed with one specific person in mind. Jews believe that the Messiah will pass through Tzfat from Mt. Meron on his way to Jerusalem. And this is the alley he'll have to take, as it's the only one in Tzfat that runs perfectly east to west, a straight shot from Mt. Meron. Bubbe Yocheved, who once lived here, set out two cups of coffee every day, based on the very sound logic that the Messiah would probably be tired and need a pick-me-up, and then it would only be polite for him to stay for a quick chat. Still visible are the handrails that the Tzfat Jewish Municipality installed for Bubbe as she got older.

🧭 Intersects Shimon Bar-Yehai St. next to house #49, with a "Van der Veen" sign. ℹ Informational placard across the street. $ Free.

BEIT HAMEIRI MUSEUM — MUSEUM

158 Keren HaYesod St. ☎04 697 1307; beit.hameiri@gmail.com

It's worth the price of admission just to see the building alone. The restored old house has 400-year-old rooms and 170-year-old rabbinical court halls but still manages to feel homey. The actual collection showcases 200 years worth of Tzfat history, covering both major historical events and the daily lives of its citizens in an eclectic assortment of odds and ends, like manuscripts, candid photos, and tin pots.

🧭 Take the British Stairs all the way down to the bottom of the street. Turn right onto Keren HaYesod St. and walk until you see the museum's sign on the right. Go up the flight of stairs into the museum's front courtyard. ℹ Gives out a good map of Tzfat. $ NIS14, students and ages 6-18 NIS9. ⏰ Open Su-Th 9am-2pm, F and holiday eves 9am-1pm.

KADOSH DAIRY — ARTISAN WORKSHOP

Yud Alef St. ☎050 729 9798

Free samples! Galore! This dairy has been in the Kadosh family for seven generations; according to family legend, Great-great-great-great-grandpa Kadosh was living in Morocco when a dream told him to come to Tzfat and start its first dairy. Now the family uses sheep's and goat's milk to make a wide range of cheeses, ice creams, and *halva* (a crunchy sesame and honey dessert). In particular, the goat's milk ice cream is an intense experience not for the faint of stomach.

⇄ Go down the British Stairs and turn right onto Yud Alef St. Continue down Yud Alef St. almost until HaAri. Look for the sign on your right. $ Cheeses NIS90 per kg. 1 scoop of ice cream NIS10; 2 scoops NIS15. ⏰ Open Su-Th 8am-8pm, F 8am-2pm.

SAFED CANDLES ARTISAN WORKSHOP

62 Israel Najara Alley ☎04 692 2557; www.p-i.co.il

Safed Candles doesn't charge an admission fee, but it could totally get away with it. There are some expensive candles for sale, but the more interesting part is the collection of large candle sculptures that aren't even for sale. Keep an eye out for the giant Noah's Ark full of comical cartoon animals. Some candles are made in the shop; others are made at home and brought in for sale.

⇄ On Israel Najara Alley, past Ashkenazi Synagogue when coming from the British Stairs. $ Tapers NIS20. ⏰ Open Su-Th 9am-7pm, F 9am-2pm.

ABUHAV SYNAGOGUE SYNAGOGUE

Yud Alef St.

Modeled on the synagogues of Toledo, Abuhav Synagogue was built more than 500 years ago by Sephardic Jews who were exiled from Spain. It's named after Rabbi Isaac Abuhav, a 15th-century Spanish mystic who never actually came to Tzfat. However, his 550-year-old Torah scroll, thought to be one of the oldest in existence, is held in the first ark on the right facing the front of the synagogue. The second ark contains Rabbi Luria's 400-year-old Torah scroll. These scrolls are only brought out on special occasions. If you're feeling tired, do not, for any reason, sit down on the infamous chair in the back of the synagogue: it's been used for over 200 years to circumcise eight-day-old Jewish boys. Yikes.

*⇄ On the right side of Yud Alef St. when coming from the British Stairs, just before the end of the street where it turns uphill. **i** Modest dress required. Kippahs and scarves on loan. $ Free, but donation requested. ⏰ Prayers at 5am, 7pm, and 8pm.*

CARO SYNAGOGUE SYNAGOGUE

Beit Yosef St. ☎050 653 4046, 050 855 0462

The beloved Caro Synagogue is one of the most well-known synagogues in Tzfat. It's named after Yosef Caro, a chief rabbi of Tzfat who studied and taught here in the 16th century. He's also the author of the famous *Shulkhan Arukh* (The Set Table), the standard guide to daily life according to Jewish law. The wall of glass cabinets in the sanctuary is full of Jewish books said to date back to the 17th century.

*⇄ On the left when coming from the British Stairs, across the street from a steep set of stairs. **i** Modest dress required. $ Free, but donations requested.*

CANAAN WEAVER'S WORKSHOP ARTISAN WORKSHOP

47 Beit Yosef St. ☎04 697 4449; www.canaan-gallery.com

If, like a raccoon, you find shiny things impossible to resist, you should avoid this workshop at all costs, lest you get sucked into buying one of the US$550 *talit* sets. Imminent danger aside, this workshop is a cool place to watch how people originally wove: no electricity, just hands, feet, and that big old loom. If they're not too busy, they'll explain to you all the intricacies of weaving that you never wanted to know. The whole process is surprisingly loud.

⇄ After the Caro Synagogue when coming from the British Stairs. Across the street from a small playground. ⏰ Open in summer Su-Th 9am-7pm, F 9am-3pm; in winter Su-Th 9am-5pm, F 8am-3pm.

MUSEUM OF HUNGARIAN-SPEAKING JEWRY MUSEUM

HaAtzma'ut Sq. ☎04 692 5881; www.hjm.org.il

This small house-turned-museum pays homage to the 2000 Hungarian-speaking Jewish communities whose culture was almost destroyed by the Holocaust. It is lovingly curated and includes such items as a homemade Shabbat apron, locks of hair, and forged documents used to smuggle Jews out of Hungary. The museum has English recordings that explain its collections, as well as a 20min. film on the culture's history. Going through this small and cramped museum may feel a little like going through your grandmother's attic (if she happens to be a Hungarian Jew), but it's a very intimate—albeit somewhat depressing—experience.

➔ Go south on Aliya Bet St. and turn left at the Wolfson Community Center. The museum is through the parking lot on the left. Ring bell to enter. $ NIS15, guided tour NIS30. ⏰ Open Su-F 9am-1pm.

LEMBERG SYNAGOGUE — SYNAGOGUE

Alkabetz St.

All that remains of this synagogue is its western wall, so it's very easy to miss. But if you dust off your glasses, you'll be able to make out the faded carving of a lion, an inscription in Hebrew, and a depiction of hands forming a blessing.

➔ On the right just before the Tourist Information Center when coming from the British Stairs.

CEMETERIES — CEMETERY

Off HaAri St.

If you're OK with a hot, dusty hike, head to the three adjoining cemeteries at the end of HaAri St. The oldest cemetery contains the 16th-century graves of the most famous Tzfat Kabbalists, including HaAri himself. At his blue tomb, you're almost guaranteed to find people praying and lighting candles. It's separated by gender (men on the left and women on the right) but easy to mix up, as there are no English signs. Also supposedly buried under the hill are Hannah and her seven sons, whose martyrdom at the hands of the Syrians is recorded in the Book of the Maccabees. If you head back uphill a little bit following the path, you'll come to HaAri's *mikveh.* This icy natural spring was the bathing place of HaAri himself and is popular with Jewish mystics, but the rabbinical court has ruled that women are not allowed in. Again, the lack of English signs is bound to make a fool out of the unsuspecting traveler. And whilst bathing in their skivvies no less.

➔ On the western outskirts of the Old City, at the end of HaAri St. $ Free.

SHEM VA'EVER CAVE — CAVE

HaPalmach St.

Good things come in small caves. This cave, one of the oldest sites in Tzfat, was the burial site of a wealthy Jewish family during the Byzantine period (fourth to fifth centuries CE), and there are remnants of the genuine stucco in half of the original 32 alcoves. This is also said to be the burial ground of three Talmudic sages and the cave where Joseph the Patriarch studied. The cave is named after Shem and Ever, descendants of Noah. Today, the entrance is fenced off.

➔ About 100m north of the HaPalmach Bridge. It's easy to miss. $ Free. ⏰ Jewish prayers daily at 2pm.

DAVIDKA MONUMENT — MONUMENT

Jerusalem St.

This large, black, and rather phallic-looking monument memorializes the weapon responsible for the Palmach's victory in Tzfat: the Davidka mortar. It's said that these duds didn't actually do much damage except make a lot of noise—enough that the Arab forces thought the Palmach had atomic weapons and fled. If that doesn't do it for you, just enjoy the view of the city from the monument.

*➔ South of the Municipal Building, across the street from the British Police Station. **i** Push the green button for an English and Hebrew voice recording about the historical significance of the sight.*

THE GREAT OUTDOORS

If staring at the mountains from a safe distance in Tzfat isn't your thing, grab a daypack and go. Natural areas of interest include **Khar Meron** (Mt. Meron), the highest mountain in the Galilee, and **Tel Khatzor**, a large archaeological site dating back to the third millennium BCE. If you're looking for something even more intense, read on, brave soul.

ALMA CAVE — CAVE

☎02 500 6261, Northern District Office 04 652 2167; www.parks.org.il

For those with sturdy constitutions and a fresh battery in their flashlights, Alma Cave offers a chance to get your spelunk on. Legend claims that the maze-like tunnels of Alma Cave connect Tzfat and Jerusalem and contain the corpses of 900,000 "righteous men," an image which is not at all creepy to think about when you're halfway through the depths of the cave. Luckily, you're more likely to find 900,000 righteous bats and, as to the passage thing, that remains unverified. If you end up at the Dome of the Rock, please let us know: *Let's Go* is always looking for the inside scoop.

The cave is officially one of the Israel Nature and Parks Authority's open spaces, but there's no specific information center for the site. You should call the Northern Regional Office for up-to-date information, and it's best to go with a guide, which will get you some safety, headlamps, and possibly a chance to rope swing over the cave entrance. For the independent adventurer, there are small metal handles bolted into the rock at the cave entrance, which help you climb (or, for the less graceful, stumble) down into the hole. Once you're about 60m in, look for two phallic rocks near the right wall to find the small hole that leads to the inner chambers of the cave. Follow the white markers on your way in and the red markers on the way out. Budget at least 1½hr. for getting in and 3hr. for getting out. Near the end of the trail, the caverns start dripping stalagmites and stalactites (hint: stalagmites *might* reach the ceiling one day, stalactites hold on *tight* to the ceiling).

🪧 Take Nateev Express bus #45 from the Tzfat central bus station. Get off at Rehunia village (don't wait until Alma village). Walk about 30min. down the dirt road across the entrance to the village. From there, walk about 1km to the green nature reserve sign on the hillside of gray stones. Head uphill to a couple of metal poles, and the cave entrance is in a gorge just beyond. Bus #45 also makes the return trip at 8:45am and 1:30pm. ℹ Wear clothes you don't mind getting dirty or ripped. $ Free. ⏰ No entry at night. Closed during the winter.

FOOD

The *midrakhov* on Jerusalem St. is lined with a combination of expensive tourist restaurants (with great views) and hole-in-the-wall falafel joints (with great prices). For groceries, go to **Bashut Zol**, on Arlozorov St. west of the HaPalmach Bridge. (⏰ Open Su-Tu 7:30am-9pm, W 7:30am-10pm, Th 7:30am-11pm, F 7:30am-2pm.) For produce, visit the fruit and vegetable store **Yoram.** (☎04 697 1789 🪧 At the intersection of Meginei Tzfat St. and Jerusalem St. ⏰ Open Su-Th 7am-10pm, F 7am-4pm.) Since all restaurants—and just about everything else in the city—close for Shabbat, you'll either have to cook for yourself or arrange and pre-pay for food to pick up. This can be pretty pricey, but if that's your thing, try **Shabbat Food** (☎054 845 1189; shabbes@drori.or).

👍 TREE OF LIFE — VEGETARIAN $$

2 HaMeginim Sq. — ☎050 696 0239

Herbivores rejoice: Tree of Life actually offers something other than the perpetual falafel. The two-room stand serves up whole wheat, vegetarian meals made fresh daily. Grab a delicious fruit shake (NIS15) to go, or enjoy your food at an umbrella-shaded table in the square. If the stuffed pepper with quinoa (NIS48) doesn't sound appealing, check the board for a list of daily specials that, if you're lucky, will include the cheesecake. Don't be surprised if the older ladies who run the place drop by your table to chat.

On the north side of HaMeginim Sq. ℹ Strictly Kosher. $ Quiche NIS45. Salads NIS40-48. Cash only. ⏰ Open Su-Th 9am-11pm, F 9am-5pm.

M BAGEL BAGELS $

Jerusalem St. ☎04 682 1441

Mmm, bagels. The bagels here are all right (though not NYC bagels, no matter what the signs promise), but the homemade cream cheese absolutely melts in your mouth. Add some delicious toppings like roasted peppers, fried onions, or tuna and you'll have a nice, filling meal at a good price.

On the midrakhov, just before the British Stairs and on the right when coming from HaPalmach Bridge. $ Bagels with cream cheese NIS16; with extra toppings NIS18; with lox NIS30. ⏰ Open Su-Th 8am-11pm, F 8am-3pm.

YEMENITE FOOD BAR YEMENITE $

18 Alkabetz St. ☎050 225 4148

Beloved by locals, the gregarious Ronen—aka The Yemenite Pizza Man—dons traditional dress to make *lachuch* (flatbread) for his clients.

Directly across the street from the Tourist Information Center. $ Lachuch NIS25-35. ⏰ Open in summer Su-Th 9am-1am, F 9am-4pm; in winter Su-Th 9am-6pm, F 9am-3pm.

when to eat what

Israelis celebrate their (mostly religious) festivals by congregating, spreading joy, and stuffing themselves. Here are some of our favorite festivities and their gastronomically pleasing accompaniments:

- **HANUKKAH:** If carbo-loading on potato pancakes isn't enough for you, keep in mind that Hanukkah celebrators eat doughnuts too! And now Israeli bakeries carry new fillings that deviate from the traditional strawberry, like chocolate, vanilla, or cappuccino. Clearly, Dunkin' Donuts was onto something.
- **TU B'SHEVAT:** Not a curse in Latin, but instead a festival for the return of spring marked by the consumption of... well... squirrel chow–nuts, berries, figs, and dates are the fare of the day. If you're discouraged by your empty stomach, you may be assuaged by the fact that Kabbalistic tradition requires you to drink four cups of wine.
- **ROSH HASHANAH:** The Jewish New Year is one of the few guilt-free Jewish holidays, so the indulgence goes overboard. Typical dishes include apples dipped in honey, honey cake (land of milk and honey, remember?), beets, pomegranates, and challah, a traditional bread spruced up for the new year with raisins and–you guessed it–drizzled honey.
- **PURIM:** A celebration of the deliverance of the Jews from the evil Haman, this holiday is marked by the giving of packages of food, usually containing nuts, sweets, and baked goods, to neighbors along with a recommended healthy serving of wine to accompany the late afternoon meal.

MAFIYAT ARIEL BAKERY $

Jerusalem St. ☎04 840 1459

This bakery has an impressive display—rolls, loaves, pitas, pastries, cakes, cookies, *bourekas*, and challah all waft that unmistakable scent of fresh baked goods. Unfortunately, that aroma and the open doors combine to attract as many flies as people.

🚶 At the beginning of the midrakhov when coming from HaPalmach St. $ 5 pitas NIS5. Pastries NIS25-32 per kg. ⏰ Open Su-Th 6:30am-9pm, F 6:30am-3pm.

FALAFEL AND SHAWARMA CALIFORNIA FAST FOOD $

Jerusalem St. ☎04 692 0678

This tiny restaurant doesn't pull any punches: it serves falafel and shawarma, and that's it. But crowds of loyal patrons swear that it's the best place in town.

🚶 Just before HaPalmach Bridge, on the left when coming from the bus station. $ Falafel NIS10. Shawarma NIS20-25. Cash only. ⏰ Open Su-Th 9:30am-10:30pm, F 9:30am-3pm.

MILANO DAIRY RESTAURANT CAFE $$

Jerusalem St. ☎04 692 2982

Prime real estate on the *midrakhov* means that this cafe is pricier than most, but the homemade bread and butter may be worth the extra shekels. Colorful murals on the walls, free Wi-Fi, and a nicely air-conditioned upstairs make this an attractive place for tourists and locals alike to linger over a nice *hafuch* (latte).

🚶 On the midrakhov, on the right before the British Stairs when coming from HaPalmach Bridge. ℹ Breakfast served all day. Free Wi-Fi. Strictly Kosher. $ Sandwiches NIS36-40. Entrees NIS40-60. Shakshuka NIS32. ⏰ Open Su-Th 8:30am-midnight, F 8:30am-5pm.

ARTS AND CULTURE

Since Tzfat's one bar was shut down and converted to a dairy restaurant, nightlife in the town has pretty much gone the way of Pop Rocks. In the past, *Let's Go* has made the wry suggestion of a night walk through the graveyards, but, if you're willing to trade in keg stands for a little culture, the following options are sure to make you feel a bit more sophisticated.

GENERAL EXHIBITION SAFED ART

Issakov Alley ☎04 692 0087

Though Tzfat was once known for producing some of Israel's best artists, the number who actually live in Tzfat today has decreased. Nonetheless, art galleries fill the neighborhood known as the Artists' Colony (you'd think creative people would've figured out a better name). You're bound to find something you like by simply wandering around its alleys and popping your head in, but, to get a sampling in one location, head to the General Exhibition. The gallery is devoted to local art and housed in the town's former mosque, which has been empty since the 1948 War. There's no organization to the displays in the large main gallery or the rooms to the side, but don a beret and fake accent and pretend you can discern one anyway.

🚶 Walking north on Arlozorov St. from the HaPalmach Bridge, turn left on Issakov Alley and the exhibition is on the right. $ Free. ⏰ Open May-Sept Su-Th 10am-6pm, F-Sa 10am-2pm; Oct-Apr Su-Th 10am-5pm, F-Sa 10am-2pm.

YIGAL ALLON CULTURAL CENTER THEATER, CLASSICAL MUSIC

HaAtzma'ut Sq. ☎04 686 9601

Since there's no movie theater in town (Tzfat kind of makes the town from *Footloose* look like L.A.), the Yigal Allon Cultural Center is the place to go to see theater, classical music, and films. To find more information, keep an eye out for posters around town or call their box office.

🚶 Next to the main post office, at the roundabout where HaPalmach St. and Aliya Bet St. intersect. ℹ Productions in Hebrew and English. $ Varies based on the event; usually from NIS20.

ASCENT INSTITUTE OF TZFAT MUSIC, SEMINARS

2 HaAri St. ☎04 692 1364, 1 800 304 070; www.ascentofsafed.com

Unlike its hostel, Ascent Institute is actually open to gentiles. That does not mean, however, that it isn't still very spiritual: free classes cover religious topics often related to Kabbalah, the few computers may only be used for checking email or learning about Kabbalah, and the library is—you guessed it—devoted to Kabbalah. The Institute offers weekday English seminars (9:15am, noon, and 8:30pm), live music events, tours of Tzfat, and nature hikes in the Galilee. They will also arrange for travelers to have dinner with a local family, although it can be more difficult to find families for non-Jewish travelers.

➜ From the bus station, go north on Jerusalem St. and take a right on HaAri St. The Institute is on the left. $ Tzfat tours NIS20. Nature hikes NIS30. Arranged dinners NIS15. ⏰ City tours July-Aug, 3 per week. Hikes July-Aug, 1 per week.

FESTIVALS

Every year, Tzfat hosts its renowned **Klezmer Festival.** This three-day event takes place in late July or early August, and, if you plan to visit Tzfat, you may want to consider timing your visit accordingly (depending on the depth of your love for Jewish music). During the festival, the city closes its roads and sets up eight or nine outdoor stages through the city. Israelis from all over come to enjoy a repertoire of music that ranges from old-world Yiddish tunes to modern Hasidic rock, though the festival is trying to return more to its Klezmer roots. The best part of the entire thing? It's all **free**—although you will have to pay for a bus into the city if you arrive after the roads close (at 4pm on the day before the festival). Accommodations may also reach astronomical prices and usually fill up well in advance. Check the city's website (www.safed.co.il/klezmer-festival-safed.html) to get the latest information.

ESSENTIALS

practicalities

- **TOURIST OFFICE: Tzfat Tourist Information Center** is run by **Livnot U'Lehibanot** and staffed by English-speaking expats, including the legendary Laurie, who is a fount of useful information. The website is simple but comprehensive. They also have an archaeological excavation that is not currently open to the public, though they might let you in if you ask nicely. (17 Alkabetz St. ☎04 692 4427, 052 431 7156; www.safed-home.com ➜ Coming downhill from the British Stairs, turn right on Beit Yosef and continue walking past Abuhav Synagogue. *i* The Livnot campus next door runs programs for Jewish foreigners. They also have a balcony open to the public that has arguably the best view in Tzfat. $ The English map of Tzfat, also available on website, is not very legible; NIS 1. 10min. movie on Tzfat's history NIS3. ⏰ Open Su-Th 8am-4pm.)
- **ATM: Bank Leumi** has outdoor 24hr. ATMs. (35 Jerusalem St. ☎03 954 4555 ➜ When walking away from HaPalmach Bridge, the bank is on the left after the *midrakhov* ends and before ChangeNet. ⏰ Bank open Su 8:30am-2pm, M 8:30am-1pm and 4-6:15pm, Tu-W 8:30am-2pm, Th 8:30am-1pm and 4-6:15pm.)
- **CURRENCY EXCHANGE: ChangeNet** changes currency without commission. (Jerusalem St. ☎04 682 2777 ➜ After the *midrakhov* ends and before the intersection with Meginei Tzfat St., just past Bank Lemui. *i* Credit cards, cash, and checks accepted. ⏰ Open Su-M 9am-2pm and 3-6pm, Tu 9am-2pm, W-Th 9am-2pm and 3-6pm.)
- **ENGLISH LANGUAGE BOOKSTORE: Eliezer's House of Books** sells mostly religious books in English, Russian, Hebrew, and other languages. (37 Jerusalem St. ☎04 697 0329 ➜ Walking up the *midrakhov* away from HaPalmach Bridge, it's on the right

after the municipal building. 🕐 Open Su-Th 9:30am-2pm, F 9:30am-1pm.)

- **LAUNDROMAT: Laundry and Dry Cleaning.** (28 Jerusalem St. ☎054 776 6580 ⚲ When walking away from HaPalmach St. past the municipal building, it's on the left at the intersection with Meginei Tzfat St. *i* Takes about 5hr. 5kg min. load Ⓢ NIS10 per kg. 🕐 Open Su-Th 9am-2pm and 4-7pm, F 9am-1pm. Hours may vary.)

- **SWIMMING POOL:** Tzfat has a public indoor pool. (☎04 692 2288 ⚲ At the southern tip of city, near the industrial zone. *i* Gender-segregated. 🕐 Women only Su 4-7pm, M 9-11pm, Tu 10am-1pm, W 4-7pm. Men only Su 7-10pm, W 7-10pm, F 7-10:30am. Both genders M 5-9pm, Tu 5-10am and 1-9pm, W 5:30am-4pm, Th 5am-10pm, F 10:30am-5pm, Sa 9am-5pm.)

- **INTERNET: Tzfat Tourist Information Center** has free Wi-Fi. **Baruch Adler's Internet Cafe** also has Wi-Fi and computers with internet access. (88 Jerusalem St. ☎052 344 7766 ⚲ By HaPalmach Bridge. *i* The proprietor also rents rooms. Ⓢ NIS10 per 30min., NIS15 per 1hr. Singles NIS180; doubles NIS250. 🕐 Open Su-Th 10:30am-2am, F 10:30am-2pm.)

- **POSTAL CODE:** 13103.

- **POST OFFICE: Main Post Office.** (87 HaAtzma'ut Sq. ☎04 692 0405, 04 692 0405 ⚲ At the intersection of HaPalmach St. and Aliya Bet St., through the parking lot on the other side of the Yigal Allon Cultural Center. 🕐 Open Su 8am-6pm, M-Tu 8am-12:30pm and 3:30-6pm, W 8am-1:30pm, Th 8am-6pm, F 8am-noon.)

emergency

- **POLICE: Town Police.** (Canaan St. ☎04 697 8444 ⚲ At the south entrance to the city.)

- **LATE-NIGHT PHARMACIES: Canaan Pharmacy.** (92 Jerusalem St. ☎04 697 2440 ⚲ Under HaPalmach Bridge. 🕐 Open Su-F 8am-1:15pm.) **Golan Pharmacy.** (39 Jerusalem St. ☎04 692 0472 ⚲ Opposite the municipal building and away from the *midrakhov.* 🕐 Open Su-Th 8:30am-7pm, F 8:30am-2pm.)

- **HOSPITALS: Sieff Hospital.** (☎04 682 8811, 077 682 8811; www.ziv.org.il ⚲ At the southern entrance to Tzfat, near Rte. 89. *i* Also known as Ziv Hospital.)

getting there
BY CAR
You can rent a car at **Eldan** in Kiryat Shmona and Tiberias, **Avis** in Tiberias and Nahariya, and **Rent-a-Car** in Sde Eliezer (☎04 693 0777).

BY BUS
Egged Bus runs from Haifa (☎*2800 ⚲ Bus #361. 🕐 Every 30min.), as well as from Tel Aviv and Jerusalem. **Nateev Express** runs buses from Nahariya and Rosh Pina. (⚲ Bus #511 from Kiryat Shmona and bus #522. Both through Rosh Pina.) **Connex** buses run from Rosh Pina and Tiberias. (☎*6686 ⚲ Bus #450 from Tiberias, through Rosh Pina.)

getting around
BY FOOT
The Old City is pretty compact, making walking the best way to navigate Tzfat.
BY CAR
Many sights outside Tzfat's Old City are also accessible by car. The streets in the Old City, however, are often too narrow or convoluted for cars to be convenient.

BY BUS

Nateev Express runs local buses, mostly for residents going to and from the outskirts of town. The main bus lines are #3, 4, and 7. Bus #45 (⏱ 25min., 9:15am and 2pm.) goes from the central bus station to surrounding villages and Alma Cave.

beit she'an   ☎04

A roadside town with few attractions, Beit She'an is not a place that people flock to. In fact, its proximity to Jordan means that most people don't even talk about Beit She'an. And even the people who live in Beit She'an don't talk about the fact that it's a major **border crossing**. If you ask about the Peace Bridge Border Crossing, the most common response will be, "Why? Are you going to Jordan?" However, there's a good chance they'll tell you about the Beit She'an National Park, home to one of the finest archaeological sites in the country—which is saying something in a country that's been inhabited practically since the dawn of civilization. Excavations at the park, which is located at the intersection of important ancient trade routes, have revealed 20 layers of settlements dating back as far as the fifth millennium BCE.

Today Beit She'an is a quiet, plain town with few pedestrians and even fewer tourists sticking it out longer than a few hours. However, Beit She'an is currently working on improving its tourist infrastructure with the construction of new sidewalks, a bus station, and a second guesthouse.

ORIENTATION

Most buses will drop you off at the northeast corner of town, at the roundabout where **Menahem Begin Street** and **HaShalom Road** intersect (at the time of writing, an actual bus station was being built there). Luckily, this section of town also has everything you'll need: the ticket office, Binyamin Mall (the tall orange building), and the requisite falafel stand. Walk a few meters south and turn right, and you'll see the courtyard of the **Saraya** (an old Ottoman government building), which houses the Economic Development Office and the tourist office. These are pretty much the only places you'll need to go for a quick trip—the national park is a short bus ride away up north. However, if you're inclined to keep exploring, walk southwest and you'll find the Beit She'an Municipality Building in the town center at the intersection of HaArba'a St. and Yerushalayim HaBira St.

the galilee

ACCOMMODATIONS

Accommodation options in Beit She'an are pretty limited. As in, there's one. You're probably better off staying in a nearby city (Tiberias does quite nicely) and taking a bus in for the day.

BEIT SHE'AN GUEST HOUSE — GUESTHOUSE $$$

129 Menahem Begin St. ☎02 655 8400

What looks a bit like a maximum security prison on the outside actually isn't too terrifying on the inside. Each clean and tidy room has a spacious bathroom with two sinks, and you can squeeze up to five beds into each room by folding out all the cots. There may not be too much personality here (if you hated high school, the hallways may feel a little too familiar), but a large dining room, basketball court, and swimming pool are nice bonuses.

➡ Walk south on Menahem Begin St. from the bus station. The guesthouse is the big building on the left. ℹ Breakfast included. Internet access NIS10 per 30min. $ Singles NIS345; doubles NIS460. Additional person NIS145. ⏰ Reception 24hr.

SIGHTS

Attractions here center on the Roman ruins of Beit She'an National Park and not much else. But a small collection of sights of natural and historical interest do dot the beautiful valley road between Beit She'an and Afula.

👍 BEIT SHE'AN NATIONAL PARK — RUINS

☎04 658 7189; www.parks.org.il

Beit She'an National Park is one of the finest archaeological sites in the country, with some sections dating back to the fifth millennium BCE and others containing vast complexes of Roman and Byzantine ruins. Although Tel al-Husn may win the "Most Ancient" award, the Roman theater garners the coveted prize for "Most Awesome." Built by Emperor Septimius Severus in 200 CE, the three-tiered theater could once seat up to 7000 fans and has now been renovated in order to be occasionally used for (more subdued) performances. Other highlights include the Ashtaroth Temple, a Byzantine bathhouse, and the Nymphaeum fountain. Be sure to walk down the 150m-long colonnaded Palladius St. to feel the grandeur of the ruins, and, on your way out of the park, don't miss the ingeniously designed public toilets where rocks jut out to make comfortable seating.

➡ Buy tickets in the Saraya, a 1min. walk from the bus stop. Look for the white paper signs. A free shuttle that runs every 10min. (closes early on holidays) will take you to the park. ℹ Better to visit in the morning, before the sun makes climbing the tel unbearable. $ NIS38, ages 5-16 NIS23, under 5 free. ⏰ Open Apr-Sep Su-Th 8am-5pm, F 8am-4pm, Sa 8am-5pm; Oct-Mar Su-Th 8am-4pm, F 8am-3pm, Sa 8am-4pm.

SHE'AN NIGHTS — SHOW

Beit She'an National Park ☎04 648 1122 *3639; www.parks.org.il

A different way to visit the national park is to take the She'an Nights tour. The night (obviously) tour begins with a 10min. presentation, then lets you walk around the park and watch the audiovisual presentations projected onto the ruins. It may be a bit gimmicky, but it's a gimmick that cost 210 million shekels to engineer.

➡ In the national park. ℹ Call in advance to reserve tickets. $ NIS50, ages 5-14 NIS40. ⏰ Open M 8pm-late, W-Th 8pm-late, Sa 8pm-late. Hours vary seasonally.

HAAZMA'UT GARDEN — RUINS

Menahem Begin St.

The hors d'oeuvre to the Beit She'an National Park's entree, the HaAzma'ut Garden (read: courtyard) is planted with historical buildings (read: ruins that aren't as cool as those in the national park). It includes the Saraya from the Turkish period (now used as the ticketing office for the park), the remains of a Crusader castle, and a Roman amphitheater. Unlike the national park, the garden is free to visitors—but, again, not nearly as cool.

1min. walk west from the bus stop.

GAN HASHLOSHA NATIONAL PARK HOT SPRINGS

Rte. 669 ☎04 658 6219; www.parks.org.il

Also known as **Sakhne,** this park features waterfalls and crystal-clear swimming holes, refreshing in both summer and winter (they remain a constant 28°C, or 82°F for you Americans). Locals like to bring the kids and swim, pitch a tent, and barbecue. Beware of weekends, when cars double park and people pack in like sardines—more specifically, pasty old sardines with moobs and screaming, splashing young sardines in floaties. If you're looking for serenity (now), head to the end of the park, where a partially hidden set of steps leads down to a more tranquil swimming spot. The park also includes the **Museum of Regional and Mediterranean Archaeology,** which houses a collection of Hellenistic and Islamic art and pottery.

On Rte. 669, which is off the larger Rte. 71. Bus #412 will bring you to the park (watch out for Shabbat schedules on F and Sa). ℹ *Admission to park required for museum entrance.* $ *NIS38, ages 5-14 NIS23.* ⏰ *Park open Apr-Sept Su-Th 8am-5pm, F 8am-4pm, Sa 8am-5pm; Oct-Mar Su-Th 8am-4pm, F 8am-3pm, Sa 8am-4pm. Museum open Su-Th 10am-2pm, Sa 10am-2pm.*

BEIT ALPHA NATIONAL PARK NATIONAL PARK

Kibbutz Heftziba ☎04 653 2004

A few min. drive into Kibbutz Heftziba will bring you to a beautiful sixth-century synagogue. The highlight of Beit Alpha is its magnificently preserved mosaic of a zodiac wheel surrounding the sun god Helios—before you get polytheistically confused, know that the prophet Elijah was often associated with Helios. The entrance fee includes a 14min. introductory film, which features a stilted reenactment of how the temple came to be. Unintentionally funny highlights include a scene about haggling over the price of the mosaic and the kerfuffle that arose when commissioners were scandalized by the inclusion of an uncircumcised schlong.

On. Rte. 669, which is off Rte. 71. Bus #412 will bring you to the park (watch out for Shabbat schedules on F and Sa). $ *NIS21, ages 5-18 NIS9.* ⏰ *Open Su-Th 8am-5pm, F 8am-4pm, Sa 8am-5pm. Last entry 30min. before close.*

FOOD

Food options in Beit She'an are also pretty limited. Right across from the bus stop is a **falafel stand,** which is run by a woman who knows everything that's going on in town, and **Betmafe** may just be the best bakery in the Galilee. There are also fast food options across the street in the **Binyamin Mall,** and, in a fit of beautiful grocery magic, a *souq* pops up near the Municipality Building every Friday.

BETMAFE BAKERY $

Yerushalayim HaBira St. ☎050 631 0483, 077 551 5610

The warm smell of just-out-of-the-oven bread wafts out into the street, luring in passersby. But, once trapped in this small bakery, there is no leaving empty handed. Betmafe specializes in *bourekas*, stuffed pastries similar to calzones. Try the especially popular tuna or cheese *bourekas*, or just go straight for the *freekasay*. We're not positive on that spelling, but we do know two things: it's nothing like a fricasee, and it's absolutely delicious, a sandwich-like creation made with fresh bread, with potatoes, eggs, and a spicy lemon garnish.

Across from the central square, near the intersection with King Saul St. There are no English signs, so look for the red plastic chairs. $ *Freekasay NIS15. Bourekas NIS32 per kg. Coffee NIS8. Credit card min. NIS26.* ⏰ *Open Su-Th 6am-8pm, F 6am-4pm.*

SHEPUDAY HAKIKAR BARBECUE $$

Yitzhak Shemesh ☎04 606 0198

Ask any local for a restaurant recommendation and the knee-jerk response will be "Shepuday Hakikar." Maybe it's the food, maybe it's the straightforwardness of the decor and the menu, but all we know is this—this barbecue joint has achieved small-town fame for a reason.

➜ At the intersection of Yitzhak Shemesh and King Saul St. The building has a big clock on top. $ Entrees NIS50-60. ⏰ Open daily noon-midnight.

ESSENTIALS

practicalities

- **TOURIST OFFICES:** The **tourist office** has free brochures and maps and can also help with border crossing information. (Menahem Begin St. ☎052 284 5731 ➜ Across from the Saraya in the courtyard. It's a smaller gray building with a Cleveland sign. ⏰ Open Su-Th 8am-6pm, F 8am-noon.) The **Economic Development Office** can also be helpful with tourist information. (Menahem Begin St. ☎050 864 2234 ➜ The white stone building is in the same courtyard as the tourist office.)
- **ATM:** Available inside the Binyamin Mall. (➜ At the corner of Menahem Begin St. and HaShalom Rd.)
- **INTERNET: Beit She'an Guest House** has computers with internet access. (129 Menahem Begin St. ☎02 655 8400 ➜ Walk south on Menahem Begin St. from the bus station. The guesthouse is the big building on the left. $ NIS10 per 30min. ⏰ Reception 24hr.)
- **POSTAL CODE:** 10900.
- **POST OFFICE:** Herzl St. ☎04 648 0810 ➜ In the Municipal Building at the intersection of Herzl St. and HaArba'a St. ⏰ Open Su 8am-6pm, M-Tu 8am-12:30pm and 3:30-6pm, Th 8am-6pm.)

emergency

- **POLICE: Local Police.** (King Saul St. ☎100 ➜ Inside the Police Garden Promenade.)
- **LATE-NIGHT PHARMACY: Sammy Pharmacy.** (HaArba'a St. ☎04 648 9300 ➜ Inside the Municipality Building. ⏰ Open Su-F 8am-1pm and 4-8pm.)
- **FIRST AID: Kupat Holim Meuhedet.** (HaArba'a St. ☎04 648 9300 ➜ Inside the Municipality Building. ⏰ Open Su 10am-4pm, M-Th 8am-7pm, F 8am-1pm.) For more serious injuries, patients are sent to the hospital in Afula.

getting there

BY BORDER CROSSING

The **Peace Bridge Border Crossing**, also known as the Jordan River or Sheikh Hussein Crossing (not to be confused with the King Hussein Crossing farther south), is one of the busiest border crossings into Jordan, so be sure to allow extra time and check the website ahead of time for updated exit fees and possible exemptions. (☎04 609 3400 for terminal operator, 04 648 0018 for customs, 04 648 1103 for border police; www.iaa.gov.il *i* You can pay online to save time. $ Exit fee from Israel NIS96, from Jordan JD5. Visas on the Jordanian side JD10. Shuttle tickets from Israeli terminal to Jordanian terminal NIS4.50, Jordanian to Israeli NIS6. ⏰ Open Su-Th 6:30am-9pm, F-Sa 8am-8pm; closed on Yom Kippur and Eid al-Hijra, the Muslim new year.) To get to Beit She'an from the border crossing, take **bus #16** ($ NIS9. ⏰ 1 per day, around 12:30pm.) or a **taxi.** (☎04 658 8455 $ around NIS50.)

BY BUS

From Afula, take **bus #411** or **412** (⏰ 30min.), run by Kavim. From Tiberias, take **bus #28** ($ NIS14.90. ⏰ 40min.), run by Connex. From Jerusalem, take Egged **bus #961.** (⏰ 2hr.) From Tel Aviv and Haifa, take a bus to Afula, then switch over.

getting around

Beit She'an is a small town and easily manageable by foot, which is the best way to get around—grab a map from the tourist office and you're golden. If, however, you prefer to be chauffeured, you can find taxis run by **Avi Taxi** (☎04 658 8455, 04 658 6480) near the main bus stop and along Yerushalayim HaBira St.

WEST BANK

Since Israeli occupation began in 1967, the West Bank has become a festering center of rage and disappointment; the highly poetic (or Poe-etic) would perhaps call it the beating black heart of strife in the region. Recent tensions between the West and Middle East aside, the situation requires careful navigation by tourists, including a highly specific vocabulary ("occupation," "Green Line," "right of return") and no small amount of doublespeak (when talking to Palestinians, call the West Bank "Palestine" while commiserating over how Palestine doesn't exist). Though set in a treacherous terrain, the Palestinian culture is one of the most open and friendly to tourists; some combination of a tradition of hospitality, concern for their image abroad, and a need to understand the opinions of foreigners causes a shocking percentage of Palestinians to strike up a conversation with you, invite you to tea, or introduce you to their friends. Women should also not worry about donning head scarves. That said, views on homosexuality are not very advanced in the West Bank, to the extent that it is simply does not exist in public life.

These days, the West Bank is calm, yet teetering on the brink of total uproar. *Let's Go* is writing before the September UN vote and after the Arab Spring, and the situation in the West Bank can change radically at any time. Make sure to check http://travel.state.gov for updates on the political situation and to read *This Week in Palestine* when you're in the West Bank, for information on everything from protests to concerts.

greatest hits

- **PARTY POLITICS.** Visit the Dheisheh Refugee Camp (p. 254) and get a feel for real West Bank culture.

- **GET LOW.** See the fossils at Tell es-Sultan (p. 273) in Jericho—the lowest city on Earth.

- **AWAY IN A MANGER.** For once that song is irrelevant. Go visit Jesus's birthplace in Bethlehem (p. 253).

- **I SAID BRR, IT'S COLD IN HERE.** Cool off with a cocktail at Snowbar in Ramallah (p. 267).

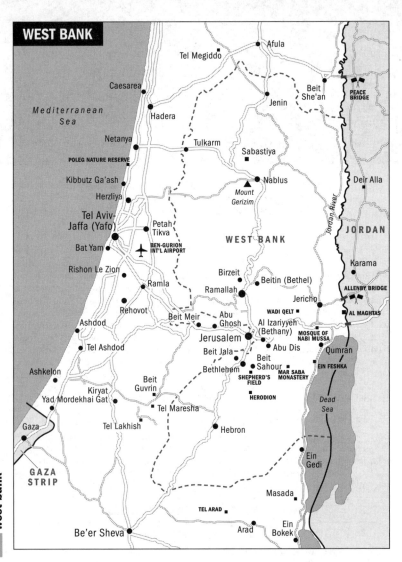

WEST BANK

Mediterranean Sea

Afula

Tel Megiddo

Caesarea

Beit She'an

PEACE BRIDGE

Hadera

Jenin

Netanya

POLEG NATURE RESERVE

Tulkarm

Sabastiya

Deir Alla

Kibbutz Ga'ash

Nablus

Herzliya

Mount Gerizim

JORDAN

Tel Aviv-Jaffa (Yafo)

Petah Tikva

WEST BANK

Bat Yam

BEN-GURION INT'L AIRPORT

Karama

Rishon Le Zion

Birzeit

Ramla

Beitin (Bethel)

ALLENBY BRIDGE

Ramallah

Jericho

Rehovot

WADI QELT

AL MAGHTAS

Ashdod

Beit Meir

Abu Ghosh

Al Izariyyeh (Bethany)

Jerusalem

Tel Ashdod

MOSQUE OF NABI MUSSA

Beit Jala

Abu Dis

Qumran

Ashkelon

Bethlehem

Beit Sahour

EIN FESHKA

Kiryat Yad Mordekhai Gat

Beit Guvrin

SHEPHERD'S FIELD

MAR SABA MONASTERY

Gaza

Tel Maresha

HERODION

Dead Sea

GAZA STRIP

Tel Lakhish

Hebron

Ein Gedi

Be'er Sheva

Masada

TEL ARAD

Arad

Ein Bokek

Jordan River

west bank

Travel in the West Bank is a total cultural immersion experience. Consider staying at the **Ibdaa Cultural Center** in the Palestinian section of **Bethlehem** and engaging the young and eager staff in conversation on daily life. Continue the immersion in **Ramallah,** where every aspect of daily life for Palestinians is evident. Don't forget to grab some cheap eats—there's nothing quite like Palestinian pizza, and **Beit Manaqish** arguably does it best. **Rukab's Ice Cream,** a local legend, is just down the road and completes the staple student pizza-and-ice-cream diet.

Last but certainly not least, dudes with an affinity for haunted houses should check out **Mar Saba Monastery** in Bethlehem, and be sure to ask about the miracles and ghost stories that shroud the place. Sorry ladies—much like the little Rascals, it's no girls allowed.

essentials

GETTING THERE

The best way to get to the West Bank is from Jerusalem. You'll find most Arab buses heading to the West Bank outside the Jerusalem Hotel. **Bus #18** is the best way to get to Ramallah, and buses **#124** and **21** go to Bethlehem. The #124 goes to the checkpoint, while #21 goes to Bab izQaq in the center of Bethlehem. You can also take a private car, though this may cause more complications at checkpoints. It is generally easier to go from Israel to the West Bank than the other way around.

GETTING AROUND

Bethlehem and Ramallah are the two most cosmopolitan cities in the West Bank and, therefore, the two major transportation hubs.

by service taxi

Unless you have a private car, the best way to travel in the West Bank is by service taxi (pronounced "ser-veece"), which is the same as the Israeli *sherut.* Service taxis can be picked up on the highway or at city transportation hubs, such as the bus station in Bethlehem and the service taxi station on **al-Nahdah Street** in Ramallah. These taxis are frequent and reliable and often lead to excited conversations between young Palestinian friends who run into each other on the same service or even cause ribald chats between jocular drivers and old ladies in headscarves. Drivers don't always speak English but can usually drop you off at any location you specify. Make sure you have some idea of where you're going before you actually arrive there—remember that there is no single central stop that a service taxi makes. Service taxi prices are fixed and always under NIS30; it helps to check whether you are paying the same amount as the people around you.

by bus

Buses are not the common method of travel around the West Bank. Generally used only to reach Israeli settlements, these buses are run by **Egged,** meaning they are a little pricier than Arab buses but are generally more reliable. They usually stop at **Jerusalem's Jaffa Road Station** as well as in the settlements themselves. **Arab buses** do not run on a set schedule but can be used in major transportation areas like Ramallah and Bethlehem; they are generally less fun, slightly cheaper, and a little faster than service taxis.

essentials

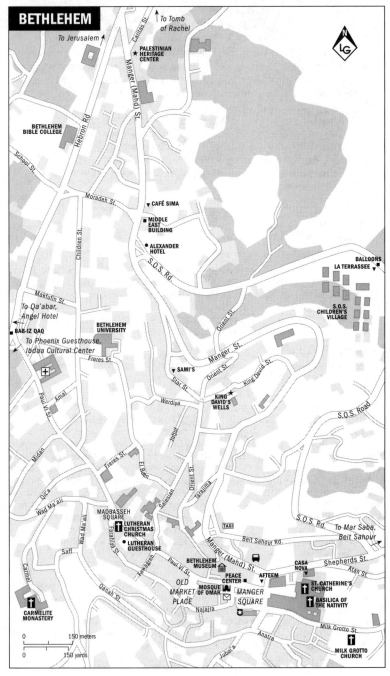

BETHLEHEM

To Tomb of Rachel ↑

Caritas St.

To Jerusalem ↑

★ PALESTINIAN HERITAGE CENTER

Manger (Mahd) St.

Hebron Rd.

■ BETHLEHEM BIBLE COLLEGE

School St.

Moradeh St.

Children St.

▼ CAFÉ SIMA

■ MIDDLE EAST BUILDING

● ALEXANDER HOTEL

S.O.S. Rd.

BALLOONS ■

LA TERRASSEE ▼

Makfulin St.

To Qa'abar, Angel Hotel

■ BAB-IZ QAQ

To Phoenix Guesthouse, Ibdaa Cultural Center

Orient St.

S.O.S. CHILDREN'S VILLAGE

■ BETHLEHEM UNIVERSITY

Freres St.

Manger St.

▼ SAMI'S

Orient St.

King David St.

S.O.S. Road

Star St.

Wardiya

♦ KING DAVID'S WELLS

Paul VI St.

Amal

Midan

Qit'a

Wad Ma'ali

Ila Ma Ma

Freres St.

El Bab

Juttut

Orient St.

Taralima

Salesian

MADBASSEH SQUARE

✝ LUTHERAN CHRISTMAS CHURCH

● LUTHERAN GUESTHOUSE

Faraliya St.

Tawwagh

Saff

Carmel

Paul VI St.

Qanah St.

OLD MARKET PLACE

Najajra

S.O.S. Rd.

To Mar Saba, Beit Sahour

Beit Sahour Rd.

TAXI

Shepherds St.

Atan St.

CASA NOVA ▼

AFTEEM

BETHLEHEM MUSEUM 🏛

PEACE CENTER ■

MOSQUE OF OMAR ✉

MANGER SQUARE ✲

Manger (Mahd) St.

✝ ST. CATHERINE'S CHURCH

✝ BASILICA OF THE NATIVITY

Milk Grotto St.

✝ CARMELITE MONASTERY

Anatra

Jubai'a

✝ MILK GROTTO CHURCH

0   150 meters

0   150 yards

N

west bank

MONEY

ATMs are less abundant than in Israel but are usually concentrated around banks near the center of town. Make sure not to take out Jordanian shekels (JD) accidentally.

bethlehem ☎02

Being the birthplace of the lord and savior of the world's most popular religion sort of gives you all-time bragging rights. If nothing else, it at least allows the vendors to utter a fervent and honest, "Thank you, Jesus," as they eye the wallets of the faithful. Bethlehem's bragging rights and its proximity to Jerusalem make it the major tourist destination in the West Bank. As such, it's also a good way to get a taste of the West Bank for those not ready for heavy hitters like Hebron; for many pilgrims in Bethlehem, the Israeli-Palestinian conflict only slightly seeps through the cracks. Tour buses avoid the contentious wall, and itineraries keep them close to Manger Sq., home to the **Basilica of the Nativity** (birthplace of Christ), the usual icon-hawking street vendors, and Afteem, one of the great falafel restaurants of the West Bank. Taxi drivers beg to take you on tours of major sights, cheap food is good and abundant, and services are centralized.

Away from all this, of course, there is a different story: anger directed toward the giant concrete slab that is the wall and poverty in refugee camps like Dheisheh. In the outskirts of the city, a large community of student volunteers affiliated with Phoenix Association and Ibdaa Cultural Center seek to better the lives of residents. Still, Bethlehem is a town that represents much of the best that the West Bank has to offer.

ORIENTATION

Manger Square is the tourism center of town, home to the Visitor Tourism Center and the Peace Center Tourism Office, the Basilica of the Nativity, and St. Catherine's Church. Adjacent to it is Manger St., the main commercial boulevard of Bethlehem, where you will find the **bus station** and the police station. On the opposite side of Manger Sq. lies the **souq**, which centers on **Najajreh Street, Saint Paul VI Road,** and **Star Street.** To the northeast is the mountainous and picturesque Beit Jala and to the west is Beit Sahour. **Bab izQaq** is a central reference point in town, only a block away from the northern section of Manger St. The gathering place for service taxis is located at the intersection of **Hebron Road** and **Bethlehem Street.**

ACCOMMODATIONS

Reportedly, Jesus was born on Christmas, which seems like something that would really interfere with present-buying. Hotel prices skyrocket during Christmas, as well as during other holiday seasons. However, the Phoenix Guesthouse and Ibdaa Cultural Center remain low year-round.

◪ PHOENIX GUESTHOUSE   HOSTEL $
Dheisheh   ☎02 275 1006; www.phoenixbethlehem.org

Phoenix provides large and exceptional facilities—and an inspiring environment—for almost no money. Naji Owdah, who runs Phoenix and helped create Ibdaa, hosts a series of projects and classes for Dheisheh youth who are usually taught by young Western European volunteers. Through their after-school programs, Palestinian youth have discovered a love for painting, applied to and been accepted at universities internationally (including Brown), and learned about women's rights, among other things. The guesthouse has dorms and a large kitchen and common area where the largely volunteer crowd cooks impromptu dinners and shares cigarettes over long talks about politics. Phoenix earns most of its money from hosting Palestinian weddings, which means that there is a wedding on the grounds nearly every single night and sometimes during the day as well. The space is intimate, fun, and productive, even if it's a bit of a hike to get to.

‡ Take a left off the main street of the Dheisheh Refugee Camp to reach Ibdaa. From there, exit and take a right. Continue to walk down until there is a large turn uphill to your right, with a small Palestinian military base 50m up on the left. Take that turn, and continue walking until you see a sign for Alfeneic on the right; go up that hill. Phoenix is on the 2nd right. i Free Wi-Fi and computer access. Free laundry. Naji can help arrange tours and homestays. $ Dorms NIS50. Cash only, but most currencies accepted. ⏰ Reception 24hr.

IBDAA CULTURAL CENTER GUESTHOUSE, COMMUNITY CENTER $

Dheisheh ☎02 277 6444; www.dheisheh-ibdaa.net

Wayward students and daytripping activists collect at this community center and guesthouse that functions as the primary location for travelers living on the cheap in Bethlehem. A restaurant upstairs offers spotty Wi-Fi and a single menu item, always for a reasonable cost (around NIS30). Ibdaa's staff are young and politically motivated Palestinians who enjoy sharing their story with Western visitors—though it's best to keep in mind that Ibdaa is one of the more pro-Palestinian establishments in the West Bank (which is saying something). Rooms are small and come with a desk, fan, and ensuite bathroom.

‡ Take a left off the main street of the Dheisheh Refugee Camp. There are no street signs, so ask a local. i Free Wi-Fi. $ Rooms NIS50. ⏰ Doors close at midnight, but you can get a number to call to be let in later.

BETHLEHEM LUTHERAN GUESTHOUSE GUESTHOUSE $$

St. Paul VI Rd. ☎02 277 0047; info@annadwa.org

The Bethlehem Lutheran Guesthouse is just one component of the **Addar Cultural Center,** which also includes a bar, restaurant, and theater. The guests have constant access to all these facilities and may also attend the monthly program of music, theater, and dance in the adjacent auditorium. Rooms are small but impeccable, with two comfortable beds, tasteful blue and beige decor, a small desk, and the constant twitter of birds outside. Each room is named after a Palestinian town or figure and exhibits artwork made by students at the nearby university.

‡ Walk 300m up St. Paul VI Rd. from Manger Sq. or the souq. i Wi-Fi in rooms. Breakfast included. $ Singles US$65; doubles US$90. ⏰ Reception 24hr.

ANGEL HOTEL HOTEL $$

al-Sahel St. ☎02 276 6880; www.angelhotel.ps

Mouth agape, hair on end, arms outstretched in exaltation, the weary budget traveler can press a simple switch and watch in amazement as the machinated window screen at Angel Hotel slowly lifts and descends on command. For the price, it is almost impossible to find a joint as sleek as Angel, with its polished marble surfaces and black leather furniture. Maybe it's so reasonable because it's in Beit Jala, far from Manger Sq. sights, or maybe the winged celestials who told shepherds of the Messiah's birth recommended they build a divinely fair hotel as well.

‡ From Bab izQaq, walk 500m, downhill and then uphill. Angel Hotel is on the left. $ Singles US$50; doubles US$90; triples US$120. ⏰ Reception 24hr.

ALEXANDER HOTEL HOTEL $$

315 Manger St. ☎02 277 0780; www.alexanderhotel.ps

Each floor is different, and each room presents its own advantages and difficulties. One room has a spectacular view over Jerusalem and Bethlehem—but pairs felt bed covers with white tile floors, a combination that will make you try to keep your eyes firmly fixed on the panorama. Another has no such view but creates a more cozy feel with comfortable bed covers and a nice carpet. The large lobby, with leather chairs and couches organized around a big TV, sometimes hosts tourist groups.

⇅ Near the roundabout on Manger St. ℹ Breakfast included. Free Wi-Fi in the lobby and on 2 of the 6 floors. $ Singles NIS150; doubles NIS125. Prices may be negotiable. ⏰ Reception 24hr.

SIGHTS

Bethlehem is clearly the best place for sights in the West Bank, boasting the birthplace of Christ and one of the most bizarre, most fascinating, and certainly oldest monasteries around in Mar Saba. The area also has an impressive set of ruins in nearby Herodion, a deep look into the hopes and difficulties of refugees in Dheisheh camp, and a case study in denominational squabbling in the multiple Shepherds' Fields.

★ BASILICA AND GROTTO OF THE NATIVITY — CHURCH

Manger Sq. ☎02 274 2425

Duck your head and crawl through the severely titled Door of Humility—built originally to keep out Muslim cavalry, not to make you feel lowly—and enter one of the oldest churches in Christianity. According to the New Testament, Bethlehem is the location of Jesus's birth, and third-century accounts specify the birthplace as the grotto where today's church stands (no manger in sight, unfortunately). The spot is considered so important that the original Constantinian church has been spared by attackers throughout history. Even the Persians, who thoroughly trashed practically every other Christian holy place during their 614 CE invasion, left it alone. The church today is therefore more a testament to renovation than rebuilding: the original mosaics are visible through half-open wooden trapdoors, the building itself and the four rows of red limestone columns are mostly from a sixth-century reconstruction by Justinian, and the gold and mother-of-pearl fragments adorning the walls are from the Crusader era. Most of the other illustrations, lamps, and adornments date back to the massive 19th-century restoration, although the icons adorning the main altar facing the front entrance were given by the Russian royal family in 1764. The patchwork appearance you see today only came into being after hundreds of years of denominational wrangling that sometimes came to bloodshed. The prayer schedule functions partially on the Greek Orthodox Church calendar and time schedule, but squabbles about the edifice continue to this day.

The main attraction at the Church of Nativity is in the basement-level **Grotto of the Nativity,** where nuns stoop in a tiny lair under an altar to light candles and polish silver with the care of a dental surgeon. The lucky worshippers who make it through the line to pray in this miniature cavern kneel and repetitively kiss the ground for a precious minute. A 14-pointed silver star—each point represents a Station of the Cross—lies at the bottom. Its inscription reads "Hic De Virgine Maria Jesus Christus Natus Est" (Here, of the Virgin Mary, Jesus Christ was born).

⇅ Coming uphill from Manger St., the church is on the right at the back end of Manger Sq. ℹ Legs must be covered. English brochure available in St. Catherine's Church. $ Free. ⏰ Church open M-Sa in summer 6:30am-7:30pm, in winter 5:30am-5pm. Grotto open M-Sa in summer 6:30am-7:30pm, in winter 5:30am-5pm.

SAINT CATHERINE'S CHURCH — CHURCH

Manger Sq. ☎02 274 2425

A modern appendage to the Basilica of the Nativity, St. Catherine's Church was built by the Franciscans in 1881 on the site where Jesus is said to have appeared to St. Catherine of Alexandria and predicted her martyrdom. The church is white, open, and airy. The newly famous bas-relief of the Tree of Jesse, made by religious sculptor Czeslaw Dźwigaj, was given as a present by Pope Benedict XVI during his trip to the Middle East in 2009. Most visitors, however, make the trip to see the two chapels that lie underneath all this. The **Chapel of Saint Joseph** commemorates the adoptive father's vision of an angel that advised him to flee to Egypt, and the **Chapel of Innocents** was built to honor the children killed by King Herod according to the Gospel of Matthew. Mass is broadcast from here on Christmas Eve every year, when it becomes jam-packed.

⚔ *Just to the left of the basilica. i Legs must be covered. English brochure available at the front.*
Ⓢ *Free. ☾ Open daily in summer 6am-noon and 2-7:30pm, in winter 5am-noon and 2-7pm.*

MAR SABA MONASTERY

St. Saba the Sanctified became a monk when he was eight years old. Ten years later, he moved to the Holy Land to live alone in a cave, supposedly on orders from an angel. Or maybe he just got sidetracked on his gap year—prodigies tend to do that. He stayed there and worked for the rest of his life, attracting a series of followers who helped him build the monastery in 502 CE. Today, the building, which is not open to women, has walls lined with faded illustrations, dim chandeliers hanging from the ceiling, and marble floors warped with wear. Considering his biography, it's not surprising that St. Saba helped create the entire monastic movement; many in the Orthodox community believe he achieved perfection and inspired other ascetics like St. Stephen the Wonderworker.

As the whole "wonderworker" thing implies, the monastery is one of the best places to hear some crazy stories. The principal miracle, which is perpetually on view, is St. Saba's uncorrupted body. That's right: St Saba's skin never fully decomposed, and his eyes and brain are reportedly intact. More then 500 years after his death, Crusaders took away his body, but they brought it back to Mar Saba after a series of popes had nightmares about St. Saba demanding a return. It is now on gruesome display when you first enter on the right. Don't question its authenticity—one woman who doubted reportedly saw the skull's head turn toward her, nod, then return to its former state. Apparently, there were many witnesses.

The Mar Saba miracles don't stop there. As you're walking around the main courtyard, know that you are standing above a giant graveyard for monks who have worked at this site, whose bodies are said to miraculously dry and stiffen without putrefaction. Creepier than this is the room across from the monastery, which exhibits skulls of martyrs from the 17th century onward, as well as a pitch-black room full of their bones. Mild-mannered and thoughtful monks can walk you through and explain all this, which sounds a lot less like sheer madness when it is directly in front of you.

⚔ *There is no way easy to walk here. Cab prices range dramatically: NIS70 for a round trip is fair, but it's reasonable to try for NIS50. i Women not allowed inside. It is preferred but not required for arms and legs to be covered. English brochures available.* Ⓢ *Guided tours free. ☾ Open daily 9am-7pm, depending on sunrise and sunset.*

DHEISHEH REFUGEE CAMP

"Refugee camp" is a loaded term, and the images it conjures are not pretty. Palestine is littered with them, and they have been around long enough to become places in their own right—meaning that former refugees now live in proper houses, not Hooverville shantytowns, and have easy access to basic services. While some Palestinian camps are punctuated by buildings that have been in crumbled heaps of stone since 1967, Dheisheh has basically solved its broken-windows theory problem and its physical landscape is ordered, though still spare, unclean, and sometimes depressing. Graffiti pleas to the outside world can be found without too much difficulty, and the works tend to have more desperation rather than the screw-you attitude of Ramallah wall art. As his own addition to homages to the right of return and lamentations about the wall separating many from their ancestral homeland, UK-based tag legend **Banksy** scrawled an infamous image of a young girl patting down a soldier, which can be found on the wall near the entrance to Bethlehem.

What makes Dheisheh unique as a refugee camp is the unbelievable efforts taken by locals to organize extracurricular programs for the camp's youth. At the Phoenix Association, volunteers from around the world teach everything from painting to how to deal with advertising, and a library, playground, sports center, and theater are all used in children's programs. Nearby Ibdaa Cultural Center has similar organizational goals and has helped to create a children's health parliament—a group of children seeking to fight the various health problems facing Dheisheh—a series of basketball teams, a traditional Palestinian dance troupe, and much more.

✈ *Service taxis (NIS3.50) regularly run to Dheisheh from the side of Manger St. heading away from the square and from around the bus station.* ⓘ *It is best to avoid walking around alone late at night. Ibdaa will sometimes offer free tours around Dheisheh—call for more details.*

BEIT SAHOUR   NEIGHBORHOOD, RELIGIOUS SITE

According to the New Testament, somewhere in this neighborhood angels proclaimed the birth of God's son to shepherds more than 2000 years ago. But where exactly? Unfortunately (or, possibly, conveniently), three different Shepherds' Fields have cropped up, each associated with a different denomination of Christianity and proclaiming itself to be the authentic site. The most popular and grandest of these sites is the **Franciscan Shepherds' Field,** which is run by a friendly group of monks. (Walk right from the Beit Sahour bus station, take a left after the second gas station, and walk past the Sahara Hotel. The field is on the right.) The **Protestant Shepherds' Field** is the newest of the group. While a convincing case can be made about the topography of this site preventing actual shepherding, the point of this site is less about accuracy and more about providing a field for all types of Protestants. In fact, the biggest draw may be the ancient cave; staff associated with the YMCA lead you through here and point out the many pockmarks that indicate the presence of oil lamps many centuries ago. (From the Franciscan Field, return to the main road and take a left. Walk 50-100m to reach a large gate.) From a touristic view, the **Greek Orthodox Shepherds' Field** is the most interesting. Simple cave mosaics are all that remain of a fifth-century monastery, and three churches have left behind broken columns, a mysterious wheel, and a large stone altar. The nearby **Greek Orthodox Church,** opened in 1989, takes the term wall mural to a whole new level: every column, ledge, and support beam has its own brightly colored biblical illustration, making for an overwhelming entrance. (Exit the YMCA and take a right. Walk along the road for 1km until you see a red sign for the Siraj Center on a building to the right. Cross the street and take the left that doesn't lead uphill. Walk for around 200m until you reach an intersection and take another slight left. Keep walking until you see the pink domes of the church. Take a left to enter.)

Outside of these tourist destinations, Beit Sahour is also a real place, and one of the most prominent Christian neighborhoods in the area around Bethlehem. Walk along Main St. to find the Alternative Tourism Group to try and schedule a guided walk.

✈ *The bus to Beit Sahour stops right behind the Peace Center (NIS2.50). Walk around 2km on Shepherd St., heading away from Jerusalem. You can also take a taxi.* ⓘ *Legs must be covered at all sites. Taxis should cost NIS15, but will probably cost closer to NIS20.* ⏰ *Franciscan Field open Su 8-11:30am and 2-5:30pm, M-Sa 8am-5:30pm. Protestant Field open daily 8am-6pm.*

TOMB OF RACHEL TOMB

The Wall ☎02 654 1142

Walk past the wall, get asked the inevitable questions at the metallic checkpoint station, make it through another mini-checkpoint, and find yourself in a concrete hangar, weaving through uniformed men with guns, sheet metal separating platforms, and bobbing Hasidim. That's right—it might seem like you've entered a third checkpoint, but you're actually in the Tomb of Rachel, a tiny room that gravitates around a central black monument representing the grave of Jacob's more beloved wife. The tomb would technically be on the other side of the wall, but some inventive construction allows it to appear on what is officially considered Israel. It takes singular religious focus not to see this sight in the political terms it has become embroiled in—the real significance of this spot hardly extends beyond its specific geographic location.

 # Go through the main checkpoint north of Manger St., then take a left when you exit and the immediate right alongside the wall. To enter Rachel's Tomb you need to be in a car. If you're walking, some travelers recommend that you just wait outside until someone drives up, and they'll usually let you hop in for a ride. As always, Let's Go recommends caution. i Men's and women's sections are separate. Kippot provided at the door. Legs must be covered. Make sure to bring your passport in order to cross the checkpoint. $ Free. ⏰ Open Su-Th 8am-6pm, F 8am-1pm.

HERODION RUINS

☎057 776 1143; www.parks.org.il

Herodion is one of the best preserved sights built by the famous king and one of the premier examples of Roman architecture in the Middle East. Under Herod's direction the mountain was molded into a cone that served as a palace, fortress, and, after the king's death, monument to Herod's rule. Control ping-ponged between the Romans and the Jews for a century and a half until a large group of Byzantines, probably monks, took up residence among the buildings in the fifth century. By then, the buildings were already ruins, and the Byzantines skedaddled around the seventh century. Herodion remained unoccupied except by the occasional group of nomadic Bedouins until excavations began again in the 1960s; now, Herodion is one of the three places in Judea and Samaria (the West Bank) that is part of the Israel Nature and Parks Authority.

Although the astounding aerial view of Herodion may only be attainable by Google search, a trip to the sight is still worth it. There's evidence of an ancient synagogue, first-century living quarters, and a *mikveh* built after Jews reclaimed Herodion in 66 CE. Most impressive is the underground tunnel system and cistern, which can be used to walk up to Herodion from the tourism office entrance. Stand on top of Herodion and look around the surrounding landscape: to your east are the bare desert mountains of Jordan, to your north Bethlehem and Jerusalem, and just to the west, Hebron. There's nothing quite like this perch to get a sense of the land and to orient yourself. It also affords the striking realization that much of the West Bank is empty space.

 # The only way to get here is by taxi. From Beit Sahour, a round trip should be NIS30; from Bethlehem and such tourist centers as Manger Sq., cabbies might not back down from NIS40 or more. i Bring water. English brochures available. $ NIS27, students NIS22, under 18 NIS14. ⏰ Open in summer Su-Th 8am-5pm, F 8am-4pm, Sa 8am-5pm; in winter Su-Th 8am-4pm, F 8am-3pm, Sa 8am-4pm.

PALESTINIAN HERITAGE CENTER MUSEUM

Manger St. ☎059 274 2381; www.phc.ps

This center is one of the more interesting versions of the standard Palestinian cultural investment, where traditional dresses and pottery are usually on display with explanations that don't necessarily go beyond their importance as symbols of a lost past. At the Heritage Center, on the other hand, Beit Sahour brides come to rent the traditional dresses for their weddings, women in refugee camps make all the goods in the gift shop, and the founder, Maha Saca, has hung pictures of herself and her prestigious family in one room of the museum.

Around the intersection of Hebron Rd. and Manger St., just a few meters from part of the wall and on the corner of the street. ***i*** *Call ahead for a guided tour or to schedule a visit at the museum when it would otherwise be closed.* $ *Free.* ⏰ *Open M-Sa 10am-6pm.*

KING DAVID'S WELLS HISTORICAL SITE

King David St.

In his long siege against the Philistines, King David is said to have yearned for water from the well in Bethlehem, and eventually his army broke through enemy lines to capture the well and bring him a drink. If this is so, it would make the three wells just off Manger St. at least 12,000 years old. Though this site has attracted attention for its possible biblical relevance since it was first discovered in the late 19th century, it is in an effectively unmarked walkway between residential streets and the Catholic Action Centre. Those with immense imaginations can see much of history in these stone openings to ancient cisterns, but most travelers might find them underwhelming.

Walk 350m up Manger St., turn left up the staircase near the King David's Wells sign and across the Catholic Action Centre courtyard and up another staircase. $ *Free.* ⏰ *Open daily 7am-noon and 2-7pm, though it can sometimes be accessed later if the Catholic Centre gates are open.*

goliath by the numbers

- **HEIGHT:** "Six cubits and a span," or 10 ft.
- **FATHERS:** Over 100. According to the Talmud, Goliath was born by polyspermy (exactly what it sounds like), leaving him with many babydaddies to choose from. No lab was used for this. Use your imagination.
- **SIBLINGS:** One. The Book of Samuel tells of a battle between Elhanan and an enemy named Goliath who later books claimed was actually the brother of David's Goliath. The two stories are remarkably similar, though, and there's still some dispute about which was the "real" Goliath. Or the many babydaddies planned the naming of their children in order to cause further confusion.
- **DEPICTIONS AS A PICKLE:** One (see VeggieTales).

TENT OF NATIONS CAMPGROUND, VOLUNTEERING CENTER

☎02 274 3071; www.tentofnations.org

Israeli law dictates that, once land has been unused for long enough, it may be possessed by the state. The Tent of Nations sits between four different settlements, and Israel has been trying to gain possession of it since 1967. The Nassar family bought the area in 1916 to produce olives, grapes, wheat, and other grains and has fought to maintain control ever since. Bishara Nassar built a youth activity hall and began a series of other projects, preventing repossession even after the Israeli government declared the property (and surrounding area) to be government-owned. His son Daoud has since taken over, and fights have continued in courts and on the land itself; in 2000 the broader Tent of Nations organization was created to fulfill the dual purpose of keeping this land under the Nassar family and Palestinian control while facilitating group activites for children from conflict areas. By bringing together young people from different cultures, the Tent of Nations seeks to foster mutual understanding. The site includes 100 acres of land for hiking and camping, caves used for meetings and worship, nine operating cisterns, an ancient cave residence, and a historic wine press that has been transformed into an outdoor theater for children and youth festivals.

 # Take a service taxi to Sabahtash (Kilo 17), then walk on the road toward Nahalin village. Tent of Nations is on the left. i Contact the Tent of Nations for tours, information about camping, and opportunities to volunteer for a few days.

FOOD

Bethlehem is the best place for cheap eats in the West Bank. Qa'abar and Afteem serve up Palestinian standbys, while **Sami's** is the best place to sit and have a coffee in a many-mile radius. Nicer options for Western fare also exist, although be prepared for a little bit of painful schlock.

🍴 QA'ABAR — BARBECUE CHICKEN $

Char'ah Tjar St. ☎02 274 1419

Qa'abar's sit-down meal of chicken and unlimited salad (NIS32) is a feast enjoyed daily by some locals. For travelers, it may be a once-in-a-lunchtime experience. The grilled chicken (the only menu item other than salads) is smoked to the core and comes from what must be the heavyweight champions of chickens—half a fowl rarely looks like this much. These poultry powerhouses are what Qa'abar (pronounced Kah-ah-bar) is famous for; quietly, however, they also dish out some of the creamiest hummus in town, and the combination struck by the smoky meat and velvety chickpea is true glory. Most locals tear into these meals with their bare hands: maybe because a knife isn't always nearby, or maybe because the food is just too good for table manners.

 # Walk toward Beit Jala from Bab izQaq and take a left. Alternatively, ask any local or taxi driver; everyone knows Qa'abar. $ Takeout grilled chicken NIS18. Small salads NIS4, large NIS10. Cash only. ⏰ Open daily 9, 10am-midnight.

turkish joe

Hankering for your American plain morning cup of Joe? Don't order a "black coffee" in Israel. What you'll get is Turkish coffee, affectionately referred to as *cafe botz,* or "mud coffee," due to the murky sediment at the bottom of the cup. Some swear by the strong, sweet flavor of this Turkish Joe, but if you're looking for a good old American version, try ordering a Cafe Americano with no milk.

🍴 AFTEEM — FALAFEL $

Afteem St. ☎02 274 7940; afteemrestaurant@yahoo.com

In Jerusalem, falafel sells faster than cotton candy in Disneyland, so budget travelers beginning their journey in J-town get spoiled with the fresh stuff all the time. Moving into the West Bank, they might notice the creeping rise of stale bricks of chickpeas, cold and hardened by the cruel cryogenics of time, filling their formerly tasty sandwiches with damp rubber. Enter Afteem, possibly the premier falafeleria in the West Bank. The only choice you make is whether you want it spicy or not—then the specialists take over. In truth, they know what you want better than you do. The smooth crunch, the spicy sweetness, the true craftsmanship that Afteem puts in a plastic wrapper and serves for only NIS5 is enough to bring even the most disillusioned falafel feeder back into the fold. Welcome home.

Walk down the hill just beyond the Peace Center as if going to the Basilica of the Nativity in Manger Sq. Afteem will be among the restaurants on the left. $ Kebabs NIS30. Shishlik NIS40. Fresh lemonade with mint NIS10. Cash only. ⏰ Open daily from 7:30am to 10 or 11:30pm.

SAMI'S COFFEE, TEA $

Off Star St. ☎059 551 3443

A portable stove, a fridge, four chairs, a bedside table, and a couple of ashtrays is all you're going to find in this tiny shop. The owner, Sami Khamis (Sammy Thursday in English), is a cheerful and inquisitive middle-aged man who brings little cups of coffee and tea to all the surrounding shopkeepers and workers on a silver platter that he effortlessly balances by clutching a central swinging pole. The coffee is rich and black, and the mint and sage for the tea are kept extremely fresh. This is hands-down the best place near Manger Sq. to stop for a midday break.

Walk on Star St. toward the Basilica of the Nativity, and take the left turn within 20m of the staircase. Sami's is on the right. $ Coffee NIS2. ⏰ Open M-Th 7:30am-4 or 5pm, Sa 7:30am-4 or 5pm.

CAFE SIMA FRENCH, INTERNATIONAL $$

Manger St. ☎02 275 2058; www.cafesima.com

Locals come to this European import to be tourists themselves, as French-trained patissier Chef Sima cooks up cakes and crepes under the quintessentially continental motto, "Life without chocolates and cakes is life lacking something important." Disgruntled taxi drivers might have a thing or two to say about that, but this is a good place to go when you're tired of political tirades and just want to see some English. After all, where else are you going to find both iced coffee (NIS10) and a Nutella crepe (NIS10)?

On the right side of Manger St., just past the intersection with Moradeh St. when you're walking toward the wall. ***i*** *No smoking. $ Frappucino NIS12. Waffles NIS15. Quiches NIS15-18. Parmesan chicken sandwich on ciabatta NIS20. Cash only. ⏰ Open Su 10:30am-8:30pm, M-Tu 10:30am-7-pm, Th-Sa 10:30am-8:30pm.*

BONJOUR CAFE INTERNATIONAL CAFE $

John Paul II St. ☎02 274 0406

Photoshop artwork that owner Marwan spends months creating hang in this cafe near Bethlehem University that plays host to students and monks alike. Low lighting, a large barista bar, and black tables easily achieve a Western aesthetic; it is more surprising that the two eggs any style (with thick Arabic bread; NIS12) also manages to do so—even though it simultaneously incorporates local flavor.

From Bab izQaq, head down Manger St. until you see Nissan Restaurant on the right. Walk past the gas station in front of it and head behind Nissan on its left, then uphill. Once you reach the street, take a left and continue to walk uphill. Bonjour is on the left. ***i*** *They deliver for a small fee. Free Wi-Fi. $ Caesar salad NIS25, large 39. Fish fillet NIS40. Beef and chicken burgers NIS20-45. ⏰ Open M-Sa 9:30am-11pm.*

CASA NOVA RESTAURANT ITALIAN, INTERNATIONAL $$

Manger Sq. ☎02 274 2798; www.casanovapalace.com

Spacious outdoor seating adjacent to one of the most famous Christian sights in the world (the Basilica of the Nativity) keeps this restaurant busy with tourists, but it remains a nice place to sit. Although technically closed on Monday, the restaurant still offers drinks and is usually pretty quiet. Boozy budget travelers will appreciate the piña colada or bottle of Maccabee for a mere NIS10.

Just to the left of the Basilica of the Nativity as you walk with your back to Star St. $ Ham and cheese sandwich NIS20. Ravioli with spinach and ricotta NIS50. ⏰ Open Su 11am-3pm and 6-10pm, Tu-Sa 11am-3pm and 6-10pm. Outdoor seating open for drinks on M.

LA TERRASSE MIDDLE EASTERN, INTERNATIONAL $$

al-Karkafeh St. ☎02 275 3678; www.balloonspizza.com

The flatscreen blares music videos, laughing relatives laugh and pass around the *argilah*, and the french fry grease glistens at Bethlehem's closest approximation to one of those feel-good, family-friendly restaurants. Sharing a building and owner with Balloons Pizza, La Terrasse serves a *sheesh tawook* (NIS40) with mounds of bread and fries that is everything you'd expect from a kebab. An amazing view of Jerusalem and the area surrounding Bethlehem is somewhat covered by flora growing all over the windows.

➔ At the roundabout on Manger St., take a left and walk downhill about 500m. $ Fried calamari NIS45. ⏰ Open daily 1-11pm.

ESSENTIALS

practicalities

- **TOURIST OFFICE: Peace Center Tourism Office** has free maps and brochures, Wi-Fi, and stores luggage during business hours. (Manger Sq. ☎02 276 6677 ➔ Walk into Manger Sq. from Star St. It's just on the left. *i* Cafe, tourism police, English-language bookstore, and other services in the same building. ⏰ Open M-Th 8am-3pm, Sa 8am-3pm.) **Visitor Tourism Center** provides maps, information, Wi-Fi, computers, bathrooms, and help with reserving hotel rooms and renting cars. (Manger Sq. ☎02 275 4234/5; celina_salman@hotmail.com ➔ On the same corner as the Bethlehem Municipality and on the opposite side of the square from the Peace Center. ⏰ Open Su-F 9am-6pm.)
- **TOURS: Alternative Tourism Group** is a very political organization that leads trips around the West Bank. Call in advance to schedule or join a tour. (74 Star St. ☎02 277 2151; www.atg.ps ➔ On the main street in Beit Sahour, through a green door within 50m from the Greek Orthodox Church that's not the one by Shepherds' Field.)
- **ATM: Bank of Palestine.** There are many throughout the city, and all have 24hr. ATMs, but the one at 573 Manger St. is the closest to Manger Sq. (➔ From Manger Sq., walk uphill on the right side of the street for around 400m.)
- **LAUNDROMATS:** Laundry can be done for free at Ibdaa and the Phoenix Center. This is usually reserved for guests, but if you call ahead of time and ask politely, you may be able to use the machines.
- **PUBLIC TOILETS:** Available in both Manger Sq. tourism centers and behind the Visitor Information Center on the right if you are facing it.
- **INTERNET: ICC (Internet Center and Coffee Shop)** offers computers, coffee, and the joy of watching young children play first-person shooter games. (645 Manger St. ☎02 276 4502 ➔ 300m from Manger Sq. on the left side of the street. $ NIS7 per hr., 3rd hr. NIS5. ⏰ Open daily 9:30am-9:30pm.)
- **POST OFFICE: Bethlehem Post Office.** (Manger Sq. ☎02 274 2668; www.palpost ➔ Walk down the staircase adjacent to the Bethlehem Municipality. ⏰ Open Su-Th 8am-3pm.)

emergency

- **POLICE:** Manger St. ☎02 274 8231 ➔ Directly behind the Peace Center in Manger Sq.
- **LATE-NIGHT PHARMACY:** There are pharmacies every 100m on Manger St., but most close by 9pm; at the latest, they are open until 11pm. Get your medicine early.
- **HOSPITAL: Al-Hussein Government Hospital.** (Hebron Rd. ☎02 274 1161 ➔ On the way to Beit Jala.)

getting there

BY BUS

The best way to get to Bethlehem from Jerusalem is by taking **bus #21,** which leaves from around Damascus Gate, puts you near the center of town, and costs NIS6. **Bus #124** makes a number of stops in Jerusalem, deposits you at the northernmost part of Manger St., and requires you to go through an arduous process to get past the checkpoint.

BY SERVICE TAXI

Service taxis are the best way to travel within the West Bank. Service taxis cost NIS11-30 between all destinations in the West Bank, and, as long as you pay during your ride, you can see how much those around you pay and pay the same. If your driver tells you a surprisingly high number, tell him you know that that isn't the price.

getting around

BY SERVICE TAXI

The six-door "stretch" service taxis of Bethlehem are arguably some of the coolest vehicles in the universe. Service taxis cost NIS3.50 and go just about everywhere in town; there should be no real reason to take a personal (or "special," pronounced spay-shull) taxi unless you are pressed for time, unable or unwilling to walk from a service taxi route to your destination, or are traveling a bit outside Bethlehem.

BY TAXI

Taxis congregate around **Manger Square,** and tend to charge more than those going up and down Manger St. Never pay more than NIS15 for a trip within Bethlehem.

ramallah ☎02

Every aspect of Palestinian life is on display in Ramallah, the cultural and political capital of Palestine. Students discuss current events in the cafes of Birzeit University, working-class Palestinians sit in all-male cafes off Main St. devoting full days to *argilah* and idle chatter, the children of the landed class flit from restaurant to bar, and refugees reside in camps outside of the center of town. High in the mountains, Ramallah was traditionally a vacation spot before that whole "constant violent unrest in the Middle East" thing began in the 20th century. The city has since become the center for Palestinian activism: the nearby university is a hub for student protest, and many peace activists base their efforts here.

Ramallah is also home to Palestinian culture, one of the few places where theater groups and art galleries have succeeded in obtaining funding. International and Palestinian art festivals, academic colloquia, and theater events are frequent, especially during the summer. While many women adhere strictly to Islamic law, there is also a large population of more self-determined (often secular) women who go to college and have careers. Conversations everywhere buzz with politics and current events, and even the most apathetic tourist may find it impossible to avoid taking a stance when approached by everyone from taxi drivers to expats.

ORIENTATION

Ramallah's beating heart is **al-Manara Square,** and most directions will refer to it. Most commerce and cheap restaurants can be found along **Main Street. Al-Bireh,** formerly an independent city and now a large part of greater Ramallah, is connected to the rest of town chiefly by **al-Nahdah Street,** which begins in al-Manara Sq. Most nightlife and high-class restaurants can be found in **al-Masyoun,** the more ritzy and fashionable neighborhood. Bars can also be found along Jaffa St. and nearby Issa Ziadeh.

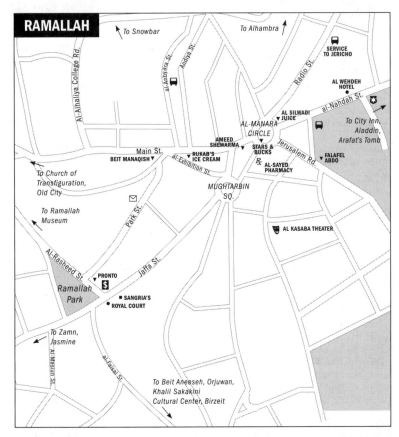

RAMALLAH

To Snowbar

To Alhambra

SERVICE TO JERICHO

AL WEHDEH HOTEL

al-Nahdah St.

To City Inn, Aladdin, Arafat's Tomb

AL SILWADI JUICE

AL-MANARA CIRCLE

Al-Athaliya College Rd.

al-Andyara St.

Andya St.

Radio St.

Jerusalem Rd.

AMEED SHEWARMA

Main St. BEIT MANAQISH

RUKAB'S ICE CREAM

al-Exhibition St.

STARS & BUCKS

Rx AL-SAYED PHARMACY

FALAFEL ABDO

To Church of Transfiguration, Old City

MUGHTARBIN SQ.

To Ramallah Museum

Park St.

AL KASABA THEATER

Al-Rasheed St.

Jaffa St.

PRONTO

Ramallah Park

SANGRIA'S ROYAL COURT

To Zamn, Jasmine

Al-Masiun St.

al-Faisal St.

To Beit Aneeseh, Orjuwan, Khalil Sakakini Cultural Center, Birzeit

ACCOMMODATIONS

Cheap places to stay aren't very easy to come by in Ramallah, which makes **Al-Wehdeh Hotel** particularly nice. In terms of the higher class options, **Royal Court Hotel** and **Alhambra Palace** are both good bets; after them, hotels can become inconvenient or exorbitant for what they offer.

AL-WEHDEH — HOTEL $$

37 al-Nahdah St. ☎02 298 0412

The plaster peels a bit and the brown decor is by no means homey, but Al-Wehdeh is ideally convenient, unbeatably cheap, and has its own appeal. Traveling students tend to choose this place to spend their few nights in Ramallah, and the fluorescent-lit common room sometimes sits on the edge of becoming an actively social space. Rooms are surprisingly large, and some even feature wall-sized windows with fantastic views of Ramallah. If Al-Wehdeh were a guy you were dating, you might not introduce him to your parents, but you would definitely have fun at all the slightly ominous pool halls he took you to.

🚶 Walk down al-Nahdah St. from al-Manara Sq. for about 50m; Al-Wehdeh is on the left. $ Singles NIS100; doubles NIS120; triples NIS150; suites NIS180. ⏰ Open 24hr., buzz after midnight.

ROYAL COURT HOTEL — HOTEL $$

Jaffa St. ☎02 296 4040; www.rcshotel.com

The more corporate feel of this hotel can be assuaged by the knowledge that it is classier than anything else near its price range. Even the cheapest rooms, while small, generally have a large balcony and small kitchenette along with a queen bed, desk, and small flatscreen TV. More expensive rooms are similar, except with more space. Royal Court is located within 5min. of Ramallah's nicer restaurants and bars and is just a short walk from al-Manara Sq.

🚶 Walk 150m down Jaffa St. from al-Manara Sq. Royal Court is on the left. ℹ Breakfast included. $ Singles NIS255-390; doubles NIS370-450. Wi-Fi NIS35 per day. ⏰ Open 24hr.

ALHAMBRA PALACE — HOTEL $$$

Irsal St. ☎02 295 6226; www.alhambra-palace-hotel.com

From the large outdoor courtyard to the broad terraces attached to most rooms, Alhambra Palace is the perfect place to lounge. It's no wonder that families sometimes host weddings outside the hotel, which may afford a good opportunity for living out that *Wedding Crashers* dream of yours. Rooms have kitchenettes and sitting areas, making Alhambra a good place to settle if you want some indoor time while in Ramallah. The price for a single (US$80 a night) may not be cheap, but it's standard for the area.

🚶 From al-Manara Sq., walk down Radio St. and then take a right on Irsal St., which can also go by Mukataa and al-Hambra. ℹ Free Wi-Fi in rooms. Breakfast included. $ Singles US$80; doubles US$100. ⏰ Open 24hr.

CITY INN HOTEL — HOTEL $$

Nablus St. ☎02 242 8081

In the Ramallah boonies, the City Inn offers beautiful views into the surrounding countryside and—apart from bordering a busy road—puts you at a peaceful distance from al-Manara Sq. It's a bit too far to walk, but the city is an easy shared taxi (NIS2.50) ride away. Some singles have pretty yellow and blue decor and desks. Larger rooms have sitting areas as well.

🚶 Very far down Nablus St., which you can cross to from al-Nahdah in al-Bireh. It is best to take a shared or private taxi rather than walking. ℹ Free Wi-Fi. Breakfast included. $ Singles NIS200; doubles NIS300; triples NIS400. ⏰ Open 24hr.

ALADDIN HOTEL — HOTEL $$

al-Bireh St. ☎02 240 7689; aladdinhotel1@gmail.com

The hallways may be dark and empty and the gray carpets may be stained, but Aladdin Hotel does provide a roof, a bed, and window without fail. So, if those are your three wishes, consider *Let's Go* your Robin Williams, er—Genie.

 # From al-Manara Sq., walk 500m down al-Nahdah and take a left. Aladdin Hotel is across from al-Quds Bank. ***i*** *No internet available. $ Singles NIS240; doubles NIS260.*

SIGHTS

After you're done sleeping off last night at **Snowbar,** you might as well go out and do something. Sure, any resident would tell you that sights are not really the point of Ramallah, but **Arafat's Tomb** is a dramatic testament to the recently deceased leader, and the **Church of Transfiguration** is strikingly designed. At the very least, it will give you something parent-appropriate to write in your postcard home.

ARAFAT'S TOMB — TOMB

Mukataa

Soldiers surround this solemn compound built out of bare Jerusalem stone and surrounded by a pool, three bare trees, and three Palestinian flags. The reverence for leader Yasser Arafat, who died in 2004, is evident, and the silence of soldiers and picturesque severity of his resting place is reminiscent of a religious site. It's located in the Mukataa, the administrative center of the Palestinian Authority that was put under siege by the IDF during the Second Intifada in 2002.

 # Walk down al-Nahdah St. from al-Manara Sq., take a left at the first traffic light and walk for around 700m until a dead end. Take a left, and you will see the entrance to the tomb on the right $ Free. ⏰ Open daily 9am-10pm.

CHURCH OF TRANSFIGURATION — CHURCH

Old City ☎02 295 6618; www.tajalli.ps

Built in 1852, this Greek Orthodox church is full of icons collected from churches destroyed in the early 19th century. In a spectacular effect, the church grows darker from its back pews to the front, leading up to an extremely tall wooden panel that spans the room, covered in depictions of biblical scenes. There is a room for monks and priests behind it, from which light emanates over the panel, silhouetting the large wooden cross centered at the top of the panel-cum-wall. In one of the icons, a beautiful olive-skinned Mary is said to shed tears of oil. We can only assume that it's extra-virgin.

 # Walk down Main St. from al-Manara Sq. until you reach a large intersection downhill. Go left at the traffic light, and you will enter the Old City. Look up to see a minaret and, next to it, a church spire. Follow the minaret and spire until you reach the church, which is next to the mosque. ***i*** *Shorts and tank tops tolerated, but with grimaces.*

BIRZEIT UNIVERSITY MUSEUM OF ETHNOGRAPHY AND ART — MUSEUM

Birzeit Univeristy ☎02 298 2976; virtualgallery.birzeit.edu

The Bizreit University Museum includes an area devoted to displaying films and objects related to Palestinian culture and politics, as well as an exhibition space for contemporary art. The museum makes for a short but unfailingly interesting visit. The rotating exhibitions may have political resonance but also stand on their own as works of art and thought. Visiting Birzeit University, a campus with beautiful views of the area and hyper-friendly students known to approach foreigners and begin conversations out of the blue, is also fun. The museum is associated with other parts of the university, including its collections of amulets, art, and costumes. For more information, inquire at the front desk.

 # The last building before the long downhill leading to the guarded entrance/exit at Birzeit. To get to the university, find a shared taxi in al-Manara Sq. or the nearby shared taxi building. Private taxi NIS30. Shared taxis are easy to find in the parking lot just outside of campus. ***i*** *Call ahead to*

ask about lectures and seminars that are sometimes offered, usually in May and June. [$] Free. ⏰ Museum open M-Th 10am-2pm, Sa 10am-2pm. Office open M-Th 8am-4pm, Sa 8am-4pm.

PALESTINIAN FOLKLORE SOCIETY MUSEUM MUSEUM

Samina Khalil St. ☎02 240 1123; www.inash.org

The historical collection here includes medicinal plants and instruments, ancient storage containers made of mud and hay, and traditional coffee-making tools. Diorama reconstructions include one of fake Palestinian bros sitting on comfy pillows, playing the *oud*, and drinking tea. Tours provide more detailed background information.

🧭 Walk down al-Nahdah St. until the large right turn; take it and veer left, and you should see Blue Sky Dry Cleaning. Go to the left of Blue Sky and walk through the white gates, then go to the end of the parking lot and walk up the stairs and through the door at the farthest point. ℹ Contact the office in advance to arrange for a tour. [$] Free. ⏰ Open daily 8am-3pm.

RAMALLAH MUSEUM MUSEUM

al-Harajeh St. ☎02 295 9561

This small museum of archaeological fragments neither offers much insight into Palestinian culture nor constructs much of a narrative. The Ramallah Museum is best visited by people with an interest in ancient pottery that is completely unaffected by the historical or sociological information that can be learned from it. The ethnographic section in the basement is more accessible, with a traditional woman's dress, a baby crib, and a washing basin used before prayer. At least with these, there are short explanations on placards.

🧭 Take the first left off Issa Ziadeh St. after the Municipality and walk down the street until you reach the Arab Bank and the gas station. The Ramallah Museum is directly in front of you, forming a triangle with the bank and the gas station. ℹ Brochure available in English. [$] Free. ⏰ Open Su-Th 9am-3pm.

OLD CITY NEIGHBORHOOD

A collection of beautiful low-lying Ottoman architecture left over from the 19th century, the Old City provides tourists with the opportunity to soak up a smaller, more residential, and slower version of Ramallah life. Old men smoke *argilah* outside all-male coffee shops, and fruit sellers flick flies.

🧭 Walk down Main St. until the intersection down the hill and take a left.

FOOD

Food in Ramallah represents the best of each different class of resident in this diverse city. **Beit Manaqish** is the ultimate cheap Arabic pizzeria, largely undiscovered by the small but slowly growing tourist crowd, while **Zamn** is clearly a high quality foreign import.

👍 **BEIT MANAQISH** PIZZA $

Main St. ☎02 295 8283

It doesn't get much cheaper or better than this pizzeria, which attracts an entirely local clientele in search of the best Arabic pizza in town (Ramallans suggest you stay away from their inferior Italian pizza options). Cheese and thyme pies, traditionally eaten in the morning, can be enjoyed in all their sticky and savory glory at any time of day. The crust is thin and doughy at once, an impressive feat of advanced pizza chemistry. If you just want to relax for a day, bring a book, eat all three meals here and occasionally wander over to nearby Rukab's for dessert.

🧭 Walking on Main St. from Rukab's, make 2 street crossings and Beit Manaqish will be just after the Big Bite sandwich shop. Walk through the gold and brown doors. [$] Small Arabic pizzas NIS5, large NIS10. Small Italian pizzas NIS7, large NIS12. ⏰ Open daily 10am-10pm.

👍 **RUKAB'S ICE CREAM** ICE CREAM $

22 Main St. ☎02 295 3467; rukab_icecream@yahoo.com

Main St. is sometimes called Rukab St. in its honor. If that doesn't prove that this place is a local institution, the ice cream will. The Rukab family has run the store since it opened in 1941 and at least one member of the clan is usually behind the counter. They speak close-to-perfect English and are extremely friendly to foreigners, making Rukab a good place to start an adventure in Ramallah. Due to an infusion of gum resin into the recipe, the ice cream congeals into an unforgettable, almost-chewy goop. Americans may scream for ice cream, but Ramallans would downright shriek for this stuff.

Coming from al-Manara Sq., walk about 200m down Main St. Rukab's will be on the left. $ Cones NIS5-14. Cups NIS8-10. ⏰ Open in summer Su-Th 8am-1 or 2am, F 9am-1 or 2am, Sa 8am-1 or 2am; open in winter Su-Th 8am-10pm or midnight, F 9am-10pm to midnight, Sa 8am-10pm or midnight.

AL-SILWADI JUICE — FRESH JUICES $

al-Manara Sq. — ☎02 295 6006

This tiny juice booth displays all its fresh fruit in crates and serves up smoothies that are the stuff of local legend. Whether you're looking to refuel during the afternoon or detox after three straight meals of shawarma grease, al-Silwadi is definitely the best healthy option around al-Manara Sq. The prices (medium juice NIS8) are almost impossible to beat. Though their list of fruits is a little too ambitious—they may be out of the one you have your heart set on—al-Silwadi has enough (bananas, carrots, oranges, mangoes, etc.) to cover a wide span of flavors.

Opposite Stars & Bucks directly on al-Manara Sq. $ Juices NIS6-10. ⏰ Open Su-Th 6am-midnight, F 8am-midnight, Sa 6am-midnight.

ZAMN — CAFE, RESTAURANT $$

al-Tireh St. — ☎02 295 0600; www.zamn.ps

Hot zamn! An aspiring chain, Zamn may only have two locations right now, but it seems primed for expansion. The fairly priced menu is full of conventional Western-style sandwiches that taste great—the chicken sandwich comes on surprisingly good whole wheat, and the meat itself is lean and crunchy—and the small outdoor sitting area is quiet and comfortable. A few buttoned-down expats and fashionable old ladies will sit here drinking tea and smoking past mealtime. Zamn is maybe the best place to sit and read in Ramallah.

Between al-Tireh's intersections with Labib Hishmeh St. and Batn il-Hanva, down Dar Ibrahim, which changes into al-Tireh. It is adjacent to the First Ramallah Group. $ Iced coffee and iced cappuccino NIS16. Zamn breakfast platter NIS35. Sandwiches NIS24-30, halves NIS15-18. ⏰ Open daily 6am-12:30am.

FALAFEL ABDO — FALAFEL $

Jerusalem St. — ☎02 295 6601

Walk through the closet-sized entrance, into and out of the kitchen, up a creaking wrought-iron staircase, into a low-ceilinged second-floor lair, and crack open some of the tidiest, tastiest falafel in Ramallah. The food is simple and the price unbeatable. The variety of accoutrements is modest and allows the high-quality chickpea flavor to come through. This place is, like the falafel itself, minimalist beauty.

Walk 50m down from al-Manara Sq. It's on the left. $ Falafel NIS4. Drinks NIS3. ⏰ Open Su-Th 9am-6pm, Sa 9am-6pm.

PRONTO — ITALIAN $$

al-Rashid St. — ☎02 298 7312; basemwkhoury04@yahoo.com

The quiet outdoor patio overlooking sleepy al-Rashid St. can be one of the best places for a slow and relaxed meal in Ramallah, with old men talking up waitresses and reading newspapers at surrounding tables. Tourists have definitely found this place, and it sometimes serves as a gathering ground for solo travelers. The food is unimpressive as far as any objective standard for Italian food goes, but it's above average for the Middle East. The pasta menu presents a selection of pastas and sauces and asks you to mix-and-match.

 # Walk down Jaffa St. to the Royal Court Hotel and then take the immediate right. Pronto is 15m away. $ Pasta NIS38. Small pizza NIS38. Cocktails NIS30-40. ⏰ Open daily 8am-1am.

falafel war

Not as fun as it sounds (no bazookas loaded with fried chickpeas, unfortunately), there was indeed a minor falafel war when a Lebanese trade union attempted to sue the state of Israel for presenting the image that falafel, in addition to hummus and *tabbouleh,* was an Israeli food. The trade union believed that Israel should pay Lebanon millions of dollars in lost revenue and attempted to trademark falafel as a Lebanese food. Seems a little crazy, until you hear about the "Greek feta precedent," in which Athens was able to prove that it was the inventor of feta cheese. The suit was unsuccessful, meaning you can eat all the untrademarked falafel you want.

AMEED SHAWARMA SHAWARMA $

Main St. ☎02 295 6093

Locals flock to this reliable and well-priced shawarma shop, which is perceptibly cleaner and more orderly than its extensive competition (that is, as long as you can ever consider a hunk of mystery meat on an open-air spit to be clean or orderly). Sandwiches are tightly packed, and the cucumber-tomato salad is fresh. There are almost always seats available along the bar.

 # Facing Stars & Bucks in al-Manara Sq., take a right to head up Main St. It's one of the 1st storefronts on the left. $ Shawarma NIS12. ⏰ Open daily 8am-2am.

STARS & BUCKS CAFE $

al-Manara Sq. ☎059 893 1233

It takes a pretty dire lack of humor to not appreciate the proximity between this Stars & Bucks location and the one on Radio St., the perfect mimicking of the logo, the endless coffee menu (29 iced coffees alone), and the other intentional and unintentional parodies of a certain Seattle chain. Some of the departures from form, such as the apple-cinnamon frappuccino (NIS15), are creative successes. Others, such as the lack of any pastry without cinnamon or chocolate, the loud pop music, and the bizarre plastic-sealed water cube delivered with each order, are less so. Regardless, Stars & Bucks is worth a stop for more than just a double take.

 # Walk 5m on Main St., then walk up the stairs coming from al-Manara Sq. i Free Wi-Fi. $ Iced coffee NIS15. Chicken sandwich NIS20. Cocktails NIS16-25. ⏰ Open daily 8am-1am.

NIGHTLIFE

Probably the best nightlife spot in Israel and Palestine outside Tel Aviv, Ramallah is home to the famous **Snowbar** and local legend **Beit Aneeseh**. Palestinians and foreign aid workers may form their own little cliques, but each are fascinated by the experiences of those traveling through. Aim to wake up the next morning with more phone numbers than memories.

★ SNOWBAR BAR, CLUB

Ein Musbah ☎059 926 4663

The reigning king of Ramallah nightlife, Snowbar has been known to throw decadent parties that go from noon to noon and draw a rotating selection of 400-500 people. DJs, bands from all over the world, jazz and hip-hop music, film screenings, and anything else owner Ameen Marouf can dream up make appearances on Thursdays or Fridays, accompanied by a large bonfire and a swimming pool larger than a city block. When it gets under 75°F during the summer (a.k.a. icy, by Ramallah standards), residents flee to indoor clubs and Snowbar can become empty. During normal summer days, however, tables are packed with lunching families. The pool (entry NIS50), meanwhile, serves as the social center for Ramallah's moneyed youth.

*⇟ Best to take a cab if coming from the center of town. To walk, go up the street opposite Rukab's, then take a left at the Palestine Bank, the next left to go downhill, then take your 1st right and go almost all the way uphill. Veer left just before the summit and go downhill until the intersection, then take a right. **i** Men without female accompaniment have been known to have trouble getting in. It's good to call in advance to find out about this and the night's activities. $ Cover NIS50-70 for big events. No regular cover. Beer NIS15-20. Argilah NIS20. ⏰ Open daily 7am-late.*

BEIT ANEESEH BAR

al-Hajjal ☎02 295 2991

USAID employees drunkenly gesticulate; kids huddle in the corner and watch high-heeled Palestinian beauties attempt to dance without falling over; and the night doesn't start winding down until the bartender drifts around the bar banging a tiny bell and shouting "last call!" The sloppy nightlife of the Ramallah glamorous doesn't get much more fun or hilarious than at Beit Aneeseh, whose polo-shirted patrons come to make the rounds with old friends, eye strangers, and get the friendliest kind of plastered. The grassy outdoor sitting area is lovely, but you shouldn't take the time to appreciate it—just grab a quick breather, then dive back into the action inside.

⇟ Walk down Jaffa St., go past the right onto al-Rashid, then take the next left. Walk on the right side of the street until you see a sign for Beit Aneeseh, which will be downhill on your 2nd right. $ Bottled beer NIS15. Glass of wine NIS20. ⏰ Open noon-midnight or 2am.

ORJUWAN LOUNGE RESTAURANT, BAR

Luthern St. ☎02 297 6870; www.orjuwanlounge.com

Home to the most interesting menu in Ramallah, Orjuwan Lounge mixes the form and ingredients of Palestinian and Italian dishes—an Italian risotto is constructed like the Palestinian *makluba* (upside-down in Arabic) with cauliflower and eggplant layered inside (NIS45), and the *musakhan* is made with focaccia dough (NIS50). On Thursdays this place becomes the hot spot for the fervent mingling of Ramallah's younger elite. However, just enjoying a drink near the outdoor fountain, or by the fire in the polished stone interior, is fun regardless of the crowd. The bar is owned and operated by the Sakakini brothers, and, if you want your night to be a bit more meaningful, find Sari Sakakini, who will be delighted to start talking spirituality. Just make sure you're wearing a monocle on your third eye.

*⇟ Take the 1st left off Jaffa St. after al-Rashid St. and then the 2nd right. Orjuwan Lounge is adjacent to the Khalil Sakakini Cultural Center. **i** Su live music. Sa international menu. $ Beer NIS15. Cocktails NIS30-40. ⏰ Open daily noon-midnight.*

JASMINE LOUNGE

22 al-Tireh St. ☎02 295 0123

This place would be just a restaurant if it weren't so preposterously popular. Ramallans have a tendency to follow the trendy, which might explain the need to make a reservation at this mostly outdoor cafe. Jasmine is the new kid on the block here, but even the cynical say that this place has the chops to stick around. An original (or just bizarre) menu of Western food includes apple cinnamon pancakes (NIS28) and mozzarella sticks (NIS32)—*Let's Go* challenges you to find another restaurant serving both of these dishes. Hordes of Palestinian youth and NGO loafers crowd tables covered in glasses of wine, *argilah*, and laptops against a backdrop of loud techno music.

*⇟ Keep walking down al-Tireh from Zamn. Jasmine is at the end of the street on the other side. **i** Free Wi-Fi. $ Cappuccino NIS12-19. Glass of wine NIS18. ⏰ Open daily 7am-1am.*

give it a rest

"And on the seventh day, God rested" (Genesis 2:2). Sounds pretty straightforward, right? But Jews, Christians, and Muslims have all managed to choose a different "seventh day" for their sabbaths, making a tangled mess of recent attempts to standardize the Israeli weekend. Although you'll find something close to the standard Western weekend in most parts of Israel—with the addition of a half day on Friday—more Muslim areas often take Thursdays and Fridays off. So, what does this mean for you? When you're looking to party in Ramallah, forget Friday night: Thirsty Thursday is the way to go.

SANGRIA'S BAR $

Jaffa St. ☎02 295 6808; www.sangrias.ps

Though older and, as a result, slightly less happening than other nightlife venues in the area, Sangria's spacious outdoor garden is the best place to go when you're tired of talking over overpowering techno beats or dealing with the constant buzz of Ramallah's more vibrant social spots. Large groups of locals and tourists share big tables in the low, smoky lighting. Waiters wearing lime green polos tucked into khakis dish out the drinks, and pink flower bushes line the seating area.

 # Walk down Jaffa St. toward the turn off to al-Rashid away from al-Manara Sq. Sangria's is on Jaffa St. adjacent to the Royal Court Hotel. [$] Taybeh NIS12. Gin and tonic NIS28. ⏰ Open in the summer daily noon-midnight.

ARTS AND CULTURE

Home to the al-Kasaba theater troupe and the internationally renowned Khalil Sakakini Cultural Center, Ramallah is the undisputed center for culture in Palestine.

AL-KASABA THEATER AND CINEMATHEQUE THEATER, MOVIE THEATER

Hospital St. ☎02 296 5292; www.alkasaba.org

The group associated with the theater has been around since 1970 but only managed to purchase its own space 12 years ago, making it the first troupe to do so in Palestine. The theater showcases everything from international theater during its annual April festival to traditional Arabic theater to music and dance. The company also runs a drama school on the premises. While the theater schedule is uncertain due to inconsistent funding, the connected cinema shows two different movies every night beginning at 6pm. Movies come from Egypt, Palestine, Europe, and America— all foreign films have Arabic subtitles.

 # Walk down Palestine St. from al-Manara Sq. and take the 1st right. Al-Kasaba is about 200m down. ℹ Tickets are usually available 10min. before a showtime. [$] Cinema tickets NIS30. Call about performances.

KHALIL SAKAKINI CULTURAL CENTER ART GALLERY

Luthren St. ☎02 298 7374; www.sakakini.org

Though its apparent function is as an exhibition space and visual arts center, Khalil Sakakini has the much broader goal of promoting Palestinian culture by supporting emerging artists and attracting new audiences. The contemporary art on display usually explores political and cultural issues, with both a Palestinian and international focus.

 # Take the 1st left off Jaffa St. after al-Rashid St., then take the 2nd right. The center is next to Orjuwan Lounge. [$] Free.

POPULAR ART CENTRE

THEATER

al-Bireh ☎02 240 3891; www.popularartcentre.org

Popular Art Centre organizes and runs the International Music and Dance Festival every summer and hosts film screenings and other cultural programs related to Palestinian heritage.

⚐ Across the street from the al-Bireh Municipality opposite the al-Ain Mosque.

---

by any other name?

Before it was officially dubbed Israel in 1948, the territory was known variously as **Palestine**, **Southern Syria**, **Kingdom of Jerusalem**, **Coele-Syria**, **Canaan**, and **Syria Palaestina**. Keep those in mind when "categories" for King's Cup come up.

ESSENTIALS

practicalities

- **TOURIST OFFICES:** The **Ramallah Tourism Agency**, as of research, is set to open in September 2011. In case it isn't, go to the 2nd floor of the Ramallah Municipality across the street. The people at the front desk will help answer any tourism questions. (Issa Ziadeh St. ⚐ Just before the intersection of Friends St. and Issa Ziadeh. Al-Rashid turns into Issa Ziadeh as you walk uphill and farther away from the Royal Court Hotel.) Alternatively, check for tourism numbers in the back pages of *This Week in Palestine*.

- **ATM:** In abundance around al-Manara Sq. The best ones are in the Palestinian National Bank just to the right of Main St. when facing Stars & Bucks.

- **LAUNDROMATS: Blue Sky Dry Cleaning** does washing, drying, and dry cleaning. (Al-Nahdah St. ☎02 240 5439 ⚐ Walk down al-Nahdah St. until the large right turn that leads to the Palestinian Folklore Center. Looking right, you will see a sign for Blue Sky about 30m away. In case you don't, just take the right and then take a left at the fork. Ⓢ Wash NIS50. Dry NIS50. ☒ Open Su-Tu 8am-9pm, Th-Sa 8am-9pm.)

- **PUBLIC TOILETS:** Ahliyyah College St. ⚐ Go 200m down Main St. from al-Manara Sq. to Ahliyyah College St. and then take a right. Take the 1st right from there and toilets will be on the right.)

- **INTERNET:** Wi-Fi is prevalent, but **Pal Soft** is one of the few places with its own computers. The price is probably the best deal in town. (Main St. ☎02 298 4021 ⚐ 50m up Main St. on the right, opposite the large buildings with the small triangle shapes on the roof. On the 5th floor. Ⓢ NIS2 per 30min. NIS7 per 2hr. NIS10 per 3hr. ☒ Open Su-Th 8am-10pm, Sa 8am-10pm.)

- **POST OFFICES: Ramallah Post.** (Park St. www.palpost.ps ⚐ Take the left heading downhill after Rukab's and walk about 50m, past the 1st right turn. The post office is on the right. ☒ Open Su-Th 8am-2pm.)

emergency

- **EMERGENCY NUMBERS: Police:** ☎100. **Ambulance:** ☎02 240 0666. **Fire:** ☎102.

- **POLICE: Ramallah Central Police Station.** (Off Main St. ☎02 295 6571 ⚐ Directly when you begin walking on Main St. from al-Manara Sq. take a right. Walk 50m down the street to reach the Police Station, which is flanked by police cars outside. ☒ Open 24hr.

- **LATE-NIGHT PHARMACY: Al-Sayed Pharmacy.** (☎02 295 6708 ⚐ On the street that runs between al-Manara Sq. and Mughtarbin Sq. ☒ Open Su-Th 8am-2am, F 10pm-2am, Sa 8am-2am.)

west bank

- **HOSPITAL: Ramallah Hospital.** (Al Ahli Hospital St. }02 298 2222 ⚕ Coming from al-Manara Sq., take the 1st right on Jerusalem St. and walk down about 300m. The street has other hospitals on it as well. ☉ Open 24hr.)

getting there

BY BUS

The best way to get to Ramallah from outside the Palestinian Territories or from the other side of the wall is by bus. Head to the bus station right outside the Jerusalem Hotel and take **bus #18.** (Ⓢ NIS6.50. ☉ 40min.) Don't be alarmed by the informality of the process—buses run regularly, and the numbers of each vehicle are clearly visible.

BY SERVICE TAXI

Within the Palestinian Territories, the preferred mode of travel is service taxi. Prices vary, but make sure to ask beforehand and never pay more than NIS35—some drivers may try and jack up the price at the end of a ride. From **Bethlehem,** service taxis should cost around NIS18, from **Nablus,** NIS15, and from **Jericho,** NIS17. The Ramallah service taxi station is located on **al-Nahdah Street** up the ramp 50m down the street on the left when coming from al-Manara Sq. To travel from Ramallah, simply go inside the station and ask any of the cab drivers where you can find the cars for your destination.

getting around

BY TAXI

If you're not going to walk around Ramallah—and most restaurants, sights, and bars in town are within walking distance—cabs are the best (okay, only) way to get around. Service taxis are used mostly for going to nearby towns, though if you find yourself in the **al-Bireh** outskirts, you might catch one to **al-Manara Square.** Taxis should never cost more than NIS10 when traveling within Ramallah and should cost around NIS30 for a trip to **Birzeit University.** Some cabbies stick to their first offers and refuse to bargain, but cabs are plentiful, and you should feel free to move off in search of a better offer. If you want to go it alone, you can rent a car from either **Petra Car Rental** (☎02 295 2602) or **Good Luck Car Rental** (☎02 234 2160).

jericho ☎02

Jericho is one of those places where you excitedly arrive to see what the fuss is about and leave thinking, "Well, everything has really gone downhill since the second millennium BCE." The local economy relies on such a mindset, which attracts more tourists than professionals and subsequently pours funds into the ancient sights rather than commercial or cultural growth. Today's Jericho is highly decentralized, with little urban life connecting the scattered sights that attract all those European and Russian Christians along with some curious backpackers.

However, vibrant local life does exist here—you just have to know where to look. The best place to find modern Jericho is in the Spanish Garden on a Thursday, when it can become packed with *argilah*-toting teenagers and picnicking families. It can also be interesting to walk around Aqbat Jaber, a neighborhood and refugee camp that was flooded with fleeing Palestinians in the wake of the 1948 War. While it can get eerily dark and potentially dangerous at night, during the day Aqbat Jaber is a place where service taxi drivers feel compelled to say hi to everyone on the street and inquisitive restaurant owners ask detailed questions about life abroad. This is a sight in itself, a glimpse into Palestinian life today just as Hisham's Palace and Tell es-Sultan provide a window into the distant past.

jericho

ORIENTATION

The **city center** is the hub of taxis, restaurants, and services in Jericho. Unfortunately, the same does not go for hotels or sights, which are dispersed throughout the city. This means you'll have to rely on taxis to get around the city. **Amman Street,** home to the Spanish Garden, and **Ein es-Sultan Street,** site of Tell es-Sultan and Elisha's Spring, are the two most important streets to know. Both extend out from the city center, as does **Jerusalem Road,** which leads to Aqbat Jaber and Sami Youth Hostel. This information, however, will only get you so far: unless you have a superhuman endurance for blistering heat, you'll probably spend most of your time in the air-conditioned comfort of cabs and restaurants.

ACCOMMODATIONS

Hotels in Jericho, like in many urban West Bank locales, tend to be expensive for budget travelers, though the Jericho Resort Village is worth every penny.

▨ SAMI YOUTH HOSTEL

HOSTEL $$

Aqbat Jaber · 02 232 4220

Sami is the best budget option in Jericho, and a great deal by West Bank standards. All rooms are triples that go for NIS120, regardless of the number of people staying in them. Curtains abound, both protecting the lobby from the outside glare and cloaking the small—and strangely seductive—staircase that leads to the rooms. The manager Iyad is almost always in his office but comes out to reception as soon as he senses that a guest needs help. This means that free coffee and tea are frequently offered, and his diligence is particularly useful when dealing with taxi drivers, as Iyad happily plays the role of mediator.

From the city center, go down Jerusalem Rd. about 3km. A sign in the middle of the road will tell you where to take a right for Sami, which is 300m down the street. ℹ Free Wi-Fi in lobby. ⏰ Reception 24hr.

JERICHO RESORT VILLAGE RESORT $$$

Qasr Hisham St. ☎02 232 1255; www.jerichoresorts.com

Tennis courts, multiple pools, sand volleyball, a children's playground, and a stately terrace grace this pleasure-universe-unto-itself. The large rooms all have their own terrace as well, along with king-size beds in simple but fully equipped singles. A foil to Jericho—which is brutally hot, characterized by serious historical and religious sites, and frustratingly sprawling—the Resort Village is a condensed oasis of pure amusement. Even the most devoted pilgrims might pick up a tennis racket, take a dip afterward, have a bite on the terrace, and suddenly realize that the afternoon has ended without their seeing a single sight.

Across the road and up the hill from Hisham's Palace. ℹ Free Wi-Fi. Breakfast included. [$] Singles with mountain view US$100, with pool view US$120; doubles US$120/140. Bungalows from US$200. ⏰ Reception 24hr.

JERUSALEM HOTEL HOTEL $$

Amman St. ☎02 232 2444; www.jerusalemhotel-jericho.com

The large terraces, huge beds, and ample natural light might not be enough to justify the high price of this out-of-the-way rest stop. Larger rooms and the addition of breakfast make this hotel especially expensive, and its competition—Jericho Resort Village and some nearby chain hotels—are better prepared for and more explicitly geared toward this price range. Unfortunately, there is no internet anywhere in the hotel.

Also called al-Quds Hotel. On Amman St., about 1.5km outside the town center. [$] Singles US$70, with breakfast US$80; doubles US$90/110; triples US$120/150; suites US$170/220. US$25 per extra person. ⏰ Reception 24hr.

SIGHTS

Jericho is the oldest of the old. In a land where anything from the last 2000 years is "only" that old, Jericho that can sell itself as the oldest city in the region, thanks to Tell es-Sultan. The ruins of ancient Jericho, the Tell dates from before the 14th century BCE. Though not as impressively geriatric, Hisham's Palace is one of the most expansive ruins you could hope to visit.

TELL ES-SULTAN RUINS

Ein es-Sultan St. ☎02 232 2935

At 250m below sea level (and with the scorching damp heat to prove it), Tell es-Sultan is officially the lowest and potentially oldest city on Earth. The pottery, fortifications, and houses that jut out of and are represented by the different strata of rock are concrete manifestations of human evolution: the transition from hunting and gathering to agriculture, then surplus and therefore free time, then the rise of culture. The town was actually deserted in the 14th century, a mind-blowingly long time ago for anything to have become obsolete, though there are also remains from Iron Age inhabitants and Persians. The potentially coolest part of the site is the vertical archaeology of the rock strata, as different eras of human history are visibly stacked on top of each other in the rock.

From the city center, follow Ein es-Sultan until its end. Signs point you to the ruins, which are around the corner from the Elisha's Spring complex. ℹ Guides are usually loitering outside the front gate waiting to be hired. English brochures available. [$] NIS10, students NIS7, ages 5-18 NIS5. Informational movie free with ticket. Cash only. ⏰ Open daily in summer 8am-6pm; in winter 8am-4pm.

HISHAM'S PALACE RUINS

Off Qasr Hisham St. ☎02 232 2522

What used to be luxury on a massive scale—think two stories of thermal baths, a fountain, two mosques, and multiple servants quarters—is now an expansive and enigmatic collection of debris. Indeed, so many remains lie on today's archaeological site that little bits of columns have been haphazardly stacked along the walls. Yet for all the antiquated clutter, it's the enormity of the emptiness that really gives a sense of the grand scale of the former complex. Ancient foundations mark out the bygone dimensions of the vast eighth-century rooms of Walid II. The site gives you free reign to walk around and imagine the grandeur that once was.

*# To reach the palace from the square, head about 3.5km north on Qasr Hisham St., following the signs that lead you to a turn at a guard post. **i** English brochures available. [$] NIS10, students NIS7, ages 5-18 NIS5. Informational movie free with ticket. Cash only. ⏰ Open daily in summer 8am-6pm; in winter 8am-5pm.*

NABI MUSA MOSQUE

Middle of the freaking desert ☎052 311 0560

Amid cascading, unending mounds of brown sand, the camouflaged Nabi Musa emerges out of a nondescript rock face, its brown stones made distinct from the landscape only by a set of large white domes. The clear blue sky that usually looks down on Jericho is most beautiful here. Nabi Musa (Prophet Moses in Arabic) was originally built in 1269 CE by the Sultan Baibars at the spot that Salah ad-Din dreamed Moses had been buried. The tomb there today, which you can only see through bars, is said to have special powers and is covered in Oriental rugs and a modest green velvet cloth. The Ottomans popularized the Nabi Musa Festival, which used to run during the week preceding Easter. Its nationalist aspects, however, have made it a point of contention between Israelis and Palestinians, and weary authorities since the time of the British mandate have prevented celebration of the festival. Bedouins revere this site in particular for its shale, which is flammable thanks to a high content of *qatraan* (tar). Ask the souvenir venders to unlock the gate across from the tomb in order to see them—barbecue enthusiasts will be delighted to discover that it looks remarkably similar to coal.

*# The only way to get here is by car. Go toward Jerusalem for around 5km until you see a sign for Nabi Musa and then turn left. Following the road uphill for another 5km or so. **i** Legs must be covered. [$] Free. ⏰ Open daily 8am-9pm.*

MOUNT OF TEMPTATION MONASTERY MONASTERY, CHURCH

☎02 232 2827

A Greek Orthodox monastery cut into the rock face serves as a memorial to Jesus's temptation by Satan. The peak of the mountain is said to be the exact spot where Jesus rebuffed Satan's offer to fall and worship him in exchange for a kingdom, and a small grotto near the church is supposedly where Jesus had fasted for the preceding 40 days and nights. And then this place in Georgia is where the devil supposedly went down...wait, different story, sorry. The earliest evidence of worship here comes from sometime between the fourth and sixth centuries CE, when a tiny cave was molded into a makeshift chapel. The view from a small terrace outside today's church looks over a vast expanse of the West Bank and attracts highly appreciated cooling winds.

*# To make the hike, which takes under 1hr. if you're fast, start climbing at the base of the mountain near Tell es-Sultan. Alternatively, take the téléphérique from the Elisha's Spring parking lot. After getting off, walk down the staircase and continue down the path and climb the staircase. **i** Legs should be covered. [$] Free, but donations welcome. ⏰ Open Su 9am-2pm, M-F 9am-4pm, Sa 9am-2pm.*

SPANISH GARDEN PARK

Amman St. ☎02 232 4977

A manmade stone pond, blasting Arabic pop music, topiary, cotton candy, and *argilah* come together in this small park, which is a nice place to sit, read, or have a picnic. A bodega/cafe sells some food and drink, and dirt walkways make for a nice short stroll. The Spanish Garden is the best place to go to engage with—or, if you're shy, observe—Jericho public life, as local families and teenagers gather in this essentially untouristic spot.

Walk down Amman St. from the city center following the wall on your left for about 500m until it ends, at which point turn left to follow it. After 50m, you will reach the entrance. $ NIS3. ⏰ Open daily 10am-11pm or midnight.

ELISHA'S SPRING — SPRING

Ein es-Sultan St.

According to the Bible, the prophet Elisha healed this once-tainted water by throwing salt into it. It is now considered holy by many residents who use it to this day. A hose runs up from the stream so you too may ingest some of this holiness yourself. This is also a nice spot to sit on the grass and admire the beautiful stone passageways that channel the water.

From the city center, follow Ein es-Sultan until its end. Signs point you to the spring, which is around the corner from Tell es-Sultan. $ Free.

FOOD

It isn't easy to find great restaurants in Jericho. **Abu Omar** is the best option, serving up delicious grilled meats in a comfortable back room at a reasonable rate. Most restaurants are located in the city center.

ABU OMAR — MIDDLE EASTERN $$

Ein es-Sultan St. ☎02 232 3429

The fact that the food is a bigger draw than the 10 fans is extremely impressive, considering how much you'll love those fans in the stifling 50°C temperatures. The meat is fresh and tender, and the amount of food you get for NIS50 is a good deal in a town where the economy seems to operate on the premise of taking advantage of tourists. The back area has large comfortable couches, and the staff are enthusiastic to answer questions about the area.

From city center, walk 10m down Ein es-Sultan. Abu Omar is on the left. $ Falafel sandwich to-go NIS3, eat-in NIS5. Grilled meat, salad, fries, hummus, and a drink NIS50. Cash only. ⏰ Open daily 6am-2:30am.

ESSAWI — MIDDLE EASTERN $$

City Center ☎02 232 2160

Caged *hassouns* and canaries line the walls of this clean coffee shop, and their back-and-forth chirping is adorable unless, perhaps, you're a PETA activist. The fresh lemonade (NIS10) is tangy and sweet, and the lamb and beef come fresh (also not okay if you're a PETA activist). The heat-sensitive should note that there are only six fans here to Abu Omar's 10, though the fan coverage to square footage ratio may well be superior at Essawi. *Let's Go* is investigating.

Opposite the police station in the city center, Essawi is on the right. It's within 10m of Petra Taxi. $ Mixed grill with salad NIS60. Shawarma NIS15. Cash only, but they accept a wide variety of currencies.

GARDEN VIEW RESTAURANT — MIDDLE EASTERN $$

Ein es-Sultan St. ☎02 232 2349

The half *musakhan* (roast chicken on bread; NIS35, whole NIS50) is thicker on the grease than the cinnamon, and there aren't many cheap lunch options, but the Garden View Restaurant is worth stopping by for its outdoor air conditioning. Choose the right seat, and you'll find yourself in the only part of Jericho that is pleasant in July. It's large, making it a good choice for big groups.

About 1km down Ein es-Sultan on the left. $ Arabic salad NIS8. Kebab NIS45. ⏰ Open daily 10am-11:30pm.

ESSENTIALS

practicalities

- **TOURIST OFFICES:** Although there is no official office, the **tourism police** are happy to help you with lost items, directions, and other questions relating to your stay. (Ein es-Sultan St. ☎02 232 4011 ⚔ Across from the téléphérique entrance and Elisha's Spring. ◷ Open 24hr.)

- **ATM:** Available at the **Cairo Amman Bank** in the city center and at the nearby post office.

- **INTERNET: Waqqad Internet.** (Ein es-Sultan St. ☎02 232 0231.)

- **POST OFFICES: Jericho Post.** (Amman St. ☎02 232 2574; www.palpost.ps ⚔ Walking down Amman St. from the city center, you'll see Jericho Post 75m down on the left. ◷ Open Su-Th 8am-2pm, Sa 8am-2pm.)

emergency

- **POLICE: Central Police Station.** (☎02 232 2644 ⚔ Between Ein es-Sultan St. and Qasr Hisham St. in the central square.)

- **LATE-NIGHT PHARMACY: Jericho Pharmacy.** (Amman St. ☎02 232 2456 ⚔ About 100m down Amman St. on the right. ◷ Open Su-Th 8am-10pm, Sa 8am-10pm.)

- **HOSPITALS: New Jericho Hospital.** (☎02 232 1968 ⚔ Head down the main highway as if you were going to Sami Youth Hostel. However, instead of taking the right to the hostel, take a left. The hospital is about 180m down on the left. ◷ Open 24hr.)

getting there

To get to Jericho from Jerusalem, take **bus #33** or **36** from the bus station outside the Jerusalem Hotel (NIS6.50) and ask to be dropped off in Jericho. The best (read: only) way to get to Jericho from elsewhere in the West Bank is by **service taxi,** which costs NIS15-35 from all locations (set a price before you leave and make sure everyone around you is paying the same amount). The sweetly simple method of payment is handing coins to the people in front of you, and service taxis don't leave until they're full anyway. Service taxis will usually stop at the city center if you ask them to, but if they will only stop at the casino, simply wait on your side of the road for another service taxi. It will most likely be a local Jericho cab heading to the city center, and the fare should only be about NIS2.50.

getting around

BY TAXI

Jericho is expansive, sparse, and extremely hot. The combination means that getting anywhere by anything other than private taxi or rented car is generally infeasible (service taxis go mostly between residential areas), though the cold-blooded and budget-conscious are free to try walking. For the mortals among us, the best place to get a taxi is outside **Peta Taxi** (☎02 232 2525 ◷ Open daily 5am-2am.), in the city center, where a number of cabbies are always waiting around and competition drives the price down. Don't feel pressured to take the first offer.

If you are staying at a hotel on the outskirts of town, it's a good idea to take a cheap cab into the center and then find the driver who will take you around for the day. A good rate for seeing a few sites is NIS60; a good rate for a whole day traveling around Jericho is NIS100. Never pay more than NIS100, but also know that keeping one driver with you all afternoon is not simply a luxury—if you want to see everything Jericho has to offer, it's a necessity. Confident and resilient bargainers may have better luck finding new cabs throughout the day, as this prevents the exorbitant rates that come from a driver waiting around.

west bank

BY BIKE

In the winter, renting a bike can also be an easy and effective way to get around (it's often too hot in the summer). Bikes are easy to find in the city center.

nablus ☎09

Nablus is known throughout history for fighting off invaders. Heavily affected by shifting balances of power from the Byzantines to the Brits, Nablus was committed to each major *intifada* but today is more famous for its bustling commercial life: it's home to the Palestinian Stock Exchange and a seemingly endless *souq* that might seem never-ending to untrained eyes. However, it is also a place of devastating unemployment in refugee camps, a problem which some have ascribed to the checkpoints just outside the city. The major checkpoint Huwwara was recently disabled, meaning that travel between Nablus and Ramallah is now unrestricted.

Nablus is not a place accustomed to tourism; Jacob's Well and Joseph's Tomb are the only two religiously significant sights here, and Tell Balata is one of the few places of historical interest. As such, locals are fascinated by people who are visibly foreign, and kids will often stare at or shout greetings to the tourists they see. Older residents will sometimes take you on short tours or invite you for a cup of tea; these experiences can be rewarding, though, as with the rest of the West Bank, they almost always have a political dimension. Be careful what you say, but also be sure to listen.

ORIENTATION

Free from a clear grid system, maps, or a tourist office, Nablus can be very difficult for visitors to navigate. Not many locals speak English, so when you find one make sure to ask a lot of questions—this can go a long way. The center of town is **Martyr Square,** which borders the edge of the *souq* and is near the locally famous Al Yasmeen Hotel. **Faisal Street,** home to the Crystal Hotel, is one of the main streets in the city.

ACCOMMODATIONS

Since the Nablus tourist population is notably lacking, the city doesn't have many hotels. Crystal Hostel is a great deal for those on a tight budget, while those with a (very, very) small hole burning in their pocket may want to try the slightly more expensive Al Yasmeen, which has great services and a classy cafe sensibility.

👍 AL YASMEEN HOTEL — HOTEL $$

Tetouan St. ☎09 233 3555; www.alyasmeen.com

Reasonable for what it offers, Al Yasmeen is small, comfortable, and mildly luxurious. Cafe seating and outlets are spread throughout the lobby, which has free Wi-Fi. The space also operates as a restaurant, which attracts *argilah* addicts at all hours. Pleasant rooms have just enough space for a large bureau, small TV, desk, and comfortable bed. The guys behind the desk speak very good English and are enthusiastic about helping guests find their way around Nablus.

➜ Coming from Martyr Sq., walk toward Hattin St. and take the 1st left after Omar el-Mokhtar St. If you can't find the tiny street signs, just ask the locals. ℹ Free Wi-Fi. Breakfast included. A/C. $ Singles US$55; doubles US$75. ⏰ Reception 24hr. Ring the bell after 1am.

CRYSTAL HOTEL — HOTEL $$

Faisal St. ☎09 233 2485; crestal_motel@windowslive.com

A modest price by Nablus standards gets you a very large room, a queen-size bed, Wi-Fi, and a large desk. Some rooms have tile floors; if you care about living space aesthetics, you can ask for a carpeted room. Unfortunately most employees do not speak very good English, so coordinating this preference could get complicated. (Just in case, *b'nishbahle qarmeeda b'shayn* is something along the lines of, "In my opinion, the tile is unsightly.")

➜ Coming from Martyr Sq., walk 50m on Faisal St., which begins in the square. ℹ Free Wi-Fi in rooms. Breakfast NIS15. A/C. Cash only. $ Singles NIS120; doubles NIS180. ⏰ Reception 24hr.

SIGHTS

Nablus doesn't have much left from its ancient past, but the undermanaged and unrestored Tell Balata is an unbelievable treasure and makes for one of the best sights in the West Bank.

👍 TELL BALATA — RUINS

Balata

Forget about the interesting but historically uncertain Biblical resonance that some endow this sight with. If it actually is Canaanite Shechem—and, therefore, the first capital of ancient Israel—that would be kind of important, but these are some of the most fun ruins to visit in the Palestinian Territories either way. The complete lack of signposts and placards may be frustrating to some, but this allows for imaginative exploration of the semi-intact foundations and broken-down towers. No prohibitive ropes or watchful guards stand in the way of interaction with the otherwise lonely rubble. Jump on it, caress it, imagine yourself in Rome—really, whatever you're into. There's a piece of a large wall that used to protect the city, which is said to date back to 5000 years ago.

➜ Coming from Joseph's Tomb, walk opposite the monument uphill until you see a large fence on your left. Walk alongside it until you reach the entrance.

TOMB OF JOSEPH — TOMB

Zut Rd.

This dilapidated memorial may or may not hold the remains of the prophet Joseph—you know, the one with the technicolor dreamcoat. As with many ancient sights, we're not positive that he's actually buried here, though a compelling case for it has been constructed from pilgrim diaries and Biblical descriptions. Unfortunately, all the he said/she said/He said about ancient religious artifacts can really get out of hand, and the alleged tomb is now one of the many points of contention between Israelis and Palestinians. Earlier this year, a group of settlers tried to sneak onto the site, prompting shots from Palestinian policemen and the death of one of the offenders. Now it is armed guards, not amateur archaeologists, who are on hand outside to escort the few tourists who stop by. The weirdest part? The marble tomb that everyone's fighting about is just a reconstruction that's less than a year old.

➜ From Jacob's Well, walk uphill 100m. Take the right after the smoothie and ice cream shop, then walk about 300m down the street, staying left. The tomb is on the right near the dead end. ℹ ID sometimes required. $ Free.

JACOB'S WELL — CHURCH, WELL

Zut Rd.

This huge, bright church has lamps and chandeliers hanging from the ceiling in illogical abundance, and its walls are lined with icons and illustrations. In the basement, however, lies an ancient well, one so old that it is said to date from the time when Jacob bought this land to make camp. The religious significance continues into the New Testament; the Book of John mentions Jesus talking to a Samaritan woman on what was supposedly this site. In case you get too lost in pondering the bygone history of this structure, there is a gift shop full of shiny objects only 4 ft. away.

➜ Walk down Main St. from the city center for about 3km until there is a fork; take a left, and the church is 50m down on the left. $ Free, but donations accepted. ⏰ Open daily 8am-noon and 2-4pm.

common grounds

Whether you're Jewish, Muslim, Christian, Baha'i, Taoist, Maoist, or nudist, it's hard not to be touched by the spiritualism of Israel—even if it's that divine presence that has made the country one of the world's main conflict zones. But holy hand grenades aside, there are a few organizations that actually attempt to foster inter-religious and interethnic dialogue.

The **Abraham's Path Initiative** (www.abrahampath.org) is dedicated to recreating the path that Abraham, the common ancestor of the monotheistic traditions, took on his travels through the Middle East. The hope is that walking the path will foster interfaith dialogue and turn fighters into friends (or at least willing negotiators). Walk in Abe's footsteps yourself in both Israel proper and the West Bank, or get involved with a cross-cultural student exchange or service learning program.

But maybe that's not enough. For the more stubborn cases of intractable conflict, the **Israel Tennis Center** (www.israeltenniscenter.com) claims to have the perfect cure—a brisk game of doubles. By bringing together doubles partners from among the Jewish and Arab populations of Israel and the Palestinian territories, the ITC hopes to nip feelings of hostility in the bud. The program has also been surprisingly effective at bringing together the youngsters' parents; apparently nothing unites adults from warring ethnic groups quite like good old-fashioned overbearing parenting.

FOOD

Food is plentiful but not necessarily good in Nablus—street fare is sometimes great but generally unreliable, and more conventional restaurants can be hard to find. **Assaraya** is the best among these, a grill joint with pleasant outside seating near the center of town. Good luck navigating the cheap eats of the *souq* if that's what your gut desires. Be sure to ask for suggestions before you dive in.

ASSARAYA — MIDDLE EASTERN $$

Hattin St. ☎09 233 5444; www.saleemafandi.ps

That Assaraya sounds a bit like the title of a reggaeton bump-and-grind track is probably an accident. A quiet and relaxed spot, the restaurant offers tender grilled meats and an outdoor sitting area away from the bustle of the nearby *souq*. Well-priced options, usually of the carnivore variety, come with large salads and smooth hummus, along with a particularly good spicy tomato Turkish salad. Assaraya is stomping ground for foreign journalists as well as for scarved local ladies.

🧭 From Al Yasmeen, walk 2 streets up toward Martyr Sq., then take a right and take your 2nd right down. Assaraya is one of the 1st storefronts on the left. $ Slice of pizza NIS15, whole pie NIS40. Arabic breakfast NIS30 in the morning. ⏰ Open daily 8am-10pm.

ZEIT OU ZATAAR — MIDDLE EASTERN $$

Tetouan St. ☎09 233 3555; www.alyasmeen.com

A sort of all-day snack and *argilah* cafe, Zeit ou Zataar hosts indolent locals and chitchatting foreigners alike. When the free Wi-Fi and transformative air-conditioning are taken into account, meal prices are reasonable, though sitting for just a drink (lemonade with mint NIS10) can be almost the same as a cheap lunch (shawarma NIS12). Try to sit in the first room on your right when you enter, since it has the best view of the *souq* and the coolest air.

🧭 In the lobby of the Al Yasmeen Hotel. $ Arabic salad NIS6. Pastry basket NIS25. ⏰ Open daily 7:30am-11:30pm.

ESSENTIALS

practicalities

- **ATM:** Abundant in the *souq*, especially on the blocks around Al Yasmeen, and along Faisal St.
- **LAUNDROMATS:** Most laundromats are in **East Nablus.**
- **INTERNET:** Internet cafes line the *souq*, but few of them have computers for public use. Tourists can usually use the computer in the lobby of **Al Yasmeen Hotel** for a reasonable amount of time.
- **POST OFFICES: Nablus Post Office.** (Faisal St. ☎09 238 7202 ⚐ 200m to the right on Faisal St. if you head straight up from Al Yasmeen.)

emergency

- **POLICE: Nablus Police Station.** (Faisal St. ☎09 238 3040 ⚐ 2 storefronts to the right of the post office.)
- **LATE-NIGHT PHARMACY: Al-Shaab Pharmacy.** (el-Ghazali St. ☎09 237 6847 ⚐ Face the front of Crystal Hotel, turn left, walk down the staircase, and then head straight. ☼ Open daily 8am-9pm.)
- **HOSPITALS:** Faisal St. ☎09 238 3599 ⚐ Toward Al Yasmeen on Faisal St., about 200m down from the post office and police station. ☼ Open 24hr.)

getting there

BY SERVICE TAXI

You can't go straight to Nablus from Jerusalem, which means the only good way of getting here is by service taxi. These should cost NIS15-35 from all locations in the West Bank; ask your driver the price before you depart, and ask the people sitting next to you whether the price seems right. Service taxis can usually stop near **Martyr Square** if you ask them to, which is the best way to get to the hotels and restaurants around town. From there, you can also walk down **Faisal Street** to the *souq*.

getting around

BY TAXI

Nablus, like many of its West Bank counterparts, is too expansive to be walked in its entirety. However, its lack of popular religious sights and consequent lack of major tourism means its cabbies are less bloodthirsty than those you will encounter elsewhere. Don't pay more than NIS10 for any one-way trip around town, and start by asking prices closer to NIS2. If you're heading up to the **Samaritan village,** be prepared to pay a bit more. Cabs are abundant on the street, and a large percentage of drivers speak just enough English to make the sale, though having your desired location written down in Arabic always helps. The three sights listed in this book can all be reached with one cab ride.

hebron ☎02

The most populated and industrial city in the West Bank, Hebron is also the most tensely fought over; it has been divided into two parts since 1997. **H1,** 80% of the city, is under the control of the Palestinian Authority and includes the New City and most commercial centers; **H2**—made up of the settlements, the Tomb of the Patriarchs, and much of the Old City—is under Israeli control. This area is inhabited mostly by Palestinians, though many have fled to make room for the fewer than a thousand Jewish settlers. Metal caged roofs surround some marketplaces to protect Palestinians from settler attack, but they are often covered with trash thrown down by aggressive settlers. Settler violence is common here, and was most dramatic in the mid-90s when Baruch Goldstein walked into the Tomb of Patriarchs and killed more than two dozen Palestinians and wounded more than 100. The vast military presence protects settlers, so there is no theoretical possibility for retaliation. The Hebron status quo, therefore, is tectonic-plates-grinding-against-each-other tense. Visible similarity to a Jewish settler or one of their supporters will earn you immediate suspicion among Palestinians; appearance as a Palestinian or foreign aid worker will earn you hate in the eyes of some settlers; and simply seeming to be a tourist will lead to relentless pursuit by beggars in the Old City.

For some, then, a visit to Hebron can be extremely troubling and dangerous. For others, however, it is the best view into the Palestinian-Israeli conflict, a sort of laboratory in which various kinds of acid are carefully dropped into a single test tube, resulting in constant minor explosions. Volunteers have endless quantities of work to do here, from fixing up broken-down homes and closed shops to helping document violence. Hebron is also home to one of the most important sights in the Judeo-Christian tradition, the **Tomb of the Patriarchs,** and has a restricted but lively commercial life along Ansara St. Hebron isn't really a tourist destination, so those who want to break through the fourth wall of travel into the irreconcilable conflicts and daily lives of some West Bank residents will find the starkest realities here.

girls with guns

Every Israeli citizen over the age of 18 must complete a term of national military service, and women are no exception—they've been a part of the Israel Defense Forces (IDF) since its inception in 1948. Whereas lovely ladies were originally assigned to be nurses, signal operators, drivers, and cooks, nowadays you can find women operating aerial defense systems, flying fighter planes, guarding the border, and undergoing combat training alongside their male counterparts. Basically, think twice before challenging an Israeli woman to an arm-wrestling contest.

ORIENTATION

Not a popular destination for Westerners of any kind—let alone big-spending tourists—Hebron has little in the way of clear maps and English street signs. Soldiers asking about and regulating movement every 300m in certain parts of the city make inquisitive wandering pretty difficult. In general terms, it is important to know that the **New City** is in the north and the **Old City** is in the south. Between them is the city center, **Bab izAwie,** whose main streets are **King Faisal Street** and **Ansara Street,** which has most of the restaurants in Hebron. King Faisal St. turns into **Ein Sarah** in the south and then **King David Street** in the Old City, and brings you to the Ibrahimi Mosque, home of the Tomb of the Patriarchs.

ACCOMMODATIONS

Tourists don't come to Hebron very often, so hotels don't host them very often. Your best option is therefore the homestay program run by Hiram Sharabati, which will get you a home-cooked meal and a great look into average Palestinian life.

HANTHALA GUESTHOUSE   HOMESTAY $$
☎059 927 1190; www.hanthalahostel.com

Usually a guesthouse as well as a homestay service, Hanthala is now in flux, currently operating only as a middle man connecting tourists with Palestinian families. The literal man in the middle is Hiram Sharabati, a Palestinian human rights activist who is extremely enthusiastic about sharing his family and work with outsiders and is usually free to take visitors on tours of Hebron on Fridays and Sundays. Lucky travelers get to stay with Hiram himself, but all the families are kind and offer home-cooked meals.

i Unmarried couples should specify their status beforehand but should be able to get a room with a welcoming family. Dinner and breakfast included. Not all families have internet access or A/C. Best to call a week in advance. No explicit maximum length of stay, but it could be hard to accommodate travelers staying for significantly longer than a week. ⑨ Stays NIS120 per night.

HEBRON HOTEL   HOTEL $$
Off King Faisal St.   ☎02 225 4240; hebron_hotel@hotmail.com

The hotel specializes in things a budget traveler can truly appreciate: not only are the rooms large and the Wi-Fi free, but each room also has a small round table and chair and a tiny shower tub, and there is one large bed, instead of multiple twins, in each single. When you're aiming to spend around NIS100 per night, every extra inch is a miracle. Hebron may not have any great hotels, but this cheap sleep beats the best budget deal in other West Bank cities.

⚑ Uphill from King Faisal St., ask locals for Pension (pronounced Pon-see-own) Hebron. *i* Breakfast included. Free Wi-Fi in rooms. ⑨ Singles US$38; doubles US$49; triples US$60. ⌚ Reception 24hr.

SIGHTS

There are two main points of interest for travelers to Hebron: the religiously and historically significant **Tomb of the Patriarchs,** and the current political situation in the Old City. Both sights mix political strife, religious history, and pretty much every other theme of Jewish and Palestinian life.

◼ TOMB OF THE PATRIARCHS   MOSQUE, SYNAGOGUE
Old City

Located above the Cave of Machpela—in which Old Testament superstars Abraham, Sarah, Isaac, Rebecca, Jacob, and Leah are said to have been buried—the Tomb of the Patriarchs is the second holiest sight in Judaism. Also revered by Muslims and Christians, the site has been home to the usual rotation of synagogue, church, and mosque. The building that finally made it—a Salah ad-Din mosque—forbade Jews from going above the seventh step of the stairwell to worship, a setup that lasted for more than 800 years, until Israel gained control of the West Bank in 1967. The series of attacks that followed the reinstitution of prayer rights were mostly on Jews until, in what is perhaps the most well-known strike, radical settler Baruch Goldstein opened fire on Palestinian worshippers, killing 29 and wounding more than 100.

The building is now divided in two mutually exclusive sides, one a mosque that Jews cannot enter and one a synagogue closed to Muslims. While monuments to Isaac and Rebecca are only in the **Ibrahimi Mosque,** each place of worship is focused primarily on the same object, the cenotaph of Abraham, which looks the same from each side, right down to the green bars that keeps viewers out of its actual room. The allegorical possibilities of this astounding effect—two different groups looking at the same object from segregated areas and investing that object with different meanings—are almost comically endless. Regardless of whether or not you see this place as a symbol of the conflict, it is a foundational site for Western religion and an unparalleled opportunity to compare the differences both deep and superficial that exist between Judaism and Islam.

⚑ Follow the signs in the Old City. The building is at the at end of the main street in the souq. *i* Legs must be covered for both sides. Women are given a full-body cloak to wear at the mosque. Have your passport ready and be prepared to talk to a lot of Israeli soldiers. ⑨ Free. ⌚ Mosque open daily in summer 8:30am-6:30pm; in winter 8:30am-4pm. Hours can vary. Synagogue hours vary, but generally open whenever services are not being held.

OLD CITY NEIGHBORHOOD

A great opportunity to see the political conflict, a walk around the Old City is troubling, exhausting, interesting, complicated, and not that much fun. Begin in the *souq* outside the Ibrahimi Mosque, where you might be doggedly followed by beggars, surrounded by closed shops, and be the only tourist around. It can be tempting to buy items from the people who follow you out of charity, pity, or the desire to be left alone, but be aware that buying one thing often leads to more heckling from others. Continue through the mosque courtyard, where you will likely encounter more beggars and unauthorized tour offers, usually from young boys. Once on the other side of the fence, walk to the left and up the hill to see the best examples of **ancient decrepit buildings.** Housing here is almost all more than a hundred years old—and can run as far back as the 13th century—and nature has clearly taken its toll on these abandoned and rickety stone structures. Though the combination of garbage and collapsed buildings can make this area look like a war zone, there have been no bombings here.

Now take it back now, y'all. Turn around and walk to **Settler's Restaurant,** adjacent to the staircase leading up to the synagogue, so you can see the photos: of its opening right after the 1967 War, of the visit by former Israeli Prime Minister Yigal Allon, and of the first Jewish wedding held in Hebron after the war. Then, continue back toward the fence that blocks off the area in front of the Ibrahimi Mosque and stay straight. Take a slight right turn at the nearest intersection, and you'll wind up in a Jewish settlement. To understand the historical background of settler claims to Hebron, follow signs to the uphill **Hebron Heritage Museum** (☎052 429 5550). To see a busy part of the Arab old city, bear left after you pass the Ibrahimi fence and you will find yourself on a commercial street. Vendors are friendly and may invite you in for tea. That said, be careful on this walk; it was not long ago that there was a military curfew imposed on Palestinian residents, and acts of violence between the two sides are infrequent but persistent. At the same time, soldiers are everywhere, and most residents are eager to talk to tourists about the situation.

*🚶 Walk down King Faisal St. away from Jerusalem through the length of the city; duration of walk depends on where you begin. **i** Leg covering is wise but not required.*

FOOD

Cheap food abounds in Hebron—especially on **Ansara Street**—but it can be hard to differentiate the top from the slop.

MALAHAMATA SHAB KEBAB $

Ansara St. ☎02 222 9669

The pictures on the meat freezer of peacefully grazing sheep and cows may seem a bit twisted—especially as fresh carcasses are being carried through the tiny front sitting area—but true carnivores (and sadists) will see the humor in it. Tomatoes, onions, beef, and lamb are all Malahamata's offers, and it's all it needs; the grease in these sandwiches (NIS6) melts in your mouth like it can only when coming from old, overused grills in close proximity to sidewalk concrete and air pollution.

🚶 From the municipality building (called Baladeiet al-Khaled, first word pronounced Bel-luh-dee-et), cross the street and walk 80m until you reach the awning with sheep and cows. [$] Tray of diced meat, tomatoes, and onions (enough for 2) NIS12.

ESSENTIALS

practicalities

- **TOURS: Hiram Sharabati,** a human rights worker and homestay organizer, can give political, historical, and religious tours around Hebron. (☎059 927 1190 🕐 Hiram is usually free F and Su, though tours can also be arranged for other days.)

- **ATM:** ATMs are easiest to find in the city center. There is one just off the square in Wadi Tufa St.

- **PUBLIC TOILETS:** Just past the checkpoint near the Ibrahimi Mosque.

emergency

- **POLICE: Hebron Police** (☎02 222 6382).

- **LATE-NIGHT PHARMACY:** The best-stocked pharmacy in the Old City is 200m past the checkpoint on the right, just below the synagogue portion of the Tomb of the Patriarchs.

- **HOSPITAL:** There is a hospital 200m past the pharmacy as you walk away from the Tomb of the Patriarchs. (☎02 223 1973 🕐 Open 24hr.)

getting there

You can only get to Hebron from within the West Bank, and the best way to do that is by service taxi. The price depends on starting point but should be below NIS30. Make sure you are paying the same amount as the people around you. Service taxis are easy to find anywhere on the West Bank highway or in city centers.

getting around

BY TAXI

Taxis should never cost more than NIS10. Service taxis do not usually go to tourist destinations, so it may be good to hire a single taxi to take you to multiple locations.

BY SERVICE TAXI

Centered on Bab izAwie off the new Wadi Tufa St. (there is also an old Wadi Tufa), service taxis head around Hebron and to other parts of the West Bank.🏕 Walk down King Faisal St. away from Jerusalem through the length of the city; duration of walk depends on where you begin. *i* Leg covering is wise but not required.

DEAD SEA

Cry me a river. And then float on it. That, my friends, is the Dead Sea.

You may feel like *such* a tourist when you inevitably get your picture taken while reading a magazine as you float on the pristine water. But hey—it's the closest you're going to get to the big guy who walked on water. After all, the Dead Sea is like no other place. You've heard it all before: it's the lowest point in the world; it's one of the saltiest bodies of water in the world; there's a nearby mountain made almost entirely of salt; everything from sulphur wells to huge crystal formations are scattered throughout the area. It's only when you pass a large sign saying sea level, then turn the corner to see whole mountain ranges whose peaks are level with you, that you realize the grandeur of the place. Beaches aside, the sun-cracked desert plateau, mist-tipped Jordanian mountains, and occasional luscious oasis make for some magnificent scenery.

What you may not expect, however, is how underdeveloped the region is. There are no cities and barely any towns here. What few places there are have become swamped by tourists, and, because it's all best accessed by car, backpackers are severely outnumbered by swarming groups. Hence the beaches are usually less about chilling out—the sun's too blazing, the water too warm and salty—and more about the novelty of floating. Basically, you may not struggle to swim, but you'll probably struggle to find a bank, pharmacy, or good food.

But what the hell—go float and take your cheesy picture. The quirks and excitement of the Dead Sea really come from the area's natural curiosities. Find solace in a remote lagoon and spy on the sullen ibexes as they totter across cliff faces.

greatest hits

- **FRANKIE SAYS.** Relax at Ein Gedi Spa (p. 288), then channel your inner pig and roll around in a mud bath. Hey, you look pretty.

- **CLIFF DIVING.** Take a trip to Qumran and see the caves where the Dead Sea Scrolls were found (p. 294). Let us know if you see any sheep.

- **WHO WEARS SHORT SHORTS.** Grab the SPF, throw on your swim trunks, and head to Kalya Beach (p. 295).

THE DEAD SEA AND ITS ENVIRONS

Kalya

QUMRAN RUINS

Hurkanya
(Kh. El Mird)

Ein Feshkha

To Kalya Beaches

N. Kidron

N. Gorfan

N. Darga

Rosh Tur

90

Metzudat Mazim

Einot Kaneh

N. Teko'a

N. Amos

Einot Samar

Metzokei Dragot

Mitzpeh Michvar

Mitzpeh Shalem Kibbutz

Mineral Beach

N. Hatzetzon

N. Kedem

Mitzpeh Kedem

Dead Sea

ISRAEL JORDAN

Nahal Arugot Reserve

N. David

Ein Gedi Reserve

Ein David

N. 'ever

HEVER CAVES

Ein Gedi Kibbutz

N. 'oled

En Gedi Spa

N. Mishmar

TREASURE CAVE

90

Ein Tzaftzafa

Ein Tze'elim

Metzada Plain

Mt. Namer

Ein Aneva

Masada

Metzada Junction

To Arad

CABLEWAY

N. Kana'im

Mt. Kana'im

N. Rahaf

N. Kidod

N. Ye'elim

0   3 kilometers

0   3 miles

Metzad 'atrurim

Ein Bokek

N. Bokek

Zohar Spa

Metzad Zohar

N. 'alamish

31

Neve Zohar

N. 'emar

N. Lot

90

Mt. Badad

N. Peratzim

Mt. Sodom

Salt Pans

To Dead Sea Works, Moshav Neot Hakikar (8km)

FLOUR CAVE

SODOM CAVE

Sodom

dead sea

student life

Sure, the Dead Sea draws hordes of beauty school dropouts to its lauded authentic mud bath, but there's plenty for students of other majors to do. Those with pale post-exam complexions can warm themselves as they bathe at the beach, while the area's history will keep any scholarly mind sharp.

So traverse the desert and learn something new. The stories behind Masada and Qumran are dramatic tales the likes of which could only happen in Israel (ancestors! sheep! tradition!), and there are always simpler pastimes to fall back on. You look smarter—and svelter—already.

ein gedi ☎08

You came for the salty, but you'll be staying for the sweet. At the geographical center of Israel's Dead Sea coast, Ein Gedi is probably the most famous resort on the lake, with a sprawling oasis that crawls up the canyons behind. The beach for your token salty-sea floating may be underwhelming, but the sweet—and freshwater—oases of the national park, dotted with waterfalls and lagoons, make for stunning hikes and refreshing swims. Just as David took refuge from Saul here, you'll find cool midday relief from the sun perched on the canyon walls.

In the generally undeveloped Dead Sea area, it's almost inevitable that anywhere that gets hyped up is going to turn out to be a little overrated. The beach and spa—the supposed jewels of the area—are probably Ein Gedi's most unexciting parts. Have a quick float, then spend your time in the park and, if you have a car, the nearby kibbutz, which has lush botanical gardens and a small zoo.

ORIENTATION

A single road passes through Ein Gedi. Along it are four main clusters of buildings: two hostels and the **national park** in the north, the **beach** 1km down, the **kibbutz** 2km farther down, and the **spa** another 3km down. Each has a bus stop, but make sure to inform the bus driver where you need to get off or else he won't actually stop. Do not try to walk between these stops—the road is exposed, making the way oppressively hot.

ACCOMMODATIONS

Thankfully, Ein Gedi has budget accommodations near the beach and national park. The kibbutz is slightly further afield, but it offers resort-level treatment.

BEIT SARAH GUEST HOUSE HOSTEL $$

☎02 594 5600; eingedy@iyha.org.il

A complex of several two-floor, motel-like buildings, Beit Sarah is the clear choice for independent backpackers. The rooms may be a little small, but they're spotless and sit on a hill with brilliant views of the sea and Jordan beyond. In the morning, ibex often wander around the premises, making for an even more picturesque sunrise.

⇄ From the bus stop, walk to the uphill access road. Beit Sarah is at the beginning of the road on the right. ℹ Breakfast included. A/C, TV, ensuite bathroom, and fridge. Wi-Fi in lobby NIS30 per 24hr. $ Dorms NIS118; singles NIS276; doubles NIS352. Dinner NIS60 (sometimes not served on Sa). ⏰ Reception daily 8am-10pm.

EIN GEDI FIELD SCHOOL HOSTEL $$

☎08 658 4288

A series of bungalows with comfortable five-bed dorms sits high on a hill over the Dead Sea, offering all the vistas you'd expect that to entail. The hostel is often booked full by groups during the winter high season, but solo travelers can usually find rooms during the summer.

 # Follow the access road past Beit Sarah. The Field School is at the end. i A/C, fridge, and ensuite bathroom. $ Dorms NIS115. July-Aug singles NIS345; doubles NIS380. Sept-Dec singles NIS430; doubles NIS470. Jan-June singles NIS430; doubles NIS470. Discounts for SPNI members.

KIBBUTZ EIN GEDI HOTEL $$$

☎08 659 4220; www.ein-gedi.co.il/en

Offering more than just a bed to sleep in, Kibbutz Ein Gedi has somehow evolved from typical cheap-stay kibbutz into near-resort commune. The buildings are situated in the middle of lush botanical gardens, there's a small zoo (with the requisite depressed-looking monkey), and guests can choose between luxury hotel rooms and country lodging. The latter is rather less rugged than it sounds—each one-room bungalow is as big and clean as a hotel room and comes with an ensuite bathroom. Every hour, a van heads over to Ein Gedi Spa, where hotel guests can pamper themselves for free and country lodgers get a 50% discount.

 # The access road branches off the main road about 3km south of the beach. i Hotel includes breakfast and dinner. A/C, TV, and ensuite bathroom. $ Country lodging singles US$92; doubles US$108. Hotel singles US$175; doubles US$222. 🕐 Zoo open in morning; hours vary.

the sweet smell of sulfur

The Ein Gedi Spa is famous for the Ein Gedi road race, also known as the Shalom Marathon or Dead Sea Half-Marathon (depending on how far you choose to run). Since its inception in 1983, the popular race has used the spa as the starting point—athletes love the course, as the air in the area has 10% more oxygen than it would at sea level. If you don't feel like running in the sulfur-scented region, you can just take advantage of the spa resources. Visitors must take a shuttle to float in the Dead Sea due to the rapid evaporation of the shoreline, but hot springs, cold pools, and mud baths are located in close proximity. The healing mud may smell noxious, but consider how much money a similar treatment would cost in an actual spa as opposed to a communal tub. And don't forget to inhale deeply—bromine, a natural tranquilizer, fills the air, providing visitors with a sense of medicated serenity that's better than any Prozac derivative.

SIGHTS

Ein Gedi most heavily promotes its beach and rugged national park, but its other attractions are also well known throughout Israel.

within ein gedi

EIN GEDI SPA SPA

☎08 659 4813; www.ein-gedi.co.il

The Dead Sea is renowned for its therapeutic effects, and this is its premier health spot. Thanks to an underground sulphur source, you can bathe in phenomenally smelly water, then go rinse in a cool outdoor pool before trucking to the mud baths. Though the mud was originally right next to the pool, the Dead Sea's shrinkage means that it's now a 1km walk to the shore. If you're really pampering yourself, you can hop on a shuttle and save yourself the 10min. walk. Much like Ein Gedi's beach, the spa seems to have suffered due to its good reputation: the place is now packed with families and tour groups and feels more like your local YMCA than a high-class spa.

About 3km south of the kibbutz. A car is necessary. $ NIS69, with lunch NIS118. 20% student discount. ⏰ Open Su-Th 9am-5:30pm, F 9am-4pm, Sa 8am-5:30pm.

ANTIQUITIES NATIONAL PARK HISTORICAL SITE

☎08 658 4285

Less a national park and more a small spot of land at the foot of the actual one, Antiquities National Park is home to an impeccably restored Byzantine-era synagogue—and that's about it. The highlight is a good-as-new mosaic, which includes the signs of the zodiac and a list of humanity's ancestors from Adam to Japheth (the son of Noah).

Heading south, make the right just before the beach and walk for about 300m. $ NIS14, students NIS7. ⏰ Open daily in summer 8am-5pm, in winter 8am-4pm.

masada

If you get bored with the sand and salt, take a trip up the road to Masada, a Herodian citadel that was most famously used as a fortress by the Zealots in 70 CE. The story is actually a pretty common one in Semitic history: Jews hide in the mountains to avoid the fill-in-the-blank oppressors until they either win (thanks, God) or are massacred. In the case of Masada, 967 Zealots retreated to this citadel and held off thousands of Roman troops for five months. When they realized that they were going to be overtaken, the leader of this small Jewish sect declared that it would be best to die "unenslaved by enemies and leave this world as free men in company with wives and children." Since Judaism forbids suicide, they chose 10 men to kill the rest of the population, and then one man to kill the other nine before falling on his own sword. This story remains one of the most important in Jewish history, even if murder-suicide pacts don't exactly make for great Sunday School reenactments.

The citadel, which is now a national park and UNESCO World Heritage Site, is about 18km south of Ein Gedi, meaning that you'll need to drive or take a bus—any of the buses that run through the Dead Sea area will stop here. To reach the ruins, you can either take a cable car or climb up one of two paths: the **Roman Ramp** in the west is steep but short (and takes about 20min.), while the longer, gentler **Snake Path** starts in the eastern parking lot and takes about 45min. to hike. The sights listed below assume that you're following the well-signed path through the ruins that starts near the **cable car drop-off** on the eastern side of the citadel. As you begin your oohing and ahhing, keep in mind that about a third of the sights are actually reconstructions and that, other than these ruins, you're not going to find much in Masada other than a hospitable guesthouse, a cheerless food situation, and the occasional light show. (☎08 658 4207 for citadel, 08 995 9333 for light show $ Park NIS27, children NIS14; with 1-way cable car NIS54, children NIS28; with 2-way cable car NIS72/41. ⏰ Open Apr-Sept Su-Th 8am-5pm, F 8am-4pm, Sa 8am-5pm; Oct-Mar Su-Th 8am-4pm, F 8am-3pm, Sa 8am-4pm. Last entry 1hr. before close. Cable car runs Su-Th 8am-4pm, F 8am-2pm, Sa 8am-4pm.)

EASTERN WALL WALL

A series of towers once lined this stretch of stone, but the wall itself is all that remains. An underground channel put in by the Zealots is even older than the wall itself. See that grove of fir trees to the left? Close your eyes and pretend it's 1988, when the copse was the site of a dramatic reenactment of the powerful battle. Or, better yet, start your own!

SNAKE PATH LOOKOUT VIEW

This ancient lookout provides sweeping views of the walls, the Snake Path, the Roman camps, the Dead Sea, and the mountains of Moab.

QUARRY
RUINS, AMMUNITION

All those stone buildings and walls had to have come from somewhere. That somewhere is this quarry, which provided most of the stone for Masada's construction. Between the western wall and the quarry, you'll see a huge collection of perfectly round rocks—most likely intended to be ammunition for catapults.

STOREROOMS
RUINS

Just before killing one another, the Zealots destroyed the fortress and most of their valuable possessions in order to really stick it to the (Ro)man. However, they left this storeroom full of food; it's believed that the Zealots wanted their oppressors to know they died to escape slavery, not from starvation.

ROMAN BATHHOUSE
BATHHOUSE

Unlike the religious ritual baths, or *mikva'ot*, that are common throughout the citadel, this was a frivolous creation of King Herod that remained unused by the Zealots.

LOTTERY AREA
BATHHOUSE

This bath was used by the Zealots for ritual cleansing and purification. The more interesting thing about this sight, however, is the pieces of broken pottery that were discovered during the excavation. These ostraca were inscribed with names, including that of Elazar Ben-Yair, leader of the Zealots. Historians believe that these were used as lots to decide who would kill the others.

NORTHERN PALACE
PALACE

Count 'em up, my friends: that's one, two, three terraces on that ancient palace. It may have been a remote fortress, but the frescoes and columns that remain prove that Herod insisted on living in style even in the boonies. On a completely unrelated note, skeletons of a man, woman, and child were discovered in the bathhouse in the lower section of this palace.

ZEALOTS' SYNAGOGUE
SYNAGOGUE

Many of the sights you see in Israel boast that they're the "oldest this" or "most ancient that." Don't believe everything you hear—it's on Masada that you'll find the world's oldest Zealot synagogue. A *mikveh* found here proves that the Zealots strictly followed biblical law, while scrolls discovered here are now on display at the Israel Museum in Jerusalem.

CASEMATE OF THE SCROLLS
RUINS

Archaeologists unearthed many relics here, including scrolls, papyri, shekels, a tallit, a wooden shield, arrows, sandals, and even keys.

WATER CISTERN PATH
PATH

The enormous cisterns scattered across the mountain are lined with almost perfectly water-repellent plaster, allowing the proud engineers to drain rainfall from the surrounding mountains into Masada's own reservoirs. This allowed the Zealots to stockpile eight years worth of fresh water.

BYZANTINE CHURCH
CHURCH

A break from the more historic remains, this well-preserved church was a hideout for Christian hermits during the fifth and sixth centuries. This is one of the most impressive (and intact) ruins; make sure to check out the mosaic floors.

WESTERN PALACE
PALACE

If you keep walking along the edge, you'll find the former site of Herod's throne room and offices of state. This was his "working palace," while the Northern Palace was his "country residence." It includes a waiting room, courtyard, dining hall, kitchen, and throne room in the southern wing and a system of water cisterns under the western wing. The northern wing surrounds a large central courtyard

dead sea

SWIMMING POOL BATHHOUSE

This pool worked double duty: first as a symbol of Herod's power—he could swim laps while the rest of the fortress inhabitants were parched—and then as a ritual bath for the Zealots.

COLUMBARIUM RUINS

Despite what some archaeologists long argued, the niches in the back left wall weren't meant for pigeons, but rather for dead people. Cremation is illegal according to Jewish law, but many of Herod's non-Jewish garrison members had their remains placed in these cubbyholes.

SOUTHERN CITADEL CITADEL

Just as it sounds, this Southern Citadel kept watch over the Masada Wadi, the Dead Sea, and many Roman encampments.

SOUTHERN WALL WALL

Sure, the whole manly citadel-siege angle is fun, but this one's for the ladies—the southern wall is home to the former site of a courtyard, ritual bath, dressing rooms, and possibly a bakery.

SOUTHEAST WALL WALL, VIEW

A memorial inscription of "Lucius" on this southeast wall probably has more to do with a Roman garrison than *Harry Potter*, so don't get too excited. You can also see four impressions of the name "Justus" in Latin and Greek. Keep your eyes peeled for a lookout, which you can climb to see the outer walls.

THE GREAT OUTDOORS

beaches

Ein Gedi's beach is, without a doubt, the focus of the area. In fact, it's probably the most famous beach on the Dead Sea. That title, however, might be somewhat misplaced.

EIN GEDI BEACH BEACH

It's the Dead Sea's main beach, but you may have trouble figuring out why. For one, there's no sand; you head down a hill to reach a small and rocky beach. Due to the crowds who flock to Ein Gedi, drawn by its famous name, this small patch of subpar coast gets incredibly packed. Litter covers the shore, and the crowds—tour groups, families, and rowdy high schoolers—don't really facilitate a relaxing nap by the sea. There's a large picnic area at the top of the hill by the parking lot, but it's usually swarmed with tourists barbecuing odd-smelling meats. By night, locals take to the parking lot and nearby greenery, pumping loud music from their cars. Theft, at any hour of the day, is not unheard of, so act accordingly.

⇟ About 1km south of the national park and field school. $ Lockers NIS5. ⏰ Lifeguards on duty daily 7am-6pm.

hiking

Hiking in Ein Gedi is done in the **national park** (☎08 658 4285 $ NIS27. ⏰ Open daily in summer 8am-5pm, in winter 8am-4pm.), which occupies two large canyons, both overflowing with lush greenery, waterfalls, secluded pools, and packs of wandering ibex. At least nine designated trails wind through the park; some of these are family-friendly, while others are relatively extreme and can involve traversing sun-baked canyon faces for up to 8hr. These hardcore hikes are usually closed during the summer and require careful planning and up-to-date information during the rest of the year. No matter what hike you're doing, it's a good idea to grab a map at the ticket office. Much of the park is exposed, so bring plenty of water—at least 1.5L for every hour you expect to be out.

WADI DAVID

Wadi David is the more northern of the park's two canyons and consists of a series of waterfalls and pools. The initial climb from the ticket office is more of a stroll than a hike, as you follow a clearly demarcated path uphill first by pavement and then across some rocks and small streams. The five lagoons you'll soon reach are usually packed with families and kids frolicking in the water as hyraxes flit between the rocks, strangely unfazed by the crowds. Halfway up the canyon is **David's Waterfall,** where a huge cliff marks the end of this first hike, which takes about 20min.

Here, you can either turn back or follow the path from the waterfall that leads up the canyon walls and along the cliff. The path isn't too steep or difficult—and eventually turns into rocky steps—but it's still possible to slip, so be careful. As you work your way around the cliff face, the views of the Dead Sea will take your breath away (if the climb hasn't done so already). Once the path levels out, continue for about 200m to reach a T-junction. If you turn left, you'll eventually reach **Ein Gedi Spring,** a knee-deep pool that is refreshing despite the fact that it's exposed. This mostly downhill trail also passes the 5500-year-old **Chalcolithic Temple,** which is perched on a high peak.

Your better bet, however, is to take a right at the junction and head to **Dodim's Cave.** This path descends into the canyon again, taking you just past the top of David's Waterfall and above the cliff face you saw as you were leaving the falls. After clambering down some rungs built into the rock, you'll find a shady cave hanging over a pristine lagoon. The lagoon is covered by rocks on all sides, so the area remains refreshingly cool throughout the day. While not completely isolated, the pool requires about 25min. more legwork from the foot of David's Waterfall, making it decidedly less crowded than the lagoons farther back down the canyon. You must leave the cave by 2:30pm.

For harder trails, take the path heading up the cliff face from the Chalcolithic Temple. You'll reach another T-junction. Turning left will take you to the Ein Gedi ascent—a grueling 8hr. climb up to the desert plateau—which is closed for most of the year. Heading right, however, will take you along the **Zaffit Path.** This skirts the edges of **Wadi David** along the seam between the lush greenery of the oasis and the desert cliff face that leads up to the plateau. It requires about 4-5hr. from the junction, but it takes you across the so-called dry canyon and dry waterfall and back around the inlet, ending with a scenic descent into the Field School.

FOOD

In Ein Gedi, you may be almost walking on water, but you won't be eating like a king of kings. Not one of the four eateries in town would come close to being gourmet, and three of them serve only OK dishes at drastically marked-up prices. Unfortunately, they're all far enough away from each other that you really have no option but the one in front of you. **Hostel Beit Sarah** also provides a self-serve dinner for guests (NIS60), and the kibbutz has a **grocery store,** so your best option may be to stock up there (or before you come) and simply cook for yourself.

PUNDAK EIN GEDI — FAST FOOD $$

Ein Gedi Beach — ☎08 659 4761

In case your wallet isn't thin enough just from staying at the kibbutz, you can starve it further at the commune's beachfront lunch stand. A no-frills self-service eatery, Pundak Ein Gedi offers a selection of meats which include such imaginative options as schnitzel and frankfurters.

➜ On the southern end of the parking lot. $ Entree and 2 sides NIS45. ⏰ Open daily 11am-4pm.

BOTANICAL GARDENS RESTAURANT BUFFET $$

Kibbutz Ein Gedi ☎08 659 4221

Sure it's pricey, but it's an all-you-can-eat buffet. Fill your plate with all the meat, salad, fruit, and vegetables that can fit. Remember: all-you-can-eat is not an offer; it's a challenge. Man up.

From the reception, head west and follow the bend in the road uphill until it curves south. Head down until it bends west again, and the restaurant is on the right. $ Breakfast NIS65. Dinner NIS100. ⏰ Open daily 7-10am and 6:30-8:30pm.

the swimming dead

The Dead Sea, one of the saltiest bodies of water in the world, borders Israel to the west. An early health resort for Herod the Great (yes, *that* Herod the Great), the Dead Sea has been the source for compounds used in everything from mummification to cosmetics. Even more morbidly called the "killer sea" in Hebrew, the Dead Sea is too salty to support any of the usual marine life. Although unfortunate for fish, this tidbit lends the Dead Sea one of its coolest characteristics: because of the high salt content, you can stay afloat in the water without any effort at all. But be aware of any small cuts or shaving nicks you may have—otherwise, you'll actually be rubbing salt into those wounds.

EIN GEDI SPA RESTAURANT SELF-SERVICE $$

Ein Gedi Spa ☎08 659 4934

If the sulfurous water is really getting your appetite going, your only choice is this self-service joint, which is essentially indistinguishable from the others in the area.

Underneath the spa on the ground floor. $ Meals from NIS52. ⏰ Open Su-Th 11:30am-4:30pm, F 11:30am-3:30pm.

EIN GEDI KIOSK SANDWICH STAND $

Ein Gedi Beach ☎08 659 4761

This kiosk, which shares a building with Pundak, gets kudos for being the only late-night joint in town, serving hot dogs and expectedly bad ready-made sandwiches.

On the south side of the parking lot. $ Hot dog NIS20. Sandwiches NIS17. ⏰ Open 24hr.

ESSENTIALS

The only amenity in Ein Gedi is the **ATM,** which has an NIS7 surcharge and can be found in the lobby of the kibbutz. However, since most places accept cards, it's pretty superfluous. Sunscreen is available for purchase at Pundak Ein Gedi, but anything else you need should be brought with you, as the first aid station is only for kibbutzniks.

getting there

Egged Bus runs several services to Ein Gedi, including the **#486** from Jerusalem ($ NIS36. ⏰ 1½hr., every hr. at 30min. past) and the **#444** from Eilat. ($ NIS45. ⏰ 3hr., 4 times per day.)

getting around

In Ein Gedi, you're going to be in one of four locations, and each has its own bus stop. As with much of the Dead Sea, however, the bus schedules are not that reliable; your best bet for a non-frustrating trip is to rent a car from Jerusalem.

kalya beaches ☎02

Perched on the northern tip of the Dead Sea, Kalya (sometimes spelled "Qalia") is the closest the Dead Sea gets to life—or, at least, to civilization. Throw in the fact that it's less than an hour from Jerusalem, and you'll quickly realize that Kalya is the perfect destination for anyone dead set on seeing the Dead Sea (get it?). Kalya doesn't offer many distractions: unlike most Israeli tourist spots, there are no ancient archaeological sites or picturesque hikes to lure you from your salt-water floating. In fact, we might even have been using the term "civilization" loosely; Kalya is less of a town and more of a handful of buildings that happen to be near each other. Each of its three beaches is accessed separately, and there's nothing much on the road between them. Kalya Beach itself is party to a constant train of tour buses heading in and out, but it's large enough to never feel crowded, making it one of the more peaceful beaches on this seriously salinated sea.

ORIENTATION

Kalya consists of three adjacent beaches; from north to south, they are **Kalya Beach, Biankini Beach,** and **Neve Midbar.** All three are accessible from the highway via a single road. A left at the first T-junction will take you to Kalya Beach, while going straight will get you to the other two, whose parking lots are right next to one another. Signs clearly point the way.

ACCOMMODATIONS

Kalya can easily be seen and done in less than a day, but, should you want to stick around, you have a few options. The middle of the three resorts, **Biankini** (☎02 940 0266), offers large wood cabins for fairly astronomical prices and a "Moroccan palace" with huge double beds and a jacuzzi over two floors. You can instead sleep on the large outdoor restaurant terrace for a meager NIS50 if you're willing to give the hovering mosquitoes a hand in their quest for dinner. If you want a guaranteed cheap sleep, Neve Midbar, the most southern resort, is by far your best bet.

NEVE MIDBAR RESORT — CABINS, CAMPING $
☎02 994 2781

Probably the most reasonably priced of the three resorts in Kalya, Neve Midbar has the best overnight options. Camping on the premises costs as little as NIS60 for an adult, and small huts are also available. These huts go back to the basics—there's no air-conditioning, the bathroom is just an outhouse, and the notion of Wi-Fi is laughable. However, they can house two people, which makes for a better value.

➜ At the T-junction, go straight and then follow signs. $ Camping NIS60, ages 2-12 NIS50. 2-person huts NIS220. ⏰ Reception 24hr.

SIGHTS

Look at the name: there's nothing to Kalya Beaches except lots and lots of shoreline. But if you're willing to go a little inland, you'll find history aplenty.

QUMRAN — NEW FRONTIERS
☎02 994 2235

Just 7km south of Kalya, Qumran provides a slightly calmer experience than the sightseeing madness of Jerusalem, but it's thanks to Qumran that we understand much of the history behind those Old City sights. After all, it's here that the Dead Sea Scrolls were discovered. Perhaps the most important artifact in terms of understanding the Bible's origins, the scrolls are a mixture of biblical and apocryphal writings that make up the oldest-known surviving copies of these religious texts. All the excitement started in 1947 when a young Bedouin was looking for a lost sheep. Cursing the futility of his quest (one sheep, lots of desert), this spry fellow threw a rock into a Qumran cave—and heard something in the depths of the cave break. He ventured inside and found a collection of dirt-encrusted jars that held something even better than sploosh: 2000-year-old manuscripts. The sheep, we can only assume, is still out there.

Historians have since determined that the authors were most likely the Essenes, members of a strictly devout Jewish sect that took refuge in the area after becoming disillusioned with the Hellenization of their bros in Jerusalem. Like other zealous and highly ascetic groups, the Essenes believed that the non-devout would soon be destroyed; more specifically, they predicted a *Star Wars*-esque struggle that would occur between the Sons of Light (themselves and the angels) and the Sons of Darkness (everyone else).

At the top of the mountain you can find some solace and relief—if not a bit of boredom—in a 5min. dramatized film depicting life as an Essene back in the day. Following the film, the screen rises to reveal a chamber through which you can access the museum and the path through the ruins. You'll get to see the famous cave, but the actual scrolls are on display at the Israel Museum in Jerusalem.

🚌 Qumran can be reached by any bus that takes you to Kalya Beaches. By car, follow the road along the Dead Sea (Rte. 90) and turn into Kibbutz Kalya. $ NIS21, children NIS9. Groups (of 30 people or more) NIS18, children NIS8. ⏰ Open daily Apr-Sept 8am-5pm; Oct-Mar 8am-4pm. Last entry 1hr. before close.

BEACHES

What else did you come here for? While one stretch of sand is basically the same as another, none, unfortunately, are free.

KALYA BEACH

☎02 994 2391

Probably Kalya's most popular beach—after all, it's become the name of the entire area—Kalya Beach is the biggest and easiest to get to, so expect a regular rotation of tour groups. The entry fee might be hefty, but it comes with chairs, umbrellas, hot showers, parking, and that Dead Sea mud. With a bar by the beach and a restaurant and cosmetics shop just inland, Kalya Beach has more amenities than any of the other beaches in the area. Your happiness, however, will depend on whether you can put up with the slightly irksome reggae soundtrack that's constantly in the background.

$ NIS47, students NIS37. ⏰ Open daily 8am-7pm.

NEVE MIDBAR

☎02 994 0281

As you head south, the beach gets a little narrower and the ratio of rocks to sand slowly increases. Nevertheless, Neve Midbar does have the least crowded beach, albeit with a bar that's hell-bent on blasting the cheese.

$ NIS40, students NIS35. ⏰ Open daily 7am-7pm. Women-only 7-9:30am on M and Th.

FOOD

Food joints in Kalya are scarce. Each beach has a single, suitably overpriced restaurant, but your best bet is to pack your own lunch—even subsisting on ice cream alone would cost a pretty penny. If you care to lug some raw meat to the shore, you can borrow a rusty grill from **Neve Midbar.**

KALYA BEACH RESTAURANT INTERNATIONAL $$

Kalya Beach ☎02 993 6332

The daily lunch buffet has heaps of meat and enough salad, so cram as much as possible on your plate and don't feel guilty. With plenty of seating and a wall-length window overlooking the Dead Sea and Jordan, it's a staple for the tour groups.

⇞ Just before the entrance to the beach. [$] Lunch buffet NIS46. Falafel lunch NIS34. ⏰ Open daily noon-4pm.

NEVE MIDBAR ISRAELI $$

Neve Midbar ☎02 994 0281

A small cafe and restaurant overlooking the beach, Neve Midbar serves the usual Israeli and beach fare.

⇞ On the left as you enter the beach. [$] Breakfast NIS42. Shakshuka NIS34. ⏰ Open daily 9am-6:30pm.

snack attack

Pizza. Tacos. Onions. Falafel. This may sound like the menu at your favorite greasy spoon, but they're also some of the flavors of Bissli, a popular Israeli snack that looks like undercooked pasta. Over 4000 tons of these crunch munchies are produced each year, often in such delightful flavors as "smoky" and "grill." Sound unappetizing? If Bissli isn't working for you, consider stocking up on Bamba, which can best be described as a peanut-flavored Cheeto. Yum.

ESSENTIALS

Kalya has absolutely nothing in the way of basic amenities. However, you're unlikely to spend more than a day here, and most places accept credit cards, so the lack of an ATM isn't dire. Stock up on any necessary supplies in nearby Jerusalem and bring any medications you might need.

getting there

Any bus going along the Dead Sea passes through Kalya, which means it's pretty easy to get there. Egged runs an hourly service to Kalya from Jerusalem's Central Bus Station. Take **bus #486** ([$] NIS26.50. ⏰ 45min.) and remember to tell the driver that you're going to Kalya Beach so that he'll stop appropriately—otherwise, you'll end up at the kibbutz, which is an unmanageable 5km walk away.

The return journey can be difficult—buses back to Jerusalem almost never come at the specified time, so it helps to be at the station 15min. before the scheduled departure, though you should be prepared to wait for up to 1hr.

getting around

The bus will drop you off at the highway. Walking to Kalya Beach is possible, but it's a solid 2km in the oppressive desert sun. Many travelers suggest hitchhiking, which *Let's Go* does not recommend.

If you plan on moving between several beaches, the walk from Kalya Beach back up the T-junction in the access road is a good 500m and then a further 2km to Biankini and Neve Midbar. This is not fun in the heat. Overall, the best way to get around the area is to rent a car in Jerusalem.

THE NEGEV

David Ben-Gurion, the first prime minster of Israel, saw the Negev as the representation of his hopes for Israel: the once arid desert would become habitable, transformed into farmland by intimate cooperative communities. With only a spade, a yarmulke, and his biceps, the farmer would build himself a state. This was the real dream of Zionism, the drive to turn a seemingly barren land into one of milk and honey, a haven for a new class of Jewish people—self-reliant, hardy, and communal.

That, uh, didn't really work out. Most Israelis live in major cities, either on the lusher Mediterranean coast or in the occupied West Bank. The Negev has not become the agricultural Disney World Ben-Gurion imagined. The more civilized Be'er Sheva aside, the area is predominantly home to small towns of dreadlocked adventurers, wacky left-wing oldsters, and small communities of artists. These settlements, which thrive thanks to hikers, are still in the process of building up the restaurants and hotels that go with their industry. Visitors won't find pristine hostels, but they can easily discover opportunities to sleep on cheap mattresses in yoga studios or eat in endless picnic space among desert ravines. Some hotels are even perched on high desert mountains, advertising themselves as places to escape electricity, noise, and the busy outside world in general. In a way, this is exactly the opposite of what Ben-Gurion hoped for—the solemn desert experience as a break for Israelis and tourists alike, a place to go to when you're getting away. This land has changed little since Abraham moved in. It's still a secluded spot to appreciate the essentials, and tourists can enjoy the modern equivalent—even if it means paying NIS80 per night.

greatest hits

- **STOP CHASING THEM.** Check out Ein Avdat National Park (p. 312) while in Sde Boker for a taste of the Amazon in the Israeli desert, a waterfall and all.

- **ALL-YOU-CAN-DRINK RED BULL AND VODKA.** Sound like a good idea? Thought so (p. 306).

- **BACK TO THE BASICS.** Get a true desert experience under the stars at Silent Arrow in Mitzpe Ramon (p. 316).

- **INTERNATIONAL JAMS.** Try Gecko's (p. 304) delicious breakfast plates.

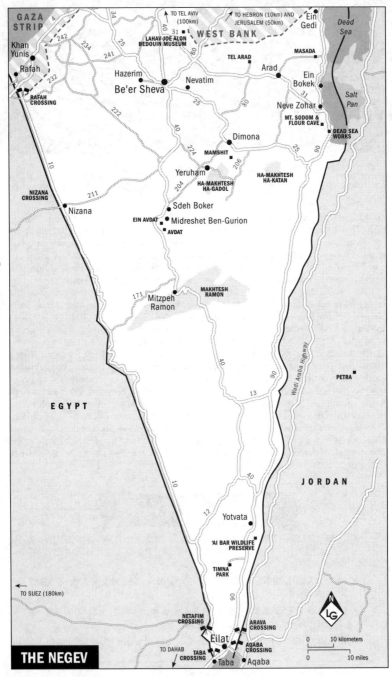

THE NEGEV

Put the books away and pack the granola; the Negev is just about the chillest place in the world. It's hard to be stressed when you're picnicking with an alpaca in **Mitzpe Ramon** or finding your inner child at the **Negev Zoo** in **Be'er Sheva.** Be'er Sheva is also the home of Ben-Gurion University, which is full of students looking for fun and frolic. **Einstein** is your best bet for a night out on the town, with a discount on shots when you buy a beer—that sounds pretty genius to us. Just remember: liquor before beer, in the clear; beer then liquor, never sicker.

Not to be left out is **Sde Boker,** the place to find your inner hippie, play some bongos, hike, and live exclusively on chickpeas (if you aren't already) at **Hummus Land.**

be'er sheva ☎08

Tel Avivian students complain that Be'er Sheva has all the problems of the desert—unremitting heat, little grass, plenty of isolation—without any of the perks. The beauty of the landscape is obscured by the concrete strip mall that dominates Be'er Sheva. It's certainly true that there's been some urban development since Abraham built a well and made a home for himself here. But not much really happened in Be'er Sheva for 11,900 years after that, until the Ottomans decided to make something of this barren stretch of Bedouin camps. They built an infrastructure: a police station, a large governor's mansion, a garden, and what is today melodramatically called the Old City. The town became a flashpoint in WWI, but development skyrocketed afterward thanks to Ben-Gurion's attempts to make the Israeli deserts bloom.

Unfortunately, it seems that development has been more focused on quantity of buildings rather than quality, and life in Be'er Sheva is more urban than urbane. Regardless, it's still the first place that travelers, especially students, should visit in the Negev. Not only does Be'er Sheva boast a burgeoning restaurant scene and the Negev's only state-recognized museum, but it's also most prominently home to **Ben-Gurion University,** one of the most popular and advanced universities in Israel. And where there are students, there are parties—everything from dive bars where the staff drink along with patrons to weekday live trance DJ bashes. And the town is only growing; residents speak animatedly of what might be here in 20 years, once the university's place has been solidified in Israel and the young professionals start having families. There is no historical or religious monument of dramatic stature, nor is there yet a vibrant culture scene, but the seeds for both lie in this concrete oasis.

ORIENTATION

When you arrive at the central bus station on Eilat St., you will be in between the three most popular Be'er Sheva locales. Behind the bus station and just outside the city proper is the **Bedouin Market,** which comes to life on Thursday mornings. To the southwest is the **Old City,** a moderately old and semi-slummy area that is home to both Be'er Sheva's nicest and its cheapest restaurants. It's bisected by two major streets, **HaAtzma'ut Street** going vertically and **Herzl Street** going horizontally. About 1.5km north is the student section of town, which is basically a series of sidestreets off **Yitzhak Rager Boulevard,** the main road in

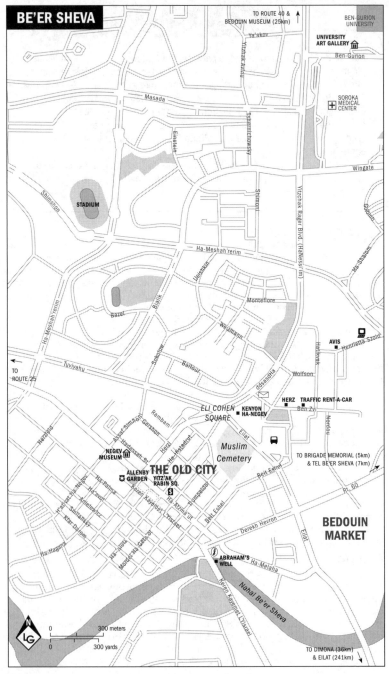

BE'ER SHEVA

TO ROUTE 40 &
BEDOUIN MUSEUM (25km)

BEN-GURION
UNIVERSITY

Ya'akov

Yitzhak Avidu

UNIVERSITY
ART GALLERY

Ben-Gurion

Masada

Tsharnichowsky

SOROKA
MEDICAL
CENTER

Einstein

Shimshon

Wingate

STADIUM

Shimoni

Yitzchak Rager Blvd. (HaNessi'im)

Golomb

Ha-Meshah'rerim

Ussishkin

Ha-Sharon

Montefiore

Bazel

Bialik

Weizmann

Ha-Meshah'rerim

Sokolov

Balfour

AVIS

Henrietta Szold

Hatikva

Tuviyahu

Ha'azzadt'Ha

Wolfson

TO
ROUTE 25

Rambam

ELI COHEN
SQUARE

KENYON
HA-NEGEV

HERZ

TRAFFIC RENT-A-CAR

Herzl

Assaf Simhon Gershon

Ben Zvi

Nordey

Hadassah St.

Herzl

Muslim
Cemetery

Eilat

NEGEV
MUSEUM

Ha-Histadrut

TO BRIGADE MEMORIAL (5km)
& TEL BE'ER SHEVA (7km)

ALLENBY
GARDEN

YITZ'AK
RABIN SQ.

Keren Kayemet L'Yisrael

Ha'Atzma'ut

THE OLD CITY

Beit Eshel

Rt. 60

Ha-Palma

Ha'aluz

Trumpeldor

Ha'avpart-Ha-Negev

Anielewicz

Sukharov

Beit Eshel

Derekh Hevron

BEDOUIN
MARKET

Ktar Darom

Ha-Haluz

Mordel Ha-Geta-ot

Eilat

Ha-Hagana

ABRAHAM'S
WELL

Ha-Melaha

Keren Kayemet L'Yisrael

Nahal Be'er Sheva

N
LG

0   300 meters

0   300 yards

TO DIMONA (36km)
& EILAT (241km)

town. If a student bar isn't on Rager, it's probably along Ben-Gurion St., and off-campus students live mainly on Bialik St. and Ya'akov Avinu St. Back near the bus station, **David Tuvyaho Street** intersects with HaAtzmaut at its genesis and leads into **Hevron Road,** which you can follow east to the **Big Center,** the main mall in a place where some residents spend most of their free time in one mall or another. That is, unless you think wide sections of the place are little more than outdoor malls, in which case few people ever leave them.

ACCOMMODATIONS

Tourism still isn't well-established in Be'er Sheva, and the poor hotel choices show it. It's possible to find students who live in apartments with extra rooms or that are between leases, but relying on this option is a bit like walking into the Negev and hoping you'll run into a pond.

NEGEV HOTEL
HOTEL $$

16 HaAtzma'ut
☎08 627 7026

Considering that it's one of the cheaper options in Be'er Sheva, the Negev Hotel's adult-sized bathtubs are an unexpected luxury. But since you're paying NIS200 for a room, it doesn't seem quite luxurious enough. A better deal for two than one—rooms cost the same either way—the Negev Hotel has large air-conditioning units, a small common area with two TVs, a fridge with beer, a chess board, and generally spacious rooms. You may not find many special perks, but you'll probably find nothing to complain about either. Except the lack of internet.

⇟ About 100m down HaAtzmaut from Herzl St. ℹ No internet. $ Rooms NIS200. Cash only.

BEIT YATZIV YOUTH HOSTEL (HI)
MOTEL $$

79 HaAtzma'ut
☎08 627 7444; www.beityatziv.co.il

This concrete monstrosity has justified its existence by housing an open university, meaning there are classes and students hanging around to study. In hotel terms, it generally stands in defiance of human standards regarding value and happiness. For NIS200, you get a tiny single room without a shower. A dead cockroach might be enjoying a 12hr. vigil in the dim beige hallway, and your air-conditioning might not work—and the elevator might not either. Despite the "Youth" in its name, Beit Yatziv is populated mostly by families who, we can only assume, didn't realize just how dire the hotel situation in Be'er Sheva could be. These pitfalls negate even the effects of free Wi-Fi, which, if this hotel dies, will probably be emphasized to St. Peter as its sole reason to get into hotel heaven.

⇟ Walk about 200m north of the Old City, and Beit Yatziv is on the left. ℹ Free Wi-Fi. Cash only. $ Singles NIS250, extra person NIS100. Nicest rooms NIS400 regardless of the number of people. ⏰ Open daily 24hr. Reservations can be made 8am-8pm.

SIGHTS

If you are awake and lucid before 5pm—a possibly unnecessary and even undesirable state in Be'er Sheva—there is no shortage of things to do, though only so much of it is worthwhile.

★ NEGEV ZOO
ZOO

☎08 641 4777; www.negevzoo.com

It's kind of hard to make an arid wasteland seem compelling, but the Negev Zoo does its best with a collection of some of the desert's most common and compelling animals: beautiful and bizarre tiny birds, huge vultures that look ominous even from their cages, and jackals that eye visitors hungrily. Gigantic ostriches strut around as exotic porcupines snack on the watermelons that are fed to seemingly every animal that could eat them.

The lack of English signs or brochures may disappoint some, but anyone who still has the slightest trace of a five-year old in the catacombs of his consciousness will use his eyes a lot more than his mind.

⚑ Bus #18 goes near the junction on David Tevyahu. Walk down the road following the signs to the zoo. *i* Guided tours available by prior arrangement for 1½hr. Ⓢ NIS23, students NIS18. Tours NIS60. Ⓐ Open July-Aug Su-Th 9am-8pm, F 9am-1pm, Sa 2-8pm; Sept-July Su-Th 9am-5pm, F 9am-1pm, Sa 10am-5pm.

edible underwear

Your English is impressive enough, but throw in a few Hebrew pick-up lines—listed here from simple to too real—and you'll be beating them off with a stick:

- **AT HAMA:** You're hot.
- **AT YAFA:** You're beautiful.
- **HATAKHTONIM SHELI AKHILIM:** My underwear is edible.
- **ANI META ALECHA:** I'm crazy about you.
- **ANI OHEV OTACH:** I love you.

BEDOUIN MARKET   MARKET

The nostalgic complain about the gentrification of the Thursday Bedouin Market, where camels and sheep just aren't bartered like they used to be. However, basic Bedouin goods have been sold here since 1905, and Bedouin and Jewish locals alike still travel here for shopping rather than spectacle. It's true that snow globes and T-shirts now dominate, but traditional Bedouin copperware, robes, and rugs are still sold in odd corners. Livestock also get their fair share of hand-changing, though the market for them is admittedly smaller among big-spending travelers. We suspect that it's mostly due to how bad goats are at air travel.

⚑ Walk down Eilat St. to the south part of the city, near the intersection with Hevron Rd. Some local buses stop here on request, and locals can point it out. Ⓐ Open Th 6am-1pm.

THE NEGEV MUSEUM OF ART   MUSEUM

60 HaAtzma'ut   ☎08 699 3535; www.negev-museum.org.il

Rotating exhibitions of both somewhat prominent artists—like Michal Rovner, whose work has appeared at the Louvre—and lesser-knowns are on display at the Negev Museum of Art, which is the only state-recognized museum in the region. Subject matter often focuses on Israel or the Negev, and many works are very recent pieces by national artists, though there is no constraint on what can be shown. The building was originally built in 1906 as the Ottoman governor's residence and has been faithfully renovated.

⚑ About 200m north of Herzl St. *i* English brochures available. Call in advance to arrange guided tours. Ⓢ NIS12, students NIS10. Tours NIS14 per person. Ⓐ Open M 10am-4pm, Tu 10am-6pm, W-Th 10am-4pm, F-Sa 10am-2pm.

TEL BE'ER SHEVA   RUINS

Off Be'er Sheva-Shoket Junction   ☎08 646 7286; www.parks.org.il

With the densely-packed layers of history typical of Israel, Tel Be'er Sheva was first inhabited in the fourth millennium BCE. No architectural ruins remain from that period, but an oven has been preserved from a second millennium BCE settlement of a few dwellings and a grain storage area.

The *tel* was most prominently used as a fortified city in the ninth century BCE, during the reign of King Herod at the turn of the millennium, by the Romans in the second and third century CE, and in the Early Arab Period from the seventh to eighth centuries. A series of somewhat intrusive Biblical inscriptions are featured on plaques around the site, and some scholars link certain ruins to Biblical stories. The foundations of many city buildings are intact, and the aerial view afforded by a raised platform really gives a sense for how this ancient place might have once looked. It also gives a great perspective on a broad expanse of the Negev.

✚ *Continue approximately 8km down Hevron Rd. until the sign for the tel appears on your right; continue down that road for another 1km, and the site is on the right. A car makes this trip significantly easier.* **i** *English brochures available.* **⑨** *NIS14, seniors and under 18 NIS7.* **⍉** *Open daily Apr-Sep 8am-5pm; Oct-Mar 8am-4pm.*

ABRAHAM'S WELL   RELIGIOUS SITE
1 Hevron Rd.   ☎08 623 4613; bavraham@ladpe.net.il

An impressively huge well stands on the location where the biblical Abraham is said to have arrived and decided to settle here. According to the Old Testament, this well caused a small dispute between Abraham and the King of Gerar; the name Be'er Sheva (meaning "well of the oath" or "well of seven") is in honor of the tiff's settlement. From a religious standpoint, this site marks a crucial turning point in the story of the Jewish people; from a historical one, it's the usual attempt to extract reality from a religious text; and from a touristic one, it's decidedly underwhelming. However, those with a deep interest in Judaism will find it extremely satisfying to see this marker of Abraham's transition from wandering herdsman to holder of the covenant.

✚ *Walk all the way down HaAtzma'ut St. until it intersects with Hevron Rd., then take a left and cross the street.* **⑨** *NIS5.* **⍉** *Open Su-Th 8am-4pm. Call in advance to visit F and holiday eves.*

---

scientific swine

According to Israeli law, it is illegal for Jews to raise pigs in the country. The task therefore falls to Arab farmers, who are responsible for supplying the small non-Jewish population with its bacon fix. The only Jewish organization that deviates from both the religious and national law is Kibbutz Lahav, which breeds over 10,000 pigs for "research purposes." We highly suspect there's some tasty research being cooked up behind closed doors.

ALLENBY GARDEN   GARDEN
HaAtzma'ut St.

The city's first public garden was originally commissioned by the Ottomans and, as with most of old Be'er Sheva, was later reappropriated—in this case in honor of the man who officially marched into Palestine and ended Ottoman rule, Edward Allenby. Allenby's capture of Be'er Sheva was a strategic turning point, and a few months later Jerusalem fell out of Arab hands for the first time in more than a millennium. Once you've gotten your fill of sitting and staring at some of Be'er Sheva's only grass, head across the street to **Gan Remez,** behind the Negev Museum. A large ceramic sculpture garden, it was created for the 1997 Ceramics Biennale, which was held in Be'er Sheva.

✚ *Across from the Negev Museum on HaAtzma'ut.*

MUSLIM CEMETERY CEMETERY

The Muslim Cemetery is buttressed by two major highways, with billboards sitting directly on the surrounding fence and a parking lot in its backyard. Inside the fence, however, is some of the only untouched desert land within Be'er Sheva, as well as some of the only untouched remnants from its Ottoman past.

 # From HaAtzma'ut St., walk up HaHalutz about 4 blocks and take a right on Rambam St. The cemetery is on the left.

FOOD

The division between student and local food is also one between price and quality. Excellent but slightly pricier fare can be found in the Old City; however, budget travelers don't have to pawn their passports just to eat well here. Lunch deals in particular combine great food with reasonable prices.

LITTLE INDIA INDIAN $$

15 Ringleblum St. ☎08 648 9801; www.bgu.co.il/littleindia

If the canoodling couples on the low-lying pillows in the student section are putting you off your food, head indoors to the comfortable wooden tables of the unnecessarily great Little India. The only Indian restaurant in Be'er Sheva (and maybe the whole Negev) offers an all-you-can-eat lunch buffet for an unbeatable value (NIS39), though dinner offerings like the yellow lentils (NIS34) are well worth the massive plate. This may be your only chance for good Indian fare on your trip to Israel.

 # Take a right onto Ringleblum St. 200m up from Ben-Gurion St., then take a left at the dead end and walk up 25m. Little India is on the left. i All-you-can-eat buffet Su-Th noon-4pm. Student discount on fish entrees. Delivery NIS10. $ Fish curry NIS54. Mango lassi NIS12. ⏰ Open Su-Th noon-11pm, F noon-3pm.

GECKO CAFE $$

13 Smilansky ☎08 628 8937; www.gecko-cafe.com

Gecko is probably one of the most cafe-like cafes in Israel outside of Tel Aviv. The French posters are modest in size and quantity, wooden planks hang from the ceiling in geometric designs, and brick columns line the walls, supporting nothing—all wonderfully superfluous for the observant and perfectly inconspicuous for the otherwise engaged. Its food is simple, fantastic, and only slightly overpriced. The best part may be the small AstroTurf square outside the cafe, where tan wooden tables and a large pink umbrella imply a mini-resort experience. Fresh apple juice (NIS14) is made in-house and goes excellently with any of nine breakfast deals, each named after the country that inspired it. Served all day, they come with a small salad, a plate of cheeses and jams, bread, and fresh juice or a hot drink.

 # In the Old City, 300m down from Herzl St. i Free Wi-Fi. $ Tunisian breakfast (2 pastries filled with eggs, onion, and cheese with salad and green tahini) NIS42. 3 pancakes NIS29. Pesto and grilled vegetable sandwich NIS31. ⏰ Open Su-Th 8am-11pm, F 8am-6pm, Sa 9am-11pm.

PITPUT INTERNATIONAL $$

Big Center ☎08 628 9888

Lucky Be'er Shevans brunch at this bougie ideal of a mid-range restaurant. Ample space separates each table; there are indoor, outdoor, and semi-outdoor areas; and the salads are the best for value in town. And this isn't just chicken salad—it's chili and sesame chicken, drizzled with a citrus vinaigrette and sitting atop a haystack of radishes, tomatoes, carrots, and cucumbers, all cut into tidy thin strips. After weeks of street food have left falafel in your stubble and tahini in your hair, bedraggled budget eaters will find sweet relief here.

✤ Coming from the Old City up Hevron Rd., Pitput is in the 1st Big Center area on the far left-hand corner. i There is also a kosher location in the Old City, with different hours and a different menu. $ House hamburger NIS59. Cappuccino NIS12. ⏰ Open daily 9am-midnight.

BILBAO TAPAS BAR TAPAS $$$

23 Smilansky St. ☎08 665 4854

Maybe the best restaurant in terms of quality, the Bilbao Tapas Bar doesn't skimp on portions or prices. If you can afford an appetizer, the crispy cauliflower florets with chili aioli (NIS34) are so well-executed that fond memories will linger for days. That and an *entrecote pincho*, cooked in red wine and beef stock (NIS46), might gastronomically cheer you up enough that you can handle a week of subsisting on shawarma leftovers. Your budget might leave you no choice anyway.

✤ 75m down Smilansky St. from Hertzl St. i Free Wi-Fi. $ Merguez sausages NIS47. Seared sirloin NIS108. Hard cider NIS29. Lychee martini NIS36. ⏰ Open M-Sa in summer noon-late, in winter 5pm-late.

GLIDA BE'ER SHEVA ICE CREAM $

Hassadah St. ☎08 627 7072; info@glidabeersheva.com

Now more than 60 years old, Glida Be'er Sheva was opened by Polish immigrant Julia Rotenberg when Be'er Sheva was just a twinkle in David Ben-Gurion's eye. Today, Glida is a small Israeli ice cream chain, but its main production center is located in the original shop in Be'er Sheva's Old City, where customers choose from 70 flavors that include a tangy mint-lemon and a thick and sweet marzipan. Glida is usually busy, especially in the summer, but you'll find yourself asking to try as many flavors as possible before the person behind the counter wants to dump curdled milk on your head.

✤ In the Old City, where HaHalutz meets Hassadah St. $ 1 scoop NIS9, 2 NIS15; additional scoops NIS4 each. Add whipped cream NIS4. ⏰ Open daily 9am-late.

KAMPAI SUSHI $$

Big Center ☎08 665 5999; www.rol.co.il/sites/eng/kampai

Kampai, located in a large black room with black wooden tables, comfortable leather chairs, and a circular black bar, is known around Be'er Sheva as the premier Asian restaurant in the Negev, and the sleek interior isn't the only reason. The fish in its well-crafted sushi are imported from abroad—even as far away as Scandanavia—two to three times a week. Typical of its fusion aspirations are the tiny vegetable tempura sandwiches (NIS35), which are aesthetically similar to its English teatime cucumber ilk. Kampai staff also claim that the restaurant has the largest alcohol menu in Negev, which, considering the bar's size, is very possible. The crowd is generally on the older side, though the restaurant becomes more of a bar after dinnertime.

✤ From the Old City, go up Hevron Rd. Kampai is up the escalator from the 1st area you'll hit of the Big Center. i Free Wi-Fi. Business lunch deal (appetizer and main course, with drink and dessert discounts) Su-Th noon-6pm. $ Business lunch NIS69-99. ⏰ Open M-F noon-1am, Sa-Su noon-1:30am.

SOYAMI SUSHI BAR SUSHI $

13 Ringleblum ☎08 649 5511; www.soyami.co.il

A major draw for students, who often sit and chat past dinner, Soyami has the cheapest sushi in town—they claim to have the cheapest prices "anywhere"—and two large outdoor platforms for munching as you watch the world go by.

✤ Next to Little India. $ Su-Th noon-5pm salad, soup, and sushi roll NIS39. Spicy roll NIS35. Beer NIS18. ⏰ Open Su-Th noon-midnight, Sa sunset-midnight.

MIDBAR INTERNATIONAL $$

Mercuz-HaNegev ☎054 633 6020

Don't let the large bar and well-polished tables fool you: this is a student's greasy spoon. Fancier dishes like the chicken salad (NIS30 before 6pm, NIS35 after) may not quite be Midbar's speed, but the large, juicy hamburger (NIS30/35) does not disappoint. Midbar's outlets hidden behind the bar and unfailing internet make it one of the better places to check email or get work done near Ben-Gurion University.

 # Walking up Yitzhak Rager, take a left on Mezada Rd., then your 1st major right turn onto Yitzhak Avinu St. The Mercuz-HaNegev building is 15m uphill on the right. **i** *Main courses NIS5 off before 6pm. Free Wi-Fi.* [$] *Eggrolls NIS10. Hamburger and tortilla NIS35. Pastas NIS30.* ⏰ *Open Su-F noon-midnight, Sa 1pm-midnight.*

NIGHTLIFE

As with most things in Be'er Sheva, nightlife is divided into the student and young adult categories. *Let's Go* focuses on the student side of things, where nightlife is cheapest and most consistent—weekdays are known to be some of the best nights for going out in Be'er Sheva, as students choose drinks and *argilah* over those annoying school duties.

MANGA BAR, CLUB

87 Yitzhak Rager ☎050 883 3170; www.einstein-bar.co.il

The packed outdoor garden is full of students, all in semi-permeable groups of friends talking and standing near the bar or half-dancing to American rock music. The more intimate indoor area has walls covered in newspaper clippings from the last 50 years, and people here are more likely to sit and stay with their groups. This combination makes Manga the best place for a tourist to visit in Be'er Sheva, a good spot to meet locals or just chill with your friends.

 # Walk up Yitzhak Rager. Manga is in the teacher's center on the left, about 75m before Ya'akov Avinu St. **i** *25% discount on food 9-10pm.* [$] *Sushi NIS23-28. Cocktails NIS31-35. Arak NIS22.* ⏰ *Open Su-Th 9pm-late, Sa 9pm-late. Usually closes around 3am.*

EINSTEIN BAR, CLUB

2 Ben-Gurion St. ☎052 500 0822; www.einstein-bar.co.il

The classiest of the student hangouts, Einstein is a slightly more mature nightspot owned by the same team that operates Manga. Cheery synth pop and a red-lit strip extending around the bar—along with chandeliers that sometimes go through wild tye-dye color shifts—lend a faintly futuristic undertone to the otherwise deep wooden bar. Like Manga, the crowd is mostly students (if you've taken an exam that day, you get a free beer), but a few older guys also come here to grab drinks with buddies and relive the good old BGU days. As it gets later, the party moves from chats around the bar to dancing in Einstein's narrow (and therefore intimate) open space.

 # Walk down Yitzhak Rager, take a left onto Ben-Gurion St., and continue until you see a parking lot and the athletic center on the left. Music and a line will be snaking out of Einstein. **i** *For a seat at the bar, arrive before 11:30pm. No English menu, but the bartenders speak English. Sa 50% discount on food.* [$] *Sushi rolls NIS24-38. Cocktails NIS30-41. Shots NIS22, with a beer NIS10.* ⏰ *Open daily 9:45pm-late, occasionally 5 or 6am.*

ROZZA BAR

Mercuz-HaNegev ☎050 904 0101

Students tablehop, suck face on the ledge outside, and get communally plastered at the most quintessentially college bar Be'er Sheva has to offer. Drinks are cheap, music isn't overpowering, and socializing (of all types) grows louder as the night wears on. This may be due to the crazy drink deals, including Sunday "Refill Night" (first beer NIS2 off, each successive beer NIS6) and Thursday "Can't-See-The-Bottom Night," where you get unlimited beer, wine, and sparkling wine for NIS53. You can add vodka and Red Bull to that laundry list for only NIS10 more. Note: *Let's Go* is not liable for any lawsuits resulting from your actions during all-you-can-drink Red Bull and vodka nights.

Walk up Yitzhak Rager, take a left on Mezada Rd., then your 1st large right turn onto Yitzhak Avinu St., and the Mercuz-HaNegev building will be 15m uphill on the right. **i** *DJs spin Su and Th, when there is a NIS20 drink minimum.* $ *Nachos NIS18. Fries NIS25. Goldstar NIS23. Gin and tonic NIS41.* ⏰ *Open Su-Th 9pm-late, F-Sa 10pm-late.*

PUBLO DIVE BAR

14 Alexander Yanai Rd. ☎052 897 1400

Down a tiny road near a sleepy set of student dorms and apartments, a Cambridge-educated metaphysical poetry MA candidate bartends while drinking with regulars. This is not an uncommon scene at Publo, the first and oldest student pub in Be'er Sheva. Staff encourage dancing on the bar during appropriate circumstances—which can arise at any time, as the couples and small groups of friends on the patio unexpectedly transforming into a beer-sodden dance party.

Walking up Yitzhak Rager, take the small road on your left across from the large road leading to the university on the right side of the street. **i** *Hamburger, sandwich, or sausages with fries, a salad, and beer NIS30. Chicken fingers or fried cauliflower with a soft drink NIS37. Buy 0.5L of beer, get a discount on a shot-sized chaser.* $ *Cocktails NIS22-30, 0.5L of beer NIS23-27. Grilled cheese NIS20, NIS3 for additional ingredients.* ⏰ *Open Su-Th 9pm-late, F 10pm-late, Sa 9pm-late. Happy hour Su-Th and Sa 9-10pm.*

MUNCHILLA HOOKAH BAR

50 Arlozorov ☎052 262 6266

A dizzyingly huge *argilah* palace, Munchilla is the premier smoke-and-chill spot in Be'er Sheva. Munchilla is so relaxed that the bar sits about 2 ft. above the ground and people lounge on low-lying couches around it. The seemingly never-ending dimly lit rooms are punctuated by multiple outdoor spots, but Munchilla never feels empty. In fact, it fills up with students most nights, though Saturday is reportedly the main event.

Walk up Yitzhak Rager and take a right onto Ben-Gurion St. After walking through the university, you'll reach a roundabout, and take a right on Arlozorov. **i** *All-you-can-drink beer and wine NIS49 on Tu.* $ *Burger, beer, and fries NIS42. Argilah NIS25.* ⏰ *Open Su-Th 9am-late, Sa 9am-late. Usually closes 2-3am.*

SHAPO RESTAURANT, BAR

81 Herzl St. ☎08 665 1811

Though definitely a restaurant by day, Shapo (a misappropriation of *chapeau*) has an outdoor garden that sports a DJ booth and pool by night. The loud music can be heard in a five-block radius, and, though the pool is somewhat plastic-tub-like, Shapo throws daytime pool parties on Fridays. The indoor area, surprisingly insulated from the noise, is a nice place to get a drink any night, especially on the wooden deck looking onto the street.

Walk toward the Old City, take a left at the intersection of HaAtzma'ut St. and Herzl St., and walk 150m. Shapo is on the left. **i** *Pool party F at noon.* $ *Eggplant lasagna NIS49. Asian noodles with seasonal vegetables NIS45. Cocktails around NIS39.* ⏰ *Open Su-Th 11am-late (usually midnight), F 11am-3pm, Sa sunset-midnight.*

DRAFT BAR AND LOUNGE BAR

Big Center ☎052 312 2120

Proximity to a gym explains a lot about Draft. Americans are supposed to feel at home due to the substantial quantity of bros who pump iron at Great

Shape by day and pound brews at Draft by night. That said, Draft is famous for its elaborate (or just plain excellent) cocktails and is basically a dance bar, so it isn't totally a US frat-import. You can count on a fit clientele.

⚜ *Under the "Great Shape" sign in the Big Center.* *i* *M 9pm-midnight Red Bull vodka and Jäger vodka NIS12. Tu-Sa 9pm-midnight, buy 1 beer, vodka and chaser, or cocktail, get 1 free. Electronica on M. Israeli and Middle Eastern music on Tu.* Ⓢ *Cocktails NIS36-38.* ⌚ *Open M-Sa 9pm-late.*

COCA   BAR
50 Arlozorov   ☎08 623 3303

Irish-themed and sticky-surfaced, Coca is divided between a large outdoor area where small groups of friends chain smoke and an indoor area where groups of girls and guys sit at separate tables talking about talking to each other. It's basically a chill spot to sample homemade beer (NIS25) while munching on margherita pizza (NIS28).

⚜ *In the cluster of bars around Munchilla.* *i* *10% off for students who took an exam that day.* Ⓢ *Roast beef on ciabatta NIS37. Chocolate whiskey NIS10. Arak NIS18.* ⌚ *Open daily noon-late.*

ARTS AND CULTURE

A student town, Be'er Sheva has a theater that students (theoretically) go to. If the Negev Museum of Art wasn't enough culture for you, this your best bet.

BE'ER SHEVA THEATER   THEATER
41 Yitzhak Rager St.   ☎08 626 6444; www.b7t.co.il

Shows typically begin at 9pm Sunday-Thursday, though there are some Saturday night plays as well. The theater's proximity to the Negev Center for the Performing Arts gives it access to a talented crop of young actors for its many different types of productions. Call in advance or check the website for details on what plays are being performed.

⚜ *Walk up Yitzhak Rager St. and take a left at HaMeshahrerim Rd. The theater is the large building on the right.* Ⓢ *Tickets NIS160, students NIS100.* ⌚ *Box office open Su-Th 9am-9pm, F 9am-noon.*

FESTIVALS

The Be'er Sheva River Park Festival, a springtime concert and street fair with the typical games and entertainment, can only get better once the town is finished constructing its 1700-acre central park. In mid-July, the town hosts **Smilansky Fest,** which involves three days of drinking, shopping, and partying on the street. There is also a wine festival along the Be'er Sheva wine route in early September, and other ones could always pop up, so ask around.

ESSENTIALS

practicalities

- **TOURIST OFFICE:** Be'er Sheva no longer has a tourist office, but at **Abraham's Well,** you can find good maps of Be'er Sheva (NIS5). The woman behind the desk is happy to help and can give advice in Hebrew, French, or Spanish (but not English).

- **ATM:** 24hr. ATMs are easy to find on **Yitzhak Rager,** especially on the few blocks after the post office.

- **LAUNDROMAT: Bubbles** offers washing, drying, dry cleaning, and folding. (Intersection of Tchernichowsky St. and Bialik St. ☎08 649 6037 ⚜ Take a left onto Bialik from Yitzhak Rager St. and walk 200m. Ⓢ Wash and dry NIS30, folding NIS10, express cleaning (done within a day) NIS15. ⌚ Open Su-Th 8am-8pm, F 8am-1pm.)

- **INTERNET:** There is no internet cafe in Be'er Sheva, but you can use free Wi-Fi in a classroom at the **Beit Yatziv Youth Hostel** or at a number of restaurants. **Gecko** is probably the nicest of these places.

- **POST OFFICE: Be'er Sheva Post Office.** (9 Yitzhak Rager St. ☎08 628 5846 ✈ About 200m north of the intersection with David Tuvyahu, across the street from a mall. It has red signs and is on the right. ☺ Open Su-Tu 8am-6pm, W 8am-1pm, Th 8am-6pm, F 8am-noon.)

emergency

- **POLICE: Be'er Sheva Police Station.** (30 Herzl St. ☎08 646 2744 ✈ Walking down HaAtzma'ut, take a left once you reach Herzl St. The entrance to the police station is through a gate on the right. ☺ Open 24hr.)

- **LATE-NIGHT PHARMACY: Super-Pharm.** (In the Big Center ☎08 625 6600; www.super-pharm.co.il ☺ Open Su-Th 9am-11pm, F 8am-5pm, Sa 8am-midnight.)

- **HOSPITAL: Be'er Sheva Hospital.** (☎08 640 0111 operator, 08 640 0345 ER ✈ The gigantic structure off Yitzhak Rager St. on Eilat St. ☺ Open Su-Th 8am-4pm, ER 24hr.)

getting there

The major transportation hub of southern Israel, Be'er Sheva is an easy place to reach. **Egged** (☎*2800) and **Metropoline** (☎*5900) both serve Be'er Sheva; the former transports travelers to Be'er Sheva from all over Israel, while the latter mostly circulates the Negev. Egged **buses #446** and **#470** both go from Jerusalem to Be'er Sheva throughout the day, and **# 370** goes from Tel Aviv to Be'er Sheva.

getting around

Can you believe that there is nowhere to rent a bike in the concrete maze that is Be'er Sheva? Neither can *Let's Go*, but there really isn't a single place to pick up a bike just for a few days. Your choices, then, are to take one of the local buses (NIS4.10) or a cab (NIS25). The two main sections of town are only about 1km apart, so the sturdy and sun-screened should have little trouble walking.

be'er sheva

palming it up

Worried about deforestation? Just take a look out the window when driving through Israel. The numerous groves of palm trees lining the side of the road are enough to calm any treehugger. In fact, Israel was the only country to come out of the 20th century with a net gain in the number of trees. Not only are trees more abundant in Israel, but they are also happier and healthier: palm trees in Israel produce over 182kg of dates per year, which is almost 11 times as much as a typical tree.

sde boker ☎08

Skateboarding tweens, dreadlocked 20-somethings, outdoorsy tour guides, and bikers approaching middle age are the most conspicuous residents of this hiking hub. The small town of Sde Boker is defined by the kind of centralized, close-knit community that David Ben-Gurion envisioned as the backbone of Israel—perhaps that's why he retired here. Town-wide open-air concerts happen occasionally on Thursdays, and the domesticated crusties of this desert outpost gather to sway in unison to *oud*, synth, base, and acoustic-guitar jam sessions. What little commercial activity exists here is contained within the small shopping center in the middle of town, which houses Sde Boker's only real restaurant, a bike rental and tour center, and a grass field where gazelles casually graze. Everything shuts down by 10pm, maybe because there is no demand for commerce by then or maybe because the lack of lights makes the stargazing better; in a town like this, the two options are equally likely.

ORIENTATION

From the roundabout outside the gates of the **Midreshet Sde Boker** (Sde Boker Institute), a right leads to the visitors center, a trip back down the road and to the right leads to **Ben-Gurion's Hut,** and going straight ahead and to the right leads to the SPNI Guesthouse and Hostel. Across the street from there and about 30m down is the **commercial center,** where you can find food and public toilets.

ACCOMMODATIONS

There is only one hotel in Sde Boker. Therefore, there are no cheap hotels in Sde Boker. Suck it up, dish out the dough, and stay at the Field School.

FIELD SCHOOL HOSTEL AND GUESTHOUSE — HOSTEL, GUESTHOUSE $$

☎08 659 2100; www.boker.org.il

Hostel rooms are spare but clean, with private baths and six beds. Guesthouse rooms have powerful air-conditioning units, televisions, and two beds. The highlight of both places, each located in its own building on the beautiful Field School Campus, is clearly the spectacular views onto the desert. Considering the price, however, that might sound pretty paltry. But that's what happens when a town has only one hotel—at least this will give you a new appreciation for trust-busting laws.

✈ From the town's entrance, follow the signs and go straight. Take a left at the dead end and then the 1st right, then head straight up on the right side. ℹ No internet. $ Hostel singles Su-Th NIS240, F-Sa NIS290; doubles NIS300/360. Guesthouse singles Su-Th NIS300, F-Sa NIS350; doubles NIS390/460. Prices subject to change with holidays. ⏰ Reception 24hr.

SIGHTS

Sde Boker is a place to go hiking, not sightseeing. However, if you are injured, are scared of hiking boots, or have a deep personal love for the diminutive David Ben-Gurion, then the old man's hut is worth a look. There is also a large collections of ruins in nearby Avdat, as well as some options for the especially enthusiastic.

BEN-GURION'S HUT — HOUSE

☎08 656 0469

Do you want to go to the house of a famous person? Is there some kind of "aura" you feel when you walk in the same place they walked? Good, because this is a worthwhile pilgrimage only if you feel that way and/or have always been really into David Ben-Gurion (what a hunk!). You can see his retirement house as he left it, absorb the inspirational quotes that line the walkways, and read about his life in the exhibit adjacent to the home.

From the bus stop in front of the gas station between Kibbutz Sde Boker and Midreshet Sde Boker, walk up to the left of the gas station and take another left when you see the museum on your left. ℹ *Guided tours are available for groups of 15 or more if you call ahead.* $ *NIS12; students, children, and seniors NIS9. Tour NIS2.* ⏰ *Open Su-Th 8:30am-4pm, F and holiday eves 8:30am-2pm, Sa and holidays 10am-4pm.*

AVDAT RUINS

☎08 655 1511

Though historically most important for its enshrinement in the 1973 classic *Jesus Christ Superstar*, Avdat dates back to the fourth century BCE. Nabateans initially used the area as a perch to spy on and supply caravans on the Petra-Gaza trade route, but it was then captured by the Romans and later used by the Byzantines. Nabateans continued to live here even after their temple was converted into a church—whose ruins remain—until the seventh century, when an earthquake destroyed the city. Residents of Avdat then turned to wine production, and wine presses are still evident here from the Byzantine period. The church, dedicated to fourth-century martyr St. Theodore, exhibits marble tombstones with Greek inscriptions on its floor.

Take bus #60, which passes Avdat on the way to Mitzpe Ramon, and make sure to tell the driver that you're going to the Nabatean archaeological site, not Ein Avdat. $ *NIS25, students NIS21, children NIS13.* ⏰ *Open Apr-Sept Su-Th 8am-5pm, F 8am-4pm; Oct-Mar Su-Th 8am-4pm, F 8am-3pm.*

BEN-GURION HERITAGE INSTITUTE RESEARCH CENTER, MOVIE, GRAVE

Ben-Gurion University of the Negev ☎08 659 2100

The movie is a little preposterous—two young adults are entered into a TV contest to answer biographical questions about David Ben-Gurion, the winner gets a scholarship to Oxford, and there are many dramatic close-ups, futuristic special effects, and the constant drone of bombastic music. Nonetheless, a visit to the revered leader's grave overlooking the desert can be a great and meditative experience. Historians also work here, doing research at Ben-Gurion's archive, which is housed at the institute.

Immediately bear right after entering the gate and keep right. $ *Free.* ⏰ *Open Su-Th 8am-2pm, Sa 8am-2pm.*

NATIONAL SOLAR ENERGY CENTER RESEARCH CENTER

Ben-Gurion University of the Negev ☎08 059 6934; www.bgu.ac.il/solar

A pioneer in solar power development and, of course, solar-powered itself, the Solar Energy Center can make for a fascinating visit if you call ahead and schedule a tour.

When you enter Midreshet Sde Boker, bear left and continue, taking a right when the road dead ends. You will eventually end up in the college complex. The solar energy center is at its end.

HIKING

Unless you're on a focused Ben-Gurion pilgrimage, your trip to Sde Boker is probably due to its proximity to the mountainous Negev. At least, we know you're not coming here for the food or luxury housing. **SPNI** and **Geofun** both offer tours of the surrounding trails and wilderness, but no matter how you approach the outdoors, it's important to remember to bring lots of water, wear head and neck coverings, and have a map. Before heading out, go to the **visitors center** for free maps, up-to-date information about the different paths, and suggestions based on your hiking preferences.

EIN AVDAT NATIONAL PARK WATERFALL, OBSERVATION POINT

☎08 655 5684; www.parks.org.il

It may be in the desert, but Ein Avdat National Park hides tropical trees, mosses, ferns, and maidenhair, pools full of algae, and steep canyons. The main trail, marked by helpful green signs, winds through all these features. Starting from the lower parking lot, you'll see palms around the Ein Mor spring and come to an intersection, at which point you can cross the river bed and walk along the river to see a natural waterfall. Head back to the intersection and climb the stairs to head to the top of the waterfall. Continue along the path and notice the high caves carved in the sides of canyons, which used to serve as the homes of Byzantine monks. Keep going until the observation point, where you can see striking cliffs.

*🚏 Go through the northern entrance between kilometer markers 130 and 131 on Hwy. 40, turn east (as a sign will tell you), then follow route delineated on the map you should get at the Parks Information Center. **i** Getting to the upper gate requires climbing ladders which you cannot go down, so allot at least 1hr. for the trip up and then another 2-3hr. for the return. If you stop at the dam and head back, you will have done a nice and easy 1.4km hike. $ NIS27, students NIS22, under 18 NIS14. ⏰ Open daily in summer 8am-3:45pm; in winter 8am-2:45pm.*

KARAKASH DESERT

This green-marked 1½-2hr. hike passes over fairly even desert terrain and culminates at an intersection with other trails. Most interesting among them is definitely **Kharim,** one of the few parks in Israel open at night. Some experienced hikers say that if you sit on the white sand at night, light from the moon allows you to read without a flashlight. To reach Kharim—marked by blue signs—take a right at the intersection and stay right as another path opens up on your way to a campground; it will take at least another 3hr. If you want to camp a little closer by, take a left at the intersection; after about 1hr., you'll reach a site.

🚏 To begin the hike, turn left on the Be'er Sheva-Eilat highway from the end of the Midreshet entrance road and walk 1km; the path is marked green on your left. There is a sign. ⏰ Open daily from 1hr. after sunrise to 1hr. before sunset, by which time you must be in a camp or off the trail completely.

EIN AKEV POOLS

If you're one of those single-minded hikers who doesn't stop walking, Ein Akev will take you around 2½hr. in each direction. Assuming, however, that you decide to chill for a while or admire the pool, it can take much longer. After walking 1km, you will reach a junction—all of its trails end up at a pool. On the way you can see desert gazelles, multiple species of vultures, and a whole host of sand creatures both rare and common. Once at the pool, feel free to swim, but don't jump in. If you head out early enough, hikers report that you can see animals drinking at the spring.

*🚏 Walk down the winding road from the Midreshet toward Ein Avdat and follow the red signs just beyond the end of the road that lead to Ein Akev. **i** This is a long hike, and it can be especially hard in the desert during the summer. If you choose to do it, bring at least 5L of water per person. ⏰ Open daily from 1hr. after sunrise to 1hr. before sunset, by which time you must be in a camp or off the trail completely.*

FOOD

Hummus Land would be one of the better restaurants in most small Israeli towns, but it's the best in Sde Boker—mostly because it is also the only restaurant. You can also eat at the Field School dining hall, but it is more cafeteria than restaurant, with the exact level of quality which that implies.

HUMMUS LAND

HUMMUS, FALAFEL $

Commercial Center

☎08 653 2118

For the only legitimate restaurant in Sde Boker, Hummus Land is unnecessarily great. The hummus is creamy, and, according to the menu, the "most popular" option is to have it with *ful* (fava beans) for NIS25. The pita is thick and warm, but the best is the falafel, fried much more thoroughly and carefully than at most other places. It always comes hot and with a few plates of sauces and vegetables. Eighties power ballads blast from speakers most of the time, which creates an atmosphere both absurd and cheery.

🚏 Across the street from the Field School. Walk past the green patch of grass to find the restaurant at the opposite end of the circular commercial zone. ***i*** *Internet available.* *[$] Falafel sandwich NIS14. Espresso NIS9.* *⏰ Open Su-Th 10am-6pm.*

five fun hummus facts

It's likely that you'll find yourself up to the neck in this chickpea dish during your time in Israel. But is this reason for complaint? Hell no! Prepare to become a hummus connoisseur with this crash course in hummus-ology.

1. Hummus is actually just the Arabic word for "chickpeas." The dish's proper name is *hummus bi tahina*, or "chickpeas with tahini."

2. The Oxford English Dictionary records that the word's first usage in English was in a 1955 cookbook.

3. Hummus has been around much longer than that. Recipes from 13th-century Egypt tell of a similar dish made from chickpeas and vinegar, while the earliest known mention of hummus as we know it dates to 18th-century Damascus.

4. As if the Middle East didn't already have enough conflict, there's a long-running dispute over which country invented the dish. Lebanon even petitioned the European Commission to give hummus protected geographic status, meaning that only Lebanese hummus would count as the real thing. This campaign was not successful.

5. Israelis eat twice as much hummus per capita as the citizens of other neighboring countries. However, Lebanon can claim the Guinness world record for largest dish of hummus ever made, weighing in at a whopping 22,994 lbs. Next up? World's largest pita pocket, so they have something to eat all that hummus with.

FIELD SCHOOL DINING HALL

CAFETERIA $$

☎08 653 2016

This place will remind you of your high school cafeteria—the only difference might be that this time your parents aren't helping you out with milk money. Food comes in tin trays and is unfailingly edible, which is probably less than you'd expect from the price.

🚏 From the guesthouse, walk parallel to the front gate past the community center. The dining hall is on the right. ***i*** *Lunch has meat, dinner is vegetarian.* *[$] Lunch NIS47. Dinner NIS42.* *⏰ Open daily 12:30-1:30pm and 6-7:30pm*

ESSENTIALS

practicalities

- **TOURIST OFFICES:** The **Visitors Center** is the best place for information about and suggestions of specific hikes. (Exit the *midresha,* take an immediate left and walk about 50m. *i* Maps and hiking gear available. Open daily in summer 8am-5pm; in winter 8am-4pm.) **Geofun Bikes** offers guided bike tours, maps, bike rentals, and detailed advice about the area. (Commercial Center ☎08 655 3350; www.geofun.co.il Across the street and about 30m up from the guesthouse. $ Bike rental NIS80 per day. Detailed map NIS55. Open Su-Th 9am-6pm, F 8:30am-2pm.) **SPNI** also organizes tours, offers advice, and sells maps. (☎08 653 2016; www.boker.org.il In the office building in front of the guesthouse.)
- **ATM:** **Tsin,** the town supermarket, offers an ATM service at the counter. (Commercial Center Across the street and 30m north from the guesthouse. Open Su-Th 8am-7pm, F 8am-2pm.)
- **PUBLIC TOILET:** There is a public bathroom in the commercial center across the street and 30m north from the guesthouse.
- **INTERNET:** **Hummus Land** is the only place in town with internet.

emergency

- **PHARMACY:** Although the town has no official pharmacy, the supermarket **Tsin** has a row of pharmaceutical goods in the back. (Commercial Center Across the street and 30m north from the guesthouse. Open Su-Th 8am-7pm, F 8am-2pm.)

getting there

BY BUS

The best way to get to Sde Boker is on **bus #60,** whose nearest hub is in Be'er Sheva. A ride to Sde Boker costs NIS15. The bus stops in three locations in the area: the first at the Sde Boker kibbutz, the second near a gas station outside of it, and the third at the Midreshet Sde Boker, on which *Let's Go* listings are centered.

getting around

BY BIKE

Rent a bike from **Geofun Bikes** (NIS80 per day). Other than that, the best ways are walking and driving. *Let's Go* does not recommend hitchhiking, but it is how many of the locals travel.

mitzpe ramon ☎08

For tourists, Mitzpe Ramon is less notable as a town and more as a crater—more specifically, Ramon Crater (Makhtesh Ramon), the largest crater in the world. It is 40km long, 9km wide, and 400m deep and is punctuated by bizarre mushroom-shaped mounds, clay hills of fantastic reds and yellows, and rainbow sands. Basically, it looks like a chunk of Mars grafted onto the planet. The stark desert landscape, home to four different climate zones, also hides rock formations that are millions of years old and like nothing else in the world. It may look barren, but as you try one of the many hikes in and around the crater, you will discover a world of life, from desert springs to stalking scorpions.

And, though it is still in an embryonic stage, the town is also growing to

accommodate the increase in tourism that is making it a worthy destination in its own right. The industrial zone, long a failed commercial venture, is becoming a neighborhood more and more crowded with small shops and art spaces. A gigantic bocce ball court is under construction; a French restaurant (run by actual French people!) opened recently; and development is evident wherever you walk.

ORIENTATION

The central roundabout borders the gas station and functions as the intersection between **Route 40** and **Ben-Gurion Avenue,** the main road in town. Most services, including restaurants, the post office, the supermarket, and the library, lie along Ben-Gurion. By going up **En Zik Street** you can reach **Ramon Street,** which is the surest path toward finding the industrial zone, home of many of the newer restaurants and art spaces in Mitzpe Ramon (referred to by residents as simply "Mitzpe"). By heading off Ben-Gurion and following the signs near the main roundabout, you can find the visitors center that is currently being renovated and nearby Bio Ramon, which is the acting information center.

ACCOMMODATIONS

Some hotels in Mitzpe Ramon are enough of a reason to come to Mitzpe Ramon. **Silent Arrow,** secluded, communal, and volunteer-operated, provides an entire lifestyle rather than just a living space, and the **Desert Eco Lodge** takes a philosophical approach to its environment; its houses are made almost entirely from recycled goods, and it relies on solar energy.

ADAMA — GUESTHOUSE, DANCE COMPANY $

4 Har Boker ☎08 659 5190; www.adama.org.il

Walk into Adama on your way to bed, and you may pass a professional dance rehearsal, children's karate class, loud party with an open bar and free sushi, group of old ladies and/or tweens sitting in a circle doing yoga, or anything else you could imagine happening in a post-industrial artistic warehouse in the desert. The outdoor sitting area is shaded with large sheets hanging from the ceiling and has low-lying couches, large round and rectangular tables, and space to stand and chat with the different groups of people flitting through Adama at all hours, making it the perfect place to unwind after a long day of desert trekking. Sleeping on a mattress may be modest, but it's the best deal for budget travelers who want to have Wi-Fi and be near the valuable little urbanity that Mitzpe Ramon has to offer.

From the main roundabout, take the 2nd left heading toward Be'er Sheva and then the next 2nd left. There is a big sign on the right. ℹ *Free Wi-Fi. Dance workshops, meals other than breakfast, and performances can be arranged by calling in advance. If staying in the dorm, bring your own linens and towel.* $ *Dorms NIS80, with breakfast NIS100. Little hut rooms (with breakfast) NIS175, for 2 NIS315.*

SILENT ARROW — HUTS $

☎052 661 1561; www.silentarrow.co.il

The lack of electricity or any nearby structure makes Silent Arrow truly silent, an unparalleled spot for stargazing, contemplation, and intimate meals. Careful construction means that the small huts have space for proper beds. The huts are cool in the summer and warm in the winter, when it sometimes snows, causing guests to huddle around the Bedouin-style stove in the common area tent. Volunteers come from around the world to help clean and maintain the site in exchange for a free bed, and it's normal to meet bearded world travelers taking a month off from adventuring for some quiet work and the chance to scrutinize the surrounding desert expanse.

Leave Mitzpe Ramon proper by going downhill on Ben-Gurion in the opposite direction of Eilat. The highway will turn into a small road. Continue for around 2km. There will be a sign on the right pointing out Silent Arrow. ***i*** *Only candles light the area at night, so bring a flashlight. Kitchen, open for guest use, has a portable stove and standard utensils. Jeep, camel, and walking tours can be arranged.* $ *Mattress in a dorm or onsite camping NIS80; private tent NIS120 per person for 2, NIS100 per person for 3-4 people. Cash only.*

DESERT ECO LODGE HUTS $$

☎08 649 1003; www.desert-nomads.com

Of the many hut-based, nature-friendly sleeping arrangements in Mitzpe Ramon, the Desert Eco Lodge is possibly the most devoted to lessening its environmental impact—so much so, in fact, that it looks like a redesigned, recycling-friendly shantytown. Huts are made with mud, scrap metal frames, scrap marble tile floors, scrap wood, and (other than a few glass windows), old glass bottles let in light. The campground is mostly solar powered, which means that greedy showerers will be limiting the amount of hot water for subsequent water-users. Large and comfortable indoor and outdoor sitting areas provide an idyllic view onto the Ramon Crater.

Just opposite Har Ardon St. beyond the industrial zone. ***i*** *Wi-Fi available in the common space and occasionally in some tents. Jeep tours, bike tours, and bike rental available.* $ *Mattress in the dorm tent NIS90, ages 2-12 NIS60; 1-person private tent NIS185, 2-person (for couples) NIS270. Prices include breakfast; ask if you would prefer a cheaper room without breakfast. Firewood is also sold at a small premium.* ⏰ *Reception 5-8pm.*

IBIKE HOTEL GUESTHOUSE $$$

2 Har Ardon ☎052 436 7878; www.ibike.co.il

Menachem and Aviva's pre-retirement project is to run this guesthouse, and, in doing so, to popularize this lesser-known region of the Negev by hosting tourists and taking them on hikes. They are both accredited tour guides and very enthusiastic about outdoor exploration, as well as about cooking breakfast for their guests.

30m down Har Ardon from Hakaze in the industrial zone. ***i*** *Massive breakfast included. Free Wi-Fi. Bocce court, coffeeshop, and subterranean fishtank all under construction at time of writing.* $ *Singles NIS345; doubles NIS420. Bikes NIS70 for a ride, NIS100 overnight. Call in advance to find out prices for tours.*

SPNI FIELD SCHOOL GUESTHOUSE HOTEL $$

☎08 658 6101

Ibex graze undisturbed around trees, the view of Ramon Crater is astonishing, and the hotel is within a 30min. walk from town yet manages to avoid urban noise. That said, NIS265 is pretty steep for the budget traveler—the rooms here are modest and cozy, but, well, you can get a mattress elsewhere for less than NIS100.

Walk about 1km down the road from Silent Arrow, then take a left at the crossroads. ***i*** *Internet is available at night in common area.* $ *Singles Su-Th NIS265, with breakfast NIS295; F-Sa NIS345. Doubles Su-Th NIS295/335; F-Sa NIS385. F-Sa breakfast included. Non-members can usually, but not always, get these member prices. Call in advance to make sure that these prices are available.*

BE'EROT CAMPGROUND CAMPGROUND $

☎08 658 6713; beerot@netvision.net

Private bathrooms, hot water, electricity, grills available for free: in camping terms, the works. So what if it's 13km from town? The only legal place to sleep in the Ramon Crater, Be'erot Campground is affordable and provides enough for complete comfort.

Travel 9km on the road toward Eilat, then take a left at the sign for Be'erot Campground and continue for 4km. $ *Camping NIS35, in Be'erot tent NIS50; 6-person cabin NIS500. Breakfast NIS40. Small meal NIS40, large NIS85. Firewood NIS35.*

SIGHTS

Hikes and animals—it's called nature, and that's what you can find at Mitzpe Ramon. When you get bored of the former (the main attraction), check out the latter. Its especially important to take advantage of what may be your only opportunity to rent an alpaca to have lunch with.

BIO RAMON ZOO

Ma'ale Ben-Tor St. ☎08 658 8755; www.parks.co.il

Beetle exoskeletons stick to the web of the black widow spider which has sucked out their insides. The shed skin of a black desert cobra hangs from a tree as the snake slithers underneath. Bio Ramon staff prod a fattail scorpion out of its daytime hibernation so that it will lift its tail and flex its claws. In short, Bio Ramon is great for anyone who appreciates the nitty behind the gritty desert. Maybe best among the desert animals here is the Old World Porcupine, whose quills—jet black near its head, bright white and sticking out far beyond its frame in the back—are homologous with its New World non-cousin.

🚌 Follow the signs to the visitors' center from Ben-Gurion Ave. at the end of town closer to Eilat. **i** *Free tours given by Bio Ramon staff can range from 20min. to 1hr. depending on interest level of visitors. Free informational movie. Botanical garden under construction.* [$] *NIS21, students NIS18, ages 5-18 NIS9.* 🕒 *Open in summer Su-Th 8am-5pm, F 8am-4pm; in winter Su-Th 8am-4pm, F 8am-3pm.*

israel national trail

Israel is obviously full of biblical sites. But you know what's also pretty biblical? Walking. Walking a lot. Fortunately, Israel's got you covered on that one too: the Israel National Trail spans the entire length of the country, from Dan by the Lebanese border to Eilat on the Red Sea. The 597-mi. trail zigzags through the country, providing an unparalleled opportunity to enjoy all that Israel has to offer, from blooming valleys and rolling fields to steep mountains and ocean bluffs. There's also a stretch of austere desert in the Negev if you want to wander as the Israelites did, preferably without getting lost for 40 years. The trail can be easily reached by car or public transportation at many points along the route, so you can pick a segment that strikes your fancy or attempt the whole route–it takes most people 40-60 days to complete. The path is clearly marked along its whole length, and has plenty of places to stop and camp out under either the stars or a hostel roof. Definitely a better deal than they got in either Testament.

ALPACA FARM FARM

☎08 658 8047; www.alpaca.co.il

Alpacas are much like oversized, slow-moving stuffed animals that take a mild interest in humans. Native to South America, the alpacas in question here were brought to Israel by enterprising vegetarians who wanted to produce wool in the Negev. Guided tours around the farm are free with entry, but much more fun (and simply hilarious) are the rides for children and alpaca picnics. Using your alpaca like a mule, the two of you walk down to a forest in the crater (NIS60) and enjoy a lunch provided by the farm (NIS20-40). You can also feed the alpacas for free—no matter how fun you find it, the lip-licking alpacas clearly enjoy it more.

🚌 Leave Mitzpe Ramon proper by going downhill on Ben-Gurion in the opposite direction of Eilat. The highway turns into a small road; continue down it for around 3km to reach a

crossroads. The Field School is to the left, and the Alpaca Farm to the right. ℹ *Horseback rides can also be arranged to the crater; call in advance for more info.* [$] *Entrance NIS25.* ⏰ *Open daily in summer 8:30am-6:30pm; in winter 8:30am-4:30pm.*

HIKING

What, you thought people only came to Israel for the religious epiphanies and falafel? The Negev desert has some of the greatest trails in the Middle East, but be warned: trails are only open from 1hr. after sunrise to 1hr. before sunset. Plan accordingly unless you want some impromptu "Kumbaya" time with desert gazelles. And remember—you're in the desert. Wear a hat, bring much more water than you think you need, and always, always get up-to-date information on trails and conditions before heading out into the wilderness.

HAR ARDON

A difficult but rewarding trail takes you on a hike that ends with the greatest view of Ramon Crater imaginable. The top of Har Ardon (Mount Ardon) is actually the center of the crater, meaning you can see rainbow sands all around you from the summit. The hike takes about 7hr., so start as early as possible in order to avoid the miserable (and possibly dangerous) midday heat.

🚏 *Drive on Hwy. 40 toward Eilat for 15-20min. and take a left at the sign for Be'erot Campground. Follow the road and continue onto Saharonim Plateau. Then take the Spice Route (also called the Incense Route) back toward Be'erot. After 1.5km, turn right onto the red trail, then take another right onto the black trail for hikers only. Your next right, onto a blue-marked trail, will lead up to the observation point.*

WADI ARDON

As if ruins from the ancient Nabateans weren't cool enough, the Wadi Ardon (Ardon Valley) path also winds around crystallized magma that marks the former insides of a long-deceased volcano. You also pass through the Parsat Nekarot river bed, where striking cliffs create small enclaves that make for ideal rest stops. Ein Saharonim, the nearby spring, rarely has water—particularly during the summer—but at we're pretty sure the millennia-old ruins will be there year-round.

🚏 *The trail begins in the Be'erot Campground. Walk along the black trail for ½km and turn right onto the red-marked dirt road. After another 1km, take the dirt road on the left (marked in black) to reach the parking lot. From the lot, continue on to Wadi Ardon. If you want to continue from here, go on the black trail immediately to the left and continue until you reach the intersection of a red and blue trail; take the blue one.*

HAR HARUT

Hike along this circular path for views of Wadi Ardon, the Saharonim Plateau, and Har Harut (Harut Mountain).

🚏 *Begin at the black trail from Be'erot, but immediately take the blue trail on the left, which leads to Har Ardon. You'll reach a crossroads; the blue trail goes to Har Ardon, and the red trail to Lavan River. Take the red trail, and at the river find the gray-marked trail that goes up Har Harut. Then head back down along the red trail where it connects with the black. Continuing on this will land you first at the Ardon River and finally at the Saharonim Plateau.*

HAR SAHARONIM

Catch a great view from the top of Har Saharonim (which means "Crescent Mountain") and then pass Ein Saharonim—an often waterless spring in the middle of this desert—on your way back down.

🚏 *Start at the western side of the crater (closest to the main road) and take a right at Be'erot Campground. Turn left onto the black-marked Petroleum Trail. After about 40min., follow the steep hill past the green trail and turn left at the green marker for Har Saharonim. From there, follow the blue path to Parsat Nekarot in reverse, or double back to the road leading to Be'erot.*

CARPENTRY PATH

Also known as HaMinsarah, this generally gentle 2-3hr. hike passes prism-like rocks that hikers think are shaped like carpenter's tools—though it's possible that they've just been in the desert too long.

Pass the visitors' center, staying on the promenade. After you pass 2 iron ball sculptures, take the green-marked trail that descends from the cliff. Continue following the green trail. A dirt road heads east toward the highway.

RAMON'S TOOTH

Ramon's Tooth (*Shen Ramon* in Hebrew) is a huge black rock formation that stands near the southern wall of the crater. It's a different color from the surrounding sandstone because, well, it's not sandstone—this **dragon**-like ridge was formed when magma cooled undergound and then rose to the surface around the same time as the crater was created. The full hike takes about 5hr.

From the green-marked Carpentry Path, take the red turnoff that heads south. The trail eventually passes the Ammonite Wall before ending at the highway.

AMMONITE WALL

Before Ramon's Crater was the parched sand and stone it is today, the area was actually under an ocean: millions of years ago, unimaginable animals wandered the deep, including ammonites and gigantic cephalopods. All that's left of these deep-sea denizens are their fossilized shells. Though the largest specimens have been stolen from this natural wall in the Ramon wasteland, impressive examples remain.

Drive south on Hwy. 40 to the edge of Ramon Crater. There will be signs on the road pointing to the Ammonite Wall. A red-marked path marks the 10-20min. hike to the wall, which is on the right.

FOOD

Most of Mitzpe Ramon's cheap eats can be found near the **supermarket** (☎08 658 8406 🕰 Open Su-Tu 8am-8pm, W 8am-8:30pm, Th 7:30am-9:30pm, F 7:30am-3:30pm.), and it doesn't take too much exploring to find a standard falafel and shawarma meal.

HAKAZE — INTERNATIONAL $$

2 Har Ardon — ☎08 659 5273

Between the smoke breaks and working on a puzzle, the Hakaze chef cooks up the best and most inventive food in town. The menu changes every day but is consistently excellent: a fresh chicken curry (NIS50) spiced to an ideal tang could come one day, while the next could feature a vegetable quiche (NIS50) thick with different vegetables and buttery crumbled bread. It's hard to make a wrong choice here—the real dilemma is just convincing yourself to leave. The peaceful outdoor garden features large couches and a beautiful view of the desert.

Har Ardon is the backend street of the industrial zone, and Hakaze is at the corner farthest from town, about 50m from the gas station. i Free Wi-Fi. $ Hummus NIS26. Soup of the day NIS25. 🕰 Open Su-Th noon-8:30pm, F-Sa noon-10pm.

CAFE NETTO — CAFE $$

5 Nahal Tsia — ☎08 658 7777; www.ert.co.il

The only legitimate cafe in town, Netto is a hub for bespectacled readers of the newspaper, aimless teenagers, and Israeli soldiers. It's the kind of place where two female soldiers may sit and talk to the old man at the next table over for hours on end as they all enjoy above-average lattes (NIS13) and crumbling chocolate pound cake (two for NIS16). Two small bookshelves contain an assortment of books in Hebrew and English—a cursory glance of the latter could find *The Swiss Family Robinson* and *Huckleberry Finn*—that are all sold for NIS20.

⇆ From Ben-Gurion Ave., walk 100m down Ziyya St. [i] Free Wi-Fi. Take-away available. Credit card min. NIS25. [$] Omelette NIS59. ⏰ Open Su-Th 8am-10:30pm, F 8am-6pm, Sa 9am-10:30pm.

CHEZ EUGENE FRENCH $$$

8 Har Ardon St. ☎08 653 9595; www.mitzperamonhotel.co.il

Just 10 months old at time of writing, Chez Eugene seeks to introduce a level of quality and price otherwise unknown in Mitzpe Ramon and the surrounding kibbutzim and towns. It does so with no small success—the Chez Eugene shawarma, constructed from grilled chicken thigh over flat beans and pureed eggplant (NIS69), is an inventive and tasty interpretation, even if purists scoff at its lack of week-old cabbage. A few local families and a good number of tourists have already caught on, and it's a worthwhile stop for those who can afford haute French-Israeli fusion.

⇆ On Har Ardon just past its intersection with Har Arif. [i] Free Wi-Fi. Menu changes regularly. [$] Soup du jour NIS32. Chocolate fondant with carmelized fruit NIS36. ⏰ Open Su-Th 7-10pm, F noon-4pm and 7-10pm, Sa noon-10pm.

HAVIT INTERNATIONAL $$

8 Nahal HaHamov ☎08 658 8229

A little overpriced for what it offers, Havit is a reliable choice; its chicken breast with vegetables and rice (NIS68) is pounded thin and cooked well, but it's more in the category of sustenance than fine dining. The real draw of the place is its great patio, which overlooks the desert and yields particularly beautiful views of the setting sun.

⇆ From Ben-Gurion Ave., walk 100m down Ziyya St. Havit is next to Cafe Netto. [$] Pizza NIS38. Duck breast sandwich NIS48. Smoked salmon plate NIS70. ⏰ Open Su-Th 9am-midnight.

ESSENTIALS

practicalities

- **TOURIST OFFICE:** At time of writing, the information center was undergoing major renovation that would take approximately another year. The **Bio Ramon Zoo** acts as the information center, and its extremely knowledgeable staff can provide information about sights, lodgings, and hikes. They offer maps of hiking and biking trails and of the city.
- **ATM:** There is a 24hr. ATM at the gas station at the edge of town. It's around the main roundabout visible when you first enter or as you head toward Eilat.
- **PUBLIC POOL:** ⇆ On Ben-Gurion Ave. on the left before the shopping center and post office. [$] NIS45, foreign students NIS35. ⏰ Open Su-Th 9am-9pm, F 9am-4-:15pm, Sa 9am-9pm.
- **INTERNET: Mitzpe Ramon Library** has a wide selection of English and Hebrew books as well as computers with internet. (☎08 658 8442, ext. 6; sifriamizpe@gmail.com ⇆ Go uphill on Ben-Gurion Ave. toward town. The library is marked by a red apple sign and is on the left before Nahal Zihor appears on the right. [$] Internet NIS10 per day. ⏰ Open in summer Su-Th 1-7pm; in winter Su 3-7pm, M-Tu 9am-noon and 3-7pm, W 3-7pm, Th 9am-noon and 3-7pm.)
- **POST OFFICE: Mitzpe Ramon Post Office.** (Ben-Gurion Ave. ☎08 658 8416; www.israelpost.com ⇆ On the left after En Zik St. and the public pool. The post office is behind a parking lot around the corner on the left. ⏰ Open Su 8am-6pm, M-Tu 8am-12:30pm, W 8am-1:30pm and 3:30-6pm, Th 8am-6pm, F 8am-noon.)

emergency

- **EMERGENCY SERVICES:** The **police station** and the **emergency medical center** are both located at 1 Nahal Hava, adjacent to the fire department, and can be reached at ☎100 and 101. They are both open 24hr.

getting there

Apart from renting a car or hitchhiking, there are two ways to get to Mitzpe Ramon: by **Egged bus #392** or by **Metropoline bus #60.** Schedules and prices tend to change, but there are usually more Metropoline buses than Egged buses. Both lines originate in Be'er Sheva: the #392 goes through the town on its way to Eilat, while the #60 ends in Mitzpe Ramon. Even after checking the schedule, it's important to note that specific times represent an approximately 10min. window; it's best to show up at the stop before the advertised arrival.

getting around

Most people walk around Mitzpe Ramon, and it is small enough that walking may be the best option. However, long trudges up hills can become painful in the afternoon sun, and walking to some of the farther sights—or from some of the accommodations—would require you to spend a large fraction of your day in transit. As such, it might be better to rent a bike, which you can do through **iBike Hotel** (2 Har Ardon ☎052 436 7878; www.ibike.co.il $ Ride NIS70, overnight rental NIS100. ⏰ iBike also operates as a hotel, so its owners should be around most of the day; call in advance to make sure.) Some travelers say hitchhiking is also a viable mode of travel in the area, but *Let's Go* does not recommend hitchhiking.

EILAT

Lick your finger and hold it to the wind: what's that strange thickness in the air? Is it humidity? Sweat? Vaporized *arak*? After about a day in Eilat, you'll realize that it's some combination of the three, and what you make of that fact seems to be more about taste and less about truth. Some treat the city as an oasis of cocktails and Coppertone in the Negev, an adventureland perfect for snorkeling through coral reefs by day and stumbling through bars by night. Families make the trek to Eilat in search of tans and tranquility. And outdoorsy purists see Eilat as the Negev's hairy backside, an overpriced urban cesspool whose only half-redeeming quality is the overpopulated beach.

Regardless, they all come. Weekends, especially in July through September when school is out, turn Eilat into a crazed zoo, and eager hotels and restaurants jack up their prices in response. The same goes for most Israeli holidays, which may be why real devotees say the city is never better than in the dead of winter, when the promenade empties out and the hustle, grease, and phone jabbering is replaced by a few contemplative beachgoers, making it an entirely new city.

greatest hits

- **GOT MILK.** Learn to milk a cow at Kibbutz Yotvata (p. 327) and try their chocolate milk. If you still want to drink milk, that is...
- **UNDER THE SEA.** Scuba and snorkel in Eilat with Eyal Diving Service (p. 328).
- **GO GOURMET.** Take that cute lifeguard to Eddie's Hide-Away (p. 331) for a much deserved (and delicious) splurge.

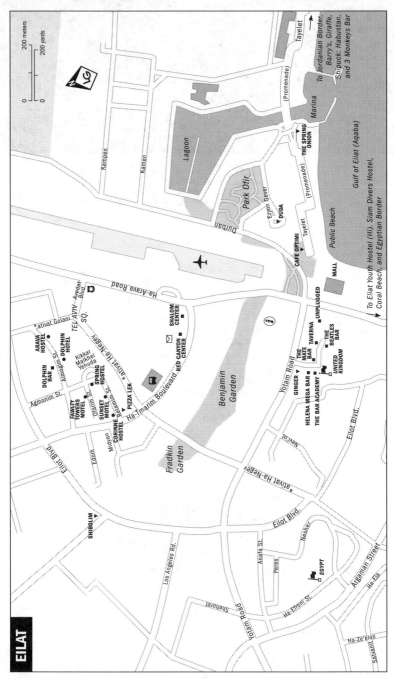

To Jordanian Border,
Barry's, Giraffe,
Shipuck: Habustan,
and 3 Monkeys Bar

To Jordanian Border, Tavelet

Marina

Gulf of Eilat (Aqaba)

THE SPRING
ONION

Ezyon Gever

DUDA

(Promenade)

Tavelet

Park Ofir

Lagoon

Durban

Public Beach

To Eilat Youth Hostel (HI), Siam Divers Hostel,
Coral Beach, and Egyptian Border

Kampen

Kamen

CAFE OPTIMI

MALL

Ha-Arava Road

TEL AVIV
SQ.

Avedat Blvd.

ativat Golani

ARAVA
HOSTEL

DOLPHIN
HOTEL

DOLPHIN
BAR

Almogim St.

Agmonim St.

Kikkar
Malkhei
Yehuda

SPRING
HOSTEL

SHALOM
CENTER

RED CANYON
CENTER

ativat Ha-Negev

Ha-Tmarim Boulevard

Ofarim St.

FAWLTY
TOWERS
MOTEL

SUNSET
MOTEL

CORINNE
HOSTEL

PIZZA LEK

Midyan

Edom

SHIBOLIM

Benjamin
Garden

Fradkin
Garden

UNPLUGGED

Yotam Road

TAVERNA

THE
MATE
BAR

GINGER

HELENA MEGA BAR

THE BAR ACADEMY

UNITED
KINGDOM

THE
BEATLES
BAR

Nevi'im

ativat Ha-Negev

Eilot Blvd.

Eilot Blvd.

Los Angeles Rd.

Nesher

Anata St.

Peres

EGYPT

Ha-Efroni St.

Argaman Street

Ha-Ela

Shenher

Yotam Road

Ha-Ze'elon

Salvanit

0   200 meters
0   200 yards

student life

For the more adventurous–and slightly more affluent–reader, Eilat is the place to explore the depths. Take your pick from the multiple diving services, snorkeling and scuba diving opportunities, beaches, boats, and even dolphins that all let you experience the **Coral Beach Reserve.**

Eilat has also created a fairly vibrant nightlife scene. **Joya** has gimmicks including rotating drink deals, Top 40 night, and live shows. If you really want to show your colors, though, take a trip into **Gaby's Pub** and see if you can keep up with the Irish. Then pass out at **Corinne's Hostel,** the ultimate Eilat youth hostel. Treat yourself to a mouth-watering burger at **Agadir** or save your shekels and go to the **Bakery,** a shop so delicious that it needs no introduction, or more complex name.

orientation

The best way to visualize Eilat is as a peace sign—and that's not just because its most frequent visitors are college students itching for a game of beach volleyball. On one side, the **airport** bisects the main part of the city and ends near the beach, which is the bottom of the peace sign. Facing the beach, the section to the right has most of the cheap hotels and restaurants in town. **HaTmarim Street** is the main boulevard; **Retamim Street,** near the airport, branches off from HaTmarim St. to enter the hotel neighborhood. One street over is **Yotam Road,** which is the entrance point for the messy conglomerate of bars, restaurants, and convenience shops that make up the town's **Tourist Center.** The other half of the peace sign has less of these places, though it can be easier to find affordable restaurants and some larger hotels here. The main street that runs along the airport on this side of town is **Durban Road.** In the lower quadrant, you will find the promenade, a series of public beaches, and the tourist information center.

accommodations

Forget seasonal prices—room rates can vary daily in Eilat, as the hotel industry attempts to ride the touristic waves. Stay away from the overpriced hotels that dot the shore, and you have a good chance of finding well-priced lodgings.

✓ CORINNE'S HOSTEL — HOSTEL $

127 Retamim St. ☎08 637 1472; www.corinnehostel.com/indexen

The low buzz of chattering 20-somethings floats through Corinne's, Eilat's ultimate youth hostel. It's also Eilat's oldest youth hostel, a fact evident from the beat-up backgammon and checker board tables at which lanky, tattooed guests get their internet fix. All dorm rooms have their own bathrooms, TVs, and bedding—all unnecessarily great additions for a place that already offers the best price in town.

➜ On the corner of HaTmarim and Retamim, just beyond the bakery and north of the bus station. *ℹ Free Wi-Fi in lobby. Kitchen open 24hr. for guest use. [$] Dorms NIS60; private rooms NIS100 per person. ⏰ Reception 24hr.*

✓ ARAVA — HOSTEL $

106 Almogim St. ☎08 637 4687; www.a55.co.il

Roadtripping post-docs, long-haired trance fans, and laptop junkies all congregate at Arava, the other premier hostel in Eilat. This dorm-room haven might have slightly older patrons than Corinne's—and the slightly higher prices to match—but the staff is unbeatably helpful, and the outdoor garden the most scenic of any cheap hotel in the city.

➡ Just 50m away from the Golani St. and the HaNegev St. traffic circle. ℹ Free Wi-Fi. Free maps. Dorms usually single-sex. Valuables stored for free behind desk. $ Dorms NIS60-100; singles NIS150-200; doubles NIS180-350. 10% discount for divers.

DOLPHIN HOSTEL HOSTEL $

99 Almogim St. ☎050 790 4594

The best living arrangement for small groups in Eilat, Dolphin Hostel offers apartment-style living for its guests; every suite comes with a laundry machine, kitchen, four distinct rooms, and a large bathroom. Their pool is actually dug into the ground—rare for hotels in this price range—though it may not actually be filled until July, and the outdoor area features a workout machine more prominently than it does greenery.

➡ From the end of Retamim St. (opposite Corinne's), take a left and walk approximately 100m. Dolphin Hostel is 20m down the street on the right. There's a sign. ℹ Free Wi-Fi. $ Rooms NIS70, in early Aug NIS100. Extra person NIS10.

AVIV MOTEL HOTEL $$

126 Ofarim Ln. ☎08 637 4660; www.avivhostel.co.il

Benefits of Aviv Motel include a small above-ground pool and larger-than-average singles, which come with small desks. There's also actually space to shower in the bathrooms—though, like most low-priced hotels, Aviv considers shower walls and curtains to be unnecessary luxuries. Suites have beach views, balconies, and kitchenettes. The staff, who clearly consider themselves Eilat veterans, are eager to answer questions.

➡ Take a left at the end of Retamim St. ℹ Free Wi-Fi. $ Singles NIS150; doubles NIS200-250; suites NIS300.

SUNSET MOTEL HOTEL $$

130 Retamim St. ☎08 637 3817; www.sunsetmotel.co.il

It may sound like Best Western's Israeli cousin, but Sunset Motel is actually one of the nicest budget options in town. A few rooms are scattered along a stone walkway buttressed by plants on both sides and along the wire trellis ceiling. Each one has a small kitchenette, which includes a microwave and fridge, and rooms for couples have large bathtubs. Israelis hang around couches in the outdoor lobby to share brews and *argilah.*

➡ 50m from Corinne's Hostel. ℹ Free Wi-Fi. 2 computers in lobby. $ 2-,4-, and 5-person rooms around NIS100 per person; may be as high as NIS175 per person.

NATHAN'S WHITE HOUSE MOTEL $$

131 Retamim St. ☎08 637 6572

A bare-chested, ponytailed, and wiry man—whom we can only assume is Nathan—holds down the fort at the front desk. He makes sure the place stays quiet: rules include no loud noises after 11pm and no looking too energetic (so put away that beer hat). Enter the hostel through a peaceful, somewhat sparse outdoor sitting area that has a laundry machine and kitchen around the corner. Rooms are spacious and cheap.

➡ At the end of Retamim St. You can also reach it via the small lane the extends from HaNegev St. ℹ Free Wi-Fi. Fridges in rooms. $ NIS75-200 per person depending on season.

sights

Eilat has beaches. And reefs. And so many tan people smiling at you. Why would you ever want to leave all that? But if you can tear yourself away from the shore for a couple hours, you'll find some worthwhile sights farther afield.

shoko-late milk

If you're walking down the street wondering what those people are drinking out of those bags, we have your answer: chocolate milk. Unlike in the United States, where the milk comes packaged in little cartons, in Israel it's sold in pouches. And this "*shoko b'sakit*" is extremely popular. As you will notice, everyone from toddlers to middle-aged men in power suits quench their thirst with this sugary, bone-healthy drink.

TIMNA NATIONAL PARK NATIONAL PARK

☎08 631 6756; www.parktimna.co.il

The 6000-year-old copper mines in Timna National Park may be the oldest such mines in the world. Copper was a major trade resource for the ancient Egyptians, and the park contains remains of workers' camps and cisterns that date from the 11th century BCE. In fact, some believe that the area had signs of civilization as early as the 14th century BCE. Walking through mutlicolored sands, visitors can also see remnants of the Egyptian Temple of Hathor and the 50m-tall King Solomon's Pillars.

⇞ Drive up Rte. 90 by way of Arava Rd. About 20min. north of Eilat, turn right onto Kibbutz Eliphas' access road and continue straight to the outskirts of Timna Park. Taxis cost NIS50; ask them to use the meter. Northbound buses stop here upon request. $ NIS44, children NIS39. ⏰ Open Su-Th 8am-4pm, F 8am-3pm, Sa 8am-4pm.

KIBBUTZ YOTVATA KIBBUTZ

☎054 979 8552; yotvata.org.il

The oldest and largest kibbutz in the area, Yotvata is a renowned producer of *shoko* (chocolate milk). Although experts originally warned that the region's climate was not conducive to cow-rearing, Yotvata reportedly produces half of Israel's milk. Call ahead to arrange a tour of the farm and kibbutz lifestyle.

⇞ Rte. 90 between Timna and Hair Bar.

water sports

Scuba diving and snorkeling are the major draw for some Eilat visitors, who see the beaches and bars as only a secondary concern to the coral. If you want to explore Eilat's reef and many aquariums comprehensively, prepare to be here for weeks (which we doubt your wallet could handle). And remember: just jet-skiing until your hair stands straight up can be fun too.

CORAL BEACH NATURE RESERVE NATURE RESERVE

Coral Beach ☎08 637 6829; www.parks.org.il

A wide variety of sea creatures, from colorful butterfly fish to giant shells, populate this underwater habitat. If you couldn't tell from the name, the highlight of the reserve is the reef itself; one of the densest in the world, it extends 1200m along the beach.

⇞ Along the road between Eilat and the Taba Border Crossing. The entrance is across from the Eilat Field School. $ NIS33, students NIS25, children NIS20. Mask and breathing tube NIS16. Flotation device NIS10. Recliner NIS10. ⏰ Open Apr-Sept Su-Th 9am-6pm, F 9am-5pm, Sa 9am-6pm; Oct-Mar Su-Th 9am-5pm, F 9am-4pm, Sa 9am-5pm

EYAL DIVING SERVICE DIVING, TOUR

☎08 633 3319; www.eilatdivers.com

Eyal Sayag is widely considered the most reliable scuba instructor and guide there is on the Eilat shore. His company supplies such high-tech gear as closed circuit rebreathers—meaning there are no bubbles when you breathe—and underwater communication masks. If you've been waiting for just the right person to initiate you into the art of underwater exploration, Eyal is your man.

⇞ Outside the Isrotel Yam Suf Hotel on Coral Beach. $ Introductory dives for uncertified divers NIS200. 2 guided dives for certified drivers NIS350. 3-day, 21hr. scuba certification courses NIS1000. 8-10hr. advanced courses for certified divers (6 dives) NIS1000. ⏰ Open daily 8am-8pm.

LUCKY DIVERS DIVING

5 Simtat Tsukim ☎08 632 3466; www.luckydivers.com

Boasting that they're the "Best Way Into the Red Sea Since Moses," Lucky Divers has the best deals on introductory and guided dives in town. They also have a strong reputation for safety and fun—and not just because they're lucky. If you're willing to dish out the dough for their five-day certification course (NIS1000), you'll have to sit through 20hr. of class but get to practice with nine open-water dives.

⇞ Lucky provides free transportation to and from your hotel. $ Guided dives NIS150; introductory dives NIS220. Both come with equipment. Textbook for certification course NIS220. ⏰ Open daily 8am-5pm.

CORALWORLD UNDERWATER OBSERVATORY NATURE RESERVE

☎08 636 4200; www.coralworld.com/eilat

An artifically constructed reef sits in a glass enclosure, yielding an excellent opportunity to understand the inner architecture and society of the ecosystem. Check out sandbar sharks and silky sharks—if you're there at 11am, you can watch them being fed. Best might be the rare fish room, which includes a dark flashlight fish room that may be the best glowstick party you ever experience.

⇞ Across the street from the Orchid Hotel. Take bus #15 and ask to stop at Coralworld. ℹ Rare aquarium fish fed at 11:30am; other feedings at noon and 2pm. $ NIS89, children NIS69. ⏰ Open daily 8:30am-5pm.

HOF HADEKEL (PALM BEACH) BEACH

This chill party beach features a seaside restaurant with idyllic places to sit, fruity drinks to imbibe, and a majestic sea of scantily clad post-adolescents to mingle with. Budget travelers should bring their own chairs and drinks—prices can be exorbitant and, as it's technically public land, the worst the Hof HaDekel staff can do is flash a killer stinkeye.

⇞ North of the port, 1km south of town center. ⏰ Open sunrise-sunset.

DOLPHIN REEF ANIMAL SANCTUARY

Southern Shore ☎08 630 0100; www.dolphinreef.co.il

Dolphins from the Black Sea—where they are frequently the victims of poaching—are protected in this small section of Eilat water. Since they don't usually breed in captivity, the fact that the animals have begun mating while remaining close to the reef may portend the revolution in human-dolphin relations that we've all been waiting for. This is no SeaWorld—the management takes a laissez-faire approach, meaning that dolphins perform tricks if so inclined but are under no obligation to do so. Also, they may not be touched. Swim around them in the sea or simply sit and watch from the beach as they jump and play and do their dolphin things.

🚏 Bus #15. Just below the stop by the port on the way to the border with Egypt; ask for Dolphin Reef. $ 30min. of snorkeling NIS280, with a private guide (necessary without certification) NIS320. ⏰ Open daily 9am-5pm.

RED SEA SPORTS CLUB DIVING

Bridge House, North Beach ☎08 633 6666; www.redseasports.co.il

Perhaps the best place for experienced divers who just want equipment and hands-off help, Red Sea Sports Club has low prices for dives and is content to continue refilling your tank as you dive all day.

🚏 Near the New Marina, off HaYam St. $ Longer dive (9:30am) and shorter dive (1:30pm) both come with equipment and cost NIS110. Self-directed dives without a diving computer NIS150; 1st tank free, refills NIS25. ⏰ Open daily 8:30am-5pm.

HOF HANANYA BOAT RENTALS

Marina ☎08 631 6348; www.h1h.co.il

The equipment offered ranges from motorboats to paddle boats to kayaks. Grab some motorized plastic and head off on an adventure—preferably one that does not involve pirates.

🚏 Face the beach from the tourist center side. Hof HaNanya is on the beach to the right of the bridge. $ Kayaks for 2-3 people NIS70 per hr. Paddle boats NIS80 per hr. Motorboats NIS180 per 30min., NIS220 per hr. ⏰ Open daily 9am-5:30pm.

hiking

If all that ocean is making you blue, head to the red sandstone gorges and ancient ruins of Eilat's nearby mountains. Contact the **SPNI Field School** first, as they provide essential information on routes, necessary equipment, the correct amount of water, and the length of time for each hike. (☎08 637 1127; eilat@spni.org.il ⏰ Open daily 8am-8pm.) Most sites are accessible via **bus #393, 394,** or **397,** and there are countless tour guide companies. If you're feeling particularly lost, get in touch with **Desert Eco Tours,** which offers mountain biking, camel rides, jeep tours, and guided hikes (☎08 632 6477; www.desertecotours.com).

MT. TZFAHOT (ZEFAHOT) MOUNTAIN

It's best to attempt the steep but short ascent up Mt. Tzfahot early in the day or late in the afternoon; save the scorching midday hours for a swim in the organically cool sea. Once you have reached the summit (which should take around 45min.), you'll be able to appreciate a sweeping panorama that overlooks the expansive Negev, Sinai in Egypt, and Aqaba in Jordan. The entire trail, which ends near Aqua-Sport, should take 2-3hr.

🚏 Begin at the Field School. A green- and white-marked trail extends to the left of the fence that separates the school from the highway.

RED CANYON CANYON

Any bus heading north on Rte. 12 goes through the **Eilat Heights,** home to Ein Netafim, Mt. Shlomo, and the striking Red Canyon. The sandstone Red Canyon is tight and winding, and the hard part is reaching it—once you're there, the walk is only a few hundred meters long. At a few points during the 1½hr. trail, the canyon is so narrow that you must use handholds. As with all hikes, it is important to call SPNI in advance, especially if you plan on making the trek during the summer.

Ask the driver of the bus to let you off at the peak of Eilat Heights. From the parking lot at the entrance of the trail, follow the green route to reach the canyon and the black one to return.

food

There are about as many restaurants in Eilat as there are shirtless guts exposed to the sun. However, it can be hard to find moderately priced places to eat. There are a few comfortable restaurants with affordable menus; if you really want to make it rain (shekels), **Eddie's Hide-Away** is widely considered the best restaurant in town. It also makes for excellent upper-crust people-watching.

BAKERY — PASTRIES $

☎08 637 5804

The name makes it clear—there are no frills at Bakery, the best place for baked goods in town. The cinnamon rolls literally melt in the mouth, and the spinach *bourekas* taste so deliciously buttery and doughy that they could replace sandwiches as the standard lunch food. But instead of seeking their well-deserved international fame, the Bakery remains on its nondescript corner, with just a few wooden tables and a tired, sweaty, cheerful staff that works long shifts to hand out the most affordable eats in town.

On the corner of HaTmarim and Retamim St., across from Corinne's Hostel. $ Pastries NIS2. ⏰ Open 24hr. but closed on Shabbat (from F sunset to Sa sunset).

DUDA — MIDDLE EASTERN $$

☎08 633 0389

It's hard to find decent Middle Eastern food in Eilat, which is surprising considering that Eilat is, you know, in the Middle East. Duda is well-priced and better than decent, as the students on tentative dates at the small tables seem to have realized. The marinated grilled chicken with sauteed onions (NIS55) comes on a steaming hot plate and is abundantly spiced.

In the Dalia Hotel, within 50m of the airport fence. $ 5 falafel NIS7. Kebabs NIS24. Entrees NIS40-50. ⏰ Open daily noon-midnight.

GULF RESTAURANT — INTERNATIONAL $$

Tarshish St. ☎08 637 4545

It's a very specific kind of cheap restaurant that can be called romantic by the very virtue of its cheapness. At Gulf Restaurant, the plants are disorganized but large; the outdoor tent is old, beat-up, and looks onto the street through inexplicable small windows; and the buzz of conversation isn't intrusive—but it's loud enough to remind you just how little personal space you've been given. Somehow, though, it all just works. In fact, dazed by this illogical and budget-beautiful maze, you may get down on one knee and propose to your travel fling: will you go to Petra with me?

Cross the bridge from the Queen of Sheba Hotel and take a right instead of walking onto the promenade. Gulf is on the right. $ Spaghetti NIS40. Beef kebab NIS45. Mussels NIS65. ⏰ Open daily noon-midnight.

GINGER — ASIAN $$

Yotam Rd. ☎08 637 2517; www.gingereilat.com

One of the better-priced choices in Eilat, Ginger has the best food near the tourist center. The chicken with fried rice (NIS49 at lunch) is delicious, and the appetizers come with three different sauces. The jet-black walls, bar, and huge leather couches may indicate that Ginger is trying a little too hard to be a lounge for the cool kids, but, to be fair, it seems like everyone is vying for their attention in Eilat.

Directly outside the square in the tourist center. [i] Free Wi-Fi. $ Business lunch NIS49-69. ⏰ Open daily noon-midnight. Business lunch noon-5:30pm.

EDDIE'S HIDE-AWAY — INTERNATIONAL $$$

8 Agmonim St. ☎08 637 1137; www.eddieshideaway.rest-e.co.il

Amazonian Aryans in 5 in. heels strut in with rotund sugar daddies, and red-cheeked American families search for a States-like feast at Eddie's Hide-Away, an undisputed leader among Eilat's higher-priced restaurants. Gourmet chicken parms (here called "chicken schnitzel breaded and baked in tomato with parmesan") are worth the NIS64, especially considering the sauteed carrots and lightly cooked potatoes that accompany them. Call in advance to reserve a table in the front room, which affords a pleasant view and seats more besotted couples than barking tourists.

Walk downhill on Eilat St. and pass Agmonim St. Turn where you see the sign for Eddie's on the right. Eddie's is in a somewhat secluded alcove about 10m off the sidewalk. $ Spaghetti bolognese NIS45. Stroganoff NIS75. Entrees around NIS90. ⏰ Open M-F 6:30-11:30pm, Sa 2-11:30pm.

SPRING ONION — ISRAELI $

Bridge House ☎08 649 6644

The best place to eat on a budget while on the promenade, Spring Onion is typified by its grilled chicken sandwich on ciabatta (NIS30), generously slathered with a tangy sauce and composed of more than a single chicken's rack. Only a week old at time of writing, Spring Onion should soon be attracting all the major student traffic in Eilat.

Adjacent to the tourism information center on the promenade. [i] Free Wi-Fi. Takeout available. $ Hummus and tahini NIS20. Falafel in pita with fries and a drink NIS25. ⏰ Open Su-Th 11am-2am, F 11am-sunset, Sa from 30min. after sunset to 2am.

GIRAFFE — ASIAN $$

Herods Promenade ☎08 631 6583; www.giraffe.co.il

The Eilat branch of this chain must have learned from its cousins in Tel Aviv and Haifa: Giraffe constructs what some consider to be the best sushi in town. Its outdoor area is small but relatively quiet, and its indoor space is powerfully air-conditioned. The servings are so large that two people can easily split a main course. Stop by for dessert and try the much-talked-about banana brulee (NIS41).

Under Herods Hotel at the eastern end of the North Promenade. [i] Free Wi-Fi. $ Salmon and avocado roll NIS33. ⏰ Open in summer Su-W 12:30pm-midnight, Th-Sa noon-midnight; in winter Su-W 12:30-11pm, Th-Sa noon-11pm.

AGADIR — BURGERS $$

10 Kamen ☎08 633 3777; www.agadir.co.il

Girls in short shorts and guys with gold Star of David chains gather at this local hamburger hole, which has also begun attracting young families. The devoted go for the thick Angus burger (NIS55), 250g of gullet-greasing glory, while cheating dieters can get the same on a whole wheat bun (that's healthier, right?).

On the other side of the airport from the city center. From the Americana Hotel, walk 50m toward the bridge. Agadir is on the right. $ Roasted eggplant with tahini NIS27. Chicken caesar salad NIS49. 10% discount on food Su-Th noon-5pm; 30% discount on drinks Su-Th 4-7pm. ⏰ Open daily noon-3am.

MIKA HAPPY SUSHI — SUSHI $$

Promenade Hotel, Royal Beach ☎08 633 7244; www.mikasushi.co.il

By far the cheapest sushi on the promenade, Mika Happy Sushi is a place to get your fish fast. Sit around the bar or in the small (and possibly scorching) area outside and enjoy the fact that raw fish is by nature cold.

➡ Fom the Tourist Center, Mika is about 300m past the 1st bridge you cross on the promenade. ℹ Free Wi-Fi. Takeout available. $ Salmon avocado roll NIS2. Maccabee NIS14. ⏰ Open Su-M noon-midnight, Tu noon-1am, W-Th noon-midnight, F-Sa noon-1am.

nightlife

Eilat nightlife is all about the bars, which are, after pavement and lampposts, the city's most prominent urban feature. These bars range from places to get sloshed with bros and listen to alcohol-soaked tales of debauchery—**Gaby's Pub** has perfected this—to dance bars like the **Three Monkey's Pub.**

👍 GABY'S PUB — IRISH PUB

Tourist Center — ☎08 637 6687

Listen to Gaby's drunken tales about his first acid trip in 1967 and how he came to serve carrots at the bar—its now-famous trait, which patrons all agree is "f***ing genius." Drinks are the cheapest in town, though your final tab might mysteriously be even lower. Customers and Gaby compare notes on classic rock and sing along as he blasts everything from The Who to Porcupine Tree. The first **Irish pub** in Eilat, Gaby's is the only joint that not only doesn't target drunken tweens, but is also actively unappealing to them. This means that it isn't always as packed as the surrounding bars, but that shouldn't deter anyone.

➡ From Beatles Bar around the Tourist Center, cross the patio with the pool tables. Instead of walking down the staircase, go right and walk through the alley in front of you. Gaby's is on the right. $ 0.5L Goldstar NIS20. Shots NIS15. ⏰ Open daily 10pm-4 or 5am.

beer with me

You walk into the bar, and realize that everything's in Hebrew. This would be confusing enough even if you hadn't pregamed at the hostel; with two drinks already under your belt, your chances of figuring out what to order are basically nil. To prevent this disastrous situation, memorize this quick list of Israeli beers:

- **GOLDSTAR.** A full-bodied lager, this is the classic Israeli beer you've been hearing about, the one for soldiers, kibbutzniks, and tourists alike.
- **MACCABEE.** The Natty Ice of the Holy Land. Let backward caps ensue.
- **TAYBEH.** The only Palestinian brew on the market, Taybeh has recently begun exporting its rich beers to the European market. Its West Bank brewery also hosts an annual Oktoberfest.
- **ALEXANDER.** Although ales have a surprisingly small market in this sweltering state, this mid-sized microbrewery cranks out such boutique brews as the Alexander Black and the Alexander Blonde.

BEAR PUB — PUB

Tourist Center — ☎08 634 9777

A younger crowd and upbeat classic rock characterize this bar where bartenders tie balloons around their ponytails and waitresses bring out candles for patrons' birthdays. Couples canoodle around the bar, and friends share *argilah* while mutually texting other friends.

➡ Across from the Tourist Center, in the square. ℹ Live DJ on W. 50% discount for women on Su. $ Chicken schnitzel and fries NIS24. 0.5L Goldstar NIS19. Argilah NIS25. ⏰ Open daily 9pm-late.

JOYA
Tourist Center
CLUB
☎054 254 4970

Joya becomes packed around midnight, when the loud electro really starts to rain down on a mix of high school students, 20-somethings in tight dresses, and burly older dudes. Energy drinks line the bar like glasses, and the bass is powerful enough to crack your back. Some plastered patrons slump on the couches, where they wearily puzzle at the alternate form of intoxication enjoyed by everyone on the dance floor.

⚡ *Walk down the staircase opposite Beatles Bar near the Tourist Center and immediately take a right.* ⓘ *Rotating drink deals on M. Top 40 night on W. Hip-hop night on Sa. W and Sa also have live shows occasionally.* Ⓢ *0.5L beer NIS22-25. Cocktails NIS40-45.* ☼ *Open M 11pm-late, W-Sa 11pm-late.*

THREE MONKEY'S PUB
Tourist Center
CLUB, BAR
☎08 636 8888

Get down on the recently renovated dance floor during the American and British rock cover sets earlier in the evening or to the standard electro beats afterward. If that's not your thing, at least amble up to the spacious bar and watch the monkey business. Although some complain that the rock's gone soft in the past few years, Three Monkey's is still one of the best-known bars on the promenade.

⚡ *On the North Promenade underneath the Royal Hotel, which owns it.* ⓘ *Cover bands stick around for a few months and play nightly 10:30pm-1:30am. Live DJ Th-Sa between sets and after the band is done.* Ⓢ *0.3L Carlsberg NIS18. Cocktails NIS32-35.* ☼ *Open daily 7pm-3 or 4am.*

BARBI'S
Tarshish Park
RESTAURANT, BAR
☎08 634 2408

A wooden deck; wine, champagne, and lowball glasses with candles floating in a blue mixture of alcohol and water; and gregarious staff make Barbi's a great place to sit. It's best to come on Friday and Saturday after 11pm, when things start to get going. Call in advance to see if there will be a live band playing during your visit.

⚡ *Cross onto Tarshish Rd. from Durban St., which hugs the airport fence.* ⓘ *Burger NIS29 after 11pm. Movies and major soccer matches shown Su at 11pm.* Ⓢ *Lasagna with vegetables NIS44. Draft beer with a shot NIS9. Maccabee NIS18. Cocktails NIS28-34.* ☼ *Open Su-Th noon-late, F-Sa 11am-late.*

PARK AVENUE
Tarshish Park
CLUB, BAR
☎08 633 3303

A black and orange bar snakes around this dancing hot spot for Eilat weekenders, where DJs spin every night after 11pm. Drinks may be a little more expensive than at the nearby Barbi's, but that might just be because this place moves a little bit faster.

⚡ *Cross onto Tarshish St. from Durban Rd., which hugs the airport fence.* ⓘ *Karaoke night on W. 25% discount on bottles of wine 7-10:30pm. Shots NIS14 with a beer. Discounts on 2nd and 3rd drinks (wine and beer excluded).* Ⓢ *Goldstar NIS22. Cocktails NIS38-44.* ☼ *Open daily 7pm-late.*

BEATLES BAR
Tourist Center
BAR
☎052 749 3638

Loud electropop and an ongoing lightshow surround flip-flopped buddies at this polished attempt at an American diner, which sports sleek black tables and a white-and-black-checkered floor. Many of the older dudes sport earrings and leave a few too many buttons unbuttoned, while the leggy hostesses stand outside and half-heartedly court passersby. If you want to make it rain (or just get trashed), get a bottle of Smirnoff and six cans of Red Bull for only NIS250 (11pm-midnight). Ah, the glamor.

⚡ *Around the corner from the Tourist Center opposite the staircase that leads down from the square to the street below.* ⓘ *Food and drink specials 7-11pm.* Ⓢ *0.5L Tuborg NIS26. Cocktails around NIS49.* ☼ *Open daily 7pm-4am.*

essentials

PRACTICALITIES

- **TOURIST OFFICE:** At the **Tourist Center,** you can find information about what to do in Eilat, which diving companies to use, how to cross borders, and everything else imaginable. (➜ On the North Promenade in the Bridge Center. ⏰ Open Su-Th 8:30am-5pm, F 8am-1pm.)
- **ATM:** ATMs are easy to find around the Tourist Center and on **HaTmarim.** If you really find yourself pressed, take a left off HaTmarim 50m down from HaNegev St. Walk through the parking lot near the bus station to find a small covered lane that has ATMs.
- **PUBLIC BATHROOM:** Located near the bus station, on the same lane as the ATMs.
- **LAUNDROMAT: The Station** has washing, drying, and a convenience store. (Almogim St. ➜ Across from the Dolphin Hostel. Walk downhill on Eilat St. and take a left at Agmonim St. $ Wash NIS20. Dry NIS10. ⏰ Open 24hr.)
- **INTERNET: Speedo Cafe** is a calm cafe with free Wi-Fi and usually a few empty tables. (☎08 637 7975 ➜ At the very end of the promenade, opposite Coral Beach. $ Iced coffee NIS18.)
- **POST OFFICE:** ☎08 637 2219; www.israelpost.co.il ➜ Just behind the bus station on Arava Rd. ⏰ Open Su-Tu 8am-6pm, W 8am-1pm, Th 8am-6pm, F 8am-noon.
- **POSTAL CODE:** 88000.

EMERGENCY

- **POLICE: Eilat Police Station.** (1 HaMeyasdim Sq. ☎08 636 2444 ➜ Across the traffic circle from Arava Hostel and adjacent to Derech HaArava. ⏰ Open 24hr.)
- **LATE-NIGHT PHARMACY: Super-Pharm.** (HaTmarim St. ☎077 888 1440 ➜ On the right on HaTmarim, 150m before you reach the end of the street at the traffic circle that interesects with Mitzrayim Rd. ⏰ Open Su-Th 8:30am-10pm, F 8am-5pm, Sa 10:30am-11pm.)
- **HOSPITAL: Yoseftal Hospital.** (☎08 635 8011 ➜ Far down Yotam Rd. about 1.5km outside the city center. ⏰ Open 24hr.)

GETTING THERE

Egged buses #444 and **445** travel from Jerusalem to Eilat a few times per day ($ NIS75. ⏰ 5hr.). However, it's slightly easier to get here from Tel Aviv: buses **#390, 394,** and **790** cost the same and take about the same amount of time as the Jerusalem buses, but they run more frequently. From within the Negev, look up the travel schedule the day before you want to leave. Bus **#392** is the main way to get through the desert to Eilat, but on Fridays there may only be one chance (and it may be very early).

GETTING AROUND

The best way to go long distances is to take **bus #15**, which stops at many of the major hotels, diving companies, diving locations, and sites outside Eilat. The schedule and prices change periodically, but the information should be readily available upon arrival. If you choose to take a **taxi,** make sure the driver is using the meter. **Hertz,** which rents manual cars for US$45 a day and automatics for US$55, is located just north of the airport entrance. (⏰ Open Su-Th 8am-6pm, F 8am-2pm.)

PETRA

More than 2000 years ago, Nabateans built a trading post in the desert, creating an odd cultural brew of Assyrian, Greek, Roman, and Egyptian features on their rockface tombs, giant columned monasteries, and cryptic inscriptions along the sides of a towering gorge. Romans later took over this town—a fact made obvious by the 4000-seat Roman theater that remains today—and the Byzantines housed important outposts of Christianity here. However, shifting world power, a series of earthquakes, and the end of the Nabatean civilization led to the abandonment of Petra, which stood for the next 1500 years as a curiosity for nomadic Bedouins and nothing more. They desecrated tombs and cleared out the remaining structures, and the ancient city faded from memory. Petra returned to the collective consciousness when Johann Burckhardt, an early 19th-century Swiss explorer, impersonated a Christian pilgrim and convinced a guide to take him to the ancient city. It has since become one of the major tourist attractions in the Middle East and may be some of the most spectacular ruins on Earth.

In fine Imperialistic style, Bedouins have since been kicked out of Petra proper and now live in a nearby housing complex, focusing most of their commercial efforts on tourism. The town of **Wadi Musa,** built up outside Petra once it became a major destination, is basically a tourist town as well, and gives a glimpse into the world of two millennia ago. But no matter how much your imagination runs away into the lifestyles of the ancients, beggar children hawking postcards and aggressive donkey rental salesmen will ground you in Petra's most recent incarnation.

greatest hits

- **A-TISKET, A-TASKET.** Pack a picnic for an afternoon at the Khazneh (p. 340), an ancient Nabatean temple, and watch the colors of the sand change.

- **FUN WITH PUNS.** Stay at the Cleopetra Hotel (p. 338) for a price far less than Elizabeth Taylor's jewelry.

- **CARBO-LOAD.** Fill up on tasty omelettes at Al-Wadi (p. 343).

- **RITUAL SACRIFICE.** Venture through the ruins of the breathtaking ancient city, and find the High Place of Sacrifice (p. 342). *Let's Go* does not endorse animal sacrifice.

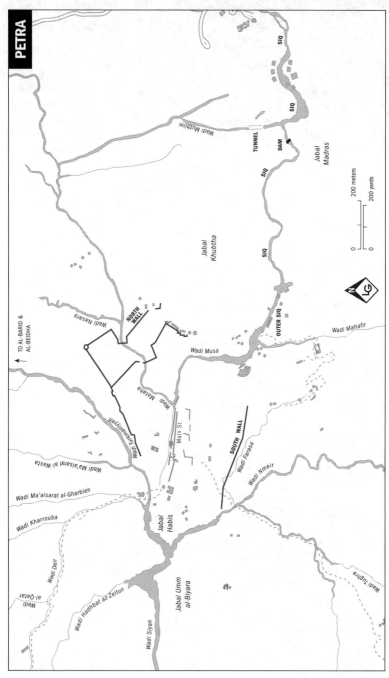

PETRA

TO AL-BARID &
AL-BEIDHA

SIQ

SIQ

TUNNEL

DAM

Jabal Madras

SIQ

SIQ

OUTER SIQ

Wadi Mahafir

Wadi Muthlim

Jabal Khubtha

NORTH WALL

Wadi Nasara

Wadi Musa

Wadi Mataha

Main St.

Wadi Turkmaniyyeh

Wadi Ma'aisarat al-Wasta

Wadi Ma'aisarat al-Gharbieh

Wadi Kharrouba

Wadi Deir

Wadi al-Qatar

Wadi Hadhbat az-Zeitun

Wadi Siyah

Jabal Habis

Jabal Umm al-Biyara

SOUTH WALL

Wadi Farasa

Wadi Nmeir

Wadi Tughra

200 meters
200 yards
0
0

N
LG

petra

Petra has a very specific appeal—Petra and the ruins that go along with it. Along with these badass ancient creations, there's not a ton to see or do. **Valentine Inn** offers a cheap place to stay and free Wi-Fi for you time in this ruin-filled city, and tons of field trips will help make you feel more like a second grader than an undergraduate.

You can also get your moderate drink on at **Cave Bar,** one of the only places in Petra with a liquor license. It's overpriced and not open very late, but you can channel ▩**Han Solo** as you down beer in the cave-like room.

orientation

The name to know here is **Wadi Musa**—the town outside Petra, it's also the official name of the ancient city and present-day sight. The town is so small that it barely matters that there are few street signs or even street names. A main road runs perpendicular to the one that leads to Petra, and the two streets connect at a three-way intersection. On the main road just 100m above the intersection is the **Shaheed traffic circle,** which is the main reference point in town. Almost all the hotels and restaurants in town are on either the main road, on a street off the traffic circle, around the three-way intersection, or near Petra itself—about a 2km walk from the traffic circle.

accommodations

A town this touristy is like a deciduous tree—you can tell just by looking at it whether it's summer or winter. If you get here at the right time, concierges will be begging to bargain, and prices will shoot down at even the ultra-fancy Amra Palace Hotel. Come during holidays at your own financial risk.

▩ **VALENTINE INN**   HOSTEL $

☎03 215 6423; www.valentine-inn.com

Staying at Valentine makes you feel like you got the cool homeroom teacher in first grade: trips and helpful Petra tips are written in marker on poster board, there are cushions with important information stitched on them, large winding couches are punctuated by fluffy pillows, and the nightly movie is decided by a show of hands. We do, however, doubt that quite so many of your fellow first-graders were bearded. Despite the many daytrips, the cheap rooms and laundry, and the unbelievably huge buffet—sometimes upward of 40 dishes in high season—served for a mere JD5 nightly, the best service provided by Valentine Inn might be their travel assistance. Important bus times are written on a board every night, and staff can arrange for buses returning from Petra to stop outside Valentine. This is not just the best way to have a real understanding of when and from where the buses leave—it may be the only way.

✦ At the traffic circle, face uphill and take a left. Walk approximately 150m, take a right uphill into a kind of driveway, then continue down the path for 80m. 3 signs direct you along the way. ℹ Free Wi-Fi in lobby. Free luggage storage. Free bus to Petra at 7 and 8am; returns from Petra at 5 and 6pm. Full-day trip to the castle, Dead Sea, mountains, and Amman JD30. Overnight trip to a Bedouin camp in Wadi Rum (dinner and breakfast included) JD35; transportation back around JD5 extra. Ⓢ Roof (not always open) JD2; large dorms JD3; small dorms JD5.50. Singles JD10-15; doubles JD15-20; triples JD21. Laundry JD2.50 per kg. Breakfast JD2.50; lunch box JD2.50. Beer JD2.50-5. Ⓣ Reception 5am-midnight.

SABA'A HOTEL

HOTEL $$

☎778 730 533; www.sabaahotel.com

The most overtly friendly hostel in Petra, Saba'a has walls covered with floral and geometric stencil designs, a spacious basement-level dorm, an amply-postered dining area, and rooms that get a fair amount of natural light. The staff are eager to help with Wadi Musa advice—some of them are even former tourists themselves. Head up to the roof to sit on daybeds and chat with some of the other guests, who tend to be on the younger side.

⇞ Face uphill at the traffic circle, take a left, and walk 80m. Saba'a is on the left. i Free Wi-Fi in the lobby. No A/C, but fans in rooms. $ Dorms JD6.50; singles JD14; doubles JD20; triples JD24; quads JD30. Prices reduced by JD1.50 if you opt not to have breakfast. Cash only. ⏰ Reception 5am-midnight.

CLEOPETRA HOTEL

HOSTEL $$

☎796 634 823; www.cleopetrahotel.com

Owner Abu Ali may instantly offer you tea and turn on BBC (an ideal routine), and the roof arrangement allows you to sleep on comfortable beds overlooking the Wadi Musa skyline. There's no better way to wake up than in the bright sun above the whole city (and there's no better way to ensure that you won't sleep past 9am). The crowd is a mix between younger backpackers and 30-something couples.

⇞ On the left, 150m uphill from the traffic circle. i Wi-Fi JD2 for whole stay. $ High-season roof beds JD8; singles JD25; doubles JD35; triples JD45. Low-season prices negotiable, usually roof beds JD5; singles JD20; doubles JD30; triples JD35. Prices reduced if you opt not to have breakfast. ⏰ Reception 5:30am-midnight.

ELGEE HOTEL

HOTEL $$

☎03 215 6701; elgeehotel@yahoo.com

At first glance, the family-run Elgee Hotel might seem a lot like other cheap hotels—nondescript sign, once-regal furniture that has become faded, etc. But Elgee has unusually excellent rooms in terms of value. The JD10 single may have no air-conditioning, but it does come with a small sitting area, and its beat-up bathroom has separate rooms for the toilet and shower. Next door, one of the JD18 singles has a four-poster bed covered fully by a curtain, an entire sitting room, and a large vanity mirror. For those who see vintage luxury as indescribably more sweet than the modern equivalent, Elgee is the place to be.

⇞ Downhill from the traffic circle on the right. Look for signs. i Breakfast included. Free Wi-Fi. Elgee also has a bar. $ Singles without A/C JD10-15, with A/C JD18-22; doubles JD18-25. Beer JD3-4. ⏰ Reception 6am-midnight.

AMRA PALACE HOTEL

HOTEL $$$$

☎03 215 7070; www.amrapalace.com

The best place for luxury in Wadi Musa, Amra Palace has singles with thick king beds supported by stately wooden headboards. A large Turkish bath and spa complex with private and communal steam rooms, a beautiful indoor pool with an oblong skylight, 1000 satellite channels, and an exceptional breakfast spread are all available for guests. Non-residents looking for a substantial morning meal will also appreciate the breakfast (served 6-9:30am; JD4), which includes fresh fruit, above-average American coffee, made-to-order omelettes, and the finest Weet-Bix. Sit at white-clothed tables on the terrace and enjoy the view of the Jordanian mountains.

⇞ Walk 245m uphill from the traffic circle. Just before Cleopetra Hotel is on the left, there is a steep downhill turn on the right. Walk down it, and Amra Palace is on the right. i Breakfast included. 3rd fl. rooms cost the same but are larger and have better views. $ Singles JD30-54; doubles JD40-64; triples JD56-85. Turkish bath with 24hr. jacuzzi use and unlimited internet NIS20, for guests NIS13. Otherwise, 1 hr. internet US$3, 7hr. US$10.50. ⏰ Reception 24hr.

PEACE WAY HOTEL

HOTEL $$

☎03 215 6963; peaceway_petra@yahoo.com

Brightly colored rugs and wood-panelling makes the lobby of Peace Way look like one of those hunting lodges used in Pendleton photo shoots. However, this is just a budget hotel in Jordan that offers rooms with bathtubs, small tables, and more than enough space to move around.

 # On the left, 100m up from the traffic circle. i Breakfast at hotel included, 15% discount at adjacent restaurant. Free Wi-Fi. In summer, live bands usually play Arabic music on F. Transport leaves from the hotel to Petra anytime you like in the morning. [S] Singles JD14-18; doubles JD20-25; triples JD25-35; quads JD40.

ROSE CITY HOTEL

HOTEL $$

☎03 215 6440

Floral wall designs and matching bedspreads and curtains cheer up this efficient hotel, which has TVs sitting on the small fridges and enough fans to make up for the lack of air-conditioning. Budget travelers will be cheered up themselves to know that a well-positioned showerhead makes room flooding substantially less likely.

 # On the right near Elgee Hotel, downhill from the traffic circle. i Free Wi-Fi in lobby. [S] Singles JD10-13; doubles JD16-20; triples JD25. Without breakfast, rooms JD2 less.

PETRA GATE HOTEL

HOTEL $$

☎03 215 6908; petragatehotel@hotmail.com

An erstwhile champion on such eminent hostel tastemakers as Hostelworld and Hostelbooker, Petra Gate Hotel has actually shed its hostel status by dismantling its dorm room and, in doing so, made itself a little less relevant for budget travelers. However, Petra Gate probably has the best roof among cheap hotels in town, with comfortable couches and *argilah* for sale.

 # On the right, 140m uphill from the traffic circle. i Free Wi-Fi in lobby. Breakfast included, though not when booked online. [S] Singles JD15-20; doubles JD20-24; triples JD25-36. Argilah JD4.50. Lunch box JD3.50; dinner buffet JD5.50. Laundry JD0.50 per item. Most prices negotiable.

SHARAH MOUNTAINS HOTEL

HOTEL $$

☎03 215 7294; sharahhostel@yahoo.com

Sharah Mountains is your typical cheap hotel: small desk, two twin beds, unadorned white walls, low lighting. However, it does set itself apart by having air-conditioning in its rooms. Doubles are a bit overpriced during the high season.

 # 220m uphill from the traffic circle. i Ask for rooms above the 1st floor; they have a better view and cost the same. Free Wi-Fi in lobby. [S] Singles NIS15-25; doubles NIS25-33; triples NIS35-45.

sights

A path leads through the main sights of the Old City, but smaller trails splinter off to small temples and inscrutable designs etched in the rock. If you want to see only the major sights and get a sense of Petra, don't spend the JD50 to hire a guide at the visitors center. However, if you plan on doing any of the farther-flung hikes, having a guide won't just be useful—it'll be required. Know before you come that Petra is extremely expensive; you have to pay JD50 for one day, JD55 for two, and JD60 for three, and there are no discounts. You'll want to have a map, but make sure to give yourself some time to simply wander around Petra. The most famous sights pale in comparison to the overall experience of walking in the almost alien landscape of the abandoned capital.

OBELISK TOMB

TOMB

Between the *siq* (main passage) and the entrance to Petra lie incredibly large rocks that the Nabateans carved smooth into unpatterned curves, making them look like extraterrestrial dunes or ancient drops from a celestial carton of yogurt. While the small ornamental steps cut into many of these bizarre rocks come from Assyrian tradition, the large Obelisk Tomb on your right is definitely an Egyptian export, and Greek and Nabatean inscriptions sit side by side on the rock face. The tomb is more than an embodiment of conflicting cultural influence, however—it's one of the most beautiful above-ground monuments in Petra.

KHAZNEH (TREASURY)   TEMPLE

Sunlight bursts through sky-level patches in the *siq*, and it is often just visible in the swimming reds and pinks across the gorge. As you walk through the last 80m, the path narrows, and little is visible beyond the deep magenta of the walls and the uninterrupted blue of the sky above. The Khazneh, then, comes quickly and shockingly, a pure pink visible in a wide courtyard that adds an exclamation point to the *siq*'s conclusion. Little is known about the Treasury other than that it was a Nabatean temple, though that didn't stop Bedouins from riddling the carved urn on the facade with bullets in the hopes that ancient treasures would come tumbling out (high-stakes piñata, anyone?). Sit at a bench facing the Khazneh, enjoy a late afternoon picnic, and watch how the setting sun casts a cycling range of reds.

arabian nights

While Bedouin rights have long been an important, if underemphasized, point of contention in Israeli politics, the reality is that few Bedouins retain their traditional nomadic way of life, and many have settled in towns in Jordan and the Negev. In the interest of the almighty shekel, however, many Bedouin families claim to offer "authentic" (read: touristy) Bedouin experiences, in which they invite you into a desert tent to feast on traditional meat and rice dishes, sip their extraordinarily sweet tea, and listen to the rhythmic sound of coffee grinding. Of course, this is all while imagining a time in which the tribes roamed the desert in search of the next oasis rather than the next unsuspecting tourist.

ROMAN THEATER   THEATER

A few hundred meters down from the Khazneh is the Roman Theater, which dates to the reign of King Aretas IV (9 BCE-40 CE). Its 4000 seats imply a city population of 24,000—Romans characteristically built one seat for each family, and the average family was said to have six people. The theater, which was recently restored to its original appearance, sits at the foot of the High Place of Sacrifice and under the red-stone Nabatean necropolis.

ROYAL TOMBS   TOMBS

Along the mountain of rock directly opposite the Roman Theater lie the Royal Tombs, grand columns and designs cut directly into the wall and suspended above ground level. The **Urn Tomb,** named for the urn that sits atop the structure (clever, right?), has a Byzantine inscription inside explaining that this former tomb for first-century king Malichus II was converted into a church in 447 CE. The adjacent **Corinthian Tomb** is another example of architectural pastiche: it bears similarities both to the Khazneh and to Nero's Golden Palace in Rome. Near here is the five-story facade of the **Palace Tomb,** which was probably used for feasts or funerals. Finally, there is the **Tomb of Sextus Florentius,** the Roman governor of Arabia who was so taken with his provinces that he asked to be buried in the desert.

THE CARDO — STREET

Originally a Nabatean road, this was reconstructed as the main street for Petra when it became a Roman outpost. Today, patches of dirt sometimes cover the paved road, which you can feel underneath; at other points, the uneven stones create small waves of road, and it's smart to look before you step. Ruins of a Nabatean gate are still visible nearby, and the columns that used to line this street live today as stumps, though a few have been restored to their former grace.

BYZANTINE CHURCH — CHURCH

To the right of the Roman street stands the Byzantine Church, one of the few sights in Petra that's notable for more than just its structure. Three apses with corresponding entrances are clear around the basilica, and the mosaic floors have been inexplicably well-preserved despite the ravages of earthquakes, storms, and looters. Mythological animals, enactments of various professions, and representations of the four seasons are all discernible in the floor designs. Indications are that the site was important in the Byzantine bishopric well into the sixth century, which seems to contradict the accepted belief that Petra was already in decline by the mid-sixth century.

THE GREAT TEMPLE — TEMPLE

Look beyond the Cardo to the left side. Thanks to the current dig, the Great Temple may look like little more than trash heap of marble and limestone rubble, but it's currently one of the most important archaeological sites in Petra. Researchers from Brown University are tiptoeing and toothbrushing for artifacts around the recently discovered complex under the stern eyes of the UNESCO World Heritage Society. Fortunately for archaeologists, excavations began before Petra attained its official UN status, and the 28-by-40m site is still open to investigation. The craftsmanship of the limestone and friezes, as well as the hexagonal white stones covering an elaborate tunnel system, indicate that this was a place of importance in Nabatean society in the first century BCE, though archaeologists think this site was also used by Byzantines.

MUSEUMS — MUSEUM

To the right of and beyond the Cardo is a small **archaeological museum**, which has coins, columns, and an elephantine water pipe fit for the Bob Marley of Nabatea. On the way to the monastery, the **Nabatean Museum** has artifacts and the only air-conditioning within miles.

$ Free. ⏰ Open daily in summer 9am-5pm; in winter 9am-4pm.

photographer's etiquette

Best times to put down the camera lens:

- **HAND SIGNALS.** If someone in your frame puts her hands over her face—or in your face—she might have a religious excuse to shy away from the camera. Don't mess with God (or the gods).
- **SIGN LANGUAGE.** Keep your hands off the shutter button in any clearly signed no-photo territory. If the English doesn't ring any alarm bells, look out for telltale warnings in Arabic or Hebrew: ممنوع التصوير or **אין צילום**.
- **SUPERMAN.** It's kind of obvious, but if you're flying, hang gliding, or otherwise in position to take aerial shots, don't point and shoot. Bizarro and Kryptonite Man might be on your tail.

hiking

It's pretty much a waste to come to Petra and not hike, because the walks contained within the ancient city are some of the most glorious you'll ever find. Grip onto ancient red stones, summit the High Place of Sacrifice and look over the surrounding landscape, and explore millennia-old tombs that have been used by three distinct civilizations and exhibit a host of other cultural influences. Hikes in Petra all occur on the site, so if you intend to do a lot of trekking, be prepared to buy a two- or three-day pass (JD55 or JD60). Tour guides can be hired at the visitors center for JD50 for 2-3hr., but hikes will take longer—you can negotiate, but be prepared to spend around JD100 for a full day. The visitors center accepts only dinars, so be prepared. The site is open in summer from 6am to 6pm and in winter from 6am to 4pm.

WADI TURKMANIYYEH

A short and easy hike weaves through the Oriental Gardens—which are full of pink flowers—on the way down to the ◪Lion Temple, where a Nabatean inscription on the tomb asks the god Dushara to protect the grounds. This was clearly an insufficient measure; like all sights in Petra, the tomb has been stripped bare. This hike also helps give you a lay of the land outside the *siq*.

AL-HABIS

One of the main sites visibly occupied by Crusaders, al-Habis is nothing more than the rubble of a once-great castle that was already in ruins when the Sultan Baibars came to Petra in 1276 CE. The path that winds around the mountain leads to beautiful views of the canyons and tombs.

⚑ *Begin at the end of the road that descends from Pharaoh's Pillar to the cliff, which is a few hundred meters left of the museum.* ⌚ *Full trip takes around 1hr.*

HIGH PLACE OF SACRIFICE

This extremely popular (and extremely satisfying) circular trail leads up the mountain Jabal al-Madhbah to the dramatically named High Place of Sacrifice. Climb the 550 steps of the staircase just to the left of the Roman Theater and bear right. Here you will see the two 7m obelisks of **Obelisk Ridge,** one of which is dedicated to the Nabatean god Dushara, and just above the ridge is the main attraction: a courtyard that contains benches, an altar, a sacrificial platform, and a basin to receive the blood of the animals. Disconcerted vegetarians can regain spiritual equilibrium at the garden on the other side of the mountain, where there's also a Roman cistern.

⚑ *Located at the top of the mountain. Trail starts at the exit of the siq and ends at Qasr al-Bint Temple.* ⌚ *Full trip takes 2-3hr.*

JABAL HARUN

Begin from the museum and go south toward Umm al-Biyara, passing the **Snake Monument,** a large snake carving probably from Nabatean times. Stay on this path for approximately another 9km. Halfway through you will reach the human-shaped hole of **Lion's Triclinium,** which you will be able to see from the staircase in a small *wadi* on the left. Named after the the two lions carved on the entrance, it was probably used for funerary banquets. Continuing upward, you will eventually reach **al-Deir** (the Monastery), which was modeled on the Khazneh and is Petra's largest monument. One of the longest-used sites in the area, all that remains of al-Deir are two benches, an altar, and some crosses carved into the back wall—though the structure predates Christian influence in Petra, it was reappropriated by monastic Byzantines. You can no longer climb to the urn at the top of al-Deir unless you want to incur the wrath of a Nabatean god (or, more likely, the nearby policeman), but if you still have energy left after that full day of hiking, continue to the **Tomb of Aaron** atop Jabal

Harun. Though biblical scholars are still arguing over whether this is the actual burial site of Moses's brother, a small dome was built here to commemorate Aaron in the 14th century.

food

Food in Wadi Musa tends to be overpriced, though a few places combine worthwhile sit-down spaces with cheap and tasty eats. Hotels are town-famous for huge buffet dinners, and small shops around the traffic circle offer rotisserie chicken at low prices. Whatever you do, don't go into Petra without a food plan; the meals here cost significantly more than the cheap accommodations.

👍 AL-ARABI

MIDDLE EASTERN $

☎03 215 7661; yhamadeen@link.net.jo

Pink tables surround a central fountain at Petra's only restaurant that undercharges for what it delivers. The *sheesh tawooq* (JD2) comes with thick, juicy chunks of spiced chicken, and the surrounding bread is thin almost to the point of translucence. The Al-Arabi smoothie (JD2) is clearly the highlight, however—the combination of milk, strawberries, bananas, and mango tastes like a sugar-coated farmers' market.

↔ On the main traffic circle. [$] Falafel and fries JD1. Arabic salad JD1. Chicken tikka JD5. Cash only. ⏰ Open Su-Th 6am-midnight, Sa 6am-midnight.

AL-WADI

MIDDLE EASTERN, INTERNATIONAL $

☎776 331 431; mashalehl@yahoo.com

While the Middle Eastern fare is similar to that of the surrounding restaurants, Al-Wadi distinguishes itself with what would accurately be called a scrambled omelette (JD2.50), an egg creation with enough vegetables, cheeses, and proteins to get your fists pumping and legs kicking in preparation for the day. A little fresh orange juice (JD2.50) doesn't hurt.

↔ On the traffic circle. [$] Kebab JD2. Mansaf (rice, lamb, and yogurt) JD8. ⏰ Open daily 9:30am-10:30pm.

SANABEL BAKERY

PASTRIES $

☎079 576 0605; yousef_tw2008@yahoo.com

With the sweetest and stickiest desserts in town, Sanabel is a bit more focused on the chocolate angle than the breakfast one. A couple of small pastries and a Turkish coffee will jolt even the most bushed backpacker.

↔ Face uphill. Sanabel is just to the right of the 3-way intersection. [$] 3 small pastries or 1 large JD1. ⏰ Open daily 6am-midnight.

MIDTOWN

JORDANIAN $$

☎03 215 9995

Midtown is one of the few restaurants around Wadi Musa that explicitly focuses on Jordanian cuisine. Slightly more expensive than its immediate competition, it makes up for the prices with inventive fare from the husband and wife home-cooking team behind the operation. Experience the serious tang of fresh OJ (JD3), and try the lamb *kabsa* (JD7.50), made with rice, spices, and yogurt.

*↔ 50m up from the 3-way intersection. Midtown is on the right up the staircase. **i** A screen and projector allows Midtown to play important soccer matches or screen a movie. Call in advance. [$] Grilled fish JD8. ⏰ Open daily 11am-midnight.*

TURKISH BBQ RESTAURANT

MIDDLE EASTERN $

☎077 624 2104

The most standard of standard restaurants, Turkish BBQ offers only the basics—and only at a reasonable rate. Chat up the friendly staff for long enough

to appreciate the broken English they can muster and, perhaps, to charm your way into a free mint tea good enough to rival any in Petra. Vegetarians should stay away—Turkish BBQ is meat-tastic.

 # Just right of the main traffic circle when facing uphill. $ Kebab JD1.50. Large plate of baklava JD2. ⏰ Open daily 10:30am-midnight.

BUKHARA — MIDDLE EASTERN $

☎03 215 4225

Rip through the well-charred skin of the renowned grilled chicken (*sheesh tawook;* JD4), which tastes even better when paired with the Bukhara special rice (JD1.75). A couple of students and the Petra archaeologist/restaurateur sit outside to smoke *argilah* and chit-chat most nights. The fan may not be powerful enough to compensate for a lack of air-conditioning at high noon, but Bukhara is cool by evening.

 # Facing uphill at the 3-way intersection, walk to the right for approximately 150m. Bukhara is on the right. $ Falafel NIS0.50. Cappuccino NIS1. ⏰ Open daily 7am-midnight.

RED CAVE — BEDOUIN $$

☎777 715 223

The cheapest proper restaurant near Petra, Red Cave offers an impressive and affordable selection of Bedouin dishes. The classic *gallayah* (JD6.50) comes on a large plate with a sweet tomato sauce. The outdoor seating is cool under the shade, though harshly facing the busy street.

 # Walking downhill toward Petra from Wadi Musa, Red Cave is 50m before the entrance on the right. $ Burgers JD3. Fried eggs JD3. ⏰ Open daily 9am-11pm.

nightlife

It isn't easy to find alcohol in Petra, which kind of puts a wrench in the nightlife.

CAVE BAR — BAR

☎03 215 6266

One of the few establishments with a liquor license in Petra, the Cave Bar is a great place to sit and get a beer with friends—as long as you accept in advance that said beer will cost about as much as your dinner did. Drink under a cave or outside looking onto Wadi Musa and listen to the *oud* playing nearby. Most of the patrons are tourists passing through, though locals also have no other choice when it comes to getting crunk in public.

 # Take the last right before entering Petra. Cave Bar is 40m uphill, directly in front of you. i Live music most nights—usually Arabic but during the high season sometimes international or DJs. Happy hour 6-8pm, 50% discount. $ Nachos JD8. Arak JD3.50. Gin JD5. ⏰ Open daily 8am-midnight.

essentials

PRACTICALITIES

- **TOURIST OFFICE:** The **Tourist Office** has a temporary location on the left side of the road to Petra, about 50m away. A new building is going up about 50m behind that. (☎03 215 6029 ⏰ Open daily in summer 6am-6pm; in winter 6am-4pm.)
- **ATM:** There is a 24hr. ATM 120m uphill from the traffic circle, on the left.
- **LAUNDROMATS:** There is a 24hr. laundry service inside the **Amra Palace Hotel,**

but it is extremely expensive; better to call **Valentine Inn** and ask if they will do your laundry, as they charge only JD2.50 per kg.

- **INTERNET:** Internet cafes litter the main road between the 3-way intersection and the traffic circle. Most charge JD1-2 per hr.
- **POST OFFICE:** ☎03 215 7613 ⚔ Uphill just before you enter Petra, on the right. 🕐 Open Su-Th 8am-6pm, Sa 8am-6pm.

EMERGENCY

- **EMERGENCY NUMBERS:** ☎199. **Police:** ☎191. **Traffic:** ☎190.
- **TOURISM POLICE:** ☎06 569 0384 ⚔ Right before you enter the *siq* in Petra.
- **LATE-NIGHT PHARMACY: Qamar Al-Wadi.** (☎03 215 7188 ⚔ 135m uphill from the traffic circle, on the left. 🕐 Open daily 8am-midnight.)
- **HOSPITAL: Petra Clinic Complex** is the health center recommended by the tourist office. (☎03 215 6360 ⚔ Facing downhill at the traffic circle, walk 20m. The clinic is on the left. 🕐 Open 24hr.)

GETTING THERE

There are three border crossings from Israel into Jordan (or vice versa): one in **Jericho** at the King Hussein/Allenby Bridge, one near **Beit She'an** in the north of Israel, and one close to **Eilat.** Travelers to Petra usually cross at the Eilat border, which is by far the most convenient. A cab from Eilat to the border should cost around NIS25—make sure that the driver is using the meter. Once at the **Yitzhak Rabin Border Station** (also called the Wadi Araba Crossing), travelers must pay an NIS101 exit tax from Israel and either get an Israeli stamp on their passport or have a sheet stamped in its place. You then walk the 1km **no man's land** through the outdoor border complex. Welcome to Jordan. Put your luggage through a metal detector and get your passport stamped. There is a **money exchange** to your right, which you will need in order to pay for the cab to Aqaba. Unfortunately, there is no ATM.

The cab to Aqaba costs JD6, and the cab driver will probably do anything to convince you to let him drive you directly to Petra or Amman for an exorbitant rate. Don't cave, even if he tells you that the buses are done for the day (they're probably not). The bus to Petra (JD5) has no official timetable, so it is wise to arrive in Aqaba as early as possible to ensure that you make it on time. There is usually one bus early in the morning, around 7am, and another in the afternoon between noon and 1pm. If you are truly too late for the bus or want to expedite your trip, don't pay more than JD50 for a cab. You can even aim to pay JD40, but be aware that few cabbies will go below this, and most won't even let you get to that price. Starting low and staying firm is the best policy—insist that you will take the bus upon arrival in Aqaba, and then relent to the lowest price your driver has offered.

GETTING AROUND

You can walk between every significant destination in Petra, but the uphill climbs can become wearying. Make sure not to pay more than JD1 for a cab during low season; during high season, it should never be more than JD1.50. Cabs are easy to find in the city—if anything, you'll wish there were fewer after a couple of hours of honking.

ESSENTIALS

You don't have to be a rocket scientist to plan a good trip. (It might help, but it's not required.) You do, however, need to be well prepared, and that's what we can do for you. Essentials is the chapter that gives you all the nitty-gritty you need to know for your trip: the hard information gleaned from 50 years of collective wisdom and several months of furious fact-checking. Planning your trip? Check. Where to find Wi-Fi? Check. The dirt on public transportation? Check. We've also thrown in communications info, safety tips, and a phrasebook, just for good measure. Plus, for overall trip-planning advice from what to pack (money and as little underwear as possible) to how to take a good passport photo (it's physically impossible; consider airbrushing), you can also check out the Essentials section of www.letsgo.com.

So, flick through this chapter before you leave so you know what documents to bring, while you're on the plane so you know how you'll be getting from the airport to your accommodation, and when you're on the ground so you can find a laundromat to solve all your 3am stain-removal needs. This chapter may not always be the most scintillating read, but it just might save your life.

greatest hits

- **EGGED ABOUT IT.** Buses are the best way to get around Israel. But do all the cool kids still sit in the back? (p. 352)

- **YOU CALL THAT A BARGAIN?** Haggling for that Holy-Land hookah just got a hell of a lot easier (p. 350).

- **NO MAN'S LAND.** You've been pushing boundaries all your life. Now learn how to cross them and not get grounded... or detained (p. 351).

- **I'LL HAVE WHAT SHE'S HAVING.** Useful phrases for ordering shawarma—with pita lightly toasted, no cucumber, and hummus on the side (p. 362).

planning your trip

DOCUMENTS AND FORMALITIES

We're going to fill you in on visas and work permits, but don't forget the most important document of all: your passport. **Don't forget your passport!**

entrance requirements

- **PASSPORT:** Required for citizens of all countries. Return ticket also necessary.
- **VISA:** Required for citizens of countries other than Australia, Canada, Ireland, New Zealand, the US, and members of the EU.
- **WORK PERMIT:** Required for all foreigners planning to work in Israel.

visas

Citizens of Australia, Canada, Ireland, New Zealand, the EU, and the US do not need a visa for entrance into Israel unless they plan to stay for more than three months—just a passport will do. Congratulations on choosing such a tourist-friendly destination! Visitor visas cost US$24 and are usually valid for three months. Visas can be purchased at one of the embassies or consulates listed below. The process can take anywhere form a week to a month.

Double-check entrance requirements at the nearest embassy or consulate of Israel for up-to-date information before departure. US citizens can also consult http://travel.state.gov.

Entering Israel to study requires a special visa that costs US$48. For more information, see **Beyond Tourism.**

work permits

Admittance to a country as a traveler does not include the right to work, which is authorized only by a work permit. For more information, see **Beyond Tourism.**

passport maintenance

Afghanistan, Algeria, Iran, Iraq, Kuwait, Lebanon, Libya, Saudi Arabia, Somalia, Sudan, Syria, and Yemen will all turn away anyone with an Israeli-stamped passport. If planning on traveling elsewhere in the Middle East, request that the customs officer in Israel not stamp your passport; after a bit of extra questioning, the official is usually happy to let you pass through without the inky proof of your time in Israel. The excuse, "I'm going other places in the Middle East" almost always suffices, so there's no need to get all shady about your reasons.

EMBASSIES AND CONSULATES

embassies in israel

- **THE AUSTRALIAN EMBASSY:** Discount Bank Tower, Level 28, 23 Yehuda HaLevi St., Tel Aviv 65136 ☎03 693 5000; www.israel.embassy.gov.au.
- **EMBASSY OF CANADA TO ISRAEL IN TEL AVIV:** 3/5 Nirim St., Tel Aviv 67060 ☎03 636 3300; www.israel.gc.ca ⏰ Open M-Th 8am-4:30pm, F 8am-1:30pm.
- **EMBASSY OF IRELAND:** 3 Daniel Frish St., Tel Aviv 64731 ☎03 696 4166; www.embassyofireland.co.il ⏰ Open M-Th 9:30am-4pm, F 9:30am-1pm.

- **NEW ZEALAND HONORARY CONSULATE:** 3 Daniel Frish St., Tel Aviv 64731 ☎03 695 1869; nz.honcon.il@gmail.com. *i* The **British Embassy** also serves New Zealanders.

- **BRITISH EMBASSY:** Miglador Building, 15th fl., 1 Ben-Yehuda St., Tel Aviv 63801 ☎03 725 1222; http://ukinisrael.fco.gov.uk/en ☒ Open M-Th 8am-4pm, F 8am-1:30pm.

- **EMBASSY OF THE UNITED STATES:** 71 HaYarkon St., Tel Aviv 63903 ☎03 519 7475; http://israel.usembassy.gov ☒ Open M-Th 9:30am-4pm, F 9:30am-1pm.

abroad

- **THE EMBASSY OF ISRAEL IN CANBERRA:** 6 Turrana St., Yarralumla, ACT 2600, Australia ☎+61 2 6215 4500; http://canberra.mfa.gov.il.

- **EMBASSY OF ISRAEL, OTTOWA:** 50 O'Connor St K1P 6L2 Ottawa, Ontario, Canada ☎+1 613 567 6450; www.embassyofisrael.ca.

- **EMBASSY OF IRELAND:** Carrisbrook House, 122 Pembroke Rd., Ballsbridge, Dublin 4, Ireland ☎+353 123 094 01; www.embassyofireland.co.il. ☒ Open M-F 10am-1pm.

- **EMBASSY OF ISRAEL IN WELLINGTON:** Level 13, Greenock House, 39 The Terrace, Wellington CBD, 6011, New Zealand ☎+04 471 0079; info@wellington.mfa.gov.il.

- **EMBASSY OF ISRAEL IN THE UNITED STATES:** 3514 International Dr. NW, Washington, D.C. 20008, USA ☎+1-202-364-5500; www.israelemb.org.

- **EMBASSY OF ISRAEL, LONDON:** 2 Palace Green, London W8 4QB, UK ☎ +44 020 7957 9500; http://london.mfa.gov.il.

shabbat and you

Since approximately 75% of Israelis are Jewish, the Sabbath (Shabbat) is a big deal in Israel. From Friday night to Saturday evening, practicing Jews are forbidden from doing work. The definition of work, though, varies depending on who you talk to. The most important things to keep in mind when traveling are that all public offices close and public transportation doesn't operate. In addition, you may find that many private businesses shut their doors and fewer people are out in the streets. Since most Orthodox Jews avoid using electricity directly during Shabbat, many hotels will have a marked elevator automatically set to stop at every floor.

money

GETTING MONEY FROM HOME

Shit happens. And when shit happens, you'll probably need some money. And when you need some money, the easiest and cheapest solution is to have someone at home deposit it into your bank account. Otherwise, consider one of the following options:

wiring money

Arranging a **bank money transfer** means asking a bank at home to wire money to a bank in Israel. This is the cheapest way to transfer cash, but it's also the slowest and most agonizing, as it usually takes at least several days. Note also that some banks may release your funds in local currency, potentially giving you a poor exchange rate, so inquire about this in advance. Money transfer services like **Western Union** are faster and more convenient than bank transfers, but they're pricier. To find the nearest of Western Union's many locations worldwide, visit www.westernunion.com or call. (☎1800 173 833 in Australia; 800-235-0000 in Canada; 0808 234 9168 in the UK; and +1-800-325-6000 in the US.) Money transfer services are also available for **American Express** cardholders and at selected **Thomas Cook** offices. The most common **banks** in Israel are Citicorp, Visa, Leumi, Bank of America (don't ask), and Barclays Bank.

us state department (us citizens only)

For serious emergencies, the US State Department can help your family or friends get money to you within hours. The money goes to the nearest consular office, which hands it over according to instructions for a US$30 fee. If you wish to use this service, you must contact the Overseas Citizens Services division of the US State Department (☎+1-202-501-4444, from US 888-407-4747). Note: buying that super-cute swimsuit in Tel Aviv does not constitute a "serious emergency."

the shekel

In 'Merica it might be all about the Benjamins, but that bland green cash hasn't really caught on abroad. The New Israeli Shekel (NIS) is a beautiful thing: not only does the transfer rate usually hover between three and four shekels per US dollar, but the cash comes in greens, purples, browns, and reds. Coins are either copper or nickel and come in quantities up to NIS10. Unfortunately, "Ten shekels for your thoughts" just doesn't roll off the tongue as well.

WITHDRAWING MONEY

To use a debit or credit card to withdraw money from a cash machine (ATM), you must have a four-digit Personal Identification Number (PIN). If your PIN is longer than four digits, ask your bank whether you can just use the first four or whether you'll need a new one. Credit cards don't usually come with PINs, so if you intend to hit up ATMs with a credit card to try to get cash advances, request one from your credit card company before you leave.

Cash is preferred in most establishments (and required in many), so it's particularly nice that ATMs litter the streets of Israel. Many of these accept MasterCard in addition to all debit cards. Keep in mind that many banks charge for money withdrawal in a foreign country. This will either be a flat rate or a 1-3% fee. Though this is by no means guaranteed in Israel, it's better to be safe than sorry, so find out from your bank before you leave.

TIPPING AND BARGAINING

While tipping 10% in the States might get you a loogie in your aperitifs, that's the standard rate in Israel, and restaurants are the only places where tipping is the norm. (It's almost never included, so keep your eyes peeled.) Cabbies don't expect it, but, hey, couldn't hurt...

For our faint-of-wallet readers, sit down: you're about to die and go to haggle heaven. You can bargain everywhere. And we're not just talking about the rough-and-tumble markets that you were born for, but also transportation, supermarkets, laundromats—everywhere.

The key to a good haggle? You've spotted the perfect gift, just lying there at the market. It can't be that expensive, right? But there's only one! You feel the urge to

essentials

pounce. "How much, how much?!" Keep cool, baby! Don't act too interested, ever. You're Lady Gaga; show off that poker face. If they won't agree to your price and you don't want to pay more, just walk away. If you stick to your price and start struttin', the salesperson will often call after you. If they don't, you can always come back later.

Another tip—always check what you're buying before you give your money away. Trickster shopkeepers often want to hoard their mediums or more common shoe sizes. Sorry, average-sized people—we all have our shopping struggles.

TAXES

The Israeli value added tax (VAT) is frequently in a state of flux due to the ever-changing political situation of the country. Most products have a 17% VAT, but it's waived for tourists on many items and services, including accommodations, hospital visits, car rentals, flights, and use of hotel saunas (you know, the necessities). For a complete list, see http://ozar.mof.gov.il/customs/eng/tourinfo.htm.

All tourists are also entitled to a VAT refund on purchases of US$100 or more at any establishment approved by the Ministry of Tourism. These stores will be easily visible by their Ministry insignia or a sign that reads "VAT Refund." You will need to present your VAT receipt at your point of departure when you leave. Fun news for resort hoppers: Eilat is a free-trade zone, which means VAT doesn't even come up.

getting there

The most common and convenient way into Israel is to fly into **Ben-Gurion International Airport** in Tel Aviv (TLV). Customs here can sometimes feel a little more like an interrogation than it does in Western airports, but just stay polite and answer honestly. Once you've made it into the terminal, you'll find that Ben-Gurion is easy to navigate. Signs in a number of languages abound and will direct you to buses, trains, and taxis.

Israel is also littered with smaller airports—many are military airbases, but some are frequented by domestic flyers. In particular, those in Eilat and Haifa are often used.

If traveling elsewhere in the Middle East, you can also get into Israel using one of the border crossings in Jordan or Egypt, two countries with which Israel is generally on peaceful terms. However, keep your eyes on the news, as the ease of border crossing depends on the political situation in the relevant countries.

Tourists can cross into Egypt from Eilat at the Taba Border Crossing. Every traveler must pay a fee of NIS68 to leave Israel and 30 Egyptian pounds to enter the country. For stays of 14 days or less in Sinai, get a Sinai-only visa stamp on the Egyptian side of the border. This visa limits travel to the Gulf of Aqaba coast as far south as Sharm al-Sheikh (but not the area around Sharm al-Sheikh, including Ras Muhammad) and to St. Catherine's Monastery and Mt. Sinai (but not sites in the vicinity of St. Catherine's). Unlike ordinary one-month Egyptian visas, the Sinai-only visa has no grace period; you'll pay a hefty fine if you overextend your stay. To get a 30-day visa that covers all of Egypt, contact the Egyptian Consulate in Eilat (68 Afraty St. Bna Betkha, Eilat ☎07 597 6115). For more information on crossing into Petra, see **Petra Getting There.**

After getting through Israeli security, you may think you've reached your limit of silly and/or exasperating questions. Welcome to border crossings. They usually go swimmingly—just remember who you're dealing with (hint: they're soldiers). Be polite. Reassure them that you have your passport and, if applicable, the proper visas.

getting around

BY BUS

The most common, convenient, and (hallelujah!) budget-friendly way to travel is by bus. It can take a few rides to get the hang of that deviously confusing process of pressing the button at the right time in order to be let off at the right spot (no, really; it's tougher than it sounds). Once you're a pushing pro, you still may want to tell the driver your stop when you get on the bus, particularly if it isn't a big travel hub.

Though the **Dan Company** in Tel Aviv and Arab buses in the West Bank are a good choice, it's the **Egged Bus Cooperative** that takes the cake. Egged runs within (and between) most major cities in the country and even has services to and from a surprising number of tiny towns. To get information on intercity travel, call ☎03 694 8888. Buses go either direct *(yashir)* or local *(me'asef)*.

If you're going on a grand Israeli tour, it's probably best to invest in a season ticket or *kartisia*, which gets you 10 rides for the price of seven. Purchase one from any bus driver and steep yourself in that clean, discounted air-conditioning.

BY TRAIN

Slightly more expensive than the bus, **Israel Railways** goes to all major cities in Israel. The company suggests you get to the station at least 10min. before your train leaves. Also, remember that railway crime isn't just for old Westerns and Hitchcock films —keep track of your possessions at all times.

BY CAR

Israel is a highway, and you're gonna ride it all night long, my friend. The country is about the size of New Jersey, and, like the Garden State, there are a lot of ugly roads in there. If you're planning on seeing the smaller towns in the Holy Land, renting a car may be your best bet.

Sadly for our younger adventurers, most places require that you be 24 to rent an automatic and 21 to get any car at all. However, these rules are sometimes flexible, requiring only a large deposit and some extra money for insurance. Ben-Gurion Airport might be the easiest place to get a car, because of all the signs pointing the way toward nearby shuttles to rental agencies. Beware, however, that there is an extra $27 airport fee if you take the car out of Ben-Gurion Airport.

In terms of braving the roads of Israel: stereotypes be damned, Israelis are crazy drivers. "Rules of the road" have neither place nor meaning. Stay alert—none of that highway hypnosis for you—and drive defensively. Americans should read up on the traffic rules regarding roundabouts, as they are plentiful and confusing. In addition to plenty of one-way streets, loops, and random curves, roads tend not to have very clear signs (if any signs at all). Oh, and those signs will probably be in Hebrew or Arabic. To sum up: get a GPS.

License plates carry special, color-coded meanings in Israel: there's yellow for Israeli civilians, black with an "m" for the army, red for police, blue or grey for members of the Palestinian Territories, and white for diplomats. The road bingo opportunities are endless.

BY TAXI AND SHERUT

Israel boasts both private taxis (à la NYC) and shared taxis called *sheruts*. City taxis operating as "special" must use a meter *(moneh)*, so make sure the driver turns it on. Keep in mind that being offered a no-meter "discount" means that you're probably being offered a rip-off. Don't be scared to haggle before getting in a cab, but always agree on the price before you start rolling.

Sheruts can make you feel like a boss. Of course, they'll first make you feel like

essentials

an idiot, and you have a good chance of getting ripped off once or twice. But once you get the hang of it, sheruts are the fastest and cheapest way to get around any city: like taxis, they have no set schedule and will drop you off right where you need to be; like buses, they are cheap and require you to share the vehicle with strangers. Even more so than with private taxis, be sure to settle on that price before you go.

not so direct-ions

Getting around the mean streets of Israel can be pretty difficult thanks to two different languages (with two different alphabets), conflicting transliterations, and a lack of street signs. *Let's Go* lists the English translations of the Hebrew street names rather than just the transliterations, so here are some helpful words to know should you find yourself faced with a mess of Hebrew words:

- **SDEROT** means "avenue" or "boulevard."
- **DERECH** means "road" or "street."
- **RECHOV** is an alternative word for "road."
- **KIKAR** means "square."
- **GAN** means "garden."

BY THUMB

Hitchhiking in Israel is more prevalent than in many places in the world, and you may see people throwing out that thumb. But along with the basic horror movie scenarios that involve being picked up by—or picking up—randos, Israel offers a few extra dangers. Keep in mind the license-plate colors mentioned above before getting into a car, and remember that *Let's Go* does not recommend hitchhiking. We beg you, even if the Kerouacian spirit strikes, just to say no to that chicken truck offering a one-way ticket to scenic industrial Afula.

safety and health

GENERAL ADVICE

In any type of crisis, the most important thing to do is **stay calm.** Your country's embassy abroad is usually your best resource in an emergency. In fact, it's a good idea to register with that embassy upon arrival in the country. The government offices listed in the **Travel Advisories** feature can provide information on the services they offer their citizens in case of emergencies abroad.

local laws and police

Depending on how you look at things, the world may seem like a much safer or much scarier place when everyone has a gun. Crime doesn't seem to be too prevalent in the country where everyone and their *bubbe* are packing heat, but that doesn't mean you shouldn't stay on your toes. Israel's police force is well respected and known for being competent and honest.

drugs and alcohol

Though we know that Israel is the place to par-tay, many devout parts of Israel have especially strict laws. Sure, you may see people tokin' in Tel Aviv, but that doesn't give you a free pass, and the use of pot is widely prosecuted. On the upside, the **drinking age** in Israel is a delightful 18. But beware, young Birthrighters: this age limit is enforced more strictly these days. Partiers of any age should avoid the loud drunk-stumble through city streets, as it's both dangerous and highly annoying.

For our more law-abiding readers, if you're bringing prescriptions with you abroad, try to always carry a copy of the prescriptions themselves.

travel advisories

The following government offices provide travel information and advisories:

- **AUSTRALIA: Department of Foreign Affairs and Trade** (☎+61 2 6261 1111; www.smartraveller.gov.au).

- **CANADA: Department of Foreign Affairs and International Trade** Call or visit the website for the free booklet *Bon Voyage, But...* (☎+1-800-267-6788; www.international.gc.ca).

- **NEW ZEALAND: Ministry of Foreign Affairs and Trade** (☎+64 4 439 8000; www.safetravel.govt.nz).

- **UK: Foreign and Commonwealth Office** (☎+44 845 850 2829; www.fco.gov.uk).

- **US: Department of State** (☎888-407-4747 from the US, +1-202-501-4444 elsewhere; http://travel.state.gov).

SPECIFIC CONCERNS

natural disasters

EARTHQUAKES

Israel is no stranger to plate tectonic motion. Almost all earthquakes occur in the Jordan Rift Valley and are too small to be felt. However, should a larger quake start to happen, make your way to a sturdy doorway, table, or desk.

SANDSTORMS

That's right, Lawrence of Arabia, some of Israel is pretty desert-y (though not as much as you might think). If you find yourself in a sandstorm in the south of Israel, cover your face with a scarf or sturdy fabric and make a run for the nearest shelter.

FLASH FLOODS

Similar to everywhere else in the world, flash floods in Israel are unpredictable and vary in seriousness. To keep safe, get to high ground immediately, particularly if you feel that your structure is susceptible to flooding, and keep your eyes peeled for rising water.

demonstrations and politics

Unfortunately, many demonstrations coincide with the high season for tourism. Ask at your hostel to find out which areas may not be safe during your visit, and then steer clear of them: generally, staying in safe neighborhoods means you stay safe. If things seem a bit volatile, check with your hostel before going out to make sure that a curfew has not been set in place.

One of the greatest parts about traveling to Israel is the opportunity to discuss some of the world's most contentious issues with the people directly affected by them. That being said, these issues mean a great deal to both Israelis and Palestinians. In Israel, politics are central to personal identity, so be smart (which we know you are—you bought this book, after all). People talk about the problems all the time, and few things are off-limits beyond the extreme—don't start telling Jews that Israel shouldn't exist or try to convince a Palestinian that they don't deserve a state. Just don't. There are a lot of other subtleties and loyalties that may be very hard to navigate—they might not be as clearly off-limits, but people do care.

Don't have an opinion unless it is an educated one, and be open to the opinions of others. If someone is offended by your opinion, back off—in the interest of politeness, not safety. Feel people out for what they will think before you talk to them, and act accordingly. Remember that almost everyone is well intentioned.

dress and etiquette

Israel is a deeply religious place. While this brings enlightenment, joy, and above-average numbers of tourists, it also means you need to bring above-average respect. Throughout our coverage we've tried to point out the places where tank tops and shorts won't fly (much less boob tubes and daisy dukes, hot as the weather may be), but stay on the lookout for how other people are acting and dressing. Ladies, carry around a shawl or sweater, particularly if you plan on going to religious sights. Gents, leave the wife-beater at the hostel; you're not Ryan Atwood, and the Old City is not the OC.

let's not go

At the time of publishing, most of the Middle East was in turmoil. You will notice that this edition does not cover Mount Sinai, the Golan Heights, and the Gaza Strip. We monitor the unrest in these places closely and make decisions based on the danger at the time. You should follow this same procedure when making travel plans for a part of Israel that was recently in a time of war or unrest.

terrorism

Since most terrorism isn't advertised beforehand, it is theoretically a constant threat. But, come on, we're all friends here. Yes, the threat of terrorism in Israel is a little more real that it is in, say, the French Riviera. Since literally the beginning of time, Israel has been a hotspot for unrest, and things have been particularly rough since it became its own state. However, we care about our readers, and we would never send you anywhere we wouldn't (and haven't) sent our own people. Don't feel terrified and helpless while in Israel; just be smart and keep your eyes on the news.

Follow the guidelines we gave in the section on **demonstrations,** and always stay aware of your surroundings. If visiting areas in the West Bank or Gaza Strip, ask around first and find out whether your trips falls near the dates of any important anniversaries or holidays, as attacks tend to take place during those times. Though it may feel inauthentic or cowardly, be careful about outward displays of religious heritage; consider trading that *kippah* for a Sox cap in heavily Palestinian areas.

Ironically, Israeli tourists are often more affected by anti-terrorist efforts than by terrorist efforts themselves. The sight of people your age toting heavy weaponry might be unnerving, but remember that soldiers are generally there for protection. It's foolish to leave your bags unattended anywhere, but in Israel unidentified luggage can be confiscated, and you could wind up being questioned. Security at sights, bus stations, and public events is almost always extensive, so if you're in a hurry or are particularly impatient, go bagless.

female and minority travelers

Needless to say, inhabitants of the Middle East look extremely, well, Middle Eastern. While this does mean that you're more likely than usual to meet a dark, handsome stranger, it also means that different complexions stand out very easily. Travelers of Asian descent in particular may experience problems with harassment. This can be avoided by traveling in groups or with at least one man in the party.

Yes, we did just say "man." Though Betty Friedan would roll over in her grave along with Susie B. and Madonna, traveling is more dangerous for women. *Let's Go* recommends wearing a decoy wedding ring to ward off creepers. It's also helpful to learn phrases like, "I'm meeting my husband," or "See that burly soldier? He's my brother, and he'll kick your ass."

PRE-DEPARTURE HEALTH

Matching a prescription to a foreign equivalent is not always easy, safe, or possible, so, if you take **prescription drugs,** carry up-to-date prescriptions or a statement from your doctor stating the medications' trade names, manufacturers, chemical names, and dosages. Be sure to keep all medication with you in your carry-on luggage. It is also a good idea to look up the Hebrew and Arabic names of drugs you may need during your trip.

immunizations and precautions

Travelers over two years old should make sure that the following vaccines are up to date: MMR (for measles, mumps, and rubella); DTaP or Td (for diphtheria, tetanus, and pertussis); IPV (for polio); Hib (for *Haemophilus influenzae* B); and HepB (for Hepatitis B). For recommendations on immunizations and prophylaxis, check with a doctor and consult the **Centers for Disease Control and Prevention (CDC)** in the US (☎+1-800-232-4636; www.cdc.gov/travel) or the equivalent in your home country.

STAYING HEALTHY

environmental hazards

Before you go out hiking and finding your roots, be sure to pack plenty of water, sunscreen, and bug spray. Israel is buzzing with mosquitoes, and you will get bitten. Fun: Oxy Pads, Clearasil, or similar alcohol-covered acne fighters also do away with that horrid itch. Stock up at Super-Pharm before taking your tour of the Dead Sea.

keeping in touch

BY EMAIL AND INTERNET

Hello, and welcome to the 21st century, where you're rarely more than a 5min. walk from the nearest Wi-Fi hot spot—even if you'll sometimes have to pay a few bucks or buy a drink in order to use it. **Internet cafes** and free internet terminals are listed in the **Practicalities** section in each city. Barring fun Digital-Bean-type establishments, almost all hostels have Wi-Fi in the lobby at the very least. For lists of additional cafes in a specific city, check out www.cybercafes.com or www.netcafeguide.com. Cyber love is going to be the best way to keep in touch while abroad, so make sure you have all the email addresses you need before you go. And, come on, not having a Facebook at this point is a lot like being that person in 2007 who still didn't text. You really are just using it keep in touch with people, right?

Wireless hot spots make internet access possible in public and remote places. Unfortunately, they also pose security risks. Hot spots are public, open networks that use unencrypted, unsecured connections. They are susceptible to hacks and "packet sniffing"—the theft of passwords and other private information. To prevent problems, disable "ad hoc" mode, turn off file sharing and network discovery, encrypt your email, turn on your firewall, beware of phony networks, and watch for over-the-shoulder creeps.

BY TELEPHONE

calling home from Israel

If you have internet access, your best—i.e., cheapest, most convenient, and most tech-savvy—means of calling home is probably our good friend **Skype** (www.skype.com). You can even videochat if you have one of those new-fangled webcams. Calls to other Skype users are free; calls to landlines and mobiles worldwide start at US$0.023 per minute, depending on where you're calling.

For those still stuck in the 20th century, **prepaid phone cards** are a common and relatively inexpensive means of calling abroad. Each one comes with a Personal Identification Number (PIN) and a toll-free access number. You call the access number and then follow the directions for dialing your PIN. To purchase prepaid phone cards, check online for the best rates; www.callingcards.com is a good place to start. Online providers generally send your access number and PIN via email, with no actual "card" involved. You can also call home with prepaid phone cards purchased in Israel.

Another option is a **calling card,** linked to a major national telecommunications service in your home country. Calls are billed collect or to your account. Cards generally come with instructions for dialing both domestically and internationally.

Placing a collect call through an international operator can be expensive but may be necessary in case of an emergency. You can frequently call collect without even possessing a company's calling card just by calling its access number and following the instructions.

international calls

To call Israel from home or to call home from Israel, dial:

- **1. THE INTERNATIONAL DIALING PREFIX.** To call from Israel dial ☎001; from **Australia,** ☎0011; **Canada** or the **US,** ☎011; and from **Ireland, New Zealand,** or the **UK,** ☎00.

- **2. THE COUNTRY CODE OF THE COUNTRY YOU WANT TO CALL.** To call Israel, dial ☎972; for **Australia,** ☎61; **Canada** or the **US,** ☎1; **Ireland,** ☎353; **New Zealand,** ☎64; and for the **UK,** ☎44.

- **3. THE LOCAL NUMBER.** If the area code begins with a zero, you can omit that number when dialing from abroad.

cellular phones

Cell phones are easy to come by in the land of milk, honey, and SIM cards. Though they sometimes run up to a few hundred shekels, pay-as-you-go phones can be found in most cities.

The international standard for cell phones is **Global System for Mobile Communication (GSM).** To make and receive calls in Israel, you will need a GSM-compatible phone and a **SIM (Subscriber Identity Module) card,** a country-specific, thumbnail-size chip that gives you a local phone number and plugs you into the local network. Many SIM cards are prepaid, and incoming calls are frequently free. You can buy additional cards or vouchers (usually available at convenience stores) to "top up" your phone. For more information on GSM phones, check out www.telestial.com. Companies like **Cellular Abroad** (www.cellularabroad.com) and **OneSimCard** (www.onesimcard.com) rent cell phones and SIM cards that work in a variety of destinations around the world.

BY SNAIL MAIL

sending mail home from Israel

Airmail is the best way to send mail home from Israel. Write "airmail" or *"par avion"* on the front. For simple letters or postcards, airmail tends to be surprisingly cheap, but the price will go up sharply for weighty packages. Surface mail is by far the cheapest, slowest, and most antiquated way to send mail. It takes one to two months to cross the Atlantic and one to three to cross the Pacific—good for heavy items you won't need for a while, like souvenirs that you've acquired along the way.

receiving mail in Israel

There are several ways to arrange pickup of letters sent to you while you are in Israel and the Palestinian Territories, even if you do not have an address of your own. Mail can be sent via **Poste Restante**, which is French for "general delivery," and therefore the obvious choice for Israel. All post offices will hold mail sent Poste Restante for up to 30 days, and all it takes to pick up said mail is a valid ID. Address letters like so:

Jesus CHRIST
Poste Restante
Nazareth, Israel

The mail will go to a special desk in the central post office in town, unless you specify a local post office by street address or postal code. It's best to use the largest post office, since mail may be sent there regardless. Bring your passport (or other photo ID) for pickup. If the clerks insist that there is nothing for you, ask them to check under your first name as well. *Let's Go* lists post offices in the **Practicalities** section of every city. It is usually safer and quicker, though more expensive, to send mail express or registered. If you don't want to deal with Poste Restante, consider asking your hostel or accommodation if you can have things mailed to you there. Of course, if you have your own mailing address or a reliable friend to receive mail for you, that will be the easiest solution.

If you're old school—or just want to mess with someone who loves old movies—you can send telegrams in Israel by dialing 171.

TIME DIFFERENCES

Israel is 2hr. ahead of Greenwich Mean Time (GMT) and observes Daylight Saving Time. This means that it is 7hr. ahead of New York City, 10hr. ahead of Los Angeles, 2hr. ahead of the British Isles, 7hr. behind Sydney, and 9hr. behind New Zealand. Don't accidentally call your mom at 5am! (But please call her. You know how she worries.)

climate

Some parts of Israel are paradise—never too hot, never too cold, light jacket at night, you know the drill. However, there's no avoiding the fact that parts of Israel are desert. Remember that whole story in the Old Testament about wandering in the wilderness for 40 days and 40 nights? There are some parts of Israel, my friends, that are very, very hot. Keep safe in the sun by investing in a touristy hat (you know you want one) and keep sunscreen on hand. Also, either track down Miriam and her moving well of water or carry water with you at all times. In terms of rain, shine, etc., on a bad day you might see a cloud, but it's usually all rays all the time.

Israel is somewhat diverse in climate. The listed temperatures are for Jerusalem, a good (but not exact) barometer for weather worries.

MONTH	AVG. HIGH TEMP.		AVG. LOW TEMP.		AVG. RAINFALL	
January	12°C	53°F	6°C	44°F	133mm	5.2 in.
February	13°C	55°F	6°C	44°F	118mm	4.7 in.
March	15°C	60°F	8°C	47°F	93mm	3.6 in.
April	22°C	71°F	13°C	55°F	25mm	1 in.
May	25°C	78°F	16°C	60°F	3.2mm	0.1 in.
June	28°C	82°F	18°C	64°F	0mm	0 in.
July	29°C	84°F	19°C	67°F	0mm	0 in.
August	29°C	85°F	20°C	67°F	0mm	0 in.
September	28°C	83°F	19°C	65°F	0.3mm	0 in.
October	25°C	76°F	17°C	62°F	15mm	0.6 in.
November	19°C	66°F	12°C	54°F	61mm	2.4 in.
December	14°C	57°F	8°C	47°F	106mm	4.2 in.

To convert from degrees Fahrenheit to degrees Celsius, subtract 32 and multiply by 5/9. To convert from Celsius to Fahrenheit, multiply by 9/5 and add 32. The mathematically challenged may use this handy chart:

°CELSIUS	-5	0	5	10	15	20	25	30	35	40
°FAHRENHEIT	23	32	41	50	59	68	77	86	95	104

measurements

Like the rest of the rational world, Israel uses the metric system. The basic unit of length is the meter (m), which is divided into 100 centimeters (cm) or 1000 millimeters (mm). One thousand meters make up one kilometer (km). Fluids are measured in liters (L), each divided into 1000 milliliters (mL). A liter of pure water weighs one kilogram (kg), the unit of mass that is divided into 1000 grams (g). One metric ton is 1000kg.

MEASUREMENT CONVERSIONS	
1 inch (in.) = 25.4mm	1 millimeter (mm) = 0.039 in.
1 foot (ft.) = 0.305m	1 meter (m) = 3.28 ft.
1 yard (yd.) = 0.914m	1 meter (m) = 1.094 yd.
1 mile (mi.) = 1.609km	1 kilometer (km) = 0.621 mi.
1 ounce (oz.) = 28.35g	1 gram (g) = 0.035 oz.
1 pound (lb.) = 0.454kg	1 kilogram (kg) = 2.205 lb.
1 fluid ounce (fl. oz.) = 29.57mL	1 milliliter (mL) = 0.034 fl. oz.
1 gallon (gal.) = 3.785L	1 liter (L) = 0.264 gal.

language

HEBREW

We can only assume that, as a *Let's Go* reader and future pioneer of Israel's vast lands, you laugh in the face of a challenge. And Hebrew, the primary language of Israel, is, in fact, a challenge, whether you're looking to know a few quick phrases or learn the language to get the authentic Israeli experience.

The letters, which will heretofore be referred to as symbols to spare our Roman-alphabet-raised readers' sensibilities, are read from right to left, not left to right—or "normally" if we want to get all politically incorrect like that. Vowels don't get their own letters, but are symbols strategically placed around the other symbols. Truth be told, most signs and translations don't even use the vowels, so—though they might one day unionize and get their rights—right now, we're going to let them be. There are also several letters that have two different symbols: one for when it falls in the beginning or middle of a word and one for when it falls at the end. Why do we have these alphabetic traditions? Why? We'll tell you. We don't know. And neither does Tevya.

alphabet

"Ach!" you exclaim upon landing at Ben-Gurion, "This is not the alphabet Elmo taught me!" Okay, okay, before you start shvitzing and planning a new trip, take a look at this handy chart:

SYMBOL	NAME	PRONOUNCED	SYMBOL	NAME	PRONOUNCED
א	alef	silent, mostly used for vowel placement	ל	lamed	*l* as in lovah
ב	bet	*b* as in boat	ם ,מ	mem, final mem	*m* as in mole
ג	gimmel	*g* as in gimlet	ן , נ	nun, final nun	n as in Nessie
ד	dalet	*d* as in dope	ס	samekh	s as in savior
ה	he	*h* as in ha-ha!	ע	ayin	silent like lasagna
ו	vav	*v* as in velour	ף , פ	pe, final pe	*p* as in pee-pee
ז	zayin	z as in zany	ץ , צ	tsadi, final tsadi	*ts* as in tsk
ח	het	*hh* as in challah-back girl	ק	qof	*k* as in kite
ט	tet	*t* as in toot	ר	resh	*r* as in rakish
י	yod	silent	ש , שׂ	sin, shin	*s, sh* as in... sin and shin
כ, ך	kaf, final kaf	*kch* as in kitch	ת	tav	*t* as in totes

numbers

Being the go-getters that they are, Jews also use Hebrew symbols as numbers. Cue handy-dandy chart part two. Zero is *efes* because—as the perennial black sheep—not only is he neither positive nor negative, but he also has no letter assignation. Always marching to the beat of his own *oud*, that one.

SYMBOL	NAME	VALUE	SYMBOL	NAME	VALUE
א	echas	1	כ	shloshim	30
ב	shnayim	2	ל	arba'im	40
ג	shlosha	3	מ	chamishim	50
ד	arb'a	4	נ	shishim	60
ה	chamisha	5	ס	shiv'im	70
ו	shish	6	ע	shmonim	80
ז	shiv'a	7	פ	tish'im	90
ח	shmonah	8	צ	me'a	100
ט	tish'a	9	ק	matayim	200

essentials

| י | assara | 10 | ש | shlosh meot | 300 |
| ר | esrim | 20 | ת | arba meot | 400 |

ARABIC

The Israeli-Arab conflict runs deep, deeper than borders, deeper than the age-old pot roast or shawarma debate—it runs down into the lines of communication. Yes, in Israel, Hebrew is a pretty important language. But Arabic is no chopped liver. In fact, it has roughly 447 million more speakers. Picking up a few phrases might be helpful.

Neither of the two languages wins the sought after "Ridiculously Hard to Read and Learn Award"—they're both equally fiendish. Arabic, like Hebrew, reads from right to left and is short on the vowels.

alphabet

The Arabic alphabet gets tricky, especially because many of the letters make very similar sounds. Sometimes you just have to accept that things can seem different but still sound the same, just like every single song by Jack Johnson. Note that the distinction between taa and thaa is very small—and then taa and thaa are repeated. The difference can really only be distinguished when heard. The different letters influence the way that the following letters are pronounced. Another example of this is the different between daal and daa—whereas "daal" is extremely similar to the Roman "d" and is pronounced like "d" in "dad," "daad" represents a sound more like the "d" in "dodge." Again, this is why we're giving you phonetic translations.

SYMBOL	NAME	PRONOUNCED	SYMBOL	NAME	PRONOUNCED
ا	alif	a as in alley	ض	daad	d as in dodge
ب	baa	b as in bed bug	ط	taa	t as in talk
ت	taa	t as in tank engine	ظ	thaa	th as in thought
ث	thaa	th as in think	ع	ayn	ayn as in Fran Drescher saying I'd
ج	jiim	j as in jim halpert	غ	ghayn	similar to the above but more gutteral, like Fran Drescher when she's angry
ح	haa	h as in how	ف	faa	f as in falafel
خ	xaa	ch as in Bach	ق	qaa	hard c as in cucumber
د	daal	d as in damn	ك	kaaf	k as in krakow
ذ	thaal	th as in that	ل	laam	l as in llama
ر	raa	r as in ra-ra-ra-ra-ra	م	miim	m as in my oh my
ز	zaay	z as in zoinks	ن	nuun	n as in now
س	siin	s as in super	ه	haa	h as in hey
ش	shiin	sh as in shh!	و	waaw	u as in under
ص	saad	s as in soot	ي	yaa	y or ee as in yes or we

numbers

SYMBOL	NAME	VALUE	SYMBOL	NAME	VALUE
٠	sifr	0	٢٠	'ishrun	20
١	wahid	1	٣٠	thalathun	30
٢	ithnan	2	٤٠	arba'un	40
٣	thalatha	3	٥٠	khamsun	50
٤	arba'a	4	٦٠	sittun	60
٥	khamsa	5	٧٠	sab'un	70
٦	sitta	6	٨٠	thamanun	80

language

٧	sab'a	7	٩٠	tis'un	90
٨	thamaniya	8	١٠٠	mi'a	100
٩	tis'a	9	٢٠٠	mitayn	200
١٠	'ashra	10	٣٠٠	thalaath mi'a	300

PHRASEBOOK

Fun fact: in Hebrew, me means who, he means she, and dog means fish. What? You wanted more than that? Fine, we've included a few of the most important phrases with the transliteration so you can converse with the masses. As in any language, a simple, "Do you speak English?" goes a long way. Or, if all else fails, consider the traveler's golden standby of frantically waving your arms around to get your point across.

ENGLISH	HEBREW	ARABIC
Hello	Shalom	As-salammu aleikum
Goodbye	Shalom	Ma' as-salaama
Could you help me?	To M: Ata yakhol la'azor lee? To F: At yekhola la'azor lee?	To M: Mumkeen Tesa'eedni? To F: Tesa'edeenee?
Good morning	Boker tov	Sabah al-kheir (Response: Sabah an-nour)
Good evening	Erev tov	Masaa' al-kheir
How are you?	To M: Ma shlomkha? To F: Ma shlomekh?	To M: Keefak? To F: Keefek?
Fine / Excellent / Not good	Beseder / Metzuyan / Lo tov	Mnih / Mumtaaz / Mush mnih
I'm tired	M: Anee ayef F: Anee ayefa	M: Ana ta'abaan F: Ana ta'abaana
Yes	Ken	Na'am / Aywa
No	Lo	La
Maybe	Ulay	Mumkin
Thank you	Toda	Shukran
Excuse me (to get one someone's attention)	Slikha	To M: Lao samaht To F: Lao samahet
Please / You're welcome	Bevakasha / Bevakasha	To M: Min fadlak; To F: Min fadlek / Afwan
I don't know	M: Lo yode'a F: Lo yoda'at	Ma ba'arifsh
What is your name?	To M: Eikh kor'im lecha? To F: Eich kor'im lach?	To M: Shu ismak? To F: Shu ismek?
My name is...	Shmi...	Ismi...
I'm a student	M: Ani student F: Ani studentit	M: Ana taalib F: Ana taaliba
Who	Mee	Meen
How do you say..?	Eikh omrim..?	To M: Keef beet'ool..? To F: Keef beet'oolee..?
I don't understand	Ani lo mevin	Ma afhamsh
I don't speak Hebrew/Arabic	M: Ani lo medaber eevreet F: Ani lo medaberet eevreet	Bah'keesh arabee
Do you speak English?	To M: Ata medaber angleet? To F: At medaberet angleet?	Tihki elengleezeeya?
Please repeat	To M: Tageed shuv pa'am bev-akasha; To F: Tageedee shuv...	To M: A'ed meen fadlak To F: A'edee meen fadlek
Please speak slowly	To M: Daber le'at bevakasha To F: Dabree le'at bevakasha	To M: Ihki shwaya meen fadlak; To F: ...meen fadlek
I'd like to make a call to the US	M: Ani rotze leheetkasher le'artzot habreet; F: Ani rotzah...	Bidee attasel al-weelayaat el-mutakheeda
Telephone	Telephon	Teeliphoon/Haatif
What do you call this in Hebrew/Arabic?	Eikh kor'im leze be'eevreet?	Keef bee'tsami haada beel'arabi?
Great/Awesome	Sababa	Mummtaz

essentials

DIRECTIONS		
Where is...?	Eyfo?	Wayn?
Straight	Yashar	Dughri
Right	Yemeen	Yameen
Left	Smol	Yasaar
How far is...?	Kama rakhok?	Ad'eish yab'ud... (masculine noun) Ad'eish tab'ud... (feminine noun)
North/South/East/West	Tzafon/Darom/Mizrakh/Ma'arav	Shimaal/Janub/Sharq/Gharb
I'm lost	Ne'ebadetee	Ma Ba'arifsh wayn ana
When	Matay	Eemta
Why	Lama	Leysh
I'm going/riding to...	M: Anee nose'a le... F: Ani nosa'at le...	M: Ana mesaafir ala... F: Ana mesaafira ala...
There is...	Yesh	Fee
There is no...	Eyn	Mafeesh
Do you know where... is?	To M: Ata yode'a eyfo...nimtza? To F: At yoda'at eyfo...nimtza?	To M: Aaref wayn..? To F: Aarfe wayn..?
Wait a second	Rak rega	Lahtha
Let's go!	Yalla!	Yalla!
PLACES		
Bathroom	Sherooteem	Manaafi
Beach/Ocean/Mountain	Khof/Yam/Har	Shaate/Bahr/Jabil
Boulevard	Sdera	Jaada
Building	Binyan	Mabnee
Center of town	Merkaz ha'ir	Markaz el-madeena
City	Eer	Madeena
Town	Kfar	Karya
Road	Kveesh	Tareeqa
Church	Kneseeya	Kaneesa
Market	Shuk	Souq
Museum	Muze'on	Matkhaf
Mosque	Misgad	Masjid
Pharmacy	Beit merkakhat	Saydaleeya
Post office	Sneef do'ar	Maktab el-bareed
Pool	Brekha	Bareekat sabaakha
Restaurant	Mis'ada	Mat'am
Room	Kheder	Ghurfa
Street	Rekhov	Shaare
Synagogue	Beit knesset	Kanees
University	Ooniverseeta	Jaami'a
TRANSPORTATION		
Central Bus Station	Takhana merkazeet	
Bus Stop	Takhanat otoboos	
Do you stop at...?	To M: Ata otzer be...? To F: At otzeret be...?	To M: Bee'tkif eend..? To F: Bee'tkifee eend...?
From where does the bus leave?	Me'eyfo yotze ha'otoboos?	Meen wayn ghaadir elbas?
I would like a ticket for...	M: Ani rotze kartees le... F: Ani rotza kartees le...	Bidee tathkara eela...
One-way	Rak halokh	Thahaban faqt
Round-trip	Halokh ve-khazor	Thahaban wa-awdatan
Please stop	To M: Ta'atzor bevakasha To F: Ta'atzri bevakasha	To M: Wa'ef meen fadlak To F: Wa'fee meen fadlek
Take the bus from...to...	To M: Kakh et haotoboos me...le... To F: Kekhi et haotoboos me...le...	To M: Khuth el-bas meen...la... To F: Khuthi el-bas meen...la...
What time does the...leave?	Be'eyze sha'a ha...yotze?	Fee ay sa'ah mghaader el...?

language

Bus/Train	Otoboos/Rakevet	Bas/Kataar
Taxi	Moneet	Taaksi/Sayyaara ajra
Car	Mekhoneet	Sayyaara
Where are you going?	To M: Le'an ata nose'a? To F: Le'an at nosa'at?	To M: Lawayn mesaafir? To F: Lawayn mesaafira?
Airport	Sde te'ufaa	Mataar
Plane	Matos	Tayyara
Tourist	Tayar	Sayih
Use the meter please (to be said adamantly to swindling taxi drivers)	To M: Teeshtamesh ba'moneh bevakasha; To F: Teeshtamshe...	To M: Eesti'mal el'adad meen fadlak; To F: ...meen fadlek

DATE AND TIME

What time is it?	Ma hasha'ah?	Addeysh e-sa'a?
At what time...?	Be'eyzo sha'a...?	Fee ay sa'a...?
Hour, time	Sha'a	Sa'a
Day/Week/Month/Year	Yom/Shavua/Khodesh/Shanah	Yawm/Usbuu'/Shahr/Sana
Early/Late	Mukdam/Me'ukhar	Bakeer/Muta'akhir
Morning/Afternoon/Evening/Night	Boker/Tzohorayeem/Erev/Layla	Sabah/Thuher/Masaa'/Leyl
Open/Closed	Patuakh/Sagur	Maftuuh/Mughalak
Today/Yesterday/Tomorrow	Hayom/Etmol/Makhar	El-yawm/Imbaareh/Bukra
Sunday	Yom Rishon	Yawm el-Ahad
Monday	Yom Sheni	Yawm el-Ithneyn
Tuesday	Yom Shleeshee	Yawm at-Talaat
Wednesday	Yom Revee'ee	Yawm el-Arba'
Thursday	Yom Khameeshee	Yawm el-Khamees
Friday	Yom Sheeshee	Yawm el-Jum'aa
Sabbath (Saturday)	Yom Shabbat	Yawm e-Sabt

ACCOMMODATIONS

Do you have a single/double room?	To M: Yesh lekha kheder yakheed/zugee? To F: Yesh lakh kheder...	To M: Eendak ghurfa leeshakhs waahid/gurhfa leeshakhseyn? To F: Eendek ghurfa...
Do you know of a cheap hotel?	To M: Ata makeer malon zol? To F: At makeera malon zol?	To M: Ti'raf funduk rakhees? To F: Ti'rafee funduk rakhees?
Hotel/Hostel	Beyt malon/Akhsaneeya	Funduk/Funduk leetulaab
How much is the room?	Kama ole hakheder?	Adeysh el-ghurfa?
I'd like a room	To M: Ani rotze kheder To F: Ani rotza kheder	Bidee ghurfa
I'd like to reserve a room	To M: Ani rotze lehazmeen kheder To F: Ani rotza lehazmeen kheder	Bidee ahjiz ghurfa
Upstairs	Lemaala	Foq
Downstairs	Lemaata	Taht
What's your special price for me?	Ma hamekheer hameyukhad shelakhem beeshveelee?	Adeysh elsha'er elkhaas lee?

FOOD

Restaurant	Mees'ada	Mat'am
Waiter	Meltzar	Naadil
Water	Mayeem	Mayaa
Bread	Lekhem	Khubz
Could I have some more...	Efshar od...	Mumkin kamaan...
Grocery store	Makolet	Bakaala
Breakfast/Lunch/Dinner	Arukhat Boker/Arukhat Tzohorayim/Arukhat Erev	Ftur/Ghadaa/Ashaa
Chicken	Off	Dijaaja
Beef	Bakar	Lahm bakr
Vegetables	Yerakot	Khathraa
Do you have vegetarian food?	Yesh lakhem okhel tzeemk-honee?	Eendkoo akel nabaatee?

I am vegetarian	M: Anee tzeemkhonee F: Anee tzeemkhoneet	M: Ana nabaatee F: Ana nabaateeya
Coffee/Tea	Kafe/Te	Ahwe/Shay
Milk	Khalav	Haleeb/Labn
Eggs	Beyzteem	Bayd
Candy/Chocolate	Sukareeyot/Shokolad	Heelweeyaat/Shookoolaat
Ice cream/Cake/Cookies	Gleeda/Uga/Ugiyot	Jilati/ Ka'aka/Ka'aka
I'm stuffed	Ana mefootzatz	Ana halloss maa ikhl
This hummus is divine	Hakhumus haze elohee	Hatha tahina el-humdelilah

EMERGENCY		
Hospital	Beyt Kholeem	Mustashfa
Doctor	Rofe	Dooktoor/Tabeeb
I need a doctor	M: Ani tzareekh rofe F: Ani tzreekha rofe	M: Ana muhtaaj ledooktoor F: Ana muhtaaje ledooktoor
Don't touch me	To M: Al teega bee To F: Al teeg'ee bee	To M: Ma talmasnee To F: Ma talmaseenee
Help!	Hatzeelu!	Eelkha'unee!
I'm calling the police	M: Anee meetkasher lameeshtara F: Anee meetkasheret lameeshtara	M: Ana muttasil a-shurta F: Ana muttasila a-shurta
Leave me alone	To M: Azov otee To F: Azvee otee	Khaleenee lawahdi
Police/Firefighters/Ambulance	Meeshtara/Mekhabey esh/ Ambulans	Shurta/El-Mutaafe/Sayaarat ees'aaf
I'm ill	M: Anee khole F: Anee khola	M: Ana mareed F: Ana mareeda
I'm hurt	M: Anee patzua F: Anee ptzu'aa	M: Ana mujreh F: Ana mujreha
Stop!	Atzor!	Waqef!
Passport	Darkon	Jawaaz safr
Israeli/Palestinian Red Cross (ambulance service)	Magen daveed adom (often abbre-viated to "mada")	Elheelal el-akhmar
Bomb shelter	Meeklat	Malja
We're all going to die!	Anakhnu koolanu holkhim lamut!	Kulna han'moot!

MONEY AND BARGAINING		
How much?	Kama?	Adeesh?/Bekem?
No way!	Eyn sikuy!	Mush mumken!
I'll give you half	Anee eten lekha khetzi	Ba'ateek nus
Money	Kesef	Masaaree
Change	Odef	Fraata/Faakaa
I want...	M: Anee rotze... F: Anee rotza...	Bidee.../Yoreed...
Tip	Teep/Tesher	Baqsheesh
You should pay *me* for this	Ata tzareekh leshaleem *lee* bishveel ze	Lazm tidfa'anee *eenta* leehada

BARS AND NIGHTLIFE		
Beer	Beera	Beera
Wine	Yayn	Khamr
Bar	Bar	Bar
Club	Mo'adon	El-naadee el-lell
Party	Meseeba	Hafla
What beer do you have on tap?	Eyzo beera yesh lakhem me'hakhaveet?	Shoo beera andek fee cubeya?
Can I have another...?	Efshar od..?	Mumkeen kamaan..?
Is there a cover charge? How much?	Yesh mekhir kneesa? Kama ze?	Bekem illa dahel?
How late are you open?	Ad eyzo sha'a atem ptookheem?	Hata ay sa'ah eentoo maftooheen?
Do you have live music?	Yesh lakhem moozeeka khaya?	Entee andak haflat museeka?

language

Drinks list	Tafreet maskha'ot	Shurub menu min fudlik
Gay night	Erev homo'eem velezbeeyot	(This does not exist formally in Arabic)
I'm drunk	M: Anee sheekor F: Anee sheekora	Ana shurrub
I'm high	M: Anee mastool F: Anee mastoola	Ana ahhlea
What do you want to drink?	To M: Ma ata rotze leeshtot? To F: Ma at rotza leeshtot?	To M: Shoo beedak teeshrab? To F: Shoo beedek teeshrabee?
I've had enough to drink.	Shateetee maspeek	Ana khaaloss maa shurub
Do you want to head out?	To M: Ata rotze lalekhet? To F: At rotza lalekhet?	Yalla beeana?
What's a girl/guy like you doing in a place like this?	To M: Ma bakhur kamokha ose bemakom kaze? To F: Ma bakhura kamokh osa bemakom kaze?	Shoo bint/waled mithl entee amel fee makkan mithl hatha?
How old are you?	To M: Ben kama ata? To F: Bat kama at?	To M: Adeysh omrak? to F: Adeysh omrek?
Where are you from?	To M: Me'eyfo ata? To F: Me'eyfo at?	To M: Entee men aaen? To F: Entii men feen?
Do you want to dance?	To M: Ata rotze lirkod? To F: At rotza lirkod?	To M: Enta yoreed el ru'kus? To F: Entee yoreed el ru'kus?
What's your phone number?	To M: Me meespar hatelephon shelkha? To F: ... shelakh?	To M: Shoo teleephoonak? To F: Shoo teleephonek?
I'm not interested.	M: Anee lo me'unyan F: Anee lo me'unyenet	Mish ayyiz
Leave me alone	To M: Azov otee To F: Azvee otee	Ammshee
I have a boyfriend/girlfriend	Yesh lee khaver/khavera	Eendee saheb/sahbe

let's go online

Plan your next trip on our spiffy website, **www.letsgo.com.** It features full book content, the latest travel info on your favorite destinations, and tons of interactive features: make your own itinerary, read blogs from our trusty Researcher-Writers, browse our photo library, watch exclusive videos, check out our newsletter, find travel deals, follow us on Facebook, and buy new guides. Plus, if this Essentials wasn't enough for you, we've got even more online. We're always updating and adding new features, so check back often!

essentials

ISRAEL 101

Israel may be kiddie pool-sized, but its depth of history and culture rivals oceans. This country, smaller than the state of New Jersey, proves acreage matters little. Dating back to biblical times, the region is a true cradle of civilization, home to multiple world religions and even more street-side falafel stands. Through a tumultuous history of religious upheaval, political overturning, and mass exodus, Israel has weathered everything thrown at it and comes out stronger. This plucky country shows size matters little; its willingness to fight for what it believes in and drive to continually redefine its global identity demonstrates its lion-hearted culture steeped in religious tradition. With so much resting on its shoulders, the biggest wonder may be as to how Israel still somehow manages to find time to go with the flow and party like a youngster.

facts and figures

- **SIZE OF ISRAEL IN SQUARE KILOMETERS:** 20,770 or 22,072, depending on whom you talk to
- **SIZE OF NEW JERSEY IN SQUARE KILOMETERS:** 22,608
- **NUMBER OF OFFICIAL ISRAELI RELIGIONS:** 5
- **NUMBER OF CELL PHONES PER PERSON:** 2.1
- **WEIGHT OF WORLD'S LARGEST FALAFEL IN POUNDS:** 24

367

history

AROUND 3000 BCE.
Jacob, grandson of Abraham, changes his name to Israel, and sets that stone a-rolling.

IN THE GARDEN OF EDEN BABY (BEGINNING OF TIME-BIBLICAL TIMES)

According to a few best-selling books, **Abraham** first joined the cool kids club when God came down to Earth to make a strangely skewed deal with him: Abraham would get as many descendants as the stars in the sky, but they would have to be persecuted for 400 years and then wander the wilderness for another 40. Unable to argue with this sound logic, Abraham agreed. After some troubles involving infertility and a rather unlucky handmaiden, Abraham ended up with two sons: Ishmael got cast out into the desert to found what is now Palestine, and Isaac was set to work making all those descendants, starting with a set of twins, Jacob and Esau.

587 BCE.
Destruction of the First Temple of Jerusalem by the Babylonians.

LET MY PEOPLE GO! (1280 BCE-1890)

True to His word, these descendants of Abraham suffered, enslaved in Egypt for several generations. After escaping in 1280 BCE, the Jewish people began an **Exodus** across the desert, then finally set down roots and built themselves a city that they called Jerusalem. Things were gravy for a few hundred years until, in 721 BCE, Israel was conquered by Assyria and subsequently Babylonia, at which point the city of Jerusalem was destroyed and the Jewish people were exiled to Babylon. However, in the seventh century BCE, the Assyrian king Ashurbanipal (try saying that five times fast) died and the Assyrian Empire collapsed, leaving the geographical Palestine open for business.

63 BCE.
Destruction of the Second Temple of Jerusalem by the Romans.

Over the next 2000 years, Israel switched hands like a hot potato—anyone who was anyone in the conquering and/or colonial set just had to have it. It bounced between Egyptian, Babylonian, Persian, and Sassanian rule until the **Ottoman Turks** laid down the law in 1516 and took control. The Ottomans kept an iron fist on the region for 400 years, even shutting down the ever-precocious Napoleon's attempts at usurpation.

ZIONISM? I HARDLY KNOWS'M! (1890-1900)

Specifically Jewish political movements finally codified in the 1890s with the emergence of **Zionism**, a movement for the creation of a Jewish country to replace the region then called **Ottoman Palestine**. The movement was precipitated by **Theodor Herzl**, a Jewish writer and journalist from Budapest. Studying in France during the late 19th century, Herzl witnessed the incredible anti-Semitism and decided that it was a societal ill that could not be changed. Rejecting the idea of assimilation, Herzl founded the idea of an entirely Jewish state, a haven for the persecuted Semites of Europe. He began to organize a collection of stockholders to help him finance this ideal and in 1897 convened the first Zionist Congress, using the event to help form the **World Zionist Organization** (minus 10 points for lack of creativity), of which he was elected the president.

1 CE.
Baffled by a rather confusing pregnancy, the medical community of the Middle East sets all calendars back to 1 to deal.

COLONIALISM IS ALL THE RAGE (1900-1945)

At the same time, in geographical Israel, the Ottoman Empire was still the big man on campus. Unfortunately for them, all things must come to an end, and the Ottoman Turks ended in a big way. In 1917, still high on the power trip of World War I, **Britain** took control of the land and formalized the boundaries of Palestine. In a rather abstract deal, Britain promised the Jewish peoples of Europe a "National Home" in the Balfour Declaration, and thousands of Jewish immigrants began to move into Palestine. Unfortunately, Britain had failed to discuss the plan with the Arab people already living in Palestine and, as the rise of Hitler encouraged many European Jews to seek sandier pastures, Palestinian Arab nationalist organizations sprouted in protest. Jewish efforts to assist in illegal immigration, coupled with the rise of militant Zionist groups, did not help the situation, and the violent **Arab Revolt** of 1936-39 added yet another reason for Britain to regret its earlier, er, altruism.

DIVIDE AND CONQUER (1945-1965)

As Jews continued to pour into the region after World War II and the British mandate drew to a close, the situation worsened. In 1947, the United Nations stepped in and split Palestine into two states: the **Jewish Israel** and the **Arab Palestine**, with Jerusalem left under international control. This move was met by reluctant acceptance from the Jews (who, after all, did get over half the land) and full-blown dissent from almost every Arab leader in the area. Both sides prepared for war, so it came as no surprise that, on May 15, 1948, the day after the State of Israel declared independence, it was promptly invaded by neighboring Arab countries.

Proving that they had learned a few lessons from David and Goliath, the **Israeli Defense Forces** managed to protect their allotted regions and conquer large pieces of Palestine. Many Arab inhabitants fled to the few areas remaining under Arab control, with refugee camps set up in the Gaza Strip, West Bank, and nearby countries. The Arabs that remained were given Israeli citizenship but placed under martial law until the 1960s, while the **Palestinian Liberation Organization (PLO),** led by **Yasser Arafat,** sprung up in response to the situation.

A HELLO TO ARMS (1965-1991)

A watched pot may not boil, but it appears that a watched region still can. Despite international attempts at diplomacy, decades of simmering violence erupted into a vigorous boil in 1967 with **The Six-Day War**, during which Israel attacked the amassed forces of neighboring Arab countries. In the **1973 Arab-Israeli War**, those countries struck back (noticing a pattern yet?). Disputed regions continued to change hands, resulting in the displacement of more Palestinian Arabs and, yes, more tension until a 1979 Israeli-Egyptian **peace treaty** left Israel with its present-day boundaries. All of the problems in the Middle East were miraculously solved.

Kidding. Palestinians were still understandably upset

1099 CE.
The Crusaders' first visit, resullting in the killing of thousands of Jews and Muslims alike and, yes, the destruction of the temple.

1973.
Yom Kippur War. Not, as one would hope, a giant, latke-driven food fight.

1985.
Sports Illustrated supermodel Bar Refaeli is born. Men all over the world rejoice.

1992.
Darwish Darwish is awarded the first all-Arab prize for musical excellence in the *oud*. It's unclear how many other people were even entered.

history

about this whole your-former-homeland-is-now-our-land business, and, after an inconvenient car accident between an Israeli armored transport and several Arab cars in 1987, violence again erupted. Palestinians responded to 20 years of military occupation with just about any weapon that they could find during the **intifada** ("uprising" in Arabic), which raged throughout the Gaza Strip and soon spread to the PLO-controlled West Bank, becoming more organized as time went on.

NOWADAYS (HOT HONEY RAG!) (1991-PRESENT)

Although the 1993 **Oslo Accords** brought the first glimmers of peace in a long time, with Israeli troops beginning to withdraw from the West Bank and Gaza Strip, tensions reignited in 1996 due to Israel's treatment of certain Islamic holy sites. **Hamas** and other militant groups continued attacks on Israelis, and Israel began constructing a giant **separation fence** along the border between the West Bank and Israel. This did nothing to prevent a second *intifada* in 2000. In recent years, small wars have also broken out on the Lebanese border and in the Gaza Strip.

These days, the status of many of the disputed regions is still unclear. The Gaza Strip is internationally considered to be Israeli-occupied territories, although Israel unilaterally withdrew from the Gaza Strip in 2005, leaving the governance of the region to the **Palestinian Authority**. Hamas has since taken over, and the area remains extremely dangerous for tourists. The West Bank is currently under joint control.

customs and etiquette

SHOP 'TIL YOU (HOPEFULLY DON'T) DROP

Haggling is an acceptable practice in Israel, although this exercise is not for the faint-of-heart. While it is generally not acceptable in smaller family-run stores, it is expected that you get sassy in order to shop savvy at **souqs,** the open markets stuffed with textiles, jewelry, food, and trinkets. Also, don't be alarmed by the large men with guns standing in the entrances to department stores checking bags; they're government soldiers mandated for your safety. Just make a point not to try the five-finger discount—there's always a chance they might be trigger-happy.

IN GOD WE TRUST

Israel is a country with a torrid political background and the birthplace to multiple major religions. Respect for religious places, symbols, and monuments is very important, and, in general, a conscientious attitude toward topics of potential conflict is recommended. This conscientiousness extends to clothing: churches, temples, and mosques often refuse entrance to those sporting bare shoulders, upper arms, backs, or legs, so save the miniskirts (and even shorts and tank tops) for the clubs of Tel Aviv. You don't need to wear a burka, but carrying a scarf to help you cover up is probably a smart move.

It's also good to remember that, while about 75% of Israelis consider themselves Jewish, the country houses the religious monuments and cultures of several other prominent religions. Islam has substantial ties to the region as do Christianity and the newer religion of Baha'i. When traveling and sightseeing, be sure to remember that sites holy to some religions, others may feel equal ownership to as well.

Another important fact is that many neighboring Arab countries will deny access to travelers who have Israeli stamps on their passports. If you're planning on making a *hajj* anytime in the near future, it might be prudent to ask the customs official to stamp another piece of paper that can be easily removed from your passport before the next set of customs.

ON THE HOT SEAT

Israelis are notorious for valuing **honesty** over politeness. Given a long history of persecution, Israelis have developed a culture in which arguing for what you believe in is worth far more than protecting the feelings of those around you, and a person's deepest personal opinions are far more interesting than his or her thoughts on the weather. Don't be offended if conversations seem personal or heated; chances are your acquaintance is genuinely interested in what you have to say.

GLBT CULTURE

Despite its reputation as fairly conservative, Israel is probably one of the most accepting of the Middle Eastern countries to gay and lesbian tourists. Several of the world's more famous transsexual and transgender musicians, performers, and public figures hail from Israel, including Sharon Cohen (better known as **Dana International**) and Aderet. Although Tel Aviv is known as a gay haven in the Middle East, GLBT travelers may want to be careful about letting that pride flag fly in the more religious parts of the country, such as the West Bank and parts of Jerusalem.

food and drink

MEATY CHOICES

Given the heavily religious background of Israeli cuisine, Tel Aviv might not be the place to find the world's best pork chop. Other options make up for the lack of oink: kebab-style beef and lamb are particularly prevalent along with *osban*—sausages filled with meat, spinach, and spices. **Turkey** has also evolved as a popular meat ever since the 1940s when, due to some worldwide crises, most meat was too expensive to be consumed with every meal. An inexpensive alternative to chicken, turkey gained popularity and is now served breaded, often with pasta, as a basic main meal.

MANNA OF HEAVEN

In the late 20th century, as part of a larger movement to help create a distinctly Israeli culture, Israelis began to incorporate more and more biblical foods into their diets. Pomegranates, honey, and something known as "prickly pear" became very popular as a tie to religious backgrounds. Just beware if anyone offers you a particularly good apple…

STANDING OVATION

If you don't have time to stop and eat, the chances of finding a **street vendor** in an Israeli city are high. Here you can purchase all kinds of wraps, pitas, and sandwiches to eat while running to your next museum stop or gawking at the sights around you. For the vegetarians, **falafel** are fried balls of chickpeas and spices often served in a pita with veggies and a tahini- or yogurt-based sauce. On the carnivorous side of things, **shawarma** is meat cooked with lamb fat on a rotisserie burner and then served in a wrap with hummus, onions, lettuce, and pickles.

LOTS OF LOX

However you pronounce it, a bagel is very different in Israel than the typical New York breakfast food. Instead of being boiled rings of dough, "Jerusalem" bagels are oblong. They are also sweeter and chewier than their American counterparts, often rolled in sesame seeds and eaten at sporting events. No need for fixings here—these babies are prime for eating on the go.

food and drink

KOSHER

As a largely Jewish nation, Israel takes its kosher laws seriously. While it is possible to find non-kosher restaurants, don't count on every establishment you visit being willing to serve you that bacon cheeseburger. Kosher laws detail dietary restrictions: first and foremost it features a list of forbidden meats including (but not limited to) pork, rabbit, and shellfish. Even animals that have been deemed acceptable under kosher law must be slaughtered humanely, prepared properly, and blessed by a rabbi before they are consumed. Meat and dairy can never be mixed.

If you're feeling particularly peckish, it might be helpful to know that in 2008 a panel of rabbis ruled that eating giraffe meat with milk is acceptable under kosher rulings. Unfortunately, hunting giraffe is currently illegal but, hey, knowing is half the battle.

fashion

HUBBA HUBBA

Israel has sent some true beauties to America lately (Natalie Portman, anyone?), and its fashion industry has become a major competitor in European shows. Schools such as the Shenkar College of Engineering and Design and the Bezalel Academy of Arts and Design prepare the new fashion elite of Israel to compete with their Milanese rivals. Since self-designed, couture clothing is cheaper in Israel than in America or Europe, treat yourself to some designer clothing to impress your friends back home!

GET THEE TO A NUNNERY

Even the fashion industry can't escape the importance of religion in Israel, and many designers feature clothing that is specifically meant to appeal to the niche market of Orthodox high fashion. New designs are premiered at women-only fairs where models strut the runway sporting headscarves and floor-length dresses, and booths abound with clothing and headwear aimed at being both modest and trendy.

SHOW SOME SKIN

On the other end of the spectrum is the Israeli swimwear industry. Bathing suits seem to be Israel's true calling, and ever since they got their hands on latex fabric it's been a love affair so intense that even Brad Pitt and Angelina Jolie are put to shame. Israel has also cornered the international market in sandals and summer footwear, so don't be afraid to put together some bodacious beach outfits while you're in Israel.

music

MY COUNTRY 'TIS OF THEE

Israel's musical passion has its roots in the early 1900s, when a desire to create a repertoire of Hebrew songs to improve Zionist pride and artistic identity inspired many composers. Until 1990, all radio and television stations were controlled by the government, playing only Israeli-written songs to foster national pride. The premium placed on music was so high that many students even carried around notebooks, ready at any minute to write down the songs that they sang with their friends, each hoping to be the next Bono.

This new Israeli style of music was inspired heavily by a mishmash of the Eastern European *klezmer* tunes and Arabian *melismatic* music, a style where each syllable has several different notes. Played mostly in the major key—a departure from the melancholic minor common to the area—it is light, playful, and highly patriotic.

LIFE IS A CABARET

Perhaps it's no accident that Liza Minelli and Israel were born within three years of each other. Cabarets are particularly popular in Israel and helped to facilitate the national identity of Israeli music. Even before the political creation of the state of Israel there were three major cabarets displaying their unique brand of performance art in Palestine: HaQumQum (Hebrew for "The Kettle"), HaMatate ("The Broom"), and Li-La-Lo ("Funny-Sounding-Name?"). With their distinctive combinations of song, poetry, and comedy (there were puppets), these cabarets helped foster a uniquely Israeli style of music and performance art.

HAPPINESS IS A WARM GUN

Israel and an active military are sort of like peanut butter and jelly, if sandwiches could carry guns. The Israeli military and music are sort of like gin and juice: delicious and dangerous at the same time. All Israeli citizens over 18 are required to perform a tour of duty in the military (known as the Israeli Defense Forces, or IDF), but those with exceptional musical talent are allowed to be a part of a performing unit in the army. The people in these units perform for other troupes, as well as on the military-run radio station in Israel, *Galey Tsahal*. The military has been key not only in fostering musical talent but also in supporting Israeli songwriters.

holidays and festivals

PURIM

March 8-9

The Jewish equivalent of Mardi Gras, Purim is the only Jewish holiday that requires you to dress up in outrageous costumes and get schwasted—if you can't read straight by the end of the festive meal, you're in accordance with Jewish law. It is traditional to read the story of the Jews' deliverance from the plotting of Haman, with the crowd booing and shaking noisemakers every time they hear the sound of Haman's name. Celebrants also march in parades and give gift baskets full of *hamentaschen*, a cookie shaped like the three-cornered hat of Haman.

moonstruck

Much like werewolves, Jews and Muslims delineate religious holidays by the cycles of the moon, so to users of the Gregorian calendar (i.e. the Western world), the holidays seem to move around every year. Since "the ninth of Tishrei" and the "15th of Nisan" are pretty meaningless to those who have grown up on good ol' September and March, we've listed the dates these holidays will occur in 2012. Be aware that most Jewish holidays actually start at sunset the night before.

PASSOVER

April 7-13

Slightly less well known than the Eight Crazy Nights of Hanukkah are the Seven Fairly Somber Nights of Passover. Much less exciting than in biblical times (but also with fewer plagues), only the first and last nights are official government holidays, although the more religious members of the population will certainly be fasting and the country may not be in quite full swing. Beware especially if you're a firstborn, as you might be forced into a ritual sacrifice to protect yourself from 🔥**God's wrath**.

ISRAELI INDEPENDENCE DAY

April 26

Yom HaAtzma'ut (Hebrew for "Day of Independence") is celebrated by most Jews, while it is considered a day of mourning by many Palestinians, who refer to it as "*al-Nakba*," meaning "The Catastrophe." Depending on which interpretation you agree with, observance of the day can range from picnics and barbecues with parades and fireworks to wearing ashes and black sackcloth. Just try to be clear about the opinion of your new friends before you plan any celebration.

HOLOCAUST REMEMBRANCE DAY

May 2

Holocaust Remembrance Day (known as *Yom HaShoah* in Hebrew) is a day recognized across Europe, but one which holds specific meaning in Israel. At 10am, sirens are sounded in all major cities in Israel, and all citizens stop what they are doing for a moment of somber remembrance in honor of those who died in the Holocaust.

VICTORY DAY

May 9

This holiday lets Israel celebrate the end of World War II and the capitulation of Germany with the rest of the Allied countries. This is the more upbeat version of the earlier Holocaust Remembrance Day, so expect parades, barbecues, and lots of adorable old men with medals.

RAMADAN

July 20-August 18

Prayer, fasting, and supplication may not make for the most exciting holiday for tourists, but the Islamic holy month of Ramadan requires just that, with adherents practicing self-denial in order to focus on worship. Although chowing down on some falafel in front of the fasting faithful is kind of in bad taste, remember—each day after sunset, they're allowed to do the same thing. Ramadan ends with a three-day blowout called **Eid al-Fitr,** during which fasting turns into feasting and parties.

ROSH HASHANAH

September 16-18

Literally translated as "head of the year," Rosh Hashanah marks the Jewish New Year, a two-day official state holiday. The day symbolizes new beginnings for people, animals, and legal contracts (perhaps this is the day for that shotgun wedding you've been planning!). Make sure to get your hands on the traditional apples and honey, but, if you're feeling adventurous, there's another, less conventional holiday delicacy: some Jews take the "head" part of the name pretty seriously and consider Rosh Hashanah the time to eat the meat of the heads of animals.

YOM KIPPUR

September 26

The holiest day in the Jewish religion is also known as the Day of Atonement. It includes a 25hr. fast, so make sure to pack a bagged lunch if you're going to be falling on the wrong side of it. While finding open restaurants and shops will be difficult at this time, take advantage of the opportunity: it's a God-given chance to be divinely forgiven for any wrongdoings over the course of your travels.

BEYOND TOURISM

If you are reading this, then you are a member of an elite group—and we don't mean "the literate." You're a student preparing for a semester abroad. You're taking a gap year to save the trees, the whales, or the dates. You're an 80-year-old woman who has devoted her life to egg-laying platypuses and what the hell is up with that. In short, you're a traveler, not a tourist; like any good spy, you don't just observe your surroundings—you become an active part of them.

Your mission, should you choose to accept it, is to study, volunteer, or work abroad as laid out in the dossier—er, chapter—below. We leave the rest (when to go, whom to bring, and how many *Arrested Development* DVDs to pack) in your hands. This message will **self-destruct** in five seconds. Good luck.

greatest hits

- **ADVOCATE** for human rights with an internship through the Faculty for Israeli-Palestinian Peace (p. 382).
- **REPORT** on the Israeli-Palestinian conflict with the NYU journalism program in Tel Aviv (p. 377).
- **LIVE LIKE A SOLDIER** by volunteering on an Israeli Defense Force base with Volunteers for Israel (p. 383).

studying

If you woke up one morning and realized that you just don't love college the way Asher Roth does, it may be time to study abroad. Hit the brakes on normalcy and accelerate to Israel. After all, when you spend a semester in Israel, study breaks suddenly include everything from swimming in the Mediterranean to picking through densely packed *souqs* for souvenirs. The aim of many of these study-abroad options is to provide coursework in Middle Eastern studies, Jewish studies, and related topics so that students can better understand the region and its conflicts. But Israel also boasts top-notch programs in the physical and social sciences, like the engineering program at the Technion Institute and the psychology track at Haifa University. Most programs also often focus on teaching Hebrew and/or Arabic at lightning speeds with language intensives called *ulpanim*. All this—and the perks of falafel and shawarma on every corner—makes Israel an ideal study-abroad locale.

UNIVERSITIES

Israeli study-abroad programs are perfect for the linguistically challenged, with many programs either conducted in English or assuming little to no knowledge of Hebrew or Arabic. Most Israeli universities also have a school specifically for international students and offer more coursework in English than universities in many other study-abroad locations.

beyond tourism

international programs

International programs can be difficult to find—mainly because Israeli universities already have excellent options for international students—but they may be your best bet if you are looking for a program that offers classes in your major (unless you happen to be majoring in Hebrew, Arabic, or Middle Eastern studies). These international programs, run by American universities, cost more and have more prerequisites than the Israeli university programs, but they include field trips. Win.

BOSTON UNIVERSITY HAIFA LANGUAGE AND LIBERAL ARTS PROGRAM

888 Commonwealth Ave., Boston, MA 02215, USA ☎+1-617-353-9888; www.bu.edu/abroad
BU's program in Israel is based in the coastal city of Haifa. In addition to Hebrew, Arabic, and Middle Eastern culture classes, this program allows college students to continue with the coursework for many majors popular in the United States, including communications, education, psychology, and sociology. Guided tours, visits to museums, and archaeological seminars are also included.
i *1 semester college-level Hebrew or Arabic required.* Ⓢ *Semester US$24,564, including housing and airfare.*

NEW YORK UNIVERSITY IN TEL AVIV PROGRAM

110 E. 14th St., New York, NY 10003, USA ☎+1-212-998-4433; www.nyu.edu/studyabroad
NYU in Tel Aviv offers a variety of social science courses and has special tracks in political science and journalism. While previous Hebrew or Arabic classes are not required, one language course must be part of your studies in Tel Aviv. If you still feel like you'll have too much free time (overachiever much?), there are excursions to natural wonders and cultural sights and an optional internship placement program.
☞ *Located in Tel Aviv, where parties don't stop until the sun rises.* Ⓢ *Semester US$27,141, including housing and a meal plan.*

FLORIDA STATE UNIVERSITY KIBBUTZ TZUBA PROGRAM

282 Champions Way, Tallahassee, FL 32306, USA ☎+1-850-644-3272; www.international.fsu.edu
This five-week summer program focuses on criminology, criminal justice, and international affairs, with all classes taught in English by Israeli and FSU faculty. Students live 20min. outside of Jerusalem on a kibbutz with nicer amenities (swimming pool, tennis courts, and a room cleaning service) than many American colleges offer.
i *Min. 2.5 GPA.* Ⓢ *Program US$7475, including housing, meals, and excursions.*

HARVARD UNIVERSITY SUMMER STUDY ABROAD PROGRAM

51 Brattle St., Cambridge, MA 02138, USA ☎+1-617-495-4024; www.summer.harvard.edu
If you think you'd dig the chance to, well, dig, Harvard offers a six-week program excavating Ashkelon, an ancient Israeli seaport. For those who aren't as enamored with shovels, sweat, and sun, the school has partnered with Hebrew University to offer a five-week program studying Israeli history in Jerusalem.
i *Both programs led by Harvard professors. Dig includes strenuous activity.* Ⓢ *Application fee US$50. Programs US$5500-6200, including housing, excursions, and some meals.*

israeli programs

Israel has as many delicious study-abroad options in its local universities as there are toppings to put on your falafel. From the cosmopolitan city of Tel Aviv to the heart of the desert, there is a university to suit everyone from sunbathers to sightseers. Each of these universities also has an international school dedicated to accommodating foreign students, all of which offer instruction in Hebrew and Arabic.

BEN-GURION UNIVERSITY OF THE NEGEV

P.O.B. 653, Be'er Sheva 84105 ☎08 646 1144; www.aabgu.org/osp
If you're looking to study somewhere hot, sunny, and sandy, BGU is for you. Located in the city of Be'er Sheva in the Negev, BGU runs the Ginsburg-Ingerman

Overseas Student Program. Foreign students can take English coursework in sustainable development and environmental justice, peace and security studies, global health, and Middle Eastern studies in addition to required language courses. To promote intercultural friendships (and maybe something more?), most students live in dorms with Israeli students.

✦ *Located in the desert, with endless opportunities for camel riding.* **i** *Housing included.* **Ⓢ** *4-week program US$1585; academic year US$16,200.*

HEBREW UNIVERSITY OF JERUSALEM

Mount Scopus, Jerusalem 91905 ☎02 588 2600; http://www.huji.ac.il/huji/eng
One of the most popular universities with international students, Hebrew U boasts the longest running study-abroad program in the country. The majority of coursework in their Rothberg International School is in Israeli, Middle Eastern, and religious studies, but there are also tracks in business, psychology, environmental studies, and the fine arts. If just studying at what many Israelis call the "Harvard of Israel" isn't good enough for you, consider applying to Spring in Jerusalem, an honors program actually affiliated with Harvard.

✦ *Prime location in Jerusalem overlooking the Old City.* **i** *Housing not included.* **Ⓢ** *Semester US$7600; academic year US$12,000.*

INTERDISCIPLINARY CENTER (IDC) HERZLIYA

P.O.B. 167, Herzliya 46150 ☎09 952 7272; www.portal.idc.ac.il/en/schools/rris
If you are desperate to get as far away from your hometown (and that high school ex) as possible, consider spending all your college years in Israel with IDC. The university has three-year Bachelor of Arts programs in business administration, government, communications, psychology, and computer science. The best part? It's all taught in English.

Ⓢ *US$100 application fee; actual price varies by program.*

TEL AVIV UNIVERSITY

P.O.B. 39040, Tel Aviv 69978 http://international.tau.ac.il
A favorite among nightlife-loving study abroaders, Tel Aviv University is the largest university in the country. Their Overseas Students' Program offers summer-, semester-, and year-long programs in Middle Eastern studies, Hebrew, Arabic, and, if you've got *chutzpah*, Yiddish. An intensive Hebrew course, however, is required for semester- or year-long study. In addition, TAU offers special programs in law and engineering. Courses are taught in English, and students live in dormitories.

Ⓢ *Semester US$11,200; academic year from US$17,450.*

BIRZEIT UNIVERSITY

P.O.B. 14, Birzeit ☎+970 2 298 2000; www.home.birzeit.edu
The Palestine and Arabic Studies (PAS) Program at Birzeit University is the study-abroad option that most strongly emphasizes the Palestinian perspective. Located near Ramallah in the West Bank, the university's program for foreign students combines Arabic lessons with English coursework focused on Palestinian and Arabic culture.

i *Considerably more basic facilities than other universities.* **Ⓢ** *US$550-650 per course. Apartment-style housing US$150-250 per month. Food and transportation not included.*

TECHNION ISRAEL INSTITUTE OF TECHNOLOGY

Technion City, Haifa 32000 ☎04 829 2111; www1.technion.ac.il/en
If you feel naked without a pocket protector and graphing calculator on your person, consider studying at the Technion, which offers courses in biotechnology, civil engineering, and environmental engineering. The Technion has a special year-long program for freshmen after which you may finish your degree in Israel or transfer the credits to one of the program's many

partners in America, where your now-well-traveled TI-89 will put all other calculators to shame.

✈ *Located in Haifa, only minutes away from the beach.* 𝒊 *Housing not included.* Ⓢ *Semester US$6000.*

UNIVERSITY OF HAIFA

Mount Carmel, Haifa 31905 ☎04 824 0766; www.uhaifa.org/letter.asp

The University of Haifa has separate courses for international students, including a psychology track, a specialty program in Peace and Conflict Studies, and an internship program. In addition, U of H offers many levels of Hebrew and Arabic programs and provides on-campus housing for a fee.

Ⓢ *Semester US$7600; academic year US$12,000. Housing additional US$1600-3400.*

ART SCHOOLS

The MASA Israel program offers various ways for young Jews to spend time in Israel. In addition to the more standard academic and volunteer options, they also have study-abroad programs focused on the visual arts and music, with almost every participant successful in securing grant funding.

BEZALEL EXPERIENCE

Mount Scopus, Jerusalem 91240 ☎02 621 6907; www.israelexperience.org.il/bezalel

There may not be many art schools in Israel, but, of the few, Bezalel Art Academy is considered the most prestigious. This program offers art classes, Hebrew language instruction, and volunteer opportunities—but good luck transferring these credits if you're pre-med.

𝒊 *Open to Jews ages 18-30.* Ⓢ *Contact MASA for prices.*

RIMON SCHOOL OF JAZZ

46 Shmuel HaGanid St., Ramat HaSharon 47295 ☎03 540 8882; http://eng.rimonschool.co.il

Rimon is Hebrew for "pomegranate," which has absolutely nothing to do with anything you'll be learning at this music school located in Ramat HaSharon, just outside of Tel Aviv. This 11-month program combines music classes at the school with Hebrew language courses and weekly volunteer work.

𝒊 *Open to Jews ages 18-30.* Ⓢ *US$18,000.*

LANGUAGE SCHOOLS

Israel has a unique option for learning Hebrew called *ulpanim* (singular *ulpan*), intensive residential programs where students are completely immersed in Hebrew and forbidden to speak anything else. It may sound pretty hardcore, but these schools undoubtedly provide the fastest way to pick up the language. While many prominent Israeli universities have ulpanim as a required part of their study-abroad programs, they also offer shorter programs for those who want to learn Hebrew at double the speed.

BEN-GURION UNIVERSITY ULPAN

P.O.B. 653, Be'er Sheva 84105 ☎08 646 1144; www.aabgu.org/osp/programs/ulpan.html

The ulpan at BGU is required for any students doing longer study-abroad programs at the school, but the four- and six-week courses offered during the summer and the winter are open to all.

Ⓢ *4 weeks US$1235; with housing US$1585. 6 weeks US$1865/2390.*

HEBREW UNIVERSITY ULPAN

Mount Scopus, Jerusalem 91905 ☎02 588 2600; http://overseas.huji.ac.il/hebrew

The Rothberg International School at Hebrew U offers an intensive winter ulpan along with more traditional Hebrew courses during the summer and academic year. Instruction ranges from beginning to upper advanced levels.

Ⓢ *Winter ulpan US$1150, with housing US$1860. Regular courses cost US$1050-1470 per session plus US$600-850 for housing.*

studying

UNIVERSITY OF HAIFA ULPAN

Mount Carmel, Haifa 31905 ☎04 824 0766; http://overseas.haifa.ac.il

The University of Haifa has one- and two-month residential summer ulpanim and also offers a non-residential Arabic program each semester.

Ⓢ *Ulpan US$1250 for 1 month, US$1800 for 2. Arabic program US$900 per semester. Registration and housing not included.*

TEL AVIV UNIVERSITY LANGUAGE PROGRAM

P.O.B. 39040, Tel Aviv 69978 ☎03 640 8111; http://international.tau.ac.il

The summer language program at TAU has 11 levels of Hebrew, five of Yiddish, and two of Arabic. There are regular and intensive options for each language, and the program offers cultural activities and trips in addition to the academics.

Ⓢ *From US$1450. Housing not included.*

volunteering

As the land which Jesus, Moses, and Ishmael once called home, it's no surprise that Israel is an especially popular location for do-gooders from around the world. Whether you work with children in the Palestinian Territories or help conserve precious environmental resources, volunteering in Israel can be physically and emotionally grueling. The most successful volunteers are determined and enthusiastic, but also flexible enough to adjust to sudden changes in projects and programming. When you get back from your trip, you'll have much more street cred than your friends who painted murals or played with dolphins.

KIBBUTZIM

Kibbutzim (singular *kibbutz*) are cooperative communities in which everyone works together and shares utilities, household duties, and living quarters. These communities were once readily open to international volunteers, providing a cheap, fun environment for people hoping to spend some time in Israel. But much like rock and roll, tie-dye, and your mother's haircut, living on a kibbutz simply isn't what it used to be, as many kibbutzim are now privatized. While they may not have held on to their socialist ethic, they are still highly regarded for their popping bars, cheap housing, and numerous volunteering and language programs.

KIBBUTZ PROGRAM CENTER

☎+1-212-462-2764; www.kibbutzprogramcenter.org

Registration through this agency is required to work at most kibbutzim for those who do not have an Israeli passport. Programs include language courses in Hebrew and Arabic, academic coursework, and volunteering options.

i *Ages 19+. 2 month min. for most programs.* Ⓢ *Price varies by program, location, and length.*

YOUTH MENTORING AND OUTREACH

Why are Israeli and Palestinian children cuter than all other children? You'll have to figure it out and get back to us.

BIG BROTHERS BIG SISTERS OF ISRAEL

84 Golumb St., Jerusalem 96903 ☎02 561 2131; ; www.bigbriothers.org.il

With locations in Jerusalem and Tel Aviv, the program matches volunteers with children from single-parent homes. Big Brothers and Sisters design weekly activities with the help of their Littles based on their shared interests—anything from movie watching to mountain climbing is fair game.

i *Ages 18+. 2hr. weekly commitment for 1 calendar year.*

SUCCESS FOR KIDS, INC.

Yedidiya Frenkel 15 St., Tel Aviv 66084 ☎54 323 2096; http://sfk.org

Volunteer opportunities with this organization include advocacy work, coordination of awareness events, mentoring, and assisting teachers in the classroom.

FARMING AND ENVIRONMENTAL CONSERVATION

With an environment as varied—and at times rugged—as Israel's, it's difficult *not* to be aware of it. This means that for those who want to take an active part in conservation efforts (or make that desert bloom), there is plenty to do. The more studious can find opportunities for research in sustainability and farming technology, while those who like to get their hands dirty can get to work through environmentally- and agriculturally-focused volunteer placements.

THE ARAVA INSTITUTE FOR ENVIRONMENTAL STUDIES

Kibbutz Ketura, DN Hevel Eilot 88840 ☎08 635 6618; www.arava.org

The Arava institute may be located in the hot desert, but its mission, at least, is pretty cool: it fosters collaboration between foreigners, native Jews, and Muslims in order to address the environmental challenges of their shared territory. Arava offers both graduate and undergraduate programs for full academic credit in the summer and academic year, with English coursework covering a range of topics from coexistence to leadership to environmental issues.

i Ready to be sweaty? Arava is in the southernmost region of Israel, where summer temperatures are often above 100°F. $ Contact Arava for prices.

KIBBUTZ LOTAN: GREEN APPRENTICESHIP PROGRAM

DN Hevel Eilot 88855 ☎08 635 6811; www.kibbutzlotan.com

Located in the Arava desert, Kibbutz Lotan has gained a reputation for maintaining the traditional kibbutz spirit of the good ol' days. Participants in the Green Apprenticeship program gain hands-on experience in designing, building, and running sustainable communities.

i Academic credit available. $ 7 weeks US$3150; 5 months US$6750. Housing and meals included.

GO ECO

☎77 552 7000; www.goeco.org/israel

This organization has ecotourism and conservation projects all over Israel. Work for a week or fill your summer with activities that range from coral reef conservation in the Red Sea to a wildlife program in the desert.

i Projects span 1-10 weeks. $ US$350 and up.

LEKET ISRAEL

P.O.B. 2297, Ra'anana 43650 ☎09 744 1757; www.leket.org.il/english

The national food bank of Israel has a number of volunteer projects from which you can choose one that matches your comfort level with nature—pick produce that farmers leave to rot, or stay inside and make sandwiches for underprivileged children.

more visa information

All non-citizens wishing to work in Israel have to obtain a one-year **work visa.** This can be difficult, since the visa is usually provided by the employer, who must explain why the job should be given to a foreigner instead of an Israeli. If you do manage to get a work visa, keep in mind that they are trade-specific: you must reapply for a work visa if you wish to switch sectors. For more information on the industries open to foreigners, check out www.gov.il/firstgov/english.

SOCIAL ACTIVISM

Helen Keller and Annie Sullivan. Paris Hilton and Nicole Richie. Palestinians and Israelis. Some of these pairs may interact more cordially than others, but the hard work of volunteers can be an important step toward healing shaky relations between cultures (not so much for squabbling stars). While formalized volunteer programs in the West Bank may be difficult to find and fieldwork can be dangerous, there are many opportunities to intern or volunteer at advocacy or human rights organizations. Securing this kind of volunteer position may entail finding your own housing in a potentially unsafe area, so, as always, *Let's Go* recommends that its readers take the utmost care.

PROJECT HOPE

29 An-Najah al-Qadim St., Nablus ☎+970 09 233 7077; www.projecthope.ps

Project Hope uses its volunteers to provide a range of services for Palestinian youth, including English and French lessons, art classes, and workshops on social justice and human rights.

Ⓢ *US$141 per month, plus US$28 for materials.*

B'TSELEM

P.O.B. 53132, Jerusalem 91531 ☎02 673 5599; www.btselem.org/English

This Israeli NGO focuses on identifying human rights violations in the Palestinian Territories and advocating for policy changes. Although many of the volunteer opportunities are meant for residents of Israel and the Palestinian Territories, B'Tselem also offers an unpaid internship program for foreigners in which participants work in the office and occasionally assist in fieldwork.

i *Competency in Hebrew or Arabic is required.*

FACULTY FOR ISRAELI-PALESTINIAN PEACE

P.O.B. 2091, Amherst, MA 01004, USA ☎+1-413-992-7355; www.ffipp.org/internships

If you don't mind spending a pretty penny for short-term summer volunteer placement, consider FFIPP. After a week of orientation coursework in human rights, justice, and peace, participants complete one-month internships with a variety of Palestinian and Israeli organizations, from research centers to foundations. Participants can apply to locations in Israel or the Palestinian Territories.

i *College students only.* Ⓢ *US$1500 for tuition and housing, not including airfare or food.*

GEORGE MASON UNIVERSITY CENTER FOR GLOBAL EDUCATION

4400 University Dr., Farifax, VA 22030, USA ☎+1-703-993-2154; http://globaled.gmu.edu

GMU offers a nine-week summer internship program with a focus on Israeli-Palestinian relations. After a week of touring and orientation, participants are placed at NGOs, private sector organizations, and peace activism groups across the region.

i *Min. 2.25 GPA. Course credit available.* Ⓢ *US$6495 for tuition and housing.*

ARMY VOLUNTEERING

If you've arrived in Israel and are wondering where all the good-looking young people are, let us help you out: they're in the army! Military service is compulsory for all Israelis after completing high school. Volunteer positions at army bases are a great way to help and celebrate their commitment to their country (and to appreciate how good they look in those uniforms).

RUACH TOVA

☎+1 700 505 202; www.ruachtova.org

This website provides a database containing all types of volunteer programs and includes a section about working on various army bases. Search options are divided by region and activity.

VOLUNTEERS FOR ISRAEL

330 W. 42nd St., Ste. 1618, New York, NY 10036, USA ☎+1-212-643-4848; www.vfi-usa.org

VFI offers a program to live and volunteer at an Israeli Defense Force base for one to three weeks. Added bonus: you, too, get to wear a uniform! While the phone and address listed are for the main New York office, there are also different offices across the United States and abroad, so contact your nearest one for more information.

Ⓢ *Application US$90. Expenses during program covered; airfare and insurance not included.*

JEWISH FELLOWSHIPS

If you thought the perks of being Jewish stopped at free food at Bar Mitzvahs and eight nights of Hanukkah presents, think again—these volunteer options are only open to Jewish young adults, and grant funding is widely available.

ORANIM TEL AVIV INTERNSHIP EXPERIENCE

P.O.B. 2135, Kfar Saba 44641 ☎+1-888-351-9897; www.destinationisrael.com

Picture the longest course catalogue you've ever seen. Now, double the number of courses, and you'll begin to have a pretty good idea of the wealth of options that the Oranim website provides, featuring programs in business, finance, communications, arts, education, politics, environment...the list goes on. The five-month long program includes numerous field trips and an intensive Hebrew language course. Shorter programs are also available.

i *Jews only. Ages 21-30.* Ⓢ *US$9200-9950, depending on start date, tuition, and housing.*

OTZMA ABROAD

25 Broadway, Ste. 1700, New York, NY 10004, USA ☎+1-877-466-8962; www.otzma.org

This 10-month program combines Hebrew language study with volunteer work. The program begins with academic coursework, which is followed by a semester of community volunteering and a three-month internship working either in a kibbutz or for a variety of non-profits in Jerusalem and Tel Aviv. The application is pretty lengthy, though, so get started early. As in, now. Trust us.

i *Jews only. Ages 20-26.* Ⓢ *US$13,000.*

working

Finding work in Israel can be difficult. Only certain sectors are allowed to offer jobs to foreigners, so if construction, welding, and agriculture aren't exactly your skill set, your best bet may be teaching, working in the hospitality industry, or doing informal short-term jobs such as private English lessons. If your ultimate goal is to make bank, your best option may be to get a job at a European or American company that has a branch in Israel. Even if you don't go this route, it is advantageous to start searching for a job well in advance.

LONG-TERM WORK

Although you may be able to find opportunities in local newspapers or online, using a placement agency or an organized teaching or internship program may save you valuable hours of internet searching that could otherwise be spent uploading cute pictures of your dog.

placement agencies

THE JEWISH AGENCY

48 King George St., Jerusalem 91000 ☎+1-800-228-055; www.jewishagency.org

Because of its extensive website, this is the most popular organization for finding work or volunteer placements in Israel. Many "work" opportunities are actually volunteer positions that include room and board.

teaching english

While your parents and professors may occasionally take issue with your grammar, in Israel your English-speaking skills are highly appreciated and desired. Although teaching is grueling work, many teachers cite their time abroad as being emotionally satisfying (if not financially so). To be a teacher, most positions require a bachelor's degree, but undergrads can normally nab internships and tutoring positions. While a TEFL (Teaching English as a Foreign Language) certification is not required, it may help you get a job and up your pay. Public schools normally require that teachers speak Hebrew or Arabic, but Israeli private schools are often on the lookout for native English speakers. You can contact schools directly or look up listings on your own (the English Teachers Network in Israel is particularly good, www.etni.org.il), but a placement organization or internship program may prove more fruitful.

SEARCH ASSOCIATES

www.searchassociates.com

Search Associates places students in paid internship positions at international schools in over 100 countries. Possible jobs include teaching, mentoring, coaching, and tutoring.

i *Program covers health insurance, airfare, housing, and provides a monthly stipend.*

INTERNATIONAL SCHOOL SERVICES (ISS)

www.iss.edu

If you are currently in college or a recent grad and can boast at least one semester of student teaching experience or K-12 teaching certification, ISS will grant you access to a database chock-full of overseas teaching opportunities—well, as long as you shell out the $185 fee, that is.

TEL AVIV TEACH AND STUDY PROGRAM (TASP)

P.O.B. 2320, Kadima 60920 ☎09 899 5644; www.tasp.org.il

College grads can intern at an Israeli public school and study for a master's degree in TEFL through this two-year program.

i *Min. 3.0 GPA.* [$] *2-year program US$24,000. Hebrew lessons, health insurance, and a monthly stipend included.*

SHORT-TERM WORK

First the rule, then the exceptions: Short-term work is illegal for foreigners in Israel. However, some foreigners have found ways to get around this by tutoring or teaching English or completing other odd jobs. In addition, sometimes it is possible to find short-term jobs in the tourist industry by accepting pay in the form of discounted room rates. The best way to find these kinds of jobs is by word of mouth, so put down your Hebrew-to-English dictionary and chat up restaurant managers and hotel workers. Note that all this information is provided simply for informational purposes, as *Let's Go* does not recommend or condone illegal activity.

tell the world

If your friends are tired of hearing about that time you saved a baby orangutan in Indonesia, there's clearly only one thing to do: get new friends. Find them at our website, www.letsgo.com, where you can post your study-, volunteer-, or work-abroad stories for other, more appreciative community members to read.

INDEX

index

index

MAP INDEX

MAP LEGEND

★	SIGHT	♜	CASTLE	▯	INTERNET CAFE	℞	PHARMACY
▪	NIGHTLIFE/SERVICE	⛪	CHURCH	▮	LIBRARY	✚	POLICE
●	ACCOMMODATION	⚑	CONSULATE/EMBASSY	Ⓜ M	METRO STATION	✉	POST OFFICE
▼	FOOD	⚜	CONVENT/MONASTERY	⛰	MOUNTAIN	🎿	SKIING
✈	AIRPORT	⚓	FERRY LANDING	☪	MOSQUE	✡	SYNAGOGUE
⌂	ARCH/GATE	(347)	HIGHWAY SIGN	🏛	MUSEUM	☎	TELEPHONE OFFICE
$	BANK	✚	HOSPITAL			♖	THEATER
⚲	BEACH		PARK	The Let's Go compass always points NORTH.		(i)	TOURIST OFFICE
🚌	BUS STATION		WATER			🚆	TRAIN STATION
✪	CAPITAL CITY		BEACH			⋯⋯⋯	PEDESTRIAN ZONE
						▨▨▨	STAIRS

The Let's Go compass always points NORTH.

map index

LET'S GO!

THE STUDENT TRAVEL GUIDE

**Let's Go guidebooks are available
at bookstores and through online retailers:**

EUROPE
Let's Go Amsterdam & Brussels, 1st ed.
Let's Go Berlin, Prague & Budapest, 2nd ed.
Let's Go France, 32nd ed.
Let's Go Europe 2012, 52nd ed.
Let's Go Europe Top 10 Cities, 1st ed.
Let's Go European Riviera, 1st ed.
Let's Go Germany, 16th ed.
Let's Go Great Britain with Belfast and Dublin, 33rd ed.
Let's Go Greece, 10th ed.
Let's Go Istanbul, Athens & the Greek Islands, 1st ed.
Let's Go Italy, 31st ed.
Let's Go London, Oxford, Cambridge & Edinburgh, 2nd ed.
Let's Go Madrid & Barcelona, 1st ed.
Let's Go Paris, 17th ed.
Let's Go Rome, Venice & Florence, 1st ed.
Let's Go Spain, Portugal & Morocco, 26th ed.
Let's Go Western Europe, 10th ed.

UNITED STATES
Let's Go Boston, 6th ed.
Let's Go New York City, 19th ed.
Let's Go Roadtripping USA, 4th ed.

MEXICO, CENTRAL & SOUTH AMERICA
Let's Go Buenos Aires, 2nd ed.
Let's Go Central America, 10th ed.
Let's Go Costa Rica, 5th ed.
Let's Go Costa Rica, Nicaragua & Panama, 1st ed.
Let's Go Guatemala & Belize, 1st ed.
Let's Go Yucatán Peninsula, 1st ed.

ASIA & THE MIDDLE EAST
Let's Go Israel, 6th ed.
Let's Go Thailand, 5th ed.

Exam and desk copies are available for study-abroad programs and resource centers.
*Let's Go guidebooks are distributed to bookstores in the U.S. through Publishers Group West
and in Canada through Publishers Group Canada.*
For more information, email letsgo.info@perseusbooks.com.

ACKNOWLEDGMENTS

LEAH THANKS: It's a truth universally acknowledged that, to make an excellent book, you need an even more excellent research manager. ✡**Amy,** you are my world. And by world, I mean mother (sorry Mom—you're great too). In fact, thanks to all my parents, adoptive and otherwise, the cause(!), the founders of Berryline, that little noise gchat makes, our three researcher-writer-badasses, Sberlow's medits, LGHQ, and Pandora for letting me listen to way more than 40hr. per month. To my friends from home for only mild guilt trips, most major deities for letting us gently mock them without any lightning strikes (yet), and my brother for Job and Maya Angelou. And to Tuesday—couldn't have done it without you. Next year in Jerusalem.

AMY THANKS: First, foremost, and always to ✡**Israel;** the stunning beauty, the warring tendencies, the deep religious roots, the connection to mother earth. An impossible to understand entity, wrapped in an enigma, painting with all the colors of the wind everyday. Of course to Sberlow, Agent Liu, Traubster, and the Fege—may you be pleased now and forever. The LG Frevolution (The Cause!) No, you still can't sit with us. Joey G. and Billy, who would win Rivals as quickly as they won my heart. Iya for kicking box and taking names. Mary for life-changing jamz, Dorothy for Tennessee understanding, Spencer for his beard and T-Jeff love. Sarah for being like that, like how you are. Kat for making sure my life stayed "outta control." Emily J. for Arabic and camaraderie. Most of all, to Mom, Dad, Nate, and the fam, for making sure I always stayed homesick. Next year in Jerusalem.

DIRECTOR OF PUBLISHING Joseph Molimock

EDITORIAL DIRECTOR Iya Megre

PRODUCTION AND DESIGN DIRECTOR Marykate Jasper

PUBLICITY AND MARKETING DIRECTOR Joseph Brian Gaspard

MANAGING EDITORS Sarah Berlow, Chris Kingston, Sara Plana

TECHNOLOGY PROJECT MANAGER Ranjit Nilacanta Venkata

PRODUCTION ASSOCIATE Whitney Adair

MARKETING AND FINANCIAL ASSOCIATE Hanna Choi

DIRECTOR OF IT Robert Cunningham

PRESIDENT Ethan Waxman

GENERAL MANAGER Jim McKellar

LET'S GO
masthead

ABOUT LET'S GO

THE STUDENT TRAVEL GUIDE

Let's Go publishes the world's favorite student travel guides, written entirely by Harvard students. Armed with pens, notebooks, and a few changes of clothes stuffed into their backpacks, our student researchers go across continents, through time zones, and above expectations to seek out invaluable travel experiences for our readers. Because we are a completely student-run company, we have a unique perspective on how students travel, where they want to go, and what they're looking to do when they get there. If your dream is to grab a machete and forge through the jungles of Costa Rica, we can take you there. If you'd rather bask in the Riviera sun at a beachside cafe, we'll set you a table. In short, we write for readers who know that there's more to travel than tour buses. To keep up, visit our website, www.letsgo. com, where you can sign up to blog, post photos from your trips, and connect with the Let's Go community.

TRAVELING BEYOND TOURISM

We're on a mission to provide our readers with sharp, fresh coverage packed with socially responsible opportunities to go beyond tourism. Each guide's Beyond Tourism chapter shares ideas about responsible travel, study abroad, and how to give back to the places you visit while on the road. To help you gain a deeper connection with the places you travel, our fearless researchers scour the globe to give you the heads-up on both world-renowned and off-the-beaten-track opportunities. We've also opened our pages to respected writers and scholars to hear their takes on the countries and regions we cover, and asked travelers who have worked, studied, or volunteered abroad to contribute first-person accounts of their experiences.

FIFTY-TWO YEARS OF WISDOM

Let's Go has been on the road for 52 years and counting. We've grown a lot since publishing our first 20-page pamphlet to Europe in 1960, but five decades and 60 titles later, our witty, candid guides are still researched and written entirely by students on shoestring budgets who know that train strikes, stolen luggage, food poisoning, and marriage proposals are all part of a day's work. Meanwhile, we're still bringing readers fresh new features, such as a student-life section with advice on how and where to meet students from around the world; a revamped, user-friendly layout for our listings; and greater emphasis on the experiences that make travel abroad a rite of passage for readers of all ages. And, of course, this year's 16 titles—including five brand-new guides—are still brimming with editorial honesty, a commitment to students, and our irreverent style.

THE LET'S GO COMMUNITY

More than just a travel guide company, Let's Go is a community that reaches from our headquarters in Cambridge, MA, all across the globe. Our small staff of dedicated student editors, writers, and tech nerds comes together because of our shared passion for travel and our desire to help other travelers get the most out of their experience. We love it when our readers become part of the Let's Go community as well—when you travel, drop us a postcard (67 Mt. Auburn St., Cambridge, MA 02138, USA), send us an email (feedback@letsgo.com), or sign up on our website (www. letsgo.com) to tell us about your adventures and discoveries.

For more information, updated travel coverage, and news from our researcher team, visit us online at www.letsgo.com.

- **ABRAHAM TOURS.** 67 Hanevi'im Street, Davidka Square, Jerusalem. ☎972 2 566 00 45; www.abrahamtours.com or tours@abrahamhostels.com

HELPING LET'S GO. If you want to share your discoveries, suggestions, or corrections, please drop us a line. We appreciate every piece of correspondence, whether a postcard, a 10-page email, or a coconut. Visit Let's Go at **www.letsgo.com** or send an email to:

feedback@letsgo.com, subject: "Let's Go Israel"

Address mail to:

Let's Go Israel, 67 Mount Auburn St., Cambridge, MA 02138, USA

In addition to the invaluable travel advice our readers share with us, many are kind enough to offer their services as researchers or editors. Unfortunately, our charter enables us to employ only currently enrolled Harvard students.

Maps © Let's Go and Avalon Travel
Design Support by Jane Musser, Sarah Juckniess, Tim McGrath, Lohnes + Wright Cartography

Distributed by Publishers Group West.
Printed in Canada by Friesens Corp.

ISBN-13: 978-1-61237-004-0
ISBN-10: 161237-004-7
Sixth edition
10 9 8 7 6 5 4 3 2 1

Let's Go Israel is written by Let's Go Publications, 67 Mt. Auburn St., Cambridge, MA 02138, USA.

Let's Go® and the LG logo are trademarks of Let's Go, Inc.

quick reference

YOUR GUIDE TO LET'S GO ICONS

👍	*Let's Go* recommends	☎	Phone numbers	↔	Directions
ℹ	Other hard info	$	Prices	⏰	Hours

PRICE RANGES

Let's Go includes price ranges, marked by one through four dollar signs, in accommodations and food listings. For an expanded explanation, see the chart in How To Use This Book.

ISRAEL	$	$$	$$$	$$$$
ACCOMMODATIONS	Under NIS80	NIS80-260	NIS260-400	Over NIS400
FOOD	Under NIS 32	NIS32-80	NIS80-145	Over NIS145

JORDAN	$	$$	$$$	$$$$
ACCOMMODATIONS	Under JD7	JD7-21	JD21-42	Over JD42
FOOD	Under JD4	JD4-9	JD9-15	Over JD15

IMPORTANT PHONE NUMBERS

EMERGENCY: POLICE ☎100, FIRE ☎101, FIRE DEPARTMENT ☎102			
US Embassy in Tel Aviv	☎03 519 7475	Israeli Tourist Police	☎03 516 5382
International operator in Israel	☎188	Egged Bus Passenger Information	☎03 694 8888

USEFUL HEBREW AND ARABIC PHRASES

ENGLISH	HEBREW	ARABIC
Hello!/Hi!	Shalom!	Marhaban!
Do you speak English?	To M: Ata medaber angleet? To F: At medaberet angleet?	Tihki elengleezeeya?
Help!	Hatzilu!	Saaydoonee!
Where is the bathroom?	Eyfo sherooteem?	Wayn manaafi?
Could you help me?	To M: Ata yakhol la'azor lee? To F: At yekhola la'azor lee?	To M: Mumkeen Tesa'eedni? To F: Tesa'edeenee?
I would like a ticket for...	M: Ani rotze kartees le... F: Ani rotza kartees le...	Bidee tathkara eela...
Leave me alone.	To M: Azov otee. To F: Azvee otee.	Khaleenee lawahdi.
How much?	Kama?	Adeish?/Bekem?

CURRENCY CONVERSIONS

AUS$1 = NIS3.6	NIS1= AUS$.275	NZ$1 = NIS2.82	NIS1 = NZ$.355
CDN$1 = NIS3.54	NIS1 = CDN$.282	UK£1 = NIS5.46	NIS1 = UK£.183
EUR€1 = NIS4.93	NIS1 = EUR€.203	US$1 = NIS3.41	NIS1 = US$.293

TEMPERATURE CONVERSIONS

°CELSIUS	-5	0	5	10	15	20	25	30	35	40
°FAHRENHEIT	23	32	41	50	59	68	77	86	95	104

MEASUREMENT CONVERSIONS

1 foot (ft.) = 0.305m	1 meter (m) = 3.28 ft.
1 mile (mi.) = 1.609km	1 kilometer (km) = 0.621 mi.
1 pound (lb.) = 0.454kg	1 kilogram (kg) = 2.205 lb.
1 gallon (gal.) = 3.785L	1 liter (L) = 0.264 gal.